# SUSTAINABLE SOLUTIONS
## DEVELOPING PRODUCTS AND SERVICES FOR THE FUTURE

Contributing Editors: Martin Charter and Ursula Tischner

# Sustainable Solutions

## DEVELOPING PRODUCTS AND SERVICES FOR THE FUTURE

CONTRIBUTING EDITORS
MARTIN CHARTER AND URSULA TISCHNER

Greenleaf
PUBLISHING
2001

© 2001 Greenleaf Publishing Limited unless otherwise stated

**Published by Greenleaf Publishing Limited**
**Aizlewood's Mill**
**Nursery Street**
**Sheffield S3 8GG**
UK

British Library Cataloguing in Publication Data:
   A Catalogue record of this book is available from the British Library.

ISBN 1874719365

# CONTENTS

# PREFACE

Most of the discussion about business sustainability to date has focused on the corporate management level, with a lack of emphasis on product and service development issues. We perceived this gap in knowledge and information and decided to invite the leading global experts from business and academia to explore the business, design and organisational issues surrounding ecodesign, eco-product development and sustainable product design (SPD). *Sustainable Solutions* is aimed at environmental directors, product developers and designers in companies and consultancies, as well as academics and students, policy-makers and NGOs. It constitutes a global state of the art and practice of SPD.

The book is business-oriented with a prime focus on the product and service development process. As product development (supply) is always dependent on demand, sustainable consumption issues are also discussed. Most of the book's authors are drawn from industrialised countries. However, as sustainable development is obviously impossible without the involvement of less developed countries, chapters and case studies have been included that explore the Southern perspective.

Most of the chapters in *Sustainable Solutions* cover ecodesign and eco-product development. SPD, which we argue expands ecodesign to incorporate wider social and ethical considerations in the process, is also referred to, and sometimes these terms are used interchangeably—which reflects the newness of the topic. The book puts an emphasis on product development and design because this phase accounts for more than 80% of the economic costs and environmental impacts (and possibly social impacts) of a product during its whole life-cycle (excavation of raw materials, production, use, recycling and disposal).

*Martin Charter*  *Ursula Tischner*
*Farnham, UK*  *Cologne, Germany*

*August 2000*

# ACKNOWLEDGEMENTS

The editors would like to thank all the authors for their thinking and hard work and the employees of The Centre for Sustainable Design, econcept and Greenleaf Publishing for co-operation and motivation. Thanks also go to our families for their encouragement and support.

# FOREWORD

*Jacqueline Aloisi de Larderel*
**Director, Division of Technology, Industry and Economics,
United Nations Environment Programme**

Regardless of recent efficiency improvements in the development of products and services, a growing population and the emergence of a dynamic global consumer culture are fuelling environmental deterioration. UNEP's *Global Environment Outlook 2000* highlights the urgent necessity for adopting sustainable practices at all levels of society, and over 100 environment ministers, gathered by UNEP in June 2000 in Malmö, Sweden, for the first global environmental forum, called for the 'development of cleaner and more resource-efficient technologies for a life-cycle economy'.

Changes in consumption and production patterns will depend on the actions of all stakeholders. Today, the business sector is increasingly expected to respond to the demands of society for improved environmental, social and ethical performance. The global sustainability debate has evolved to the point where businesses must consider the impacts of products and services throughout life-cycle and supply chains. This 'calling' for change is the fundamental rationale behind business and governmental support for moving corporate responsibility issues to the forefront of the global agenda.

At the 1999 World Economic Forum in Davos, UN Secretary General Kofi Annan proposed a 'Global Compact' to ensure that there is 'a human face to the global market'. He urged companies to commit themselves to apply recognised principles and standards in three areas: human rights, labour standards and environmental protection.

The business sector is beginning to realise that financial and social benefits will arise from incorporating practices of sustainability. Energy efficiency, recycling and maximising the use of raw materials can all deliver profitable returns, as can clean, efficient production processes and innovative 'sustainable' products. The power of consumption—as a driving force towards sustainable development—is in many ways greater than the power of legislative and regulatory measures, hence the escalating attention among decision-makers worldwide for the concept of sustainable consumption.

Since the Rio Earth Summit in 1992, UNEP has been catalysing the implementation of 'Cleaner Production and Sustainable Consumption' throughout the world. This remarkable book demonstrates that solutions are available and that innovative thinking, drawing from current technological changes, can lead to considerable improvements towards sustainability.

*Sustainable Solutions* successfully demonstrates the enormous business opportunities relating to ecodesign and sustainable product design (SPD). UNEP congratulates the authors of this publication which emphasises a variety of innovative examples that are drawn from both large and small companies and from both developed and developing countries. Decisively, *Sustainable Solutions* approaches the elements of consumption and production in an integrated manner. With the adoption of a 'life-cycle economy' remaining as a considerable global challenge, this book will carry us somewhat closer to a sustainable future.

# INTRODUCTION

*Martin Charter*
The Centre for
Sustainable Design, UK

*Ursula Tischner*
econcept, Germany

**SUSTAINABLE SOLUTIONS** ARE PRODUCTS, SERVICES, HYBRIDS OR SYSTEM changes that minimise negative and maximise positive sustainability impacts—economic, environmental, social and ethical—throughout and beyond the life-cycle of existing products or solutions, while fulfilling acceptable societal demands/needs. Sustainable solutions require multi-stakeholder engagement and involve changes or shifts in consumption and production patterns. The aim of sustainable solutions is to create a positive net sustainable value (positive impacts should outweigh negative impacts) for all stakeholders in the delivery process. Changes may be incremental at the product level or radical if system shifts are needed.

Ecodesign has evolved primarily from the engineering and life-cycle assessment (LCA) communities and has therefore often been technically rather than business or organisationally focused. The first phase of greener product development has tended to produce 'one-off' eco-(re)designs within research and development (R&D) departments, with relatively few companies implementing environmental considerations throughout the product development process. As a result, ecodesign management systems have remained immature. The reasons for this are manifold, but include a lack of corporate vision, perceived high costs, weak market awareness and the risks associated with being too far ahead of the market.

Ideally, each stage of the product development process should receive environmental consideration. However, these stages are often owned by different internal stakeholders with different interests and objectives. For example, the marketing function is a key player in the product development process but, because of a lack of environmental awareness, market research on sustainability issues is rarely commissioned. Designers are also key role players in the product development process but again generally have little awareness and knowledge of environmental issues, because of the lack of integration of ecodesign modules into design college or university curricula. This means that materials reduction, recycling or energy-efficiency opportunities are unlikely to be considered unless they are in 'the brief'. In addition, to date there has been a limited ecodesign toolbox for product developers.

The business climate is, however, beginning to change. A growing number of companies are now sending questionnaires to suppliers requesting detailed information about hazardous materials usage, product recyclability and life-cycle impacts. Enacted, or soon-to-be-enacted, legislation on producer responsibility and the development of environmental product policies in countries such as the Netherlands, Austria, Germany, Sweden and, more recently, Japan—coupled with the increasing global importance of standardisation—are all having a growing effect. A good product environmental profile may not yet win a company new business but a bad profile, or a failure to provide detailed information on the life-cycle performance of a product, is likely to result in lost customers.

Increasingly, business is also having to account to an ever-growing array of stakeholders on social and ethical performance. The wider societal dimensions of the sustainability debate have been recently highlighted by concerns related to Shell and the company's involvement in Nigeria, by controversy over food ethics and genetically modified organisms (GMOs) and by the demonstrations in Seattle against the power of the World Trade Organisation (WTO). Such concerns are being accelerated by the increasing sophistication of environmental and developmental non-governmental organisations (NGOs), the growth of the 'CNN world' and the communications power of the Internet. This means that the corporate 'radar' will need to scan not just the environmental but also the social and ethical impacts of products and services throughout life-cycle and supply chains. The need to take this overview will produce a set of new questions and different perspectives and is likely to generate new opportunities and ideas. The next ecodesign paradigm will focus on three areas: the greater understanding and communication of business benefits for ecodesign; a more widespread implementation of organisational approaches to eco-product development; and an extension of this thinking to the broader social and ethical implications of sustainability for product and service development.

What in this book we call sustainable product design (SPD) will need to stretch the envelope way beyond ecodesign to a more integrated model that considers all aspects of the 'triple bottom line'. New thinking on SPD is now starting to emerge but remains primarily centred on ecological or 'closed-loop' issues. The future will mean exploring the development of products and services that contribute to sustainable development throughout their life-cycle. For those companies that take a first-mover position on implementing such systematic approaches there will be a significant range of commercial benefits. These will include not only direct impacts on the bottom line through cost reduction and revenue generation but also less quantifiable benefits to brand and corporate image.

## Book structure

*Sustainable Solutions* is divided into three parts. The first part provides background discussion of sustainable development, production and consumption issues on a macro level (societal, national and international). In the second part, ecodesign, eco-product development and sustainable product and service development are explored at the company level. The third part introduces case studies from a range of countries and companies worldwide. Additionally, at the end of the book, there is a comprehensive list of websites relevant to ecodesign, eco-product development and SPD.

In Chapter 1 Spangenberg gives an overview of the concept of sustainable development from a systems viewpoint, with a particular focus on housing, nutrition and mobility. Sustainable development has become a *lingua franca* for politicians and environmentalists, but the concept remains vague for many business people. There are many visions of sustainable development. Is it a more dematerialised world with a relatively higher consumption of services and more use of the Internet or is it a more localised world where producers and consumers act locally, sourcing and producing raw materials, components and products and services within their locality? Each scenario produces its own set of opportunities and problems. Spangenberg argues convincingly that sustainability requires consideration of the international trade regime and that there is a need to take account of global supply chain issues. In other words, sustainability is unachievable without change to the system, not only generating incremental changes but also creating total system solutions including changes in infrastructure and shifts in consumption patterns.

In Chapter 2 Robins and de Leeuw focus on the issues surrounding sustainable consumption—a much more complex debate than that related to green consumerism and niche green products. The global dimension includes considerations such as satisfying basic human needs in the South and sufficiency in the North, as well as social and ethical aspects such as the use of child labour and fair wages in, for example, the textile industry in Bangladesh. Companies from the South may respond to market needs with 'design-for-necessity' strategies as there is no concept of waste, with all materials considered to be resources.

In Chapter 3 Lentz gives an overview of the North–South issues that pervade the whole debate on sustainable development and discusses the possibilities for SPD in less developed countries (LDCs). The author provides an overview and analysis of the context of the development of SPD within LDCs, at state, regional and business level, highlighting opportunities and obstacles. The relationship between environmental management and SPD is also explored and illustrated with various examples from Bolivia.

Next, in Chapter 4, James highlights the business implications of sustainability. In order to enable the more effective implementation of either ecodesign or the broader concept of SPD, there is a need for the development of an integrated model of business sustainability that takes account of the 'triple bottom line' and consideration of the sustainable value chain. James highlights both progress and dilemmas in developing such an approach.

To integrate the management of the demand and supply side of 'product and environment' issues into governmental policy, a new policy approach is being developed by the European Commission: integrated product policy (IPP). Discussion over IPP and national governmental approaches to environmental product policy (EPP) is included in Chapter 5, by Charter, Young, Young and Belmane. Some European countries have already established national approaches to EPP, but often the emphasis is on particular aspects of the toolbox such as eco-labels, ecodesign and green taxes and not on a holistic approach. Charter *et al.* go on to ask what is beyond IPP and what sustainable integrated product policy (SIPP) might look like.

The second part of the book covers the practicalities of implementing ecodesign, eco-product development and SPD. In Chapter 6 Tischner and Charter discuss the differences between the terminologies used in *Sustainable Solutions* and provide some ideas about the incorporation of broader environmental, economic, social and ethical issues into product development. Best practices incorporating ecologically driven SPD are high-lighted in their chapter as are the problems and dichotomies with a holistic version of SPD. For example, a computer may be purchased in the USA that incorporates 95% recycled plastic in its casing. The same computer, however, may have had subassemblies sourced from Sweden, that in turn have components from an Indonesian factory, which may have high environmental and good health and safety standards but employs child labour, which in turn enables a family of ten to live! Tischner and Charter argue that sustainable value is currently very difficult to see.

McDonough and Braungart continue this theme in Chapter 7 with the argument that the need to create sustainable value may require such radical change that it should be compared with the Industrial Revolution. They provide a new model for product development in a more sustainable society. To establish such a society will also require a move beyond eco-efficiency to what McDonough and Braungart dub 'eco-effectiveness'. This new paradigm will include the replacement or delivery of products by new eco-service development.

This trend is explored more fully with numerous examples by Stahel in Chapter 8. Product service systems (PSS)—products that come packaged with far higher levels of service—are now starting to emerge as a new strategy for delivering sustainability.

To determine environmentally sensible options, companies need robust and practicable measurement instruments. Fiksel gives an overview of the issues surrounding the measure-ment of ecodesign and SPD performance in Chapter 9. Metrics for ecodesign are now start-ing to be used by some larger companies, but broader SPD metrics are still in their infancy.

But ecodesign is not only practised by large companies. In Chapter 10 van Hemel provides an analysis of the results of a study on the implementation of ecodesign among small and medium-sized enterprises (SMEs) in the Netherlands. Generally, SMEs face a lack of customer and legislative pressure for ecodesign, which has resulted in little activity outside of 'niche green' companies and products.

Continuing this theme, experience is indicating that there is a need for simpler ecodesign tools that busy designers can use, as well as 'hands-on' practical training. In Chapter 11 Masera provides an overview of SPD, drawing on experience from a project among micro and small companies in Mexico. His experience highlights the need for practice-based rather than classroom approaches to ecodesign training.

If ecodesign is to be planned and implemented systematically the process has to be managed. In Chapter 12 Charter gives an overview of the management of ecodesign and consideration of 'soft factors' such as organisational structure, systems, communications and corporate culture—all of which are particularly important when executing eco-product development.

Next, in Chapter 13, Brezet and Rocha present details of product-oriented environmental management systems (POEMS). Experience generated from Dutch projects indicates that, unless ecodesign is built into environmental management and/or more general management systems, then such initiatives and projects tend to be 'one-off' exercises. For ecodesign to be successful there is a need to build in environmental considerations alongside costs, quality and feasibility if it is going to become part of mainstream product development.

Tools are also helpful in that process, and in Chapter 14 Tischner provides an overview of ecodesign tools. Eco-product development requires a range of tools at different stages of the product development process. Most of the first phase of ecodesign tools has tended to focus on environmental evaluation. These tools include LCA, which illustrates the existing focus on eco-(re)design. Tischner concludes that there is a need for new tools and new processes to enable eco-innovation (environmentally considered new product and service development) and a broader toolbox to satisfy the needs and interests of different business functions.

Finally, ecodesigned products have to be marketed and communicated. In Chapter 15 Polonsky provides the big picture of the motivations, practicalities and the dos and don'ts of green(er) marketing. Marketing has a key role to play in ecodesign but to date has shown little appetite for environmental issues.

The third part of this book provides 12 case studies from around the world, focusing on both transnational and SME examples. First, in Chapter 16, a case on the eco-(re)design of a dishwasher range is presented by Gertsakis. This is one project out of a series of products that have been eco-(re)designed in Australia, incorporating eco-efficiency principles throughout the product development process.

Next, in Chapter 17, Allenby highlights the environmental implications of eco-service development using the example of teleworking. He illustrates that there are real opportunities to deliver greener services but that at this stage there are very few tools available to measure the relative eco-impacts.

In Chapter 18 Cramer and Stevels give examples of eco-innovation at Philips. Experience there indicates that there are various ecodesign opportunities ranging from incremental improvements, redesign, and onwards to systems change, each with its own set of business sustainability challenges and benefits.

In Chapter 19, Baynes et al. provide ecodesign examples from Sony. The company's approach focuses on integrating environmental considerations throughout each stage of the product development process.

Thompson and Sherwin, in Chapter 20, then give an example of an academic–business partnership on ecodesign. The project focused on green concept development, matching the research skills of a university with the 'real-life' practicalities faced by a company.

In Chapter 21, Rohn and von Proff-Kesseler focus on a kitchen system integrating sustainability considerations. Kambium is an example of an SME that is implementing eco-efficient product design at a local level.

Burchardt, in Chapter 22, highlights 'design-for-longevity' issues promoted by the catalogue company Manufactum, which provides an example of a company focused on delivering quality products, with consequent environmental and customer benefits.

In Chapter 23, Paulitsch highlights activities undertaken by Germany's largest natural clothing retailer aimed at integrating sustainability into business processes. Hess Natur illustrates the need for an integrated ecodesign approach focusing on supply chain considerations.

Kälin, of Rohner Textil, provides in Chapter 24 a case study on the development of the Climatex® Lifecycle™ textile range. This eco-innovation was generated through the application of ecological design principles created by McDonough Braungart Design Chemistry.

In Chapter 25, Ax gives details of a craft-based project on shoes. The application of simple ecodesign tools has helped develop more durable and customised products at affordable prices.

Guimarães and Steward describe in Chapter 26 the development of an 'ecobroom' from Brazil. The case gives an example of entrepreneurial ecodesign where a product derived from waste has generated a range of sustainability benefits.

Finally, in Chapter 27, Masera provides an example from Kenya of carving using renewable timber.

The aim of *Sustainable Solutions* is to demonstrate in one source the huge business opportunities relating to ecodesign and SPD. The contributions give a variety of innovative examples drawn from both large and small companies from both North and South. Of course, there are huge problems. The challenge of satisfying a growing global population with less environmentally and socially harmful products and services is real and will require a raft of new ideas and innovations. The achievement of 'factor $x$' reductions in energy and materials will require substantial changes in the way that production and consumption is organised at a product and systems level. But the 'rebound effect'— increased consumption of more eco-efficient product and services—must be acknowledged. This will mean policy-makers, businesses and other stakeholders will need to move into the contentious and fuzzy area of the links between consumption and quality of life. However, for those companies that are prepared to take the necessary leadership and organisational risks associated with the development of *Sustainable Solutions*, we believe that the benefits may well be incalculable.

# Part 1
## BACKGROUND TO SUSTAINABLE CONSUMPTION AND PRODUCTION

# SUSTAINABLE DEVELOPMENT
## From catchwords to benchmarks and operational concepts

*Joachim H. Spangenberg*
Sustainable Europe Research Institute, Germany

The terms 'sustainable development' and 'sustainable consumption and production' are used by different actors with diverging definitions and sometimes biased interpretations. For the sake of clarity, the historical development of the concept is briefly summarised (Section 1.1), before a number of frequently used definitions and measurements on the macro level are described (Sections 1.2.1 and 1.2.2). Then a macro-level concept is presented, including sustainable production and consumption and links to the micro level (Section 1.3). Finally, the barriers to political implementation and some key issues for ecodesign are introduced (Section 1.4).

## 1.1 The history of development of the sustainability concept

The term 'sustainable development' was first introduced into the international policy debate by the World Conservation Strategy (IUCN/UNEP/WWF 1980). It became established as a new global paradigm only after *Our Common Future*, the final report of the Brundtland Commission, had been published (WCED 1987) and the preparatory work for the United Nations (UN) Earth Summit 1992 had begun.

However, despite all the attention devoted to the concept, the perception of its core message regarding the integration of environment and development remained ambiguous. In the North sustainable development was predominantly understood as one more new environmental concept, like environmental modernisation, greening the industrial metabolism or safeguarding biodiversity as the common heritage of humankind had been beforehand. In much of the South, however, the term 'sustainable development' was taken as meaning poverty alleviation and economic development. These diverging perceptions are not only the result of differing priorities, but are also the result of controversial interpretations of environmental problems arising since the early 1970s.

During the 1970s, *Limits to Growth*, the report to the Club of Rome (Meadows 1972), was shaping the debate in the North, stressing the need to change the current development path in order to maintain a safe resource base for human societies. In the US, this contributed to the perception of population growth as the main future risk, whereas in Europe the focus was more on individual and industrial consumption patterns (strengthened by the subsequent oil price crisis). The South, however, understood the argument as an attempt to deny the 'right to development' they had been promised (e.g. in the Human Rights Charter). Regarding resource consumption, they saw the challenge not in terms of 'limits to growth' but in a fair distribution of wealth: according to Mahatma Gandhi the world has enough for everyone's need, but not for some people's greed. This position was most clearly stated in *Limits to Misery*, a report in response to *Limits to Growth* and produced on behalf of the Bariloche Foundation, Argentina (Herrera and Skolnik 1976). It resurfaced in the sustainability discussions in the late 1980s and led to the statement in Agenda 21 that the 'excessive demands and unsustainable lifestyles among the richer . . . place immense stress on the environment' (UN 1993: 31).

One of the key objectives of the Brundtland Commission was to reconcile these two positions. It tried to do so by updating the environmental dimension by focusing on global environmental systems and their absorptive and carrying capacities and by embarking on a globalist view concentrating on the interdependencies of North and South. It highlighted their shared responsibilities, without ignoring the factual inequality in power, influence and responsibility. The Commission succeeded in avoiding much of the polarisation of the 1970s by organising the debate around the term 'sustainable development', which by its very definition ruled out trade-offs between environment and development, leaving only the question how to create the win–win situations envisaged.

The problems encountered in the process of developing a broadly shared view became even more obvious in the preparatory phase of the UN Conference on Environment and Development (UN 1993). Officially it was a consensus-oriented discourse about the best solution for the world's problems. Politically, it was a power battle. On one side there was the extreme version of neoliberal deregulation politics (represented by the US government, members of the Organisation of Petroleum Exporting Countries [OPEC] and major businesses). Their opponents followed an ordo-liberal[1] responsible capitalism approach including social and environmental standards represented by social-democratic leaders from Latin America and Europe as well as by the US Democrats (Roddick 1998). Nevertheless, the compromise reached in the end was praised globally for its landmark quality, but it necessarily meant sacrificing some goals for all parties involved. Rio 1992 was a kind of watershed: whereas before environmental issues had been shaping

---

1    Ordo-liberalism combines a liberal market regime with framework regulations that safeguard the social cohesion and—as a more robust development—environmental integrity. It is the theoretical basis of the European continental regulated capitalism approach ('Rheinish Capitalism').

the public discourse in many parts of the world for some time, soon afterwards the globalisation and deregulation discourse began to dominate. This change also resulted in a certain reluctance regarding the implementation of the UNCED decisions, in particular from those who felt that the current balance of power was more favourable to them than the results obtained in 1992.

## 1.2 What is sustainable development?

Given the underlying conflicts, the unanimous agreements of Rio de Janeiro 1992 and, before that, the consensus of the Brundtland Commission are all the more remarkable. It is thus most plausible to start elaborating on the meaning of sustainable development by unfolding the description given by the World Commission for Environment and Development (WCED).

### 1.2.1 Sustainable development: a definition

The WCED has given the most frequently quoted criterion for sustainable development by characterising it as 'development that meets the needs of the present without compromising the ability of future generations to meet their own needs' (WCED 1987: 43). This statement is as close to a definition of sustainable development as the Brundtland Commission has come but it is frequently considered as being too vague to provide any operational value. Nonetheless, it immediately illustrates that sustainability is not environmentalism dressed up for the new millennium but is essentially a new way of seeing the world (see Fig. 1.1), based on considerations of intergenerational and intragenerational justice and shared responsibility.

Human needs (not only material ones!) should be met and the opportunity to lead a dignified life should be granted not only to specific groups but also to the population at large. This criterion calls for an equitable sharing not only of the benefits of the consumer society but also of the risks it immanently produces (Beck 1986). It provides an interesting point of departure for ecodesign, because, obviously, contributions to sustainability cannot be limited to marketable products but need to start from human needs and to look for the most sustainable ways to satisfy them. This can be achieved by products, by eco-efficient services or even by social processes. Furthermore, accessibility and affordability even beyond pure market concerns become important criteria for ecodesign.

For future generations, the opportunity to meet their own, self-defined needs (probably differing from those of the current generation) has to be assured. This criterion requires freedom of choice to be granted to generations to come. It includes the preservation of nature and its resources in such a way that future generations will still find a sufficient basis for their preferred lifestyles, based on possibly different value systems.

Based on this understanding of sustainability, measurements have been developed. Since criteria such as ecosystem resilience, poverty and income distribution are defined

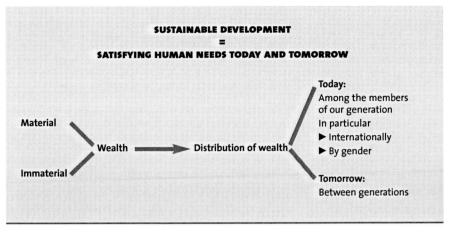

*Figure 1.1* **The goal: sustainable development**

on the macro level, they are macro measures. Only after such a macro measure has been agreed can the micro effects influencing be explored, be it in terms of household consumption (Section 1.3) or entrepreneurial activities.

### 1.2.2 Macro measurements

Grounded on these core elements of sustainability, a number of attempts have been made to assess quantitatively the sustainability of a given development path (for an overview, see Guinomet 1999), based on the conceptual bases provided by different disciplines and sub-disciplines.

On the one hand physical data has been aggregated to derive quantitative indicators or even indices of sustainability. These tend to describe the input of the 'industrial metabolism' (Ayres and Simonis 1994) in terms of energy and material flows from a resource economics perspective. The output is predominantly treated according to toxicological and ecological criteria, including an analysis of the state of the respective environmental systems (e.g. Eurostat 1999; for an overview, see Walz *et al.* 1995). Many of the methodologies suggested suffer from the fact that, because of the diverging geographical outreach of different environmental problems, the indicators derived also apply to different geographical scopes, rendering them quite problematic as a basis for political decision-making. One way to overcome this problem is to develop rough measures such as the 'ecological footprint' (Rees and Wackernagel 1994) or the sustainable process index (SPI; Eder and Narodoslawski 1999), both based on land-use analysis, or the 'ecological rucksack' (Schmidt-Bleek 1994), based on material flow accounting. For energy, a number of measures have been developed: for example, emergy accounting (Odum 1996), exergy measures (Ayres *et al.* 1996) or embodied energy analysis (King and Slesser 1994). All of these suffer from the fact that land, material and energy have no common denominator, so a combination of these three numeraires as included in the environmental space concept (Spangenberg 1995; Weterings and Opschoor 1992) provides less biased and more comprehensive information. Furthermore, environmental space combines the definition of a maximum threshold for resource use, derived from carrying capacity analysis, with a socially defined minimum criterion for access to resources as a core element of sustainable development.

On the other hand, monetary valuation of environmental assets and damages and, in some studies, of social achievements as well, is suggested (for an overview, see van Dieren 1995). This can be done within the framework of national accounting systems (Bartelmus 1999) as an attempt to derive an environmentally adjusted gross domestic product (or only partially monetarised in the system of integrated environmental and economic accounting [SEEA]). Other options are to calculate the damage cost in monetary terms, based on a valuation of the damage to humans, goods and the environment, but there are severe difficulties in particular in assessing future damage potentials. The same holds true for avoidance cost calculations, which not only need a comprehensive analysis of the damages caused but also a reliable estimate of the potential cost invoked by avoiding the damage. This is not easy for damages already detectable, and it becomes all the more challenging when future damages as well as future technologies and their respective cost are concerned. Most approaches concentrate on the valuation of environmental damages, with little attention paid to the social impacts.

Another economic approach does not focus on the damages but starts from the notion of capital stocks (Pearce *et al.* 1990). In this approach, the capital stock of the economy (assets, equipment, infrastructure) is called 'man-made capital', the stock of environmental resources (sometimes extended to functions such as the atmospheric sink capacity for carbon dioxide [$CO_2$]) constitutes 'natural capital', and the personal skills of people are termed 'human capital'. Few studies recognise the value of institutions, i.e. interpersonal structures such as norms, laws and organisations (the social capital) for sustainability as well as for the economic process (World Bank 1997).

According to economic theory, non-declining capital stocks can provide a long-term reliable income. Consequently, a sustainable income can be achieved by not depleting the stock, which implies limits to the maximum extraction of resources from the stock, called the sustainable yield. Furthermore, regular investment is needed to compensate for the depreciation of capital stocks. In this approach sustainability could be defined as a state of non-declining stocks of capitals.

A controversy shaping much of the economic debate has arisen over the question whether in this definition each capital stock has to be maintained independently (strong sustainability) or whether the sum of all capital stocks has to be at least constant (weak sustainability). In other words: in the former case, a constant or growing stock of natural capital would be a minimum condition for sustainable development, whereas in the latter case material goods, savings or education could compensate for a diminishing stock of natural capital (Pearce and Turner 1991).

On the one hand, this economic view is enlightening because it makes clear that:

- The preservation of social and environmental assets is an economic necessity.

- The productivity of using manpower and natural resources is one key factor of sustainable income generation.

● Part of the revenues gained throughout the production process must be reinvested in all four capital stocks.

On the other hand, the notion of 'capital stocks' comes with a number of economic concepts attached to it (Hinterberger *et al.* 1997). In particular, if the capital stock is considered quantifiable in monetary terms, there can be no limits to substituting one form of capital with another. Consequently, scarcities are considered to be relative not absolute (unlike those foreseen by the more 'physical' approaches of researchers from Malthus to Meadows), a perception that makes little sense in any non-economic perspective (Ehrlich *et al.* 1999). Since these problems play only a minor role in ecological, sociological and political sciences, they seem to be more characteristic of the challenge that sustainability poses to economics by integrating non-market goods and services and placing them on an equal footing than of the economic challenges of sustainable development (Spangenberg and Lorek 2001).

Scientifically, it is obvious that to a certain degree substitution of resources is a common process in the co-evolution of species and their ecological niches; however, there are a number of essential resources (water, minerals, etc.) that cannot be substituted, i.e. replaced by a different but functionally equivalent item. The different compartments of ecological systems do not have a common denominator that would permit substitution, nor do human ingenuity, social cohesion, economic productivity and environmental resilience. Furthermore, from an ecological point of view it is quite obvious that it is not the stock of resources but the functioning of the ecosystem (i.e. its resilience and viability) that needs to be sustained. Given the character of ecosystems as dynamic, non-linear systems (which is true for social and economic systems as well) the predictability of system behaviour is limited not only because of the current lack of knowledge but also for fundamental reasons. An approach following the precautionary principle is thus called for, including a sound scepticism regarding future contributions of technological progress: such contributions will be significant and crucial for sustainable development but will certainly not solve all sustainability problems, environmental or social.

Investment in social, human and natural capital cannot be seen as monetary investment as it is for man-made capital; the very nature and composition of these types of capital requires other 'currencies' of investment (Spangenberg 2001a). For all capital stocks patterns of consumption must be developed by which their sustainable use and self-reproduction become mutually reinforcing processes instead of producing deadlocks. Together with the precautionary principle this forces one to rethink the current orientation towards the use of natural and human resources: the goal must not be to determine these resources precisely (which is not possible) and then to exploit the resources up to the limit, but to stay clear of the limits as much as possible, to maximise and not minimise the safety margin.

A mixed approach attempting to integrate social, economic and environmental criteria is the calculation of (disputable) quantitative welfare indices such as the index of sustainable economic welfare (Daly and Cobb 1990; Jackson and Marks 1994), the genuine savings index (World Bank 1995) or the human development index (HDI; UNDP

1994). Here, the relevance of the elements included is disputed from the economic, the social and the environmental point of view, as are the methodologies of aggregation.

Although these indices do not refer to the capital stock approach, most of them are also dependent on monetary valuation of environmental and social services in order to be able to aggregate them. This causes a number of problems, in particular regarding the value of essential resources, goods and services not traded in the market and the resulting impression of unlimited substitutability. Like capital stock accounting they are well suited for demonstrating the importance of non-economic factors for the economy but they have significant weaknesses when it comes to their core intention: quantifying sustainability.

Given the inherent weaknesses of all single-disciplinary approaches, a definition based on systems science is suggested here that allows one to accommodate a variety of different measures from different disciplines of science and humanities.

## 1.2.3 The concept and its limits

The basic theme of sustainability is to maintain functioning systems in the long run, to avoid irreversible damages and to leave to future generations the choice of how they wish to use their heritage to provide the kind of quality of life they prefer. This not only refers to the natural systems underlying all industrial economies but also to social, economic and, in particular, institutional systems (see below). The concept of quality of life is based on, but not restricted to, a certain standard of living. It includes non-monetary values such as a healthy environment, equal opportunities and the level of social cohesion of society. Furthermore, standard of living is determined not only by monetary income but also by all kinds of goods and services—purchased, donated and self-made, individually or collectively—that humans take advantage of in their everyday lives. Sustainability in this sense can be understood as consisting of four dimensions (UNCSD 1996), as visualised by the prism of sustainability (Fig. 1.2).

The environmental dimension is quite clearly defined to be the sum of all bio-geological processes and the elements involved in them. It demands preservation of the viability of ecological systems as the natural base sustaining human civilisation.

The social dimension consists of the personal assets of individuals, their experiences, dedication and resulting behaviour. It calls for human development, for improved health standards and skills, for the absence of poverty and misery.

Institutions contain the explicit and implicit rules of societal decision-making and the means (organisations, mechanisms) of implementing these rules. Thus the institutional dimension includes political organisations and civil society groups as well as the legal and administrative system, traditions and basic social orientations such as democracy. From a sustainability perspective, a maximum of participation, equal opportunities with no social, ethnic or gender-based discrimination, equity in the justice system, a not overly corrupt administration and so on are desirable.

The economic dimension is singled out as one specific subsystem of society because of its inherent characteristics such as its logic of economic efficiency, short time-frames and its perception of human beings as profit-maximising individuals. Sustainability calls

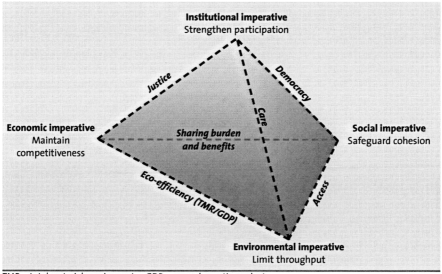

TMR = total material requirement    GDP = gross domestic product

*Figure* 1.2  **The prism of sustainability**

for an economic system that meets the needs of its 'customers', provides enough jobs and is able to rejuvenate itself in order to provide these services in the long run. To meet these demands, the competitiveness of the economic system must be part of the sustainability concept. This analysis should not be understood, however, as denoting the permanent interactions of the economic, social, institutional and environmental dimension of all human activities.

In this sense, the search for a sustainable society can be understood as a multi-criteria optimisation process in a complex system consisting of four dimensions of sustainability. As is well known from systems analysis, only in exceptional cases do such processes have one, clear-cut solution. The usual result is a range of options depending on the weights attributed to the different goals and the balancing mechanisms taken into account. Consequently, there cannot be a standard model of a sustainable future, but necessarily political choices have to be made on which way to go based on the preferences dominant in the respective society. Put differently, sustainability delivers no ready-made vision of how the world should be; rather, it helps in defining targets by providing criteria based on a diversity of goals. There can be no such thing as a blueprint of a sustainable society. This understanding of sustainable development contradicts the monetary approach that is based on cost as the sole criterion for determining one optimal solution.

Sustainability criteria are effective in detecting unsustainable trends and effects, thus identifying unsustainable policy approaches (e.g. policies increasing resource use or societal disparities). For ecodesign this is a challenge: criteria can be helpful, but the responsibility of designers, producers and consumers is not contested. There is not one sustainable lifestyle or consumption pattern, but myriads of them, as different as people's individual preferences.

# 1.3  What is sustainable production and consumption?

Consumption is not a well-defined concept but is a term used with a variety of meanings (Lorek and Spangenberg 2001; Princen 1999). In the widest possible sense the concept of consumption is considered as characterising the total amount of resources extracted from the environment. These resources are used partly for economic purposes, but the larger share is immediately disposed of as waste and waste-water (the 'ecological rucksack' of any product). Since these flows are also environmentally relevant they are included when the total throughput of the economy (the total material requirement [TMR]) is calculated. Production, then, is the process of transforming the resources not immediately disposed into useful goods and services, and waste. Seen this way, all environmental issues are production and consumption issues.

## 1.3.1  *Measures of consumption*

The most widely spread definition of consumption is based on the economic under-standing that all products are produced to meet the demands of consumers. It is formalised in the system of national accounts, which defines household consumption, state consumption, intermediate use and storage and exports as fields of final demand. In this system, all valuables are accounted for and resource consumption is attributed to the final user, whose demand stimulated the production. From this perspective, the economic process can be characterised as a turbulent but linear flow of physical resources from extraction via production to private consumption (including exports), followed by a few recycling loops before the final stage of waste deposition is reached. These physical flows are complemented by cyclical monetary flows from the employer to the employee, who spends that money as a consumer, thus channelling the money back to the producer who again uses it for new production. As intermediate business consumption and storage supply future production, and as state consumption is needed to produce services that in the end are consumed by individual citizens (security, education, medical treatment, etc.), from this point of view all consumption except for the trade balance can be allocated to consumers. Interestingly the theoretical basis behind this standard economic approach is that of demand-driven economic development, exactly the opposite of the dominant supply side-oriented beliefs and politics.

Obviously, although this methodology can be helpful to provide an understanding of the volume, structure and direction of the flows through different economies, it does not give any product-specific information.[2] At least in principle, for all goods and services consumed an impact assessment over their entire life-cycle would be needed to produce full information on the impact of consumption. However, as a complete life-cycle assessment is too complex, time-consuming and expensive, in particular for small and

---

2   Another frequently used approach is to assess the household inventory of equipment without taking the resource consumption caused by the use of the machinery into account (Cogoy 1999). This approach is product-specific, but it tends to underestimate the environmental impact of households because the monetary and physical running costs are neglected. In some cases, however, it can overestimate their role by not taking into account the limits of choice caused by the lack of alternatives.

medium-sized businesses, simplifications have been developed and tested. These offer what is to some degree a 'quick and dirty' methodology but it still provides a life-cycle assessment of the main environmental impacts (Fussler with James 1996; Spangenberg and Kuhndt 1996).

None of these methodologies is able to identify the relevant actors and their respective influence, a key precondition for developing effective policy measures and management tools. This is the objective of another approach to consumption: from an actor-based perspective (Cogoy 1999) it asks who can influence the monetary and thus the physical flow of resources. In this view, consumption is a micro-level activity consisting of two components: commercial activities (resource consumption by business, for raw materials as well as for intermediate products) and household activities. To some degree these compete with each other (food cooked at home compared with that produced at a restaurant; neighbourhood collaboration in place of commercial services; and so on), but mainly they overlap ('missed work'; Hildebrandt 1999). Consumer preferences, including those for certain product designs, shape what households consume, but they have only limited influence on the process design (i.e. on how sustainably goods and services have been produced). Although there is still some demand-side influence on the composition and production process of consumer products (e.g. by boycotting textiles that have been produced by children), this is not the case for intermediate goods (e.g. enzymes used in food production may be produced by genetically modified organisms) and even less for investment goods. The same is true for state services such as defence or education.

Whereas business and state shape the supply side of the economy, consumer preferences determine the demand; for a transformation towards sustainable consumption, both sectors have to change. However, the mechanisms shaping the supply side are quite different from those on the demand side, and so are the means to influence them. The role of design is vital to both spheres, but very different in each.

Given the highly differentiated patterns of influence in different markets, regions, price segments, etc. and the overlapping domains of influence without any clear dominance structure, no quantitative estimates of the impact per actor can be produced on a sound scientific basis. Nonetheless, options available to each actor and their respective effects can be elaborated (Lorek and Spangenberg 2001).

## 1.3.2 Business and state consumption

The environmental challenge for the production system is easy to define: if it is agreed that Western societies are already close to the limits of nature's carrying capacity (on either side of the limits), following the precautionary principle industrial economies should reduce the total throughput of resources. The main social sustainability goals, given the urgent concern about high levels of unemployment and poverty in many parts of the world, are employment generation and income distribution.

On the micro level, the main driving force of business is the motive of maintaining and increasing market shares and of maximising profits; at least in theory, share values should reflect the prospects regarding future profits. Competition is then either about providing better products and services at competitive prices (quality competition) or about offering equivalent products at lower prices (cost competition). Whereas for companies following a cost competition strategy—often the last resort of 'dinosaur' industries with no options for quality improvements available—sustainability is economically attractive only if a sustainable mode of production is cheaper than a non-sustainable one, the situation is different in the case of quality competition. Here, not only can the use characteristics of the final product be optimised (e.g. through better resource efficiency of production equipment and through gender sensitivity in the consulting provided) but also an environmentally or socially friendly way of production can be part of a corporation's identity and marketing strategy. Thus products and processes need to be designed according to three main criteria to succeed in quality competition: added value, customer demand and, last but not least, cost. As long as customers appreciate sustainable production and consider this an added value, even (modest) cost increases can be justified for sustainably produced goods and services. Cost increases are held in check by savings from increased resource efficiency and higher motivation resulting in higher productivity of the labour force. This way, conscious management and consumer preferences can be mutually supportive along the production chain (Fussler with James 1996; WBCSD 1999).

Intelligent marketing, product and process design, engineering and social as well as technical innovations are the main tools to implement such strategies, but these are always restricted by cost concerns. These tools provide standards to measure against in cases of competition strategies oriented towards cost cutting (strategies which, if applied at the macro level, are comparably less successful in providing jobs, income and relief for the environment; see HBS 2000). Eco-efficient design can be supported by such cost-cutting strategies, but only if the cost of investment to increase resource productivity are overcompensated by cost savings in the short run (i.e. if the return on eco-efficiency investment is higher than for other investments, including at the stock account). Thus the relative prices of resources, labour and money play a crucial role in determining the investment strategy, and sustainable development can be stimulated by getting the prices right (i.e. by making the 'prices tell the environmental truth'; see von Weizsäcker 1994) by increasing resource prices to make them reflect the true social and environmental cost that they cause. The most prominent instrument supporting this objective is eco-tax, but other charges or tradable permits are tools to achieve the same end.

Once these instruments are in place, normal market processes should increase the affordability and/or the attractiveness of new, innovative solutions and foster their implementation. If the costs incurred are high, sufficiently broad and predictable in the long run the resulting processes of efficiency increase and resource substitution will initiate a modernisation of the capital stock that will offer significant opportunities for redesigning products and processes.

### 1.3.3 Household consumption

The situation is more complex for household-based activities that constitute the demand side of consumption. They consist mainly of buying goods and services from the market, but include non-market productive activities such as gardening, cost-free neighbourhood co-operation and do-it-yourself work.

Environmentally relevant consumption patterns can be identified by assessing the life-cycle energy and material flows activated by final demand (including consumption of public services by households) based on the national accounting mechanism. Household consumption can then be disaggregated into ten consumption clusters that cover more than 95% of the total impact (see Table 1.1). An analysis of their respective resource consumption identifies the most environmentally relevant clusters.

| Consumption clusters | Can be influenced by private households | Is environmentally relevant |
|---|:---:|:---:|
| Clothing | ✓ | |
| Education/training | | ✓ |
| Food | ✓ | ✓ |
| Healthcare | | ✓ |
| Construction/housing | ✓ | ✓ |
| Hygiene | ✓ | |
| Cleaning | ✓ | |
| Recreation | ✓ | |
| Social life | | ✓ |
| Transport | ✓ | ✓ |

*Table 1.1* **Where households can make a difference**

However, not all of these are equally subject to influence by consumer decisions. In the health sector, for example, the products and services are consumed by households and individuals which have little influence on the type, quality or eco-efficiency of the services offered. Three such clusters can be identified that consist primarily of state consumption: healthcare, education and training and social life. Since households as customers have only limited influence on the frequency of consumption of these services and hardly any on the resource consumption per service provided, these clusters cannot be considered priorities for consumer action, regardless of their undisputed environmental significance. These sectors are not open to the 'demand pull' of consumer preferences; they can only be influenced by 'push measures' such as eco-taxation, public planning or legal standards.

Clusters of prior environmental importance as fields of household decision-making are those that are both environmentally relevant and accessible to significant influence by consumer choice. Three clusters can be identified that meet this condition: construction and housing, food, and transport. Their total resource requirement adds up to about 70% of total material extraction, energy consumption and land use in Continental European economies such as Germany. Each of these clusters represents more than 15% of total energy and material consumption. It is these fields where the ecodesign of consumer products can have the most significant impacts.

The remaining four clusters (hygiene, clothing, cleaning and recreation [without transport]) that can be influenced by households actually account for—if measured in detail—less than 5% of total resource consumption each (Lorek and Spangenberg 2001). Consequently, these sectors can be considered as environmentally secondary, although they include products of high symbolic or emotional value such as recycled paper or second-hand clothing.

Unfortunately, the sustainability of household consumption beyond the environmental dimension has gained much less attention. Given the broad definition of sustainability suggested in Section 1.2.1, participatory decision-making in consumption decisions, a fair sharing of tasks between men and women, affordable supply of goods and services necessary for a dignified life and internationally fair prices are other aspects of sustainable consumption that pose additional challenges to decision-makers as well as to designers. Although economic growth cannot be an end in itself, it may be a necessary means to achieve these objectives. Therefore criteria are needed to distinguish sustainable from unsustainable patterns of growth.

## 1.3.4 Sustainable growth: minimum benchmarking conditions

Sustainable growth has been stated as a policy goal in the European Union's Maastricht Treaty as well as by national governments and the Organisation for Economic Co-operation and Development (OECD). However, all too often the criteria suggested are that growth should be continuous, steady and non-inflationary—that is, sustained growth with no reference to social and environmental criteria (e.g. see the draft set of integrated OECD sustainability indicators; OECD 1999a, 1999b). Proper criteria would qualify which patterns of growth are sustainable regarding all the dimensions of sustainable development. They would provide benchmarks identifying the minimum growth needed, and the maximum growth affordable, as the following example demonstrates.

If at any given growth rate of the economy the volume of products and services generated from a certain amount of resources grows faster than the economy as a whole, then the total resource consumption is decreasing (an environmental sustainability condition). Only if in a given period of time the resource productivity or eco-efficiency increases faster (or drops slower) than the volume of output is an absolute reduction of resource consumption achieved. This implies that economic growth can only be environmentally sustainable if it is accompanied by resource productivity increases that are higher than the growth rate.

If per capita production grows slower than the economy as a whole, more people will be needed to do the work and thus employment increases. Per capita production depends on the output an employee produces per hour of working time (i.e. the labour productivity) and the average number of hours worked per capita. To generate a growing number of full-time paid jobs, the working time must decrease sufficiently to offset increases in labour productivity unless the increase in hourly labour productivity stays below the growth rate of the economy. The employment effects of shortened weekly working time, early retirement, part-time jobs, etc. are captured here through their effect on the average working time.

Thus a necessary precondition for sustainable growth is that the growth rate is somewhere between the growth of per capita production and resource productivity. This may be termed the *minimum condition of socio-environmental sustainability.*

If the main concern is not employment but income distribution, more equity is achieved if the share of the lower-income segments of the population increases beyond the economic growth rate. The condition for economic growth to be sustainable would then be that economic growth must be below the growth rate of resource productivity, and that the income growth for the poorer segments of society must be above the average (i.e. above the growth rate of the economy). Equivalent benchmarking conditions can be defined for other key problems of sustainable development.

## 1.4 Applying the concept of sustainability

Sustainability and its measures as developed above are macro-level concepts, defining benchmark conditions for business as well as household or community strategies towards sustainable consumption. However, sustainability criteria on the micro level with consumers and companies as actors cannot simply be derived by applying the macro measures to companies. Micro strategy development needs identification of goals that are more specific. As for the macro level, they may be structured as a prism representing the four dimensions of sustainability. Sustainability goals could include reduced resource consumption or eco-efficiency (i.e. declining resource consumption per value added; WBCSD 1999) for the environmental dimension, and competitiveness (i.e. non-declining market shares) for the economic dimension. These aims may be conflicting in terms of reducing resource consumption if a business grows while improving its eco-efficiency: the result may still be growing resource consumption if growth over-compensates efficiency gains. However, if that eco-efficient product substitutes a number of more resource-intensive competing products, the overall effect may be positive again. A strong criterion might be that a new product contributes to reducing the overall resource consumption of its business sector even if it experiences increasing sales. Although some such guidelines can be given, much still depends on a case-by-case assessment. This is also why life-cycle assessment (LCA) in the development phase of new products and services is helpful to find out early on whether or not a product or service has a potential to contribute to sustainability. In order to fully explore such a potential, however, the analysis cannot be restricted to the environmental and economic situation but has to take into account the social and institutional goals and criteria. Given the cost, time and capacity constraints that small and medium-sized enterprises (SMEs) in particular are confronted with, simple but robust measures are needed, such as the corporate human development index (CHDI) for the social dimension (Spangenberg and Bonniot 1998) and the material input per unit of service (MIPS) (Schmidt-Bleek 1994) or the ecological footprint (Wackernagel and Rees 1996) for the environmental dimension.

## 1.4.1 *Sustainability metrics for the micro level*

This section briefly illustrates the application of the basic concepts of sustainability to the micro level and suggests a set of corporate sustainability indicators (for more details see Chapter 9).

### 1.4.1.1 Economic sustainability criteria

As of today, the dominant economic concepts tend to reduce business to profit-maximising and cost-minimising entities by stressing the role of costs in competition. This, however, is exactly the opposite aim of strategic sustainability management, which should proactively identify the environmental and social as well as the economic risks and see the opportunities for new products and markets in the changes induced. Proactive corporate management towards sustainability includes efforts beyond legal compliance and active lobbying for a proper institutional framework supporting the implementation of medium-term to long-term sustainability targets. They should be made explicit as a constitutive element of the corporate identity and translated into annual improvement goals. Consequently, for a company to actively support a move towards sustainability, new management tools are needed that provide the necessary information on the strategic level to keep business operations 'on track' (i.e. corporate sustainable development indicators).

In market economies, economic sustainability is usually defined as a firm's ability to maintain its market share under competition. The core group of indicators for assessing performance according to this narrow definition of economic sustainability consists of liquidity and solvency ratios, profitability ratios and growth ratios. However, the exclusively monetary quantification of flows and stocks at the micro level is not only unable to reflect a firm's level of sustainability but also may lead to a misguiding assessment. So, for example:

- Investments in end-of-pipe technologies are *de facto* embodied resources and therefore represent resource consumption, but they are accounted for as increasing the firm's value by investment.

- Investments aiming at reducing environmental impacts at the source of the damages (e.g. by redesign of production processes and/or products) are accounted as costs.

- De-investment processes relating to material goods (such as those affecting means of production) are accounted by firms as a monetary capital deprecia-tion and therefore lead to a monetary depreciation of the material flows embodied in the good, although the amount of flows from the ecosystem remains the same. De-investments are particularly influenced by a short legal depreciation time of means of production and by the possibility of tax deductibility, which plays a major role in determining their real life-span.

Furthermore, preservation of available human and social capital as represented in Figure 1.3 obviously also constitutes an element of a firm's sustainability but is not accounted for in the mainstream approach.

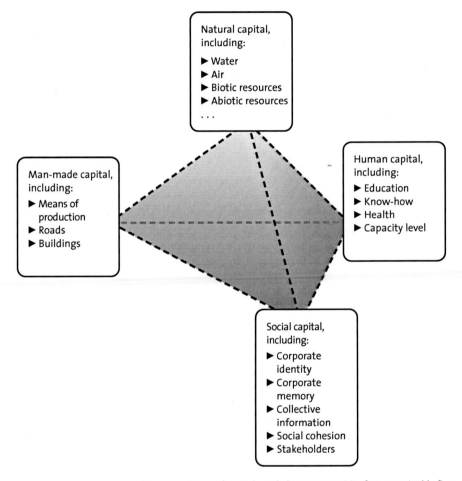

*Figure* 1.3 **Types of capital needed as a prerequisite for a sustainable firm**

### 1.4.1.2 Environmental sustainability criteria

So far, no standard corporate ecological indicators exist.[3] However, a number of promising attempts to measure sustainable development have been presented (e.g. in the work of the World Business Council for Sustainable Development [WBCSD] and its

---

3 The European Union Eco-management and Audit Scheme (EMAS) or standards such as the ISO 9000 and 14000 series provide only reporting frameworks.

member firms on systems of eco-efficiency indicators, efforts in environmental bench-marking, ranking and social indicators development). Furthermore, a multitude of companies' own indicators have been developed, either as management tools to monitor the compliance with environmental legislation norms and standards or as communi-cation tools for environmental reporting and public relations.

Besides these, indicators of material consumption are generally used by firms for cost evaluation (e.g. regarding water consumption, energy consumption, material consump-tion and waste generation). Since derived for a financial purpose, only the total amount of natural resources bought is reported as being important. The use of free goods such as air is not taken into account, and even less so the total amount of materials activated by a certain production process (the ecological rucksack). If these were included, a comparison between material input used for production of a firm with the average of its sector could give a first impression of its relative environmental performance.

The material intensity (Schmidt-Bleek *et al.* 1998) can be calculated as tonnes of material input per tonne of product, or per service generated (MIPS). In a similar way, indicators can be calculated for the intensity of energy or land use or, as an important socio-environmental disturbance indicator, transport intensity. The lower these intensi-ties, the better the (environmental) sustainability performance of the respective com-pany. Thus any attempt to operationalise macro-level resource use reduction by demanding firms to curb growth may turn out to be counterproductive: those firms winning growing market shares for products with a particularly high resource efficiency as compared with their competitors are actively contributing to the overall resource efficiency of a national economy. The absolute capping of resource consumption can only be enacted on the national level, enforcing competition on the access to scarce resources and providing a first-mover benefit to the leading companies, resulting in a competitive advantage.

Together with a firm's resource efficiency, the existence of a means to safeguard the allo-cative efficiency of the economy has to be assessed. For example, a clear regulatory frame-work is needed, without loopholes, with undisturbed, non-monopolised markets and with prices that to some degree reintroduce the externalities into economic decision-making.

### 1.4.1.3 Economic productivity of resource use

In order to assess not only the efficiency level of resource use but also the correlated income creation, the returns per material input expressed as returns in monetary units per material input in tonnes, along a firm's value chain, is a valuable indicator. It can be used for comparisons between different production processes for functionally equiva-lent goods or services in terms of their respective economic attractiveness for a company.

### 1.4.1.4 Resource productivity of investment

For firms willing to invest in reducing resource consumption, this indicator measures the effectiveness in financial terms of the steps planned. It is expressed by material input savings in tonnes per investment in monetary units. The indicator can also be used as a tool for investment choice between several options to reduce resource consumption.

### 1.4.1.5 Social and institutional sustainability

As at the macro level, improving social sustainability at the firm level requires simultaneous improvement of social and human capital (see Fig. 1.3). The maintenance and development of human capital is concerned with the knowledge and experience of individuals. Social capital refers to the institutional interaction between individuals on all levels of a company, a process that constitutes the social system known as a 'firm' and which determines its coherence. Corporate human capital and social capital are strongly dependent on each other, for instance in innovation processes (CPE 1986; Gaffard 1990: 325-82; HBS 2000). For this reason, human capital development cannot be de-linked from organisational and institutional aspects. Both the social dimension and the institutional dimension are at least to some degree captured in the corporate human development index (CHDI; see Section 1.4.2).

Furthermore, social sustainability cannot be thought of as independent of culture and history (van Dieren 1995: 121). Cultural identity, ethical codes and the working atmosphere are constitutive parts of the social sustainability of each company, but they are dependent on factors outside the companies' own reach. Consequently, dealing with social capital of the firm requires one to take into account processes on the meso level. With regard to company–society relations, it should be emphasised that staying in touch with stakeholders is a *conditio sine qua non* for a firm to maintain the legitimisation of its existence, understood as a tacit or explicit acceptance of a firm and its business practices by the society at large (i.e. by consumers, employees, credit institutes, trade unions, etc.).

## 1.4.2 *The corporate human development index (CHDI)*

Although corporate social capital and human capital are extremely helpful concepts to understand the driving forces behind a company's success, they are hardly quantifiable— the same problems apply as on the macro level. In order to provide at least a certain degree of measurability regarding a firm's progress towards sustainability, the corporate human development index (CHDI) has been proposed (Spangenberg and Bonniot 1998). It is based on and inspired by the criteria the United Nations Development Programme (UNDP) has developed for the quantitative assessment of the human development of nation-states as reflected in the human development index (HDI). Adding to the information for shareholders, this index intends to inform stakeholders about the attitudes of a company and its behaviour towards staff members.

The three main components of the HDI are longevity, knowledge and material standard of living. Their micro equivalents might be:

- Quality of industrial relations and labour conditions, measured in terms of
    - Personnel rotation (fluctuation of the personnel, average duration of employment) and average duration of a contract; these act as indicators of the reliability of employment from the employees' perspective; personnel rotation also measures corporate memory
    - Amount of regular work hours annually lost as a consequence of labour conditions (i.e. accidents, job-induced diseases, early retirements, and so on)

- Education (input and maintenance of human capital), measured as
    - The quantity of 'embodied education' brought into a firm by the employees ('purchased' human capital), measured by the average duration of school, university or other educational enrolment among employees
    - The level of consideration of the maintenance or improvement of human capital; this is expressed as the average number of hours invested in education and skills training per year and per capita (e.g. through provision of in-house seminars and workshops, external training and educational holidays including personality development other than training for the job)

- Income level and distribution
    - The income level is best judged by expressing the minimum income paid by the company as a multiple of the national social aid standard; income represents here the sum of all monetary contributions during a year.
    - To represent income distribution within a firm, a figure could be reported representing the relative size of the income of the chief executive officer or board member as compared with the average shop-floor worker.

As for the HDI, there could be adjusted versions and amendments. One obvious adjustment, again based on the HDI, would be a gender-adjusted CHDI, taking into account income inequities as well as female representation in top decision-making positions. The educational indicators might be improved by developing a measure of how a firm's organisation influences learning (e.g. through structures allowing exchange of experiences). This would reflect the need for a company to be a 'learning organisation' as a precondition for long-term competitiveness as well as for the successful management of the transition towards sustainability.

The CHDI as proposed here, combined with eco-efficiency measures and economic indicators, provides a coherent approach to a comprehensive set of indicators that link business performance on sustainability to the overall performance of a country (see Fig. 1.4). However, the CHDI does not cover all aspects of corporate sustainability. For instance, in the institutional dimension more participation has been a key goal at the macro level. On the company level this would spell co-decision, shareholding by employees and other participatory elements. This and other indicators could be added to the CHDI if considered necessary.

# 1.5 Supporters, opponents and the role of ecodesign

## 1.5.1 Supporters and opponents

It must be considered that there is nothing more difficult to carry out, nor more doubtful of success, nor more dangerous to handle than to initiate a new order of things. For the reformer has enemies in all those who profit by the old order,

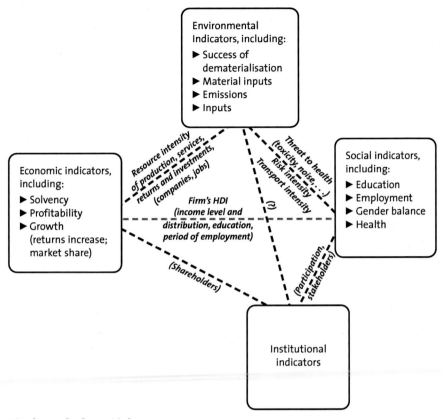

HDI = human development index

*Figure* 1.4 **A comprehensive system of sustainability indicators for the micro level**

and only lukewarm defenders in all those who would profit by the new order, this lukewarmness arising partly from fear of their adversaries, who have the laws in their favour; and partly from the incredulity of mankind, who do not truly believe in anything new until they have had actual experience of it (N. Machiavelli 1513: ch. VI).

When the winds of change start to blow, some people begin to build wind-breakers, but others build windmills (public wisdom).

Sustainability is a multifaceted concept, and so are its supporters multifaceted. For environmental reasons, national and international non-governmental organisations (NGOs) have engaged in support of sustainability strategies, although others have rejected the concept as not radical enough. In particular, organisations from the South have aired concerns that sustainability could be just another attempt to shift the burden from the North to the South and to deny the developing world the benefits of future economic growth (ELCI 1997).

Regarding the social dimension, trade unions, churches and social development groups would be expected to support this aspect of sustainable development enthusiastically. However, whereas for a number of actors this is exactly the case, many have not yet realised how the concept of sustainable development could strengthen their point by integrating it into a broader framework. Instead they either perceive sustainability as an environmental issue with no links to their case or they are afraid their specific goals could be watered down and lose focus by this integration. Also, in particular for trade unions, some trade-offs between environment, growth and employment do exist, as illustrated by the minimum condition of socio-environmental sustainability mentioned in Section 1.4.1.2.

A similar situation is evident in significant parts of the business sector: although many companies, multinational corporations and SMEs could be winners in the socio-environmental modernisation process, for the time being most of them see the threats, not the opportunities. Part of the problem may be the predominant neglect of the social dimension and the complete neglect of the institutional dimension as driving forces for innovation processes.

A serious conflict arises where ideological questions are concerned. Proponents of the neoliberal theory expect that with increasing wealth the pressure on the environment will automatically be diminished and thus that unrestricted economic growth is the most efficient way to solve all kinds environmental problems (this is termed the Environmental Kuznets Hypothesis). This is not only in contradiction with the sustainability benchmarks discussed in Section 1.3.4, it has also been shown that the empirical basis claimed is more a methodological artefact than a trend that could provide solid ground for policy development (for further references, see Spangenberg 2001b). So far, economic growth has been more or less closely correlated with increasing resource consumption (Adriaanse et al. 1997) and as a result the consumption patterns of the rich are significantly more resource-intensive than those of the poor (Spangenberg and Lorek 1999). Nonetheless, it can be expected that this kind of argument will find its way into the political debate. Sound or not, it serves the interests of those who want to get rid of any kind of environmental policy, either because they would be losers in the environmental modernisation process or because they have not yet realised how they could become winners. Even potential winners are held back by the inertia of individuals and institutions, making any reform approach (also towards sustainability) a challenge to implement, even if it is beneficial for the vast majority of actors (a phenomenon noticed earlier by Machiavelli).

The emphasis on social and institutional aspects embodied in the concept of sustainable development provokes the resistance of those who see the world only in economic terms, trusting in the 'invisible hand' of the market (but ignoring the problems of those who feel its elbow).

## 1.5.2 *Some key strategies and the role of ecodesign*

In recent research projects a number of different sustainability strategies have been compared to identify what might be their common core. Although highly differentiated when it comes to the practical details of implementation, five fields could be identified that are common to all these approaches on the macro level (HBS 2000). None of them represents a need for completely new policy approaches, but all of them call for strengthening some and reducing other incentives and institutions. This should result in a political framework that does not hamper the innovative capacities of markets driving permanent structural change but should give that change a preferred direction towards sustainable development. The following five items are required:

- Environmental incentives (e.g. green fiscal reform and subsidy reform, environmentally motivated investment programmes) to direct the market towards eco-efficiency

- Regulations and institutions for social security (such as basic social security provisions or basic income and social infrastructure) to improve on the institutional dimension, including gender equity

- Innovation through increased expenditure on research and education, life-long learning, greater participation in planning and decision-making and provision of more time for innovative processes

- Changes to working hours, reductions in labour time and provision for an appropriate degree of flexibility, taking into account the preferences of the labour force

- Changes to consumption patterns, in particular by making sustainable goods and services economically more attractive, providing socially and environmentally sound alternatives, providing information through education, advertisements and mandatory product labelling, etc.

A strategy comprising these elements will significantly enhance labour and resource productivity (eco-efficiency) and thus sustainable economic growth while reducing resource consumption.

Ecodesign can contribute to most of these goals, be it in terms of promoting eco-efficiency and resource productivity or in terms of the production of environmentally and socially sound attractive goods and services (ecodesign should also read as 'economically viable design'). It can help to modify consumption patterns, as with a changing fiscal framework ecodesigned products will probably be cheaper than conventional ones: markets and production volume will soar, and businesses now reluctant will hasten to buy into the concept.

Obviously, any such development is dependent on political efforts to correct the economic framework. With this condition given, ecodesign is the main tool for exploiting the new possibilities resulting from changed framework conditions; without it, ecodesign can only use the limited room for manoeuvring within the given cost structure and the business and marketing strategies based on it. Any suggestion from ecodesigners to improve the product performance according to sustainability criteria will only be fruitful if the change either reduces the total cost (that is why eco-taxes are so important) or is considered as an added value consumers are ready to pay for (this is why consumer preferences are so important).

These concerns refer to changing product design (e.g. to achieve reduced resource consumption over the life-cycle). The even more challenging task is to realise that products shape the patterns of their use, and ecodesign should try to make use of that fact. User- and maintenance-friendliness, 'upgradability', etc. are just some of the catchwords that will be elaborated in other chapters of this volume.

Going even one step further, it is not only use patterns that count but also the institutional framework shaping individual behaviour (VROM 1995). Ambitious eco-designers should thus focus not only on good products and services but also on systems design. However, such a focus would go significantly beyond their current education and training and would require additional skills and intensive collaboration with other professions involved. So far, the complexity of the task is obvious, but no clear pattern of sharing tasks has emerged.

## 1.6 Outlook

It is remarkable that the need for more transparency, better public accountability and more public understanding is discussed in a number of social and natural sciences at the same time. Physical, engineering and juridical experts, just like people in the design professions, are discussing how to provide more openness and become 'fit for the future' (i.e. sustainable). Similar developments seemed to emerge in (small) parts of the economic community after the 'Seattle Shock' of NGOs and third world countries bringing down attempts to initiate a new round of the World Trade Organisation, as well as in parts of biosciences suffering from public resistance. Although no organised communication process exists between these processes so far, they may have to come together to bridge the gap between expert system developments and the public at large (Giddens 1996).

These parallel discussions seem to indicate a common problem: citizens no longer believe unquestioningly in experts, but they are helpless without them when confronted with the complexity of decisions to be taken. Here, the common discussion of disciplines could contribute to the development of new participatory approaches of 'post-normal' (Funtowicz and Ravetz 1993) science. This includes the co-operation of different scientific disciplines and the involvement of non-scientific knowledge (e.g. from citizens' groups or representatives from civil society institutions) from the phase of problem definition (i.e. the development of questions to be asked) to the final result.

Such an approach is particularly needed when it comes to a concept as multifaceted as sustainability. Designing for sustainability thus requires a broader perspective, broader collaboration and new skills as compared with traditional design concepts. These qualifications and knowledge must be the result of the interaction of a variety of sectors. This is true for the eco-efficient design of intermediary products and services in the business sector and is even more so regarding consumer demands. The ultimate demand for such new approaches, however, results from the imperative that ecodesign should contribute to problem-solving ('meeting the needs of the present without compromising the ability of future generations to meet their own needs'). This calls for innovative solutions, including social, institutional and technical innovations instead of incremental improvements based on existing technologies. A technology fix is certainly not sustainable.

Since it is not clear which discipline will take what stance (is the input of a synthetic sociologist, an institutions engineer or a communication process designer more appropriate?), designers should evaluate where their strengths lie. If identifying the patterns of consumer preference and perception and the shaping of goods and services to make them 'digestible' to citizens are some key qualifications, designers might have a key role to play. This would include not only the shaping of products and services but also communicating sustainability demands to the business sector, engineers and investors. Thus designers would act as a translator between disciplines, as the spider weaving the sustainability web. To do this effectively, however, would also require that the other actors take the contribution of designers serious enough to accept them in this role of increased importance.

Obviously, there is no consensus about what sustainability really is. However, the vagueness of the concept is one of its strengths and offers room for creativity, fantasy and innovation. Companies should not hesitate to grasp the opportunity.

**2**

# REWIRING GLOBAL CONSUMPTION
## Strategies for transformation*

*Nick Robins*
Henderson Global Investors, UK

*Bas de Leeuw*
Ministry of Housing, Spatial Planning
and the Environment, Netherlands; United
Nations Environment Programme, France

## 2.1 The consumption explosion

Almost 40 years ago at the height of the post-war economic boom, Vance Packard sounded perhaps the first warning note about the downside to the modern consumer society. In *The Waste Makers*, Packard argued that the USA had become 'a force-fed society with a vested interest in prodigality and with no end in sight to the need for ever-greater and wasteful consumption' (1960: 173). Coining the phrases 'planned obsolescence' and the 'throw-away society', Packard pointed to the serious social, economic and environmental consequences of an unchecked expansion in consumption. At the time, few paid attention to his critique. But now, 40 years on, the need to make consumption patterns sustainable has risen to the top of the global environment and development agenda.

The reasons for this turnaround are clear. The scale of global consumption has expanded dramatically, growing as much as fourfold since 1960, reaching US$24 trillion in 1998. However, this consumption explosion has put unprecedented burdens on the environment, leading Norway's former premier, Gro Harlem Brundtland, to conclude in 1994 that

> it is simply impossible for the world as a whole to sustain a Western level of consumption for all. In fact, if 7 billion people were to consume as much energy and resources as we do in the West today we would need 10 worlds, not one, to satisfy all our needs.

\* The authors wrote this chapter in their personal capacity and it does not necessarily reflect the opinions of Henderson Global Investors, the Dutch government or UNEP.

But not only are today's dominant consumption patterns unsustainable, they are also highly inequitable. The world's richest countries make up only a fifth of global population, but account for 45% of all meat consumption, 58% of total energy use, 84% of paper use and 87% of vehicle ownership. At the other end of the spectrum, the poorest fifth of the world's population—more than one billion people—still lack food, shelter, housing, water and sanitation and access to electricity (UNDP 1998). To be sustainable, global patterns of consumption will not only need to be decoupled from material and energy consumption, but will also need to be more focused on achieving a high quality of life for all, particularly for the world's poor.

After a decade of dialogue and dispute, sustainable consumption has now arrived as a global policy priority. The Agenda 21 agreed at the 1992 Earth Summit laid out the first internationally agreed strategy for 'changing consumption patterns'. More recently, the United Nations Development Programme (UNDP) has outlined a seven-point agenda for action (see Box 2.1), and the United Nations Environment Programme (UNEP) has established a new sustainable consumption programme. In addition, the Oxford Commission on Sustainable Consumption was launched in early 1999, bringing together a group of 20 international figures to act as a catalyst and facilitator for action by key players and communities to move towards more sustainable patterns of consumption. The need for such co-ordinated efforts to reform consumption became increasingly important during the 1990s as globalisation gathered pace.

1.  Ensure minimum consumption requirements for all
2.  Develop eco-efficient goods and services
3.  Remove perverse subsidies and restructure incentives
4.  Strengthen public action for consumer protection
5.  Strengthen international mechanisms to manage consumption's global impacts
6.  Build strong alliances between consumer, poverty and environment movements
7.  Foster synergies between civil society, the private sector and government

*Box 2.1* **UNDP's seven-point agenda for action**

*Source:* UNDP 1998

## 2.2 Consuming the globe?

Globalisation is starting to blur the traditional distinctions between North and South. A global consumer class is emerging, sharing common lifestyles despite being separated by great distances—and generating similar environmental impacts (Barnet and Cavanagh 1994). For Hans-Peter Martin and Harald Schumann (1998: 12),

> [there is] no doubt about it: if humanity had to vote today on a choice of lifestyle, it would know what to do. Uniform pictures on a billion television screens nurture the same longings on the Amur, Yangtse, Amazon, Ganges and Nile.

One estimate suggests that in 1996 the emerging middle class of China, India, Venezuela, Brazil, Argentina, South Korea, Taiwan, Indonesia, Malaysia and Thailand amounted to roughly 750 million people—almost as many as the 880 million consumers in the industrialised countries, not all of whom are affluent (Brandsma 1996). Already the richest fifth of Chileans and Malaysians enjoy higher incomes than the average German or Japanese person (Barnet and Cavanagh 1994). Indeed, East Asians are now 'leaders of postmodern consumerism', renowned for their extravagance in luxury goods and recently prompting the establishment in Korea of a National Campaign against Excessive Consumption (Gong 1999).

In China alone, by 2020 the spread of car ownership could reach levels similar to those currently present in the United Kingdom. This would mean 400 million more cars, doubling global iron ore use and massively increasing landscape destruction, local pollution and greenhouse gas emissions (NCM 1999). Despite the recent shock to living standards in Asia, there is no reason to believe that the upward surge in consumption will not continue in emerging economies over the long term. Meanwhile, the poorest fifth of the world's population continues to be left out of global consumption, with the average African household consuming 20% less than it did 20 years ago.

Given these extremes, today's global pattern of consumption remains structurally skewed in favour of 'private affluence and public squalor', to use the phrase of Packard's contemporary John Kenneth Galbraith (1958). For example, to bring basic healthcare and nutrition to all would cost about US$13 billion a year; more than US$17 billion is spent on pet food in Europe and the USA alone (UNDP 1998). The task ahead, according to Ashok Khosla, president of Development Alternatives in India, is to 'raise the floors, bring down the ceilings and plug the leaks'—in other words, meet the needs of the poor, limit excessive consumption by the rich and ensure all consumption respects environmental limits (quoted in Turaga 1998).

Globalisation and the growing integration of consumption patterns worldwide is therefore creating an unprecedented collective dilemma. As the US writer William Greider (1997: 448) has put it:

> If industrial growth proceeds according to its accepted patterns, everyone is imperilled. Yet, if industrialisation is not allowed to proceed, a majority of the world's citizens are consigned to a permanent second-class status, deprived of the industrial artefacts that enhance life's comfort, the tools that multiply human choices. The world has entered new ground, a place where people have never been before. We will have no choice but to think anew.

The world is faced with a consumption crunch: either both North and South move together—recognising the primary responsibility of the affluent to change—or the global prospect looks bleak.

## 2.3 Re-linking consumption and quality of life

During the 1990s two main approaches to sustainable consumption emerged: eco-efficiency and eco-sufficiency. Eco-efficiency aims to get the same (or more) goods out of less material; eco-sufficiency seeks to get the same welfare out of fewer goods and services (Carley and Spapens 1998). Eco-efficiency has been widely adopted by governments and business as a way of linking environmental improvements with global competitiveness. But there has also been growing recognition of the need for a parallel agenda to address the ways in which consumption enhances or detracts from quality of life.

The transport sector highlights the need for this twin-track approach. A new model of the Ford Ka, for example, produces only 2% of the $NO_x$ (nitrogen oxide) emissions of a 1976 model of the Ford Fiesta (UNCSD 1999). But these qualitative improvements at the micro level have been more than outpaced at the macro level by the volume growth in car use and ownership. According to a recent report by the Nordic Council of Ministers, achievement of the necessary reductions in pollution and material use will require 'considerable changes in individual and social values as well as regulatory regimes' (NCM 1999: 35). This means that policy-makers are now being forced to broaden their gaze beyond technical solutions to encompass the messy and contentious social realm of consumption—and in particular to re-examine the links between consumption and quality of life.

Research has shown that 'there is no consistent relation between national or individual income and happiness'—largely because expectations rise with income whereas satisfaction does not (Carley and Spapens 1998). As Juliet Schor (1998) has shown in the USA, the contemporary 'cycle of work and spend' can bring high social costs, not least in terms of rising consumer debt. Over 80% of Americans believe that they 'buy and consume far more than [they] need' (MFF 1996). Although there is evidence that a growing number of Americans (and some Europeans) are 'downshifting' to simpler and more sustainable lifestyles, many others feel stuck on a treadmill of pressures to conform to ever-rising consumption, largely as a result of inflexible working practices (Ghazi and Jones 1997). Global expenditure on advertising now amounts to US$435 billion per annum and is a powerful force for continued consumption, potentially neutralising the parallel growth in environmental awareness among consumers.

As a result, according to the Organisation for Economic Co-operation and Development (OECD 1997a: 47), central to strategies for sustainable consumption is a new societal conversation on the 'wider vision of welfare in which the satisfaction of needs, rather consumption per se, is the aim'. Leading US thinker Amitai Etzioni (*Financial Times* 2001) has also called for a 'grand dialogue' launched by public leaders to question whether material consumption and economic growth are the right basis for personal fulfilment. Ultimately, these are ethical questions, something that governments in postmodern, pluralistic societies find extremely hard to address; according to a recent report on ethics and consumption (Michaelis 2000), 'modern society is reluctant to impose any one vision of the good life on its citizens'.

Yet there does appear to be a willingness for people to enter into a dialogue to work out lifestyle choices with others, informed by robust information on what works, what doesn't work and why. Indeed, as UNEP executive director Klaus Töpfer has observed, 'it is becoming more and more evident that consumers are increasingly interested in the "world behind" the product they buy: they want to know how and where and by whom the product has been produced'.[1] This is evident in the global campaigns against sweatshops, deforestation and genetic modification, spawning a range of civic and corporate initiatives (such as SA 8000 and the Forest Stewardship Council) to provide citizens with some assurance over the sustainability of what they consume. For Naomi Klein (2000: xviii), who has traced the origins of these protests, 'as more people discover the brand-name secrets of the global logo web, their outrage will fuel the next big political movement, a vast wave of opposition squarely targeting transnational corporations'.

## 2.4 From niche to system

It is now clear that sustainable consumption has grown far beyond the 'green consumer' movement of the late 1980s and early 1990s. Then, the emphasis was on providing eco-products for niche markets serving affluent consumers, supported by modest policy initiatives such as eco-labelling. Now, the focus is more systematic, emphasising the need to

- Make goods and services serve sustainable development: meeting basic needs, improving quality of life, raising efficiency and regenerating the environment

- Reform the underlying patterns of demand, such as market forces, demographics, social and cultural values, technology, regulation and infrastructure

- Use the demand side to lever long-term social, economic and environmental benefits in use and along the product chain

- Influence the purchase, use and disposal choices made by corporations (i.e. in the supply chain) and public authorities, not just the choices made by individual consumers

- Identify innovative political, cultural and market approaches to comprehending and changing complex patterns

Sustainable consumption is thus best seen as a strategic perspective. It seeks to tackle the 'hidden wiring' of demand that ultimately determines the success or failure of micro-level improvements to product design and marketing. The task is to create the conditions that improve the capacity to choose, use and dispose of goods and services sustainably: in other words, to bring alternatives in from the margins and institutionalise them so that there is a fusion of individual choice with equity and sustainability requirements. The issue is now one of strategic design: rewiring the consumption system.

1  United Nations Environment Programme press release, August 1999.

As a result, many of the solutions to unsustainable consumption lie in collective choices. Governments have the primary responsibility for putting in place the framework that shapes consumption choices and have a profound steering role through utility regulation and public expenditure in many critical consumption clusters, such as food, energy, water and transport. This means finding new ways of thinking about consumption and wellbeing, new services to fulfil these needs and new approaches to communicate and inspire change. Given the physical, economic and cultural bottlenecks to change, sustainable consumption will need to become popular and politically attractive. This will mean going beyond the moralistic approach that has dominated many efforts to date. This can appear threatening, implying 'giving up' for the affluent and 'losing out' for the poor. Instead, an emphasis on improving quality of life for all could prove more successful, stressing the value that individuals and institutions can achieve through changes in consumption behaviour. Sustainable consumption has to add up to a lifestyle that people want and that is within their reach—that is, 'low-impact affluence', in the words of Germany's Wuppertal Institute (Sachs *et al.* 1998).

UNEP is tackling this issue of the desire for sustainable consumption on several fronts, including advertising and youth. UNEP is working with the advertising industry to seek its help in defining the sustainable consumption message more clearly and in using communication tools more effectively. The work has also explored responsible business practices within the industry itself (UNEP 1999a). UNEP has also launched a youth programme and is collecting information about consumer trends among young people through global surveys (UNEP 1999b).

## 2.5 Achieving the global shift

What separates today's efforts to achieve sustainable consumption from Vance Packard's proposals for reform in the 1960s is not necessarily any change in the content of what is required. In fact, there is an eerie sense of *déjà vu* reading Packard's five points for more 'enlightened consumption' (see Box 2.2); what has changed dramatically is the arena for action, which has been transformed by globalisation. This does not mean that local and national action is no longer necessary or important; instead it requires four changes in the ways we approach consumption (Robins and Roberts 1998).

1. Restoring pride in prudence, tackling built-in obsolescence
2. Restoring pride in quality, ensuring better product labelling
3. Respecting the eternal balance, protecting the environment
4. Facing the unmet challenges, targeting social needs
5. Achieving an enduring style of life, balancing consumption with values

*Box 2.2* **Developing enlightened consumption patterns**

*Source:* Packard 1960

First, it requires an extension of responsibility in the North. In the global economy, consumers and producers will have to take a far broader view of their responsibility for increasingly distant impacts. Upstream there is already mounting pressure to improve standards along the supply chain; downstream, businesses are increasingly required to take a life-cycle responsibility for the emissions and wastes their products cause. But, at a more strategic level, the post-industrial economies of the North will need to accept responsibility not just for the direct environmental impacts of their consumption patterns but also for the demonstration effect these have on aspirations in emerging economies. Achieving this will require a considerable imaginative leap for consumers, business and policy-makers. A first step would be to focus on the sustainability of the goods and services—and not just on the production processes—of multinational corporations in emerging economies; these multinationals, according to the Third World Network, are 'responsible for most of the world's resource extraction, pollution and generation of consumer culture' (TWN 1997).

Second, 'leapfrogging' in the South is required. In many ways, the South has not yet invested in the physical infrastructure, technological capital, lifestyles and regulations that drive unsustainable consumption in the North. In India, the Tata Energy Research Institute (TERI) has recently assessed the country's environmental performance in the 50 years since independence and has projected future trends. One of its key conclusions is that 'it is vital that we are not locked onto paths that lead to a sub-optimal dependence on a particular technology', such as the automobile (TERI 1998). The issue for developing countries is therefore to take preventative action, to 'leapfrog' over conventional consumption patterns. But to leapfrog you need legs, and many of the developing countries lack the ability in terms of institutions and expertise to analyse the situation, assess their needs and implement strategies to change course (Wijkman 1999). New forms of international co-operation are clearly required to help fill these gaps.

Third, the generation of new cultures of consumption are needed. Linked closely to the leapfrogging imperative for the South is the importance of re-evaluating the role of traditional lifestyles and values in the face of mounting consumption. According to Josefa Bautista, vice-president of the Development Academy of the Philippines, the critical issue is to 'to look back to our ancestors' culture and reinculcate its treasure of sustainable living' (quoted in Carley and Spapens 1998: 54). For TERI in India, market signals can certainly drive home the environmental implications of consumption. But these need to be reinforced through 'an assertion of traditional Indian values. Blind aping of the West will lead us to disaster, environmentally, economically and socially' (TERI 1998). The question is how developing countries can develop hybrid cultures of consumption that combine eco-efficient technologies with traditional ethical approaches to nature and society. For the North, where traditional values of frugality and caring for nature have been more thoroughly replaced by the current consumer culture, the task of reinvention is that much greater. One possible route is to encourage more links between the generations. For example, in the community of Steigen, in the north of Norway, the Local Agenda 21 process has helped to regenerate traditional knowledge about local food and materials by establishing a Generation Café, where older people can share their skills with others.

Last, there is a need to build confidence and trust. Running through the global policy dialogue on sustainable consumption is a sense of deep distrust by the South of the North. Sustainable consumption is seen as a way of denying developing countries the fruits of development and also posing new green protectionist trade barriers against their exports. The industrialised world is also seen to have reneged on the Rio Earth Summit bargain in terms of increasing the volume of financial assistance to support the transition to sustainable development in the South. Given the increasingly global nature of the consumption crisis, practical mechanisms are needed that will help to build up trust between governments, business and civil society internationally. UNEP is organising a series of informal expert meetings across the world and has launched the 'sc.net' forum,[2] and the Oxford Commission is focusing on empowering communities to develop their own action plans for change.

## 2.6 Conclusions

This chapter has attempted to show why the transformation of consumption has to be at the heart of any strategy for sustainable development. The environmental burden from consumption is growing and eco-efficiency improvements at the product level are proving insufficient to cope with volume growth at the macroeconomic level. The role of consumption in delivering quality of life is also being questioned, and globalisation is both highlighting the inequalities in consumption across the world and resulting in high-consuming sectors within many emerging markets.

The sustainable consumption agenda has moved on from the green consumerism of the 1990s and seeks to tackle the 'hidden wiring' of demand which ultimately determines the success or failure of micro-level improvements to product and service design. Many of the solutions to unsustainable consumption lie in collective choices, and the challenge for governments is now to develop new conversations with society to jointly resolve the embedded nature of the problems.

The transformation of consumption is now a global concern and this chapter closes with four priorities for building greater co-operation internationally. First, the affluent industrialised countries need to take an extended sense of responsibility for their consumption patterns, not just for the direct impacts but also for the aspirations and models they generate elsewhere. Second, the South too has an opportunity to take preventative action and 'leapfrog' over conventional consumption patterns. Third, the dominant culture of consumption will need to be re-evaluated, perhaps in the South by drawing on traditional values and in the North by a more thorough reinvention. Last, at the political level, confidence and trust need to be built up through programmes of joint analysis and learning.

Much has been achieved in the global debate on sustainable consumption over the past decade. The need to change consumption—a highly contentious political issue—is

2   www.sustainable-consumption.net

now accepted. Although many problems remain, 'sustainable consumption is only as difficult as we make it', according to one of the participants at the 1998 workshop on 'Consumption in a Sustainable World' in Kabelvåg, adding 'there are many things which could be put into action now—let's do it!' (Robins and Roberts 1998).[3]

# SUSTAINABLE SOLUTIONS IN LESS INDUSTRIALISED COUNTRIES
## The conditions and actors at state and company level for sustainable product design

*Roland Lentz*
**Intercambio, Germany**

Improving the socioeconomic and industrial development of the South and the East is an important pillar in designing a sustainable world. A world that provides sufficient wellbeing for current and future generations while not further compromising its resource base will be a more sustainable world. The so-called 'developing' countries play an important role in establishing more sustainable economies, because:

- 80% of the world population lives in these countries, with a still-dynamic population growth.

- Today, they use only 20% of the world's resources.

- In some regions of these developing countries there are major untouched natural resources which still provide an important balance in natural cycles.

Today, with the globalisation of the international economy we are at a crossroads. The global industrial players are entering 'developing' markets with their products and production technologies. Will infrastructure and production process development in less industrialised countries (LICs) copy the wasteful societies of the North, with a resulting exponential growth of global environmental impacts? Or will those societies take the opportunity of following a different path towards the design of a new sustainable production economy that depends less on limited non-renewable resources and energy and which values the skills of its young people?

Sustainability is a common goal for the 'developed' countries in the North and 'developing' countries in the South and the East and is explored in a range of other chapters in the book (for an overview, see the Introduction). Sustainable development is a goal both for industrialised countries and for LICs; however, there are different development paths to achieve this goal which have to reflect the different socioeconomic potentials, eco-geographies and cultures of individual societies.

In this chapter I will explore the different socioeconomic settings and potential strategies for sustainable product development and design (SPDD) in LICs. LICs in the South and the East face a range of different socioeconomic and eco-geographic conditions so there is no panacea to suggest, but recommendations will be given based on my experiences in some LICs in Latin America. This may act as a useful starting point to identify SPDD tasks and strategies in other LICs.

Environmental management (EM) on a societal level is described as an overall framework for SPDD in LICs. Total quality environmental management (TQEM) is a well-defined management concept and is just one part of EM on a societal level. Therefore, it will only be touched on in this chapter, in the context of discussing stakeholders' needs of EM in a society.

The following sections highlight the particular environmental impacts of an LIC (Section 3.1.1), the different areas of action in a complex socioeconomic system (Section 3.1.2) and identify the actors that should be involved in a management system (Section 3.1.3). Based on work that I conducted in South America (Lentz 1997, 1998) the discussion in Section 3.1.4 focuses on obstacles and opportunities to establish SPDD or broader EM. Environmental legislation as one of the prerequisites of EM and SPDD is discussed, taking Bolivia as an example (Section 3.1.5). Potential strategies for implementation are presented in Section 3.2. Some conclusions are drawn in the final section.

## 3.1 Environmental management as a framework for sustainable product development and design in less industrialised countries

Environmental management (EM) on a state as well as a company level as defined in this text is a precondition for sustainable product development and design (SPDD) because it identifies local and global environmental pressures for LICs that should be given priority and provides opportunities for change. The actors and areas for action should be recognised early on to enable the more efficient allocation of national socioeconomic resources (capital, people, time). A well-organised management process facilitated through co-operation between central government, local authorities, industry associations and non-governmental organisations (NGOs) should be established to address key priorities and opportunities. Hurdles and barriers to the establishment of a new sustainable economy paradigm should be identified early on and tackled proactively.

### 3.1.1 Basic ecological rules

Pressures on the environment in a given region are simply a function of population size and the technology employed to satisfy the needs of the people (Bossel 1994; see Fig. 3.1).

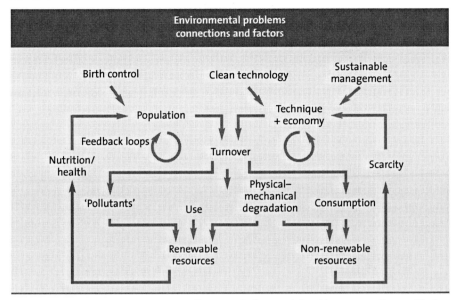

*Figure 3.1* **Environmental problems: connections and factors**

Both parameters determine the use of renewable and non-renewable resources, the degradation of the landscape and the contamination of natural resources by pollutants. There are also important feedback loops in this industrial ecosystem network that can result in exponential growth of population and technology with the consequence of accelerated deterioration of the environment. But one must also recognise that these positive feedback loops will negatively impact societies when population and technology growth exceed the availability of resources.

The ecological pressures in most LICs are different from those in industrialised countries. Industrialised countries are characterised by relatively stable populations and social infrastructure. Ecological impacts are driven mainly by the exponential growth of technology and product supply, which are resource-inefficient, despite their acknowledged progress in closing production cycles.

In contrast, the dominant factors in LICs are population growth and a less developed technology and product supply. Technology in many production sectors is outdated and inefficient but, because of the relatively minor business success and the greater importance of small and medium-sized enterprises (SMEs) in LICs, they generate far less global environmental impacts (e.g. global warming, ozone depletion, chemical pollution) than do SMEs in industrialised countries.

Ecological pressures in LICs are still mostly local; however, the global impact of converting old forests into agricultural land should not be ignored. Heavy impacts no longer known in industrialised countries on the local environment and on the health of local people and production workers still occur in LICs as a result of inefficient management of natural resources (forests), uncontrolled exploitation of mineral resources (mines, heavy metal contamination) and poorly controlled agricultural practices (pesticide contamination). Urban development cannot keep pace with population growth and migration. In the fast-growing metropolitan areas the local environment is heavily polluted by air emissions from local industry and from vehicles, from uncontrolled dumping of all sorts of hazardous wastes and from the contamination of local rivers.

In short, ecological pressures in LICs are primarily a management and infrastructure problem, and there is a major challenge to satisfy the growing demands of the population with sustainably designed products and advancements in production technology.

## 3.1.2 The environmental impact equation

As discussed above, environmental impacts are primarily a result of population size and growth and of technology development. These parameters can be further analysed in order to identify the actors and areas of action required to improve the environmental situation. Even a simple production system in an LIC can be broken down into three main interdependent factors (Fig. 3.2). These are the manufacturing system organised by the producers, the infrastructure organised by society and/or government and the demand for the utility of the product expressed by the customers or the market. Only the optimisation of all three factors will result in real ecological improvements. An SPDD manufacturer in an LIC with no market or environmental infrastructure will produce as little benefit to the environmental situation as an environmentally conscious consumer with no products available to buy.

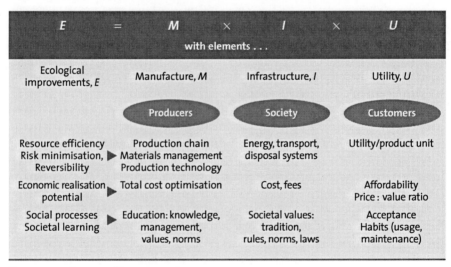

*Figure 3.2* **Environmental impact equation**

The range of ecological improvement measures must address not only technological changes in manufacturing in terms of resource efficiency and infrastructure development for energy, waste and transport systems, but also customer utility and service. In addition, it must 'factor in' the economic and implementation potential of producers, the state and the consumers.

Societal education and learning is another factor often neglected in environmental management schemes. Societal values and education are reflected in management styles and education of the workforce, the development of legislation and the acceptance and environmental consciousness of the local general public.

These factors are discussed and analysed in more detail below, highlighting that the availability of capital, technology and infrastructure development are major hurdles towards the establishment of SPDD.

## 3.1.3 The management framework

In LICs as well as in industrialised countries, EM at the state and company level is more than the implementation of a single product design method that has been successfully established somewhere else or the establishment of a law which may be called a 'law of sustainability' or 'law of the environment'—as has already been done in some LICs. The successful implementation of SPDD or broader environmental management requires an interdependent combination of measures (Fig. 3.3; Table 3.1). Successful EM at the state or at the company level requires:

- A clear goal and vision

- Motivation of and information for all actors involved

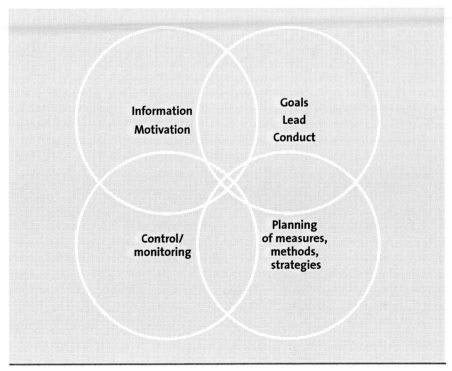

*Figure 3.3* **Integrated bundle of measures**

| Area | Type | Implementation |
|---|---|---|
| ► Legal measures<br>► Economic incentives<br>► Institutional agreements | ► Traditional command-and-control measures<br>► Provision of information<br>► Mechanisms of benefits<br>► Measures of co-operation | ► Compulsory measures<br>► Voluntary measures<br>► Incentives, fees, punishments |

*Table 3.1* **Integrated bundle of measures in environmental politics and management**

- ▓ Definition via feedback systems of the scope of management and steering

- ▓ Observation of the framework of actors and driving forces

- ▓ Planning of measures and methods

- ▓ Control and monitoring, with subsequent establishment of new goals and measures

Political environmental decision-making and management can address different areas and use different types of measures (Wilson 1995), as is shown in Figure 3.3. Typically, no single measure will be successful in reaching the goals identified. A bundle of voluntary and compulsory measures provides the required flexibility to steer a complicated societal or environmental product system.

The first step of EM at the state or company level is the establishment of clearly defined environmental goals. The motivation and involvement of all actors to reach these goals is needed, and this has to be supported by a continuity of good quality information. As well as determining goals and standards (e.g. in laws, which are binding), economic measures and regulations can support the efficient use of resources and decrease environmental impacts. This framework of measures must be supplemented by a continually revised controlling procedure. Goals and measures must be evaluated and monitored (e.g. by means of audits). Box 3.1 provides a checklist of potential measures for environmental management and political environmental decision-making.

The designers of a new sustainable environmentally oriented economy in LICs have to act as the regulators and authorities overseeing the system, as do various societal actors such as large industries and small enterprises, industry associations and NGOs (e.g. trade unions, environmental pressure groups). Only the concerted action of all these actors will ensure success in implementing new paradigms of environmental management and sustainable development. Economic incentives and rewards—in addition to a regulatory framework of environmental goals, rules and fines—must be used to motivate the involvement of all actors in society. Market-based competition for the most efficient production processes can support environmental goals. Masera discusses in Chapter 11 of this book one such example and provides a method of how different actors can be involved.

**INFORMATION AND MOTIVATION**
- Environmental objectives or goals at the national or regional level
- Programmes of information (consumers, industry, education)
- Environmental curricula in science careers and schools
- Environmental labels for products and companies
- Environmental statistics and national environmental accounts
- The right to free information
- Duties of authorities to inform public

**GOALS: LEAD-MANAGEMENT**

**Compulsory measures**
- Taxes (on products, resources, waste)
- Deposits (for packages, containers)
- Liability for environmental damage
- Polluter-pays principle (in infrastructure, recycling, disposal)

**Financial aids**
- Subsidies (for projects, investments)
- Credits (low interest rates)
- Sales promotions (in markets, for recycled products)
- Environmental awards (federal environmental foundation)

**Political–legal measures**
- Proceedings for registration of new substances
- Environmental permits for production
- Environmental impact analysis (EIA)
- Limits of use and prohibition of, for example, substances, products, packages
- Mandatory fractions for, for example, recycling, recycled material
- Determination of process selection (production, disposal)

**PLANIFICATION OF MEASURES**

**Organisational**
- Product or producer responsibility
- Inter-institutional co-operation
- Voluntary agreements on environmental goals
- Regional plans for waste management and area planning

**Technical**
- Adequate provision of recycling or disposal facilities
- Provision of necessary infrastructure
- Multiple and/or parallel solutions

**CONTROL AND SUPERVISION**

**Organisations**
- Environmental authorities for surveillance, handling of permits and for dealing with equipment, funds, training
- Laboratories (state, private)
- Environmental science organisations

**Statistics**
- Environmental statistics
- National environmental accounting
- Regional and/or industry sector waste balances

**Supervision**
- Environmental monitoring
- Physicochemical analysis of waste and emissions
- Supervision of transport and hazardous waste disposal

*Box 3.1* **Checklist of potential measures in environmental politics
and management on a societal level**

## 3.1.4 Drivers and obstacles for sustainable product development and design in less industrialised countries

Today only a few drivers of environmental business management and SPDD in LICs can be identified. These include the implementation of new environmental laws (see below and Section 3.1.5) and, to a lesser extent, the goals of companies operating in international markets or under ownership of multinational enterprises aiming at reaching the highest environmental standards worldwide.

A survey of SMEs in Bolivia (Lentz 1997) indicated that only a small number of companies had a positive attitude towards environmental protection. These companies tended to be those that use modern production technology or follow the internal environmental standards of the large multinational companies that own them. In addition, companies that focused on exporting saw environmental protection measures as an opportunity or even a need for certain markets. Many of those companies had already established a quality management system based on the ISO 9000 series and some were preparing for ISO 14001 certification. Some companies were obliged by local authorities to have prepared a plant environmental energy and materials balance and had consequently identified areas for possible major potential energy and materials savings.

But the majority of companies saw a need only to develop their quality management systems but did not see a requirement or benefit to establishing environmental goals linked to quality systems. Environmental protection and the achievement of inter- nationally recognised environmental management standards were not believed to be relevant for those countries in 'development'. Most medium-sized companies think that environmental protection is related to large investments in environmental end-of-pipe technology for which no capital is available.

Legislation should be developed according to the needs and potential of LICs and is essential to the formation of minimum environmental standards. However, there is a need for representatives of government, authorities and business to look for opportu- nities to co-operate in the development of voluntary approaches to environmental protection based on mutually agreed goals that provide benefits for economic and ecological development.

The series of environmental management standards developed by the International Organization for Standardization (ISO), the ISO 14000 series, primarily reflects the organ- isational structure, size and economic potential of companies in the more industrialised Northern countries. As such they are not directly applicable to SMEs in LICs. Such SMEs lack financial resources, research and development (R&D) capacity, environmental devel- opment and experience and education and they operate in economies that do not pro- vide the infrastructure and market demand to drive environmental management systems.

### 3.1.4.1 Opportunities for sustainable product design and environmental management in less industrialised countries

A tiered and simple approach focused on environmental considerations will provide companies with opportunities to save energy and materials with a fast return on investment. Typically, in most LICs the local economy is driven by the extraction and basic refinement of mineral resources, the exploitation of biotic resources such as timber and leather, the production of agricultural crops and the provision of simple products for construction, housing and nutrition in the local market. Highly refined products in the technical sector (machinery, computers) and the chemical sector (chemical resins, production aids, pesticides, etc.) are often imported at international prices. In contrast to the situation in industrialised countries, imported technology and equipment represent a major cost for companies, whereas salaries, water and waste fees are low in comparison.

Although the production processes are often basic and simple in nature, quite a number of companies rely on the import of additional technology. Leather production, ore mining and agriculture all require highly sophisticated chemicals to achieve the quality standards required by internal and external customers. In relation to the turnover of SMEs, expensive chemicals are imported from abroad, which end up in the products in only minute amounts owing to losses occurring as a result of poorly controlled processes (e.g. leather tanneries could rapidly amortise investments if they were to recycle and control the usage of tanning chemicals [Lentz 1998]). With an improvement to resource flow in the local economy, reliance on the import of expensive pre-products could be reduced (e.g. the beverage-bottling industry imports PET [polyethylene terephthalate] granules from abroad to replace worn-out returnable plastic bottles; and ground PET waste is exported at an additional cost). There is an enormous opportunity to build up a basic recycling technology and to convert the PET waste into a useful product for the local market. A major hurdle is the lack of start-up capital.

With a growing orientation of nationally based industries in LICs towards export, there is an increasing need for compliance with international management standards. TQEM offers companies in LICs a series of opportunities for environmental improvement while safeguarding the long-term survival of the firm. Systematic planning that takes account of the opportunities of eco-oriented production may provide the leap towards more power in a globalised economy.

### 3.1.4.2 Obstacles to the implementation of environmental management

There is a lack of environmental consciousness among the general public in most LICs. Low income, financial constraints, little environmental education and tradition results in the wasteful consumption of natural resources. End-consumers do not exert any power on manufacturers when choosing products, and influential consumer associations, 'green' press and environmental organisations tend not to exist. The macroeconomic and socio-demographic conditions do not support increased environmental consciousness, as the basic needs of the population are not satisfied.

As most of the gross national product (GNP) is produced in the local market, there is relatively little environmental pressure from the international market. Also, a major hurdle for clean production is the international division of labour. Most LICs are restricted to primary production of raw materials and semi-finished materials from ores. This primary production is known to require a high energy input and to emit a large variety of waste. Highly industrialised countries have relocated these production steps from their own territory because of high labour costs and, to some extent, growing environmental demands. The LICs that produce these primary products are in a weak position to ask for the higher prices that are needed to make investments in environmentally friendly technology.

In addition, the production technology of most SMEs in LICs is antiquated. Consequently, major gains in production efficiency that are now possible from technological advancements cannot be achieved in LICs because the existing capital infrastructure is outdated. Low salaries for the workforce and cheap or government-funded energy and water supply compensate for the inefficient production structure. The primarily local market for products manufactured in LICs means that there is no demand for more efficient and or higher-quality processes. There is insufficient money to replace old machinery, a lack that also relates to the failure to reinvest profits.

Furthermore, recent environmental legislation in some LICs is a major barrier to proactive environmental management. The rules of environmental legislation provide too few incentives for companies. The fees for waste-water discharges and solid waste disposal are not designed to promote environmental responsibility, and energy efficiency, for example, is not stimulated because electricity prices are often government-funded. Waste disposal fees are calculated based on electricity consumption as there is no technical infrastructure available to weigh waste or to calculate its volume. Sewage fees are based on the consumption of potable water, despite the fact that most companies with high water consumption in the production process drill their own groundwater wells.

Most production companies have almost no knowledge about their impact on the environment (Lentz 1997, 1998). The necessary technical controls as well as simple materials accounting systems are missing. In addition, supervisory authorities have no equipment available to monitor and control wastes and emissions.

SPDD and EM requires a management system that defines goals, evaluates the company's performance and socioeconomic condition and which has available a set of methods to re-evaluate the processes and activities of the company. SMEs in LICs are based on strongly hierarchical, often family-based, management styles, and tradition means that often new product or process designs are not sought.

The educational level of the workforce is another obstacle to EM in such companies. Employees in production do not have any specific responsibility for caring for the resources they use. They have no understanding of waste and hazardous materials (Lentz 1997, 1998), even when the supervisory engineers try to be more conscious of these issues.

### 3.1.4.3 Infrastructural deficiencies

Companies with greater environmental responsibility are confronted with the obstacle of the absence of environmental infrastructure, such as for waste disposal, effluent treatment, collection of hazardous wastes and transport of hazardous substances. In LICs the infrastructure for waste disposal and effluent treatment is often poorly organised or may even be non-existent. For example, there are often insufficient local sewage treatment plants to collect the effluents of SMEs. Waste-water is discharged without any control in most rural areas and, on the outskirts of fast-growing urban areas, it is sent into small streams and even into natural crevices which are washed only in the rainy seasons.

The installation of efficient collection systems and treatment plants typically by state or municipally owned water companies generally cannot keep pace with the rapid settlement of SME production facilities in rural or even urban areas. Even in so-called 'industrial parks', sewage collection and treatment systems have not been planned to match the amount and kinds of effluents discharged by the local companies. Ecologically and economically it does not make any sense to have SMEs install their own collection facilities. They do not have the required capital and they lack the knowledge to run such installations properly.

Recyclables from solid waste are also generally not collected in a systematic way. Although paper is typically sorted and returned to local paper mills, all other recyclable waste is often not valued. Such waste is carried to unmanaged landfills where some scavenging of plastics and other valuables takes place by landfill dwellers who make a living from it.

In any industrial production some hazardous waste is generated. In LICs there is little concern over the careful management of such waste. Authorities typically do not provide for the efficient collection and disposal of hazardous waste.

A major obstacle to the establishment of SPDD is the lack of start-up capital for investment in better equipment, training and disposal infrastructure. Even when the management of an SME calculates that an environmentally oriented investment might have a short return on investment, the necessary capital is difficult to find in the financial markets.

## 3.1.5 *The role of legislation*

Environmental legislation in LICs is a prerequisite for SPDD. Even those companies at the forefront in establishing environmentally responsible production processes cannot act in limited markets alone without any benefits or acknowledgement of their specific efforts. The companies need a basic set of environmental ground rules to provide a level playing field for each competitor. They also need a reliable environmental infrastructure covering solid waste disposal and effluent treatment; such infrastructure often can be initiated only by the state or the local administration on the basis of enabling legislation.

Environmental legislation has been rare or scattered in most LICs. Recent years have seen some efforts in a number of LICs to establish basic environmental laws at the state, regional or municipal level. This has resulted in better control of emissions to the environment and has required companies to construct installations, controlled by the authorities, for the management of hazardous materials. This legislation often follows similar legislation in industrialised countries that has been driven by international negotiations and economic development plans or in response to growing concern over local environmental pollution.

### 3.1.5.1 Example: environmental legislation in Bolivia

Relatively recently established environmental law in Bolivia (*Gaceta Oficial de Bolivia* 1992)—Law 1333, on environmental management—could be considered to be a typical example of the opportunities and difficulties of environmental legislation in LICs (cf. Lentz 1997).

This Bolivian environmental law was established by the Ministerio de Desarrollo Sostenible y Medio Ambiente (Ministry for Sustainable Development and Environmental Management) using international standards as examples and using the advice of national and international experts. The law aims at the integration of sustainable development into all environmentally relevant areas. It also documents the general environmental policy aims of Bolivia based on the principles of sustainable development that emerged at the United Nations Conference on Environment and Development (UNCED) at the Rio Summit in 1992:

- Consideration of environmental issues in all governmental activities

- Support of sustainable development considering equity and social justice for different cultural diversities

- Maintenance of biological diversity and ecosystems

- Improvement of resource efficiency

- Support of environmental education and environmental science

- Improvement of infrastructure

Of particular importance to Bolivian industry are those rules regarding approvals of new production plants and the control of existing production plants. The fixed values for maximum concentration of environmentally relevant substances are likely to be problematic for most sectors of industry. The limits have been taken from international regulations and have not been analysed as to their applicability to Bolivia.

Environmental impact analysis (EIA) is obligatory for all new projects and plants and for most manufacturing companies. Only service companies and small traders are excluded. The law requires that the EIA cover all environmental and health impacts and resource consumption. However, there are no guidelines for governmental administrators on how to evaluate the EIAs carried out by companies themselves.

When carrying out an EIA, companies are required to undertake a material and energy balance, to identify their emissions to water and air and their waste and to develop plans for monitoring and reducing emissions. Companies are encouraged to seek advice from officially registered external environmental experts. However, the rules for the registration of environmental consultants are very vague.

The environmental legislation also contains fines and disciplinary measures for companies that do not fulfil the demands of the law.

The 'new' law has the potential to improve the environmental situation in Bolivia, but it creates a series of problems and obstacles for Bolivian companies:

- The requirements of the law are too ambitious for most companies because companies are not able to rapidly change their existing production technology and cannot afford to buy expensive end-of-pipe technology.

- There is a lack of knowledge and resources in the administrative sector as well as in the scientific sector; thus the necessary environmental analyses, advice and development of appropriate environmental management systems cannot be completed.

Therefore, the rapid implementation of the 'new' law endangers its success and creates bureaucratic administrative structures which companies regard as problematic.

In 1997 I carried out a survey in which I interviewed representatives of small and medium-sized companies, chambers of industry, universities and consultants about their opinion of the implementation of the environmental law (Lentz 1997). The findings were as follows.

- Most representatives of companies and chambers of industry complained that they were not involved in the development of the law, although participation is one of the formulated principles of sustainability.

- There was a lack of understanding of the environmental value of such a law and poor general environmental knowledge among the company representatives. They see the law as another administrative burden that they can deal with in the 'traditional way'. They do not see any benefit in dealing with the requirements in a proactive way.

- The representatives of the government recognised the 'wait-and-see' and delaying tactics of most of the companies.

- Most of the companies lack the financial and staff capacities to implement the law, there is no governmental support (e.g. through funding) and there are no incentives (e.g. through changes to the tax system).

- Environmental consultants do not have the knowledge and education to support companies in the establishment of environmental management systems (EMSs), ecodesign or other operational issues.

- There are no clear criteria for environmental performance evaluation, which makes an objective evaluation impossible and opens the door for corruption.

- Fast turnover of governmental administrative staff and the need to co-operate with several different administrative offices makes company co-operation with administration much more difficult.

- The representatives of the government are aware of these problems but they expressed a hope that the law will start a process that will promote greater environmental protection among companies over the long term.

Specific problems for SPDD or EM in SMEs in LICs are:

- Unrealistic standards, with procedures imposed by national law not reflecting national characteristics

- Inapplicable international environmental standards and norms

- The absence of financial incentives and support to encourage and enable environmental product stewardship

- A lack of evaluation of environmental impacts, of priority setting and of licence schemes (e.g. awarded by local authorities for particular processes)

- A lack of EM experts and consultants

- Insufficient planning of industrial infrastructure

- Inadequate environmental education in industry and the authorities

- A lack of industrial management processes (e.g. basic process control)

- A lack of analytical tools in qualified laboratories

# 3.2 Potential strategies for implementation

Several parallel developments are needed to nurture the development of EMSs at the state (national), regional and company level. Other societal actors (science, consultancies, industry associations) can facilitate the transition process towards a sustainable economy.

## 3.2.1 State level

Existing environmental legislation has to be extended towards the promotion of voluntary systems and incentives based on the market economy. Box 3.1 (page 63) highlights several incentives. These might include improved tax deduction systems to reward environmental investment, an adequate fee system for energy, water and waste disposal, the establishment of a national environmental foundation to acknowledge excellence through a national award that provides grants for national initiatives in SPDD and environmental education.

A national environmental dialogue should be initiated by government, involving representatives from industry, science and the general public with the aim of identifying national environmental priorities. The pressing ecological needs of a country will need to be identified from the state down to the regional level. National science institutes should be sponsored to produce specific national and regional indicators of sustainable development to account for the specific geographical settings and potential of the country. Corresponding environmental statistics and monitoring systems will need to be set up.

With support from national NGOs, environmental education in schools, universities, companies and for the general public has to be stimulated. Respective curricula should be developed.

## 3.2.2 *Regional level*

State-based regional authorities also have a responsibility to design and manage environmental infrastructure, to guarantee the environmentally responsible disposal of solid waste and effluents. SPDD should aim for reduced use of toxic chemicals and reduced generation of hazardous wastes, and authorities should contribute their part to the process by establishing procedures and by building hazardous waste sites for orderly disposal. Technical feasibility, financial and ecological efficiency are criteria that should be regarded with equal importance. Employment opportunities for landfill dwellers should be developed in an organised way.

Representatives of government and authorities have to be sensitised towards a politics of realistic environmental goals and priorities. All political measures and commandments should be evaluated against a broad set of holistic environmental and socio-economic criteria. Infrastructure planning should take into account the potential of saving energy and resources and reducing waste-streams instead of setting up waste disposal facilities to cope with waste-streams from inefficient production processes. Financial resources should be allocated to those initiatives that provide the most benefits. End-of-pipe treatment may not always be the first choice. There should be funds set aside for better process control in SMEs and adequate resource flow management, with higher valorisation of valuables in the waste-streams.

## 3.2.3 *Company level*

The establishment of SPDD and EMSs in SMEs in LICs requires a cautious revaluation of international development in industrialised countries. The direct transfer of EMSs is not guaranteed.

A typical SME in Bolivia is a small enterprise with few employees, little capital and a limited number of trained management employees. To enable the implementation and use of the ISO 14000 series in LICs more experience has to be developed. Training manuals for each industry sector need to be prepared to provide management with an easy-to-comprehend and convincing introduction to SPDD methodology. Demonstration projects as described in Chapter 11 in this volume or by the ZERI waste initiative (Pauli 1998) also proved to be an economic success. Specifically, industry associations should provide specific support through personnel and material resources to help those interested companies to identify the opportunities and, even better, the market potential for environmentally designed products and processes.

Environmental protection is understood by some managers in LICs to mean high-cost, end-of-pipe waste treatment, and international aid is sought to finance such capital-intensive environmental technology. Such investment often does not provide the benefit initially sought, as equipment cannot be maintained properly in the country concerned owing to a lack of spare parts or a scarcity of trained people to operate the environmental technology. The second steps are typically completed before the first (i.e. instead of searching for low-cost and low-tech alternatives, expensive designs and overly sophisticated high-technology solutions are used).

Before low-cost, easy-to-maintain and easy-to-run end-of-pipe installations are introduced, other possibilities should be considered. For example, options of preventing environmental impacts should be examined that are embedded in the opportunities and market position of the specific industrial sector in question and the type of product the company produces. To identify these options, there is a need for simple forms of material and energy balances and other ecodesign tools.

## 3.2.4  Consultancies

Environmental consultancies could play an important role in helping companies establish adequate EMSs. In addition, they could provide services to measure and manage the environmental impacts of companies and provide laboratories to increase the company's and government's knowledge about the influences of a company's activities on the environment.

However, there is little experience among environmental consultancies in corporate environmental management. Better training is needed; training programmes should be set up to enable consultancies to spread knowledge among the companies.

Today, in most companies in LICs production processes are not well controlled as even simple analytical measurements do not exist. Companies are not aware of waste and effluent composition and thus production losses of valuable materials are not recognised. In most LICs analytical laboratories do not exist in smaller companies and even on a national level the existence of laboratories to carry out process control and environmental monitoring is very rare. The existing labs are not qualified in good laboratory practice and thus may produce unreliable results.

A number of analytical laboratories with different areas of specialisation to meet the needs of different industrial sectors should be set up. There is no need for highly advanced analytical capabilities; even rapid tests offered on the market at low cost would do.

## 3.2.5  Industry associations

Chambers of commerce can play an important role in establishing appropriate environmental protection strategies adapted to the needs of local industry. This is extremely important in LICs where SMEs do not have the power or ability to take the first move. The chambers could co-ordinate, motivate, inform, educate and convince companies that a proactive approach to voluntary EM is far better than being forced by governmental rules that sometimes are not the most sensible. The chambers could support pilot projects and communicate best-practice examples.

Dialogue with government and the public and the formulation of industry-specific environmental standards and guidelines are important tasks for chambers of commerce, as European examples show (Table 3.2; ASPRI/CNI 1998).

Another interesting role for chambers, especially in LICs, could be to support the establishment of the environmentally sound infrastructure that government has failed to establish. The chambers could provide financial support and know-how for private

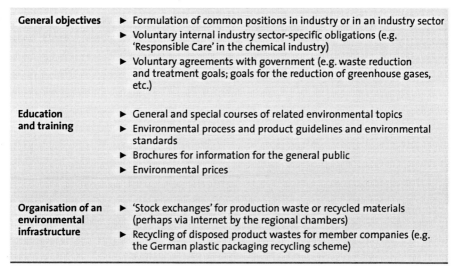

| | |
|---|---|
| **General objectives** | ▶ Formulation of common positions in industry or in an industry sector |
| | ▶ Voluntary internal industry sector-specific obligations (e.g. 'Responsible Care' in the chemical industry) |
| | ▶ Voluntary agreements with government (e.g. waste reduction and treatment goals; goals for the reduction of greenhouse gases, etc.) |
| **Education and training** | ▶ General and special courses of related environmental topics |
| | ▶ Environmental process and product guidelines and environmental standards |
| | ▶ Brochures for information for the general public |
| | ▶ Environmental prices |
| **Organisation of an environmental infrastructure** | ▶ 'Stock exchanges' for production waste or recycled materials (perhaps via Internet by the regional chambers) |
| | ▶ Recycling of disposed product wastes for member companies (e.g. the German plastic packaging recycling scheme) |

*Table 3.2* **Examples of environmental projects undertaken by chambers of commerce**

companies in the infrastructure development sector and organise joint recycling and disposal organisations, and so on.

To play an active role in the move towards a more sustainable economy, the first steps of the chambers should be to set environmental goals and formulate an environmental policy in co-operation with their members and to ask members to sign those standards. For example, in Bolivia the nine regional chambers of commerce and the national chamber of commerce have formulated a common environmental policy (ASPRI/CNI 1998) which is headed by the motto *Ecoeficiencia es Competitividad*—eco-efficiency is competitiveness!

On the basis of an analysis of strengths and weaknesses, the chambers could then formulate short-term and long-term tasks and a strategy to reach those tasks. This should be individually adapted to the specific industry sectors and for specific company sizes. The establishment of an environmental task force and working groups involving all the important stakeholders (e.g. consumers, companies, NGOs, government) is necessary. Obviously, the chambers will therefore need to employ well-educated environmental experts and provide the necessary resources for the kinds of activity mentioned above. The establishment of national centres of excellence might be a successful measure to use the available resources effectively.

Finally, the external communication of each chamber's environmental activities is important. In addition to public relations and advertising they could organise environmental awards and support projects carried out by environmentally oriented NGOs, and so on.

## 3.2.6 Establishing an environmental information system

The exchange of experience related to EMs and easy access to environmentally relevant data are key factors in the move towards more sustainable companies. This information is needed by companies, consultants and scientists. It covers, for example, environmental regulations and standards, environmental technology, addresses and services of experts, national and international funding and support programmes, databases on the environmental profile of different materials and so on.

However, information of this kind is not available in LICs. But the fast development and rapid spreading of the use of the Internet and computer technology offers an excellent opportunity to fill this gap. Computer equipment is available in most companies, industry chambers and universities in LICs and there are local Internet providers. Thus the establishment of an Internet site that offers and links all the relevant information and that is regularly updated and maintained might be a successful way to enable local actors to use information and keep up with international knowledge and technology.

In Bolivia such an electronic and Internet-based environmental information system has been built by the national industrial chamber of industry, Cámara Nacional de Industrias (CNI 1998; Lentz 1998; Fig. 3.4). The service consists of a wealth of environmentally relevant information such as international and national databases on environmental protection, information about addresses and services of governmental organisations, experts on product integrated environmental protection, environmental technology and EM.

*Figure 3.4*   **Homepage of the environmental information system of the Bolivian national chamber of industry, Cámara Nacional de Industrias, www.bolivia-industry.com/sia/home.html**

The CNI formulated three main aims for establishing this Internet service:

● To ease and speed up access to environmental data within and between the different chambers of industry

● To support companies on environmental issues and activities and to allow the exchange of company experiences

● To support the public relations activities of the chambers and to offer the public (e.g. universities) access to environmental data

## 3.2.7  Programmes for international technical aid

Although Bolivia is a small country, there is a surprisingly large number of different internationally funded projects to support environmentally sound activities (see Box 3.2). The total figure of the invested capital adds up to several million dollars.

● EP3: an environmental pollution prevention programme, funded by the US Agency for International Development (AID)
● ASPRI: a project integrated consultancy to the private sector by GTZ, the German society for technical co-operation
● PAIB: a project of environmental protection for the Bolivian industry funded by ASDI, the Swedish agency for international development co-operation
● MEDMIN: a programme of integral environmental management in the small mining industry funded by COSUDE, the Swiss agency for co-operation and development
● PMAIM: an environmental project in the general and mining industry funded by the Nordic Fund of Scandinavian countries
● ETNA: Environmental Technology Network for the Americas, funded by US AID
● CPTS: Centre for the Promotion of Sustainable Technologies, funded by the World Bank and US AID
● ESMAP: an energy-efficiency programme in the energy sector, funded by the World Bank

**These programmes:**
● Offer education and training on the ISO 14000 series (EP3, PAIB, ASPRI),
● Offer support from international experts for the evaluation of product integrated environmental protection activities in different industry sectors (EP3)
● Aim at developing best-practice examples of environmental management in selected companies (PAIB, ASPRI)
● Aim at improving the availability of information on sustainable technologies and environmental management by using the Internet (ASPRI, ETNA) and demonstration centres
● Develop technical solutions for specific industry sectors, for example mining (MEDMIN, PMAIM) or energy (ESMAP), and offer know-how and support
● Aim at improving the performance and capacity of environmental laboratories (PAIB, PMAIM)
● Offer an improved basis for the formulation of industry-specific limits by analysing the waste-water quality of companies (PMAIM)

| | |
|---|---|
| ASPRI | Proyecto de Asesoría Integrado al Sector Privado |
| EP3 | Environmental Pollution Prevention Programme |
| ESMAP | Energy Sector Management Programme |
| GTZ | Gesellschaft für technische Zusammenheit |
| MEDMIN | Manejo Integrado del Medio Ambiente en la Pequeña Minería |
| PAIB | Protección Ambiental en la Industría Boliviana |
| PMAIM | Proyecto Medio Ambiental de Industría y Minería |
| US AID | US Agency for International Development |

*Box 3.2*  **Examples of competing international aid for 'cleaner production' projects in Bolivia, as of 1998, and their aims**

All the projects listed in Box 3.2 define 'cleaner production' as producing a combination of economic and environmental benefits. They are obliged to produce integrated environmental protection and offer excellent education and training opportunities for industry and the chambers of commerce in LICs. However, the specific needs of companies in LICs are often neglected by the organisers of these programmes. They fail to adapt the sophisticated EM schemes as formulated in ISO 14001 ff. to the basic structures of SMEs in less developed countries and thus are not able to offer practical help. Companies in LICs often need very concrete, pragmatic and simple guidelines to evaluate and manage their business processes.

Another aspect for potential improvement is the co-ordination and co-operation of the different programmes with each other. A central national clearinghouse to eliminate redundant activities and to facilitate exchange of experiences and information between the different development aid organisations would be helpful. This would enable the integration of the specific needs of the national industry into the design of development aid programmes.

## 3.4 Conclusions

SPDD requires advancements in production technology, higher management efficiency as well as better-developed environmental infrastructure and government control systems. In many LICs major efforts are starting to be undertaken to decrease local environmental pollution while better satisfying the needs of the local population. The addressees of legislation and international demand for pollution control in LICs are not simply the companies. Central government and local authorities in LICs have a major responsibility to develop standards and procedures that match the economic and management potential of SMEs and give them sufficient flexibility and backing to identify the SPDD potential in local and global markets. Sufficient support should be given also by international technical aid programmes, and the different needs of those LICs should be more recognised.

# TOWARDS SUSTAINABLE BUSINESS?

*Peter James*
**University of Bradford, UK**

Many people believe that the phrase 'sustainable business' is an oxymoron. But it is hard to implement the ideals of sustainable development if they cannot be applied to the business world. Section 4.1 examines some of the issues that arise in doing this. Section 4.2 describes the elements of a sustainable value chain (i.e. the organisational activities that contribute to the objectives of sustainable business). Section 4.3 discusses the importance of values to sustainable business, and Section 4.4 identifies ways in which business sustainability can be evaluated. Finally, Section 4.5 considers the future of sustainable business and the relevance of the concept to the emerging 'new economy'.

## 4.1 What is sustainable business?

The three central pillars of sustainable development are:

- **Economic development:** the generation of wealth (especially for poorer people) in ways that are compatible with the other pillars

- **Environmental protection:** avoiding adverse impacts on natural and social systems from pollution and other environmental impacts

- **Social inclusion:** avoiding gross inequalities of wealth, health and life chances

However, it is very hard, if not impossible, to apply these at the firm level and define a sustainable business. The reasons for this are:

- Sustainability is a property of systems (e.g. the economy) rather than of system components (e.g. companies).

- The nature and importance of sustainability varies between sectors: chemical companies, for instance, have more pervasive and longer-lasting impacts and tend to be more enduring entities than, for example, hairdressers, and so must be judged by different criteria.

- It is still unclear what sustainability means, both because of a lack of data and because of social and cultural disagreement.

On the third point, the consultancy SustainAbility has observed, in a briefing paper for Shell International, that:

> A key question which will face any company deciding how to respond to the sustainability agenda focuses on which of the two following options to adopt:
>
> - A social accountability process largely driven by stakeholder-defined targets and indicators of performance; or
>
> - A triple bottom line process focusing on targets and indicators relevant to each Shell business—and specifically designed to build competitive advantage and long-term shareholder value.
>
> This is probably going to be a case of both/and, rather than either/or, but the emphasis chosen will be crucial (Shell 1998b: 1).

This distinction tends to reflect another, which is the difference between 'strong' and 'weak' notions of sustainability. Advocates of strong sustainability tend to see environmental protection and social inclusion as absolutes and are unwilling to trade them off against economic development. The hallmark of weak sustainability is its willingness to accept such trade-offs.

Despite these difficulties, the following sections nonetheless attempt to define some distinguishing features of firms that are at least becoming more sustainable, even if they can never reach an ultimate destination or satisfy all of their stakeholders.[1] This chapter draws on a growing literature on the topic (see e.g. Elkington 1997; Frankel 1998; Romm 1999; Willums 1998).

## 4.2 A sustainable value chain

The fundamental purpose of a private-sector business is to create value for its customers so that its financial stakeholders can be rewarded. This is equally true of a sustainable business, which has to meet established criteria of business 'fitness' if it is to survive in the long term. The creation of economic value also has a broader social benefit in that it provides a growing stock of financial capital which can be deployed by future generations.

---

1   For convenience, however, the term 'sustainable business' is used in the remainder of this chapter.

However, a sustainable business also has other objectives (which some will see as being equal in importance to profitability, others as subsidiary to it). Two of these follow directly from the definition of sustainable development. The first is environmental protection, which can be seen as at least maintaining, and preferably enhancing, the stock of natural capital. The second is social inclusion, which can be seen as improving the stock of social capital. As economic development increasingly rests on human knowledge and skills, many would also add a fourth sustainability objective, that of enhancing the stock of human capital through education, training and other means.

Michael Porter's concept of the value chain provides a well-known model of the key elements of a business that create value for customers (Porter 1985). The central square of Figure 4.1 adapts this model to take account of the additional sustainability objectives identified above. It supplements Porter's original eight elements with five additional ones

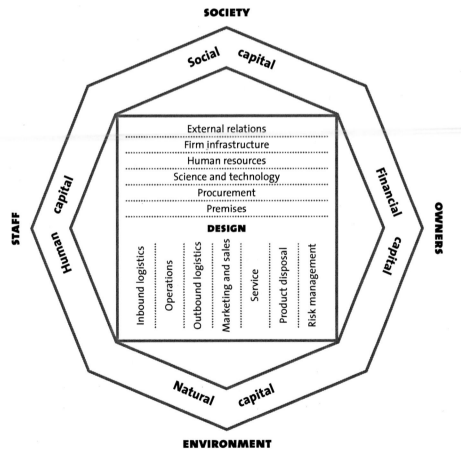

*Figure 4.1* **The sustainability octagon**

*Source:* Adapted from Porter 1985: 37

that are especially significant for sustainable business: external relations, premises, design, product disposal and risk management. The following sections discuss each in turn.

### 4.2.1 External relations

Many companies have a long tradition of community involvement and/or contributions to charity. In general, however, the initial business response to sustainability concerns—especially those created by specific incidents such as environmental disasters—was to treat the issue as a public relations problem. As the company was 'obviously right', the aim was to demonstrate that opponents were wrong. With time, however, at least some companies have come to see that a more productive approach is to engage in a dialogue with their sustainability stakeholders.

This approach grew out of the application of quality principles to environmental management during the 1990s. Total quality management (TQM) extended the definition of 'customer' from its original meaning of a buyer of goods and services to include any user of business processes or outputs. The 'total quality environmental management' (TQEM) movement added a further refinement by considering regulators, communities, environmental groups and other external stakeholders to be important customers for business environmental management activities.

The next stage in this process has been its extension to the social arena and the creation of dialogue mechanisms with stakeholders such as non-environmental non-governmental organisations (NGOs), community groups, local government and other activities.

These mechanisms have been increasingly underpinned by external reporting of actions and progress. The first environmental reports by business were published during the late 1980s and early 1990s. Their evolution of environmental reporting has been tracked in a sequence of reports produced by the 'Engaging Stakeholders' research partnership between the Industry and Environment initiative of the United Nations Environmental Programme (UNEP) and SustainAbility (SustainAbility/UNEP 1996a, 1996b, 1997, 1998a, 1998b, 1999a, 1999b). One point that emerges from these and many other publications on the topic is that corporate environmental reporting remains an unsystematic activity with a wide variation between the leaders and the rest. And, even though the amount of reporting is increasing, it continues to be only a small proportion of total companies and is likely to be confined to larger organisations as long as it remains voluntary.

Social reporting, which dates back to the 1970s, has tended to focus on employment issues (Gonella et al. 1998). A second stage began in the early 1990s when a number of organisations such as The Body Shop and Traidcraft started to produce a variety of disclosure formats to discuss issues of social performance. A third stage began in the late 1990s when mainstream companies began to issue social reports. Some common threads are large companies that have operations in potentially controversial industries and/or a significant impact on social life in particular countries or regions and/or traditions of consumer feedback. However, these reports are as prone to inconsistency as environmental ones, and, in many cases, set aspirations that are not achieved in practice.

Of course, the logic of companies committing to sustainable development is that they should create sustainability reports that integrate all the 'triple-bottom-line' issues of economics, environment and society into a holistic view of their progress towards sustainability. The first example of this was the 1998 publication that helped to bring the issue of sustainability reporting into the mainstream, Shell International's *Profits and Principles* report (Shell 1998a). This model has now been emulated by a number of large multinational corporations (MNCs).

Of course, not everyone is convinced that such reports make a difference. One commentator on Shell's report, for example, observed that:

> It is clear that Shell is serious about responding to the increasing demand for greater corporate accountability . . . However, one is tempted to ask whether all this work represents an especially sophisticated way for Shell to repair its battered corporate reputation, justify the continuation of its core business-as-usual, and renew its 'licence to operate'. Shell's problem is that it has not yet managed to set up a rigorous process by which it can claim to be interacting meaningfully with its stakeholders. The suspicion lingers that it is more interested in using stakeholder consultation for 'issue management' purposes than for genuinely understanding the impact of its activities and perhaps changing its priorities (Mayhew 1998: 10).

One cause of this suspicion was an aspect of the report that others might perhaps see as quite radical: the attempts to account for environmental and social value (see Section 5.4).

The move towards full sustainability reporting will be further encouraged by the development of the Global Reporting Initiative, a partnership of NGOs, MNCs and other bodies. This is developing a common format for what should be reported and how.[2] However, the standardisation of a basic format may be accompanied by much more variability in the vehicles used for reporting, which will increasingly include websites and 'one-off' outputs such as reports on the environmental impacts of products and product lines.

Of course, reports alone are empty vessels—they need to be filled by a process of dialogue with the stakeholders they are aimed at. Until recently, the development of such processes was driven more by NGOs and advocates of accountability than by business itself. These external pressures are always likely to be important. But in recent years more executives have started to see sustainable development as being synergistic with broader business trends (DeSimone and Popoff 1997). For example, most business gurus foresee a future in which relatively self-contained organisations are replaced by more fluid network structures. These involve a great deal of outsourcing, partnerships—both ad hoc and long-term—and discussion with a variety of customers, suppliers and other organisations. The resulting flexibility and variety can allow firms to learn and respond more effectively to fast-changing markets than they could with traditional structures. Sustainability stakeholder dialogues and partnerships can be a valuable training ground for the management skills needed in this world of 'virtual organisation'. They can also provide

2    Further details can be obtained from www.globalreporting.org.

a 'window into the future' about changing social values and trends which can be valuable for business development, marketing and other mainstream business purposes.

However, companies will always have a problem in handling such processes as long as the stakeholders are 'out there'. A 'them and us' situation can be avoided by bringing stakeholder views into the organisation. One means is the appointment of people who represent stakeholders as non-executive or (more rarely) executive directors. Another possibility is to institute a high-level advisory group. In the longer run, initiatives such as these can be reinforced by introducing new criteria for promotion, with much more emphasis on the ability to understand and communicate with the general public and NGOs.

## 4.2.2 *Firm infrastructure*

A company's sustainability performance is determined by the extent to which environmental and social issues are an important consideration in its internal business processes. The starting point for this is clear structures of responsibility for achieving good performance, and mechanisms to monitor outcomes. This needs to begin at the top, with good corporate governance. At least one board member should be personally responsible for sustainability matters. In addition, it is important that sustainability issues feature on the board agenda, ideally supported by a regular report on progress against key targets and indicators. These need to be set out in a clear policy. While many companies have environmental policies, fewer have policies for the more contentious areas of social sustainability, such as protection of human rights, business ethics and animal rights. Fewer still heed the demands of some external stakeholders that sustainability should shape their business portfolio.

One of the trickiest problems facing large companies today is how to cascade their high-level policies into divisions, subsidiaries and joint ventures. The difficulty is that best-practice management dictates a lean headquarters and granting of maximum autonomy to lower tiers. Implementation and co-ordination is usually difficult enough within a single country but is even more so when national cultural differences and sensitivities have to be taken into account. The problems are compounded with joint ventures because decisions have to be agreed with another partner, who may well have management control. The tendency to greater outsourcing and collaborative partnerships can also make it difficult to identify which organisation is responsible for long-term issues such as sustainability.

One common response to this situation is a formal management reporting structure in which the chief executive or other board member of a lower-level entity has to provide formal assurance to senior management that sustainability issues have been addressed.

The need to build sustainability into everyday operations makes it important to assign ultimate responsibility to line managers. But they obviously need to be supported by specialist sources of advice and support. With the environment this is relatively straightforward. Most large, environmentally sensitive, organisations now have a network of environmental units at higher levels (often both at corporate and at business unit level) and designated environmental champions at lower levels. One variable is usually the relative responsibility of the different units (with a constant tension between the desire of corporate environmental staff for oversight and co-ordination and the desire of business units for maximum autonomy). There can also be differences in the extent to which they are stand-alone or integrated with other activities such as health and safety and risk management and in the precise reporting route into senior management. Generally, environmental staff who report directly to a main board director have more 'clout' than those that do not.

With social sustainability, the pattern is much less clear. Social issues are not usually integrated into line responsibilities to the same degree as management but are often handled by a central unit for social responsibility, community affairs or similar. While this does give them a high profile, it can mean that they are relatively isolated from day-to-day operations.

There is also no real social equivalent of the environmental management system, which provides a formal means of controlling and integrating environmental actions. Two standards are now available for such systems—the International Organization for Standardization (ISO)'s ISO 14001 and the European Union's (EU's) Eco-management and Audit Scheme (EMAS). Both define the elements of a good system: for example, assigning responsibility, defining and documenting progress and measuring outcomes. They also provide opportunities for companies to be independently assessed as to whether they have met the standard.

Many companies have claimed that systems meeting the standard's requirements have created substantial improvements in environmental performance. Some have also found that winning a 'badge' can be a useful marketing tool (although, of course, the more companies that have it, the less unusual it is). However, environmental management systems have also been criticised as being prone to excessive bureaucracy, focusing on processes rather than actual performance and ignoring the broader issues of sustainable development. (The latter criticism could be removed if Project Sigma, an initiative by the British Standards Institution to develop a sustainability management system, is successful.)[3]

An alternative, or complementary, approach is available to companies using the European Quality Award for business planning purposes. This provides a standardised template that can be used to assess the overall performance of an organisation. The template allocates points (with a possible total of 1,000) for different aspects of performance. A total of 60 of these points are allocated to 'impact on society', which incorporates environmental and social impacts. Some have seen this 6% as being inadequate. Others argue that it at least forces organisations to pay attention to the issue and that there is no reason why environment cannot be dealt with under other categories as well as 'impact on society'. Indeed, this has been the approach of several past winners.

The precise form of sustainability infrastructure chosen matters less than the processes undertaken within it. In particular, sustainability will be taken seriously in most companies only if the business case can be demonstrated—which usually means demonstrating that there can be financial costs and benefits. This is difficult to achieve for the social dimensions of sustainability but a great deal of work has been done on

3   www.projectsigma.com

integrating environment into business financial infrastructure, such as the management accounting system and investment appraisal (Bartolomeo *et al.* 1999). One of the best-known examples of this is the healthcare company, Baxter International, which produces an 'environmental financial statement' to assess its environmental costs and benefits. Every statement produced has demonstrated that the financial benefits created by environmental programmes considerably exceed their costs.

## 4.2.3 *Human resources*

In the long run a company's recruitment, development and reward practices strongly influence its values and priorities (Wehrmeyer 1996). Ideally, issues of sustainability might be stressed to new and young employees and form a component of performance appraisals and bonuses. Encouragement—such as time in lieu—can also be given to voluntary and other forms of participation in community activities. Many believe that this can create a virtuous circle, in which a good environmental and social image assists in the recruitment of new staff and improves the morale of existing employees.

Most definitions of social sustainability also place great emphasis on human resource issues. One aspect of this is the creation of equal opportunities for disadvantaged groups—which in many areas of employment includes women as well as minority groups. As well as removing discrimination, action in this area has the further advantage of creating a more diverse workforce. Many would argue that this is essential for dealing with the social complexities of today's business world.

As noted, the maintenance and enhancement of human capital is an important objective of a sustainable business. It is perhaps unrealistic—and, in some fast-moving industries, perhaps undesirable—in today's world to expect guarantees of permanent employment. But most people with an interest in sustainable business would argue that staff should not be made redundant except as a last resort. Maximum opportunities should also be available for staff to enhance not only their employable skills but also their own personal development.

These questions are especially important in developing countries, where there are more opportunities to be exploitative of staff. At a global level, there are a number of international conventions that have been signed by most countries to deal with these matters. These include the United Nations Universal Declaration of Human Rights, the Organisation for Economic Co-operation and Development (OECD)'s Guidelines for Multinational Enterprises, and a number of examples from the International Labour Organisation. Despite recent campaigns, few companies as yet have reshaped their business policies to reflect these issues. One practical problem is cultural and political differences. For example, some argue that the trade-off between economic development and high environmental standards (assuming this trade-off exists) has to be different in poor developing countries from that in the West. Others see this as an example of the rich world exporting environmental problems. Nonetheless, a sustainable business should be doing much more than the norm to implement such conventions into its operations as well as taking other measures to ensure that real contributions are being made to the human capital of developing countries.

One issue in human resources is the role of trade unions. Most advocates of sustainable business would probably hold that this is incompatible with restrictions on union membership. Where unions exist, they can obviously be an important ally and conduit in building staff awareness of, and commitment to, sustainability initiatives. Historically, unions' interest in the topic has focused on the specific topic of employment, but in recent decades many union organisations—and their members—have shown a more positive interest in broader sustainability issues, particularly health-related environmental impacts and equal opportunities.

## 4.2.4  Science and technology

Leading-edge environmental thinkers—and a growing number of policy-makers—believe that sustainable development will require a 'factor 4' improvement in the environmental performance of goods and services. This means reducing by at least 300% over the next 20-30 years the amount of resources needed and pollution generated to deliver goods and services to consumers (von Weizsäcker *et al.* 1997). As progress in recent decades has not approximated to this rate of improvement—for example, the fuel efficiency of cars—one implication is that new 'clean' technologies and/or new social–technical systems are required. There are many possible options for such new technologies, but they often fail to inform thinking in research and development (R&D) and other functions or they meet external barriers, so that their potential is not realised (Hawken *et al.* 1999).

However, recent controversies about the implications of genetic engineering technologies indicate that some care is needed to determine exactly what these technologies might be and to ensure that they do not have unintended consequences which would work against sustainability.

It is also important that any new technologies developed are compatible with the social requirements of sustainable development and are transferred to developing countries wherever possible.

## 4.2.5  Procurement

One of the key elements of sustainable business is a life-cycle perspective. This means an acceptance of some degree of responsibility for the environmental impacts of suppliers of inputs and the consumers of outputs (Russell 1998). Often the impacts of these upstream and downstream stages of the chain outweigh the impacts of the organisation itself, particularly for service industries. In some sensitive industries, failure to identify and improve the environmental and social performance of suppliers can also compromise the saleability of the company's product or service. McDonald's and Nike are just two of the organisations that have faced consumer boycotts for allegedly failing to, respectively, conserve tropical rainforests and insist on reasonable working conditions at suppliers in developing countries.

The environmental performance of suppliers has been the focus of a number of collective and single-company initiatives. One of the best known of these is that of the

UK-based retailer of 'do-it-yourself' (DIY) products, B&Q. In 1992 the company initiated a programme to raise the environmental awareness of its suppliers and award them a rating. More action was also taken to inform customers about the environmental implications of the products the company sells. In 1998 the company announced a further stage in its programme, with a target of all its suppliers understanding the key impacts over the life-cycles of their products and developing an action plan to deal with them.

Most companies have paid less attention to the social performance of suppliers, but this is now being addressed through initiatives such as SA 8000 (see Section 4.4).

The evidence is that concerted initiatives of this kind by business customers can drive considerable environmental and social improvement among their suppliers. However, this is normally expected to occur in addition to rather than instead of other procurement criteria such as price and quality. Further, as more procurement moves to electronic e-commerce platforms, some of the bonds between buyer and seller are broken, with the possible result that it will become more difficult to put pressure on for better—or even to assess accurately—sustainability performance.

## 4.2.6 Premises

A company's factories, offices and other buildings and sites have a considerable environmental and social impact. Their construction alters the landscape and consumes raw materials, their operation uses energy, water and other inputs, creates internal and external emissions and other impacts and influences employment and transport patterns. At the end of their lives, demolition affects amenity and generates waste, some of which may be hazardous. And at all times they are one of the most visible manifestations of a company's existence and therefore a major influence on its public image.

Environmentally friendlier premises management has three principal aims:

- Minimal impacts from emissions, noise, visual intrusion or other causes

- More efficient use of inputs such as energy and water

- Projection of a clean image to employees, customers and communities

These objectives are most easily achieved in the design stage. However, there is much that can be done to make existing premises more environmentally friendly. Substitution of chlorofluorocarbons (CFCs) and other harmful substances, repainting, screening, provision of sound insulation and other measures can greatly ameliorate direct impacts. Improved insulation, electronic energy-management systems and other measures have already reduced energy consumption and costs for many companies, and research demonstrates that there is still enormous potential for cost-effective measures. Conservation and recycling measures offer similar potential for the increasingly expensive commodity of water.

In today's networked world, one emerging question is whether a sustainable business actually needs premises, or at least very much of them. If staff can telework, and many business activities can be conducted through electronic means, why incur the transport and other impacts of bringing people together? When such costs can genuinely be avoided, this is obviously the best option. But some caution is needed as teleworking does not necessarily reduce transport in the longer term. What often happens is that people adjust their living patterns to, say, live further from work, and the more time spent at home the more people are likely to invest in home extensions and related energy consumption which offsets any savings in office space (cf. Chapter 17).

### 4.2.7 Design

Design is placed at the centre of Figure 4.1 for two reasons. In the narrow sense, the design stage typically determines most of the lifetime environmental and social impacts of products and services. In many ways this makes it the most important business function for long-term sustainability. As later chapters have extensive discussion about the topic of sustainable product and service design, this is not repeated here (see Chapters 6, 7 and 8).

However, there is also a broader sense of design—that of putting the elements of sustainability and good business together so that sustainable business is possible. Sections 4.3 and 4.4 include more discussion of this topic.

### 4.2.8 Inbound and outbound logistics

The movement of materials, components, products, etc. both within companies and between them and their suppliers and customers has major environmental and social impacts. The main environmental impacts are consumption of fuel, pollutant emissions and noise. These impacts can be ameliorated by minimising distances travelled through locational, procurement and other decisions, by substituting other modes of transport for less eco-efficient transport modes (especially the substitution of train for road freight) and by using them more efficiently: for example, through 'reverse logistics' (using vehicles to carry goods on return trips when they would otherwise be empty). The social impacts include noise and contributions to congestion and other systemic impacts.

### 4.2.9 Operations

ISO 14031, a guidance document, provides a framework for assessing operational (as well as other aspects of) environmental performance. It identifies eight operational performance areas that companies need to take account of: materials, energy, service inputs, facilities and equipment, logistics, products, service outputs, and emissions and waste.

#### 4.2.9.1 Materials

The extraction and processing of materials creates major environmental impacts. Sustainable companies will therefore focus on reducing their consumption, both in their own operations and in their supply chains. One way of doing this is through 'dematerialisation' (i.e. redesigning processes and products so that they consume smaller quantities of materials). Another way is through 'revalorisation' (i.e. re-use, remanufacturing and recycling). By avoiding the impacts associated with production of virgin materials, recycling can potentially reduce environmental impacts. Whether this actually happens in practice depends on the impacts associated with recycling itself. These can sometimes exceed the impacts avoided, as when cars are used to ferry small amounts of paper to recycling points.

The company Electrolux deals with this objection by using what it terms a 'recycling index' which relates the financial value of raw materials going into a product with the anticipated financial value of disassembled components and materials at the end of the product's life. The higher the recycling value, the more likely it is that end-of-life disassembly for recycling or re-use will be economically feasible. The indicator therefore highlights the importance of considering the end-of-life of products during the design stage.

### 4.2.9.2 Energy

As with materials, energy production and consumption have major environmental impacts and are a significant business expense. Most studies suggest that, despite long attention to the issue, there remains considerable scope for cost-effective improvements in energy efficiency in most organisations.

### 4.2.9.3 Service inputs

Service inputs to many activities can often be as or more environmentally significant than material or energy inputs. An example is airports, which create considerable indirect environmental impacts through transport of passengers and staff to and from their site. One indication of their sustainability is the number of non-connecting passengers using public transport to reach the airport.

### 4.2.9.4 Facilities and equipment

Many aspects of facilities and equipment affect environmental performance: for example, modern versions tend to perform better than old versions, and emissions can often be dramatically reduced through effective maintenance.

### 4.2.9.5 Logistics

Logistics have already been discussed, in Section 4.2.8.

### 4.2.9.6 Products

As already discussed in Section 4.2.5, a life-cycle perspective requires attention to be paid to the environmental and social impacts of products. In the environmental area, there are now a number of generic and company-specific schemes that identify key areas to be managed. One example of a company-specific scheme is the environmental product profile developed by Volvo, which was first applied in 1998 to its S80 2.9 passenger car. The profile assesses 12 parameters in four categories (ENDS 1999). Each parameter has a total score of 100, and the overall profile was certified by the verification agency, Lloyds Register.

There have been fewer attempts to define frameworks for assessing either the social performance or the overall sustainability of products. One example, developed to provide a first-order assessment, is the 'sustainability wheel' (Bennett and James 1999). This identifies four key parameters: customer value, physical environmental impacts, product attributes and social impacts. The environmental parameter has six components. Three of these relate to inputs: energy, materials and water; and three to outputs: hazardous substances and radiation, non-hazardous wastes and environmentally critical substances such as CFCs or carbon dioxide. The third parameter deals with attributes of products that are major determinants of the physical environmental impacts of the product itself and/or society as a whole and that can be influenced by designers.

Three broad kinds of product attribute are identified:

- **Transport:** the total use of transportation over the life-cycle

- **Revalorisation:** the extent to which the product can itself be recycled, re-used or remanufactured, or can use inputs or components that have been recycled, re-used or remanufactured

- **Service intensity:** the provision of additional services to customers in ways that potentially reduce environmental impacts; this includes product substitution, increased intensity of use, life extension, product augmentation, multi-functionality and integration with other products and services to produce synergistic effects

The social parameters are enhancement of individual life chances, meeting the basic needs of the world's most disadvantaged peoples, challenging social norms, enhancing human capital and enhancing autonomy and community.

### 4.2.9.7 Service outputs

The output of an increasing number of organisations in today's service-intense economies is a service, either to other businesses or to final consumers. Much current thinking has stressed the potential to further substitute services for physical processes, thereby creating dematerialisation and other environmental and social benefits. A recent research project (Hopkinson and James 2000) has identified eight basic types of eco-efficient service (defined as services that directly or indirectly increase the eco-efficiency of customer's activities). These are:

- Activity management, such as end-of-life disposal of materials and products, or facilities management of energy provision to buildings

- Advice and consultancy: for example, on energy or water efficiency

- Information, such as provision of systems that make use of a global positioning system (GPS) to control tractor spraying of fertilisers or to support reverse logistics through better vehicle tracking

- Intermediation, as with e-commerce portals which enable buyers to be found for unused capacity

- Product extension, as with maintenance, repair and other after-sales services (see Section 4.2.11)

- Product result services, where suppliers guarantee levels of performance and do all that is necessary to achieve this (e.g. demand-side management in energy)

- Product utility services, as when goods are hired or leased rather than sold

- Substitution, when electronic services are substituted for physical processes

### 4.2.9.8 Emissions and waste

Emissions and waste indicators are ubiquitous because they are often required by regulators and deal with what are usually highly visible phenomena. For these reasons, and also because targets can easily be set and understood, they can be powerful drivers of improvement. This is especially true if they encourage efforts to adopt pollution prevention approaches rather than simply the 'bolting on' of equipment to control the pollution.

There are now a number of schemes for identifying key emission and waste measures, for example, the guidance document on environmental performance evaluation, ISO 14031. However, this document also makes clear that what matters for sustainable business is not the emissions and waste in themselves but their effect on environmental conditions.

## 4.2.10 Marketing and sales

Brands are often the most valuable component of a company's assets. A brand has many elements, but there are few that can be effective if they are associated with poor environmental or social performance. Conversely, good performance can create very positive feelings among actual or potential customers.

Experience suggests that success in branding and other marketing issues, and in day-to-day selling, is most easily achieved, and consumer scepticism neutralised, when environmental concern permeates a company. This requires marketing and sales to be integrated into the sustainability value chain rather than being a superficial add-on (Charter and Polonsky 1999).

However, experience over the past decade has shown that products that are based on customers paying a 'sustainability premium' can succeed in niche markets but are unlikely to succeed in the mainstream. This is particularly true in the B2C (business-to-consumer) area, where the interest that many express in opinion polls does not translate into buyer behaviour. The key to success is to offer products and services that offer a 'sustainability bonus' without asking customers to pay more for that bonus.

Several aspects of social sustainability are also relevant to marketing and sales. For international companies, decisions have to be made about whether products should be sold in countries with oppressive regimes and also—as in the case of some health products—whether it is important to provide access for a large proportion of the population.

### 4.2.11 Service

After-sales service is particularly important for environmental performance. For example, correctly explaining how a product is to be used can prolong its life and also enhance its environmental performance. Servicing through effective repair and reconditioning can also greatly lengthen a product's life, and can improve the efficiency with which it operates. Cars that have become out of tune, for example, waste fuel and emit greater amounts of toxic gases. However, they can be re-tuned easily and inexpensively.

Service can also be a critical issue in developing countries where local skills may not be sufficient to repair products or keep them at optimal performance.

### 4.2.12 Product disposal

The development of cradle-to-grave responsibility has been driven by the rising impacts and costs of product disposal. It is already a statutory requirement for many products at least in some countries and will be so in more areas in future. Companies have a choice between developing more effective forms of disposal (such as providing the option to return products to undergo supervised disposal by the manufacturer or to manufacture products with maximum use of biodegradable materials) or recycling for alternative use. Many companies and experts believe that, when the complete life-cycle of the product is carefully analysed, well-managed disposal can be more environmentally benign than recycling. However, environmental groups and much of the general public believe that the latter is more desirable. It is likely therefore that stringent legislative targets and consumer preference will require business to design products for full recyclability and develop recycling infrastructures.

### 4.2.13 Risk management

Recent decades have seen a succession of disasters that imposed severe costs on, and in some cases threatened the very existence of, the responsible companies. The *Exxon Valdez* oil spillage has cost Exxon almost US$10 billion in clean-up costs, compensation and fines, has greatly damaged its public acceptability and has consumed an inordinate amount of management time. Union Carbide paid out significant compensation for the Bhopal chemical emission disaster and might well have been bankrupted if the court cases had been decided under US rather than Indian jurisdiction. And Coca-Cola and Perrier are only two of the many companies to have lost millions of dollars in sales and forfeited public trust as a result of contamination of products.

These and other disasters have directed business attention to the extent and complexity of sustainability-related risks. In addition, their magnitude and frequency is being considerably increased by the adoption of strict liability for both future and past environmental damage in the USA, and the likelihood is that the European Community will move the same way. As a result, US business is already liable for over US$100 billion of clean-up costs for land that has been polluted in the past.

One response has been a drying up of liability insurance and a much greater caution by third parties such as banks and carriers about their own potential liability. These and other parties are now adding to internal pressures for companies to adopt a more systematic approach to the analysis of risks, to phase out the use of hazardous materials, to introduce safety control systems and to take other measures to reduce risks. However, production and marketing disasters will always happen and sensible companies now have crisis management plans and training programmes to mitigate their worst effects.

## 4.3 Winning hearts and minds for sustainable business

The sustainable value chain implements a company's strategic objectives. But strategy is more than objectives, important as these are. It must also create a shared vision of where the organisation is going and help create an organisational culture which is supportive of sustainable business (Rowledge *et al.* 1999). The former chief executive officers of Dow and 3M have defined an 'eco-efficiency business strategy mind-set' as being about (DeSimone and Popoff 1997: 45):

- An emphasis on performance that meets genuine needs rather than a focus on products alone

- Deriving competitive advantage from consideration of the entire product life-cycle

- A recognition that eco-efficiency is more a process than a once-and-for-all objective

- Integrating sustainability into the overall business so that it forms a core competence

- External collaboration to gain information, to influence debates and to identify business opportunities

Of course, many would see sustainable—as opposed to eco-efficient—business strategy as placing more emphasis on the social pillar of sustainable development. Some would also like to see more emphasis on a longer time-perspective and on the implications for the kinds of business a company undertakes.

Also, values are useless unless they are accepted—and lived—by the people within an organisation. This is particularly true of senior managers, who influence the short-term situation through their actions and the medium-term to long-term situation through their legacy in areas such as business activity and the people who have been recruited into influential positions.

Barrett (1998) has developed a framework that can be used to assess corporate sustainability values and which has been implemented within SustainAbility (1999). It involves individuals choosing from a list of values: those that most represent their personal views, those that best describe how they feel their organisation should operate and those that best describe how it actually operates. The degree of alignment between the three areas can then be identified and the results plotted onto a model of value development and a 'balanced needs scorecard'. The scorecard has six categories: 'survival' (profitability and shareholder value); 'fitness' (productivity, efficiency and quality); 'customer and supplier relations'; 'evolution' (innovation, products and services); 'culture' (trust, creativity and employee fulfilment); and 'society and community contribution'.

In many ways, becoming a sustainable business is as much a process of change as a concrete set of activities, and sustainability-based change is like any other: it involves abandoning the comfort of the known for the uncertainty and fear of the unknown. Leaders at all levels therefore have to heed the words of Martin Luther King:

> If you want to move people, it has to be towards a vision that is positive for them, that taps important values, that gets them something to desire, and it has to be presented in a compelling way that they feel inspired to follow (quoted by Walter Stahel).

Of course, the cynicism of middle and junior managers after decades of change initiatives of one kind or another is one of the principal impediments to any kind of movement. This is a particularly serious problem when, as with the natural environment, the changes require a great deal of time and effort to understand and implement.

Ultimately, the spark of leadership is useless without the tinder of enthusiasm for sustainability-related actions among all the workforce. Fortunately, a good number of employees, especially those who are young and well educated, already accept the basic rationale for change and indeed may be pressing for it. Many companies have been pleasantly surprised by the extent of the enthusiasm and commitment that their sustainability policies have unleashed. Indeed, many see core values that tap into employees' broader concerns and values—which typically include environmental and other sustainability—as the glue that will increasingly hold organisations together in an ever more virtual world.

Enthusiasm is fostered by an understanding of the reasons why change is necessary. One problem with sustainability is the complexity of the issues, and the widespread feeling that individuals cannot make a difference. Hence, mechanisms to create a sense of connectedness are important. These may include in-house awareness-raising schemes, recycling schemes, etc. However, care is needed to ensure that their relevance is not undermined by changing environmental fashions (e.g. on the merits and demerits of some kinds of recycling). One, more scientifically based, means of creating this awareness is by using the ideas of The Natural Step. This organisation originated in Sweden, with extensive discussion among scientists and other professionals to define consensus principles of sustainable development. However, although they have been endorsed by and have formed the basis of training programmes in a number of companies, the principles appear to have been more successful in their originating cultural milieu of Scandinavia than elsewhere in the world.

## 4.4 Evaluating sustainable business

One approach to evaluating the sustainability of business is to separately assess important elements in economic, environmental and social performance. Such assessments can make use of the evaluation frameworks that have been developed in the individual areas.

There is, of course, a well-developed framework to assess the financial sustainability of a company. Several reports have also highlighted the importance of measuring parameters such as human capital and/or the health of key business relationships, which include those with important social stakeholders (see e.g. CTC 1998).

One response to this has been attempts to adapt existing business performance measurement activities to take account of sustainable development: for example, that summarised in Table 4.1. The developers of this framework argue that:

> The new, value-related measures will lead a company away from commodity products and toward a search for ways to differentiate products through branding, upgrading function, or building with services. These measures reward delivery of value to the customer—translated into sales or value added—and the simultaneous reduction in environmental footprints. The older measures, in contrast, reward increases in throughput, capital investment, and production (Arnold and Day 1998: 9).

Of their six new measures, knowledge intensity and focus on function are the most challenging. The first is related to the question of measuring intellectual capital, which is attracting growing interest in conventional business performance measurement circles. The best-known example is that of the Swedish insurance company, Skandia, which has put a financial value on such capital in recent financial reports (Skandia 1994). Focus on function is concerned with attempts to build a greater service component into sales. However, there are few indications at present on how it can be measured.

There is also a well-developed literature on environmental performance evaluation (summarised in Bennett and James 1999). A decade's practical experience has been condensed into the ISO 14031 guidelines which, despite some limitations, provide a comprehensive framework for assessing environmental impacts.

| Old measures | New measures |
| --- | --- |
| Volume intensity | Knowledge intensity |
| Volume output | Value per volume output |
| Capital investment | Value per unit of capital invested |
| Material throughput | Material per customer served |
| Virgin material and energy | Recovered material and energy |
| Focus on product | Focus on function |

*Table 4.1* **Changing measures of resource productivity**

*Source:* Arnold and Day 1998: 9

Although there is an even longer history of interest in social performance (e.g. as summarised in Zadek *et al.* 1997), there has been much less detailed discussion of how it can be evaluated compared with environmental sustainability. Indeed, David Wheeler, the former head of ethical audit at The Body Shop, believes that practice in the social area is 5–6 years behind that in the environmental area, largely because of the complexity and intangibility of many social issues (quoted in BATE 1999). Nonetheless, the US Council on Economic Priorities has developed SA 8000, a social accountability code of conduct for sites. It is based on the various international conventions described in Section 4.2.3 and therefore focuses on issues such as child labour, forced labour, health and safety, discrimination, disciplinary practices, working hours, compensation and management systems, and freedom of association and right to collective bargaining.

One step forward from this separate evaluation is the construction of 'sustainability indices', which take the form of dimensionless numbers calculated from a number of weighted individual parameters. The key design issues are therefore which parameters should be included and how they should be weighted. One approach is to do this in a 'bottom-up' manner, with parameters defined by the organisation. The other is to use a 'top-down' method, with parameters developed by government or other parties. There is considerable experience of constructing such indices in the environmental area (summarised in Bennett and James 1999).

An alternative, or complementary, approach is to develop integrated indicators that encompass two or more parameters of sustainability. Most companies that have attempted to address this topic have utilised the concept of eco-efficiency (DeSimone and Popoff 1997). This means creating greater economic value from activities that also minimise environmental impacts or that, at worst, maintain impacts at no more than their current level. These parameters can be measured, and several initiatives have sought to develop standardised eco-efficiency indicators. However, some of these attempts—and particularly those associated with the World Business Council for Sustainable Development (WBCSD), a business association that brings together many leading MNCs—have been criticised by some sceptics, who argue that this is a narrow interpretation of sustainability which tries to distract attention from issues of eco-justice and/or leads in practice to a focus on incremental improvement rather than radical innovation (Gray *et al.* 1996; Welford 1996).

A more radical approach to measuring sustainability is to place a financial value on an organisation's consumption or enhancement of natural and/or social capital. This is the approach being adopted by Shell, which is working with SustainAbility and Arthur D. Little to develop 'triple bottom line accounting' (Shell 1998b). The main argument for such an approach is that it provides information that is readily understandable by management and financial stakeholders and that can easily be compared with economic value added. The Prince of Wales Business Leaders' Forum, in collaboration with the World Bank and UN Development Programme has, for example, developed the concept of 'social value added' as an equivalent of shareholder value added (Nelson 1998). Others are also seeking to operationalise the concept of 'social capital' developed by Fukuyama (1995) and others. However, attempts to create such valuations are always controversial. One critic has argued that

The concept misleads companies into thinking that by somehow aggregating economic, social and environmental 'value-added', they can claim both responsibility and sustainability.

The delusion is that they compensate for the 'value' they are subtracting from one bottom line—the environmental, say—by 'adding value' to another 'bottom line'—for example the economic—even though the two forms of value are of a very different nature . . .

The problem with such technocracy is that it obfuscates rather than clarifies. The metrics may provide some semblance of rationality to empower corporate decision-making in the short term, but it is likely to alienate rather than include many stakeholders. This approach will therefore do little to bring about a more consensual way of working or to minimise risk (Mayhew 1998: 10).

## 4.5 The future of sustainable business

If it is relatively easy to identify the characteristics of sustainable business, does this mean that they will be inexorably adopted by all companies? Unfortunately, survey and other evidence suggests that only a minority of companies are doing much to move towards it (see e.g. Cowe 1999; Suranyi 1999). The reasons for this include:

- Weak financial incentives, with environmental taxes and resource costs being at relatively low levels

- Weak commitment by managers

- The complexity of many sustainability issues, which can be beyond the capacity of many organisations to even understand let alone respond to

- The development of 'virtual' business, which makes it more difficult to understand, identify responsibility for and manage overall product chains

- Limited pressure from consumers in terms of actual buying behaviour

Moreover, the need to continually respond to changing market conditions means that it is difficult for any company to maintain constant improvements over time. Witness, for example, the tribulations at The Body Shop in recent years as it has faced pressure on its profitability and margins.

In the light of these barriers, sustainable business is likely to be a tender bloom and will always require a supportive framework to be established by governments and others. One necessary condition of this framework is that prices for resources should reflect their real environmental and social costs. If this is achieved, smaller companies will not need to pay quite so much formal attention to sustainability issues but will simply incorporate the prices into their financial calculations. Another condition is the need for smart regulation, which uses a combination of carrot and stick—especially financial incentives and disincentives—to steer companies towards the long-term changes required. However, the final change is a broader social requirement, which is the need for changing attitudes towards consumption. As long as consumers want high mobility and resource-intensive goods and services then almost every business—however sustainable it is and however much it tries to guide consumer attitudes—will have to provide those goods and services.

Could these judgements be changed by the 'new economy' of electronic networks and social fluidity which has been alluded to at several points in this chapter? Are the dot.coms, telcos and other beneficiaries of this world more sustainable than their old economy counterparts? Supporters of this view certainly argue that environmental impacts could be greatly reduced by the opportunities for better control and optimisation, by electronic substitution for physical processes and by new ways of working. They also argue that the information democracy created by the Internet can overcome many traditional geographic and social disadvantages. Perhaps, ultimately, virtual reality is the only antidote to today's inexorable demand for mobility.

However, global networks can easily enable globalised economic patterns that will generate additional demands for transport and reduce local autonomy. They also increase opportunities for consumption, and may create a digital divide between those with access to the networks and those who are excluded. The increased ease and automation of procurement—and a related expansion of the supplier base—can also make it more difficult to introduce a life-cycle perspective into supply chains. And if Wall Street is already difficult to reconcile with sustainability time, what are the implications of Internet time in which even a year is often said to be long-term?

In conclusion, the first battle for sustainable business—on the physical terrain of the old economy—has been, at best, drawn. The ground is now shifting to the next, perhaps decisive, encounter in the wires and waves of cyberspace.

# 5

# INTEGRATED PRODUCT POLICY AND ECO-PRODUCT DEVELOPMENT

*Martin Charter, Alex Young,*
*Aleksandra Kielkiewicz-Young and Inga Belmane*
The Centre for Sustainable Design, UK

Integrated product policy (IPP) is an initiative at the European Union (EU) level aimed at reducing the environmental burden of products and services throughout their life-cycles by using a toolbox of policy instruments to 'green' markets through 'greening' both the demand side (consumption) and the supply side (product development). IPP is part of a growing trend within environmentally advanced countries in Europe towards product-oriented environmental policies. As such, it represents a new shift in thinking towards 'front-of-pipe' solutions (e.g. the greening of product development and design). Generally, existing environmental policy approaches have tended to focus on point sources of pollution (i.e. production sites and production processes), using 'end-of-pipe' technologies and 'middle-of-pipe' solutions such as waste minimisation, cleaner produc-tion and pollution prevention. By focusing on the product development and design phase, IPP aims to tackle the stage at which many of the environmental burdens of products are determined, thus reducing non-point source problems further in the life-cycle. IPP considers the product development process from idea generation to product management and reverse logistics (i.e. 'end-of-life' management [EOLM]).

IPP also aims to green the consumption side of the market by focusing on the way that customers (individual, business-to-business, distributors and governmental) choose, use and discard products and services. The aim here is to reduce the environmental impact of products during their use and to ensure their appropriate disposal at the end of their life. Consumption-side measures can also help to give important feedback to product designers and developers to design, produce and supply greener products to the market by encouraging customers to chose environmentally friendlier products (i.e. through green procurement programmes, eco-labelling schemes, etc.).

IPP is not envisioned to be a new, stand-alone policy but to be integrated into already-existing EU policies and objectives. Its purpose is to develop an overall framework for all stakeholders involved in specific product groups to manage products in a more environmentally friendly manner. For this reason, IPP aims to be based on stakeholder involvement, market orientation and to take a life-cycle perspective. However, IPP formulation at the EU level is still in its early stages and national approaches at the member-state level are more advanced in some countries than in others. In reality this holistic model of IPP is yet to be implemented at the EU or national level.

The purpose of this chapter is to examine developments in the IPP initiative and how it may influence the development of 'greener' products (i.e. eco-product development [EPD]). The chapter will begin by examining the background, definition, objectives, principles, strategies, components and potential toolbox of IPP. This examination is not supposed to be definitive but instead looks at some of the main discussion points in the IPP initiative. The chapter then goes on to briefly examine environmental product policy (EPP) in Denmark as an example of a national approach. The purpose of this is to examine how some aspects of IPP may be expected to operate in reality. From this, a simplified perspective for IPP is proposed. Finally, the chapter looks at the relationship between IPP and eco-product development in companies, using the electronics sector as an example.

# 5.1 Background

It is important to make a clear distinction between integrated product policy (IPP) and environmental product policy (EPP). IPP is an EU initiative currently being developed by the Directorate General on the Environment (DGXI) aimed at the formulation of a common product-oriented environmental policy at the EU level. EPP is a more generic term referring to product-oriented environmental policies at a national level inside and outside Europe.

EPPs are receiving increasing attention from policy-makers both nationally and internationally. At the international level, activities such as those carried out by the Organisation for Economic Co-operation and Development (OECD; e.g. the Green Goods conferences and its work on public procurement and producer responsibility) and the International Organization for Standardization (ISO; e.g. its work on environmental labelling and life-cycle assessment and, more recently, on integrating environmental aspects into product development) highlight the international context of EPP.

Within the EU, the antecedents of national EPP activities and IPP reach back to the 1980s, if not before (see Box 5.1 for highlights of the key milestones in the development of IPP). However, it was not until the 1990s that EU member states began to formulate product-oriented environmental policies. The most prominent among these countries are the Netherlands, Denmark and Sweden, which are considered to be the leading countries, followed closely by Germany and Austria. EPPs are also starting to emerge in Belgium, the United Kingdom and Finland. Countries such as France, Italy, Spain, Portugal, Greece and Ireland seem to be lagging behind.

| | |
|---|---|
| **1987** | The Brundtland report, *Our Common Future*, was published, introducing sustainability as a principle of environmental policy. |
| **1987** | The French prize 'Ecoproduit' (Eco-product) was created, rewarding environmentally more benign products. |
| **1992** | The 5th European Environmental Action Programme (EAP) was published; although it does not explicitly mention product-oriented environmental policy, numerous references are made to instruments and measures that are considered to be IPP measures. |
| **1992** | At the Rio de Janeiro Summit, Agenda 21 stressed the importance of a change in production and consumption patterns. |
| **1993** | ISO TC 207 'Environmental Management' was founded, with subcommittees on, for example, Environmental Management Systems, Life Cycle Assessment, and Environmental Labelling. |
| **1993** | The Swedish 'Eco-cycle' Commission was founded, which delivered its final report, *A Strategy for Sustainable Materials and Products*, in 1997. |
| **1993** | The first international conference on 'Green Goods' in the Hague, The Netherlands, took place from 30 September to 1 October; this workshop was the start of a tradition of conferences in the product policy field: since 1993, in total five 'Green Goods' conferences have taken place. |
| **1994** | The *Policy Document on Products and the Environment* was published by the Dutch Ministry of Housing, Spatial Planning and the Environment (Ministerie van Volkshiusvesting, Ruimtelijke Ordening en Miieubeheer [VROM]). |
| **1992–95** | The conceptual report, *Product Policy in Europe: New Environmental Perspectives*, of Oosterhuis *et al.* (Germany) and 'Instituut voor Milieuvraagstukken' was published, with the support of DGXI within the 'Environment and Climate' programme. |
| **1995** | The OECD's Pollution Prevention and Control Group started its activities in the field of IPP; its important output includes the *Preliminary Results of (Sustainable) Product Policy Survey*. |
| **1996** | The Finnish Ministry of Trade and Industry published a discussion paper on *Production, Products and Consumption Patterns in Sustainable Development*. |
| **1997** | A Nordic IPP group (consisting of representatives from Denmark, Finland, Norway, Sweden and Iceland) and the first Nordic IPP workshop were founded. |
| **1997** | The 'common position' of the Council of the EU, *Towards Sustainability*, was published, listing diverse product-related issues and supporting sustainable production and consumption patterns. |
| **1997** | The Belgian Federal State of the Law for the Co-ordination of the Federal Policy on Sustainable Development was adopted; this was a first attempt to manage classical policy approaches (from process to product) in an integrated way. |
| **1996–98** | The Ernst & Young and the University of Sussex's Science Policy Research Unit (SPRU) study on IPP was carried out, with the major report being published in March 1998. |
| **1996–97** | The discussion paper, *An Intensified Product-Oriented Environmental Initiative*, was published by the Danish Environmental Protection Agency in 1996; in 1997 the report *A Product-Oriented Environmental Initiative* was published. |
| **1998** | The UK Department for the Environment, Transport and the Regions (DETR) published a consultation paper, *Consumer Products and the Environment*. |
| **1998** | The Belgian Federal State of the new Law on Product Standards Aiming at the Promotion of Sustainable Production and Consumption Patterns to Protect Health and Environment was adopted. |
| **1998** | An IPP workshop was organised in December by DGXI in Brussels, with approximately 180 participants; this was the first major stakeholder discussion of the IPP concept. |
| **1999** | An informal meeting of EU environment ministers took place in Weimar, Germany, 7–9 May; this included a background paper and discussion paper on IPP prepared by the BMU (Bundesumweltministerium für Umwelt, Naturschutz und Reaktorsicherheit [German Federal Ministry for the Environment, Nature Conservation and Nuclear Safety]); the conclusion of the meeting was an endorsement for DGXI to further develop IPP. |
| **2000** | An IPP workshop jointly organised by the BMU and the BDI (Bundesverband der Deutschen Industrie [Federation of German Industries]) was organised for 1 February. |
| **2000** | A second Nordic IPP workshop was organised by the Nordic Council of Ministers for 9–10 February, with the presentation of a 'Proposal for a Common Nordic IPP'. |

*Box 5.1* **The chronology of IPP developments**

*Source:* Adapted from BMU 1999

Although there are significant similarities among the national policies developed so far, different elements and measures have been developed and different product groups targeted, which has resulted in a fragmented picture across Europe. One of the reasons for introducing a common EU approach to environmental product policy (i.e. IPP) is the necessity of harmonising these national approaches. Therefore, the concept of IPP was introduced as a joint initiative between two European Commission Directorate Generals—for the Environment (DGXI) and for Enterprise (DGIII)—as a blueprint for EPP harmonisation in Europe.[1]

The concept was originally based on the issues highlighted in a report by Ernst & Young and the University of Sussex's Science Policy Research Unit (SPRU), which was commissioned by DGXI and published in March 1998 (Ernst & Young/SPRU 1998). Since then, several activities have helped to further develop the IPP concept. However, despite these developments, the debate on IPP is still very much at its initial stage and IPP needs to be further clarified and elucidated. The next major step in the development of IPP will be the green paper that is currently being prepared by DGXI and which is expected in December 2000 (a year behind schedule). Until then, it appears that DGXI will make no major decisions. In addition, there appears to be a 'wait and see' attitude among the majority of stakeholders, particularly business, as they wait for the publication of the green paper (Belmane and Charter 1999a).

## 5.2 Integrated product policy

This section covers the most relevant developments of the IPP initiative without attempting to cover all aspects or underlying issues associated with it. The section includes an examination of the definition, objectives and conceptual approach, principles and strategies, and building blocks proposed for IPP, and the instruments and measures that may potentially make up an IPP toolbox.

### 5.2.1 Definitions

As yet, there is no official definition of IPP. However, working definitions have been put forward for discussion. The first of these was in the *Integrated Product Policy* report (Ernst & Young/SPRU 1998: 8). This report proposed to define IPP as 'public policy which explicitly aims to modify and improve the environmental performance of product systems'. This definition was followed by a second definition advanced by the German Federal Ministry for the Environment, Nature Conservation and Nuclear Safety (Bundesumweltministerium für Umwelt, Naturschutz und Reaktorsicherheit [BMU]) as part of its background paper on product-related environmental policy, prepared for the May 1999 informal meeting of environmental ministers in Weimar, Germany (BMU 1999: 1). According to this publication, 'integrated product policy is public policy which aims at

---

1   DGIII subsequently dropped out of the process early on, leaving DGXI to continue alone.

or is suitable for continuous improvement in the environmental performance of products and services within a life-cycle context'. The new elements in this definition include:

- The addition of services

- An explicit statement of the life-cycle perspective

- The incorporation of the principle of continuous improvement

The major change in this definition is the inclusion of services, which represents a significant increase in the scope of IPP. Initially, the report by Ernst & Young and SPRU proposed a very narrow focus on physical products rather than on services. However, the IPP workshop in December 1998 identified the need to consider services as well, and this has been followed up in subsequent IPP discussions. The consequences of including intangible products (services) in the definition and scope of IPP will, at the very least, require a longer time-frame to formulate IPP strategies for services, as more research is needed to fill the significant knowledge gaps regarding the service sector and its environmental impacts. Of greater concern is the potential danger that the formulation of IPP may become unmanageable because of the high level of complexity of the issue.

The other changes in the definition (i.e. life-cycle thinking and continuous improvement) are not as major, in that they are explicitly stating what was already implied in the first definition. However, they also highlight the importance of the conceptual relationship between IPP on the one hand and quality and environmental management systems (EMSs) on the other.

### 5.2.2 Objectives and conceptual approach

Ernst & Young and SPRU propose that IPP should be a new field of policy in the EU, clearly limited to objectives that explicitly deal with resource efficiency and the environmental impact of products (Ernst & Young/SPRU 1998). The BMU and the Nordic countries take a different approach to IPP. According to the Weimar background paper (BMU 1999) and the proposal for a common Nordic IPP (COWI/ECON/ÖRF 1999), it is proposed that IPP should not be a stand-alone policy with its own separate objectives. Instead, IPP should be an overall framework for those parts of existing EU policies (environment, health, trade and industry, waste, chemicals, etc.) that are relevant to the environmental aspects of products and services. Furthermore, IPP should be based on existing EU environmental (and social and economic) objectives, such as those laid out in the EU Fifth Environmental Action Programme, with the ultimate goal being sustainable development. IPP should, therefore, be a policy framework for existing policies and objectives rather than a separate policy with its own objectives and targets.

The differences in these two conceptual approaches correspond to the two main tendencies in national EPP approaches found by Ernst & Young and SPRU: that is, the incremental and comprehensive approaches. In the incremental approach, an initial policy framework is developed, which is then incrementally filled in with specific product policies that are separate from existing policies and contain their own objectives and targets. Ernst & Young and SPRU take this approach in their report. In the comprehensive approach, product policy is not seen as a separate and independent policy but as a framework to integrate existing policies and objectives with a product orientation. The Weimar background paper and the Nordic proposal take this approach.

### 5.2.3 Principles and strategies

IPP is to be based on three fundamental principles (BMU 1999; COWI/ECON/ÖRF 1999), namely:

- Market orientation

- Stakeholder involvement

- Life-cycle perspective

This means that IPP should work with the market and involve all stakeholders in continually improving the environmental performance of products and services from a life-cycle perspective. To do this, it is envisioned that IPP should develop an overall framework for all stakeholders in specific product groups to perform integrated product management (IPM) in a co-ordinated manner. IPM differs from IPP in that IPP is a strategy for governments and authorities to encourage IPM, whereas IPM concerns the actions and measures taken by the different stakeholders (e.g. suppliers, manufacturers, distributors, retailers, customers, waste collectors, recyclers, disposal firms, financial institutions, consumer and environmental organisations, etc.) involved in the life-cycle of a product (or service) (BMU 1999).

From this perspective, IPP can be seen as a way for governments and authorities to instigate, facilitate and/or co-ordinate the actions of stakeholders in the product life-cycle to improve the environmental performance of product services, whether this involves 'greening' their design and development, production, distribution, use or recycling and disposal.

### 5.2.4 Building blocks

The IPP building blocks represent common aspects of product-oriented environmental policy that have been observed in many national EPP approaches. The building blocks are composed of clusters of policy instruments that can be used in varying contexts to achieve the stated goals of the building block. Since product groups and their environmental impacts vary considerably, a building block approach, as opposed to a policy instrument approach, allows for the construction of consistent and integrated policies across varied product groups.

The *Integrated Product Policy* report (Ernst & Young/SPRU 1998) highlighted five key building blocks:

- Managing wastes (e.g. take-back obligations)

- Green product innovation (e.g. stimulating research and design [R&D] and ecodesign)

- Creating markets (e.g. public procurement)
- Transmitting environmental information (e.g. eco-labelling, product declarations)
- Allocating responsibility (e.g. producer responsibility)

The Weimar background paper (BMU 1999) added two more IPP building blocks:

- Sustainable consumption
- Chemicals management

In our opinion, the addition of these new building blocks adds confusion to what is still an emerging topic without adding significantly to the value of the building block concept. Both new building blocks were already covered under those proposed by Ernst & Young and SPRU. Furthermore, sustainable consumption could be considered one of the overarching concepts behind IPP rather than as just being one element in it. However, it is easy to see the political motivation for including these new building blocks as they add emphasis to important political objectives. For example, relatively little research has been carried out on the 'greening' of consumption, compared with the 'greening' of products, and much remains to be done to understand and gain experience in this issue.

### 5.2.5 Integrated product policy toolbox

Until now, product policy tools have generally been applied within national and regional EPP approaches in an unco-ordinated manner, which appears to have produced sub-optimal results. Eco-labelling is a good example of this. In certain geographical areas (e.g. Scandinavia, Germany) and product markets (e.g. white goods, laundry detergents, office paper) eco-labels have had an impact on the greening of consumption and product development. However, in the other locations and/or markets the results have been more questionable. For example, eco-labelling schemes have not been as successful in countries such as the United Kingdom, France and Belgium. This is largely because of the varying contexts in which the eco-labelling instrument has been applied and the presence or lack of supporting measures (governmental, non-governmental and within the supply chain), such as consumer education. It is now understood that such policy instruments rarely work efficiently if they are not part of a wider policy approach.

The IPP concept proposes to remedy this situation by applying a range of policy instruments in a co-ordinated, integrated and complementary manner. Therefore, in the example used above, education and information campaigns to raise customer awareness, along with other instruments, would be used in conjunction with eco-labelling to ensure the effectiveness of the scheme. Furthermore, it has been realised in stakeholder discussions (Belmane and Charter 1999b; DGXI 1998; Ernst & Young/SPRU 1998) that there will not be a 'one-size-fits-all' solution and that the mixture of instruments will need to vary depending on the product group, the objectives and the shape of the market. Policy instruments will, therefore, need to be applied on a case-by-case basis.

The instruments would come from a large toolbox of different policy instruments, ranging from voluntary agreements to direct legislation. (Table 5.1 gives examples of

| Instrument | Including |
|---|---|
| Voluntary instruments | ▶ Voluntary agreements<br>▶ Self-commitments<br>▶ Industry awards |
| Voluntary information instruments | ▶ Eco-labels<br>▶ Product profiles<br>▶ Product declarations |
| Compulsory information instruments | ▶ Warning labels<br>▶ Information responsibility<br>▶ Reporting requirements |
| Economic instruments | ▶ Product taxes and charges<br>▶ Subsidies<br>▶ Deposit/refund schemes<br>▶ Financial responsibility |
| Regulatory instruments | ▶ Bans/phase-outs<br>▶ Product requirements<br>▶ Mandatory take-back |

*Table 5.1* **Examples of possible instruments in the integrated product policy toolbox**

possible instruments in the IPP toolbox.) This toolbox will not be exhaustive. New instruments should continually be developed to suit specific purposes and situations.

## 5.2.6 Uncertainty surrounding integrated product policy

There are still many questions and uncertainties surrounding IPP that need to be addressed. These include, among others:

- What are the objectives and best approach for IPP?
- What are the priorities?
- How will IPP be implemented?
- What implications will IPP have for different stakeholders: national and local governments and authorities, industry, consumers, retailers and environmental non-governmental organisations (NGOs)?

The question as to 'What is IPP?' is still being asked among stakeholder groups and a clearer vision and a practical interpretation of IPP needs to be formulated (Belmane and Charter 1999a; DETR 1999).

# 5.3  Environmental product policy: Denmark's approach

The Danish environmental product policy (EPP) approach illustrates how EPP can be tackled at a national level and provides lessons for IPP at an EU level. Denmark represents one of the leading countries in the implementation of national EPP programmes and is a good example of the comprehensive approach to product policy.

The objectives of the Danish EPP are:

- To intensify the development and marketing of cleaner products in order to reduce the total environmental impact from production, use and disposal of those products

- To consolidate the competitiveness of Danish trade and industry in a future market which increasingly brings environment into focus and calls for cleaner products (DEPA 1997)

An evaluation of Denmark's environmental policy by the OECD indicates that the relatively stringent Danish environmental policy does not pose barriers for economic competitiveness or growth and is actually considered to be an important sales argument for Danish industry.[2] Denmark's main work areas have included:

- Accumulation of know-how, methodology and competence

- Information tools

- Green taxes

- Subsidies

- Green public procurement

- Establishment of product area panels

These will each be discussed in turn.

## 5.3.1  Accumulation of know-how, methodology and competence

The Environmental Design of Industrial Products (EDIP) project, initiated by the Danish government, has had a budget of approximately DKr40–50 million. The major outcome of the project has been the creation of a detailed environmental assessment tool for products, including supportive databases and software that can be used for product design and also software development.

## 5.3.2  Information tools

The Danish Environmental Protection Agency (DEPA) is working on an overall product information strategy. The Consumer Council and the National Consumer Agency of

2   *Danish Environment* online (June 1999): www.mst.dk/magazine/contents/index8.htm

Denmark are exploring the inclusion of environmental considerations into product comparisons and information on the environmental impact of different products. These information tools include:

- Environmental guidelines
- Eco-labels
- Environmental product declarations
- Environmental manuals

These are discussed below.

### 5.3.2.1 Environmental guidelines

These are designed to be an information tool for purchasing professionals and are intended to improve environmental decision-making. At the same time, they are intended to encourage suppliers to develop 'greener' products. There will be around 50 guidelines published by 2000 and they are widely distributed to public-sector purchasing managers. The guidelines mainly target products with significant environmental impacts (e.g. office equipment, office furniture, cleaning agents, paint, lighting, transport equipment, kitchen hardware and equipment, and food products) and describe the environmental issues that should be considered when purchasing. Information about undesirable substances is also included (DEPA 1998).

### 5.3.2.2 Eco-labels

There are two eco-labelling schemes in Denmark, the 'Nordic Swan' (also operating in Sweden, Norway, Finland and Iceland) and the EU 'Flower' eco-label. The Nordic Swan has worked successfully on the Danish market; however, the EU eco-label has not been a success. There is also a special eco-label for organic food (DEPA 1997).

### 5.3.2.3 Environmental product declarations

Product declarations aim to provide information about the most significant environmental impacts of a product during its life-cycle but not necessarily to provide information about the environmentally 'best' or 'worst' products on the market. It is not clear how these declarations will be used in the Danish environmental information strategy (DEPA 1997).

### 5.3.2.4 Environmental manuals

Manuals are intended to provide information to final users about how to use, maintain and dispose of a product. The Danish EPA is examining the need for environmental manuals among different product groups and whether there should be mandatory environmental manuals required for specific product groups: for example, washing machines (DEPA 1997).

### 5.3.3 Green taxes

There are several environmental taxes and charges in Denmark, mainly connected with raw materials (e.g. sand, gravel, clay) and products and waste (e.g. batteries, cars, leaded petrol, disposable tableware, light bulbs, chlorofluorocarbons [CFCs] and halons, and pesticides). In 1996 Denmark was considered to be at the forefront in the application of environmental taxes and charges (Oosterhuis *et al.* 1996). However, a recent report commissioned by the Danish EPA gave a mixed assessment of existing Danish product taxes and charges, reflecting success for some and yet failure for others that lacked data or that were set at an insufficient level to influence demand (COWI 2000). The Danish EPP action plan considered an inter-ministerial committee to evaluate existing green taxes and use the results when considering the development of new taxes and charges (DEPA 1997).

### 5.3.4 Subsidies

In 1999 the Programme for Cleaner Products was launched by the Danish government. It is intended to give subsidies for the development and marketing of cleaner products, including the development of know-how and methods for product development, greener marketing, and waste and recycling systems. The programme will run until 2002.[3]

### 5.3.5 Green public procurement

Since 1994 activities related to greener public procurement have been promoted in the Action Plan for Sustainable Public Procurement Policy. In 1995 the Danish government sent a memorandum on green public procurement to all state institutions and state-owned and state-controlled companies specifying that environmental considerations must be taken into consideration alongside price and quality factors. The preliminary results show that the memorandum has been positively received and has resulted in a change in purchasing behaviour.

### 5.3.6 Establishment of product area panels

The Danish EPA has established product area panels made up of relevant stakeholders within specific product groups. The stakeholders are brought together and given a free hand to establish a dialogue and to strengthen co-operation in order to facilitate the development and marketing of cleaner products. The first three pilot product groups were electronics, textiles and transportation. Each of the product area panels had developed an action plan by the end of 1999, with a list of initiatives, time-schedules and possible funding sources. For example, the electronics product panel developed the following initiatives (DEPAP 1999):

3   DEPA 1997; and personal communication with M. Hounum, Danish Environmental Protection Agency, 1999.

- Product development guidelines, containing developmental concepts and methods and criteria relating to component choice for use by electronics designers and developers

- Component data sheets, covering the environmental properties of electronic components

- International standards, mapping how environmental issues are incorporated in international standards

- Energy reduction, encouraging co-operation with research institutes and companies to set up a limited number of surveys and development projects aimed at demonstrating the relationship between competitiveness and energy reduction during use

- Recycling technology: to develop appropriate techniques and methods to increase the material recovery rate for electronics to above 90% in three years and to help promote the export potential of Danish recycling technology

- Communication with product developers, to organise conferences and seminars to raise the awareness of electronic product developers of ecodesign, to assess training needs and develop training activities, to incorporate the product development guidelines into the higher education curriculum, to involve the media in spreading the message and to develop a web page with information on the environmental properties of components

- Public procurement: to examine the information and financial resource needs of public purchasers in buying environmentally friendly electronics

- Labelling: to develop a simple labelling scheme for household purchasers that gives comparable information on life-cycle impacts, including design (content of hazardous materials), use (energy consumption) and disposal (disassembly and recyclability potential)

## 5.4 Integrated product policy: a different perspective

The debate on IPP is new and evolving, and DGXI has been seeking input from stakeholders for discussion on the further development of IPP. We would like to present our thinking as input in this process.

The Centre for Sustainable Design (CfSD) has evolved a much simpler perspective on IPP compared with the current DGXI approach. CfSD defines IPP as 'public policy aiming at greening the marketplace through the integrated use of supply and demand side tools'. In this context, and based on the principles of a life-cycle perspective and stakeholder involvement, the key building blocks are:

■ Green(er) consumption

■ Green(er) product development

From this perspective, IPP is a policy initiative that includes both the supply side and the demand side of the equation. Governments or policy-makers can influence both sides of this equation by using various instruments from the IPP toolbox. By using a mixture of supply- and demand-side tools, it is possible to stimulate, facilitate and co-ordinate various actors along the product chain to engage in activities to reduce the impact of products throughout the product life-cycle. Table 5.2 gives examples of supply- and demand-side measures.

It should be noted that the instruments listed in Table 5.2 are not exclusive to their particular side of the equation. They do overlap and feed back to each other, which are key attributes in the greening of the marketplace. For example, public purchasing has the dual effect of greening the consumption side as well as sending a strong signal to producers and product developers to supply greener products.

From this perspective, however, it can be seen that business has little control over the consumption side, except through brand, product or corporate communications (e.g. advertising). Because of this, there may be a misperception in business that IPP covers only the supply side (e.g. eco-product development). To avoid perception gaps, which are already starting to emerge, the continued and balanced use of a consultative approach by DGXI, incorporating a wide range of stakeholder input, will be essential.

| Eco-product development (supply) side | Consumption (demand) side |
| --- | --- |
| ▶ Regulatory bans/phase-outs | ▶ Consumer information: |
| ▶ Product requirements (content, quality, performance) | – Eco-labels<br>– Product profiles<br>– Product guidelines<br>– Information centres |
| ▶ Take-back requirements | |
| ▶ Grants/subsidies for eco-product development | ▶ Indirect taxation |
| ▶ Eco-design competitions/awards | ▶ Public purchasing |
| ▶ Environmental management systems (EMS)/product-oriented environmental management systems (POEMS) | ▶ Deposit/refund schemes |
| ▶ Standardisation | |
| ▶ Information and reporting | |
| ▶ Voluntary agreements | |

*Table* 5.2 **Examples of supply- and demand-side measures**

# 5.5 Integrated product policy and eco-product development

From a life-cycle perspective, the greening of the product development process is key to reducing many of the environmental impacts of products (and services). Therefore, the product design and development phase is a crucial issue for IPP, as many of the environmental impacts of products are determined at this stage (Ernst & Young/SPRU 1998; Oosterhuis *et al.* 1996). For example, products that are designed to be inefficient or difficult to dismantle and recycle limit the ability of downstream stakeholders, such as customers and recyclers, to reduce product-related environmental impacts.

However, at present, ecodesign has not been widely adopted by industry (Clark and Charter 1996), particularly among small and medium-sized enterprises (SMEs; Clark and Charter 1999), and eco-product development (EPD)[4] is rarely found as an integral part of a company's business strategy. This is because many companies, on the one hand, lack knowledge of environmental issues and ecodesign strategies and tools and, on the other, feel little legislative, business-to-business or market pressure to incorporate environmental issues into their product development process.

This is likely to change with the broader implementation of product-oriented environmental policies, such as IPP, as they will act as drivers for greater EPD implementation. Pressures for EPD would come not only through the threat of possible new regulation but also, more probably, through market pressure from customer demands for greener products or through the supply chain from voluntary initiatives, such as environmental management systems (ISO 14001 or the EU Eco-management and Audit Scheme [EMAS]) and product stewardship.

Therefore, in a new IPP landscape, those who have developed EPD approaches will be better prepared for the opportunities arising from greener markets as well as for threats from new regulations and economic measures and demands from the supply chain.

Even without a fully articulated and implemented IPP at the EU level, national EPP approaches are moving fast.[5] Furthermore, many product policy tools (e.g. greener purchasing, national eco-labelling schemes, consumer education, green taxes, 'producer responsibility', etc.) are being applied irrespective of overall EPP or IPP frameworks. This means that companies will have to be prepared for emerging policies in nation-states regardless of how IPP develops in the future at the EU level.

## 5.5.1 *Focus on the electronics sector*

The electronics sector represents an excellent example of the challenges facing IPP and EPD. The electronics industry has received considerable attention recently from policy-

---

4  Eco-product development can be defined as the integration of environmental considerations into the entire product development process, from product strategy and idea generation to reverse logistics and end-of-life management.

5  For example, with the statement 'We are not waiting for the EU' (Ahlner, Swedish Environmental Protection Agency, personal communication, 1999).

makers because of its rapid technological rate of change and subsequent high rates of product obsolescence and growing problems from waste products throughout Europe and other parts of the world. As a result of these problems, the sector is under considerable pressure from a number of proposed and already active environmental regulations at both the EU and national levels. At the EU level, the proposed Waste from Electrical and Electronic Equipment (WEEE) Directive and the Restriction on the Use of Hazardous Substances in Electrical and Electronic Equipment Directive are in the process of being passed,[6] and there is a newly proposed 'New Approach' Directive from DGIII (Electrical and Electronic Equipment [EEE] Directive) focused on ecodesign issues. At the national level, a number of countries have already implemented legislation on waste electrical and electronic products and others have proposals drafted.

Owing in part to the intensity of policy initiatives already focused on the sector, DGXI has highlighted electronics as a key sector for potential IPP pilot projects (BMU 1999). This will mean significant pressure to incorporate ecodesign and eco-product development at the company level.

From CfSD's initial research in the electronics sector there appears to be the following key issues in EPD:

- Supply chain management
- Communications
- EPD and environmental management systems
- Innovation

### 5.5.1.1 Supply chain management

IPP discussions have not really directly addressed supply chain issues. However, supply chain management (SCM) is becoming more and more important in EPD. For instance, many electronics companies, especially in Western Europe, are no longer 'manufacturers' as much as they are 'systems integrators', and significant environmental impacts result from their supply chains.

Companies may influence their suppliers in a number of ways. For example, some business customers now demand that their suppliers are ISO 14001- or EMAS-certified (Barthel 1999), or they may send detailed questionnaires or work closely with them in training programmes. Box 5.2 contains examples of tools and strategies for supply chain (environmental) management.

As a part of the Ecodesign and Training for Manufacture, Use and 'End-of-Life' for SMEs (ETMUEL)[7] project, the following points and questions have been raised in discussions with electronics companies regarding supply chain issues:

---

6   The European Commission adopted the proposed WEEE and Restriction of Substances Directives on 13 June 2000. They have now been sent to the EU Parliament and the Council of Ministers.

7   ETMUEL is a project run by CfSD and funded by the Adapt programme of the European Social Fund. It is a two-year training programme focusing on the implementation of environmental considerations in product development and design (ecodesign) in the electronics sector. Further details can be found at www.cfsd.org.uk/etmuel/index.html.

- Communicating environmental expectations through written policies and communication materials (letters, brochures, articles, web-based materials)
- Providing questionnaires or the carrying out of audits
- Organising supplier meetings
- Offering supplier training and providing technical assistance
- Carrying out collaborative R&D projects
- Restructuring relationships with suppliers (e.g. implementing 'reverse logistics')
- Demanding suppliers to be ISO 14001- or EMAS-certified

*Box 5.2* **Tools and strategies in supply chain (environmental) management**

*Source:* Adapted from Lippmann 1999

- Regarding the international aspects of the supply chain, where are the majority of electronics component suppliers located? The CfSD's research shows that it has been hard to find component manufacturers based in the United Kingdom (Clark and Charter 1999). The work in the Danish electronics product area panels indicates that the majority of component manufacturers are in the Far East.[8]

- Should companies educate and train their suppliers worldwide (e.g. producing ecodesign checklists in Chinese) if they are going to reduce environmental impacts in national markets?

- Can suppliers worldwide comply with European standards? For instance, is it possible for a component manufacturer in South-East Asia to 'design for dismantling', as implicitly suggested by the proposed EU WEEE Directive (DGXI 2000)?

- Who should be responsible for raising awareness of environmental issues in electronics products? Research by DGXI (DGXI 2000) has also shown that among electronics component suppliers there is very little or no awareness about 'business and environment' issues, ecodesign, or even the proposed WEEE Directive.

- How is information to be passed down the supply chain? Are manufacturers of final products able to educate all their suppliers about environmental issues (when there may be thousands of components in the final electronic product or equipment), and what are the costs and benefits?

- How can the supply chain be harnessed to influence SMEs? The supply chain is potentially a powerful channel to influence SMEs to improve their environmental performance, since SMEs are more likely to listen to their customers (Clark and Charter 1999).

8   Personal communication with J. Jakobson, Danish Environmental Protection Agency, 1999.

### 5.5.1.2 Communications

Poor communications inside and outside companies have been major barriers to selling ecodesign (internally) or eco-products (externally). Generally, EPD has been an isolated activity within environmental management or R&D and has rarely been treated as a mainstream management issue.

**Internal communication**
A major obstacle to the development and management of 'greener' products (EPD) is that communication with customers is often carried out by the marketing and sales functions, which are two of the least 'green' business functions. In addition, marketing usually has significant influence on product decisions (Clark and Charter 1996). This has resulted in poor internal marketing of EPD to internal stakeholders (e.g. selling of ecodesign).

**External communication**
In order to establish customer needs, better dialogue with the market is necessary. Conventional market research has tended not to address environmental issues and this has led to a lack of knowledge about customer needs and expectations. For instance, Rank Xerox has two questions on environmental issues in the main yearly customer survey that have displaced two marketing questions. The environment director lobbied hard for the questions and has to report back on business benefits resulting from asking those questions (Charter 2000a).

Most EPD has focused on improving the internal eco-efficiency of the product, with little attempt to understand the use phase of products. Where this has been undertaken, there are cases of real eco-improvement. For example, with the Kambrook (Axis) kettle it was only when the researchers and designers observed how consumers used the kettle that they started to define environmental improvements (Sweatman and Gertsakis 1997; see also Chapter 16).

In addition to this, lack of awareness, lack of understanding and poor communication may be some of the reasons for the emergence of 'rebound effects'—the situation where improved environmental features in the product cause increased consumption. Good examples are light bulbs and washing machines, where cost savings have encouraged customers to increase consumption—e.g. to leave the lights on or to wash clothes more often (see Chapter 12).

### 5.5.1.3 Eco-product development and environmental management systems

EMSs, such as ISO 14001 and EMAS, have predominantly been focused on site-related issues. However, a number of companies are beginning to use their EMSs to focus on product-related issues and to implement ecodesign in their companies. The concept of linking EPD to EMSs is also the basis of the product-oriented environmental management system (POEMS) initiative in the Netherlands that aims to embed EPD in EMSs or broader management systems.

Separately, an ISO working group has organised a number of expert workshops to examine ways to integrate environmental aspects into product development. From these, it was concluded that there is a need for an ISO document that highlights environmental aspects at each stage of the product development process—ISO 14062. A technical report 'for information purposes only' (Lehmann 1999) will be completed by the end of 2001. The working group agreed that the report should be informative and provide guidance to companies but should not be an ISO standard. Discussions are continuing within the ISO TC 207 committee on environmental management systems and national standards bodies.

### 5.5.1.4 Innovation

Product innovations are considered to be necessary in order to expand and maintain a company's market share (Ousterhuis *et al.* 1996). Innovation is one of the major business drivers for the electronics industry, combined with rapid technological change. For instance, market research in consumer electronics indicates that there is a need for fundamentally new products since in many Western European countries consumer electronics products have low volume growth and low profitability (RBI 1998). Innovation is a key challenge for industry if eco-efficiency (e.g. 'factor 4' and 'factor 10') goals are to be achieved. Therefore, it is important to explore how to combine innovation with EPP instruments that differ in relation to their ability to stimulate innovation. Subsidies for R&D probably have the most direct potential influence on eco-innovation, although other instruments (e.g. taxes and charges) may have an impact (Oosterhuis *et al.* 1996).

## 5.6 Concluding remarks

Nine major conclusions may be drawn.

1. The IPP approach is new, and discussions are still in their infancy. The main questions are:
    - What are the objectives and priorities of IPP?
    - How it will be incorporated in legislation and other policy measures?
    - How can the success or progress of IPP be measured?

2. IPP is a government policy approach to green the market by greening product development (supply) and consumption (demand). However, manufacturers have little or no control over the consumption side. Environmental product policies (EPPs) often appear to be focused more on the 'greening' of the supply side rather than on the consumption side. The recognition of the importance of the consumption side in achieving sustainability goals is becoming more and more important.

3. The majority of stakeholders have adopted a 'wait and see' approach to IPP until the green paper is published by DGXI (expected in December 2000).

4. The synergies and overall benefits resulting from IPP will be achieved through the integration of supply- and demand-side measures. The development of greener products without greener markets is sub-optimal.

5. Companies should develop their own EPD programmes, which can bring financial benefits and generate new ideas and business opportunities. However, the issue needs to be managed and new tools need to be developed to enable environmental considerations to be integrated into product development from the idea generation phase to the 'end-of-life' management (EOLM) phase. Companies with EPD in place will be better prepared for new policy developments (e.g. new market opportunities, product liabilities, etc.) that might emerge from the EPP or IPP debates at either national or EU level.

6. There seem to be several key issues in EPD: supply chain management, communications, links to environmental management systems (EMSs) and innovation:

   – *Supply chain management* (SCM): SCM might provide a real opportunity to reduce eco-impacts since overall environmental performance is closely related to how EPD is managed up and down the supply chain. Additionally, supply chains hold a large potential to 'green' SMEs.

   – *Communications*: poor environmental communication both internally and externally has been one of the major obstacles to developing and promoting 'greener' products. Can IPP help to tackle these issues?

   – *Environmental management systems* (EMSs): the integration of EPD into existing EMS schemes is being tried in the Netherlands (i.e. POEMS). Similar discussions are evolving within the ISO, where an ISO information and guidance document will be produced on EPD. However, it is too early to derive any major conclusions from these initiatives since the work has just started.

   – *Innovation*: innovation is an important business driver in the electronics sector as well as one of the key eco-efficiency challenges on the supply side. Eco-innovation should be regarded as one of the strategic elements in greening the supply side.

7. There are several ways that governments can help progress the EPD process, such as through funding and subsidies, public information and education campaigns, co-ordination of information flows and support for greener purchasing. It has also been realised that increased environmental considerations can result in competitive advantage so there is more room to link environmental requirements to industrial development.

8. It is important to remember that all stakeholders must 'buy into' the IPP process, since IPP is based on 'shared responsibility' rather than 'producer responsibility'.

9. The IPP at the EU level is progressing slower in comparison to national EPP approaches in different EU countries (e.g. Sweden, Denmark, Austria, Germany, the Netherlands) and non-EU countries (e.g. Japan, Norway). Therefore it is important for companies to develop and to continue to work on their own EPD programmes without waiting for developments at the EU level.

# Part 2
# SUSTAINABLE, ECO-PRODUCT AND ECO-SERVICE DEVELOPMENT

# SUSTAINABLE PRODUCT DESIGN

*Ursula Tischner*
econcept, Germany

*Martin Charter*
The Centre for Sustainable Design, UK

Sustainable development will become an increasingly prominent issue in this decade. Present patterns of development and consumption cannot be sustained in a world of growing population, rising human aspirations and limited carrying capacity. To move towards a more sustainable society there will need to be fundamental changes to avoid serious risks to human wellbeing and natural systems. Although still weak in implementation, the principles of sustainable development (Box 6.1) are established and widely accepted among governments and various other stakeholders. These principles embrace social and ethical as well as economic and environmental dimensions: for example, the need to balance economic development with environmental protection, in the context of human needs for improved 'quality of life' and ethical issues such as social justice and the rights of future generations. It is becoming increasingly clear that sustainable development is not a remote future concern but one where progress and solutions are needed now if serious problems are to be avoided in the future.

Sustainability poses many challenges and opportunities for business. If governments or societies as a whole take action or move towards lifestyles and technologies that contribute to sustainability, this will have profound implications for all stakeholders at both a local and a global level. There are tremendous benefits for businesses that spot these trends and develop more sustainable products and services: for example, products and services designed to consider economic, environmental, social and ethical issues throughout their life-cycle (from excavation of raw materials to manufacturing and use, recycling and final disposal). The role of products and services is central to the sustainability debate, and a series of fundamental questions will need to be asked, such as:

- What is a sustainable product?

- How does one 'develop and design' sustainable products?

- How does sustainable product design (SPD) differ from ecodesign?

**SUSTAINABLE DEVELOPMENT IS 'A DEVELOPMENT THAT MEETS THE NEEDS OF THE** present without compromising the ability of future generations to meet their needs' (WCED 1987: 43). It is a process leading to the goal or result of sustainability. It is not a static situation but a state of dynamic equilibrium between human and natural systems. The document in which this principle is laid down is that of 'Agenda 21', the blueprint for sustainable development where tasks for the fields of production, consumption and policy (i.e. society as a whole) are formulated and possible steps suggested. Although a broad and complex issue, there are six principles that describe how a sustainable community should interact with other communities and with nature.

- **Environmental protection.** The resources and life-support systems needed for continuance of human wellbeing and all life must be protected.
- **Development.** 'Quality of life' should be improved, with economic development as one of the objectives, not the sole objective.
- **Futurity.** The interests of future generations should be considered in what we leave behind.
- **Equity.** Sustainability will not work if the world's resources are unfairly distributed or if the poor pay a disproportionate part of the costs of the transition to sustainability (as everyone has a part to play).
- **Diversity.** Diverse environmental, social and economic systems are generally more robust and less vulnerable to irreversible or catastrophic damage; diversity also allows individuals to chose more sustainable options.
- **Participation.** Sustainability cannot be imposed but requires the support and involvement of all sections of the community and all communities; this requires ensuring opportunities for participation in decision-making.

Sustainable development is a process with the following features:

- **Conservation of resources**
- **Respect for all stakeholders' viewpoints**
- **Use of the precautionary principle**
- **Encouragement of subsidiarity**, with decision-making at the lowest practicable level
- **Promotion of personal freedom**, meeting needs without harming the environment or people
- **Addressing aesthetics**, protecting and creating places and objects of beauty

*Box* 6.1  **Principles of sustainable development**

*Source:* UN 1992

SPD means thinking through complex issues such as meeting the basic needs of the world's poor while reducing global inequalities and producing profitable solutions. A major challenge is how to infuse sustainability issues at the 'front of the pipe', where new ideas and concepts are generated. Business is starting to undertake eco-(re)design of existing products, but approaches to eco-innovation (environmentally driven new product and service development) and broader sustainable product innovation are new. Companies are particularly struggling with the implications of the 'soft side' of the sustainable agenda (e.g. social and ethical issues) as an integrated business sustainability model is yet to be developed.

## 6.1 What is sustainable product design?

Terms such as 'sustainable product design', 'ecodesign', 'design for environment' and even 'product design' are often confused and are not clearly defined or well known. The following definitions aim to help distinguish between the different areas (see also Fig. 6.1).

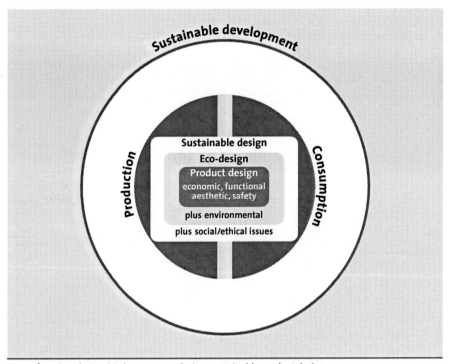

*Figure* 6.1   **The relationship between ecodesign, sustainable product design and sustainable development**

*Source:* Tischner 2000

### 6.1.1 *Product design*

Product design professionals are responsible for designing profitable products that meet the needs of users and producers of products. They form the interface between 'the user' and 'the product'. The product design and development phase influences more than 80% of the economic cost connected with a product, as well as 80% of the environmental and social impacts of a product, incurred throughout its whole life-cycle. Therefore product design and development has a pivotal role to play within sustainable consumption and production discussions as it significantly influences the ways that products are produced and consumed in terms of, for example:

- Fulfilling socially acceptable demand

- Meeting users' needs

- The materials and production technologies used

- The product lifetime

- Recycling and disposal of the product

## 6.1.2 Ecodesign and design for environment

Ecodesign and design for environment (DfE) are terms for strategies that aim to integrate environmental considerations into product design and development. They involve life-cycle thinking, which means the integration of life-cycle considerations into product design (see Chapter 14). The overall goal is to minimise the consumption of natural resources and energy and the consequent impact on the environment while maximising benefits for customers. If environmental aspects are taken into account during the earliest phases of product development, then it is more likely that lower environmental impacts can be 'built into' the final product.

Various strategies and tools have already been developed to help implement ecodesign. This approach is now being undertaken by some leading companies (e.g. Philips and Electrolux; see Chapters 12 and 18). Many studies are indicating that companies implementing ecodesign are able to reduce costs, produce more innovative products and achieve more secure market positions than their less eco-sensitive competitors (see e.g. ADEME 1999).

## 6.1.3 Sustainable product design is more than ecodesign

At present, where sustainability is considered in product design and development it is typically regarded as being the same as ecodesign. But sustainable product design (SPD) is more than ecodesign, as it integrates social and ethical aspects of the product's life-cycle alongside environmental and economic considerations—aiming for the so-called 'triple bottom line'. Sustainable product development and design is concerned with balancing economic, environmental and social aspects in the creation of products and services (see Box 6.2).

Some companies have started ecodesign activities, but social and ethical aspects are not usually integrated into product development processes. Only a few leading-edge companies appear to have grasped the wider social and ethical issues related to sustainability and have progressed beyond ecodesign. At present, there is little guidance on the product implications of business sustainability and very little information on applying SPD. Therefore it is difficult to develop, communicate and train designers and product developers in the concept of SPD.

SUSTAINABLE PRODUCT DEVELOPMENT AND DESIGN IS CONCERNED WITH balancing economic, environmental and social aspects in the creation of products and services. Sustainable product development and design looks to minimise adverse sustainability impacts and maximise sustainable value throughout the life-cycle of the product, building or service. To create sustainable products and services that increase stakeholders' 'quality of life', while at the same time achieving major reductions in resource and energy use, will require a significant emphasis on stimulating new ideas through higher levels of creativity and innovation.

Box 6.2 **Sustainable product development and design**

Source: Charter 1998b

## 6.2 Drivers and obstacles for sustainable product design

Some key SPD questions that companies are dealing with today and will increasingly be asking in the future are:

- What is our environmental and social performance?
- What environmental regulations are on the horizon?
- Which types of material are more environmentally friendly?
- What *shape* of product design uses the smallest amount of resources?
- What kind of production technique saves us money while at the same time reduces environmental impact?
- How environmentally aware is our target group (the possible buyers of the products or services)?
- Are our suppliers socially acceptable? For example: Do they employ children? Do they release their waste-water, waste and emissions into the natural environment without proper treatment?

These questions are also increasingly being asked by customers (domestic, 'business to business' [B2B], government, distributors) as they become more and more environmentally and socially conscious. In addition, companies will increasingly be forced by laws and regulations to implement 'producer responsibility' throughout the whole life-cycle of the product. Companies such as Nike have employed a sustainability manager, SC Johnson Wax have appointed a director of sustainable product innovation and other companies, such as Sony, have environment product laboratories (see Chapters 12 and 19). In addition, many companies are now starting to express the need for environmentally literate product designers but are having major difficulties in recruiting the right people, as traditional product designers have not been trained to deal with sustainability or even environmental issues.

There are growing drivers for ecodesign and SPD worldwide. Some examples are listed in Box 6.3.

- 'Curve balls'. These are societal concerns such as those regarding genetically modified organisms (GMOs) or regarding Shell and the disposal of the Brent Spar oil platform. They have illustrated that sustainability issues are not just about eco-efficiency.

- The Integrated Product Policy (IPP) initiative of the European Union (EU): a green paper to be published in 2000

- The Directorate General for the Environment (DGXI), of the Commission of the European Communities) commissioned two major studies on the 'state of the art' in ecodesign, as part of the development of the IPP green paper (1999).

- Sweden will set IPP as a key element of their environmental agenda in their presidency of the EU (2001).

- Environmental product policy (EPP) is developing in advanced 'green' countries in the EU (e.g. Denmark).

- There are EU directives that focus on 'end-of-life' issues but which also have major implications for ecodesign ('design for dismantling', 'design for recycling'), such as:
  - End of Life Vehicles (EOLV) Directive
  - Waste from Electrical and Electronic Equipment (WEEE) Directive

- The Directorate General for Enterprise (DGIII), of the Commission of the European Communities, is proposing a new directive on ecodesign that initially will be focused on the electronics sector but will then potentially be extended to other sectors.

- There is a International Organization for Standardization (ISO) working group that has been formed to cover 'environmental aspects in product development'.

- A range of eco-labels has been developed worldwide.

- Several governments and companies are starting to establish green procurement initiatives.

- There is a growing amount of research into ecodesign and SPD issues in universities worldwide.

- Japan has a major programme on ecodesign driven by the Ministry of International Trade and Industry (MITI).

- There is a range of ecodesign activities within multinational companies: for example, Lucent Technologies recently developed a programme using ISO 14001 that involved the training of 400 designers on ecodesign issues.

*Box* 6.3 **Emerging drivers for ecodesign**

*Source:* Charter 2000c

## 6.2.1 *Changing patterns of consumption and production*

It is clear that sustainable development will require a substantial increase in efficiency of resource and energy use (referred to as 'factor $x$' as no one really knows the magnitude of the change required) and a commensurate reduction in pollution and other environmental damage. Chapter 4 of Agenda 21 covers changing patterns of consumption and highlighted that present consumption levels are causing serious environmental problems. However, consumption drives the creation of income and export markets needed to promote worldwide prosperity. The replication of present consumption patterns by developing countries is not a viable solution to the sustainability conundrum. However, levels of consumption must be increased to improve overall 'quality of life'. Therefore, strategies for eco-efficiency and waste minimisation are essential (see UN 1992). The move towards eco-efficiency clearly has to start in the industrialised countries, because they consume more than 80% of the world's resources and generate 80% of all waste, although they only contain 20% of the world population.

The Rio+5 Conference in New York in June 1997 reinforced the growing need to develop more sustainable patterns of consumption and production. One of the outputs was an initiative on eco-efficiency with a target of achieving a 'factor 10' level of productivity improvement in the long term, with a possible 'factor 4' increase among industrialised countries in the two or three decades from 1997. Governments also agreed to promote measures to internalise environmental costs and benefits in the pricing of goods and services and to consider shifting the burden of taxation to focus on unsustainable patterns through, for example, reducing and eliminating subsidies to environmentally harmful activities.

## 6.2.2 Changing technologies

Some argue that the key to many (but not necessarily all) sustainability problems lies in developing new technologies that contribute to, rather than threaten, sustainability. At this point, various technologies offer great potential for dematerialisation: that is, they reduce the quantity of materials and energy required to meet a need. In particular, the increasing speed of information flows, accelerated by the rapid development of telecommunications, opens up the possibility of extensive substitution of products by services. However, the holistic environmental impacts of such shifts are still unclear. How new information and communication technologies (ICT) and the 'new economy' will influence production and consumption patterns is still unclear:

- Does it mean movement to an intermediate, appropriate or low-technology scenario of producing and consuming locally?
- Does it mean a high-technology scenario of information technology products and services dominated by dematerialisation?
- Does it mean a shift to a world dominated by lower consumption and 'more from less', with wider implications for employment, changing work patterns and 'quality of life'?
- Or does it mean a hybrid of all three? This scenario is probably the most likely.

Social behaviour patterns and technological development can move rapidly, and they represent powerful agents of change and a potential area of optimism. But, of course, technology is only as 'good' as the people who use it: one can waste much energy and a large quantity of materials by using new ICT to buy goods from all over the world, causing millions of transportation kilometres, and so on.

## 6.2.3 Changing economic and social patterns

The principles of sustainable development suggest that there will need to be many economic and social changes. There are many uncertainties, but such changes imply, for example:

- Relative shifts in power and economic bases from North to South and from West to East as demands for increased equity and 'quality of life' are met

- Increased regionalisation in government and localisation in choices about lifestyle, providing greater opportunities to choose more sustainable patterns of development

- 'Downshifting' or other changes in lifestyle whereby people meet needs in other ways than through conspicuous material consumption

Against these directions are current trends such as globalisation, the existence of political systems and business practices that are often counter to sustainability and which exacerbate the rich–poor divide and other problems. There will be growing tensions as such patterns become increasingly untenable as the 'haves' hold on to what they have. The result, besides conflict, is likely to be a diverse hybrid of patterns depending on the situation, region and locality.

Existing economic and accounting systems do not take account of wider environmental, ethical and social factors and there is a need for more holistic and inclusive costing mechanisms, which will require a change in economists' and accountants' mind-sets and language. There is a need to develop, at a minimum, environmental accounting and, at an optimum, sustainability accounting. An opportunity might be to implement temporary eco-taxes on products or services, as flags to reduce or change consumption towards more sustainable products or services. This could include incentives for successful behaviour (e.g. subsidies or 'tax breaks' to develop solar technologies) and penalties for harmful activities (e.g. carbon taxes to reduce carbon dioxide [$CO_2$] emissions).

A fundamental part of the problem is the lack of overt markets and demand for sustainable products and services. Behind the lack of demand for SPD lies a range of possible factors, which are considered below along with further thoughts on possible solutions.

### 6.2.3.1 Stakeholders

Mind-sets need to be engaged within each stakeholder group, with a key question being, 'Do stakeholders feel a stake in and/or engagement with the sustainability discussion?' If not, the question is 'Why not?' There is a need to work on peer pressures within and between stakeholders: for example, within multinational corporations (MNCs) through organisations such as the World Business Council for Sustainable Development (WBCSD) which can influence companies down through global supply chains. The potential for change through the supply chain is significant as major MNCs source raw materials, subassemblies and components globally—therefore the impact will not necessarily be at the point of decision, manufacturing or service delivery but could be anywhere in the world!

### 6.2.3.2 Education

There is a general lack of awareness and understanding of sustainability, with the concept often applied to the maintenance of economic longevity (i.e. sustainable economic growth). This is true of customers and other stakeholders and especially so in most businesses. The process of product development starts with an idea and grows into a concept. Therefore, if those individuals whose responsibility it is to generate and manage the creation of new products have no awareness and understanding of the concept of sustainability, then there will be only random and incremental advances in sustainability, not stepwise changes towards 'factor $x$' or sustainable solutions.

The general lack of awareness or interest in sustainability issues may be because:

● Sustainability issues are seen as too long-term and abstract and/or the preserve of academia and government, with the thinking inaccessible to most people.

● Economic and environmental issues are seen as being difficult enough without confusing the issue with complex, 'value-laden' social and ethical issues.

● Wider social and ethical issues are seen as being irrelevant to the debate.

If more sustainable solutions are going to be 'designed and developed', there will need to be more understanding of the practicalities of the concept and of the underlying issues. A key issue is to integrate an understanding of sustainability into strategic planning, even before the earliest stages of product development. This process may highlight far-reaching opportunities such as fundamental shifts from offering products to providing services (e.g. 'product service systems'). These shifts will require strategic-level decision-making within business and possibly a redefinition of business in terms of delivering increased value through high-quality stakeholder services. Education and re-education will be needed among all stakeholders to re-orient the product development process towards sustainable solutions.

### 6.2.3.3 Information

At present, there is no clear theoretical or practical framework as to what SPD means for companies within the industrialised world. For example, what does SPD mean for a company with 10,000 products, with 1,000 key suppliers, which manufactures and sells worldwide? Is this fundamentally unsustainable or are there strategies that can be employed to reduce the sustainability impact of products and services? At present the pressure to reduce 'time to market' and perceived costs are key constraints to ecodesign or, more broadly, SPD. Environmental and social information should focus on the needs of the stakeholders in the process. However, the collection of data is often seen as a complex, time-consuming process, and analysis is believed to be likely to slow down the product development process. To enable the effective implementation of ecodesign or, more broadly, SPD, information will have to be packaged more effectively for product developers, designers and other business functions. There should also be wider stakeholder involvement in the process, with sustainability thinking injected as early as possible, particularly through greater input from customers and suppliers (participation). Considering the issues at the detailed design stage is too late, as many decisions will have been made and opportunities missed.

# 6.3 Sustainable product design strategies

## 6.3.1 From repair to rethink: the four Rs

Looking at history and present developments one can identify four main steps or approaches to environmental protection: repair, refine, redesign, rethink. They are not mutually exclusive and may exist in parallel but will require some fundamental shifts if 'factor *x*' or sustainable solutions are to be achieved. At present the emphasis is on 'end-of-pipe' or repair modifications to existing products, with some movement towards increasing the eco-efficiency of existing products—the refine approach. The next fundamental shift will need to be towards the redesign of products, especially through new technologies and materials so that products meet our needs with greatly reduced environmental impacts. The next, more radical, shift will be towards rethinking: that is, towards new breakthroughs leading to new ways of living and doing things, and towards achieving needs through different means. This is likely to involve new strategies such as the replacement of products with information and travel by communications and to involve different patterns of consumption from the present.

Each of these shifts, especially towards redesign and rethink, will require high levels of creativity and innovation in product development and design. Innovation by business may drive social change, or it may result from a business response to social and environmental changes and pressures, or there may be a combination of influences. However it develops, the need for innovation in product design and development is becoming increasingly clear, as is the need to involve a range of disciplines and business functions, both to generate ideas and to give product design and development appropriate strategic prominence.

## 6.3.2 Eco-innovation

'Factor *x*' levels of reductions in energy and resource consumption will not come about through incremental change but will require radical new solutions. Eco-innovation or environmentally considered new product development focuses on environmental and economic issues but neglects social and ethical considerations—its use will produce new solutions but probably not the breakthroughs needed to move towards sustainability (Box 6.4).

To enable a shift from eco-innovation to sustainable product innovation will require the creation of new processes to produce new solutions that provide customers with more sustainable value and significantly reduced sustainability impact. This will necessitate a new corporate framework to manage product and service innovation. The more significant the change required the closer to the 'front of pipe' and the more strategic the

**DOW ELANCO WORKED WITH PEST CONTROLLERS TO RECONFIGURE DELIVERY** services. it succeeded in reducing by 99% the amount of material needed to provide termite protection.

*Box* 6.4 **Eco-innovation: 99% reduction in materials**

*Source:* Fussler with James 1996

decisions will need to be (cf. Schmidt-Bleek and Tischner 1995). However, at present most changes are at an operational level (i.e. incremental ecodesign changes are made to existing products). Within the sustainability context, innovation should not create new substitute markets unless they create more sustainable value and reduced unsustainable impact. Typical SPD concerns are listed in Table 6.1.

| Economic Issues | Environmental Issues | Social/ethical issues |
|---|---|---|
| ▶ Technological feasibility<br>▶ Financially feasibility<br>▶ Short- and long-term profitability<br>▶ Adequate pricing | ▶ Waste minimisation<br>▶ Cleaner manufacturing<br>▶ Cleaner materials<br>▶ Eco-efficiency<br>▶ Less materials<br>▶ Less energy<br>▶ Renewable resources<br>▶ Renewable energy<br>▶ Recycling | ▶ Fair trade<br>▶ Equitable policies<br>▶ 'Good' employment<br>▶ Conditions of work<br>▶ Investment in communities<br>▶ Support for regional economy<br>▶ Cruelty-free<br>▶ Satisfaction of real needs<br>▶ More customer value<br>▶ Better systems<br>▶ Participation<br>▶ Equality (gender) |

*Table* 6.1 **Typical sustainable product design concerns**

Business has seen sustainability primarily as a threat rather than a series of opportunities, and there is a clear need for new perspectives and tools to enable stakeholders to see the opportunities. This 'seeing' is unlikely to come only through systematic market analysis; there is a need to take more imaginative approaches. To enable this, tools such as scenario planning, Delphi techniques (expert think-tanks) and backcasting (considering desirable future scenarios and working backwards to determine what needs to be done to get there) should be used. Once new ideas and concepts have been developed there should be some positive stimulus towards thinking about more sustainable solutions as early as possible in the product development process. A 'sustainability screen' should be incorporated into the new product development process to evaluate progress. A proposed matrix to screen the performance of existing and new solutions is shown in Table 6.2, and an SPD checklist is provided in Table 6.3.

| Life-cycle phases | Economic issues | Environmental issues | Social issues | Ethical issues |
|---|---|---|---|---|
| Pre-production | | | | |
| Production | | | | |
| Transportation | | | | |
| Use | | | | |
| Disposal | | | | |

*Table* 6.2 **Sustainability screen**

Source: Charter 1997b

| Compulsory requirements Please tick if met | Desirable requirements Please tick if met | Is information lacking for a decision? If yes, who researches? |
|---|---|---|
| *Economic aspects* | | |
| Satisfies customer/user needs | Offers customer a new and obvious advantage Encourages environmentally responsible user behaviour | Find out about customer and user needs including environment-related customer needs |
| Promises success on the market | Better than all competitor products; advantage clearly evident, well communicable | Research market situation, compare with competitors |
| Does not affect costs | Lowers costs, including costs borne by the customer | Find out probable costs over entire life-cycle |
| Technically feasible for the company (additional development work needed) | Technically easy to realise (without additional development work) | Inquire about R&D in the relevant area; what technical alternatives are there? |
| *Environmental aspects* | | |
| Environmental impact is reduced | Environmental impact is drastically reduced | Analyse the environmental impact of the new solution in relation to the existing solution |
| Complies with environment-related legal requirements | Over-fulfils environment-related legal requirements | Find out about environment-related legal requirements, laws, ordinances, standards |
| *Social/ethical aspects* | | |
| Complies with the corporate image; 'politically correct' | Improves the corporate image | Define (internal) corporate image, analyse public corporate image; analyse potential public reception of the new solution |
| Conditions of work in the company itself and along the supply chain are acceptable | Conditions of work in the company itself and along the supply chain are good | Check conditions of work upstream and downstream |

*Table 6.3* **Sustainable product design checklist**

*Source:* Tischner 2000

The BayGen radio (Box 6.5), developed by the inventor Trevor Baylis, illustrates the complexities related to balancing sustainability impacts in the delivery of a new solution. In its original form the radio used human-powered (renewable) energy systems and was assembled by disabled workers in South Africa, but it is a large, material-intensive design. Later models are smaller and less resource-intensive, making use of solar cells. However, this innovation generated a ripple effect in the global market and major transnational corporations, including Philips and Sony, have developed similar products.

 THE ENERGY FOR USING THIS RADIO IS provided by human power via a crank, which is wound prior to the radio's operation. Transmission, storage and steady delivery of operating energy are effected purely by mechanical means, as in a clock that requires winding to work. There is an upgrade of the radio which makes use of solar cells, sparing the listener physical exercise, at least when the sun is shining. Originally, the radio was designed for use in developing countries, but in the meantime it also sells well in other markets. The BayGen radio won the BBC Design Award in the UK on account of its innovative design.

Box 6.5 **The BayGen radio**

# 6.4 **Sustainable solutions**

**SUSTAINABLE SOLUTIONS** ARE PRODUCTS, SERVICES, HYBRIDS OR SYSTEM changes that minimise negative and maximise positive sustainability impacts—economic, environmental, social and ethical—throughout and beyond the life-cycle of existing products or solutions, while fulfilling acceptable societal demands/needs. Sustainable solutions require multi-stakeholder engagement and involve changes or shifts in consumption and production patterns. The aim of sustainable solutions is to create a positive net sustainable value (positive impacts should outweigh negative impacts) for all stakeholders in the delivery process. Changes may be incremental at the product level or radical if system shifts are needed.

Box 6.6 **'Sustainable solutions'**

Source: M. Charter and U. Tischner

## 6.4.1 *Sustainable product design models*

At present there are few SPD models that go beyond eco-efficiency and dematerialisation. The approaches that have been developed tend to be ecologically oriented and do not address wider social or ethical issues, complex systems, technology or supply chains. In Sections 6.4.1.1 and 6.4.1.2 two SPD models are introduced: the cyclic–solar–safe principles and the McDonough Braungart principles (see also Stuart Walker's principles of design listed in Section 6.4.1.3).

### 6.4.1.1 The cyclic–solar–safe principles

Edwin Datschefski, the founder of BioThinking International,[1] has developed five design requirements for sustainable products.

- **Cyclic.** The product should either be made from organic materials and be recyclable or compostable or it should be made from minerals that are continuously cycled in a closed loop.

- **Solar.** The product should use solar energy or other forms of renewable energy that are cyclic and safe, both during use and manufacture.

- **Safe.** The product should be non-toxic in use and disposal, and its manufacture should not involve toxic releases or the disruption of ecosystems.

- **Efficient.** The product, in manufacture and in use, should require 90% less materials, energy and water compared to products providing equivalent utility manufactured in 1990.

- **Social.** The product's manufacture and use should not impinge on basic human rights or natural justice.

The first three requirements mimic the protocols used by plant and animal ecosystems, the fourth requirement is based on the need to maximise the utility of resources in a finite world and the fifth requirement is about maximising human happiness and potential.

Datschefski's (2000) research of 400 products has indicated that 99% of environmental innovations are characterised by one or more of the following 10 principles:

- **Cyclic-mined.** The product becomes more cyclic by making use of recycled metal, glass or plastic, by becoming more recyclable, or both (e.g. Patagonia's fleece jackets made from recycled polyester).

- **Cyclic-grown.** The product becomes more cyclic by making use of grown materials such as wood, leather and wool, by becoming more compostable or both (e.g. bamboo bike).

- **Alternative energy in use.** The product becomes more solar by using renewable energy in use, sometimes by using solar-generated electricity (e.g. Husqvarna solar lawnmower; alarm clock powered by solar cells).

- **Alternative energy in manufacture.** The product becomes more 'solar' by using a renewable energy source for its manufacturing process (e.g. shampoo made in wind-powered factory).

- **Substitution of materials.** The product becomes safer as a result of the substitution of toxic materials or components by safer materials or components (e.g. consumer electronics products using lead-free solder).

- **Stewardship sourcing.** The product becomes safer—in the habitat-preservation sense—by getting raw materials from low-impact sources (e.g. wood from FSC-

1 See www.biothinking.com.

approved forests, dolphin-friendly and albatross-friendly tuna) and also more social by getting raw materials from fairly traded sources (e.g. Fair Trade coffee).

- **Utility.** The product becomes more efficient by providing greater utility for the user, such as in multi-function products (e.g. Black & Decker Quattro Drill–Sander–Saw–Screwdriver) or in rented products (e.g. Electrolux's 'pay-per-use' washing machine).

- **Durability.** The product becomes more efficient in material usage as it lasts longer (e.g. Spacepen Millennium II contains a lifetime's worth of ink).

- **Efficiency.** The product becomes more efficient in its use of energy, water and materials, both in manufacture and in use (e.g. IKEA's SoftAir inflatable chair).

- **Bio-everything.** The product becomes more cyclic, solar and safe as a result of using living organisms or biomimicry techniques (e.g. Rohner's naturally coloured textiles; see Chapter 24).

### 6.4.1.2 The McDonough Braungart principles

William McDonough and Michael Braungart from McDonough Braungart Design Chemistry argue that there are two different metabolisms: biological and technical (see Chapter 7). 'Products of consumption' are consumed in a biological metabolism and 'products of service' circulate in a technical metabolism. A 'product of consumption' should return to the soil safely and a technical 'product of service' should feed back into a high-quality industrial cycle. The principles are to:

- Equate waste with food
- Use current solar income
- Respect diversity

The traditional criteria are:

- Cost (can I afford it?)
- Performance (does it work?)
- Aesthetics (do I like it?)

Additional criteria are:

- Is it ecologically intelligent (do its materials comply with the principles)?
- Is it just (is everything equitably considered)?
- Is it fun (do I get up in the morning and want to do it)?

### 6.4.1.3 Experiments in sustainable product design

Building on an original thinking of Victor Papanek (Papanek 1994), Stuart Walker has created a series of SPD prototypes (Walker 1998). These experimental 'products' are designed for local production (an important facet of sustainability) by using 'off-the-shelf' parts, simple tools and local labour rather than mechanised production. The artefacts represent a hybrid design category that includes elements of mass production, semi-mechanised production and hand fabrication. The collection covers a chair, radio, telephone, box and lamps. As a result of his experiences, Walker has developed four SPD principles:

- **Economics.** Focus on simplicity of design, the use of inexpensive and locally available materials, ease of production, incorporation of 'off-the-shelf' parts, provision of local employment opportunities, and use of low capital production equipment.

- **Environment.** Use natural materials that can be maintained and repaired, re-used parts, fasteners that allow disassembly and reassembly, water-based paints and finishes and other components that are used for aesthetic considerations and that contribute to product longevity, and low-energy production methods.

- **Ethics.** Employ responsible use of human and natural resources. Designs should incorporate considerations significant to environmental stewardship and social equity. These sustainable principles should be expressed in the aesthetic resolution of the products—the designs begin to 'add value' to the product beyond merely being utilitarian. This encourages care and maintenance of the material environment and contributes to product longevity. In turn, this starts to address the problems of excessive consumption and the 'unethical' implications of selfishness, greed, vanity and immoderate attitudes.

- **Social.** Provide local employment through local production, repair and maintenance. The evolution of local designs, expressing a local aesthetic, helps create a sense of cultural identity. Local-scale production fits well into scenarios of more sustainable ways of living that have been developed by urban planners. These scenarios emphasise the importance of 'community' and include mixed-use developments incorporating residence, production, retail and recreation.

## 6.4.2 Examples of sustainable product design

There are various examples of SPD in the chapters forming the first part of this book and in the case-study section, including Kambium kitchens (Chapter 21), Hess Natur (Chapter 23) and Climatex textiles (Chapter 24). Some further examples of SPD are presented below.

### 6.4.2.1 FRIA: an eco-efficient cooling concept for households

The FRIA concept was designed by one of the authors as an answer to the question of how to store foodstuffs in households in a more environmentally friendly and sustainable manner (Tischner and Schmidt-Bleek 1993). Today's refrigerators consume a huge amount of energy, contain problematic substances such as cooling agents and last for only 10–15 years. FRIA instead is designed for longevity and to use drastically less energy and material and to be used in an eco-efficient service system (instead of simply being sold).

### The concept

FRIA is a hybrid between a traditional storage room and a modern refrigerator (i.e. it is a cooling chamber; see Plate 6.1). FRIA is installed in a wall niche in a kitchen or in an unheated room near a kitchen and does not require any material inputs apart from a little energy and some spare parts. FRIA should be installed near the (northern) exterior wall to use outside air for cooling in winter. Cold air is conducted into the cooling compartments if the outside temperature is low enough, which reduces the amount of energy needed for cooling.

*Plate 6.1* **FRIA cooling chamber, designed by Ursula Tischner**

FRIA contains three cooling compartments and two uncooled compartments, which can be used to store canned food, etc. The user can control the cooling temperatures from the outside and vary the cooling volume, leaving one compartment uncooled if the space is not needed. The cooling system that is used in the warmer months of the year could be an ordinary compressor unit. New greener technology might also be used, as the cooling system is installed independently from the cooling chamber, which makes it easy to exchange. Thus technical improvements can be installed at convenient intervals, whereas the cooling chamber itself retains a very long life-span.

When being installed into a wall niche FRIA can be insulated with alternative materials that are free of chlorofluorocarbons (CFCs), such as blown concrete, cork, aerogel or recycled paper. This, combined with the cold outside air being conducted into the cooling chamber in winter and the possibility of decreasing the cooling volume individually, reduces FRIA's energy consumption to at least 50% of a conventional fridge with the same cooling technology. As a result of its longevity, FRIA's material consumption is lower by an estimated 'factor 4' or 'factor 6' compared to a normal refrigerator (e.g. if only one FRIA per flat or house is installed).

**A new marketing strategy**

FRIA must be built into the house by hand, with the components produced industrially but with assembly and service being delivered by decentralised and service-oriented retail outlets which are responsible for maintenance, service and repair. FRIA uses a leasing strategy (e.g. the producer retains possession of FRIA and the user rents the 'cooling' service and pays a charge for installation plus a monthly rent). The responsibility for maintenance, repairs and disposal also rests with the producer, whose interest is then to value a long-lasting and efficient refrigeration system. In addition, the producer knows which parts were used to build FRIA and, at disposal, the firm can develop strategies to re-use and recycle the components. The advantage of FRIA to the user is he or she will:

- Save money by reducing energy consumption
- Buy only one product instead of five (or only buy the service)
- Have no responsibility for the disposal of FRIA
- Have the security of using a well-functioning, energy-saving and eco-friendly refrigerator

It is also conceivable that house builders might install FRIA in apartments and that residents might pay the costs together with the monthly rent for the accommodation.

### 6.4.2.2 Growing packaging

Goods need to be packaged to enable transportation and to be sold to customers. However, packaging designers are generally unaware of the amount of resources required for product packaging and the associated environmental and social impacts throughout the life-cycle of the product. A common rule of thumb is that packaging should either be easily recyclable to close industrial cycles or should be made out of natural materials that can be disposed of without causing any problems to natural cycles. Unfortunately, there are few projects that focus on the latter (creating biological cycles) and often these are not seen by industry as viable alternatives. Those that do experiment with unusual materials or develop their own production techniques still tend to be driven by individuals or small firms.

The Dutch designer Jan Velthuizen grows gourds in special negative moulds. When they reach a certain size the gourds are then dried and cleaned. The results are organic containers for liquid and non-liquid foodstuffs or cosmetics such as bath oils and soap powder. If the negative mould contains lettering or logos the gourd shell reflects this (see Plate 6.2). Using such gourds for storage and transportation purposes is not new but the design idea is new.

*Plate* 6.2 **Gourd packaging grown in negative moulds, grown by designer Jan Velthuizen**

There is also enormous potential from natural fibres that can be shredded, softened and pressed or poured into a mould (the use of recycled paper in egg cartons is just one example). Other examples of this technique come from less industrialised countries: for instance, fibre bowls made by a Filipino company using banana plant waste and the bark of the coco-palm. Organic waste is cleaned, boiled and pulverised by using a wooden hammer to produce a fibre paste. The latter can then be dyed as desired—preferably with natural dyes—and then passed through a sieve. Strips of this paste are then placed in a mould, resulting in containers with a highly decorative, irregular fibre structure.

### 6.4.2.3 Solar intelligence: the 'Solar Mower' from Husqvarna

Inspired by sheep grazing, designers and engineers at Husqvarna (a subsidiary of Electrolux) invented a completely new type of lawnmower which requires neither manpower nor fossil energy—a solar mower (Plate 6.3).

Driven by solar energy, the Solar Mower 'eats' its way through the lawn day by day, slowly, steadily and silently. In this way noise does not become a nuisance for neighbours. A built-in computer with sensors ensures that the Solar Mower recognises and navigates its way around obstacles. In addition, it only stays in the shade for as long as its stored energy permits; it then goes back into the sun. The mower is small and cuts the grass into such small pieces that clippings can be left on the lawn as fertiliser.

*Plate* 6.3  **The 'Solar Mower', manufactured by Husqvarna (a subsidiary of Electrolux)**

However, this innovation does have its price: at present, the Solar Mower costs around US$3,000. Husqvarna is currently trying to reduce the price and at the same time transfer the insights gained with this innovative project to other product lines (Bakker 1997).

## 6.5 Conclusions

Ecodesign is already being practised in some companies. However, what are missing are methodologies, metrics and tools that take account of, and integrate, wider social and ethical considerations alongside eco-efficiency into product and service development.

There is a need for an objective operational model of business sustainability. The model should incorporate all economic, environment and social and/or ethical considerations throughout the life-cycle of the product. Part of this process will be to develop a more holistic view and to manage the product development process more effectively to ensure sustainability is embedded at each stage. The role of designers as facilitators of creativity and innovation could become central once sustainability imprints itself more firmly in the corporate and design mind-set.

A key issue is how to move the agenda from a focus on sustainability based on eco-efficiency to a focus on holistic sustainability incorporating 'triple-bottom-line' thinking. Design has an important role to play in producing more sustainable solutions, but it must first realise this!

There is a need to gain commitment from senior management and to facilitate discussion between economic, environmental, marketing, product design and brand management, as well as from a broader range of internal and external stakeholders. In addition, there is a need to develop a broader understanding of the interaction between environmental and social systems and to look for 'closed-loop' opportunities to extend existing products and re-use waste—managing both 'front-of-pipe' and 'end-of-pipe' developments, not to work in an either/or situation.

Companies will also need to improve their understanding of the 'triple-bottom-line' impacts of products from 'cradle to cradle'. This includes the 'hard' issues of eco-efficiency but also 'soft' social and ethical considerations.

There must be increased education, awareness and training of all stakeholders in the product development and consumption process. A key issue will be educating and re-educating businesspeople and particularly marketing personnel about the opportunities arising from the sustainability agenda. If SPD is to move from the 'think-tank' to 'real life' it is essential to understand the organisational reality of the concept and generate business benefits in relation to the development of products, services and 'hybrids' (i.e. products extended through services).

Clearly, product developers and designers need to have a basic eco-literacy before they will be able to generate greener or more sustainable solutions. However, sustainability requires a broader understanding, beyond environmental education. Designers will need to understand the business and environmental benefits of new concepts, to enable them to effectively sell new products to internal and external customers.

There are likely to be different levels of environmental awareness, expertise and learned knowledge within different companies, industries and countries, which will mean the need for flexible approaches. To achieve balanced solutions to the complex and evolving agenda of sustainability, managers, product developers and designers will need to evolve the ability to 'think out of the (green) box'! Clearly, this is not 'business as usual', and new structures, systems, skills and tools will have to be developed.

Companies have to make profit to survive, and sustainable solutions have to sell. Thus the task is to create sustainable value through SPD that satisfies company objectives and customers' needs. Designers, engineers and marketing personnel will need to think creatively and must have encouragement to take up the challenge.

# THE NEXT
# INDUSTRIAL REVOLUTION*

*William McDonough and Michael Braungart*
McDonough Braungart Design Chemistry, USA

When considering the concept of sustainable solutions, one is immediately confronted with the fundamental question: What are the problems—not just the apparent symptoms, but the deeper, underlying flaws? One of the most significant problems humans face is the outdated infrastructure of industrial practices and methods that arose as a result of the first Industrial Revolution.

Design can really be seen as the first signal of human intention. 'Intention' means to be deliberate and strategic—to intend something to take place. Did early engineers and industrialists intend to set in motion a system that depletes the environment in ways we see today? Clearly not. It was a different time, with different assumptions, goals and scientific facts. The environmental tragedies at this point in our history are both unintentional and the result of not intending more, but they are embedded in the present system. With such dramatic design flaws it will not be enough to work within that existing system and render it slightly less bad over time. This is why we feel the predominant strategy of change adopted by modern industries and environmentalists, 'eco-efficiency', will not rise to the occasion. It is time for a new paradigm for industry and a new way of making things: a 'Next Industrial Revolution'.

## 7.1 Why eco-efficiency won't work

In the spring of 1912 one of the largest moving objects ever created by human beings left Southampton and began gliding toward New York. It was the epitome of its industrial

* Before this chapter was originally published in the *Atlantic Monthly* (October 1998), it was subjected to a comprehensive fact-checking process by the researchers at that magazine. All of the facts and figures in the chapter were strictly accounted for.

age—a potent representation of technology, prosperity, luxury and progress. It weighed 66,000 tons. Its steel hull stretched the length of four city blocks. Each of its steam engines was the size of a townhouse. And it was headed for a disastrous encounter with the natural world.

This vessel, of course, was the *Titanic*—a brute of a ship, seemingly impervious to the details of nature. In the minds of the captain, the crew and many of the passengers, nothing could sink it.

One might say that the infrastructure created by the Industrial Revolution of the 19th century resembles such a steamship. It is powered by fossil fuels, nuclear reactors and chemicals. It is pouring waste into the water and smoke into the sky. It is attempting to work by its own rules, contrary to those of the natural world. And, although it may seem invincible, its fundamental design flaws presage disaster. Yet many people still believe that with a few minor alterations this infrastructure can take us safely and prosperously into the future.

During the Industrial Revolution resources seemed inexhaustible and nature was viewed as something to be tamed and civilised. Recently, however, some leading industrialists have begun to realise that traditional ways of doing things may not be sustainable over the long term. 'What we thought was boundless has limits', Robert Shapiro, the chairman and chief executive officer of Monsanto, said in a 1997 interview, 'and we're beginning to hit them' (Magretta 1997: 82).

The 1992 Earth Summit in Rio de Janeiro, led by the Canadian businessman Maurice Strong, recognised those limits. Approximately 30,000 people from around the world, including more than 100 world leaders and representatives of 167 countries, gathered in Rio de Janeiro to respond to troubling symptoms of environmental decline. Although there was sharp disappointment afterward that no binding agreement had been reached at the summit, many industrial participants touted a particular strategy: eco-efficiency. The machines of industry would be refitted with cleaner, faster, quieter engines. Prosperity would remain unobstructed, and economic and organisational structures would remain intact. The hope was that eco-efficiency would transform human industry from a system that takes, makes and wastes into one that integrates economic, environmental and ethical concerns. Eco-efficiency is now considered by industries across the globe to be the strategy of choice for change—the shibboleth to a sustainable world.

What is eco-efficiency? Primarily, the term means 'doing more with less', a precept that has its roots in early industrialisation. Henry Ford was adamant about lean and clean operating policies; he saved his company money by recycling and re-using materials, reduced the use of natural resources, minimised packaging and set new standards with his time-saving assembly line. Ford wrote in 1926, 'You must get the most out of the power, out of the material, and out of the time'—a credo that could hang today on the wall of any eco-efficient factory (Romm 1994: 21). The linkage of efficiency with sustaining the environment was perhaps most famously articulated in *Our Common Future*, a report published in 1987 by the United Nations World Commission on Environment and Development (WCED 1987). *Our Common Future* warned that, if pollution control were not intensified, property and ecosystems would be threatened and existence would become unpleasant and even harmful to human health in some cities. In its agenda for change, the WCED (1987: 213) stated:

> Industries and industrial operations should be encouraged that are more effi-
> cient in terms of resource use, that generate less pollution and waste, that are
> based on the use of renewable rather than non-renewable resources, and that
> minimise irreversible adverse impacts on human health and the environment.

The term 'eco-efficiency' was promoted five years later by the Business Council (now the World Business Council) for Sustainable Development, a group of 48 industrial sponsors, including Dow, DuPont, Con Agra and Chevron, who brought a business perspective to the Earth Summit. The council presented its call for change in practical terms, focusing on what businesses had to gain from a new ecological awareness rather than on what the environment had to lose if industry continued in current patterns. In *Changing Course* (Schmidheiny 1992), a report released just before the summit (and published as a book), the group's founder, Stephan Schmidheiny, stressed the importance of eco-efficiency for all companies that aimed to be competitive, sustainable and successful over the long term. In 1996 Schmidheiny said,

> I predict that within a decade it is going to be next to impossible for a business
> to be competitive without also being 'eco-efficient'—adding more value to a good
> or service while using fewer resources and releasing less pollution (1996: 51).

As Schmidheiny predicted, eco-efficiency has been working its way into industry with extraordinary success. The corporations committing themselves to it continue to increase in number, and include such big names as Monsanto, 3M and Johnson & Johnson. Its famous three Rs—reduce, re-use, recycle—are steadily gaining popularity in the home as well as the workplace. The trend stems in part from eco-efficiency's economic benefits, which can be considerable: 3M, for example, has saved more than US$750 million through pollution prevention projects, and other companies, too, claim to be realising big savings. Naturally, reducing resource consumption, energy use, emissions and waste has implications for the environment as well. When one hears that DuPont has cut its emissions of airborne cancer-causing chemicals by almost 75% since 1987, one cannot help feeling more secure. This is another benefit of eco-efficiency: it diminishes guilt and fear. By subscribing to eco-efficiency, people and industries can be less 'bad' and less fearful about the future. Or can they?

Eco-efficiency is an outwardly admirable and certainly well-intended concept but, unfortunately, it is not a strategy for success over the long term because it does not reach deep enough. It works within the same system that caused the problem in the first place, slowing it down with moral proscriptions and punitive demands. It presents little more than an illusion of change. Relying on eco-efficiency to save the environment will in fact achieve the opposite—it will let industry finish off everything quietly, persistently and completely.

The conflict between industry and the environment is a design problem—a very big design problem. In this context, eco-efficiency might be seen as bailing out the *Titanic* with teaspoons. Yes, one slows down the disaster, but the sinking ship still sinks.

## 7.1.1 A retroactive design assignment

Many of the basic intentions behind the Industrial Revolution were good ones, which most of us would probably like to see carried out today: to bring more goods and services to larger numbers of people, to raise standards of living and to give people more choice and opportunity, among other things. But there were crucial omissions. Perpetuating the diversity and vitality of forests, rivers, oceans, air, soil and animals was not part of the agenda.

If someone were to present the Industrial Revolution as a retroactive design assignment, it might sound like this:

Design a system of production that

- Puts billions of pounds of toxic material into the air, water and soil every year
- Measures prosperity by activity, not legacy
- Requires thousands of complex regulations to keep people and natural systems from being poisoned too quickly
- Produces materials so dangerous that they will require constant vigilance from future generations
- Results in gigantic amounts of waste
- Puts valuable materials in holes all over the planet, where they can never be retrieved
- Erodes the diversity of biological species and cultural practices

Eco-efficiency instead

- Releases fewer pounds of toxic material into the air, water and soil every year
- Measures prosperity by less activity
- Meets or exceeds the stipulations of thousands of complex regulations that aim to keep people and natural systems from being poisoned too quickly
- Produces fewer dangerous materials that will require constant vigilance from future generations
- Results in smaller amounts of waste
- Puts fewer valuable materials in holes all over the planet, where they can never be retrieved
- Standardises and homogenises biological species and cultural practices

Plainly put, eco-efficiency aspires to make the old, destructive system less so.

Reduction, re-use and recycling slow down the rates of contamination and depletion but do not stop these processes. Much recycling, for instance, is actually what we call 'down-cycling' because it reduces the quality of a material over time. When plastic other than that found in such products as soda and water bottles is recycled it is often mixed with different plastics to produce a hybrid of lower quality, which is then moulded into something amorphous and cheap, such as park benches or speed bumps. The original high-quality material is not retrieved, and it eventually ends up in landfills or incinerators.

The well-intended, creative use of recycled materials for new products can be mis-guided. For example, people may feel that they are making an ecologically sound choice by buying and wearing clothing made of fibres made from recycled plastic bottles. But the fibres from plastic bottles were not specifically designed to be next to human skin. Blindly adopting superficial 'environmental' approaches without fully understanding their effects can be no better than doing nothing.

Recycling is more expensive for communities than it needs to be, partly because traditional recycling tries to force materials into more lifetimes than they were designed for—a complicated and messy conversion, and one that itself expends energy and resources. Very few objects of modern consumption were designed with recycling in mind. If the process is truly to save money and materials, products must be designed from the very beginning to be recycled or even 'upcycled'—a term we use to describe the return to industrial systems of materials with improved, rather than degraded, quality.

The reduction of potentially harmful emissions and wastes is another goal of eco-efficiency, but current studies are beginning to raise concern that even tiny amounts of dangerous emissions can have disastrous effects on biological systems over time. This is a particular concern in the case of endocrine disrupters—industrial chemicals in a variety of modern plastics and consumer goods that appear to mimic hormones and connect with receptors in human beings and other organisms. Theo Colburn, Dianne Dumanoski and John Peterson Myers, the authors of *Our Stolen Future*, a ground-breaking study on certain synthetic chemicals and the environment, assert that 'astoundingly small quan-tities of these hormonally active compounds can wreak all manner of biological havoc, particularly in those exposed in the womb' (Colburn *et al.* 1997: xvi).

On another front, new research on particulates—microscopic particles released during incineration and combustion processes, such as those in power plants and auto-mobiles—shows that they can lodge in and damage the lungs, especially in children and the elderly. A 1995 Harvard University study found that as many as 100,000 people die annually as a result of these tiny particles (Regan 1996: 119). Although regulations for smaller particles are in place, implementation does not have to begin until 2005. Real change would be not to regulate the release of particles but to attempt to eliminate dangerous emissions altogether—by design.

## 7.2 Eco-effectiveness

'Produce more with less', 'minimise waste', 'reduce' and similar dictates advance the notion of a world of limits—one whose carrying capacity is strained by burgeoning populations and exploding production and consumption. Eco-efficiency tells us to restrict industry and curtail growth—to try to limit the creativity and productivity of humankind. But the idea that the natural world is inevitably destroyed by human industry, or that excessive demand for goods and services causes environmental ills, is a simplification. Nature—highly industrious, astonishingly productive and creative, even 'wasteful'—is not efficient but effective.

Consider the cherry tree. It makes thousands of blossoms just so that another tree might germinate, take root and grow. Who would notice piles of cherry blossoms littering the ground in the spring and think, 'How inefficient and wasteful'? The tree's abundance is useful and safe. After falling to the ground, the blossoms return to the soil and become nutrients for the surrounding environment. Every last particle contributes in some way to the health of a thriving ecosystem. 'Waste equals food'—this is the first principle of the Next Industrial Revolution.

The cherry tree is just one example of nature's industry, which operates according to cycles of nutrients and metabolisms. This cyclical system is powered by the sun and constantly adapts to local circumstances. Waste that stays waste does not exist.

Human industry, however, is severely limited. It follows a one-way, linear, cradle-to-grave manufacturing line in which things are created and eventually discarded, usually in an incinerator or a landfill. Unlike the waste from nature's work, the waste from human industry is not 'food' at all. In fact, it is often poison; thus, the two conflicting systems—a pile of cherry blossoms and a heap of toxic junk in a landfill.

But there is an alternative—one that will allow both business and nature to be fecund and productive. This alternative is what we call 'eco-effectiveness' (Fig. 7.1). The concept of eco-effectiveness leads to human industry that is regenerative rather than depletive. It involves the design of things that celebrate interdependence with other living systems. From an industrial-design perspective, it means products that work within cradle-to-cradle life-cycles (Fig. 7.2) rather than cradle-to-grave life-cycles.

## 7.2.1 *Principle 1: waste equals food*

Ancient nomadic cultures tended to leave organic waste behind, restoring nutrients to the soil and the surrounding environment. Modern, settled societies simply want to get rid of waste as quickly as possible. The potential nutrients in organic waste are lost when they are disposed of in landfills, where they cannot be used to rebuild soil. Depositing synthetic materials and chemicals in natural systems strains the environment. The ability of complex, interdependent natural ecosystems to absorb such foreign material is limited if not non-existent. Nature cannot do anything with the stuff by design: many manufactured products are intended not to break down under natural conditions.

If people are to prosper within the natural world, all the products and materials manufactured by industry must after each useful life provide nourishment for something new. Since many of the things people make are not natural, they are not safe 'food' for biological systems. Products composed of materials that do not biodegrade should be designed as technical nutrients that continually circulate within closed-loop industrial cycles—the technical metabolism.

In order for these two metabolisms to remain healthy, great care must be taken to avoid cross-contamination. Things that go into the biological metabolism should not contain

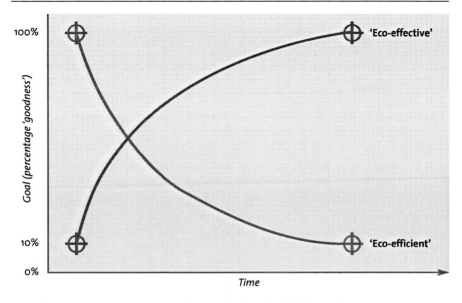

Eco-efficiency is a strategy that tries to be better by being less 'bad'. Eco-effectiveness is a strategy that begins by imagining what 100% good might look like and charts the progress towards that goal.

*Figure 7.1* **The eco-effective business model**

*Source:* © 1998 McDonough Braungart Design Chemistry

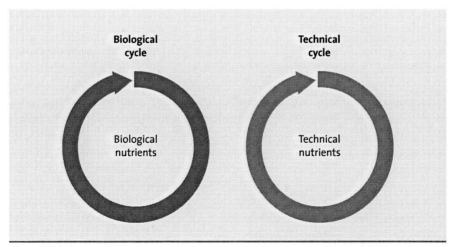

*Figure 7.2* **Cradle-to-cradle life-cycle design**

*Source:* © 1998 McDonough Braungart Design Chemistry

mutagens, carcinogens, heavy metals, endocrine disrupters, persistent toxic substances or bioaccumulative substances. Things that go into the technical metabolism should be kept well apart from the biological metabolism.

If the things people make are to be safely channelled into one of these metabolisms, then products should be considered to contain two kinds of materials: biological nutrients and technical nutrients.

Biological nutrients will be designed to return to the biological cycle—to be literally consumed by microorganisms and other creatures in the soil. Most packaging (which makes up about 50% by volume of the solid waste-stream) should be composed of biological nutrients—materials that can be tossed onto the ground or the compost heap to biodegrade. There is no need for shampoo bottles, toothpaste tubes, yoghurt cartons, juice containers and other packaging to last decades (or even centuries) longer than what came inside them.

Technical nutrients will be designed to go back into the technical cycle. Right now many people can simply dump an old television into a landfill, but the average television is made of hundreds of chemicals, some of which are toxic. Others are valuable nutrients for industry, which are wasted when the television ends up in a landfill. The re-use of technical nutrients in closed-loop industrial cycles is distinct from traditional recycling, because it allows materials to retain their quality: high-quality plastic computer cases would continually circulate as high-quality computer cases, instead of being downcycled to make soundproof barriers or flowerpots.

In the alternative system proposed here, customers would buy the service of such products, and when they have finished with a product, or when they simply want to upgrade to a newer version, the manufacturer would take back the old product, break it down and use its complex materials in new products.

This strategy is already being applied to several products, including carpeting. Ordinarily, a customer who has finished using a traditional carpet must pay to have it removed. The energy, effort and materials that went into it are lost to the manufacturer, and the carpet becomes little more than a heap of potentially hazardous petrochemicals that must be toted to a landfill. Meanwhile, raw materials must continually be extracted to make new carpets.

A typical carpet consists of nylon embedded in fibreglass and polyvinyl chloride (PVC). After its useful life a manufacturer can only downcycle it—shave off some of the nylon for further use and melt the leftovers. The world's largest commercial carpet company adopted our technical nutrient concept with a carpet designed for recycling. When a customer wants to replace such a carpet, the manufacturer simply takes back the technical nutrient—either part or all of the carpet, depending on the product—and returns to the customer a carpet in that customer's desired colour, style and with the desired texture. The carpet company continues to own the material but leases and maintains it, providing customers with the service of the carpet. Eventually, the carpet will wear out like any other, and the manufacturer will re-use its materials at their original level of quality or at a higher level of quality.

The advantages of such a system, widely applied to many industrial products, are twofold: no useless and potentially dangerous waste is generated, as it might still be in eco-efficient systems, and billions of dollars' worth of valuable materials are saved and retained by the manufacturer.

### 7.2.1.1 Selling intelligence, not poison

Currently, chemical companies warn farmers to be careful with pesticides, and yet the companies benefit when more pesticides are sold. In other words, the companies are unintentionally invested in wastefulness and even in the mishandling of their products, which can result in contamination of the soil, water and air. Imagine what would happen if a chemical company sold intelligence instead of pesticides—that is, if farmers or agro-businesses paid pesticide manufacturers to protect their crops against loss from pests instead of buying dangerous regulated chemicals to use at their own discretion. This would, in effect, be buying crop insurance. Farmers would be saying, 'I'll pay you to deal with boll weevils, and you do it as intelligently as you can.' At the same price per acre, the chemical company could still profit, but the pesticide purveyor would be invested in not using pesticide, to avoid wasting materials. Furthermore, since the manufacturer would bear responsibility for the hazardous materials, it would have incentives to come up with less dangerous ways to get rid of pests. Farmers are not interested in handling dangerous chemicals; they want to grow crops. Chemical companies do not want to contaminate soil, water and air; they want to make money.

Consider the unintended design legacy of the average shoe. With each step of your shoe the sole releases tiny particles of potentially harmful substances that may contaminate and reduce the vitality of the soil. With the next rain these particles will wash into the plants and soil along the road, adding another burden to the environment.

Shoes could be redesigned so that the sole is a biological nutrient. When it breaks down under a pounding foot and interacts with nature it will nourish the biological metabolism instead of poisoning it. Other parts of the shoe might be designed as technical nutrients, to be returned to industrial cycles. Most shoes—in fact, most products of the current industrial system—are fairly primitive in their relationship to the natural world. With the scientific and technical tools currently available, this need not be the case.

## 7.2.2 *Principle 2: respect diversity*

A leading goal of design in this century has been to achieve universally applicable solutions. In the field of architecture, the International Style is a good example. The International Style was conceived at the turn of the century by architects such as Mies van der Rohe, Walter Gropius and Le Corbusier to provide a healthy, modern, utilitarian alternative to the hodgepodge of decorative styles prominent during the Victorian era. The intentions were social as well as aesthetic; these architects hoped for the global replacement of unsanitary and inequitable housing—squalid tenements for the poor, lavish buildings for the rich—with clean, affordable buildings exemplifying social progress. New materials such as large sheets of glass and concrete blocks gave architects and engineers the tools to raise such buildings anywhere in the world. Unfortunately, the International Style has evolved into bland, uniform structures constructed primarily for their cheapness and ease. Such buildings reflect little of a region's cultural and natural distinctiveness, and they are usually sealed off from natural energy flows.

As a result of the widespread adoption of the International Style, architecture is now uniform in many settings. An office building can look and work the same anywhere. Materials such as steel, cement and glass can be transported all over the world, eliminating dependence on a region's particular energy and material flows. With more energy forced into the heating and cooling system, the same building can operate similarly in vastly different settings. Unfortunately, however, all places are beginning to look the same. The interiors of such buildings are usually sealed off from natural energy flows, intensifying problems with poor indoor air, and they are often unpleasant and uninspiring to work in, as if they had been designed for the computers, telephones and air-conditioning systems, not for the people inside.

The second principle of the Next Industrial Revolution is 'respect diversity'. Designs will respect, maximise and even enrich the regional, cultural and material uniqueness of a place. Waste and emissions will regenerate rather than deplete, and designs will be flexible, to allow for changes in the needs of people and communities. For example, office buildings will be convertible into apartments, instead of ending up as rubble in a construction landfill when the market changes.

### 7.2.3 Principle 3: use current solar income

The third principle of the Next Industrial Revolution is 'use current solar income'. Human systems now rely on fossil fuels and petrochemicals and on incineration processes that often have destructive side-effects. Today even the most advanced building or factory in the world is still a kind of steamship, polluting, contaminating and depleting the surrounding environment and relying on scarce amounts of natural light and fresh air. People are essentially working in the dark, and they are often breathing unhealthy air. Imagine, instead, a building as a kind of tree. It would purify air, accrue solar income, produce more energy than it consumes, create shade and habitat, enrich soil and change with the seasons. Oberlin College in Ohio is currently working on a building that is a good start: it is designed to make more energy than it needs to operate and to purify its own waste-water.

## 7.3 Equity, economy, ecology

The Next Industrial Revolution incorporates positive intentions across a wide spectrum of human concerns. People within the sustainability movement have found that three categories are helpful in articulating these concerns: equity, economy and ecology (Fig. 7.3).

Equity refers to social justice. Does a design depreciate or enrich people and communities? Shoe companies have been blamed for exposing workers in factories overseas to chemicals in amounts that exceed safe limits. Eco-efficiency would reduce those amounts

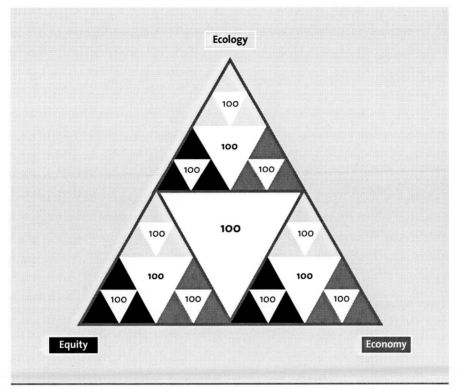

*The famous triad for sustainable design—economy, equity and ecology—rendered as a tool for eco-effective design. Designers should seek to optimise every component of the tool.*

*Figure 7.3* **Fractal ecology model for a sustainable design**

*Source:* © 1998 McDonough Braungart Design Chemistry

to meet certain standards; eco-effectiveness would not use a potentially dangerous chemical in the first place. What an advance for humankind it would be if no factory worker anywhere worked in dangerous or inhumane conditions!

Economy refers to market viability. Does a product reflect the needs of producers and consumers for affordable products? Safe, intelligent designs should be affordable by and accessible to a wide range of customers and be profitable to the company that makes them, because commerce is the engine of change.

Ecology, of course, refers to environmental intelligence. Is a material a biological nutrient or a technical nutrient? Does it meet nature's design criteria: does waste equal food, is diversity respected and is current solar income used?

### 7.3.1 A new design assignment

The Next Industrial Revolution can be framed as the following assignment:

Design an industrial system for the next century and beyond that

- Introduces no hazardous materials into the air, water or soil

- Measures prosperity by how much natural capital we can accrue in productive ways

- Measures productivity by how many people are gainfully and meaningfully employed

- Measures progress by how many buildings have no smokestacks or dangerous effluents

- Does not require regulations whose purpose is to stop us from killing ourselves too quickly

- Produces nothing that will require future generations to maintain vigilance over

- Celebrates the abundance of biological and cultural diversity and solar income

Albert Einstein wrote, 'the world will not evolve past its current state of crisis by using the same thinking that created the situation' (1934: 156). Many people believe that new industrial revolutions are already taking place, with the rise of cybertechnology, biotechnology and nanotechnology. It is true that these are powerful tools for change, but they are only tools—hyper-efficient engines for the steamship of the first Industrial Revolution. Similarly, eco-efficiency is a valuable and laudable tool, and a prelude to what should come next, but it too fails to move us beyond the first revolution. It is time for designs that are creative, abundant, prosperous and intelligent from the start. The model for the Next Industrial Revolution may well have been right in front of us the whole time: a tree.

## 7.5 Conclusions

For this Next Industrial Revolution, we imagine looking not just for sustainable but for sustaining solutions. Rather than making the existing industrial infrastructure 'less bad' such solutions will be actively restorative and regenerative, providing a healthy engagement with the natural world and leading to an abundance of safe industrial and natural systems for generations to come.

# SUSTAINABILITY AND SERVICES

*Walter R. Stahel*
**The Product-Life Institute, Switzerland**

Imagine a shop that lends you a camera, for a small fee, for the short time that it takes to shoot 24 snapshots while on holiday. Then you give the camera back to a photolab at home that will deliver your finished prints. The camera will be checked, refilled and lent to another user who will give it back to yet another shop. This is the concept of the single-use camera that is 'disposable' and made of plastic but nevertheless a truly ecologic product sold as a service.

## 8.1 Sustainability as a vision

The vision of sustainability can be compared with the problem of crossing a shallow river in which stepping stones are hidden. In the past, society has found the first three stepping stones, leading us to the present vision of an eco-efficient economy. Now, we are standing in the middle of the river and need to find more stepping stones in order to reach the goal, the other riverbank of sustainability (Fig. 8.1).

### 8.1.1 Crossing the first borderline to a sustainable economy

After the first two stepping stones (the pillars of nature conservation and of health and safety), society crossed a borderline before reaching the third stepping stone of a higher resource productivity. To recognise this border is important because the societal drivers towards sustainability differ from the 'old' side of the border to the new one: protecting the environment in the past, innovation and competitiveness in the future.

Achieving a higher resource productivity also means a departure from the theories of the industrial economy. Yet the fundamental changes that this borderline implies have not yet been widely accepted, neither by policy-makers nor by economic actors:

| THE FIVE PILLARS OF SUSTAINABILITY |
| --- |
| 1. Nature conservation (precautionary principle) |
| 2. Health and safety, non-toxicity (qualitative) |
| *The first borderline: from protecting the environment (doing things right)* *to increased economic competitiveness (doing the right thing)* |
| 3. Increased resource productivity (reduced throughput, quantitative) |
| *The second borderline:* *from a sustainable economy to a sustainable society* |
| 4. Social ecology (jobs and wants, sharing and caring) |
| 5. Cultural ecology (the choice between sufficiency and efficiency) |

Figure 8.1 **The five pillars—or stepping stones—of sustainability, and the first and second borderline**
Source: PLI 1995b

- The new goal is to de-couple corporate success as well as gross domestic product (GDP) from resource consumption, to create more wealth while consuming considerably fewer resources.

- The new drivers are money, technology and competitiveness rather than the motivation to 'save the environment'.

- The main framework condition is a product responsibility 'from cradle to cradle' through a series of loops and spirals—witness the single-use camera.

- The key tool is 'wild' innovation supported by free-market safety nets instead of a 'command-and-control' approach dictated by laws and regulations (Stahel 1997a).

- Speed of action becomes as important as scientific correctness, as knowledge increasingly becomes private property.

- The reward is a first-mover advantage leading to a higher competitiveness rather than a feeling of 'green and good' leading to eco-awards.

On the supply side, the key actors to achieve a higher resource productivity through a more sustainable production are technology managers and innovators. The strategic priority for managers is to 'do the right thing'. 'Doing things right' (e.g. clean production, as set out in the European Union's Eco-management and Audit Scheme [EMAS] and by the International Organization for Standardization [ISO]) is still important, but it will not open up new markets.

This first borderline thus also implies changes in economic thinking. Economists have only just started to accept that 'economy of scale' goes hand in hand with 'dis-economy of risks' and that industrial ecology may lead to a technology lock-in and stranded investments and thus to a loss of competitiveness. One example of this was the economy of the former German Democratic Republic (GDR; East Germany), the demise of which was triggered by the disappearance of the Iron Curtain. Other examples include the possible collapse of centralised electricity production in those countries that have privatised their state monopolies and BSE probably caused by re-use of animal waste.

## 8.1.2 Crossing the second borderline to a sustainable society

On the demand side, a higher resource productivity can be achieved by means of more sustainable consumption, such as sufficiency. This means crossing a second borderline, from a sustainable economy to a sustainable society. Behind this second border lies the next stepping stones to reach the sustainable bank of the river: the stepping stones of 'social ecology' and 'cultural ecology'.

Sufficiency solutions are, from a sustainability point of view, the most efficient strategies. Sufficiency means changing the 'wants' and 'wishes' of people, the behaviour and attitudes of individuals and the values of society through changes to the 'social and cultural ecology':

- The new goal is to create a sustainable society: ecologically, socially and economically desired, encompassing both consumption and production.

- The driver must be people's desire for sustainability—something that is utterly lacking so far.

- The framework conditions need to focus on performance and results rather than on products and technologies; standards and legislation must specify desired performances instead of 'legal technology' (e.g. the aim should be clean air instead of catalytic converters for vehicles).

- The key tools are cultural leverages—sustainability values that are appealing to people who will apply them in order to increase their own quality of life.

- The reward is happiness de-coupled from resource consumption—a truth that has been identified by many philosophies, from Taoism to Seneca to those of today.

The service economy is the junction where sustainable production and sustainable consumption meet, for sufficiency solutions are of interest only to economic actors in a service economy, where they enable an income without resource consumption (e.g. re-use of towels in a hotel bathroom is not only beneficial to the environment but also reduces the operating costs of running the hotel).

In a service economy, social actors can compete with economic actors in the production of results and performance. For example, one can hire a car for a day, borrow a car from a friend or rent a car from a car-sharing co-operative. Social innovation now competes with economic innovation—something that was difficult to achieve in manufacturing.

New solutions can also be fostered on a conceptual, policy level. Policy-makers thus have a new leadership role, as the old safety barriers and framework conditions (legislation, regulation and technical standards) are of limited use or may even hinder innovation in a non-linear development. The key to a more sustainable mobility, for instance, lies in town planning and systems optimisation, not in vehicle technology. Tony Garnier, a French architect who worked in Lyon around 1900 and who was possibly the first modern town planner, integrated many of the ideas of a sustainable town in his work, such as in the American quarter and hospital.

By using innovative technology in combination with innovations in the field of logistics and marketing, economic and political actors can greatly contribute to a more

| Sale of a performance (service economy) | Sale of a product (industrial economy) |
|---|---|
| The object of the sale is performance, customer satisfaction, the result. | The object of the sale is a product. |
| The seller is liable for the quality of the performance (usefulness). | The seller is liable for the manufacturing quality (defects). |
| Payment is due pro rata if and when the performance is delivered (a no-fun, no-money principle). | Payment is due for and at the transfer of the property rights (an as-is, where-is principle). |
| The work has to be produced *in situ* (service), around the clock, no storage or exchange is possible. | The work can be produced centrally or globally (production); products can be stored, re-sold, exchanged. |
| Property rights and liability remain with the fleet manager. | Property rights and liability are transferred to the buyer. |
| Advantages for the user:<br>▶ High flexibility in utilisation<br>▶ Little own knowledge necessary<br>▶ Cost guarantee per unit of performance<br>▶ Zero risk<br>▶ Status symbol as when buying product | Advantages for the buyer:<br>▶ Right to a possible increase in value<br>▶ Status value as when buying performance |
| Disadvantages for the user:<br>▶ No right to a possible increase in value | Disadvantages for the buyer:<br>▶ Zero flexibility in utilisation<br>▶ Own knowledge necessary (driver's licence)<br>▶ No cost guarantee<br>▶ Full risk for operation and disposal |
| Marketing strategy = customer service | Marketing strategy = publicity, sponsoring |
| Central notion of value: constant utilisation value over long-term utilisation period | Central notion of value: high short-term exchange value at the point of sale |

*Table* 8.1 **Selling performance versus selling products**

*Source:* Stahel 1994

sustainable and eco-efficient service economy. But examples for innovations in social and cultural ecology are still rare and little researched, even if their number is increasing, sometimes in unexpected cases. Most Europeans associate 'green thinking' with northern European countries—but it was Italy that introduced 'automobile-free' Sundays in spring 2000! Little research has been done so far to detect the patterns of cultural ecology, which would enable policy-makers to use cultural leverage in order to promote sustainable solutions (PLI 2000a).

# 8.2 The service economy: selling performance instead of goods

The key differences between the commercial strategies of selling performance and selling products, which are also the differences between the industrial economy and a service economy, are summarised in Table 8.1.

The present manufacturing or industrial economy has a linear structure (Fig. 8.2), and its success, both on a micro level (annual revenue) and on a macro level (GDP), is measured as the monetary flow at the point-of-sale (POS), which is directly linked to the flow of goods or resources (or throughput) of both matter and energy—it might be called a 'river economy'.

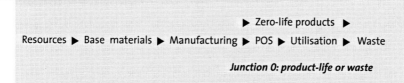

|  |  |
|---|---|
| *POS* | Point-of-sale |
| *Zero-life products* | Normal goods that have never been used (e.g. stock clearances, over-supply) |
| *Junction 0* | The decision by an economic actor to sell 100% of its production for use, or to dispose of it at least partly in order to increase profits |

*Figure* 8.2  **The linear structure of the industrial (or 'river') economy**

*Source:* Stahel and Reday 1976

It has been shown that a generalisation of the present per capita resource consumption (the 'ecological footprint') of industrialised countries on a worldwide level is not possible—it would lead to a collapse of the ecosystem. In order to become sustainable, the economy of industrialised countries will have to operate at a much higher level of resource productivity (i.e. be able to produce a higher 'utilisation value' out of a greatly reduced resource throughput). One way of doing this is through an 'economy in loops' (Fig. 8.3)—which might be called a 'lake economy'.

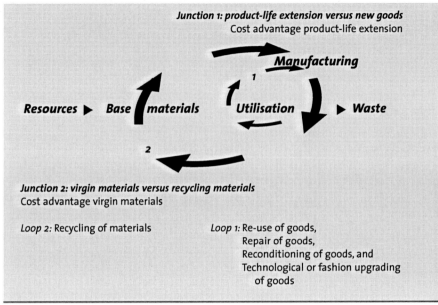

*Junction 1* The decision by an economic actor to scrap or remanufacture a used product
*Junction 2* The decision by an economic actor to re-use or dispose of the materials of a used product

*Figure* 8.3 **Closing the material loops: the loops of a self-replenishing, more sustainable service (or 'lake'), and the junctions between these loops and a linear economy**

*Source:* Stahel and Reday 1976

It has been calculated that industrialised countries need to reduce their resource flows by a factor of 10 in order to enable less developed countries to multiply their per capita resource input to a comparable level. At the same time, world resource throughput must drop to a sustainable level (see F10C 1994).

This objective cannot be achieved by dematerialised product design methods alone but calls for changes to corporate strategy (Fig. 8.4). The service economy uses utilisation value as its central notion of economic value and measures its success in terms of asset management by revalorising the existing stocks of goods and by optimising their utilisation (i.e. the lake economy). This new focus thus enables one to de-couple corporate success from resource throughput. But the maintenance of wealth with less resource consumption also means facing new risks in the emerging service economy (Giarini and Stahel 1989).

For proactive entrepreneurs, there lies a considerable untapped economic potential ahead that can be harvested only through technical and commercial innovation. The objective of achieving wealth with less resource consumption (Stahel 1997b) has been of little interest to the industrial (river) economy, as it would have led to economic disaster (as measured in resource throughput). But companies that recognise and

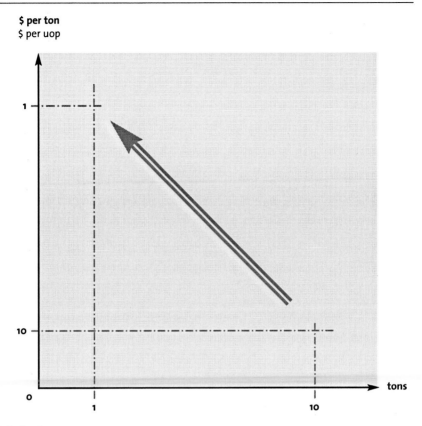

**$ per ton**
$ per uop

uop Unit of performance

*Figure* 8.4 **The solution of dematerialisation of production by factor 10**
**without loss of income to economic actors: 10 × 1 = 1 × 10**

*Source:* PLI 1995b

successfully develop the new opportunities will greatly increase their competitiveness: if customers pay an agreed amount per unit of service (with service equalling performance translated into customer satisfaction), service providers have an economic incentive to reduce resource flows. Their profits will increase twofold: procurement costs for materials and energy will go down as will distribution and waste elimination costs. Examples of this are the Xerox life-cycle design programme for photocopiers, re-treading of tyres, rail-grinding services, DuPont's voluntary programme to take back and de-polymerise its plastics and all remanufacturing activities. A number of major manufacturing companies, such as General Electric and lift (elevator) manufacturers, already earn 75% of their revenue from services linked to the utilisation of their products, and only 25% from production.

## 8.3 Policies for more sustainable solutions

There is a need for a fundamental change in political thinking, from ecology versus economy (and state versus industry) towards ecology with economy (and state with enterprises). Such a new industrial policy can best promote sustainability by removing obstacles that hinder sustainability and by creating incentives that foster innovation towards more sustainable solutions. The state still has to determine the need for safety barriers to protect people and the environment, but it should not provide this protection itself nor carry the costs of accidents. Instead, it should wherever possible foster free-market safety nets, such as mandatory insurance. The acceptance of environmental impairment liability and product liability insurance, as alternatives to legislation and mandatory technical standards, would speed up radical technological innovation and simultaneously ensure that new technologies are chosen by internalising the costs of accidents and failures (Stahel 1997a).

At a time when tax authorities increasingly leave it to the stock exchanges to define valid accounting guidelines (because banks and stock exchanges have a prospectus liability and therefore a self-interest to verify the figures they are given), the state should define the aims of, but not the strategies leading to, a higher resource productivity. In addition, the state should create framework conditions that make sure that economic actors who innovate get rewarded and promoted; those actors caught cheating (or their safety net or insurance) must pay up. By doing this, the state would become considerably leaner and more efficient. The application of the principle of insurability of risks, which defines the borderline between nation-states and the market economy, would automatically introduce the precautionary principle into the economic mechanisms to choose between possible technologies—both present and future.

## 8.4 Strategies for more sustainable solutions

Some of the strategies leading to a higher resource efficiency are summarised in Table 8.2. The solutions at the top of the table have the highest resource productivity; those at the bottom have the lowest. The entries are taken from a collection of 300 examples of higher resource productivity, where they are explained in full detail (see PLI 1995b; table entries are discussed briefly in the following sections). For proactive entrepreneurs, the main benefits of these strategies include a higher long-term competitiveness through reduced costs, a higher product quality and customer loyalty as well as a 'greener' corporate image. The main risk is the increased uncertainty resulting from the introduction of the factor 'time' into the economic calculation. This uncertainty can, however, be substantially reduced by appropriate design strategies, such as modular system design for interoperability and compatibility between product families, as well as component standardisation for ease of re-use, remanufacture and recycling. Products designed to prevent losses and abuse will further increase profitability—a strategy that would lead to reduced sales in the manufacturing economy.

| Increased resource productivity through: | Closing the material loops Technical strategies | Closing the liability loops Commercial/marketing strategies |
|---|---|---|
| **SUFFICIENCY SOLUTIONS** | | |
| | Near-zero options Ploughing at night Loss prevention (vaccination) | Zero options Towels in hotels, Non-insurance (for rear-end accidents [California]) Draught beer |
| **EFFICIENCY SOLUTIONS** | | |
| *System solutions* | | |
| Reducing *volume and speed* of the resource flow | *System solutions* Krauss-Maffei plane transport system Skin solutions Accessibility | *Systemic solutions* Lighthouses Selling results instead of goods Selling services instead of goods |
| *More intensive utilisation* | | |
| Reducing the volume of the resource flow | Eco-products Dematerialised goods Multi-functional goods | Eco-marketing Shared utilisation of goods Sale of utilisation instead of goods |
| *Longer utilisation of goods* | | |
| Reducing the speed of the resource flow | Remanufacturing Long-life goods Service-life extension of goods and of components New products from waste | Remarketing Discurement services Away-grading of goods Marketing of fashion upgrades for goods in the market |

*Note:* entries at the top of the table have the highest resource productivity; those at the bottom have the lowest; for a full explanation of each example, and for further examples, see PLI 1995b.
'Discurement': the reverse process to procurement; 'away-grading': export for re-use

*Table* 8.2 **Strategies for a higher resource productivity**

Source: Adapted from Giarini and Stahel 1989

## 8.4.1 *Sufficiency solutions*

Sufficiency and prevention solutions are the most efficient strategies to achieve a higher sustainability and 'wealth without resource consumption'. Witness a hotel: by offering its guests the opportunity to 'save the environment' by re-using towels for several days, the hotel does indeed reduce the consumption of water and detergents. But it also reduces its laundry costs and extends the useful life of towels and washing machines, thus increasing its profit margin. Zero options (sufficiency) such as this are among the most ecological solutions, and they also offer the highest economic savings (for other examples, see Table 8.2).

Ploughing at night reduces the number of weeds—and thus the need for herbicides— by 90%. The reason is a biological one: the germination of weeds is triggered by a natural light impulse when they come to the surface. In the absence of such an impulse—at night—they do not germinate. This and other examples of near-zero options are listed in Table 8.2.

## 8.4.2 Efficiency solutions

### 8.4.2.1 Systems and systemic solutions

Systems and systemic solutions are the most effective among the efficiency strategies, as they enable a reduction of volume and speed of the resource flows (Table 8.2). Witness the plane transport system (PTS) invented by German engineering company Krauss-Maffei. It is based on the wisdom that the weight necessary to provide sufficient friction to 'pull' an aircraft does not necessarily have to be embodied in the tractor itself but can be 'gained' by lifting the front wheel of an aircraft. Another case concerns providing accessibility instead of mobility, which means moving bytes instead of tonnes. The invention of lighthouses produced a quantum leap in shipping safety. Yet lighthouses are also the cheapest, most durable and efficient way to make dangerous cliffs permanently visible. Equipping all ships with a technology which would let them 'see' the cliffs in a storm would be considerably more expensive—if it were available. Yet another strategy of system solutions is to sell performance instead of goods.

### 8.4.2.2 More intensive utilisation

A more intensive utilisation, through a shared utilisation of goods, reduces the volume of the resource flow (Table 8.2). A number of people sharing in the utilisation of a pool of goods can draw the same utilisation value through a more intensive utilisation of a substantially reduced number of goods, thus achieving a higher resource productivity per unit of service. Examples for this are (in addition to 'public' infrastructures such as roads, concert halls and railways) taxis, car pools and hitchhiking, the 'Charter Way' concept of DaimlerChrysler for trucks (selling transport capacity at a cost per ton-kilometre to haulage companies), as well as textile leasing (e.g. uniforms, towels and hospital linen); 'public' does not designate ownership here, but access to goods.

Multi-functional goods also enable a dematerialisation effect through a more intensive utilisation of units. Examples are the Swiss Army knife and electronic goods such as the fax–scanner–printer–copier first commercialised by Siemens in 1992.

A shared utilisation is possible in the (monetarised) economy through rental services and the sale of services instead of goods (laundry and dry-cleaning), as well as within communities (non-monetary) through lending and sharing. The former take place within the legal framework of society; the latter's principles of sharing and caring are based on community values (trust and tolerance) which are part of sociocultural ecology. There is a great variety of forms in between (local exchange trading schemes [LETS], co-operatives, etc).

Some of the issues involved in the sharing of immaterial and material goods are open to misinterpretation because they incorporate values of both society (law) and community (trust). Distrust normally leads to increased individual consumption, conflict or failure. A shared utilisation of immaterial goods has two major advantages: a great number of people can profit from the goods simultaneously, and immaterial goods are by definition dematerialised. The technology shift from analogue to digital or virtual goods will further enhance shared utilisation, even if the main reason for the shift to virtual goods is competitiveness, not ecology.

Wealth with less resource consumption is further possible by dematerialisation strategies, such as substituting maintenance-free long-life products that deliver high-quality results for disposable products. Modern examples include music compact discs [CDs] and the use of supercondensers instead of batteries in electrical goods. CDs are also a point in case for the resulting shift in income from manufacturers to distributors (second-hand sales and rental shops) if the manufacturers themselves do not become service providers themselves, selling music instead of CDs. With material goods, this would have demanded a structural change from global manufacturing to local rental services. Downloading music from the Internet gets around this problem, but leads to issues of proprietary rights and rental fees per 'unit of listening'.

### 8.4.2.3 Longer utilisation of goods

A longer utilisation of goods through product life extension services (loop 1 in Fig. 8.3), as well as dematerialised product design, also increases resource productivity but goes against the logic of the linear economy (Fig. 8.2). From a sustainability point of view, doubling the useful life of goods reduces by half the amount of resource input and waste output and in addition reduces the resource consumption in all related services (distribution, advertising, waste transport and disposal) by 50%. Furthermore, product life extension services are often a substitution of manpower for energy, and of local workshops for (global) factories, thus enhancing social ecology, for 75% of all energy embodied in a manufactured product is used in the production of materials, and only 25% during assembly. The figures for the labour input are reversed: 75% of all labour is used in assembly, and only 25% in material production (Stahel and Reday 1976). Product life extension activities consist mostly of services associated with disassembly and assembly operations.

Product life extension services of analogue (mechanical) goods lead to a regionalisation of the economy, whereas digital and virtual goods enable producers to stay global, by providing solutions (e.g. the technological upgrading of goods) through do-it-yourself activities. This gives producers direct access to the customer; it also eliminates distributors and distribution costs. The coming change to digital television, accompanied by long-life hardware combined with later technological upgrading through software, is an example of this trend—pushed by operational leasing, voluntary take-back schemes by industry and take-back legislation.

Economic success now comes through an understanding of the logic inherent in a 'lake economy' based on services: to optimise utilisation demands a proximity to the customer and thus a regionalisation of the economy. As the stock of goods in the marketplace is the new focus of economic optimisation (the assets), these goods become the new 'mines' or resources. They cannot be centralised economically—an efficient service economy has to have a decentralised structure (service centres, remanufacturing workshops and 'mini-mills'). Service centres ideally are accessible 24 hours a day, such as the emergency department of a major hospital. (Further examples of longer utilisation of goods are provided in Table 8.2.)

## 8.5 The shift from manufacturing to a service economy

'Service is the ultimate luxury' according to publicity by the Marriott hotel group. The shift to a service economy (e.g. product rental instead of purchase) encounters few problems of acceptance on the demand side. The consumer-turned-user gains a high flexibility in the utilisation of goods (something ownership can never give) as well as guaranteed satisfaction at a guaranteed cost per unit of service. And there is no loss of status: the marketing of the industrial economy has wrongly created the idea that status symbol value is linked to ownership—in reality, it has always been linked to leasehold. The driver of a red Ferrari gets the same attention from bystanders whether that car is bought, rented or stolen.

Ownership therefore only makes economic sense in cases where durable goods increase in value, normally through an increase in rarity, such as antique furniture, vintage cars and real estate. Ownership only makes ecological sense for individuals interested in asset management. In many countries, an increasing number of individuals live, mentally, in a multi-option society: they do not want to commit themselves in the medium or long term, either to goods or to other people (Gross 1995). They want new toys all the time—and can afford them. Only a service economy can fulfil their needs without creating an avalanche of waste, by selling them performance and services instead of goods, by offering flexibility in utilisation instead of bondage by property.

Most of these strategies of a higher resource productivity also offer the customer a reduction in costs. Sufficiency solutions based on a better (scientific) understanding of a problem reduce resource flows and costs: ploughing at night, for instance, reduces weeds and thus herbicide costs by 90%; remanufactured goods cost on average 40% less than equivalent new goods of the same quality; sharing goods also means sharing costs. But sufficiency and efficiency solutions often demand that the users-cum-customers develop a new relationship with goods and/or people—knowledge and community become substitutes for resource consumption (PLI 2000b).

## 8.6 The way to sustainable solutions: benchmarking

The term 'sustainable solutions' was first used in the Austrian ecodesign competition of 1995. It indicates a change in the role of industrial designers which is part of a more fundamental change in actors and issues that occurs when society evolves down the 'sustainability pillars' (see Fig. 8.1) from nature conservation and health and safety to resource productivity. In the past, biologists and chemists have been the driving force through use of command-and-control regulations in order to conserve nature and limit toxicology, in the name of nation-states. Now, engineers and industrial designers, marketing personnel and business people will take the lead through innovation in order to achieve increases in resource productivity by a factor of 10 and more. Innovation by enterprises and an industrial policy to promote sustainability become the future key strategies not only towards a sustainable society but also towards competitiveness! A new programme of the World Business Council for Sustainable Development (WBCSD) is called 'Sustainability through the Market' and points the same way.

The gist of these ideas leads to a new, sustainable, definition of quality, which takes into account simultaneously technical efficiency, preventative engineering and time in order to define quality as system performance over long periods of time (Fig 8.5).

For an increase in resource productivity well beyond factor 4, or even factor 10, innovative strategies for new solutions are needed, attacking problems on a systems level instead of on a product level, starting from a new understanding of the underlying need

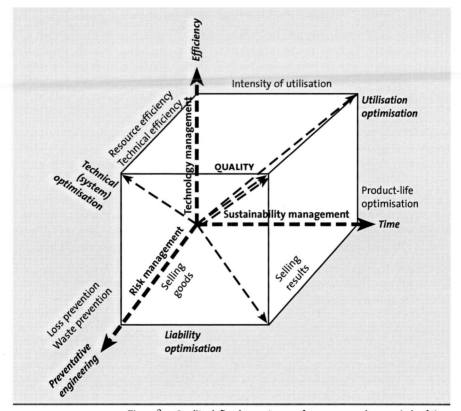

*Figure* 8.5 **Quality defined as system performance over long periods of time**

*Source:* PLI 1995b

or by using new technology (PLI 1995a). However, many traditional solutions have already reached a high degree of sustainability. An Austrian cabinet-maker who uses timber from the local forests to produce furniture and toys for the regional market, repairs broken products and heats the workshop in winter with waste timber will have difficulty improving sustainability even by factor 4. The same goes for a local brewery in Wales that buys its raw material from local farmers and sells barrels of beer to the local pubs that sell draught beer with 'zero packaging'. The fact that these firms cannot improve their ecological efficiency by a large factor does not mean that they are working in an unsustainable way—quite the contrary!—but these examples do show the necessity to establish benchmarks in order to define priorities and objectives in the quest for a higher resource productivity.

There is a need for benchmarks of sustainable solutions for nation-states, such as the 'ecological footprint' (see e.g. van Dieren 1995). This approach has existed for some time but has not led to a significant change in the course of national policy; again, this is a cultural issue, not a technical problem.

Benchmarks are also necessary for technologies. In some cases people can be used as yardsticks. For example, sustainable mobility can be defined as any method of mobility that enables a person to move faster and with less human energy input than by walking, such as the bicycle for horizontal mobility and the lift (or elevator) for vertical mobility. The chances that improvements to the motor car will ever reach the standards of the human yardstick are low.

For other products, the benchmark is the quality of the result achieved, such as in coffee brewing. During a coffee-tasting competition in 1998 organised by EU consumer associations, one of the best results was achieved by the Bialetti espresso machine. This is an eco-product designed in 1930 and still in production. Hundreds of other coffee machines have been designed since, all more expensive, more recent and more material-intensive, yet none improving on the desired result: a cup of coffee.

Benchmarks can therefore be used to indicate areas of eco-mature solutions, as well as to focus research and design on solutions of a higher sustainability. But very few strategy design tools exist today that can guide designers and engineers in order to develop new solutions. An example of such a design tool is the Vienna decision trees (PLI 1995a).

The most difficult job for designers in the coming years may well be to find their niche in helping society to establish the most eco-efficient strategies of prevention and sufficiency solutions into the marketplace. In order to succeed, these efforts will have to take place within the context of the emerging service economy.

# MEASURING SUSTAINABILITY IN ECODESIGN*

*Joseph Fiksel*
Battelle Memorial Institute, USA

As the new millennium dawns, many leading companies in the USA, Europe and Japan are responding to the challenges of global population growth and environmental pressures by adopting a commitment to 'sustainability' (Hart 1996). Business leaders speak of sustainable development, sustainable growth, sustainable products, sustainable processes and sustainable technologies. Many have launched proactive programmes that include life-cycle accounting, design for eco-efficiency, community outreach, clean technology development and a variety of other initiatives. In 1999 a group of US companies, including DuPont and General Motors, collaborated in supporting a high-visibility national town meeting on sustainability. Their motivations were not purely altruistic—recent research has demonstrated that pursuit of sustainability by a firm may not only result in environmental improvements and societal benefits but also increase economic value for that firm (Dixon 1999; Kiernan and Martin 1998).

Despite the recent flurry of public pronouncements, few, if any, companies can respond definitively to the question, 'Which of your products are sustainable?' Answering this question requires the ability to measure product sustainability in a quantitative, or at least qualitative, fashion. However, measuring product sustainability entails several formidable challenges. First, this concept is relatively new, so there is a lack of commonly accepted or mandated measurement standards. Second, sustainability is complex and multifaceted, covering a broad spectrum of topics from habitat conservation and energy consumption to stakeholder satisfaction and financial results. Last, measurement of sustainability extends beyond the operations of a single company and typically addresses the performance of upstream suppliers and downstream customers in the value chain.

* Portions of this chapter are based on the paper by J. Fiksel, J. McDaniel and C. Mendenhall (1999) 'Measuring Progress towards Sustainability: Principles, Process, and Best Practices', presented at the Eighth International Greening of Industry Network Conference, Chapel Hill, NC, 14–17 November 1999.

There is an old adage that states 'what gets measured gets managed'. By implication, a fundamental element of any successful ecodesign programme is the establishment of measurable goals and performance indicators. Without a concrete basis for measuring success, policy statements are ineffectual, accountabilities are ambiguous and design evaluation remains subjective and imprecise. Therefore, this chapter focuses on the emerging field of sustainability performance measurement (SPM). Although sustainability as a business practice is still at an embryonic stage, a viable approach toward measuring sustainability can be forged by building on the general principles of performance measurement and on the lessons learned by companies during the 1990s in establishing environmental performance evaluation systems.

This chapter surveys the current state of SPM, sets forth some fundamental principles and practices and illustrates the application of these principles by leading companies that have already begun their journey towards sustainability, including The Body Shop, BP Amoco, Collins & Aikman Floorcoverings, Monsanto and Volvo. It is hoped that the information presented here will help other companies to develop and improve their SPM practices, enabling a more rapid and widespread transition towards sustainable products and processes. Inevitably, the pressures of population growth, economic development and resource scarcity will eventually compel all companies to address sustainability issues. Achievement of worldwide sustainable development will be possible only if companies begin to routinely seek competitive advantage through the design and introduction of products that are measurably superior in their environmental, economic and social performance.

# 9.1 State of the art

Efforts to evaluate each aspect of the 'triple bottom line' of sustainability have progressed somewhat independently and have reached different levels of sophistication. Corporate reporting practices for these three aspects have evolved over vastly different time-frames. Corporate financial reporting has been providing information on economic performance since the beginning of the 20th century, while corporate environmental reporting has been practised for less than a decade. Corporate social reporting was first attempted in the 1970s and has recently been revived. Corporate sustainability reporting, which combines elements of all three aspects of the triple bottom line, has been attempted only in the past few years and is still in an exploratory phase. This section briefly discusses the current state-of-the-art in each of the three dimensions of SPM:

- Economic performance evaluation
- Environmental performance evaluation
- Societal performance evaluation

It then discusses briefly the emergence of sustainability reporting as a business practice.

### 9.1.1 *Economic performance evaluation*

Economic performance evaluation has been practised for almost a century, although it is perhaps better known as financial reporting. Standards for externally reporting financial results are highly developed, and a variety of rigorous guidelines and standards exist for these financial indicators. In contrast to this high level of standardisation for external financial accounting, firms can choose from a wide variety of managerial accounting practices to support internal decisions. Since the 1980s the introduction of new accounting methods such as activity-based accounting and economic value-added (EVA) accounting has helped to reveal the underlying drivers of economic performance and shareholder value (Blumberg *et al.* 1997).

To address the full scope of sustainability, economic performance evaluation must evolve beyond traditional techniques based solely on profitability and cash flow. Specific issues include (Epstein 1996):

- Quantification of hidden costs associated with the utilisation of material, energy, capital and human resources

- Estimation of uncertain future costs associated with external impacts of industrial production and consumption

- Understanding the costs and benefits incurred by various stakeholders (customers, employees, communities, interest groups, etc.) across the life-cycle of a product or process

A host of new research in life-cycle accounting, environmental accounting and full-cost accounting has introduced new techniques that serve to highlight costs and benefits that are not explicitly addressed with conventional approaches. One of the leading practitioners of these new approaches is DaimlerChrysler. For example, in designing several new automotive components, Chrysler engineers considered the direct, potentially hidden and contingent costs associated with each design option. Direct and potentially hidden costs were evaluated with activity-based costing methods, and contingent costs were estimated with proprietary risk factors developed by Chrysler (Armstrong and White 1997).

### 9.1.2 *Environmental performance evaluation*

Corporate environmental performance reporting has been practised since at least the 1990s. Recent research has demonstrated a plausible connection between improved environmental performance and increased shareholder value (Feldman *et al.* 1997), and a growing number of corporations have begun voluntarily to report their product and company environmental performance (Blumberg *et al.* 1997). These reporting efforts have in turn led to an increased demand for standard environmental reporting criteria, similar to those for financial reporting. For example, in 1992 the Public Environmental Reporting Initiative (PERI), a consortium of global firms, developed an influential set of guidelines for environmental reporting. The types of performance indicator typically presented in conventional environmental reports include wastes and emissions, employee lost-time injuries, notices of violation, spills and releases and so on.

With the introduction of the ISO 14000 series of standards, an international consensus was developed on the elements of an environmental performance evaluation process, documented in ISO 14031 (Fiksel 1997). An even more recent standardisation initiative is the Global Reporting Initiative (GRI). Launched by the Coalition for Environmentally Responsible Economies (CERES) in autumn 1997, the objective of GRI is to standardise the methodology and format of corporate environmental and sustainability reports; a set of initial guidelines was published in June 2000. Although the standardisation debate continues, one indicator of environmental performance has been used by more than 20 companies to measure environmental–economic relationships: eco-efficiency, generally defined as a measure of environmental performance relative to economic input or output. Several current initiatives are seeking to standardise eco-efficiency measurement; for example, Canada's National Round Table on the Environment and Economy (NRTEE) has enlisted a number of firms in a pilot-test of material and energy intensity indicators (NRTEE 1999).

### 9.1.3 Societal performance evaluation

In the 1970s many organisations began developing standards for corporate social accounting (Epstein 1996). Although interest in social evaluation faded in the 1980s efforts to measure and report social performance resurfaced in the late 1990s. This change is in part because of the need for societal indicators in the evaluation of sustainability and in part because of increased media interest in the social impacts of corporate operations. Recently, the Council on Economic Priorities (CEP) proposed SA 8000, a set of social accountability (SA) standards designed to follow in the path of other 'quality' standards. CEP hopes that, like the ISO 9000 and ISO 14000 series, SA 8000 will become the *de facto* standard for evaluating the quality of a company's social performance. Although SA 8000 makes significant advances in standardising the evaluation of corporate commitment to human rights issues, such as worker safety and equality, the issues covered by the standards include only a limited subset of the issues implied by sustainability (Ranganathan 1998). It is clear that the scope of sustainable product design must move beyond eco-efficiency to consider societal impacts, including issues such as quality of life and social equity. However, in general, the societal dimension of the triple bottom line remains the least explored and the most difficult to quantify.

### 9.1.4 Sustainability reporting

As standards and accepted methodologies have evolved in economic, environmental and societal performance evaluation, a few companies have begun to publish integrated sustainability reports. In 1997 Interface, a US carpet manufacturer, published what is believed to be the first sustainability report. This early reporting effort demonstrates that Interface is committed to sustainable development and has taken initial steps to identify potential sustainability indicators. However, this initial report did not clearly indicate any framework that would be utilised in future performance measurement and progress evaluation. Monsanto, a life sciences company, also published an early sustainability report which proposed an initial framework for product sustainability evaluation. However, this framework was never fully implemented and the company was subsequently restructured. More recently, a second wave of companies have issued sustainability reports influenced by the aforementioned GRI standard, including Shell, General Motors and Baxter Healthcare, all with a greater emphasis on quantitative indicators of progress. These early attempts at integrated sustainability measurement highlight the need for a general framework that facilitates selection and measurement of appropriate sustainability performance indicators.

## 9.2 Sustainability measurement principles

Four fundamental principles can help companies address the challenges associated with measuring and reporting product sustainability. These are:

- Address the dual perspectives of resource consumption and value creation
- Include economic, environmental and societal aspects of the product
- Systematically consider each stage in the product life-cycle
- Develop leading and lagging indicators of product performance

### 9.2.1 Resource and value

> The first principle of sustainability measurement: evaluations should address the dual perspectives of resource consumption and value creation.

A sustainable product should strive to minimise resource consumption while maximising value creation; in other words, one should 'do more with less'. Here, resources are defined broadly to be natural or anthropogenic stocks that are required for the creation, use and disposition of a product or service. Examples of resources include materials, energy, labour and land. Value is defined as a condition, attributable to a company's activities, which benefits one or more of the organisation's stakeholders (Fiksel *et al.* 1998). Examples of value creation include increased profitability, reduced pollution, improved nutrition and liberation of time. Table 9.1 lists general categories of performance associated with resource consumption and value creation—these provide a foundation for any company to select appropriate performance indicators.

### 9.2.2 The 'triple bottom line'

> The second principle of sustainability: evaluations should include economic, environmental and societal aspects of the product.

| Resource | Value |
|---|---|
| Resource | Value |
| Energy | Functional performance |
| Material | Information content |
| Water | Customer satisfaction |
| Land | Environmental quality |
| Waste | Economic value added |
| Cost | Business competency |
| Human capital | Human health |
| Investment capital | Social welfare |

*Table 9.1* **Resource consumption compared with value creation**

Effective sustainability measurement should consider the complete 'triple bottom line' of economic, environmental and societal performance (Bennett and James 1999). These aspects need to be integrated and balanced in order to obtain a comprehensive understanding of product (or service) sustainability from the perspective of different stakeholders. For example, an automobile consumes economic resources in terms of operation and maintenance costs, environmental resources in terms of fossil fuel and societal resources in terms of personal time spent driving. It also creates economic and social value, although it may detract from environmental quality. Today, most performance measurement frameworks focus exclusively on economic or environmental performance; very few address societal concerns (James 1997). However, given the recent resurgence of attention on social responsibility one may anticipate an increased focus over the next decade on measuring the societal impacts of products and services.

## 9.2.3  Life-cycle consideration

> The third principle of sustainability measurement: evaluations should system-
> atically consider each stage in the product life-cycle.

Resource consumption and value creation take place throughout the life-cycle, including the supply, manufacturing, use and disposal of a product. Historically, companies have focused almost exclusively on their internal manufacturing and distribution operations and have not considered the implications associated with the activities of their suppliers or customers. Yet an evaluation that focuses exclusively on one life-cycle stage (e.g. manufacturing) may fail to capture significant product benefits or impacts that occur upstream or downstream stages (Fiksel 1996). Referring again to the automobile example, designers have recently begun to consider the end-of-life stage and the potential impacts of disassembly, recycling, recovery, refurbishment and re-use. In applying life-cycle thinking it is important to consider not only the physical life-cycle of the product, from 'cradle to grave', but also the life-cycles of relevant facilities and capital equipment both inside and outside the enterprise.

### 9.2.4  Leading and lagging indicators

> The fourth principle of sustainability measurement: evaluations should combine leading and lagging indicators of product performance.

Lagging indicators (also referred to as outcome indicators) are measures of the results or outcomes (e.g. reduction in material intensity) that are attributable to product design improvements. Most companies use lagging indicators to report results, and they are preferred by the general public and regulators because they are meaningful and easy to understand. However, lagging indicators represent a retrospective view of performance and do not provide managers with foresight about future performance expectations. A more proactive approach, increasingly common among innovative firms, is to augment lagging indicators with leading indicators (also referred to as business process indicators), which measure internal product development practices that are expected to improve future product performance (e.g. use of life-cycle design tools which help improve material efficiency). In other words, these indicators help managers monitor their progress toward achieving their sustainability objectives. Note that it is important to have a balanced set of both leading and lagging indicators; neither is sufficient on its own.

## 9.3  Sustainability indicator selection process

The selection of appropriate performance indicators is imperative for successful ecodesign. Performance indicators form the basis for initial product definition, including requirements and specifications for material content, design architecture and product performance. In addition, indicators are important for the tracking and reporting of product performance results. Therefore, most leading companies pursue a careful, deliberate process for the selection of performance indicators. Based on common practices, the following describes a series of steps whereby ecodesign teams can select appropriate indicators.

- **Step 1: consider stakeholder needs.** The company's sustainability policy typically addresses the needs and expectations of various stakeholders and may also identify sustainability goals. This generally provides a useful starting point for aspect identification.

- **Step 2: identify major product aspects.** The ecodesign team addresses the question, 'What aspects of this product are most important in fulfilling our commitment to sustainability?'

● **Step 3: establish objectives.** By choosing a selected subset of those aspects identified in step 2, the ecodesign team establishes a small number of key product objectives.

● **Step 4: select indicators and metrics.** To select appropriate performance indicators, the team assesses how each of the major life-cycle processes (e.g. product use by customers) contributes to the selected objectives (e.g. reduced energy consumption). Quantitative or qualitative metrics must then be associated with each selected indicator.

● Step 5: determine targets. The team establishes specific, measurable, targets that will represent milestones for short-term and long-term sustainability improvements.

The four principles presented in Section 9.2 should be considered as each of these steps are implemented. Further implementation guidance is provided below.

## 9.3.1 *Step 1: consider stakeholder needs*

Stakeholder concerns typically range over a large number of different product aspects. For example, community groups might be concerned about air emissions or other releases from manufacturing plants, whereas employees have interests ranging from safety to the company's image and stewardship activities. Insurers and lenders may be concerned about environmental costs and potential liabilities, whereas non-governmental organisations (NGOs) and interest groups are concerned with issues such as labour conditions, greenhouse gas releases and the use of renewable energy sources. Finally, shareholders and investors are interested in new technology investments and in how sustainable products create economic value for the firm.

Although stakeholders are important, a company retains a great deal of discretion regarding the emphasis of its sustainability initiatives. The company's overall business strategy should influence how its product sustainability objectives are chosen. For example, a company that has developed a strong brand identity might consider focusing on environmental and social issues that could damage their image. As examples, Nike and Levi-Strauss revamped their product responsibility efforts after receiving negative media coverage related to the activities of major suppliers. Synthesis of stakeholder concerns with business strategy issues enables the selection of appropriate sustainability objectives.

## 9.3.2 *Step 2: identify major product aspects*

During the second step, companies evaluate how their products (or services) can support (or hinder) progress towards sustainability. This step ensures that the performance indicators address important economic, environmental and societal concerns. As illustrated in Table 9.2, the list of potential sustainability aspects for products is quite extensive (Fiksel *et al.* 1998). Although beyond the scope of this chapter, there are a variety of sustainability aspects that are not associated with specific products or processes but

| Economic | Environmental | Societal |
|---|---|---|
| *Direct* | *Material consumption* | *Quality of life* |
| ▶ Raw material cost | ▶ Product and packaging mass | ▶ Breadth of product |
| ▶ Labour cost | ▶ Useful product lifetime | availability |
| ▶ Capital cost | ▶ Hazardous materials used | ▶ Knowledge enhancement |
| | | ▶ Employee satisfaction |
| *Potentially hidden* | *Energy consumption* | *Peace of mind* |
| ▶ Recycling revenue | ▶ Life-cycle energy | ▶ Perceived risk |
| ▶ Product disposition cost | ▶ Power use in operation | ▶ Complaints |
| *Contingent* | *Local impacts* | *Illness and disease reduction* |
| ▶ Employee injury cost | ▶ Product recyclability | ▶ Illnesses avoided |
| ▶ Customer warranty cost | ▶ Impact on local streams | ▶ Mortality reduction |
| *Relationship* | *Regional impacts* | *Accident and injury reduction* |
| ▶ Loss of goodwill as a result of customer concerns | ▶ Smog creation | ▶ Lost time injuries |
| | ▶ Acid rain precursors | ▶ Reportable releases |
| ▶ Business interruption as a result of stakeholder interventions | ▶ Biodiversity reduction | ▶ Number of incidents |
| *Externalities* | *Global impacts* | *Health and wellbeing* |
| ▶ Ecosystem productivity loss | ▶ $CO_2$ emissions | ▶ Nutritional value provided |
| ▶ Resource depletion | ▶ Ozone depletion | ▶ Food costs |

*Table 9.2* **Aspects of product sustainability**

rather pertain to overall company practices. Examples of such company-wide aspects include management system implementation (e.g. ISO 14001), auditing programmes, educational outreach and community development.

Companies have applied a variety of approaches to review and select the aspects that are most important for product definition. One recommended approach involves a sequence of three tasks:

▣ Identify all aspects of sustainability that are potentially important

▣ Assess or estimate the magnitude of these aspects by means of available indicators

▣ Rank the aspects in terms of relative importance

Completion of the first task requires activities such as brainstorming sessions, reviews of previous successes and problems and interviewing stakeholder organisations. To carry out the second task—assessing the magnitude of the sustainability aspects identified— requires either quantifying them in terms of resource or value metrics or, at least, qualitatively rating them on a semantic scale. Finally, the product team is left to determine the most significant environmental aspects by assessing their relative importance, which can be accomplished through various group voting techniques. Having determined which aspects are most significant, the team can then proceed to select the few that merit establishment of specific objectives.

### 9.3.3 *Step 3: establish objectives*

Based on the company's sustainability policy and the determination of significant product aspects, a set of annual and/or longer-term objectives is established. Objectives should be consistent with the company's sustainability policy and quantifiable where practical. However, at this point objectives are stated in a general, qualitative fashion. Examples include:

- Eliminating usage of toxic materials

- Reducing the economic burden of product waste disposition

- Dramatically reducing the product size and mass (dematerialisation)

- Reducing or eliminating the need for maintenance supplies

- Converting to a leased product concept with closed-loop recovery

- Enhancing working conditions during product manufacturing

- Creating opportunities for product access in lower-income, developing economies

As shown by these examples, sustainability objectives should collectively address the triple bottom line and should be oriented towards either resource conservation or value creation.

### 9.3.4 *Step 4: select indicators and metrics*

Once the ecodesign team has agreed on the critical product sustainability objectives, members can proceed to select the performance indicators and accompanying metrics. The indicators and metrics are necessary both to support the detailed design and engineering efforts and to demonstrate a tangible commitment to external stakeholders.

A sustainability performance indicator (SPI) is defined as a quantifiable attribute of a product that characterises the potential contributions of the product toward the company's sustainability objectives. There are hundreds of possible indicators that might be selected for any given product. Box 9.1 illustrates some commonly used types of indicator.

A performance metric defines a specific means of measuring and tracking a performance indicator. In general, a variety of metrics can be chosen for any given performance indicator. For instance, potential metrics for solid waste include annual volume (tonnes per year), annual improvement (percentage reduction) or quantity avoided (tonnes recycled per year).

Metrics can be classified in several different ways. For example, qualitative metrics are those that rely on semantic ratings based on observation and judgement, whereas quantitative metrics are those that rely on empirical data. A second important distinction is between absolute and relative metrics. Absolute metrics are defined with respect to a fixed measurement scale (e.g. total quantity of annual hazardous waste generated). Relative metrics are normalised with respect to another metric or parameter (e.g. total hazardous waste generated per unit of product created). Another approach is to use time-

**Source volume**

- Product mass
- Useful operating life
- Fraction of packaging or containers recycled

**Material usage**

- Total mass of material consumed per unit of product
- Ratio of waste material to product output
- Percentage of recycled or renewable materials used as input to product

**Energy usage**

- Total energy consumed during the product life-cycle
- Renewable energy consumed during the life-cycle
- Power used during operation (for electrical products)

**Water usage**

- Total fresh water consumed during manufacturing
- Water consumption during product end-use (for electrical products)

**Recovery and re-use**

- Product disassembly and recovery time
- Percentage of product recovered and re-used
- Purity of recyclable materials recovered

**Waste and emissions**

- Toxic or hazardous materials used in production
- Total industrial waste generated during production
- Hazardous waste generated during production or use
- Air emissions and water effluents generated during production
- Greenhouse gases and ozone-depleting substances released over life-cycle

**Environmental impact**

- Ambient concentrations of hazardous by-products in various media
- Estimated annual population incidence of adverse effects in humans or biota
- Reduction in natural stocks of scarce resources

**Economic impact**

- Average life-cycle cost incurred by the manufacturer
- Purchase and operating cost incurred by the customer
- Cost savings associated with design improvements

**Social impact**

- Reduced accident potential
- Production worker quality of life
- Increased nutritional value

*Box* 9.1 **Some commonly used performance indicators**

based relative metrics (i.e. those that compute the change in a particular quantitative metric over a given time-period, e.g. the percentage reduction of total hazardous waste generated per unit of product created, from 1999 to 2004).

## 9.3.5 Step 5: determine targets

After the indicators and metrics have been identified, the team is ready to commit to short-term or long-term targets, which establish what level of performance it intends to achieve. In brief:

- Indicators designate a measurable dimension of performance.

- Metrics provide a means of quantifying the indicators.

- Targets provide a basis for tracking and assessing improvement.

It is not essential that targets be set for every performance indicator, as that might overconstrain the ecodesign process. In fact, companies frequently decide not to set targets until they have established a baseline performance level against which progress can be measured. However, the choice of targets is important as they will generally command highest priority in influencing design decisions. The relationship between sustainability objectives, SPIs, metrics and targets is illustrated in Table 9.3.

| Objectives | SPIs | Metrics | Targets |
|---|---|---|---|
| *Reduce or eliminate waste* | Total waste and emissions | ▶ Weight (e.g. lb) per year <br> ▶ Weight (e.g. lb)/ product unit | ▶ Reduce by 30% annually |
| *Develop 'green' products* | Recyclability of obsolete product | ▶ Percentage recovered and recycled | ▶ Achieve 95% recycling |
| *Reduce life-cycle cost* | Costs at each life-cycle stage | ▶ Cost (e.g. US$) per year <br> ▶ Cost (e.g. US$)/ product | ▶ Reduce to US$7,500 per unit |
| *Conserve energy* | Energy usage over life-cycle | ▶ Energy (e.g. BTU) to produce one unit <br> ▶ Power use | ▶ Reduce by 10% annually <br> ▶ Reduce below 30 W |
| *Conserve natural resources* | Recycled content in products | ▶ Percentage by weight of product materials that is recycled | ▶ Recycle at least 30% <br> ▶ Achieve 30% recycled plastics |

*Table* 9.3 **Examples of objectives, sustainability performance indicators (SPIs), metrics and targets**

# 9.4 Best-practice companies

A recent review of recognised sustainability leaders has shown that at least a few companies are applying SPM principles and process steps similar to those described in Section 9.3 (Fiksel *et al.* 1999). As only a small number of companies have publicly stated a sustainability commitment, other companies will find the experiences of these leading companies valuable as they progress on the path towards sustainability. Five companies have been chosen for this analysis, representing different industries: BP Amoco (petro-chemicals), Collins & Aikman (floorcoverings), Monsanto (biotechnology), The Body Shop (cosmetics) and Volvo (automobiles). Each of these companies has demonstrated innovative approaches to sustainability measurement and most have been able to realise business value from their sustainability efforts. The one significant exception is Monsanto, which has encountered public resistance to its introduction of genetically engineered seeds. An important caveat is that this analysis was based exclusively on publicly available data (i.e. the companies' annual reports and websites [see the list of case-study company websites and other sources at the end of this chapter]).

## 9.4.1 *Company profiles*

A brief summary of each company's sustainability measurement programme is provided below.

- The Body Shop has expressed its proactive environmental stance since it began business in 1976. The Body Shop's aim is to become a sustainable business, and its widely publicised *Environmental Values* report in 1997 was the first of its kind. The report, consisting of three independently verified statements on the company's environmental, animal protection and social/stakeholder performance, was recognised by an award from the United Nations Environmental Pro-gramme (UNEP).

- BP Amoco is committed to making a positive contribution to society. It takes environmental precautions and supports community development for areas in which it operates. BP Amoco believes that there is not a trade-off between financial performance and standards of care, but rather believes that the two areas are mutually reinforcing. Environmental issues considered by BP Amoco include climate change, air quality and renewable energy technologies.

- Collins & Aikman Floorcoverings (hereafter referred to as Collins & Aikman) has demonstrated that environmental sustainability can also yield advantages in cost-effectiveness. It is the only carpet manufacturer in the world reclaiming old carpet and recycling it into new, high-performance carpet. Collins & Aikman understands the importance of addressing the triple bottom line and has instituted several programmes to improve performance. It has also formed a 'sustainability laboratory' composed of outside experts.

- Monsanto has embraced sustainable development as part of its core strategy, and a few years ago it spun off its chemical manufacturing operations to focus on businesses based on the life sciences. To create value for stakeholders, Monsanto is designing products that use fewer raw materials, produce less waste, require less energy and enable users to be more productive. Moreover, the company hopes to use its product development expertise to create new markets for sustainable products in agriculture and nutrition.

- Volvo has been working towards becoming a world leader in the transportation equipment industry, based on its performance in the areas of safety, environmental care and quality.[1] The company intends to gain competitive advantage and contribute to sustainable development through environmental programmes that are characterised by a holistic view, continuous improvement, technical development and resource efficiencies.

## 9.4.2 *Applying the principles*

The study has revealed that each of these best-practice companies has applied the four SPM principles, although their approaches vary. For example, all of the companies track and report how their product-related operations consume resources and generate value for stakeholders and all consider the full product life-cycle in their evaluation of product performance. Thus, these companies are able to demonstrate how their product sustainability initiatives support their overall company goals, such as profit growth, employee opportunity and customer satisfaction. For example:

- The Body Shop reports societal indicators, including the results of ethical auditing, Institute of Social and Ethical Accountability (ISEA) principles, social auditing and customer, employee and stakeholder satisfaction surveys. The company has established a life-cycle analysis scheme that consists of six sections: origins of feedstocks, methods of extraction and/or cultivation, processing, resource consumption, waste generation, and distribution.

- Volvo has developed an environmental product declaration, with selected indicators corresponding to four life-cycle stages: environmental management methods, the environmental impact of manufacturing, the environmental impact of driving the car, and the environmental impact of scrapping the car.

- Collins & Aikman, through a five-year effort, created a carpet-backing system that is made with 100% reclaimed content. This flooring product is the first that is recyclable back into itself in a closed-loop fashion.

- Monsanto has been working with the US Department of Agriculture to convert corn hulls, a low-value by-product, into a health-promoting food source that does not require any incremental use of natural resources.

---

1   The Ford Motor Company recently acquired the automotive division of Volvo. This analysis is based on Volvo's activities prior to the acquisition.

In contrast, the environmental performance criteria of most companies tend to measure only the conventional environmental, health and safety indicators associated with manufacturing operations and do not address value creation over the product life-cycle.

Figure 9.1 shows the proportion of each company's performance indicators that correspond to the three dimensions of the triple bottom line. The study has revealed important differences and similarities among the types of indicator publicly reported by these companies.

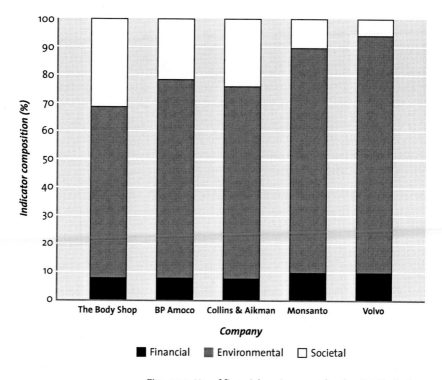

Figure 9.1 **Use of financial, environmental and societal indicators**

All of the companies emphasise environmental performance, as environmental indicators comprise 50% or more of the total indicators reported. The Body Shop more than the other companies emphasises societal indicators. The practice of measuring societal performance re-emerged during the late 1990s and many companies are now grappling with how to measure this dimension of performance (Zadek *et al.* 1997).

Financial indicators receive relatively little attention. In some ways, the lack of focus on economic performance is understandable because these companies are public corporations and therefore produce a separate annual financial report with in-depth accounting results. However, this lack of financial indicators is indicative of the fact that many companies do not adequately convey the costs and benefits of their environmental and sustainability programmes. These programmes can increase revenues, lower operating costs and improve asset utilisation, but relatively few companies have developed the capability to track and report those benefits effectively.

Finally, all of the companies report the use of both leading and lagging indicators (not shown in Fig. 9.1). As leading indicators tend to be focused on internal business processes it is not surprising that the majority of externally reported indicators were in the lagging (i.e. outcome-oriented) category. For example, Volvo's leading indicator is the number of research and development (R&D) programmes addressing material recycling, and related lagging indicators include the total quantity of material throughput and the number of parts recycled.

### 9.4.3 Applying the indicator selection process

Before deciding which indicators to track, each of the five companies underwent a process of considering stakeholder needs and evaluating how its products, processes and business activities could and did affect society and the environment. The aspects that they selected are summarised in Table 9.4. Although their process for determining which aspects were the most significant was not publicly disclosed, several important findings emerged from their published reports:

- Only two companies (BP Amoco and Collins & Aikman) track the revenues associated with their sustainability efforts.

- Although all of the companies report at least one dimension of economic performance, none is currently tackling the complex issue of measuring the externalities associated with the company.

- All of the companies track a wide variety of environmental indicators, ranging from greenhouse gas emissions to solar energy production.

- All of the companies are attempting to measure employee satisfaction but generally have few other societal indicators.

- Two unique efforts are Collins & Aikman's tracking of the impacts that its products have on indoor air quality, and Monsanto's measurement of access to medicinal drugs.

- The data visualisation methods of BP Amoco and Volvo are noteworthy because they clearly communicate the level of achievement relative to their targets.

It is important to note that nearly all of the sustainability aspects reported by the companies had corresponding objectives, indicators and metrics for tracking performance. This seemingly obvious connection is often not made—many companies have identified important environmental and societal aspects but have not developed the means to measure their performance relative to those aspects. Selected examples of sustainability objectives are listed in Table 9.5.

Table 9.6 lists examples of innovative metrics that are able to convey the company's progress toward its sustainability objectives more effectively than conventional metrics.

| | Aspect | The Body Shop | BP Amoco | Collins & Aikman | Monsanto | Volvo |
|---|---|---|---|---|---|---|
| **Environmental** | Direct | | Solar power revenues | Green product revenue | | Environmental R&D |
| | Hidden | Environmental costs; stock disposals | Environmental costs | | Environmental costs | |
| | Contingent | | Environmental disasters; fines | | Fines and Superfund sites | |
| | Relationship | Customer satisfaction | Public concern | | | |
| | Externality | | | | | |
| **Environmental** | Material | Water recycling; LCA | Water recycling | Water and waste recycling | Water recycling; LCA | Water recycling; LCA |
| | Energy | Energy; fuel; renewable energy | Energy; solar energy; clean fuel | Energy; non-fossil fuels | Energy; fuel | Energy; fuel |
| | Local | Effluent discharges; landfill; spills | Discharges; oil spills; habitat loss; hazardous waste | Dyeing wastes | Hazardous waste; spills | Hazardous waste |
| | Regional | Incineration | Hydrocarbon emissions; injection wells | Air emissions | Air emissions; injection wells | $NO_x$; $SO_2$; solvents |
| | Global | $CO_2$ | Greenhouse gases; $CO_2$ | $CO_2$ | $CO_2$ | $CO_2$; $CFC_{11}$; greenhouse gas |
| **Societal** | Quality of life | Employee; customer | Employee | Surveys; retention; promotion | Assessments; teams | Surveys |
| | Peace of mind | Social audit | | | | |
| | Illness | | | Indoor air quality | | |
| | Accident | Absences | Absences | | | |
| | Health and wellbeing | | | | Medicinal drug access | |

LCA = life-cycle assessment

*Table 9.4* **Sustainability aspects examined***

* Many of these indicators could fit into two or more aspect categories. For example, air emissions could certainly influence stakeholder satisfaction and financial performance but are included in the environmental category.

| Company | Financial objective | Environmental objective | Societal objective |
|---|---|---|---|
| The Body Shop | | To increase the proportion of recycled plastic accessories | To follow social and ethical best practices<br><br>To provide learning and development programmes |
| BP Amoco | | To reduce greenhouse gas emissions | To reduce fatal accidents in operations |
| Collins & Aikman | To make the industry's first 'green' competitive product | To increase overall materials efficiency | |
| Monsanto | To create value while reducing waste | To improve soil quality | To enable better health, better nutrition, improved quality of life |
| Volvo | To track environmentally related investment and product development costs | To take account of the entire product life-cycle | To involve all employees in environmental activities |

*Table 9.5* **Triple-bottom-line objectives**

| Indicator | Conventional metric | Innovative product metric |
|---|---|---|
| Waste production | Tonnes/year | Percentage produced compared with industry benchmark per unit of product (Collins & Aikman) |
| Energy | kWh per annum | Relative and percentage reduction (Volvo) |
| Wildlife habitat | Donations to conservation organisations | Percentage increase in yield from seeds (reducing the need for more farmland; Monsanto) |

*Table 9.6* **Examples of innovative performance metrics**

For example, a unique feature of Monsanto's programme is its approach to measuring the company's ability to conserve habitat. Most companies use annual contributions to conservation organisations as their indicator for 'wildlife habitat preservation'. Instead of using this leading indicator, Monsanto quantifies the increase in yield from using its seeds and thence calculates the amount of land that can be protected rather than used for farmland.

Although the use of innovative indicators and metrics might be the preferred choice for company decision-makers, many external stakeholders advocate that companies standardise their sustainability performance reporting process. Unlike financial reports, sustainability results generally cannot be easily compared between companies or industries. As shown in Table 9.7, a comparison of the results of the best-practice companies would be fairly difficult. One recent study of eight companies[2] which tested a set of standard indicators concluded that some indicators, such as energy intensity, are widely applicable, whereas others, such as material intensity, are more sector-specific and often more burdensome to measure (NRTEE 1999).

| Indicator | Metric 1 | Metric 2 | Metric 3 | Metric 4 |
|---|---|---|---|---|
| **$CO_2$ emissions** | Company total (tons) (The Body Shop) | Company total (billion pounds) (Monsanto) | Total including equity partners (million tonnes) (BP Amoco) | Normalised amount (lbs/yd$^2$ of carpet) (Collins & Aikman) |
| **Energy consumption** | Relative reduction (%) (Volvo; Collins & Aikman) | Normalised use (kWh per 1,000 units) (The Body Shop) | Total (million gigajoules) (Monsanto) | |

*Table 9.7* **Comparing sustainability performance with use of four metrics**

In summary, although each of these companies' measurement programmes is commendable, some important differences exist:

- As expected, the choice of measures of value generated by company activities varies widely; for example, Collins & Aikman measures air quality improvement in terms of reduction of volatile organic compounds (VOCs), whereas Monsanto measures soil conservation in terms of improved agricultural practice.

- Only one company, The Body Shop, has applied an extensive stakeholder auditing process to measure societal performance and is attempting to quantify many societal indicators by measuring stakeholder perception.

- The specific indicators used by companies vary considerably and thus the measurement results are not directly comparable.

- Only two companies—BP Amoco and Collins & Aikman—publicly track the revenues associated with their sustainability efforts.

- One company, Monsanto, states few targets for company-wide future performance because of significant variations between the types of value created and wastes generated by the different business units.

2  3M Canada, Alcan Aluminum, Bell Canada, Monsanto, Noranda, Nortel Networks, Procter & Gamble, and Pacific Northern Gas (representing West Coast Energy) participated in the study.

Finally, one of the dominant themes that emerges from these similarities and differences is the continued focus of sustainability measurement on the environmental dimension. This focus is a legacy of historical practice and continues to occupy most of the attention of external stakeholders. As mentioned earlier, the practice of societal reporting is relatively new and being led by a few path-breaking companies, including The Body Shop.

With regard to economic performance measurement, financial reporting is well established but generally focused on business performance as defined by generally accepted accounting principles (GAAPs) and driven by the finance organisation. In contrast, environmental reporting among large corporations is usually the responsibility of the environmental, health and safety organisation. An important step in moving toward triple-bottom-line integration will be the recognition that economic impacts need to be addressed through a life-cycle accounting framework that extends beyond traditional financial boundaries.

## 9.5 Integrated product development

The need to distinguish those products that are 'sustainable' poses new challenges for the design community, extending far beyond the traditional scope of product development. Perhaps one of the most formidable difficulties is the challenge of business integration. To successfully develop sustainable products, a company must learn how to effectively integrate sustainability concepts into its product development process. Sustainable product design cannot be practised in isolation; rather, it must be one facet in a multifaceted approach that considers cost, ease of use, functional performance, 'manufacturability' and other key product requirements.

However, attempts to achieve this type of integration raise both organisational and technical issues, as summarised in Table 9.8. Organisational issues include the establishment of appropriate company policies and incentives, modification of existing business processes, capture and dissemination of sustainable design knowledge via training and information technology and achievement of consistent practices across diverse business units. Technical issues include the implementation of various design strategies—e.g. modifying the material composition of products so that they generate less pollution and waste, or changing the assembly requirements so that fewer material and energy resources

|                | Strategic | Tactical | Operational |
|----------------|-----------|----------|-------------|
| **Organisational** | Company policy and commitment | Reward systems and accountability | Performance indicators and targets |
| **Technical** | Next-generation R&D strategy | Key design concepts and features | Design evaluation and improvement tools |

*Table* 9.8 **Scope of sustainable product design issues**

are consumed per product unit—as well as systematic adoption of sustainable design guidelines, metrics and tools.

Although a number of performance indicators have recently been developed to measure eco-efficiency, little work has been done in a less tangible aspect of sustainability: namely, measuring the socioeconomic impacts of products. Most organisations that have published sustainability indicators have focused on macro-environmental features for a particular community or society as a whole. In contrast, product developers need more focused indicators that address the beneficial or adverse impacts associated with particular design innovations.

The examples of best-practice companies discussed in Section 9.4 focused on company-wide metrics that are reported externally. However, for sustainable design to be adopted in a meaningful way it must be fully integrated into the product development process. This requires an understanding of the primary product design drivers, including reduction in product development cycle time, continuous improvement in product quality and responsiveness to the 'voice of the customer'. As an example, certain sustainability characteristics—e.g. durability, modularity and waste elimination—are naturally synergistic with cost of ownership, which is an increasingly important customer criterion.

To capture these types of synergy, an ecodesign organisation must incorporate sustainability awareness systematically into the daily work of development teams. This is a logical extension of the modern practice of integrated product development (IPD) whereby cross-functional teams begin at the conceptual design stage to consider life-cycle issues, including quality, manufacturability, reliability, maintainability, environment and safety. For example, many companies use a 'stage-gate' process, requiring that a product satisfy a variety of performance criteria before passing on to the next stage of development. The best-practice companies noted above, as well as most other leading practitioners, have made an effort to weave sustainability considerations into their product development processes and the associated stage-gate criteria.

To enable this type of integration, ecodesign teams must be equipped with tools that facilitate sustainability measurement and improvement. The ecodesign tools that are being used today tend to be relatively simple, ranging from rudimentary 'advisory' systems that provide online design guidance to performance tracking tools that represent multi-dimensional indicators. A number of companies have developed internal systems, although they are seldom fully integrated into the design automation environment. For example, a 'green index' software tool was developed by AT&T to assess a product's overall environmental performance. Hughes Aircraft has implemented a similar system called the 'Green Notes Environmental Rating and Measurement System', which is used to automatically provide ratings as designers develop their product and process specifications. A few companies are using streamlined life-cycle assessment tools to provide somewhat more rigorous product evaluations.

In today's exploratory phase, simple tools are preferable to help the rapid establishment of sustainable product design with minimal disruption to existing business processes. Eventually, new types of information technology, such as 'intelligent assistant' design tools, will facilitate the transformation from traditional ways of doing business to a more integrated approach. Once sustainability principles become embedded into decision-support software tools, they will become more accessible to the vast majority of companies that are extremely busy meeting the needs of their stakeholders and that do not have the time or resources for developing new processes and systems. These companies will be primarily interested in practical applications of sustainable design, to the extent that it contributes to their success in the marketplace.

## 9.6 The strategic importance of sustainability measurement

The new-found awareness of sustainability within the business community signals an emerging synthesis between traditional business values and the concepts of environmental and social responsibility. However, for sustainability to become integrated into company strategies and operations, a systematic performance measurement process is essential. To support this transformation, this chapter has presented a set of principles, a systematic process and a number of best-practice examples. This research has demonstrated that:

- Sustainability performance measurement (SPM) is a rapidly evolving practice.

- SPM is valuable for demonstrating progress to internal and external stakeholders.

- Leading companies are already addressing many of the challenges associated with measuring and reporting economic, environmental and societal performance.

- More importantly, SPM helps ecodesign teams make decisions that reduce resource consumption while creating value across their supply chain.

The SPM principles, process and best practices outlined in this chapter can help companies as they take on the complex task of moving from resource-intensive operations to more eco-efficient, value-maximising organisations. SPM practices will play an increasingly important role as environmental and societal considerations begin to permeate business activities. Already, companies in the automotive, chemical, energy, food production, packaging and other industries are using this type of information to improve their decision-making efforts. For example:

- Designers assess how the sustainability profiles of competing product concepts compare.

- Marketers analyse how their product or service satisfies their customers by lowering the cost of ownership and creating tangible and less tangible benefits.

- Production managers apply life-cycle costing methods to quantify hidden environmental costs.

- Strategic planners assess the consequences of environmentally driven scenarios.

As global pressures intensify, the need for sustainability awareness is becoming an imperative. The world population will soon surpass six billion, and concerns about climate, water, land and habitat preservation continue to mount. Rapidly developing economies around the world are creating growing markets for goods and services. These conditions are creating opportunities for companies to fundamentally change how they engage suppliers, operate facilities and service customers. In addition to new technologies, new production methods and new management systems, these companies will need a new language to communicate their performance goals and progress. A well-conceived SPM process will respond to that final, fundamental need.

## Case-study company websites and source material

### The Body Shop
'The Values Report, 1997' (23 June 1999)
www.the-body-shop.com/usa/aboutus/values.html

### BP Amoco
'Environmental and Safety Report, 1998' (21 June 1999)
www.bpamoco.com/reports/enviro/

'Health, Safety, and Environmental Data, 1998' (22 June 1999)
www.bpamoco.com/reports/enviro/

### Collins & Aikman Floorcoverings
M. Bridger (1999) 'Carpet In/Carpet Out: The Continuing Journey at Collins & Aikman' paper presented at *Industrial Ecology IV: The Future 500 Conference*, 29 April 1999

*Catalyst: Elements of Change* (1998)

'Environmental Statement, 1999' (24 June 1999)
www.collinsandaikman.com/environmental/index.html

'Practical Vision' (1998) *Interiors and Sources Magazine*

### Monsanto
'Sustainable Development Report, 1997' (15 June 1999)
www.monsanto.com/monsanto/about/sustainability/default.htm

### Volvo
'Environmental Report, 1998' (17 June 1999)
www3.volvo.com/environment/index.htm

# WHAT SUSTAINABLE SOLUTIONS DO SMALL AND MEDIUM-SIZED ENTERPRISES PREFER?

*Carolien G. van Hemel*
Delft University of Technology, Netherlands

Since the 1980s industry worldwide has been working more and more conscientiously in the direction of sustainable development. By now, environmental and social concerns in product development are no longer perceived as a responsibility of 'the others' but as a self-evident business element and even as a manifestation of corporate governance. In this process larger companies have taken the lead, strongly stimulated by regulation, competition and interest from various societal stakeholders.

'Smaller companies will follow naturally' was the line of reasoning. It has slowly become recognised that small and medium-sized enterprises (SMEs) need specific support. Fortunately, in the early 1990s the Dutch government recognised this and initiated the innovation centre (IC) ecodesign project of the IC network in the Netherlands (Böttcher *et al.* 1997). The aim of this project, which ran from 1995 to 1998, was to increase the level of awareness in Dutch industrial SMEs with regard to design for environment (DfE). For the author of this chapter it offered a unique opportunity for an empirical study on the DfE behaviour of a considerable group of SMEs (77 in total; van Hemel 1998).

One of the research questions asked concerned the preferences of the participating SMEs with regard to implementation of DfE. In other words: 'What sustainable solutions in the field of DfE do SMEs prefer?' This chapter suggests an answer to this question.

In Section 10.1 arguments are put forward for why SMEs need specific support in implementing ecodesign. Next, Section 10.2 describes how the DfE preferences of SMEs participating in the IC ecodesign project were studied. Section 10.3 reveals some of the results of the study, listing the differences in success of 34 DfE principles that were distinguished in a typology of DfE strategies and principles. The conclusions and a set of recommendations (Section 10.4), derived from this study, conclude the chapter.

## 10.1 Why do small and medium-sized enterprises need specific support?

The Dutch government stated that SMEs need specific support if they are to start greening their business. Literature supports this line of thinking; various authors claim that SMEs do lag behind their larger counterparts in terms of environmental performance. One often-mentioned reason is that SMEs generally lack sufficient staff, time and funding to lead their business towards sustainable solutions (see e.g. De Bruijn *et al.* 1992; Hutchinson and Chaston 1994). The main reason, however, is that SMEs are less subject to external stimuli that prompt them to take environmental initiatives compared with larger businesses (De Bruijn *et al.* 1992; van Hemel 1998).

In a study on the behaviour of 77 SMEs that were helped to apply ecodesign principles to their products, the question was raised as to why certain SMEs turned out to be successful whereas others lagged behind. It was found that the proactive SMEs were most motivated by internal stimuli (innovational opportunities, a drive to increase product quality and the desire to seek new market opportunities) rather than by external stimuli (customer demands, governmental regulation and industrial sector initiatives). Based on the literature, the opposite was expected (Groen 1995; Hutchinson and Hutchinson 1995; Winter and Ledgerwood 1994). What is the reason for this? The answer may be that SMEs are not sufficiently subject to convincing external stimuli: the existing regulation focuses on larger industries, as do consumer organisations and environmental agencies (De Bruijn *et al.* 1992; Dogson and Rothwell 1994).

SMEs tend to work with more ad hoc and with short-term objectives than do larger companies, which apply strategic management and set longer-term goals in comparison with SMEs (Hutchinson and Chaston 1994). Therefore SMEs are less likely than are larger companies to believe in the concept of 'pollution prevention pays' (Winter and Ledgerwood 1994) and less enthusiastic about the possible long-term commercial benefits of environmental management (Hutchinson and Chaston 1994).

## 10.2 Studying design for environment preferences in the innovation centre ecodesign project

### 10.2.1 The innovation centre ecodesign project

The intention of the IC ecodesign project was to boost awareness in SMEs regarding DfE and to show them the commercial potential of DfE. In 1994 a DfE implementation approach was developed specifically for this project (Böttcher *et al.* 1997). An essential element of this approach was the 'environmental innovation scan', intended to enhance the amount of knowledge in a company on DfE and its motivation to apply DfE to one of its products.

The environmental innovation scan made it possible for the IC consultants to contact and discuss the subject of DfE with a large number of SMEs. The second stage of the scan offered both the company and the IC consultant involved the opportunity to go into more detail. The result of this approach was that the companies became acquainted with DfE and the product life-cycle approach without being immediately forced to make extensive life-cycle assessments (LCAs).

The outcome of the environmental innovation scan was a company-specific DfE action plan, listing a set of DfE improvement options suggested by the IC consultant. The number of DfE improvement options for each of the DfE action plans ranged from 3 to 17.

A total of 22 persons (IC consultants and IC assistant consultants) were responsible for carrying out the environmental innovation scans in the 77 SMEs studied in this research. All 22 were employed at one of 17 regional innovation centres.

### 10.2.2 *Participating companies and products involved*

In 1995 a total of 94 SMEs participated in the IC ecodesign project; 77 of which were included in the study reported in this chapter. The participating companies had to meet the following selection criteria:

- They had to belong to the SME sector (i.e. have a maximum of 200 employees).

- They had to be 'self-specifying' (self-defining the specifications for the products they produced).

- Their products had to be designed and produced in the Netherlands.

- Their products had to be physical, tangible products.

Finding companies that both wanted to participate and that met these criteria was more difficult than expected.

Many branches of industry were represented; the most common were those manufacturing metal products, machinery and wood and furniture, followed by those working with rubber and synthetics, electronics and the textile industry. As many as 70% of these companies employed at least one in-house product developer. Most companies were self-specifying and most companies developed end-products. In general, until the start of the project the companies had taken few environmental initiatives; 75% of the companies had no experience with DfE.

The products the participating companies submitted for the environmental innovation scan were diverse, ranging from packaging to a coach. They differed in terms of material, production techniques, packaging, function, type and size of market, lifetime, and so on.

### 10.2.3 *Classifying the design for environment improvement options*

Before attempting to understand which sustainable solutions the SMEs studied preferred it was necessary to know how to identify and record the SMEs' DfE preferences. To this end the DfE 'strategy wheel' was applied, enabling classification of the DfE options prioritised by the companies as a result of the IC ecodesign project (van Hemel and Brezet 1997).

The strategy wheel is based on a typology of potential DfE strategies and principles and has been developed to enable DfE initiatives to be classified. The typology distinguishes 34 so-called DfE principles—possible ways to improve the environmental profile of a product system, taking all the stages of its life-cycle into consideration. On the basis of literature analysis and current DfE experiences, these 34 DfE principles were clustered *a priori* into eight DfE strategies. The original idea behind the DfE strategy wheel was simply that it should function as a frame of reference for the researcher, giving an overview of possible ways to improve environmental product profiles. The DfE strategy wheel is illustrated in Figure 10.1. The strategy new concept development is called 'DfE Strategy @'. The symbol '@' emphasises the innovative character of this specific strategy. It refers to the electronic mailing system, which is perceived as highly innovative from the functional as well as environmental perspective.

While drawing up the DfE action plans for the participating companies, the IC consultants categorised the suggested DfE improvement options at DfE strategy level. At a later stage, all options were classified again at the more detailed DfE principle level in order to create a database of DfE improvement options. This database would then help IC consultants to generate new DfE improvement options for other companies. For the research described here it was necessary to ensure that all options were classified consistently in the DfE strategy typology. Therefore, the classification of all DfE improvement options suggested to the SMEs was checked by the researcher.

### 10.2.4 Success rate of the design for environment improvement options

The first task was to determine to what extent the DfE improvement option had been realised. In other words, what was the success rate of the specific DfE improvement option? A total of nine levels of success were distinguished, as shown in Table 10.1. A DfE option could either be 'rejected' (success rate 0), 'of interest' (success rates 1, 2 or 3), 'prioritised' (success rates 4 or 5), 'realised' (success rate 6) or 'not considered' (success rates 7 or 8).

### 10.2.5 The newness of the design for environment improvement options

The next task concerned the additional value of the DfE improvement option to the SMEs, or, in other words, it was necessary to ask about the newness of the specific DfE improvement option to the SMEs. This question was asked to verify the assumption that DfE principles that are already familiar to SMEs are more successful than DfE principles that are perceived to be new. Three degrees of newness were distinguished:

- **Limited.** The company would have studied or implemented the DfE improvement option even if it had not participated in the IC ecodesign project.

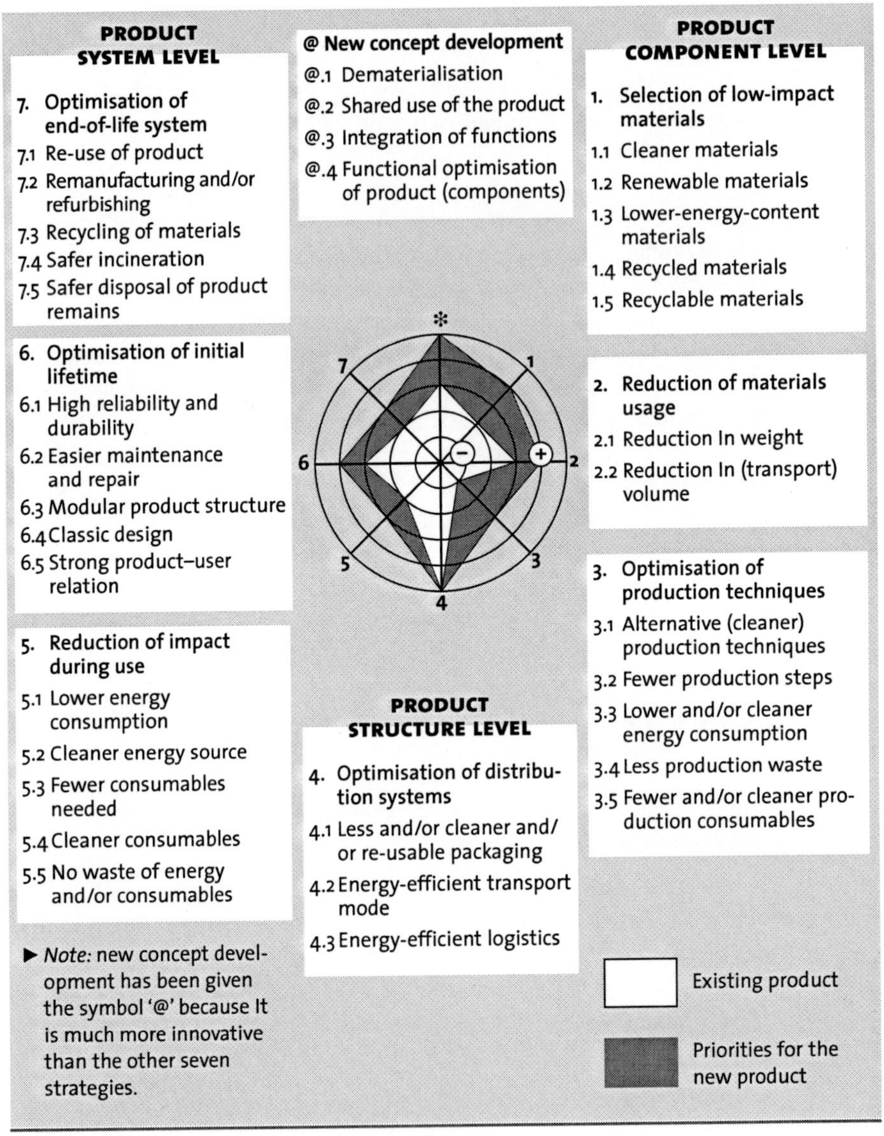

**PRODUCT SYSTEM LEVEL**

7. Optimisation of end-of-life system
7.1 Re-use of product
7.2 Remanufacturing and/or refurbishing
7.3 Recycling of materials
7.4 Safer incineration
7.5 Safer disposal of product remains

6. Optimisation of initial lifetime
6.1 High reliability and durability
6.2 Easier maintenance and repair
6.3 Modular product structure
6.4 Classic design
6.5 Strong product–user relation

5. Reduction of impact during use
5.1 Lower energy consumption
5.2 Cleaner energy source
5.3 Fewer consumables needed
5.4 Cleaner consumables
5.5 No waste of energy and/or consumables

▶ *Note:* new concept development has been given the symbol '@' because it is much more innovative than the other seven strategies.

**@ New concept development**
@.1 Dematerialisation
@.2 Shared use of the product
@.3 Integration of functions
@.4 Functional optimisation of product (components)

**PRODUCT STRUCTURE LEVEL**

4. Optimisation of distribution systems
4.1 Less and/or cleaner and/or re-usable packaging
4.2 Energy-efficient transport mode
4.3 Energy-efficient logistics

**PRODUCT COMPONENT LEVEL**

1. Selection of low-impact materials
1.1 Cleaner materials
1.2 Renewable materials
1.3 Lower-energy-content materials
1.4 Recycled materials
1.5 Recyclable materials

2. Reduction of materials usage
2.1 Reduction In weight
2.2 Reduction In (transport) volume

3. Optimisation of production techniques
3.1 Alternative (cleaner) production techniques
3.2 Fewer production steps
3.3 Lower and/or cleaner energy consumption
3.4 Less production waste
3.5 Fewer and/or cleaner production consumables

☐ Existing product

■ Priorities for the new product

*Figure* 10.1 **The design for environment strategy wheel**

Source: van Hemel and Brezet 1997, based on van Hemel 1994

■ **Fair.** The company had been considering the DfE improvement option, but without the IC ecodesign project it would not have considered it any further.

■ **High.** The DfE improvement option was totally new to the company.

| Cluster | Success rate | Description |
|---|---|---|
| Rejected | 0 | The option had been rejected; moreover, it was of no future interest to the company. |
| Of interest | 1 | The option had been studied in more depth; realisation had still been rejected. |
| | 2 | The option had not yet been studied; it was assured of the company's future interest. |
| | 3 | The option was still being studied; realisation was still not certain. |
| Prioritised | 4 | The option was being implemented; realisation was expected within three years. |
| | 5 | The option was being implemented; realisation was expected within one year. |
| | 6 | The option had already been implemented or would be implemented very soon (the option realised). |
| Not considered | 7 | The option had not been given special attention as it was regarded as a bottom-line matter in product development and therefore already had the company's continuous interest. |
| | 8 | The option had not been studied because it had become irrelevant. |

*Table* 10.1  **The nine levels of success (0–8) reflecting the extent to which a design for environment improvement option had been implemented**

## 10.3  Results: types, success rates and newness of the studied design for environment options

As many as 596 DfE improvement options were suggested in the DfE action plans for the 77 companies studied. Only after each of the 596 DfE improvement options had been classified did it become possible to generate an overview of the frequency of the suggested DfE improvement options. This overview is shown in Figure 10.2 in which the columns are stacked according to the success rates of the DfE improvement options.

Figure 10.2 shows that a total of 183 (31%) of the 596 DfE options suggested by the IC consultants were given a success rate of 6 meaning that these options had already been realised or would be realised very soon. 'Realised' here means that the DfE option suggested had been incorporated in the product's design, packaging or production processes. It also means that the environmentally improved product was already being marketed or the company was convinced that it would be launched very soon.

Furthermore, as many as 247 (41%) of the 596 DfE options suggested by the IC consultants were prioritised and given a success rate 4, 5 or 6, and were thought to be realised within three years of the research project. Some 183 of the options have already been realised (as discussed above) or should be realised within one year (success rate 5) or three years (success rate 4).

### 10.3.1  The most frequently suggested design for environment principles

As expected, considerable differences are found regarding the absolute numbers of DfE options belonging to a certain type of DfE principle. The 10 most frequently suggested DfE principles are shown in Table 10.2.

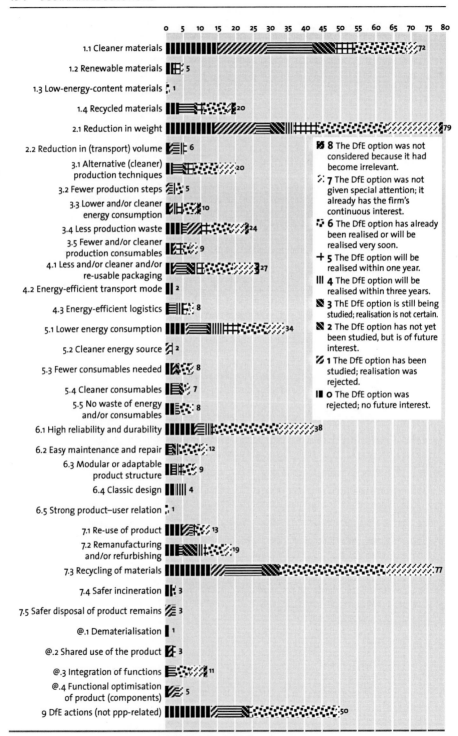

*Figure* 10.2 **The number of suggested design for environment (DfE) improvement options, categorised according to the typology of DfE strategies and principles; stacked according to level of realisation**

| DFE principle | | Frequency of suggestion |
|---|---|---|
| 2.1 | Reduction in weight | 79 |
| 7.3 | Recycling of materials | 77 |
| 1.1 | Cleaner materials | 72 |
| 6.1 | High reliability and durability | 38 |
| 5.1 | Lower energy consumption | 34 |
| 4.1 | Less and/or cleaner and/or re-usable packaging | 27 |
| 3.4 | Less production waste | 24 |
| 1.4 | Recycled materials | 20 |
| 3.1 | Alternative (cleaner) production techniques | 20 |
| 7.2 | Remanufacturing and/or refurbishing | 19 |

*Table* 10.2 **The ten most frequently suggested design for environment principles**

The data shows that these 10 DfE principles were suggested far more frequently than the other DfE principles. Regarding the number of times the 34 different DfE principles were suggested, there is indeed a considerable difference in terms of their 'popularity'.

## 10.3.2 The most successful design for environment principles

Are those DfE principles suggested most frequently also the most successful? In this study a DfE option was regarded as successful only if it was prioritised by the company concerned: the DfE option was attributed with success rate 4, 5 or 6, implying that it would be achieved within a period of three years. A DfE principle is therefore successful if a relatively large number of DfE options of the specific type of DfE principle had been prioritised and had thus been given a success rate of 4, 5 or 6.

To establish the success of a specific DfE principle the number of prioritised DfE options (success rate 4, 5 or 6) must be compared with the number of DfE options that were suggested. Let us first of all concentrate on the ten most frequently suggested DfE principles, listed in Table 10.2. The percentage of prioritised DfE options in this group are shown in Table 10.3. From Table 10.3 it can be seen that the 10 most frequently suggested DfE principles were also the most successful principles. However, the most frequently suggested DfE principles are not automatically the ones that were most frequently prioritised. For example, whereas options of DfE principle 2.1 (reduction in weight) or 1.1 (cleaner materials) were often suggested, they were prioritised less frequently.

## 10.3.3 Comparison with other studies

Do these findings match others reported in literature? Smith *et al.* (1996: 24) carried out interviews in 16 British, US and Australian companies, ranging from small to large in size,

| DfE principle | Description | Suggestion frequency | Percentage of DfE options prioritised |
|---|---|---|---|
| 7.3 | Recycling of materials | 77 | 47 |
| 6.1 | High reliability and durability | 38 | 45 |
| 1.4 | Recycled materials | 20 | 45 |
| 5.1 | Lower energy consumption | 34 | 44 |
| 7.2 | Remanufacturing and/or refurbishing | 19 | 42 |
| 3.4 | Less production waste | 24 | 38 |
| 3.1 | Alternative (cleaner) production techniques | 20 | 38 |
| 2.1 | Reduction in weight | 79 | 37 |
| 1.1 | Cleaner materials | 72 | 28 |
| 4.1 | Less and/or cleaner and/or re-usable packaging | 27 | 26 |

*Table* 10.3 **The percentages of prioritised design for environment (DfE) options and the suggestion frequency for the ten most frequently suggested types of DfE principle**

selected on grounds of their 'green product initiatives'. They concluded that the companies in question were most often concerned with:

● Choice of materials (corresponding to DfE strategy 1: selection of low-impact materials)

● Reducing the environmental impacts of production (corresponding to DfE strategy 3: optimisation of production techniques)

● Reducing the energy and pollution impacts of the product in use (corresponding to DfE strategy 5: reduction of impact during use)

● Recycling materials at the end of the product's life (corresponding to DfE principle 7.3: recycling of materials)

Comparing these four foci in DfE with the DfE principles listed in Table 10.3 it is clear that the four foci are indeed represented in the group of 10 DfE principles suggested most frequently and prioritised in the present study (Table 10.4). There are some differences as well: first, the ranking is different. For example, in the present study, DfE principle 7.3, recycling of materials, was more dominant than in the UK study. Furthermore, some DfE principles that were given a great deal of attention in the IC ecodesign study were not included in the four foci mentioned above.

There are many reasons for these differences. They might be a result of geographical differences or different national legislation. They could be a result of the fact that the IC ecodesign study focuses on companies employing a workforce of up to 200, whereas the

| DfE principle | Description | van Hemel | Smith *et al.* | Hanssen |
|---|---|:---:|:---:|:---:|
| 7.3 | Recycling of materials | ✓ | ✓ | ✓ |
| 6.1 | High reliability and durability | ✓ | | |
| 1.4 | Recycled materials | ✓ | | ✓ |
| 5.1 | Lower energy consumption | ✓ | ✓ | |
| 7.2 | Remanufacturing and/or refurbishing | ✓ | | |
| 3.4 | Less production waste | ✓ | ✓ | |
| 3.1 | Alternative (cleaner) production techniques | ✓ | ✓ | |
| 2.1 | Reduction in weight | ✓ | | ✓ |
| 1.1 | Cleaner materials | ✓ | ✓ | ✓ |
| 4.1 | Less and/or cleaner and/or re-usable packaging | ✓ | | |

*Table* 10.4 **Comparison of the most successful design for environment principles found by van Hemel (1998), Smith *et al.* (1996) and Hanssen (1997)**

UK study included small as well as large companies. Alternatively, and this is the most probable reason, they could be a result of differences in the typologies of DfE options that were applied. However, a more detailed comparison of the two studies is not justified because of the divergent research methods and companies studied.

Hanssen (1997) reports the results of the Nordic Project on Environmentally Sound Product Development, formulated to stimulate six Nordic companies to apply DfE. In Table 1 of the last paper of his thesis he lists the 'proposed or realised options for improvement of analysed products'. A total of 15 options were listed for six products. Three concerned improvements that did not relate to product design—change external system conditions (mentioned twice) and change voltage in distribution system (mentioned once, for electric cables). The following options, focusing on product improvement options, were listed:

- Substitution of raw materials (five times), corresponding to DfE strategy 1 (selection of low-impact materials)

- Use recovered material (three times), corresponding to DfE principle 1.4 (recycled materials)

- Recover material after use (twice), corresponding to DfE principle 7.3 (recycling of materials)

- Use less materials (once), corresponding to DfE strategy 2 (reduction of materials usage)

● Increase the wattage of individual fluorescent tubes so fewer fittings are required per unit (once), encompassed in DfE strategy 2 (reduction of materials usage)

A comparison of these improvement options with Table 10.3 shows that the these option types are also represented in the group of ten most frequently suggested and successful DfE principles (Table 10.4). Here again, differences in ranking and number of successful DfE principles are recorded. Owing to differences, among other things in typology of the DfE improvement options used and the number, type and size of companies investigated in the two studies, to make any further comparison would not be sensible.

Table 10.4 summarises the findings of the IC ecodesign study with those of Smith *et al.* (1996) and Hanssen (1997). This table shows that the three studies agree only on the point that dominant DfE principles are 7.3 (recycling of materials) and 1.1 (selection of cleaner materials). Three DfE principles were found to be important in the IC ecodesign project but were not mentioned in the other two studies. This concerns the DfE principles 6.1 (high reliability and durability), 7.2 (remanufacturing and/or refurbishing) and 4.1 (less and/or cleaner and/or re-usable packaging). However, as mentioned above, the comparison should not be taken too far. This would not be justified because of the considerable differences in research methodology, the DfE typologies used and the number, type and size of the companies investigated in the three studies. To enable comparison in future research on DfE implementation, the use of a common typology of potential directions for DfE improvement is recommended.

### 10.3.4  Successful but less frequently suggested design for environment principles

Figure 10.2 reveals DfE principles which, although they were not suggested very often, were prioritised with a relatively high frequency. The very successful but less frequently suggested DfE principles were

● 3.2: fewer production steps

● 3.3: lower and/or cleaner energy consumption

● 6.2: easier maintenance and repair

● 6.3: modular or adaptable product structure

● 4.3: energy-efficient logistics

● 3.5: fewer and/or cleaner production consumables

This implies that, whenever such a DfE option was suggested, the likelihood of it being prioritised was high.

In conclusion it can safely be stated that 16 DfE principles are obviously more successful than the other 18 DfE principles distinguished in the typology of DfE strategies and principles used in this study.

## 10.3.5 Newness or additional value of the design for environment options

In addition to their frequency and success rate, the extent to which the 596 DfE options were new for the companies was investigated. In the case where a company's representative perceived a DfE option as 'new', implying that the option had not been thought of before, then that option had a high additional value (newness 3). Conversely, if the company stated that it would have considered the DfE option in question whether or not it had participated in the IC ecodesign project, the option had a low additional value (newness 1).

The research data showed that in general the additional value of most DfE options was 'fair' to 'high'. In total, as many as 227 of the suggested 596 DfE options (38%) were said to be totally new to the companies (newness 3); 169 (28%) were said not to be new but would not have been reconsidered if the company had not participated in the IC ecodesign project (newness 2).

Focusing on the 247 prioritised DfE options, 62 (25%) were totally new (newness 3) and 91 (37%) were reconsidered as a result of the IC ecodesign project (newness 2). Thus, in total 62% of the prioritised 247 DfE options were prioritised partly as a result of the IC ecodesign project.

This conclusion, in combination with the high number of prioritised DfE options (41%), justifies the conclusion that on the whole the Dutch IC ecodesign project resulted in substantial additional value.

The number of DfE options per DfE principle with newness 1 is indicative of the extent to which the companies were already familiar with the DfE principle in question. Some DfE principles seem to be relatively new for the companies concerned; others being relatively familiar. Table 10.5 lists the new DfE principles next to those that are more familiar.

It is obvious that DfE principles such as 2.1 (reduction in weight), 3.2 (fewer production steps), 6.1 (high reliability and durability) and @.3 (integration of functions) are already familiar to many SMEs. They represent product requirements that are common in product development, even beyond the perspective of environmental considerations. It is expected that many of these DfE principles (leading to synergy with more familiar product requirements) will be prioritised. Furthermore, the DfE options of those types of DfE principle that are relatively new to the companies are expected to obtain relatively lower success rates.

Table 10.5 also shows the percentages of DfE options prioritised per DfE principle. It is only natural that the percentages in the right-hand column are—with some exceptions—higher than those in the left-hand column. This supports the assumption that DfE principles that are less compatible with 'traditional' product requirements have a lower chance of being prioritised than have DfE principles that lead to synergy.

| New DfE principles (newness 3) | | Familiar DfE principles (newness 1) | |
| --- | --- | --- | --- |
| *DfE principle* | *Percentage of options prioritised* | *DfE principle* | *Percentage of options prioritised* |
| 1.1 Cleaner materials | 28 | 2.1 Reduction in weight | 37 |
| 1.2 Renewable materials | 20 | 3.2 Fewer production steps | 60 |
| 2.2 Reduction in (transport) volume | 33 | 3.3 Lower and/or cleaner energy consumption (during production) | 60 |
| 3.5 Fewer and/or cleaner production consumables | 44 | 4.1 Less and/or cleaner and/or re-usable packaging | 26 |
| 6.2 Easier maintenance and repair | 58 | 5.1 Lower energy consumption (during use) | 44 |
| 6.4 Classic design | 25 | 5.3 Fewer consumables needed during use | 50 |
| 7.1 Re-use of product | 23 | 5.5 No waste of energy and/or consumables (during use) | 38 |
| 7.4 Safer incineration | 33 | 6.1 High reliability and durability | 45 |
| | | @.3 Integration of functions | 36 |

*Table 10.5* **New design for environment (DfE) principles (newness 3) versus familiar (newness 1) DfE principles**

# 10.4 Conclusions and recommendations

The central question of this chapter was: 'What sustainable solutions do SMEs prefer?' The answer to this question has been given in detail and is summarised in Figure 10.3, visualising which DfE principles were preferred by the SMEs studied.

According to this study, the companies investigated gave most of their attention to end-of-life issues (recycling of materials; remanufacturing and refurbishing), to reducing product weight and to the use of cleaner (non-hazardous) and recycled materials. Other important topics concerned increasing product durability, reducing the product's energy consumption and use of cleaner technology (less production waste and cleaner production techniques). Finally, product packaging was also regarded as an important environmental concern.

DfE strategies that were clearly given less attention were DfE strategy 5 (reduction of impact during use; with the exception of DfE principle 5.1 [lower energy consumption during use]) and DfE strategy @ (new concept development).

Figure 10.3 also summarises the answer to another research question asked in this study (but not elaborated on in this chapter): 'Why are certain DfE principles more successful than others?' The study has shown that the most influential internal stimuli were the innovational opportunities of a DfE option, an expected increase in product quality and potential new market opportunities. Personal environmental commitment (assumed to

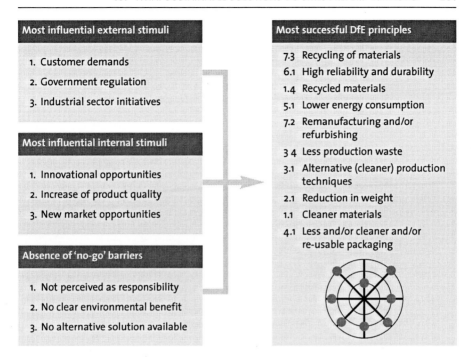

**Most influential external stimuli**

1. Customer demands
2. Government regulation
3. Industrial sector initiatives

**Most influential internal stimuli**

1. Innovational opportunities
2. Increase of product quality
3. New market opportunities

**Absence of 'no-go' barriers**

1. Not perceived as responsibility
2. No clear environmental benefit
3. No alternative solution available

**Most successful DfE principles**

7.3 Recycling of materials
6.1 High reliability and durability
1.4 Recycled materials
5.1 Lower energy consumption
7.2 Remanufacturing and/or refurbishing
3 4 Less production waste
3.1 Alternative (cleaner) production techniques
2.1 Reduction in weight
1.1 Cleaner materials
4.1 Less and/or cleaner and/or re-usable packaging

*Figure* 10.3  **The most influential stimuli and barriers, and the ten most successful design for environment (DfE) principles**

*Source:* van Hemel 1998

be an influential driver for the implementation of a DfE option) apparently had little significance. The research showed quite clearly that by far the most important external stimuli to adopt DfE are customer demands and government legislation. Furthermore, this study revealed that three of the eleven barriers distinguished must be characterised as 'no-go' barriers: their existence obstructs the DfE options in question from being implemented. The other eight barriers were only 'initial' barriers. If driven by several influential stimuli, DfE options with an initial barrier were still implemented.

The study, partly presented in this chapter, has led to many suggestions for further improvement of programmes such as the IC ecodesign project. Box 10.1 lists a selection of these.

**Recommendations for intermediary organisations promoting design for environment (DfE) in industry**

- Consultants should be selected carefully and be given proper training. This study has made it clear that the role and influence of consultants with respect to DfE is very important. Whether this depends on the consultant's knowledge, his or her consulting style or attitude towards the subject of DfE is not clear. A point for future concern and research is how this influence can be explained and what characterises those consultants who arouse significant DfE performance.

- Companies for participation should be selected carefully. The intermediary organisations (such as the innovation centres) are recommended to be more selective when choosing the companies to participate in a project such as the IC ecodesign project. Companies that regard product development as their core activity and that at the moment of intervention have high ambitions to innovate are to be preferred.

- Extensive follow-up support should be provided. Programmes such as the IC ecodesign project could be improved by ensuring more extensive follow-up support for the companies by the consultant involved.

**Recommendations for developers of policy for promoting design for environment (DfE) in industry**

- More demonstration projects. Governments should continue stimulating DfE with demonstration projects such as the IC ecodesign project. This study has shown that the approach used in the IC ecodesign project is very effective in the sense that it actually raised awareness and boosted activities connected with DfE among SMEs.

- Financial support schemes should be raised. Financial support schemes are effective instruments for lowering the threshold for SMEs to invest in DfE after the DfE intervention. SMEs sometimes find it difficult to apply for financial support from existing financial schemes, probably because of time-schedules and the necessary administration. It is therefore recommended that such schemes are adjusted to bring them more into line with day-to-day practice in SMEs.

- Commercial opportunities related to DfE should be promoted. This study has shown that DfE obviously has commercial opportunities, especially for end-products. Spreading this idea is a good way of stimulating other companies to apply DfE. In addition to the promotional activities of the intermediary organisations, government should ensure the promotion of eco-design at national level.

- Strong and consistent external stimuli should be provided. The SMEs studied implement mainly those DfE options that generate commercial benefit. How can one motivate companies to realise DfE options that have greater environmental benefit but that have less interesting commercial opportunities? The empirical findings imply that in order to boost the application of DfE in SMEs the amount and variety of external pressure could be increased. Market pull could be given a boost to increase the amount of external pressure. Furthermore, eco-benchmarking by consumer organisations seems to have a strong influence on the DfE behaviour of manufacturers and should be continued. Although it is more or less non-existent at this moment, government task-setting is believed to offer important external drivers towards DfE as well, especially for companies that 'wait and see'. Government task-setting in connection with DfE (e.g. the EU labelling scheme for energy efficiency of household appliances) could have a direct influence on the environmental initiatives of SMEs and an indirect influence by promoting DfE application in larger companies which in turn will pass their DfE demands to their SME suppliers.

- A move should be made from eco-(re)design to ecodesign. So far, the companies studied revealed DfE results that can be typified as 'eco-(re)designs' or 'incremental green designs'. For the future, it would be worthwhile approaching SMEs with a programme that is focused more clearly on promoting 'ecodesigns' or 'sustainable product designs', learning from experience with the existing eco-(re)design approach. By doing this, industry could benefit even more from the innovative potential of DfE.

*Box* 10.1 **Suggestions for further improvement of programmes such as the IC eco-design project**

# SUSTAINABLE PRODUCT DEVELOPMENT
## A strategy for developing countries

*Diego Masera*
EU Micro-Enterprises Support Programme
and Ecodesign Consultant

Developing countries face the double challenge of the economic and social development of the local population and the preservation of their natural resource base. Over the years these two objectives have been seen as mutually exclusive. Even now, most economic development policies tend to pay little attention to their environmental implications.

The limited income possibilities of most people in developing countries makes long-term planning difficult. However, the desperate and unsustainable living conditions of the rural population call for an urgent search for alternatives.

Whereas in developed countries the challenge is to change consumption patterns and the materials and energy level used, in developing countries the challenge is to reach a sustainable balance between conservation of natural resources and socioeconomic development of rural communities.

Micro and small enterprises (MSEs) play an important role in achieving these objectives because they are the backbone of the private sector. MSEs constitute over 90% of enterprises in the world and account for 50%–60% of employment (UNIDO 1999: 2). In developing countries MSEs often offer the only realistic prospects for increases in employment and value added. MSEs make a vital contribution to the development process because:

- They are labour-intensive and tend to lead to a more equitable distribution of income than do larger enterprises; they play an important role in alleviating poverty, often providing employment opportunities at reasonable rates of remuneration to workers from poor households and to women, who have few alternative sources of income.

■ They contribute to a more efficient allocation of resources; they tend to adopt labour-intensive production methods and thus more accurately reflect the resource endowments in developing countries where labour is plentiful and capital scarce.

This chapter is based on the proposition that the current lamentable environmental, social and economic situation of many communities in developing countries can be improved by introducing and implementing sustainable product design (SPD) among local MSEs.

# 11.1 A sustainable product development strategy

A successful SPD implementation strategy for developing countries needs to encompass planning, manufacturing and marketing. It has to provide alternatives to the entire production cycle, including the sustainable management and supply of natural resources, improvements in the manufacturing process and a search for alternative marketing opportunities. It needs to depart from the sustainable production of raw materials and plan for the whole life-cycle of manufactured products. A key element for success in implementation of SPD in developing countries is to find and work towards win–win conditions, conditions where reduction of environmental impact results in an increment of economic benefits at the local level.

The starting point of this SPD strategy is the position that, in order to attain sustainable development, there is a profound need to change the current patterns of production and consumption from both the technological and the behavioural point of view. This SPD approach is based on participatory development, which presents the underlying philosophy that local people are taking the initiative to improve their own conditions from inputs available to them.

The SPD strategy for a selected geographical area is divided into two main phases:

■ The assessment phase

■ The implementation phase

## 11.1.1 Assessment phase

The need for an assessment phase is based on the belief that to contribute to improving the existing situation it is essential to understand the current relationship between people and the environment. Several development initiatives have failed because they do not understand and/or do not incorporate the concrete demands of MSEs and the local population. The needs of the local MSEs and the population, who in many cases own the natural resources, are usually left out. This situation tends to lead to conflicts in the use of resources. In this context, the proposed SPD strategy tackles the problem by integrating natural resource conservation and restoration needs with the multiple demands of the local population and MSEs.

In the case of forest areas, a central element of the approach is the characterisation of the forest system, which includes the demand of different species on the system and the species and parts of trees used by small and large enterprises and the local population. It identifies and defines the different types of MSE, studies their geographical connections and analyses their impact on the vegetation.

The proposed assessment methodology has a wide focus for the investigation of the impact and consumption of MSEs in a selected area. Criteria used include: the tree species used, the part of the tree that is used, the type of wood used, relationships among enterprises (inputs and outputs), results from biomass flow analysis, mean annual increment (MAI), geographical distribution, products made and technology used. The analysis is centred on the biomass consumption of MSEs with particular attention to the relationships among enterprises and their inputs and outputs. The present methodology permits the identification of products and by-products of MSE sectors which together with the raw materials used constitute essential information for the SPD process.

In the case of forest areas, the analysis begins with the identification of demand for forest products for all biomass users of the forest area. It estimates their number, geographical distribution and their total and direct annual wood demand and studies their connections (to provide biomass flowcharts; see Fig. 11.1).

The second step in the analysis is to estimate the supply by studying the conditions and growth potential of the forest areas by species. Finally, the analysis compares the demand and the supply and produces a forest resource balance, which indicates the level of use of forest resources.

This analysis permits:

- The identification and easy visualisation of the relationships between enterprises and the regional biomass flow

- The identification of the products made by the various enterprises

- The identification of the technology used

- The types of raw material used by the different enterprises

- The quantification of the consumption of selected natural resources by different manufacturing sectors

- An understanding of the characteristics of enterprise sectors and the areas in which they have an impact

- An understanding of regional natural resource consumption dynamics

- A general assessment of the status of the selected natural resources in the region

## 11.1.2 *Implementation phase*

The proposed SPD strategy takes into consideration all actors and elements involved in the production process of MSEs, from raw material production to the users of the products. In establishing its stakeholder involvement in decisions on natural resource

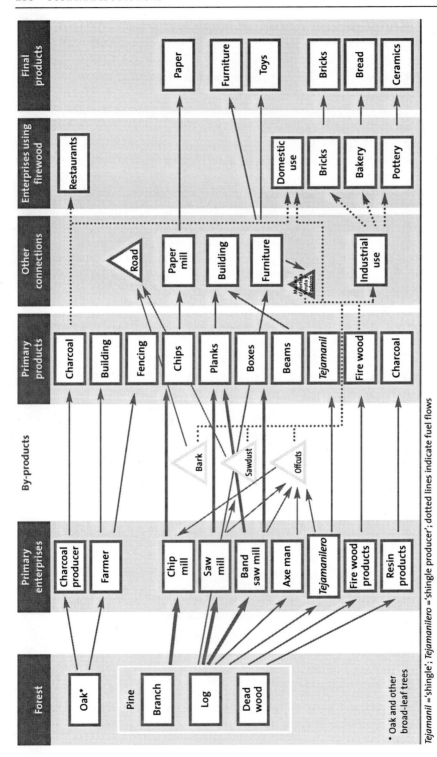

*Tejamanil* = 'shingle'; *Tejamanilero* = 'shingle producer'; dotted lines indicate fuel flows

*Figure 11.1* **Biomass flowchart for the Purépecha region, Mexico**

management, SPD needs to follow a participatory methodology that helps to build consensus and achieve results that are acceptable to everyone.

In order to tackle all the production stages and system nodes in the process and to solve the problems and the conflicts associated with them, the proposed SPD strategy presents a threefold implementation approach (see Fig. 11.2).

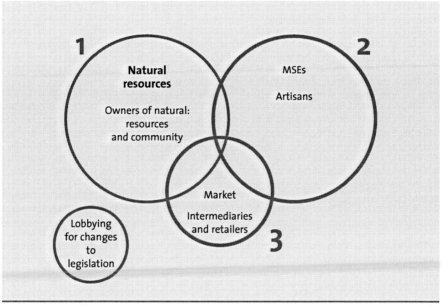

MSE = micro or small enterprise

*Figure* 11.2 **A threefold impression approach (for a description of activities 1–3, see Section 11.1.2)**

- **Step 1: extract the raw materials.** This step is implemented mainly by the forest owners (community and/or individuals) and through the participation of the community at large (including artisans[1]) and aims at attaining a sustainable management of the natural resources.

- **Step 2: carry out manufacturing activities at the workshop level.** This step is implemented by artisans. The search for alternative solutions at this level is based on resource-use efficiency, product quality, streamlining of production processes and end-of-life planning.

- **Step 3: market the products.** This step is to be implemented by the artisans, some intermediaries and retailers.

---

1 Throughout this chapter, artisans are taken to be technically skilled people who work in micro or small enterprises.

However, there is an important cross-cutting issue that also needs to be considered:

● **Lobby for changes in the legislation to better protect the interests of all stakeholders and the environment.** This is a parallel activity that needs to be carried out throughout the process and involves individuals and all organisations that have an interest in the use and/or conservation of natural resources. Effective channels for lobbying need to be found for each particular case.

According to Upton and Bass (1996: 5, 6):

> Institutional failures can explain many of the root causes of forest problems and are strongly related to policy failures . . .
>
> . . . Weak and/or inappropriate tenure . . . together with conflicts between land use policies and local rights, these lead often to forest problems concerning weaker groups.

The three main steps will be discussed in more detail below, in Sections 11.1.2.1–11.1.2.3.

### 11.1.2.1 Sustainable natural resources management: the case of forest management

The sustainable management of natural resources is a management that maintains the biodiversity and the flow of goods and environmental services in the long term. In the case of forest areas, the implementation of a management plan to achieve sustainability requires a broad focus. It needs to address the biological aspects but also must incorporate the social and economic elements linked to the forests, such as the income opportunities of the people living in the area and their perception and expectations from the forest. It is a common failure of management plans not to incorporate a consideration of products such as firewood used by villagers and MSEs. This creates a crisis of interests in the long term that threatens the sustainability of the resource.

Community participation is especially relevant in today's forest management because of the rapid losses of traditional indigenous knowledge of forest uses that have tended to incorporate a multi-use cultural focus on the resources. Some of the most effective mechanisms to promote the sustainable use of forests and the conservation of biodiversity is the strengthening of social participation in the management of resources (Becker and Ostrom 1995; Cernea 1995; Putz 1994). People's active participation can ensure the incorporation of their needs, interests and values as well as responsibility over the forest in the management plans.

> The sustainable management of forests depends on three main factors: the way the management is implemented, the communal productive activities that influence the decisions over the land use, and the needs and internal organisation of the people that use the forest (Lélé 1993: 19).

### 11.1.2.2 Sustainable product development at the level of the micro or small enterprise

SPD is a key element that determines the impact that an enterprise will have on the environment, and it is an element that depends directly on the artisan. It is inherent to the manufacturing process, the technology used and way the production is organised.

In the context of MSEs in developing countries, SPD is the process that creates product designs that are sustainable in terms of the environment and resource use while considering the need for the product. It is the process of planning and designing that integrates the following elements into a product:

- **Resource-use efficiency.** This applies to the energy and materials used in the manufacturing, component production and user phases and includes the selection of materials, favouring the use of local, renewable, recycled and low-energy materials and avoiding those that are scarce or toxic.

- **Product quality.** This includes the use, need for and function of the product, its durability, its optimal life-span, its energy efficiency and the proper use of materials and finishing.

- **Production organisation and efficiency.** This includes optimisation of human and technical manufacturing processes in terms of resources, labour and machinery, and the use and development of appropriate technologies and renewable energy.

- **Local culture and capacities.** This includes the understanding and application of local culture and indigenous knowledge and local people's needs, traditions, tastes and abilities (technical and economic) throughout the whole process, with use of local products and favouring local consumption.

- **Market.** This includes the analysis of and search for market opportunities that can make the process economically sustainable.

- **End of life.** This includes considerations regarding the possible re-use, dis-assembly, recycling and final disposal of the product.

In summary, SPD considers the intensity and optimisation of resource use for product design, involving local culture and tastes, and it addresses the overall production efficiency while simultaneously improving the product's quality in order to increase market opportunities. The incorporation of long-term environmental, social and economic implications in each step of the process gives it a new dimension in terms of sustainability. Moreover, SPD recognises the central responsibility designers bear in helping to prevent global pollution, the destruction of tropical forests and the emission of greenhouse gases, through the products they design.

The introduction of SPD can contribute to the development of MSEs in developing countries in eight different ways.

- By expanding and creating new national and international markets for newly designed products. Product quality improvement, simplification of product manufacturing processes, reduction of production time and costs and product redesign or new product design (not necessarily implying an increment of product prices) can all contribute to the expansion of the market or can create or fill a niche in the market.

- By promoting import substitution by manufacturing quality products to replace the imported products that consumers would normally buy. Quality products do not necessarily mean expensive production processes and machinery that are not available to the majority of the MSEs. The production of quality goods can be achieved by using or adapting existing appropriate affordable technology. However, the design of a quality product should be done with the existing technological capacity in mind; copies of inappropriate designs from a different context will not help.

- By developing locally made goods that are more appropriate to the specific needs and conditions of the country. Every product reflects the way of living and the production environment of the culture for which it was designed. Participatory training of local artisans in SPD will enhance the local culture expressed in the products and consequently increase the sales of those new products, which will better respond to the customer's needs and way of life.

- By fostering the job creation process. As a result of the local market creation and expansion through SPD, more artisans will join the sector, more apprentices will be required in each workshop and new jobs will be created.

- By introducing and disseminating appropriate manufacturing technologies. New or improved product ideas will in most cases lead to the need for technological improvements or to a new technology, and vice versa.

- By reducing the environmental impact of MSEs by making product and processes more efficient, by linking them to the sustainable management of local forests and by reducing the use of toxic materials.

- By increasing the average income of artisans by improving the product quality and market channels as well as by reducing raw material consumption.

- By contributing to the achievement of sustainable development by reducing the environmental impact of MSEs, enhancing community participation and contributing to a better 'quality of life' in rural communities.

**Introducing sustainable product development to micro and small enterprises**
Owing to lack of resources, information, limited education and isolation, most artisans in developing countries tend to reduce economic risks by copying what others are producing. The development of new products tends to be the result of a random process rather than a continuous and guided activity. According to van Gelder and O'Keefe (1995: 8):

> Today, faced with rapid change, rural people are faced with situations they have not previously encountered. In many cases, they have reached the point where they cannot sustain their livelihood systems within the frame of their existing knowledge, resources or institutions. In a wide range of situations rural people need assistance to maintain the sustainability of their local bio-mass economy.

SPD, as any new activity that implies a change in the current production patterns of MSEs, requires a process of understanding and training that needs to be initiated and promoted by organisations that are devoted to this purpose and that include professionals trained in the subject (designers). The role of designers in SPD training and MSE development needs to be recognised and enhanced. The presence of designers during training is a key element to its success. It is surprising to notice that many training projects around the world that tackle product development are carried out by general trainers or professionals who do not have a design background. This is because design schools tend to focus on the formation of designers who will suit the needs of large industries. Hence there is a limited number of designers working with MSEs in developing countries. Moreover, there is a lack of recognition and awareness about the design profession in developing countries.

Owing to the only recent acknowledgement of the value of SPD in the development of MSEs in developing countries there is very little experience in SPD training. Training in SPD can be provided to single artisans, groups of artisans, co-operatives and artisan associations. A combination of on-the-job sessions with visits to peers and marketplaces, with a few theoretical presentations, have proved the most successful in Mexico and Kenya. In this new approach, the notion that facts are taught is rejected. Instead, experience is encouraged. The training is organised with artisans working in the same sub-sectors (e.g. woodworkers and metalworkers). The visits to peers and marketplaces increase the artisan's exposure to new products, production processes and customers. This is critical for artisans who have limited access to information.

The SPD training process should:

- Be as practical and participatory as possible, based on the artisan's own experience and knowledge

- Take the participants away from their work as little as possible, as they rely economically on their own labour

- Stimulate a process of thinking and designing, not lead to only a single product solution

- Be conducted in the language of the participants, not of the trainer

- Encourage feedback from the participants

- Work with groups of artisans from the same sub-sector (e.g. carpenters)

- Be taught by a qualified trainer with a background in industrial design and/or relevant SPD experience

- Be on-the-job training or should use some other practical training techniques in preference to classroom training sessions

- Expose participants to the market

**Sustainable product development contributions to micro and small enterprises**
Figure 11.3 presents the way an active involvement of MSEs in SPD can contribute to improving the conditions of forests and help to promote sustainable development. It was developed by using the oval diagramming technique. Oval diagramming describes a

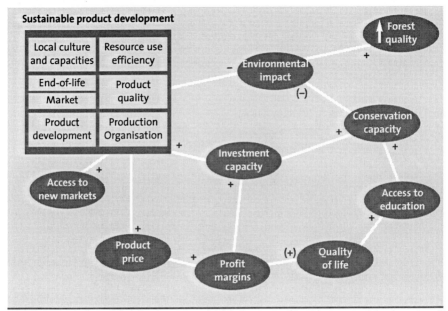

Variables are placed in ovals, with relationships indicated by '+' or '–'; for example, an increase in product price will result in an increase in profit margins. The use of brackets around a sign indicates a direct threshold effect: profit margins must increase significantly before quality of life will also increase; conservation capacity must increase significantly before environmental impacts will decrease. The vertical arrow represents an irreversibly increasing relationship.

*Figure 11.3* **The impact of sustainable product development on micro and small enterprises, economically, socially and environmentally**

problem as a set of complex relationships among system variables and variables in the system environment and provides an explicit statement of cause and effect relationships within a system and between the system and its environment. Variables are placed in ovals, and the connecting lines link them together. It allows the analysis of complex causes and effects in sequences that start from a key variable.

The diagram can be read starting at the SPD box (top left):

1. The implementation of SPD increases the possibilities of accessing new market channels and of augmenting prices by improving product quality and design.

2. The resulting increment in product price (maintaining the production costs by improving production organisation and technology) increases profit margins, which at the same time increase the investment capacities of the artisans and the possibilities of carrying out SPD activities. In this sense the process tends to be economically self-sufficient by increasing the artisans' possibilities of paying for SPD activities.

3. A continuous increment in profit margins can in the long run increase the quality of life of the artisans by allowing them to have access to better housing and services and by increasing their access to education.

4. Education, together with the increment in investment capacities, augments the possibilities of enhancing the capacity to preserve local natural resources by improving people's understanding of the environment and in many cases enabling them to go back to local traditions of forest use and management.

5. The increment of the community's conservation capacity together with the implementation of product development activities reduces the environmental impact of the MSEs, which has a direct effect in improving forest quality.

Figure 11.3 also underlines the impact of product development in social, economic and environmental terms. The economic aspects are represented by product price, access to new markets, profit margins and the investment capacity. The social aspects are represented by two variables: a very general one, quality of life, and access to education. Finally, environmental aspects are represented by conservation capacity, environmental impact of MSEs and forest quality.

The SPD process represented by Figure 11.3 is limited by the production volume of MSEs, which is determined by the sustainable production potential of the local forests. The local production volume of MSEs should not be larger than the sustainable forest potential. If the production of MSEs increases to a level that requires more wood than can be produced sustainably, the process will be reversed. However, this final scenario should be avoided by the introduction of sustainable forest management plans that limit the production volume of timber to the forest sustainable capacity.

### 11.1.2.3 The marketing of products

The third stage in the SPD strategy is the marketing of products and involves the artisans, some intermediaries and retailers. Apart from tackling local market needs and potentialities, the newly designed environmentally sound products can contribute to the creation of local preferential markets and give access to foreign markets. Although local markets in developing countries, both regional and national, tend to be less attentive to 'green products', the improvements to production efficiency and product quality resulting from the introduction of SPD can reduce a product's price and thus increase the producer's competitiveness. In local markets, improved products will have an edge over existing products if pricing is correct.

The type of market that an enterprise will be able to reach depends on a number of factors. These include the production orientation of the workshop, the entrepreneurial abilities of the artisan, the technical capacities of the producers, the quality and design characteristics of the products, the investment capacities of the artisan, support from other training and credit organisations and the ability to interpret the needs of the market.

In order to better know the market, marketing research is essential. It can help producers (entrepreneurs) discover latent demand and can indicate ways to convert that demand into effective demand, directing producers to develop marketable goods and suggesting more effective distribution channels.

The entrepreneurs should be able to build and maintain mutually beneficial relationships with their target market. To operate successfully, therefore, entrepreneurs must continually appraise the wider business situation and devise new and better ways of satisfying market opportunities by developing the right products.

An important and positive result of SPD activities is the possibility for MSEs to access a preferential market for 'green products'. By manufacturing products in a sustainable manner MSEs can apply for eco-labels that can open new market opportunities.

## 11.2  Case study: furniture production in the Purépecha region of Mexico

An example of the results of SPD training can be seen in the improved furniture developed by local artisans in the Purépecha region of Mexico. The Purépechas, the largest indigenous group of the Michoacan state in Mexico, have a long and established tradition in handicrafts. It is estimated that more than 150,000 people rely on the production of furniture, wooden toys, copper handicrafts, pottery and a variety of other products. On average, one out of four of all residents, and in many villages all residents, work in such MSEs, and most earn meagre wages (Castañon 1993). The area is endowed with important natural resources (estimated to be 79,000 ha of forest resources; mostly pine and pine–oak associations). Local forests are highly diverse for a temperate area, presenting more than 10 species of *Pinus* and 12 of *Quercus*, among many other tree species. Currently, however, a rapid deforestation process, reaching close to 2% per year (1,880 ha per year), and the degradation of a large fraction of the forested area are taking place (Alvarez-Icaza and Garibay 1994; Caro 1990). Large portions of formerly forested land have been completely eroded.

The large number of MSEs (more than 10,000 among which 2,800 are furniture workshops) as well as their regional concentration, low product quality and diversity, inefficiencies in manufacturing processes, lack of technical training, lack of support from official institutions, lack of organisation and training opportunities and lack of financial resources all combine to create a very competitive context that reduces profit margins to the minimum possible and poses serious threats to the sustainability of the forest resources in the region. The search for cheaper prices for raw materials has favoured the use of illegally harvested timber because of its lower price. These circumstances are also reflected in the products, which tend to be of poor quality and very similar in shape and style.

In the region, in co-operation with a local non-governmental organisation (NGO) called Grupo Interdisciplinario de Tecnologia Rural Apropiada and with the active participation of local artisans the author worked in a project aimed at implementing an SPD strategy. As a result of SPD training, several products were developed. Plate 11.1 shows a chair design that was developed by artisans of Casas Blancas, a small village in the Purépecha region devoted to the production of chairs. The chair was produced as a response to the recognition of the critical economic and environmental situation, as made clear after the initial phases of SPD training. The chair presents a series of

*Plate* 11.1 **Casas Blancas chairs**

improvements from the technical, environmental and design point of view (compared with other regional products). This has been reflected in its rapid success among the public.

In order to analyse the characteristics of the newly designed Casas Blancas chair, a comparative method was used. To determine the level of improvement and reduction of environmental impact of the new product, the Casas Blancas chair was analysed in relation to other similar models. This comparative analysis provided information on the new chair but also placed it into context by referring to other similar products that are regularly produced in the region. The comparisons include a series of ad hoc indicators such as: material intensity (the extent to which materials are used in production), profit margins and cost (in pesos) by board foot of timber used.

The material intensity reflects whether or not an optimal or economic use has been made of the material(s) involved. It also refers to the amount of material per unit of product. The material intensity is particularly relevant in the context of a region with limited natural resources such as the Purépecha region which thus needs to make production processes more efficient. Taking into consideration that the products (old and new) are almost entirely made out of timber (in some cases originating from sustainably managed forests), the amount of timber used is a good indicator of their environmental impact at the production level.

The cost in pesos per unit of material used is an important indicator of the economic sustainability of MSEs. It relates directly to the increment in the artisan's income (see Fig. 11.4). The market success of the chair is also an indicator of the product quality and the accuracy of its market orientation. The increment in profit margin indicates an improvement in production efficiency and resource use.

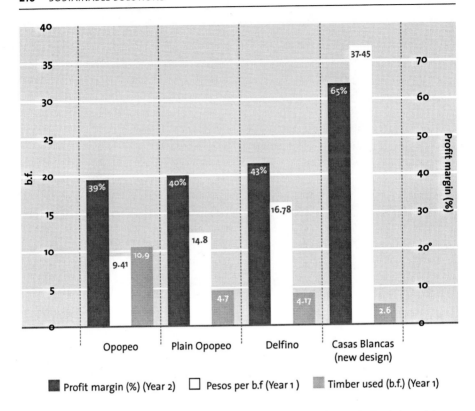

*Figure* 11.4 **Timber consumption: pesos by per board-foot (b.f.) and profit margins by chair model**

In terms of end of life, considerations were made in the new chair to ease the replacement of the seat and back by using simple screws in the assembling process.

The new chair consumes four times less timber than the common Opopeo model and between a half and two-thirds that required for the other locally produced chairs. In terms of pesos per board-foot used, the returned value per unit of timber used was between two and four times higher than that of other models. Finally, the profit margin achieved with the Casas Blancas chair was 65% compared to an average of 41% for the other models (i.e. Opopeo 39%; Plain Opopeo 40%; and Delfino 43%).

The analysis used focuses on the environmental impact during the manufacturing stage of the products and the economic benefits for the producer because it has been carried out from the perspective of the local artisans. Moreover, considerations were made to reduce the volume during transportation and to ease repair and disassembly. All the products analysed are produced with use of local materials (wood), do not have any chemical finishing and are distributed regionally.

The Casas Blancas chair is just one example of the potential benefits that the introduction and dissemination of SPD training can have in developing countries. Indeed, the production and marketing of new environmentally sound products that

*Plate* 11.2 **New products**

double the profit margins of local entrepreneurs are also essential to reinforce the commitment of the local artisans to work towards forest conservation.

## 11.3 Conclusions

SPD strategies are essential tools to attain a sustainable future for human and natural resources in developing countries. Unlike in developed countries where there is consumer and legal pressure to move towards sustainable alternatives, in developing countries MSEs facing an uncertain future can become the driving force to move towards sustainable solutions. The need for SPD comes from the producers, who have little or no income alternatives and who are witnessing a rapid depletion of their environment and sources of raw materials.

In spite of their resourcefulness, MSEs have not been studied in depth. Very few methodologies exist to help us comprehend the overall system in which they operate.

SPD strategies in developing countries need to include the whole production process of MSEs, from raw material production to marketing and final disposal of their products. Because environmental data tends to be scarce and unreliable, SPD strategies need to depart from an assessment of the prevailing natural resource use and work towards a sustainable production and use of raw materials. Also, the active involvement of all stakeholders during SPD implementation is essential for sustainability purposes.

In developing countries there is little professional experience on SPD. Universities in many countries do not offer degrees in industrial design or other relevant subjects. Therefore there is a general need to improve local knowledge through training. This training should be aimed at MSEs' artisans and possibly to a higher professional level such as university students.

The proposed SPD strategy includes the entire natural resource transformation cycle, from raw material production to the final disposal of products and integrates all the phases in order to reduce fragmentation of activities. By integrating all activities, this SPD strategy aims at generating the maximum amount of employment opportunities and income generation within the local community. Its main objectives are: environmental protection, creation of job opportunities and an increase in artisans' income. It optimises the use of local natural and human resources to promote economic and social growth within communities. One of the central elements of SPD is to increase the added value of products by improving their design, quality and finishing and by limiting their number and overall consumption of raw material by MSEs.

Most people in developing countries depend on MSEs for their living. However, the markets being served by small producers tend to be saturated by low-quality and material-intensive products and suffer from lack of product diversification. This situation leads to a reduction of the profit margins of producers and to increased pressure on environmental resources.

The market orientation of SPD is based on the new opportunities that product quality, increased production efficiency, certification of sustainable natural resource use, product certification and alternative markets (export and local markets) offer to environmentally sound products. Access to the market is improved by creating the possibility of establishing continuous and profitable communication among all interested actors through effective forums, by participating in fairs and exhibitions, by exploring the possibilities for export and by training in accounting and marketing.

Few studies have focused on the role of SPD in improving the low performance of MSEs and the way in which designers can participate in the process. Furthermore, the environmental impact related to MSEs' production has also received limited attention. In this context this chapter should be seen as an initial stage towards a more comprehensive understanding of the benefits that the implementation of SPD can bring to MSEs in developing countries and the role that designers play in the process. Four main points of the analysis should be underlined:

- SPD training is essential in the reduction of the environmental impact of MSEs in developing countries; it contributes to this aim by:
  - Considering the intensity and optimisation of resource use for product design
  - Involving local culture and tastes in the process
  - Looking at the overall production efficiency while simultaneously improving the product's quality to increase market opportunities
- Artisans require training to be able to improve their current situation.

- Designers should get more actively involved in SPD training for MSEs in developing countries.

- The results obtained in Mexico are encouraging and should be replicated in other areas.

# MANAGING ECODESIGN

*Martin Charter*
The Centre for Sustainable Design, UK

There are various definitions surrounding environmental considerations of products and services: ecodesign, green design, design for environment (DfE) and sustainable product design (SPD). Ecodesign can be termed the integration of environmental aspects into product development. Initially, ecodesign evolved from an engineering perspective but it is now becoming an organisational as well as a technical and design issue. To manage ecodesign requires appropriate organisational structures and systems, particularly if the firm is distributed worldwide and has a range of business units. In transnational corporations (TNCs) ecodesign policy decision-making is likely to be centralised, and a key issue is the relationship between the head office, divisions and national subsidiaries. This is a complex issue, particularly with the uneven distribution of environmental awareness, societal concerns and legislation worldwide. A range of eco-product pressures is starting to emerge in some sectors, particularly where producer responsibility is becoming an issue. This includes national European approaches to environmental product policy (EPP) and integrated product policy (IPP; see Chapter 5). There is also growing customer pressures, particularly in some 'business-to-business' (B2B) markets where large companies are beginning to incorporate environmental aspects into purchasing and supply chain management. In response, several leading-edge companies, including Electrolux and Philips (see Chapter 18), are publicly starting to promote the financial benefits of ecodesign in terms of both revenue and cost. For ecodesign to progress in the firm, leadership and senior-level commitment to the implementation of environmental management are essential.

The shape of ecodesign or eco-product development depends on the company, its culture and its products and markets. There needs to be a clear set of objectives, strategies and programmes for ecodesign to be successful. To enable companies to improve the management of these issues, several companies are now starting to link ecodesign activity to ISO 14001 and environmental management system (EMS) development. The Dutch are also developing product-oriented environmental management systems (POEMS) to embed ecodesign within firms on a continuous rather than an ad hoc project-by-project basis (Charter 2000b; see also Chapter 13). Those companies that are working on eco-product development appear to be developing competence through internal training and a range of tools (see Chapter 14). For example, a major telecommunications company has added various downloadable ecodesign tools to its intranet site for designers and external business partners. A number of these tools have been designed for the relatively low levels of ecodesign awareness within the company. There is also a growing move away from full life-cycle assessment (LCA) to cut-down life-cycle tools and simpler ecodesign tools (because of cost and time issues).

Supply chain issues are now becoming an increasingly important product development consideration as a result of global shifts in manufacturing, assembly, raw material, component and subassembly sourcing. Many original equipment manufacturers (OEMs) are moving away from manufacturing to outsourcing, assembly and systems integration. This means that supply chain executives are now becoming increasingly important stakeholders in the eco-product development process and are in effect becoming potential ecodesigners. For example, if the firm is an assembler it may decide to incorporate environmental criteria into supplier evaluation questionnaires and then form partnerships with suppliers to raise environmental awareness of product-related issues. Therefore existing ecodesign material is becoming less relevant for many businesses, as it is usually written for manufacturers.

Establishing ecodesign in many companies and sectors is a difficult and complex task against the backdrop of the growing number of mergers, acquisitions, disposals, new product launches, company reorganisations and leadership changes. The speed and erratic nature of change can also produce a lack of continuity for ecodesign development. The advent of 'dot.com' companies, 'e-commerce', new information communications technologies (ICTs) and the increased use of the Internet is quickening the speed of change. This is starting to affect markets and buying behaviour, with e-commerce beginning to influence purchasing in B2B markets and in some consumer markets. However, the implications of e-commerce are as yet unclear in relation to environmental aspects of product development.

At present, broader approaches to SPD (see Chapter 6)—for example, the balancing of the 'quadruple bottom line' (environmental, economic, social and ethical considerations) in product development—do not appear to have been developed or implemented. This chapter gives an overview of the organisational issues associated with the management of eco-product development, drawing on the results of recent research and industry case studies.

## 12.1 Where are we now?

The key conclusion arising from six recent surveys (Charter and Clark 2000; Tukker and Haag 2000; Charter and Clark 1997; Charter and Sherwin 1996; Chick and Sherwin 1997; Fiksel 1995b) into the management of ecodesign is that programmes are still in the early stages of development, even in some of the world's largest companies. Ecodesign objectives and strategies exist but often seem to be vague and unclear. It appears that ecodesign is usually owned and driven by environmental management rather than by marketing personnel who have considerable power in the process. Legal and customer pressures appear to be the most important external drivers, with ecodesign in certain market sectors becoming a competitive issue. Major obstacles are perceived to be cost and organisational inertia—with individual motivation often being a important factor in eco-product development both from a management and from a product design perspective. However, generally, eco-issues do not appear to be percolating down to product designers, as external and internal (e.g. marketing) clients are not incorporating environmental considerations into briefs.

## 12.2 The organisational context of ecodesign

Research (Charter and Clark 2000; Tukker and Haag 2000; Charter and Clark 1997) has indicated that many TNCs now have established centralised units to develop ecodesign strategies and programmes, which are then communicated and implemented at a local level in different countries. However, some companies have developed specialist eco-design units. IBM has an ecodesign centre in the USA that acts as a central processing unit (CPU) for internal and external information. After analysis, policies, guidelines and tools are distributed to business units worldwide (Charter 1997b). Hewlett-Packard (HP) has developed a 'virtual worldwide network' of product stewards who have responsibility for ecodesign issues. To facilitate this, HP has established an intranet-based information system called Fountainhead that includes a range of information on eco-labels, research and conference papers (Charter 1997b).

Below are three organisational models for environmental management which also reflect certain companies' approaches to ecodesign (Charter 1997b):

- **Autonomous companies.** These tend to delegate full responsibility to business units and exert little formal control over business units; the organisation acts like a holding company and manages its portfolio based largely on financial performance and 'strategic fit'.

- **Centralised companies.** These tend to delegate only partial responsibility to business units and exert substantial control over them; the company actively sets improvement goals, prescribes management methods and monitors business unit performance.

- **Influenced companies.** These delegate a high level of responsibility to business units but still try to strongly influence the practices of the business units; the company maintains significant staff capabilities in specialised disciplines and encourages business units to utilise expertise effectively.

In some companies, ecodesign emerges as a 'bottom-up' process, with interest arising from one or two motivated individuals. It is essential that these individuals are able to gain 'quick wins' for the business to enable management to have confidence in progressing ecodesign. Small companies are often able to implement ecodesign more quickly than TNCs. For example, if the managing director of a 30-person company decides that the firm is going to take up ecodesign, then a team can be brought together quickly, particularly if all the key people work in the same location. This team may include the designer (who may be a technical manager or engineer), the procurement manager, and customers and suppliers. Many large companies are also made up of many smaller companies and it is important that subsidiaries and business units 'buy into' a common vision of ecodesign to ensure that approaches are not fragmented. Setting the boundaries and co-ordinating programmes and activities are important for success.

Both in large and in small companies there will be a need for awareness-raising activities as most employees are likely to have low levels of awareness and understanding of ecodesign. The opportunity is to move individuals from zero awareness and understanding of ecodesign, to basic, intermediate and advanced understanding in a phased manner (ZBIA principle; Charter 2000b). It is important to start people at the level that they are at! For example, it is pointless to highlight complex LCA tools if the designer has never received any environmental education. For the majority of business functions, personnel are likely to have low levels of awareness and understanding of ecodesign and therefore there is a need for simple thinking tools (e.g. checklists and workshops to 'open people's eyes'; see Chapter 14). These tools and processes must be translated into the language of the business function if the issues are to be owned, accepted and adopted. For example, the company may load ecodesign tools onto an intranet, but unless designers and others have received some ecodesign training then tools are unlikely to be used. Ecodesign needs to become part of 'business as usual'. There is a need for ecodesign to be built into a formal or informal management system if it is to be successful, and several companies have already started to utilise ISO 14001 to implement ecodesign, e.g. IBM, Lucent (BATE 2000). A key issue is how and at what point ecodesign is launched within the company (internal marketing) and the speed and extent to which integration is progressed.

When implementing ecodesign there may be a range of internal barriers to development which will need to be overcome:

- Limited resources for starting new projects

- Poor communications

- Organisational structures, cultures and inertia tending to favour 'business as usual'

- Individual inertia

- Lack of expertise, awareness and understanding of environmental issues by managers and employees

- Perceived costs of change

- Lack of time

- Existing accounting systems being inadequate to reflect environmental value

- Design teams having a fear of compromising product quality or production efficiency

To enable successful implementation, strategies will need to be established to overcome these barriers. These might include (Charter 1997b):

- Establishing cross-functional teams to help ensure that there is early consideration of environmental aspects in product development (this will also encourage various other business function personnel to speak to each other about ecodesign issues)

- Establishing clear objectives, targets and performance criteria to help to ensure environmental considerations are placed in the right context

- Training and awareness raising to help in
    - Communicating and selling the business benefits of ecodesign (which is likely to encourage improvement of environmental performance)
    - The application and integration of ecodesign into management decision-making, information and tools to help with the practical application of ecodesign

Some key questions to be answered in forming an ecodesign management strategy are listed in Box 12.1.

## 12.3 Organisational integration of ecodesign

The extent and level of integration of ecodesign in a company will depend on a range of issues, including extent of senior-level vision and commitment, the extent of legislative and customer pressures and the degree to which the ecodesign business model has been proven within the firm.

### 12.3.1 Ecodesign: seven-stage model

A company may move through seven stages of implementing ecodesign (Charter 2000b):

1. **Ecodesign ignorance.** The company is unaware of ecodesign issues.

2. **Ecodesign starter.** The environmental manager is in the process of selling the business benefits of ecodesign within the company.

3. **Green research and development (R&D) projects.** A pilot green project is being developed in R&D.

**WHEN DEVELOPING AN ECODESIGN STRATEGY A RANGE OF ISSUES SHOULD** be considered.

- From a business perspective, what strategic, tactical and operational issues should the organisation take account of?
- What sectoral issues should the firm be aware of?
- What is the appropriate approach to managing an ecodesign programme worldwide?
- How should an ecodesign information system be structured?
- What ecodesign information sources are available?
- What ecodesign issues should be considered when managing different product–business mixes?
- What are appropriate business objectives for the ecodesign programme overall?
- How do you get other business functions involved in ecodesign?
- How you sell ecodesign internally, avoiding hitting the 'green wall'?
- How do you ensure that the ecodesign process is integrated into new or existing product development processes?
- Should in-house expertise be 'built up' or should consultants and universities be used?
- Who needs ecodesign training?

*Box* 12.1 **Key questions for developing an ecodesign management strategy**

4. **Technical integration.** Environmental criteria are being built into engineering procedures.

5. **Semi-ecodesign integration.** The company has integrated environmental considerations from idea generation throughout the complete product development process in one business unit or throughout the product family.

6. **Total ecodesign integration.** The company has integrated environmental considerations from idea generation throughout the complete product development process across all products and/or services.

7. **Green strategism.** The business has integrated environmental opportunity searches into corporate and business strategies (pre-product development).

As ecodesign becomes an increasingly strategic and competitive issue, recruiting and retaining skilled people will be essential. At present ecodesign skills tend to evolve within businesses rather than being produced via academia. Ecodesign training is generally completed in-house within companies, as courses and expertise are generally not available out of house (Tukker and Haag 2000). There are few specialist ecodesign courses or modules in existing undergraduate or postgraduate engineering, industrial design or management courses within universities and design schools. Therefore ecodesign awareness, knowledge and skills have generally to be learned within the firm (Tukker and Haag 2000; Charter and Clark 1997).

A major issue is how to grow and nurture ecodesign competence within the firm. This includes the need to systematically document ecodesign data and information so that knowledge does not leave the firm when key people leave (e.g. to go to a competitor or to a new area in the firm). It is important that good internal information and communications systems be developed by the individual who has responsibility for managing the ecodesign process. The information system should be focused on separate strategic, tactical and operational needs.

A key issue will be the development of information and tools for those involved in the eco-product development and design process. At present ecodesign tools tend to focus on environmental evaluation (e.g. LCA). However, a broader set of tools needs to be developed to cover each stage of the product development process (see Chapter 14). A key part of this is enabling the flow of ecodesign information to the right people, at the right time and in the right format. Designers should be in a position to ask environmental specialists more detailed environmental questions, as most designers are unlikely to want to become ecodesign specialists. However, the dilemma is that many environmental managers tend to be under-resourced and have to deal with a diverse set of questions from a range of external and internal stakeholders. So the question is likely to become: How does the organisation manage this information issue? Should designers be encouraged to develop or be provided with a network of specialists and/or information through an intranet? Alternatively, or in addition, should the capacity of personnel performing the environmental management function be extended to provide ecodesign information. Access to the *right* information is essential. Some key questions that need to be considered before ecodesign is implemented are listed in Box 12.2.

---

**BEFORE IMPLEMENTING ECODESIGN IT IS IMPORTANT TO THINK THROUGH THE** organisational context:

- What is the importance of company culture in the development of ecodesign?
- What are the organisational relationships with respect to ecodesign?
- What are the business benefits of ecodesign?
- What are the key characteristics of a successful ecodesign programme?
- What metrics should be developed to measure ecodesign?
- What are the key obstacles to the development of ecodesign programmes? Are they internal or external?
- How can awareness of ecodesign be increased among:
  - Senior management
  - Environmental managers
  - Product designers
  - Marketing personnel
  - Workers performing other business functions?
- What are the key lessons learned from eco-(re)design of existing products?
- How can innovative solutions in ecodesign be stimulated?

Box 12.2 **Key questions before the implementation of ecodesign**

## 12.3.2 *Ecodesign managers and ecodesigners*

In many firms environmental managers have weak relationships with those involved in the product development process, and designers and other business functions are unlikely to have received any form of environmental education (Tukker and Haag 2000).

At present ecodesign tends to be managed by environmental directors and managers, whereas marketing personnel tend to have considerable power over product development (Tukker and Haag 2000; Charter and Clark 1997). So, at best, the environmental function may have an influencing role over product development in some companies. This indicates that, at present, ecodesign tends to be a 'bolt-on' activity, e.g. at the green R&D stage, although various companies are starting to integrate environmental considerations alongside other criteria at each stage of the product development process (Tukker and Haag 2000; Charter 1997b).

To progress this some companies are now starting to highlight ecodesign, design for environment (DfE) and sustainable product design (SPD) in specific job titles:

- Director, Sustainable Product Innovation, SC Johnson Wax, USA

- Senior DfE Manager, Lucent, USA

- Senior Ecodesign Consultant, Philips, the Netherlands

These specific job titles and responsibilities may satisfy several goals for the firm. They indicate to the rest of the organisation and outside that ecodesign is being launched and/or becoming recognised as a business issue within the firm. However, in many firms ecodesign tasks are being hidden in various existing job titles (e.g. technical manager, design engineer, environmental manager). There may be a range of employees involved in the ecodesign process, some working on tasks 80% of their time, and others 30% or 5% of their time. It is important to identify and co-ordinate all those involved with ecodesign 'tasks' to enable a unified approach to be taken.

Depending on the organisation, its culture and its commitment to ecodesign, various job functions are likely to evolve (which may not be reflected in job titles):

- Ecodesign managers, who will steer and manage the process

- Ecodesigners (or engineers), who will deal with the internal design aspects of the product

- Ecodesigners (industrial or product designers), who will deal with the exterior design aspects of the product

- Hybrid ecodesigners, consultants with experience of management and design aspects

The role of the ecodesign manager—whether it be 100% or only part of the environmental manager's role—will become a central focus for the ecodesign process, particularly in the short and medium term. Part of the ecodesign manager's responsibilities will be to co-ordinate and analyse external ecodesign information and translate and shape this to the internal needs of the organisation. This will mean the need to develop ecodesign policy, objectives, strategy and programmes. The ecodesign manager should ideally have experience of the product development process, as well as being literate in environmental management and, particularly, business. Electrolux developed the role of ecodesign co-ordinator to integrate ecodesign activities into product design practices. The person's background was as a trained industrial designer, with around ten years' experience of the business, its product development and design processes and with an interest in environmental issues. Key steps toward ecodesign management are listed in Box 12.3.

---

**THERE ARE A SERIES OF STEPS THAT COMPANIES SHOULD FOLLOW WHEN** developing a process to manage ecodesign:

- Define strategic, tactical and operational issues
  - Review environmental issues facing the company, its products and processes, including market and regulatory issues
  - Identify opportunities and threats
  - Identify implications for the business and its operations
- Set appropriate objectives for the ecodesign programme
  - Ensure top-level commitment
  - Make the relevant management accountable
  - Link the programme to company environmental and business policy and objectives
  - Set environmental performance criteria for products
  - Ensure objectives are challenging but achievable and measurable
  - Relate the programme to the adaptation of existing products as well as the design of new products
- Establish an appropriate organisation: for each geographical or product area, as appropriate:
  - Establish a cross-functional team consisting of, as relevant, environmental, marketing, production, engineering, quality and design functions
  - Appoint an ecodesign champion whose role is to ensure the effective incorporation at the earliest stage, of all relevant design issues
- Ensure appropriate environmental training and awareness
  - For designers
  - For people working in other business functions involved in ecodesign decisions
- Ensure adequate information and support, with:
  - Access to external sources of information and tools
  - Internal sources (e.g. data on materials)
  - External two-way communications (e.g. feedback from customers)

To be effective, it is important to integrate all of these aspects. The relative complexity will depend on many factors, including:

- Product and sector
- Product mix
- The size of the company and the company's geographical structure
- Level of decision-making

---

*Box 12.3* **Key steps in ecodesign management**

# 12.4 Eco-product development

Businesses are likely to have formal or informal product development processes, and the formalisation of the process is likely to be a function of the size of the organisation—the larger the organisation the more formal the process is likely to be. The shape of the process will depend on strategic considerations—what business the company is in or what business the company wants to be in. The dynamics of this will depend on issues such as leadership style, mission, corporate culture, technology changes, laws, market trends and competitive activity.

Consideration of environmental aspects in product development should be included in the firm's environmental policy. Companies may also consider it useful to benchmark and develop an internal environment product policy that highlights its relative 'green' position *vis-à-vis* its products. This should also be translated into objectives, strategies and programmes.

The identification of environmental business and product or market opportunities may come from use of strategic environmental tools such as environmental trends analysis (ETA) and green SWOT (strengths, weaknesses, opportunities and threats) analysis (Charter 2000b). Product development is about the creation of new products and the adaptation or redesign of existing products for new or existing markets, and environmental considerations should become simply one important aspect of business analysis. Product ideas may evolve from various sources, such as past ideas, competitive products, marketing research and various creativity techniques

Product development models are likely to vary, depending on the characteristics of product and market sectors (e.g. PC [personal computer] assembly will be different from the manufacture of perfumes, but the stages of product development are likely to be broadly similar). There will be various stages to the product development process, and environmental considerations should be integrated at each stage or 'gate'. The difficulty is balancing and prioritising the importance of environmental considerations against other factors, such as cost, quality and performance.

## 12.4.1 Conceptualisation

There are broadly four levels of integration of environmental considerations into product development, each with its own set of implications in terms of potential opportunities, control, risks, cost and stakeholder involvement (Stevels 1997):

- Level 1: products are improved incrementally
- Level 2: existing products are redesigned
- Level 3: functionality is fulfilled in an alternative manner (new concepts are created)
- Level 4: functionality concepts are conceived so as to fit completely into a sustainable society

The business needs to define which level of eco-innovation it wishes to pursue.

An alternative but related perspective comes from Electrolux (Charter 1998a); it is possible to aim for:

- Level 1: continuous improvement (e.g. production of an fuel-efficient lawnmower)
- Level 2: technology adjustment (e.g. production of a more fuel-efficient lawn-mower with a catalytic converter)
- Level 3: new concepts (e.g. production of a solar-powered lawnmower)

Environmental considerations may be included early on in the idea generation stage as a stimulus to new or 'out-of-the-box' thinking and/or it can be used as part of a conceptual refinement process. Inclusion of environmental aspects at this stage has significant potential to reduce life-cycle impacts (e.g. in the supply chain, manufacture, use and end-of-life phases). There are few specific tools or processes to incorporate environmental considerations at the idea generation or conceptualisation stage. Three tools in the public domain are:

- STRETCH: strategic environmental challenge, at Philips (see Chapter 18)
- Eco-compass, at Dow (Fussler with James 1996)
- Creativity techniques, e.g. lateral thinking, brainstorming, etc. (Birch and Clegg 1995)

## 12.4.2 *Evaluation*

Ideas should be evolved into concepts which then should be refined iteratively; environmental considerations may help shape or reshape concepts. Once a concrete product idea emerges then concepts should be evaluated against a series of criteria. These might include:

- Environmental criteria
- Marketability
- Technical feasibility
- Financial considerations
- Performance
- Quality

This process will start to indicate the technical feasibility and manufacturing requirements of the product. It will also define which manufacturing strategy the company should use—for example, whether it should manufacture the product itself, use contract manufacturers or assemble the product, with greater emphasis on supply chain management.

The importance of the criteria will depend on the organisation and its own priorities. However, the crucial point is that environmental aspects should become one of the key criteria that new products are assessed against in the product development process. The importance of environmental considerations—broadly and specifically—will depend on the environmental priorities of the organisation and the predicted environmental impacts associated with the product. Matrices and weightings should be developed to help determine the overall decision (yes/no) to progress to the next stage of the product-development process.

The use of specific environmental evaluation tools (e.g. full or streamlined LCA) is likely to depend on issues such as 'time to market', available environmental expertise, costs and product development culture. The firmer the concept becomes, the lower the 'degree of freedom' to influence the environmental impact of the product (see Chapter 14).

### 12.4.3  Refining concepts

There should be cross-functional participation and well-organised information exchange between the different role players in the product development process (PDP). The use of cross-functional teams is an important part of this process. This may be facilitated through internal meetings, teleconferencing and/or Internet-based activities. A key issue is to develop a strong culture of environmental information sharing, while building in a series of 'checks and balances' to ensure that projects are kept on track. The above stages should be considered as horizontal and should be integrated at each stage of the PDP. For example, at each stage of the product development there will be different stake-holders (both 'influencers' and 'decision-makers') and there will be a need for informa-tion to be collected, analysed and presented to enable decisions (yes/no) to be made prior to moving to the next stage of PDP. Lucent has attempted to build ecodesign into mainstream PDP processes and uses a series of checklists at each stage of the process that must be completed before the next stage can be moved to (BATE 2000). A series of feedback loops should be established to ensure environmental aspects are being continuously incorporated into the PDP.

### 12.4.4  Prototype, test marketing and manufacturing

Once concepts have been fully formed, models will need to be created and then part- or fully functioning prototypes. Prior to full-scale manufacturing and as part of the ongoing evaluation and review process, the business may decide to complete market testing of the product: for example, it may test launch a product in a certain geographical area or complete concept test research. This is likely to involve a range of marketing research techniques depending on the product or market. As a result of market testing the company will then need to decide if it will manufacture or further re-develop the product, service or technology. The company will need to establish whether it will use existing manufacturing facilities, whether it needs new machinery and tools or whether it is going to contract out manufacturing.

### 12.4.5  Market launch

Once the company has decided to launch the product it will then need to determine how it is to get the product to the market (distribution), with consequent implications related to the environmental impact of transportation. Will it sell direct through e-commerce or catalogues, through wholesalers, distributors or retailers?

Prior to launch, the organisation will need to have considered the integration of the environmental aspects into the product's or brand's marketing strategy (Charter 1992; Charter and Polonsky 1999). It will need to consider its:

- Pricing strategy
- Communications strategy
- Distribution strategy
- Product development strategy

Where necessary, product or brand management personnel are likely to need to receive some form of environmental training to enable them to deal with stakeholder enquiries.

A clear product-related environmental communications programme should be developed that is coherent with the environmental positioning of product groups or brand families as well as with the organisation's strategic environmental communications plan. Environmental messages should be clear and follow international and national guidelines. The programme should cover areas such as:

- Packaging
- Information (e.g. eco-labels, environmental declarations, etc.)
- Literature (e.g. brochures, leaflets, etc.)
- Media advertising
- Sales promotion
- Direct sales (e.g. the sales force or retailers may need training in environmental aspects of the product)
- Internet

There should be a series of internal and external feedback loops. Internal monitoring should cover issues such as costs, material and so on. External feedback through intelligence systems and market research should be generated on the product's environmental performance in the market, and the organisation should adapt its product to any external changes (e.g. technology, legislation, customers). Where the organisation has implemented a take-back strategy there should be programmes established for remarketing (e.g. getting products back from customers). The organisation may decide as a result of new information (e.g. new producer responsibility legislation) that it will develop a new product and/or adapt or redesign an existing product.

## 12.5 Implementation of ecodesign

The following section gives examples of how five companies:

- Hewlett-Packard
- IBM

- Kodak
- Electrolux
- Body Shop International

have approached ecodesign and is based on research undertaken in 1996–97 (Charter 1997b).

## 12.5.1 Hewlett-Packard

### 12.5.1.1 Profile

Hewlett-Packard (HP) is a multinational company that designs and manufactures a wide range of electronic products (over 10,000). In 1995 it employed 108,300 people worldwide, with an annual revenue of US$31.5 billion. The company is organised into three main business areas:

- Computer products
- Testing and measurement
- Healthcare

### 12.5.1.2 Environmental policy

HP views environmental management as part of a wider commitment to corporate social responsibility and simply 'the right thing to do'. HP's approach to environmental management has evolved over the past three decades:

- 1970s to early 1980s: it sought 'end-of-pipe' solutions to pollution.
- Late 1980s: it worked on pollution prevention.
- Early 1990s: it took a product stewardship view.

HP defines product stewardship (PS) as:

> A philosophy and practice of designing products and their associated accessories and processes to prevent and/or minimise adverse health, safety and ecological impacts throughout their life-cycle, i.e. design, manufacturing, distribution, use, take-back, disassembly, reuse, recycling and ultimate disposal of constructive parts and materials.

### 12.5.1.3 Environmental management structure

Product stewardship is an integral part of HP's environmental management structure. HP has:

- A director of corporate environmental management
- An environmental steering committee, at the executive level
- A product stewardship council (PSC)

- A corporate PS manager
- A virtual PS network
- PS managers

To measure the effectiveness of PS, HP use a range of internal metrics, including material conservation and energy efficiency.

### 12.5.1.4 Communications and networking

An intranet-based PS network has been developed to facilitate the work of the PS managers. The network is supported by the PSC and headed by the corporate PS manager. The aim is to ease the transfer of knowledge and expertise. Each business unit has a PS manager who is responsible for managing, co-ordinating and developing his or her PS programme. The PS process has six elements:

- Customer-enquiry tracking and communication
- Global assessment and tracking
- PS self-assessment
- Public policy and influence
- Supplier evaluation
- Product end-of-life management

### 12.5.1.5 Ecodesign guidelines

Within the PS process, ecodesign guidelines have been developed that aim to:

- Minimise energy use
- Reduce waste
- Minimise emissions from manufacturing
- Reduce material use
- Increase use of recyclable materials
- Increase opportunities for re-use or recycling

### 12.5.1.6 Working with suppliers: a holistic approach

HP views working with its suppliers as part of a more holistic approach to reducing environmental impact and focuses on a range of areas of supplier environmental performance:

- Manufacturing
- Waste disposal
- Information and labelling

- Reduction of packaging

- Recycling and re-use

- Elimination of ozone-depleting chemicals

### 12.5.1.7 Obstacles to ecodesign

HP sees three key obstacles to ecodesign:

- Financial barriers: initiatives cannot increase product prices.

- Business-related difficulties: national or market sectors have different levels of environmental awareness.

- Technical problems: financial value derived from recycling is declining.

## 12.5.2 IBM

### 12.5.2.1 Profile

IBM is a worldwide manufacturer of advanced information technology, with sales of US$75.9 billion (1996) and a workforce of 225,000 employees.

### 12.5.2.2 Environmental policy and benefits

In 1971, IBM established its corporate environmental policy (CEP). In 1990, the CEP was widened to acknowledge 'producer responsibility', including the development of 'environmentally conscious products' (ECP). IBM see a range of benefits from ECP, which includes:

- Tangible benefits: lower costs

- Intangible benefits: good public relations, greater responsiveness to legislative developments and so on

### 12.5.2.3 Environmental management structure

Within the environmental management structure, ecodesign expertise is focused in the Engineering Centre for Environmentally Conscious Products (ECECP) in the USA. In each operating unit there is an ECP strategy owner, with responsibility for developing ecodesign targets.

### 12.5.2.4 Ecodesign guidelines

IBM's key ecodesign focus is on five areas:

- Materials reduction

- Recycled content

- Plastics labelling
- Reduced energy consumption
- Ease of disassembly

### 12.5.2.5 Effectiveness of environmental policy

Ecodesign performance measures are built into the early stages of development. The method used examines attributes, each supported by design guidelines or targets. Each attribute is scored with use of a formula based on:

- Part count (i.e. the percentage of parts in the product meeting specification requirements)
- Character count (i.e. the percentage of features used in the ecodesign of products; this is also being used as a mechanism to work with suppliers)

### 12.5.2.6 Ecodesign and eco-redesign

IBM has developed ecodesign approaches to the redesign of existing products and the development of new products:

- Redesign: personal computers have a small 'window of opportunity' to make eco-driven redesigns because of the short development time-scales when compared with mainframes, which have a longer product life.
- New product design: a product environmental profile is used throughout the product development and design cycle.

### 12.5.2.7 Ecodesign tools

IBM uses three main ecodesign tools:

- Life-cycle inventories
- Product environmental profiles
- Corporate standards (environmentally conscious design)

### 12.5.2.8 Obstacles to ecodesign

IBM has faced five prime obstacles in progressing ecodesign:

- Economic barriers: cost–benefit justification
- Education: lack of awareness
- Lack of understanding of environmental issues among the marketing function personnel and among customers
- Technical problems: the 'trade-off' between real and perceived costs
- Quality: issues relating to recycled materials

## 12.5.3 *Kodak*

### 12.5.3.1 Profile

Eastman Kodak is a multinational provider of photographic materials and related services, employing 90,000 people worldwide. The company has nine business units, with four key areas:

- Consumer imaging
- Health imaging
- Office imaging
- Kodak Professional

### 12.5.3.2 Environmental policy

Following the publication of its first environmental report in 1989, Kodak developed a structured worldwide environmental management programme. There are five corporate policies relating to HSE, each with nine specific HSE guiding principles. Guiding principle 4 focuses on product and service modification and on process modification. It states:

> [The goal is to] develop, produce and market products and materials that can be manufactured, transported, used and disposed of safely and in a way that poses no undue environmental impact, and to provide services in a safe and environmentally sensitive manner.

### 12.5.3.3 Environmental management structure

Environmental management is directed through the Kodak Health, Safety and Environment Management Council which is chaired by the executive vice-president and managed by the vice-president. HSE goals are operationalised through environmental managers within product lines, with specific HSE performance expectations.

### 12.5.3.4 Ecodesign guidelines

Ecodesign is built into environmental management systems and covers:

- Product inception
- Technology
- Design
- Shipping
- Manufacturing
- Product discontinuation

### 12.5.3.5 Ecodesign strategy and effectiveness

To help business units drive environmental performance into product development and commercialisation, an environmental strategy has been developed that focuses on ecodesign issues. It is a basic requirement that new products or services should be more environmentally benign than those they replace. Ecodesign performance is measured through:

- Business-unit HSE evaluation
- Market success of products
- Product data requirements
- LCA data

### 12.5.3.6 Ecodesign tools

To implement the ecodesign methodology a range of tools and approaches are used. These include:

- Guidelines
- Toxicological risk assessments
- Life-cycle cost models
- LCA
- Business-unit evaluation guides

### 12.5.3.7 Research and design

As a result of environmental programmes within research and development (R&D), a range of innovative products and services has been produced. The 'green' screen of R&D includes evaluation of:

- Materials
- Energy consumption
- Regulations
- Costs
- Ease of disposal
- Waste production
- Noise production
- Legal compliance
- Ease of recycling
- Sustainability

## 12.5.4 *Electrolux*

### 12.5.4.1 Profile

Electrolux is a major producer of household products, commercial appliances and forestry and garden products. The company employees 112,000 staff worldwide and had a turnover of SEK110 million in 1996.

### 12.5.4.2 Environmental policy

In 1992 Electrolux developed an environmental vision statement. This incorporated a reference to product development: 'We are going to meet our customer's expectations for safe, environmentally-sound products, and we will actively distribute information aimed at stimulating demand for these products.'

### 12.5.4.3 Environmental strategy

Electrolux's environmental strategy is a business strategy. It has led to competitive advantage, market opportunities and resource efficiency. In production terms, it means cost efficiency. The company set a plan to have all 150 factories accredited to the international environmental management standard ISO 14001 by 2000. Additionally, European companies within the group may register for the Eco-management and Audit Scheme (EMAS).

### 12.5.4.4 Environmental management structure

There is a clear environmental management structure driven from the top. The senior vice-president for environmental affairs acts in an advisory capacity on environmental strategy issues to the group chief executive officer. Environmental affairs operational activities are channelled through the household-products business unit. To operationalise the environmental policy within the group a worldwide network of 70 co-ordinators has been developed, positioned within each of the 20 product lines.

### 12.5.4.5 Effectiveness of environmental policy: measurement tools and responsibility

Environment-related targets for products are set within each product line. Measurement is the responsibility of the environmental affairs division, and a series of tools has been developed, which include:

- Assessment of 'environmental leadership' of the product
- Assessment of the profitability of the product
- Annual improvement of product range
- Recycling properties of products

Key issues include recognition and management of life-cycle impacts and 'adding value' through the supply chain. Within each product line, the R&D department has a key role to determine potential and existing environmental problems and generate new solutions. Product-line purchasing departments are responsible for assessing suppliers. Since 1996, supplier environment assessment has become a prerequisite for all business areas.

### 12.5.4.6 Ecodesign tools

In 1995 the environmental affairs division developed an environmental change programme as a strategic tool to support the implementation of environmental strategies and business development. At the start of the product development cycle, new product concepts are assessed against business and environmental strategies before they are progressed.

Electrolux has now incorporated ecodesign into an integrated product development process. Tools have been developed to aid this process:

- Design guidelines
- Ecodesign checklists
- Checkpoints in the development process

### 12.5.4.7 Obstacles to ecodesign

A key issue for the development of ecodesign and environmental business strategies is the differing levels of environmental awareness and concern around the world. In addition, the uncertainty surrounding trends in national and international 'green' legislation poses problems in product design and development.

### 12.5.4.8 Benefits of ecodesign

A range of improvements has resulted from applying ecodesign to the following business areas:

- Household products
    - Significant improvements have been made to the life-cycle 'use' phase
    - Products have been well received in more environmentally aware markets

- Commercial appliances
    - Improvements have been made to resource efficiency
    - A competitive edge has developed

- Forestry and gardening products
    - Ergonomics have been improved
    - Emissions have been reduced

## 12.5.5 Body Shop International

### 12.5.5.1 Profile

Body Shop International (BSI) is a manufacturer and retailer of cosmetics based in the UK.

### 12.5.5.2 Environmental policy

BSI's corporate philosophy has ensured a leading position on environmental, social and animal protection issues in business. In 1989, BSI developed its first environmental policy driven from the top by its founder, Anita Roddick (this policy was later revised in 1992).

In 1991–92 it developed a formal environmental management system (EMS), and published its first environmental statement in line with the European Eco-management and Audit Scheme (EMAS). Product stewardship was introduced into its EMS, incorporating:

- Product life-cycle analysis
- Supplier accreditation
- Risk assessment (of supplier impacts)
- Buyer environmental guidelines

### 12.5.5.3 Strategy and tools

In 1992 BSI decided that product-related LCA should be built into its EMS. LCA was used to determine environmental and social impacts from 'cradle to grave' and has become an essential tool for sourcing 'appropriate' products and materials.

### 12.5.5.4 Environmental management structure

The ethical audit department manages the environmental and ethical policies and guidelines, with daily support provided by individuals and specialists throughout the company. The EMS is audited by the ethical audit department. There is a range of different departments involved in the product development process, with specific environmental briefs:

- Product marketing (including accessories)
- R&D
- Technical issues
- Packaging technology
- Purchasing

### 12.5.5.5 Working with suppliers: a holistic approach

Supplier evaluation and accreditation is undertaken through the technical and purchasing departments. Evaluation is undertaken through two questionnaires and a detailed data-acquisition sheet including a flowchart displaying each supplier's cradle-to-grave impacts. BSI has found a range of benefits from supplier evaluation, which has enabled a more holistic approach to be taken to the incorporation of environmental, social and ethical considerations in product design and development.

### 12.5.5.6 Benefits of having a well-formed, operationalised environmental policy

- A positive reaction from stakeholders
- An increased understanding of environmental issues internally and externally, leading to increased efficiency
- Increased morale

- Improved two-way communications
- A commitment to continuous improvement

## 12.6 Conclusions

A firm must define what sustainability means for its business—environmentally, economically, socially and ethically—as its approach to product issues will be dependent on its vision, commitment and product or service type (e.g. IBM's strategy is different from that of Body Shop International). Ecodesign issues should be embedded into mainstream organisational and environmental management processes. A key issue is to define who owns the ecodesign process (e.g. environmental management or personnel in product design, engineering or strategy). Ecodesign will need to provide tangible and intangible business benefits if it is going to progress within a firm. Objectives and performance measures should be established early on, and it is essential to understand and then focus on the key environmental impacts of the firm's products or services. This should be both at the corporate and at the business unit level. Development of a management framework, clear communications systems, practical ecodesign tools and appropriate guidelines for designers is essential to successful ecodesign.

Pressures are growing for business to reduce the environmental impacts of products and services. A key issue will be the extent to which, and the speed with which, companies start to integrate environmental considerations into product development alongside cost, quality and performance. Part of the speed of integration will depend on the development of appropriate organisational structures and systems. It is essential that the company has a clear view of what it is trying to achieve. Initially, this is likely to mean raising awareness within the organisation and the development of a common vision, particularly for large and complex businesses. A key issue will be the education, management and co-ordination of internal and external stakeholders in the product development process.

Successful implementation of ecodesign requires appropriate organisational and management structures based on solid internal and external information systems. When developing ecodesign programmes it is important to consider the 'soft issues' surrounding corporate and business-unit cultures, and clear communications strategies should be developed aimed at gaining involvement from business functions.

# TOWARDS A MODEL FOR PRODUCT-ORIENTED ENVIRONMENTAL MANAGEMENT SYSTEMS

*Han Brezet*
**Delft University of
Technology, Netherlands**

*Cristina Rocha*
**National Institute of Engineering
and Industrial Technology, Portugal**

## 13.1 Introduction

Over the past few years growing attention has focused on the unsustainability of current production and consumption patterns in industrialised societies, from the environmental, economical and social points of view. This issue concerns governments, researchers, industry and other economic sectors, non-governmental organisations (NGOs) and the public in general.

Initially moved by local water and air pollution problems and ecological disasters such as those at Bhopal, Seveso and Chernobyl, the different actors of our society have gradually become aware of less visible or less immediate threats such as persistent toxicity, lost of biodiversity, desertification, over-exploitation of natural resources and potential climate change. Scientific evidence on environmental degradation has gained wider acceptance and several studies (Matthews *et al.* 2000; EEA 2000) and publications have shown that the world's resources are limited and that pollution, through emissions to air, water and soil, results in irreversible effects on ecosystems. Some of the effects of human activities on the planet and its population's health are very complex and not yet fully understood.

The responses of governments and industry to these concerns have taken four different paths, which can be summarised as follows:

- From curative to preventative
- From processes to products

● From reactive to proactive and from command and control to self-regulation
● From technological to managerial

### 13.1.1 *From cure to prevention*

This approach to tackling pollution evolved conceptually from a curative approach. As a result of increasingly costly add-on (end-of-pipe) technologies, preventative approaches (designated as cleaner production, cleaner technologies or pollution prevention) have been adopted that avoid or minimise waste and emissions at source. In many countries cleaner production programmes have been developed with the aim of demonstrating the effectiveness of this strategy in reducing pollution and, simultaneously, the consumption of resources, as well as saving money.

The United Nations Environment Programme (UNEP), which launched the concept of cleaner production in 1989 (following previous activities in the USA), has been particularly active in this domain. Several governments have included the promotion of the UNEP pollution prevention strategy in their environmental policies.

In 1992 the Business Council for Sustainable Development (BCSD) created the eco-efficiency concept, which is close to the cleaner production concept but puts more emphasis on creating additional value for customers through environmental actions. In simple terms, this means 'producing more with less' while improving rather than diminishing customer service and satisfaction (Fussler with James 1996). The 'eco' prefix of the eco-efficiency concept has a double meaning: ecological and economic. In the words of Fussler and James, 'it is an integration of sustainable development with business consideration' (1996: 133).

### 13.1.2 *From processes to products*

Although the cleaner production concept embraces processes and products,[1] in practice it has been mostly process-oriented. The product approach was, as a concept, already a part of preventative activities at the end of the 1980s, but the methods used were not suitable for product development (Brezet 1998a). Environmental product development,[2] however, has proven to be even more effective in terms of environmental outcomes because the approach is to prevent pollution along the whole life-cycle of the product and to identify opportunities for environmental improvements at first source—the product design phase. Several demonstration projects have been undertaken in the area of ecodesign, which is increasingly being addressed by governments. For instance, many European countries have been focusing on product-oriented environmental policies for some years now, which will probably leading to an EU-wide policy.

---

1 Products are defined here as mass-produced industrial goods for consumer and professional end-markets.
2 Environment product development is also referred to as ecodesign or design for environment (DfE). In this chapter these designations are used interchangeably.

## 13.1.3 *From reactive to proactive and from command and control to self-regulation*

A small but growing number of companies are taking strategic control of the environmental agenda. These firms have adopted a proactive approach to environmental management, designed to move ahead of growing regulatory burdens, environmental liabilities, market or supplier demands and negative public opinion. Their number is small, certainly less than 5% of all firms, but it is in these companies, both large and small, that the outlines of the end of the command-and-control era are to be found (Rejeski 1997).

It has been observed that environmental strategies move from 'complying' with environmental regulation to 'innovative' or 'compliance plus' and 'environmental excellence' strategies (Roome 1992; den Hond 1996). These various classifications have in common that they denote corporate environmental strategies that are aimed at doing better than the regulatory authority requires and/or at outperforming competitors in reducing the firm's environmental impact (den Hond 1996).

From the government side there are signs of change in policy and strategy style, from command-and-control types of environmental legislation to other forms of operationalising environmental policies. Although environmental regulations have stimulated change and, if properly designed and applied, will continue to motivate some companies to improve (Michael Porter 1990, quoted by Rejeski 1997), it is generally recognised that this kind of approach has limitations and does not lead to significant environmental improvement in the long run—in fact, environmental problems are still growing both in the EU and worldwide.

In the mid-1980s a new policy approach was set up, aiming at encouraging companies to assume their own responsibility in the area of the environment, through the definition of objectives and targets that the companies should achieve in their own ways. This was referred to as 'self-regulation' (Cramer 1997a) and is the approach taken in the case of negotiated agreements between companies and governments.

At the EU level, the range of instruments of environmental policy was broadened to include market-based instruments (such as the Eco-label and the Eco-management and Audit Scheme [EMAS]), which are expected to harness the creative energies of companies and direct them to improving the environmental performance of products and processes in a way that has remained untapped by the normative style of environmental legislation (Hillary 1996).

## 13.1.4 *From technological to managerial*

Business leaders are nowadays fully aware that effective environmental action requires not only adequate technology but also, mostly, an integrated approach of technological and managerial measures. The appearance of standardised environmental management systems (EMSs) was a stepping stone to the further development of environmental management in companies.

Based on the Deming cycle of plan–do–check–act, EMSs aim for continuous improvement of environmental performance. The first EMS standard was the British Standard (BS)

7750 (published in 1992; BSI 1992), followed by several national initiatives. The European Commission adopted the voluntary EMAS regulation in 1993, which became applicable in 1995 and is currently under revision. To prevent the proliferation of national standards for EMS the International Organization for Standardization (ISO) issued ISO 14001 in September 1996 (ISO 1996).

## 13.2 Environment-oriented innovation and ecodesign

Gouldson and Murphy (1998) considered the relationship between economic development, innovation and environmental performance at the level of the firm, from three interrelated perspectives:

- From a technological perspective, highlighting the importance of a shift from reactive control technologies to anticipatory clean(er) technologies

- From an organisational perspective, stressing the need for a shift in the position of environment from the periphery to the core of business decision-making

- From a strategic perspective, establishing that, as well as focusing on incremental change, there is a need to assess the potential for radical change

Incremental innovations consist of the adaptation or improvement of existing technologies, whereas radical innovations involve the development or application of significant new technologies or ideas, of totally new ways of producing products or services (Moors *et al.* 1998). These definitions focus on technological innovations, but the same conceptual thinking can be applied to social innovation, by challenging ideas, values, practices and institutions and, more comprehensively, to systems, understood as the dynamics of technology and society.

The argument for the need for radical environment-oriented innovation relies on the challenge of achieving the right balance between production and population growth, on the one hand, and the Earth's carrying capacity on the other. Experts estimate that, in order to reduce the level of pollution to 40% of the current level, an improvement in eco-efficiency by a factor of 20 is required over the next 50 years (Jansen and Vergragt 1992). This means that the environmental impact of human activities must decrease twentyfold and that the use of raw materials and energy must become 20 times more efficient. As an interim target, it has been argued that within 15 years eco-efficiency must be improved by a factor of 4 (von Weizsäcker *et al.* 1996; see also Fussler with James 1996). The achievement of such leaps forward in eco-efficiency requires a different approach from companies than the continuous improvement process. Strategic choices have to be made concerning product and process innovations (Cramer 1997a).

From these trends, the ecodesign concept (the integration of environmental aspects into product development) has evolved. It is a broader concept, described as sustainable product innovation,[3] and includes more radical innovations to the product, questioning its function and thus influencing the existing patterns of consumption, expected to offer a far bigger contribution to sustainable development.

According to the types of change undertaken and the eco-efficiency level attained, efforts to introduce ecodesign (understood in a broad sense) can be divided into four types (Brezet 1998b; Rathenau Institute 1996):

- Product improvement
- Product redesign
- Function innovation
- System innovation

Product innovation involves partial changes and improvements to products already existing in the market. The product itself and the production techniques stay, in general, the same. The achieved improvement in eco-efficiency is, at the most, considered to be of factor 2–3.

In product redesign, although the existing product concept stays the same, the components of the product are fully improved or replaced, aiming at use of non-toxic materials, recycling and disassembly, improved distribution, re-use of parts and energy-use reduction with respect to all components over the life-cycle of the product. The environmental benefit of this type of ecodesign may achieve factor 5, but it remains limited in the possibilities offered by the existing product concept.

Function innovation is not restricted to the existing product concept. In this case, the way the function is fulfilled is changed. The general shift from physical products to dematerialised services belongs to this category. For this type of ecodesign, the environmental performance in fulfilling the desired function is considered to have an improvement potential of factor 10.

In system innovation the entire technological system (product, production chain and associated infrastructure and institutional structure) is replaced by a new system. It is believed that with this type of innovation an improvement in eco-efficiency of factor 20 is possible.

The improvement in eco-efficiency over time related to these four types of ecodesign is shown in Figure 13.1.

Most current environment-oriented product policies are focused on type-1 and type-2 improvements. Many companies already 'have their hands full' with these types of product innovation. Design decisions made for type-2 improvements do not usually require significant interference or involvement from the strategic or top management level of a company. With the usual environmental support from management they could be considered to be mainly engineers' work and responsibility. However, within the research and development (R&D) programmes of leading product development industries, more and more attention is being given to the development of innovation of types

---

3   Product innovation is defined as changes to the product–market–technology combination. A completely new product innovation is realised when the product, market and technology are all changed (Kruijsen 1997).

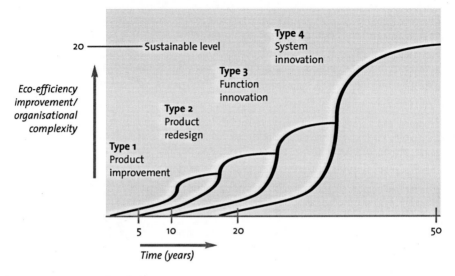

20 ——————— Sustainable level

Type 4
System
innovation

Type 3
Function
innovation

Type 2
Product
redesign

Type 1
Product
improvement

*Eco-efficiency
improvement/
organisational
complexity*

5    10          20                              50

*Time (years)*

*Figure* 13.1  **Four types of ecodesign**

*Source:* Rathenau Institute 1996

3 and 4, referred to as 'sustainable product and system innovation', in contrast to the more short-term-oriented 'ecodesign'. These further-reaching types demand policy changes from top management, sometimes including the establishment of new sustainable business units and 'green coalitions' outside the existing companies in order to be successful.

## 13.3  Why use product-oriented environmental management systems?

One often-mentioned limitation of the success of the ecodesign concept is the pilot project character of many existing initiatives in this field. It is recognised that the effectiveness of ecodesign activities will be limited if they are not integrated into the strategic management and daily operation of companies in a dynamic process of continuous improvement of environmental performance. However, this has been rarely accomplished to date. In general, after completing an ecodesign project, companies tend to return to 'business as usual', and the improvement process loses its continuity. In the Netherlands, a country recognised for its ecodesign experiments, it is estimated that approximately 1,000 ecodesign pilot projects in small and large industries have already been undertaken. It is therefore important to seek mechanisms to make ecodesign efforts encouraged in these projects to become 'normal business' in the companies involved and to avoid the significant loss of know-how gained during such projects.

However, in order to deal with the challenging changes that underlie the sustainable product innovation concept as described above, companies will have to drastically change the way they address environmental product development and its management. Actions taken so far in the majority of companies seldom involve a willingness to experiment, improve and substitute products, except under public or regulatory pressure (Cramer and Schot 1993). Cramer and Schot state that an innovative strategy should aim at improving the company's capability to produce environmentally sound products. It should, for example, seek to:

- Incorporate environmental considerations into the business strategy of the whole firm, including departments responsible for innovation (such as R&D and marketing divisions)

- Create organisational conditions for synergy between the environmental function and other functions involved in formulating the business strategy

- Promote co-operation among firms; the way firms interact on environmental aspects of products may be termed 'environmental co-makership' and consists of two steps:
  - Exchange of information between firms
  - The setting of demands on suppliers by user firms

It is pertinent to explore the potential role of EMSs in attaining such objectives, for five reasons. First, standardised EMSs are appealing to industry as they are increasingly becoming recognised as providing an adequate structure for implementing a company's environmental strategy (i.e. for putting strategic principles and objectives into practice, for evaluating the results and redefining the path), aiming for continuous improvement of environmental performance. An EMS provides order and consistency for companies to address environmental concerns through the allocation of resources, assignment of responsibilities and ongoing evaluation of practices, procedures and processes.

In spite of its relative newness and the initial resistance shown by companies, the uptake of EMAS and ISO 14001 within industry is showing a significant increase. In October 1995 only 15 companies were registered under EMAS; in April 2000 that number had risen to over 3,300. Regarding ISO 14001 (which is applicable to all types of organisation and not only to industrial sites), there were over 15,000 companies certified at that same time.[4]

Second, ecodesign can be seen as a continuous improvement process in line with the EMS. The ISO 14001 structure can be applied to achieve product impact reduction. In specific cases, the process of incremental improvement is accelerated by a product innovation or breakthrough.

Third, there is a growing awareness within industry that the traditional focus in EMSs on production processes only may no longer be appropriate. As a reaction, companies and branch organisations are developing 'environmental product care systems'. These new management tools are built around a cyclic process of continuous ecodesign improvements to products and will provide insight into what extent these goals have been reached.

---

4  For figures on uptake of EMAS and ISO 14001, see ISO InfoCenter, at www.iso14000.com/.

Fourth, some companies are taking the lead in fostering a systematic approach of their environmental product development efforts by implementing standardised EMSs that integrate environmental product development issues. This is the case, for instance, of Philips Sound and Vision (Cramer and Stevels 1997) and the Dutch companies ATAG Kitchen Group (Noordhoek and van Hemel 1999) and DAF Trucks (Rocha and Brezet 1999). This approach applies not only to large companies but also to small and medium-sized enterprises (SMEs). A research study conducted on the ecodesign project of Dutch innovation centres, aimed at 77 SMEs, showed that an EMS could be a stepping stone towards DfE, and vice versa (van Hemel 1998; see also Chapter 10). The findings of this study showed that companies active in the field of DfE had often already established a (partial) EMS. Furthermore, these companies were inclined to establish a link between their EMS and DfE initiatives.

Last, both at the EMAS committee level and at the ISO level, actions are being undertaken to seek a closer relationship between EMSs and ecodesign activities. There is the recognition that the environmental performance of a product should receive increasing importance in assessing the environmental performance of the organisation that manufactures that product. This aspect is being discussed both in the context of the revision process of EMAS and within ISO, where an ad hoc group on 'Integrating environmental aspects into product development' (ISO 14062) has been established.

In spite of the potential and opportunities that EMSs bring to promote products that are more eco-efficient, it is recognised that such systems, as currently defined in the EMAS regulation and particularly in ISO 14001, are not a guarantee of optimal environmental outcomes. The extent of their contribution to environmental optimisation and innovation of processes and products depends on companies' strategic choices (Cramer 1997b). The fact that they do not establish requirements for environmental performance beyond legal compliance and continuous improvement, together with the fact that cleaner production and life-cycle thinking are not objectively required, have been strong points of criticisms with regard to the effective contribution of these systems to the pursuit of the objective of sustainable development.

EMSs are still in the process of development. Depending on the country and the specific sector of industry concerned, experiences regarding the introduction of these systems may differ. Until now, however, all EMSs have had a common primary focus on processes. The integration of environmental issues into product design strategies (in the context of EMS implementation) has received limited attention (Cramer 1997b).

Based on the three points of departure—that EMS can be the carrier to make ecodesign a part of a company's strategies and daily practices, that EMS may enable environmental product innovation and that present EMS standards are not sufficient to adequately address environmental aspects in product development processes—the question is what a product-oriented environmental management system (POEMS) should look like, given that a POEMS is understood to be an environmental management system with a special focus on the continuous improvement of product eco-efficiency (ecological and economic efficiency) throughout the life-cycle of a product through the systematic integration of ecodesign in the company's strategies and practices (see Chapter 13). The core elements of a POEMS are:

- The consideration of the eco-efficiency of the company's products at a strategic level through definition of an environmental product policy

- An evaluation, on a regular basis, of the environmental performance of products (throughout the life-cycle)

- The consideration of environmental criteria in product development processes

- The formulation of goals to ensure that, in addition to compliance with environmental regulations, the company continuously improves the eco-efficiency of its products, in co-operation with other companies of the product chain

In the following sections, a case study of a truck-manufacturing company is described, and a Dutch initiative to promote the adoption of POEMS by companies is presented in Section 13.5.2.

# 13.4 Case study of a truck manufacturer

## 13.4.1 Introduction

Company T, a large European developer and manufacturer of trucks, has for some years been addressing environmental aspects in product design as a consequence of legal requirements and market demands. Such initiatives have resulted in trucks with low-emission exhausts, low-noise engines and reduced fuel consumption, which is translated into lower costs during the use phase, the main concern of customers.

Whereas these aspects are already integrated in the company's product creation process, the new opportunities that the ecodesign concept brings are still to be explored. In 1997, an official ecodesign project was set up, resulting in a number of actions (including a pilot project on plastics recycling, the definition of ecodesign guidelines in a dedicated tool and an ecodesign newsletter) for the environmentally conscious development of its products and related components.

The ecodesign project is aimed at bringing additional environmental requirements and opportunities (such as the use of eco-efficient materials, re-use and recycling, the involvement of suppliers, etc.) to product design, with an integrated life-cycle perspective, translated into increased cost efficiency, improved quality, improved customer satisfaction and increased market share. This is a recent initiative in the company and the opportunities of attaining such benefits (ecological and economic) are not yet fully perceived. Among product developers there is some resistance to ecodesign, perceived as an extra burden in the product development process.

Company T implemented an EMS that was designed to address primarily the environmental aspects of its production processes and attained ISO 14001 certification in 1998. For the company, the rationale for exploring the link between the EMS and ecodesign was as follows:

- The company's present EMS model and its elements (which are in accordance with the ISO 14001 standard) are considered to be a sound managerial structure to support continuous improvement to the company's environmental performance.

- As company T is ISO 14001-certified, it makes sense to extend the scope of the existing EMS to ecodesign activities; it was agreed as a basic principle that integration of ecodesign into the business should not become a burden to the company and that therefore POEMS should not form a separate management system.

- At present, the existing EMS formally includes those requirements that are suggested for ecodesign, and there is a controlling system in place that will ensure that the required activities are performed and their results evaluated.

In order to optimise the potential of its ecodesign strategy, company T undertook a project with TU Delft Design-for-Sustainability Programme. The goal was to explore the possibilities of integrating ecodesign activities in the framework of the existing EMS by means of a POEMS. It was the intention that POEMS would not only formalise the current and planned activities in ecodesign but would also be a catalyst for future activities in this domain.

## 13.4.2  *The product development process and ecodesign*

The product development process has been formalised at company T. It offers the possibility for parallel, more effective, work by cross-functional teams instead of following the traditional 'department-to-department' sequence, with the aim of speeding up the product development process and ensuring that functionality, quality and cost are considered from the very beginning of the design process.

Taking into account ecodesign models and the best practice of companies in this field, TU Delft suggested a number of ecodesign activities for the different stages of the product development process (Table 13.1). All these functions and activities were considered to be necessary for effective ecodesign, with prioritisation in time made according to the company's specific needs.

It should be noticed that within company T, at the end of the concept stage, the product's programme of demands is in principle fixed and the investment plan approved. This means that the content of the project, the timing, the risk and the financial and technical aspects would need to be completely defined. At this point, product targets and specifications are set up and the people involved in the project have agreed on all the consequences of the project. Therefore, ecodesign requirements should be defined and proven to be achievable at this stage, otherwise they will not be integrated into the product development process.

Suppliers play an important role in product development in the company. Approximately 70%–80% of trucks are made from bought components; therefore close co-operation and information exchange between the company and its suppliers is essential for the success of ecodesign.

| Stage | Ecodesign activities |
|---|---|
| **1. Orientation phase** | ▶ Form ecodesign objectives<br>▶ Form 'green' marketing objectives |
| **2. Definition stage**<br>▶ Translation of market and other requirements into a concept programme of requirements for the new product | ▶ Involve and gain support of ecodesign staff<br>▶ Carry out environmental benchmarking<br>▶ Collect information on suppliers<br>▶ Collect information on other stakeholders (government, EU, recyclers, users, environmental organisations)<br>▶ Generate 'green' options (assess environmental innovation potential)<br>▶ Validate 'green' options<br>▶ Draw up an ecodesign R&D agenda<br>▶ Form a concept environmental programme of requirements (input to concept programme of requirements) |
| **3. Concept stage**<br>▶ Define the programme of requirements<br>▶ Specify the concepts of product and process engineering<br>▶ Carry out concept styling<br>▶ Define the suppliers | ▶ Gain ecodesign support for environmental specifications and product concepts<br>▶ Consult environmental material databases and other sources of ecodesign expertise (i.e. carry out an inventory)<br>▶ Gauge the 'green' perception (i.e. the emotional response)<br>▶ Draw up an ecodesign R&D agenda (technical specifications)<br>▶ Formulate an environmental programme of requirements |
| **4. Engineering stage**<br>▶ Detail product and process engineering requirements<br>▶ Prepare and start market introduction<br>▶ Prepare after-sales introduction<br>▶ Suppliers: start serial production | ▶ Consult environmental material databases and other ecodesign expertise (i.e. optimise procedures)<br>▶ Seek environmental validation (in terms of production, use, end-of-life, regulations)<br>▶ Form a tactical green marketing and communication plan |
| **5. Volume validation**<br>▶ Test by dealers and customers a small number of series produced trucks<br>▶ Minor adjustments<br>▶ After-sales introduction | ▶ Draw up an ecodesign after-sales plan (compose user or dealer instructions, etc.) |
| **6. Evaluation stage**<br>▶ Evaluate the project<br>▶ Evaluate the market response | ▶ Evaluate the product-oriented environmental management system (in terms of procedures, expertise, support)<br>▶ Obtain feedback on ecodesign goal-setting |

*Table* 13.1 **Suggested ecodesign activities in relation to the six stages of the product development process**

Within the experiment at company T it was found that several of the activities described in Table 13.1 already exist, or exist in part, or could be easily integrated in the product development process. The questions to be answered are therefore:

- How can the activities be made systematic rather than ad hoc events?

- How can the activities be fully integrated into the product development process, therefore moving ecodesign from a satellite position to a core part of the business?

- How can progress be tracked, existing objectives be rethought and the eco-efficiency of the trucks be improved?

With these aspects in mind a general POEMS model was developed by TU Delft and is presented in the next section. It includes:

- Activities that lead to the concrete definition of environmental objectives and performance criteria for the product as well as to tracking progress

- Activities that ensure capability to apply ecodesign (including a consideration of resources, know-how, allocation of responsibilities, development of tools, etc.)

- Activities that ensure control and routinisation (in the sense of making it a systematic effort) of ecodesign

## 13.4.3 Towards a model of product-oriented environmental management systems

As stated in Section 13.4.1, company T is willing to rely on the existing EMS for the expansion of its ecodesign activities. Therefore the POEMS model developed in this experiment optimises the contents of the EMS (from an ecodesign point of view) while relying on the structure that ISO 14001 offers (Fig. 13.2). Therefore, the model follows the plan–do–check–act cycle, and it is possible to establish a parallel with ISO 14001 requirements.[5] The model is presented in Figure 13.3 and is discussed in Sections 13.4.3.1–13.4.3.3.

The structure of the model combines an operational cycle, oriented to the improvement of products' features through ecodesign (the sequence in the centre of Fig. 13.3) with a managerial cycle, oriented to provide the managerial support for ecodesign (the sequence on the left).

### 13.4.3.1 Plan

As commonly accepted and experienced in environmental management, the optimal results of an EMS require the attuning of the business strategy with the environmental

---

5   ISO 14001 requirements are those activities, documents and registers that have to be in place for a company to attain certification.

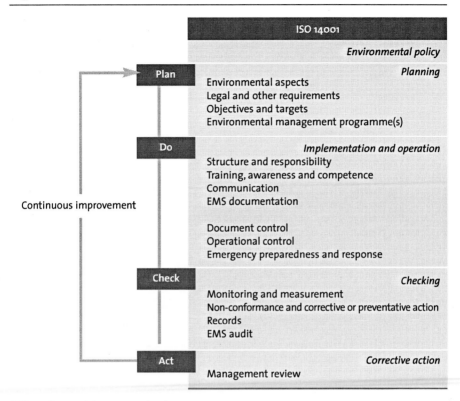

EMS = environmental management system

*Figure* 13.2 **The continuous improvement cycle and ISO 14001 requirements**

policy so that the environmental dimension is made part of the company's core values and so that resources for operationalisation are provided. When considering products, which are the core of a company's business and the most visible interface between the company and the outside world, the need for such attuning is even more obvious. In addition, a product-oriented environmental policy should provide a framework for deriving objectives for eco-efficiency improvement in the relevant phases of the entire life-cycle of the product.

Primarily in the first POEMS cycle, but also in further cycles, an analysis of and reflection on the current situation is needed. The analysis phase encompasses the product's environmental profile and existing management structures for ecodesign.

The definition of the product's environmental profile should take into account legal requirements, an evaluation of the impacts throughout the product life-cycle and other stakeholders' demands and opportunities (e.g. where the company stands in comparison to competitors, whether the company has the necessary environmental information on supplied parts and materials, whether customers' environmental concerns are being fulfilled, and so on).

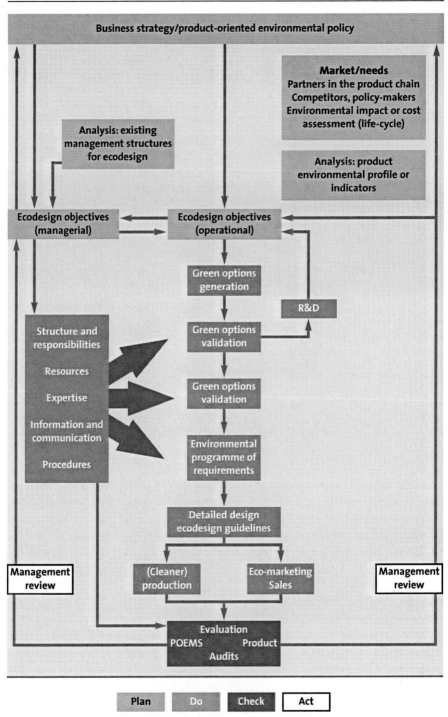

POEMS = product-oriented environmental management system

*Figure 13.3* **POEMS model**

A life-cycle assessment (LCA) or other tools should be used for an evaluation of the environmental impacts of the product; it is recommended that the results of the LCA be combined with the results of an assessment of the environmental costs throughout the life-cycle. This allows the identification of those areas that are most eligible from an environmental and economic point of view.

The results of the LCA or other assessment studies can be integrated into a comprehensive environmental performance indicator system for internal management and benchmarking, from which concrete objectives can be derived. ISO has recently released the final draft standard on environmental performance evaluation (ISO 1998) to assist companies in evaluating performance against environmental policy, objectives, targets and other environmental performance criteria in the context of the companies' EMSs in general and in relation to product-related aspects in particular.

The analysis of existing management structures for ecodesign includes the review of practices, procedures, organisation and resources and the evaluation of the ability of existing structures to support ecodesign in the company.

The analysis phase is intended to decide where to focus in terms of organisation and environmental (and economic) aspects of the product's profile; the next step is the definition of objectives, which can be either managerial or operational.

In terms of the factors that determine operational objectives (e.g. reduction of total weight by $x$%, or increase in use of renewable materials by $y$%), stakeholders' views should again be taken into account. Feasible operational objectives and targets will be translated into product characteristics and therefore will have a direct impact on consumers' expectations of and responses to the product and on the company's positioning in the market. This aspect is one of the important differences between environmental management oriented towards production processes compared with that oriented towards products.

Managerial objectives and targets aim at building capability and routines into the regular implementation of ecodesign and the exploration of its potential. Therefore, the planning stage of the development of a database of the environmental characteristics of materials used in the production process, the planning of an LCA or the definition of the required level of expertise in ecodesign among the company's designers, all fall into this category.

### 13.4.3.2 Do

In the operational cycle, the 'do' phase is directly related to the product development process. In this context, the generation of 'green' options and validation activities will help to identify improvement opportunities in line with the defined operational objectives. Depending on the availability of accurate information and on the technological implications, some of these may be feasible in the shorter term and be translated directly into the environmental programme of requirements; others will require the undertaking of R&D projects in which their environmental innovation potential will be explored. The results of these R&D projects may later be translated into new objectives and be operationalised in future product development processes.

The detailed design phase not only will require specific guidelines to assist the designers regarding environmental aspects but will also require the consultation of materials databases and other sources of information and expertise. An environmental validation of the new product may take place during this phase.

Often, the decisions taken during the design phase have important implications in the production stage. As mentioned in Section 13.4.2, company T has defined cross-functional teams for the product development process, which include the production manager. This enables dialogue between designers and the production manager at an early stage so that, once potential trade-offs are worked out between the environmental burden at this stage with that of the other phases of the life-cycle of the product, the objectives of ecodesign can be fruitfully combined with cleaner production objectives.

Regarding the managerial cycle, in order to build capability for ecodesign it is necessary to allocate appropriate resources, to assign responsibilities within the context of an adequate structure, to build expertise (including not only training but also the development and application of adequate tools, as mentioned above) and to promote internal and external communication. External communication regarding the improved or innovated product falls, of course, within the context of the (eco-)marketing strategy of the company and is therefore a very important element of a POEMS (see Chapter 15).

In order to guarantee environmentally sound management, operating methods in the form of written procedures for ecodesign should be established. Procedures clearly define the methods of operation to be followed and guarantee continuity when people change jobs or when new staff are hired. Existing product development process practices have to be taken into account as a point of departure in order to make the process work. The procedures should be established to support ecodesign activities that are agreed as 'standard' in the company and it is recommended they should also be integrated into existing EMSs and quality procedures as much as possible.

### 13.4.3.3 Check and act

Both cycles end with a phase for reviewing the process and for setting future directions (described in ISO 14001 as a management review). The aim is to address the possible need for change to policy, objectives and other elements of the POEMS in light of the results of audits and product evaluations and in light of changing circumstances and the commitment to continuously improve the environmental performance of the product. The POEMS is again analysed at a strategic level as part of an ongoing process.

## 13.4.4 Consequences of the product-oriented environmental management system at company T

The project was the initiator of a number of activities at company T. The following were defined as being of highest priority.

- At policy level:
    - Make the board of directors aware of the current situation regarding ecodesign implementation and of the results of the project and request

a clear statement on the strategic importance of the POEMS and the level of ambition of environmental objectives for product development; this was considered a crucial aspect of POEMS success in the company

–   Include a product-oriented environmental statement in the company's vision

● Analysis of the product environmental profile:

–   Assess the performance of a truck through a detailed LCA

–   Undertake eco-benchmarking, which is already a known technique (e.g. for fuel consumption), but also address other ecodesign aspects

● Ecodesign objectives:

–   Define strategic ecodesign objectives, in line with the company's vision

–   Define short-term ecodesign targets for the new heavy line truck

● Managerial support for ecodesign:

–   Define procedures for ecodesign in product development

–   Develop a training and communication programme for ecodesign, building on the existing ecodesign newsletter and guidelines

Follow-up research on company T's activities shows that approximately 15 feasible green options have been generated and will gradually be implemented.

# 13.5 The future of product-oriented environmental management systems

### 13.5.1 Conclusions from the experience at company T

The following, indicative, conclusions can be drawn from the case study:

● From an existing ISO 14001 environmental management system as a point of departure it is feasible for product-developing companies to apply the same management structure in an effective and efficient way to integrate environmental considerations into its product development processes.

● Application of TU Delft's list of ecodesign requirements within the POEMS model readily gives insight into the weak and strong points of a company's ecodesign programme.

● By means of its managerial and learning cycles, the POEMS model gives systematic direction to the continuous improvement of existing strong and weak points and to the improvement of potential, future projects.

● As the POEMS implementation programme at company T reveals, the model enhances the opportunities for environmental product innovation (i.e. it encourages the systematic generation of new 'green' options).

Altogether, the experiment shows that, by combining existing environmental management systems (EMSs) with existing product development procedures and functional ecodesign requirements, an effective POEMS model for companies can be developed.

Appropriate application of the model not only guarantees a company's sufficient 'ecodesign capability' but also improves the chance of discovering product innovations that are relevant to both the environment and the business economy.

## 13.5.2 *Other case studies*

Other studies from TU Delft show the attractiveness and feasibility of the POEMS approach. In particular, some first results of the POEMS (*Productgerichte milieuzorg* [PMZ]) programme annex subsidy scheme of the Ministry of Housing, Spatial Planning and Environment in the Netherlands (VROM 1998) should be mentioned. A study, undertaken by TU Delft and the National Institute of Engineering and Industrial Technology (INETI), Portugal, is not of the action research type but concerns an evaluation *ex post facto* of the experience of 40 companies with POEMS.

The VROM's concept of product-oriented environmental management encompasses, as its core elements, life-cycle thinking and continuous improvement. Also, as the programme was open to all types of organisation, the term 'product' was understood in a broad sense as comprising goods and services. This is in line with the definition of the term 'product' in quality management (ISO 9000 series) and, implicitly, in environmental management systems (as ISO 14001 and 14004 and the new EMAS apply to all types of organisation, not simply those from industry). One could say that POEMS, as defined in Section 13.4.3, is an example of a particular case devoted to product-developing companies, giving emphasis to the major role of these firms in defining the environmental profile of their products; in contrast, the influence of the other elements in the product chain is far more limited. Nevertheless, a life-cycle perspective can and should be applied by all partners in a the product chain, and the eco-efficiency principles discussed in this chapter apply to production processes, products and services, even if they do so with different mechanisms for operationalisation.

Our evaluation study (Brezet *et al.* 2000) shows that:

- The POEMS approach—in a broad variety of practical models—can be applied to sectors oriented towards producing intermediate goods or non-material goods, such as the chemical industry, the building-materials industry, the rubber and raw materials industry and the recreation sector.

- Main driving factors of co-operation in the PMZ subsidy scheme were:
  - Learning opportunities
  - Environmental considerations
  - Anticipation of future regulation

- The large majority of participating companies (72.5%) will continue with further implementation of the POEMS systems; most of them expect to receive concrete benefits from POEMS, but only in the long run.

● In particular the following ecodesign activities were adopted during the project:
  - LCA performance
  - The definition of an organisational structure and responsibilities
  - The definition of POEMS procedures
  - The development of tools (LCA, databases, materials lists, etc.)

● Of the ten EMS-certified companies participating, five will continue to integrate product development into their EMS (the others either already have their POEMS system in place or consider the introduction of the life-cycle perspective into EMS to be less relevant).

● The most frequently mentioned benefits from the PMZ project were:
  - The improvement of environmental knowledge
  - The improvement of the internal organisation
  - An increase in technical knowledge

  The main drawbacks were seen as the considerable resources (time and money) needed for implementation

● Although not fully comparable with the model as developed in the action research project at company T, the evaluation shows to a large extent the generic feasibility of the POEMS approach.

# 13.6 Conclusions

As discussed in this chapter, it makes sense to explore the role of environmental management systems in fostering ecodesign activities and in promoting environmental product innovation. We suggest that existing EMS 'standards' (ISO 14001 and EMAS) could provide the structure for a product-oriented environmental management system (POEMS), although specific requirements for product development and innovation are necessary.

A case study performed by TU Delft with a truck manufacturer provided encouraging results with regard to the role that the POEMS model might play in the systematic implementation of ecodesign, and the project provided a 'kick-off' point for a number of activities and feasible product improvement options in the company. So far, no major conflicts between the existing environmental management system, its extension towards a comprehensive integration of product development activities by means of a POEMS and the product development process have been identified.

In the Netherlands, the Ministry of Housing, Spatial Planning and Environment (VROM) is already active in this field and has launched a funding programme to foster the development of POEMS, with the participation of several organisations. An evaluation study (Brezet *et al.* 2000) of the results and experiences of 40 companies from different sectors, ranging from raw materials producers to service providers, has shown that:

- The companies were positive about implementing a life-cycle perspective in their environmental management.

- The most important benefits of this experience were an increase in internal knowledge of environmental issues and an improvement of the internal organisation and management of environmental aspects of products and services.

Other possible benefits, reflecting an external response to the POEMS implementation, are expected in the long run. A pre-condition for this is the establishment of an adequate policy framework to foster (eco-)improvement of and innovation in the products and services. Nevertheless, most companies will continue with the implementation of POEMS.

In their research programmes, TU Delft, INETI and their international partners will further test the POEMS model in close co-operation with product-formulating companies. POEMS seems to be promising for companies that consider ecodesign to be their responsibility and see it as a strategic issue. However, more research is needed to gain a better understanding of the specific circumstances, driving factors, obstacles in the way of adoption and diffusion and the specific contents needed for an effective and efficient adoption of the POEMS concept in companies in Europe and elsewhere.

# TOOLS FOR ECODESIGN AND SUSTAINABLE PRODUCT DESIGN

*Ursula Tischner*
**econcept, Germany**

This chapter introduces findings of the author's research and practical experience in the field of ecodesign and sustainable design, in particular the findings of a research project on ecodesign approaches (tools and methodologies) that econcept carried out with other organisations on behalf of the German Federal Environmental Agency.[1]

Ecodesign means environmentally conscious product development and design, or design for environment (DfE). These terms describe a systematic approach which aims at embedding environmental aspects in the product planning, development and design process at the earliest possible opportunity. This means that 'environment' is added as a criterion of product development alongside other classical criteria of functionality, profitability, safety, reliability, ergonomics, technical feasibility and, last but not least, aesthetics. The term 'ecodesign' also expresses in an elegant way that it aims at linking ecology with economy through professional development and design activities.

However, the term 'sustainable design' is closely bound up with the guiding principle of sustainable development and goes beyond the concept of environmentally conscious design. Sustainable design takes account of environmental, social and ethical issues (the 'triple bottom line') in addition to the common design requirements during the development and design process (see Chapter 6).

Various methods and tools have already been developed which can help to reach the goal of a more environmentally sustainable economy by, for example, minimising the consumption of natural resources and the possible burden on the environment while maximising benefits for human beings. Some of these methods and tools are presented in this chapter. Nevertheless, this chapter concentrates mainly on tools for ecodesign, because tools for a holistic sustainable design are still missing and less developed.

Product planning, development and design play a particularly important role in ecodesign and sustainable design. More than 80% of all product-related costs and

---

1   The results of the project are published in German and English; see Tischner *et al.* 2000.

environmental impacts of a product during its manufacture, use and disposal are determined during the product planning phase. If environmental aspects are taken into account during the earliest phases of product development, then it is more likely that reduced environmental impacts can be integrated into the final product. This will increase the potential long-term economic success of the company (win–win–win strategy).

Over and above the motive of merely protecting the natural environment, there are many other good reasons for initiating and practising ecodesign and sustainable design, such as

- It pays, because reducing material and energy consumption, as well as waste and contaminants, saves money.

- It improves the image of the company and its products, which can result in better sales.

- It improves legal compliance and anticipates upcoming regulations, and, by acting voluntarily and proactively, companies reduce the need for regulatory pressures.

- It is an investment in the future because it improves innovation capabilities and long-term success strategies.

Once the decision to implement ecodesign and sustainable design has been made, the following steps are usually a key part of activities:

- Investigating where environmental and social problems exist both in the company and along the entire life-cycle of a product (from extraction of raw materials through production and use to recycling and disposal)

- Thinking through the steps required to solve these problems and determining the goals:
    - Determining areas of responsibility
    - Starting and establishing a pilot project
    - Acquiring the necessary information and working materials and adapting them to needs
    - Setting up co-operative ventures (e.g. with suppliers or with waste-disposal agencies)

- Evaluating experience gained from the pilot project and the initial ecodesign and sustainable design activities and setting up a systematic step-by-step strategy including continuous improvement

- Communicating ecodesign and sustainable design successes inside and outside the company and motivating and training the workforce (see Chapter 12)

One goal of ecodesign and sustainable design is that the relevant company departments such as product development, design, purchasing, etc. continuously work out environmental and social improvements in the existing product line (redesign). Another aim is that the company's management makes it a principle to evaluate the company's products and services from an environmental and social or ethical point of view and develop strategies that might go further than redesign towards changing the whole system behind the product (systems innovation). The latter often leads to more radical results. In particular, the marketing department and associated experts should be involved in these activities, because experience shows that a lack of marketing involvement can be a strong obstacle to ecodesign or sustainable design in a company.

## 14.1 Key aspects of sustainable design

The following three considerations are particularly important when implementing ecodesign:

- Environmental and social or ethical considerations
- Life-cycle thinking
- Consideration of the core benefits of a product

First, environmental and social or ethical considerations should be introduced into product planning as early as possible. Environmental aspects should also play a major role in such basic issues as deciding which customer needs are to be satisfied, or what product or service is to be offered to which target group. The earlier environmental concerns are integrated into these decisions, the greater the potential for cost saving, for increasing profits and for reducing the environmental impact at the same time. The company's management, marketing experts and strategic planners will play an important role in this process.

Second, an important feature of ecodesign is that it considers the environmental aspects of a product or service over its entire life-cycle. It endeavours to determine possible environmental impacts (material consumption, energy input, pollutant content, waste, etc.) of a given product or service, starting from the supply of raw materials through manufacturing to final disposal. This life-cycle thinking is also highlighted in terms such as 'from cradle to grave' or 'from cradle to cradle'. The latter emphasises recycling considerations and the concept of a 'closed-loop' recycling economy, which has and will become binding on companies through the enactment of national and European regulations (e.g. 'producer responsibility').

Last, before starting an ecodesign project, the first question should concern the benefit of the intended product from the user's or buyer's viewpoint:

- What function(s) or what solutions to a given problem does the user expect?
- Of what benefit is the product to the user?
- How does the user use the product?

Quite often it turns out that there is more than just one way of satisfying an identified need of a user group and more than just one product with which to achieve this (Fig. 14.1)

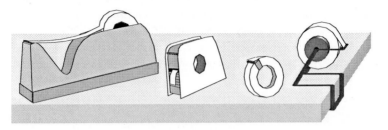

*The service of 'tearing off a strip of adhesive tape' can be accomplished by diverse products with different dimensions, rates of material consumption, etc. and consequently with different environmental impacts.*

*Figure 14.1* **Sellotape roller**

*Source:* Tischner 1995

and that alternative options can be significantly different from the current solution. Before starting to make plans it is advisable to define what is termed the 'service unit' of the intended product or service. This means thinking in terms of solutions to problems (make tasty coffee), not of products (make a coffee machine).

By combining these three aspects, ecodesign leads to

> products, systems, infrastructures and services, which require a minimum of resources, energy and land area to provide the desired benefit in the best possible way while at the same time minimising pollution and waste arisings over the entire life-cycle of the product (Schmidt-Bleek and Tischner 1995).

## 14.2 The product development and design process

The process of ecodesign (see Fig. 14.2) is not essentially different from conventional product planning processes (common planning schemes can be found in Bürdeck 1991; VDI 1993)—however, its aim is to integrate environmental aspects into existing planning processes wherever this is meaningful and possible. This chapter describes a systematic ecodesign process. In practice such a process will rarely be encountered in precisely this form; however, the structure of this chapter illustrates where tools can be applied to solve problems arising at specific points in the product development process. The tasks highlighted in the following section are likely to be reminiscent of the types of issue that design and product development professionals have encountered in their own work. This provides readers with ideas and tools for dealing with these issues.

This planning flowchart should be thought of as a flexible framework. In practice, the individual phases will be given different priorities depending on the type of company, task at hand, budget and time. The flowchart features loops to allow single or several steps to be repeated in the event that a specific phase, or the entire process, yields unsatisfac-

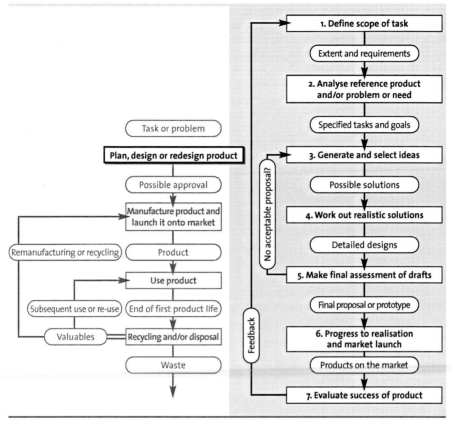

*Figure* 14.2 **The ecodesign process in relation to a product's life-cycle**

tory results. The seven steps summarised on the right-hand side of Figure 14.2 may be broken down into more detail as follows.

- Step 1: identify the task and appraise how radical the approach can be
  - Analyse the task and its scope
  - Define the internal and external factors that influence the planned project
  - Specify resources and responsibilities
  - Formulate a brief for product development

- Step 2: analyse a reference product and the given task or problem
  - Identify the most important environmental weaknesses and potential improvements, as well as other factors influencing the product under planning and the product system

- Define the functional targets for the products, the main environmental aspects related to its functions and the main environmental impacts to be expected
- Integrate knowledge in product specifications

- Step 3: generate and select ideas
    - Develop new solutions that integrate environmental and social considerations and meet product specifications and requirements
    - Try also to think about radical innovations
    - Evaluate the ideas and identify the most promising ones to develop further

- Step 4: work out realistic solutions
    - Work out the solutions selected as most promising according to the defined project-specific priorities, appropriate to the given overall strategies and integrating the set environmental and social goals and requirements
    - Collect necessary information along the product life-cycle and co-operate with suppliers, the purchasing department, end-of-life actors, etc.

- Step 5: make a final assessment of drafts and carry out testing and prototyping
    - Evaluate the product regarding the environmental and social requirements and technical feasibility, marketability, etc.
    - Amend and adapt if necessary, and make a final decision to realise or go back to the idea generation and design phase

- Step 6: progress to realisation and market introduction
    - Plan manufacturing, produce the new product and introduce it to the market
    - Determine whether the target group is sufficiently environmentally conscious to appreciate the ecological benefits of the new product
    - Decide if the product's environmental benefits can be used in advertising and other marketing communications
    - Use environmental product labelling, develop environmentally sound logistics and product take-back systems when appropriate

- Step 7: keep products and services under review after their market introduction
    - Use feedback and criticism from customers and other stakeholders as a resource for current and next product planning activities
    - Monitor whether planned environment-related product qualities prove to be valid in practice (e.g. are the expected energy savings during use really achievable?)
    - Establish measures to secure customer loyalty and maintain the product

In the following section a selection of tools for the different stages and tasks of the development process are offered that facilitate ecodesign and sustainable design activities.

## 14.3 Tools for sustainable design and ecodesign

At all steps in the product development and design process tools can be used to ease and speed up the process. They help one to analyse, collect information, be creative, decide, communicate, monitor, control and review. In the following discussion important and useful ecodesign tools are presented; these have been taken from current literature and practice or have been developed at econcept. Figure 14.3 shows how these tools can be categorised according to their purpose and complexity.

There are four categories of ecodesign tool:

- Analysis of environmental strengths and weaknesses

- Priority-setting and selection of the most important potential improvement

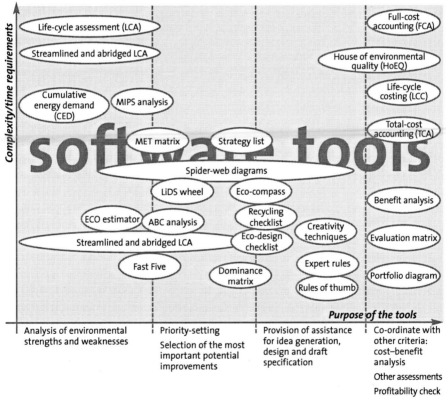

ABC   classification system (A = serious problems, action required;
      B = no direct action required but should be monitored; C = not a problem)
LiDS  Life-cycle Design Strategy
MET   Material, Energy, Toxic emissions
MIPS  material input per service unit

*Figure 14.3* **Classification of tools that are useful for ecodesign and sustainable design and their use in the product development process**

- Provision of assistance for idea generation (brainstorming), design and draft specification (these are examples of implementation tools)

- Co-ordinate with other important criteria: cost–benefit analysis, economic feasibility studies and so on

These will be discussed in more detail in Sections 14.3.1–14.3.4.

## 14.3.1 Analysis of environmental strengths and weaknesses

The analysis stage involves the identification, quantification, evaluation and prioritisation of environmentally harmful issues in relation to a product, a product system, a service or a concept. Analysis should be completed depending on planning constraints (e.g. time, personnel and financing).

This may involve a very thorough analysis: for example, drawing up a life-cycle assessment (LCA) including the goal and scope definition, inventory, impact assessment and evaluation steps. Here the factors with a negative impact on the environment are first ascertained, and then their importance is determined on the basis of their effect on the more fundamental environmental criteria.

In the case of other analysis tools, analysis and assessment may be combined in one process (e.g. material input per service unit [MIPS]; cumulative energy demand [CED]). In this case, the assessment of the harm to the environment is based directly on the evaluation of individual, environmentally relevant, factors (e.g. material or energy input).

Identical underlying conditions must always be taken as a basis for comparative analyses of several products. This applies to the services or functions that are offered through the product but also in specific circumstances (e.g. geographical factors). For example, there is little point in comparing the assessment of a beer keg with that of a beer can unless in both cases a relationship is established with their filling volume.

Similarly, when undertaking product comparisons, erroneous estimates can result if different scenarios for electricity generation are used that have been completed on the basis of averages excluding specific data for specific places of production. It is important to recognise that calculation of emissions and material flows depends on the origin of the current used (e.g. from a coal power station or a hydroelectric power station). If calculations are carried out with one scenario for one product version and with a different scenario for another, a distorted image results, which means that comparison is considerably hampered.

The following tools can be used for analysing environmental strengths and weaknesses:

- Detailed and streamlined LCAs that
    - Use process flowcharts to determine product-related inputs and outputs (raw materials, energy, waste, emissions) quantitatively and as comprehensively as possible
    - Classify weight inputs and outputs with respect to their environmental impact (e.g. ozone depletion, climate change, toxicity, soil acidification, etc.)

- – Calculate, in some cases, an overall index to facilitate comparison between several products (which offer the same benefit)

- Numerous software tools that are available to facilitate analysis, especially LCA

- CED analysis, which enables the determination of the energy demand of a product over its entire life-cycle and which can be used as a measure of environmental impairment

- MIPS analysis, which enables the quantitative determination of the material and energy input required for a product across its entire life-cycle; the energy input is converted into units of material expenditure, and environmental impact is then expressed in terms of total material input in relation to actual or potential units of service

- Checklists and matrices (e.g. the MET [Material and Energy inputs/outputs, Toxic emissions output] matrix; Brezet and van Hemel 1997) for analysis of environmental strengths and weaknesses, which enable estimations of the environmental impacts of a product within the shortest possible time (in the event that accurate data is not available)

## 14.3.2 Priority-setting and selection of the most important potential improvements

Once the potential environmental impact of the product, system or service under consideration has been determined, priorities must be set for further design work. It is rare that all environmental problems can be considered simultaneously. This establishment of priorities determines which environmental impacts are greatest in importance and should be dealt with first. In addition, an important question is: 'What improvement possibilities lie within the sphere of influence of the company?' Consideration should also be given to current and future external issues (e.g. regulatory requirements and customer needs).

Tools that support priority-setting and decision-making include:

- Spider diagrams and portfolio diagrams, such as the LiDS (Life-cycle Design Strategy) wheel (Brezet and van Hemel 1997) and the eco-compass (Fussler with James 1996), or the portfolio of Gertsakis *et al.* (1997); these
  - – Enable a qualitative classification and presentation in a diagram of the environmental qualities of a product on the basis of the most important criteria (e.g. material input, energy demand, production method, logistics and transport, product use, durability)
  - – Provide a representation (in an easily understandable diagram) of the improvement potential in relation to individual criteria

- Decision matrices, such as ABC analysis, in which one lists the most important criteria for evaluation and asks the user to evaluate each single criterion; in case of ABC analysis the user has the choice of using the classification A (serious problems, action required), B (no direct action required but should be monitored) or C (not a problem) for evaluation

■ The dominance matrix, which

  – Facilitates the definition of priorities and determination of the most important improvement options

  – Ranks criteria and potential improvements on the basis of a systematic comparison of all relevant environmental criteria and improvement options

## 14.3.3  Implementation: provision of assistance for idea generation, design and draft specification

A practical approach starts with the application of simple ecodesign tools, such as spider diagrams, rules of thumb and expert rules, and ecodesign checklists. Without a lot of analysis, they help to define appropriate ecodesign strategies and ideas, offer ecodesign criteria in a more or less situation-specific manner, present these briefly and to the point and dispense with in-depth examinations of the background.

In general, this provides a good overview of ecodesign, enabling stakeholders in the ecodesign process to absorb quickly the important aspects of environmentally appropriate product design and development. Where product development schedules are tight and finances and personnel are in short supply, this action-oriented approach still enables the topic of environmental quality to receive appropriate consideration during the product planning process.

For this purpose, checklists, expert rules and rules of thumb can be helpful for systematically integrating environmental aspects into the product along the entire course of its future life-cycle. These checklists are designed to ensure that nothing is forgotten, as when packing suitcases for a journey!

Checklists can be developed for almost any kind of problem that can occur during the design phase. The most common types are:

■ General ecodesign checklists

■ Checklists for ecodesign strategies

■ Checklists for environmentally oriented material selection and lists of hazardous materials

■ Checklists for recycling-friendly design and ease of disassembly and assembly

■ Checklists for avoiding waste and pollutants

Catalogues of requirements, expert rules and rules of thumb serve to:

■ Communicate the product brief and defined requirements to everyone participating in the planning process

▨ Keep in mind the general environmental criteria and requirements for design while generating ideas

▨ Present inspiring examples and alternatives

Tools for stimulating creativity are not only useful for ecodesign but also for mainstream product development. Creativity techniques, such as brainstorming, morphological boxes, etc., facilitate the process by

▨ Creating a relaxed atmosphere

▨ Initiating brainstorming and creative processes by virtue of their structured approach

▨ Generating a greater diversity of ideas by more or less systematic variation of existing proposals

## 14.3.4 Co-ordination with other important criteria: cost–benefit analysis and economic feasibility studies

Design approaches must be re-evaluated at different stages of the planning process, and assessment criteria should not only be considered from an environmental and social point of view but also with regard to profitability, marketability and technical feasibility. This is enabled through multi-criteria tools:

▨ House of (environmental) quality (HoEQ): this tool uses a multi-dimensional matrix to assess the different ways in which the various product properties and requirements influence each other in a negative or positive sense

▨ Environmental cost accounting methods enable
  – Understanding of the costs that a product will incur during its development and production phase (marketing, planning, construction, procurement, transport, production, distribution, service) and balancing these against the environment-related improvements it provides
  – Determination of the (environment related) costs a product will incur in the course of its entire life-cycle (i.e. all costs, including those that arise during its use, recycling and disposal phases [costs in general, not only those borne by the producer])
  – A rough estimation of the profitability of eco-improvement measures by keeping account of the associated costs

Table 14.1 gives an overview of a broad range of tools helpful for sustainable design, some of which are introduced in this chapter. With the help of the table it is possible to choose the tools according to their recommended use in the design process, as introduced above, and the purposes of the tools.

| Tool | Carry out environmental analysis of reference product or problem (Phase 2) | Find ideas and select solutions (Phase 3) | Work out selected solutions (Phase 4) | Carry out final assessment of solutions (Phase 5) | Observe production and market (Phase 7) |
|---|---|---|---|---|---|
| **Tools for environmental analysis and instruction** | | | | | |
| LCA | ☆ | | | ☆ | |
| MIPS method | ☆ | | | ☆ | |
| CED method | ☆ | | | ☆ | |
| MET matrix | | ☆ | | ☆ | |
| Spider-web and polar diagrams | ☆ | ☆ | | ☆ | ☆ |
| Sony Polardiagram | ☆ | | | ☆ | |
| Eco-compass | ☆ | ☆ | | ☆ | |
| LiDS wheel | ☆ | ☆ | ☆ | ☆ | |
| Spider diagram, econcept | ☆ | ☆ | ☆ | ☆ | ☆ |
| Checklists | ☆ | | ☆ | ☆ | ☆ |
| ABC analysis | ☆ | | | ☆ | |
| Eco estimator | ☆ | | | ☆ | |
| Ecodesign checklist, econcept | ☆ | | ☆ | ☆ | ☆ |
| Philips's Fast-Five | ☆ | ☆ | | ☆ | |
| WEEE Directive checklist | ☆ | | | ☆ | |
| Strategy list | | ☆ | ☆ | | |
| Expert rules and rules of thumb | | ☆ | ☆ | | |
| Brainstorming | | ☆ | | | |
| **Creativity techniques** | | | | | |
| Brainwriting 635 | | ☆ | | | |
| Heuristic principle | | ☆ | | | |
| Bionics | | ☆ | | | |
| Morphological box | | ☆ | | | |
| Progressive abstraction | | ☆ | | | |
| **Setting priorities, decision-making** | | | | | |
| Checklist for selecting new solutions | | ☆ | | ☆ | |
| Ecodesign matrix | | ☆ | | ☆ | |
| Ecodesign portfolio | | ☆ | | ☆ | |
| Quality profile | ☆ | ☆ | | ☆ | |
| Dominance matrix | ☆ | ☆ | | ☆ | |
| House of environmental quality | ☆ | | ☆ | ☆ | ☆ |
| **Cost accounting** | | | | | |
| Total-cost accounting | ☆ | | | ☆ | |
| Life-cycle costing | ☆ | | | ☆ | |
| Full-cost accounting | ☆ | | | ☆ | |
| Environmental cost accounting | ☆ | | | ☆ | |
| Matrix for cost estimation | ☆ | | | ☆ | ☆ |
| Benefit analysis | ☆ | | | ☆ | |

LCA = life-cycle assessment; MIPS = material input per service unit; CED = cumulative energy demand;
MET = Material, Energy, Toxic emissions; LiDS = Life-cycle Design Strategy;
WEEE = Waste from Electrical and Electronic Equipment

*Table 14.1* **Overview of ecodesign tools**

# 14.4  Example of a development process using ecodesign tools

A producer of household appliances (white goods) wants to optimise a refrigerator with due consideration of the product's environmental impacts.

## 14.4.1  Definition of goal and scope

A rough analysis of the existing product by means of an ecodesign checklist shows that it has the following main weaknesses:

- It has extremely high energy consumption during use.

- It has a relatively short life-span.

- It uses ozone-depleting cooling gases that also increase the greenhouse effect.

- The method of construction and the materials used are not good for recycling.

- It is difficult to dispose of.

The product management decides to improve the product by putting emphasis on those aspects that also generate user benefits and thus could be used for advertising (e.g. reduced energy consumption during use, increased life-span). These aspects are included in the brief for the product development team.

## 14.4.2  Developing first ideas

The product development team, including marketing and purchasing experts, gets together in a first brainstorming session, discusses the requirements given by management and develops ideas for a totally new refrigeration system, drawing up the following list:

- The refrigerators should not be built to travel: a hybrid between a storage room and a refrigerator could be built into the kitchen to stay there as long as the house exists, using appropriate long-lasting insulation material.

- The cooling compartments should be located in a convenient position for loading the refrigerator or for searching for food.

- There should be no big door; drawers and smaller doors should be used instead in order to keep loss of cooled air to minimum.

- The cooling machine should be separate and located in a separate place for easy access, repair, or replacement and upgrading (it should probably be owned by a firm specialising in cooling machines).

- The heat released by the cooling machine could be utilised (e.g. water pre-heating) and discarded during the summer months through piping.

● During winter months, cold air from the outside should be used for cooling and for discarding unwanted hot air; use of cold air should be accomplished automatically by intelligent sensors.

● It should have transparent front panels and inside compartments if possible (at least the interior temperature should be visible from the outside; e.g. through a display).

● Drawers and doors should close automatically.

● There should be no refrigeration, as it would not be used often unless for specific reasons, but a built-in device should still be usable for storing food (with the size of compartments to be adaptable to customers' needs).

● The external design of the refrigerator should be variable to follow the changing aesthetic needs of the user.

The team uses a decision matrix (Table 14.2) to specify the most important improvement options, asking for environmental improvements, technical feasibility, cost and customer benefits.

| Idea | Environmental improvements | Technical feasibility | Cost | Customer benefits |
|------|---------------------------|----------------------|------|-------------------|
| 1 | | | | |
| 2 | | | | |
| 3 | | | | |

Table 14.2 **Basic decision matrix**

The team decides to follow up the idea of a built-in refrigeration system and defines areas where research is necessary, such as which cooling technologies and which materials could be used and what kind of construction enables repair and maintenance as well as upgrading of the system aesthetically and technically. Experts are made responsible to research the fields and a timetable is set up.

## 14.4.3 Research and compilation of environmental data sheets

The material expert compiles a preliminary environmental data sheet for every material researched, putting an emphasis on the plastics and insulation material that could possibly be used for the new refrigerator and investigating the longevity and recyclability of the materials as well as function-specific aspects such as insulation potential, acid resistance, etc. The other experts do the same for their fields (cooling technologies, possible construction principles, etc.).

## 14.4.4 Developing a detailed design

These items of information get circulated on the internal intranet, and the core product development team gets together to develop and discuss the detailed design. For the detailed design phase they use an ecodesign checklist that lists all the environmentally relevant requirements and questions for the whole product life-cycle, enabling them to integrate those aspects into their design drafts. The overall design idea leads to specific product specifications for the following detailed design phase, integrating environmental aspects such as maximum energy consumption permitted, use of detachable joints, the maximum number of different materials permitted, the requirement that all materials be recyclable, etc.

The core team also decides which modules already exist and can be purchased and which modules will need to be developed by the development team. The product specifications for the purchased parts are forwarded to the purchasing experts.

The product developers then design the modules of the new refrigerator using a computer-aided design (CAD) system that connects all single modules and enables the designers to keep informed about the other modules their colleagues develop. The ecodesign checklist is shown in Box 14.1.

## 14.4.5 Final evaluation

After the detailed design phase the developed product gets through a final evaluation phase, where the product development team uses a 'spider-web diagram' (Fig. 14.4) and a supporting questionnaire. With the help of the spider-web diagram the existing product is compared with the new solution regarding the most important specifications as identified in the product brief.

The new design proves to be a very good solution, increasing customer and environmental benefits as well as being an innovative and promising product for the company, especially because it improves the image of the company as a whole in an environmentally sensitive market.

## 14.4.6 Realisation and market launch

A prototype is built and tested under real-life conditions, and final amendments are made. In parallel to this, marketing has developed a marketing strategy and has planned a test launch of the new product. Because of the special feature of the new design, which gets built into a house, it is more like a piece of architecture than a stand-alone refrigerator. Therefore marketing starts to establish new co-operation with architects and building companies as well as local crafts companies in the test area to use them as promoters and service providers for the new refrigeration system in addition to the normal retail system of such a unit.

Thus by integrating environmental considerations and ecodesign tools into the normal product development and design process the company has generated an improved product that meets the demands of customers and company; it is hoped it is successful

**EXTRACTION OF RAW MATERIALS, CHOICE OF RAW MATERIALS**

- Minimising material input
- Minimising energy input
- Minimising land use (raw materials extraction, production)
- Avoiding input or emission of hazardous substances
- Avoiding emissions (e.g. by transport)
- Minimising waste production, recycling materials
- Preferring local raw materials
- Using renewable raw materials produced using sustainable methods
- Using socially acceptable substances that will pose no health hazards
- Using recycled materials

**PRODUCTION**

- Minimising material input
- Minimising energy input
- Minimising land use
- Avoiding input or emission of hazardous substances
- Avoiding emissions (e.g. by refinement procedures)
- Minimising pre-consumer waste production, recycling materials
- Preferring local suppliers along the whole supply chain
- Minimising packaging
- Using renewable ancillary materials produced by sustainable methods
- Using socially acceptable processes that will pose no health hazards

**USE/SERVICE**

- Creating excellent customer benefits
- Appropriate design for target group
- Minimising complaints and returns
- Keeping service available

*The following alternative strategies might be discussed*
- Design for longevity (***strategy 1***)
  - Timeless design
  - 'Long life' guarantee
  - Robust, reliable wear-resistant design
  - Design for easy repair and maintenance
  - Possibilities of combination
  - Variability, multi-functionality

*Box 14.1* **The econcept ecodesign checklist** *(continued opposite)*

*Source:* Tischner *et al.* 2000

- Possibility of re-use and shared use
- Design for update to the best available technology

*or*

- Design for short-lived products (*strategy 2*)
  - Fashionable design
  - Design for product take-back
  - Design for recycling
  - Design for environmentally friendly disposal, e.g. compostable

- Understandable design for the user
- Design for self-controllable and optimisable functions
- Dirt-resistant, easy-to-clean design
- Minimising material and energy input during use
- Avoiding input or emission of hazardous substances

### RE-USE/RECYCLING (CLOSING TECHNICAL MATERIAL AND ENERGY CYCLES)

- Recycling strategy in place?
- Guarantee for take-back in place?
- Re-use of the complete product (e.g. second-hand, recycling cascade)
- Recycling of components (e.g. upgrading, re-use of components)
- Recycling of materials
- Dismantling of products
- Separability of different materials
- Low diversity of materials
- Low material and energy input for re-use/recycling

### FINAL DISPOSAL

- Compostable, fermentable products (closing biological cycles)
- Combustion characteristics
- Environmental aspects at deposition

*Box 14.1 (continued)*

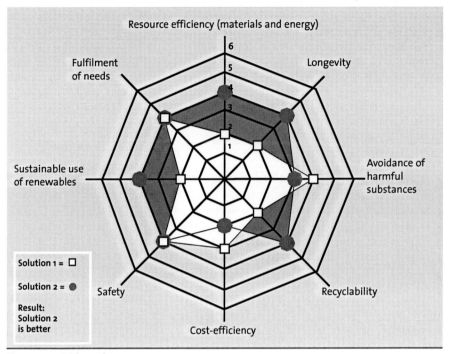

*Figure 14.4* **Spider-web**

on the market while drastically reducing the environmental burden of refrigeration systems in private households.

## 14.5 Conclusions

Although ecodesign is a complex field and adds environmental aspects to the 'normal' design requirements, it should be seen as a positive challenge by companies, as a motor for innovation and as a strategy to secure business success. There are already a number of helpful tools for ecodesign available that enables companies to deal with these complex issues in an appropriate time and cost-effectively. Experience shows that companies that use a selection of the tools and adapt them to their own needs are able to achieve very good results.

Although most of the ecodesign tools currently in use aim at the integration of environmental issues in product development and design, there are only very few that also facilitate social or ethical considerations (i.e. sustainable design). Given the definition of sustainability as the three-dimensional approach to development, which takes into account environmental, economical and social requirements, tools for sustainable design have to take a multi-criteria approach: for example, in matrices and checklists to analyse problems and design solutions that meet the 'triple bottom line'. There is still a lack of tools developed specially for sustainable design and of indicators and measures for business sustainability (what you cannot measure you cannot manage). This is a field where research is urgently needed.

Small and medium-sized companies particularly express a need for simple tools (see Chapter 10). Most of them cannot afford to run full life-cycle assessments (LCAs) for their products, because these take a lot of time and are expensive. Therefore it is recommended that they start with simple tools such as checklists, decision matrices, spider-web diagrams and increase their environmental awareness step by step through training of staff and through pilot projects (involving external experts as appropriate).

An ideal ecodesign and sustainable design approach involves top-down and bottom-up strategies: that is, top management should provide motivation, guidelines and the recommendation to implement ecodesign and sustainable design programmes, and the experts in product development and marketing should use tools and develop ideas and expertise in ecodesign and sustainable design projects. This should involve the search for short-term 'quick wins' (projects with immediate economic and environmental success) as well as long-term strategies.

With the increasing use of the above-described ecodesign tools (and a greater wealth of sustainable design tools that have to be developed) it will become easier to integrate environmental and social aspects into product development and design. These tools are likely to be part of good design practice in the future.

# GREEN MARKETING*

*Michael Jay Polonsky*
University of Newcastle, Australia

Green marketing is often incorrectly associated with superficial 'green hype' such as 'new improved and friendly to the natural environment'. Organisations (for-profit, non-profit or not-for-profit and governmental) using these types of 'claim' frequently try, with varying degrees of success, to associate themselves and/or their products with an environmental image without substantially improving the environmental characteristics of the organisations' practices and/or products. While such inappropriate behaviour is on the decline, its early use has caused irreparable harm to genuine environmentally responsible marketing actions, as many consumers are generally sceptical of all green marketing activities (Cude 1993; Davis 1994).

Green marketing encompasses much more than simple 'marketing hype' (Menon and Menon 1997), although there is no universally accepted definition of green marketing. Any definition must include the fact that there is voluntary exchange between organisations and consumers that achieves both parties' objectives, while attempting to minimise the negative environmental impacts of these exchanges, and ensures activities are sustainable. Green marketing can therefore be undertaken by all types of organisation, including consumer marketers, business-to-business (B2B) marketers, suppliers, retailers and even governmental bodies.

Green marketing is more involved than simply promoting a product's or organisation's green attributes or activities. It requires organisations to carefully evaluate the very nature of organisation–consumer exchange through a modification of the traditional marketing mix variables (product, price, promotion, and place or distribution) as well as other activities. This may require a complete paradigm shift in organisational thinking to address sustainable behaviour that moves beyond simply eco-efficiency (i.e. reducing environmental harm). As such it may involve radical changes in marketing processes that

*   I would like to thank Philip J. Rosenberger III (University of Newcastle, New South Wales, Australia) and Martin Charter (The Centre for Sustainable Design, Farnham, UK) for their helpful comments in revising this work.

could even go as far as asking: 'Do consumers need to actually "own" products, or are there other ways of delivering want-satisfying capabilities?' (Peattie 1999). Take the example of Toyota, which has been working with the Japanese government to develop a trial programme where people purchase transportation without owning automobiles. Instead, people buy access to a fleet of electronic automobiles that can be used to travel short distances to shops and/or connect with traditional public transportation, which is also accessed as part of the transportation package. In this way, green marketing has removed the need for individual ownership of cars while still allowing people to have their core need for transportation met. Toyota therefore is 'seizing the day' and shifting corporate activities, taking advantage of environmental opportunities, rather than waiting to be pushed by regulation or other external pressures.

## 15.1 Why green marketing?

Although most readers will be familiar with many of the environmental motivations for 'going green' (i.e. the responsible use of limited resources; van Dam and Apeldoorn 1996), this section will briefly discuss some of the motivations for greening marketing and organisational thinking. Unfortunately, many organisations do not incorporate environmental activities into their core evaluative criteria (Kilburne 1998) and when they undertake green marketing activities they do so to increase profits, return on investment, market share, etc. rather than to achieve a sustainable competitive advantage. Some organisations, however, do 'go green' for more altruistic reasons, although this growing number of organisations is in the minority (Drumwright 1994).

Understanding organisational motivations for greening is important, for it shapes how an organisation undertakes its specific green marketing activities. For example, organisations that undertake green initiatives simply to comply with regulations may choose to undertake minor changes to their production processes that will prevent them from being prosecuted. In contrast, organisations that choose to target niche green market segments may be required to significantly modify their environmental activities across a range of functional areas. Although many organisations see government-required greening as a constraint, more forward-thinking organisations see it as an opportunity to maintain a sustainable competitive advantage (Porter and van der Linde 1995).

For example, Toyota has established an 'eco-technologies' division which is developing technologies designed to exceed existing emission and fuel efficiency regulations and thus is an environmental leader rather than an environmental follower. It has adopted this approach because it realises that environmental issues must be considered and addressed today if organisations are to continue operation in the future. In this way Toyota is reshaping its direction and is designing traditional engines that are more fuel-efficient, as well as developing a range of new automobiles, including electric and hybrid electric–combustion automobiles, which may ultimately replace petrol engines (Toyota 1997). Even governmental bodies have seen the need to gain competitive advantage through greening their activities. For example, Newcastle City Council (Newcastle, New South Wales, Australia) has a mission to become one of the greenest councils in Australia, as it believes that this will not only improve the general quality of life in the area but will draw new industries and technologies to the region (NCC 1999).

In some cases organisations undertake greening initiatives in reaction to consumers seeking out new greener products or services. Adopting a demand-driven approach unfortunately assumes that the customer is always right (i.e. customers know which environmental improvements are most appropriate), which may not be the case. Customer-oriented or market-oriented greening can take a number of different forms, such as when organisations produce new, less environmentally harmful, products alongside their 'traditional' goods; in other cases organisations might modify products to address particular consumer concerns. For example, McDonald's replaced its poly-styrene clamshell packaging with waxed paper directly in response to consumers' concern over chlorofluorocarbons (CFCs) produced in the production of polystyrene (Gifford 1991). Unfortunately, it is unclear whether waxed paper is in fact less environmentally harmful than new-generation CFC-free polystyrene. This highlights the fact that respond-ing to customers' wants may not result in the best environmental outcome (Oleck 1992). As such, the analysis of the environmental impact of a product or process is a complex process and may require detailed life-cycle assessment (LCA) to identify the most environmentally responsible course of action. This may result in organisations selecting alternatives that on the surface (i.e. to consumers) do not appear to be the least environmentally harmful.

Competitive pressures may also force organisations to introduce green marketing activ-ities, and there is sometimes a chain reaction within an industry. For example, in the late 1980s consumers became concerned with the numbers of dolphins being killed as a result of tuna fishing. Starkist, one of the major tuna marketers in the USA, announced it was going 'dolphin-friendly', which forced all competitors to follow suit or lose market share (*Advertising Age* 1991). In another example, when one laundry detergent manufacturer in Australia introduced a concentrated formula or package, others quickly followed suit in the fear that they would be left behind (*CHOICE* 1990). In yet another example, when one German refrigerator manufacturer introduced CFC-free refrigerators, all other manu-facturers quickly followed, even though they had all initially opposed this innovation (Hartman *et al.* 1999). This required a complete shift in the market practices of these German firms and brought about strategic change across the industry (i.e. no CFC-based refrigerators). However, in some cases, changes to organisational 'environmental' behav-iour may only be tactical in nature. For example, detergent manufactures did not sub-stantially shift corporate environmental thinking or behaviour but rather simply added a 'green product' alongside their less friendly environmental alternatives.

Suppliers and downstream channel members may also pressure organisations to change their environmental behaviour. In the Starkist tuna example, suppliers were required to modify their behaviour or face losing a major customer, Starkist (Rice 1990). In another example, firms complying with the ISO 14000 series of standards are required to evaluate the environmental performance of their suppliers. In this way, complying organisations pressure their suppliers to meet appropriate environmental standards, and these suppliers, in turn, pressure their suppliers to comply. This may have implications for national and international trade: for example, IBM and Volvo already require that all their suppliers worldwide must have appropriately approved environmental management systems in place (Zuckerman 1999).

The above motivators suggest that changes can occur as a result of external pressures on the organisation. However, this is not always the case and there are several situations where changes are internally motivated because of pressures such as a financial rationale (i.e. costs) or a philosophical stance. The cost perspective is driven by the realisation that there are savings associated with greening activities that may give organisations a competitive advantage in the marketplace (Porter and van der Linde 1995). Organisations operating in a less environmentally harmful way typically increase efficiency and save by using fewer materials and producing less waste and pollution. For example, more efficient fan or blower motors use less electricity and can improve the production process, as typified by the Greenville Tube Company, who installed a new motor vector drive into their tube-making process. The company has since realised a US$75,000 saving per year from the reduction in wasted material and a 30% saving on their energy bill. In addition, they also do not have to run the process for as long, further saving on fuel and maintenance and reducing polluting emissions (*CHOICE* 1999).

The other internally motivated type of greening reflects a 'responsible' organisational philosophy, where environmental issues are given equal weighting to financial objectives. Such philosophies are often transferred from an organisational founder down to management, which are then integrated into all organisational activities (Drumwright 1994). For example, the founder of Blackmores, an Australian firm that produces and markets nutritional supplements and healthcare products, incorporated environmental issues as a core focus of the company's activities before it was fashionable to address these issues:

> In 1967, long before environmental issues were a concern, Blackmores founder, Maurice Blackmores, spoke of the importance of conservation and the effect of pollution on the environment when he stated: 'If man persists in ignoring or defying the recycling laws of Nature he will not avoid pollution, malnutrition or starvation . . . Nature does not know how to handle pollution or preserve the balance of nature in the face of it.'[1]

In the Blackmores example, environmental values were adopted because they were part of top-management philosophy. However, it is possible that a concern for the natural environment develops over time and slowly becomes a centrepiece of organisational philosophy. For example, Toyota's newest president, Hiroshi Okuda, has stated that he wants Toyota to have a strategy that promotes 'harmonious growth in the next century, balancing the needs of people, society and the global environment' (Toyota 1997: 3). Thus, even global organisations can integrate environmental issues into overall organisational philosophy because they believe it is the 'right thing to do' and because it is a sustainable practice.

---

1   Blackmores (1999) www.blackmores.com.au/content/co_enviro.htm

## 15.2 Levels of green marketing

In the green marketing area, a number of catchphrases have been used, including: green marketing, sustainable marketing and responsible marketing. As discussed earlier, the definitions of all of these terms involve satisfying organisational objectives and consumer needs while at the same time ensuring that the world is not made worse off and, ideally, trying to make environmental improvements. The ramification of such an approach is substantial and requires organisations to think globally about their activities. That is, no one is green if they simply strive to keep their own country clean but undertake environmentally harmful activities, either directly or indirectly, in other countries.

In green marketing, organisations ask themselves: 'How can organisational and consumers' objectives be achieved in more environmentally responsible and sustainable ways?' The motivations for undertaking green marketing activities, discussed in the previous section, will be likely to impact on the strategies and tactics that are used to address environmental issues. (These will be discussed in more detail in the next section.)

True green marketing involves environmental issues becoming as much a strategic organisational focus as are issues such as quality or customer service, and this will most probably require a change in the organisational mind-set as well as in organisational behaviour. Menon and Menon (1997) have suggested that the greening of marketing activities can occur at three levels within organisations. It can be:

- Strategic
- Quasi-strategic
- Tactical

Strategic greening requires a substantial and fundamental change in organisational philosophy. For example, the Australian firm CarLovers designed its entire car-washing process on a closed-loop system in which water is recycled. In this way, environmental issues are a core part of its business philosophy and practice.

Quasi-strategic greening requires a substantial change in practice. For example, some hotels promote the fact that they are trying to minimise their environmental impact. In an attempt to reduce water consumption associated with washing linen, these hotels ask guests to indicate when they want their towels washed by leaving them on the floor or in the bathtub.

Tactical greening is typified by shifts in functional activities such as promotion. For example, in times of drought, water authorities encourage consumers to behave in a more responsible fashion. In this case there is little if any change in organisational activities other than a short-term reallocation of promotional resources.

These three levels can be used to identify the amount of change required by an organisation and may reflect the degree of 'commitment' to various environmental objectives. Take the example of a jeans manufacturer who, in the early 1990s, promoted the fact that it would donate a proportion of each sale to support the planting of trees. Such a tactical activity might be viewed with intense scepticism, as there is no logical link between these activities (i.e. manufacturing jeans and planting trees). However, a similar programme by a paper company that explains the links between its activities and the natural environment, the specific environmental issue being addressed as well as how this programme will assist in improving the environment would most probably be seen as an appropriate tactical activity.

However, any strategic greening activity will require an extensive long-term financial investment as well as a shift in organisational behaviour and mind-set. As such, effectively implemented strategic greening would rarely be seen as superficial. Take, for example, Wilkhahn, a German furniture manufacture, which has undertaken substantial environmental activities that shape its fundamental philosophy and activities. These include designing long-lasting products that either use recycled materials or minimise the use of virgin products and which are produced in an environmentally designed factory that is also ergonomically designed (Wilkhahn 1996).

## 15.3 Green marketing strategies and tactics

When thinking of green marketing many people tend to incorrectly focus on promotion or product design activities. Although these aspects are important, green marketing is an integrated approach that continually re-evaluates how all types of organisation (for-profit, non-profit or not-for-profit and governmental) can better achieve their objectives and consumer needs while reducing the long-term environmental harm of these activities. As such green marketing requires ongoing improvements across a diverse range of activities (McDaniel and Rylander 1993) and has evolved since its initial conception within the mainstream business community in the early 1970s (Kilbourne and Beckmann 1998). Extensive information has been written on a range of related topics, including:

- Targeting
- Green pricing
- Green design and product development
- Green positioning
- The greening of logistics
- The marketing of waste
- The greening of promotion
- Green alliances

Each of these topics will be briefly examined in Sections 15.3.1–15.3.8, and some guidance will be provided as to how organisations can utilise green marketing activities as strategic, quasi-strategic and/or tactical activities.

### 15.3.1 *Targeting*

As mentioned earlier, consumers frequently push organisations to develop green products, such as dolphin-friendly tuna or energy-efficient light bulbs (Wong *et al.* 1996).

Although there are substantial numbers of environmentally concerned consumers, organisations would be ill advised at times to develop products solely targeting these consumers, and, in fact, the number of 'green' consumers seems to change over time (Ottman 1997a). Of course, there are some exceptions, with firms such as The Body Shop doing reasonably well targeting environmentally responsible consumers.

Although substantial numbers of consumers report to be 'green' (Ottman 1997a), it is unclear whether they purchase goods and services solely on environmental grounds. That is, they may expect 'green' goods to be competitively priced, as well as perform to a satisfactory level. What this means for organisations targeting green consumers is that a product's level of greenness is often used to differentiate two relatively equal goods and then environmental performance can become a key point of differentiation when comparing these goods with non-green alternatives.

Take, for example, the less environmentally harmful Kyocera Ecosys laser printer (Cottam 1994). When it was first introduced in Australia it was heavily promoted as a 'green' laser printer. The promotion was slowly shifted over time to emphasise product quality as well as the fact that it was less environmentally harmful than competitors and cost less to operate on a cost-per-page basis. In this way, Kyocera sought to broaden its appeal from simply targeting green consumers and organisations to targeting all types of consumer. In this way they broadened their appeal and moved away from a narrow niche segment.

This is not to suggest that there are not opportunities to solely target green consumers, and, in fact, there may be increasing opportunities as a result of new technologies (e.g. the Internet). In the past, economically targeting green consumers required that there were fairly high concentrations of these consumers and/or appropriate distribution and communication networks to access them. However, the Internet allows environmentally focused organisations to globally target green consumers, without the need to develop extensive distribution and communication networks. In fact, environmentally oriented consumers may be better able to seek out such organisations. There are a number of companies available that assist marketers of green goods in going global through the Internet. For example, Ecomall is a company on the World Wide Web[2] which provides promotion for a diverse range of environmentally oriented organisations. The Ecomall website has company listings under 68 different product categories, ranging from air purification to wood products. In this way, organisations using the Internet may be able to target green consumers in an effective fashion that was previously unavailable. For green consumers, however, this may cause a dilemma, as it may be difficult to accurately validate information being provided by an unknown producer on the other side of the world.

In targeting green segments organisations should not overlook business-to-business (B2B) customers and/or governmental bodies, as these groups are also seeking to purchase less environmentally harmful products and processes. There is increasing internal and external pressure within organisations to adopt environmental purchasing behaviour (Drumwright 1994; Earl and Clift 1999; Polonsky et al. 1998) and, in fact, some governmental organisations and businesses have incorporated environmental characteristics into their buying criteria (Drumwright 1994; NCC 1999). Organisations that

2   www.ecomall.com/biz/

proactively seek out greener alternatives need to be assured of the product's environmental credentials and that the product is of an appropriate quality, as the cost of product failure for organisational buyers is high. That is, product failure could potentially force an entire organisation to temporarily stop operation. Thus, for organisational consumers, quality and performance concerns may in the short term prevent modifications to organisational purchasing behaviour. Research suggests that, traditionally, business consumers have generally had a somewhat poor perception of recycled or remanufactured goods (Earl and Clift 1999; Polonsky *et al.* 1998). Thus, marketers must ensure that, if this is the case, they can overcome incorrect and/or outdated perceptions of poor or low-quality products. As will be discussed in Section 15.3.5 on reverse logistics, the marketing of recycled and/or remanufactured goods may require the development of rigorous quality and testing procedures. These quality assurance procedures will be used to eliminate any actual risks to industrial consumers and may be used to assure industrial consumers about product quality to counter any perceived risks to the consumer.

## 15.3.2 Green pricing

Although green products are often priced higher than traditional goods, this does not always mean that they cost more, especially when one considers all the costs associated with green goods. What this means is that initial out-of-pocket expenses for green goods is frequently higher, but the long-term costs of these goods are lower. For example, over their life, long-life compact fluorescent light bulbs are substantially less expensive than traditional light bulbs. However, given the relatively long payback period, many consumers still do not purchase these more responsible alternatives because of the relatively expensive upfront costs. In addition, there is difficulty getting consumers to distinguish between the consumption of these goods and an investment in more energy-efficient (i.e. less environmentally harmful) lighting.

In some cases, it may be easier to demonstrate cost savings associated with less environmentally harmful alternatives. Take, for example, the less environmentally harmful Kyocera Ecosys laser printer discussed in the previous section. The Ecosys laser printer is competitively priced and uses less energy and toner than many other comparable products. Thus it is easy to demonstrate that it is less expensive than traditional products in both the long term and the short term (Cottam 1994).

Those traditional goods that harm the environment unfortunately are not priced to include all the environmental costs of their production. In most cases externalities associated with production and consumption are subsidised by society and result in lower prices for consumers. In contrast, less harmful products are not subsidised by society and all costs associated with their development are passed on to consumers, usually in the form of higher prices. Thus, in some cases, less environmentally harmful products may cost more in both the short term and the long term, without there being any additional financial return, even though there is an environmental return.

Although consumers' report they will pay more for less environmentally harmful products, practice and advanced research has found that they are actually only willing to pay a small price premium (Kapelianis and Strachan 1996). In addition, as mentioned above, they also expect these 'green' products to perform as well as 'traditional' goods. Although this expectation may be reasonable, it may not be possible for some of these new green goods to match the performance of environmentally harmful products because changing the composition of a product may reduce its performance (Schwepker and Cornwell 1991).

Green pricing is thus a complex process. For if organisations are 'selling' green goods they need to ensure that environmental value is important to consumers and that when this value is built into the price this practice is also communicated to consumers. Organisations may, however, find that through renting, contracting and leasing their products or services consumers can 'purchase' need satisfaction at a significantly lower price than they would when buying the assets associated with need satisfaction. Such a strategy may make 'marginal' green products and processes economically viable. In this way pricing becomes an important part of the marketing mix but may require significant changes within other organisational activities.

### 15.3.3 Green design and product development

The incorporation of environmental attributes into products and processes is something that needs to be undertaken during the initial stages of new product development (Bhat 1993). This is not a revolutionary idea, as organisations are increasingly realising that other issues, such as quality, also need to be designed in to products. The level of green design varies across organisations. In some cases, solving environmental problems has generated a whole industry of new products, technologies and services. For example, catalytic converters were developed to reduce automobile pollutants. This type of end-of-pipe solution is an important development, although it simply deals with an existing problem rather than addressing the cause of the problem. Alternatively, automobile manufacturers could have developed lighter cars with smaller, more efficient, engines. More radical technologies could have even been considered, which might have included the use of alternative power sources (i.e. non-petrol automobiles), or organisations might even have tried to reduce consumers' demand for automobiles. Toyota's project in Japan, described in Section 15.1, is a good example of two organisations (corporate and governmental) working together to develop complex, integrated solutions. Designing such programmes is, of course, more complex, as all relevant stakeholders (consumers, governmental bodies and organisations) need to work together to address the specific environmental problem (Lober 1997).

The design stage is critical for considering the environmental impact of a product and its associated production, with Ashley (1993) suggesting that decisions made during this stage contribute 70% of a product's environmental harm. As such, it is in the initial development stages that organisations need to ensure that environmental impacts be considered and minimised (Sharfman et al. 1997). One way that this can be addressed is through an LCA of a product's environmental impacts, where environmental aspects are considered at each stage of production, including pre-production and post-production (Oakley 1993). This approach frequently allows organisations to identify alternative methods of designing or producing goods. However, it may also be equally applicable to incorporate environmental criteria into the new development process, where certain technologies and processes are not even considered as environmentally viable; thus environmental factors become a core part of the research and development process. Regulations to phase out materials may partly motivate this shift in behaviour. For example, the possible future ban of lead in soldering has pushed many firms to develop new technologies within the electronics industry (Roos 1999); thus the process rather than the products change.

A fundamental question still needs to be asked, which is: 'Can new marketing processes be developed to satisfy consumers' needs?' This is an important question for, as was discussed above, it may not be necessary for consumers to purchase goods; rather, they might be able to purchase need-satisfying capacity and thus rent goods rather than purchase them (Belz 1999). This means that organisations need to rethink their activities. For example, it has been suggested that a shift in focus from selling the products themselves to selling the performance of the products (i.e. their need-satisfying capacities) may actually increase an organisation's return on investment (Belz 1999). However, these shifts require change not only on the part of the organisation but also on the part of consumers, as they too need to realise that their needs can be satisfied without their having to buy products. Bringing about organisational and consumer changes at the same time may be a difficult request. Thus, although most appropriate from an environmental design perspective, it may be more difficult in practice.

Designing less harmful 'traditional' products and processes may also require innovative thinking. Hoover's New Wave line of washing machines incorporated a number of innovations to improve environmental efficiency. The machines were designed so that they needed less water by using a redesigned water-injection system, and were also designed to be disassembled and thus be easier to repair and recycle. Finally, various components were designed to be less environmentally harmful: for example, machine cabinets were pre-coated rather than spray-painted (Roy 1999). This example highlights the integrated and complex process needed to design less environmentally harmful products. Some changes may be relatively minor; however, others require substantial engineering changes to the operation of the product and thus environmental issues need to be incorporated in the earliest design phases.

## 15.3.4 *Green positioning*

In some ways, green positioning is an issue that needs to be raised early on in an organisation's development. That is, what are its underlying environmental values and behaviours? Truly integrated green marketing organisations demonstrate strategic greening: that is, all activities and behaviours thoroughly incorporate environmental values into the organisation's decision-making processes such that it considers environmental criteria to be as important as, if not more important than, financial criteria. Such organisations are rare, although several organisations mentioned previously (i.e. The Body Shop [Section 15.3.1] and Blackmores [Section 15.1]) do attempt to adopt this environmental positioning.

Any organisation taking this stance must perform in accordance with these expectations and needs to be sure that all activities support this image. This is sometimes difficult and, in many cases, controlling all activities is beyond the organisation's control. For example, what happens if an appropriately environmentally responsible source of raw materials disappears? The organisation must either produce these inputs itself, find an equally acceptable alternative, stop producing the products requiring the input or select the next best environmental alternative. Unfortunately, the practicalities of most situations would result in the organisation selecting the next best environmental alternative, at least in the short term.

Any deviations from stated organisational values would usually generate extensive negative publicity, even if it were not within the organisation's control. As such, it often seems that organisations promoting themselves as performing in an environmentally responsible manner seem to be held to a higher standard than others who do not uphold the same values. This has resulted in some organisations undertaking strategic greening activities without using these for positioning purposes. Take the example of SC Johnson, which markets a diverse range of cleaning products. The company has as one of its core values a concern for the natural environment and has won environmental awards from the United Nations and the US Environmental Protection Agency (EPA).[3] However, in positioning its products this focus is not emphasised, even though it obtained competitive advantage in greening activities long before competitors. In contrast, The Body Shop incorporates its environmental image into its overall image and uses this to differentiate itself in the market.

### 15.3.5 The greening of logistics

Organisations traditionally have been concerned with moving goods to the consumer, which involves considering all aspects of transportation, wholesaling and retailing as well as moving materials from consumers back to manufacturers (i.e. reverse logistics). The physical movement of goods has been one of the first areas that organisations have focused on to minimise environmental costs, for in many cases this involves non-consumer-related changes. Consumers are not traditionally concerned with how products arrive at retailers but with whether they are available and in working order. Thus changes to shipping procedures, packaging and physical transportation are internal activities which do not extensively involve external consumers, even though these activities may significantly impact on organisations' other marketing activities, such as product design.

Some logistical changes may be as minor as the use of modified shipping packaging to reduce the raw materials used, which often also reduces the associated costs of distributing goods. For example, shipping pallets have become a valuable commodity, with the firms that produce them leasing them rather than selling them (Gooley 1996). These firms then collect, repair (when necessary) and redistribute the pallets, thus reducing environmental costs (i.e. no new trees are needed to produce pallets) and

---

3   SC Johnson (1999) www.scjohnson.com/welcome1.asp

financial costs (i.e. no new pallets need to be bought; Auguston 1996). In fact, retailers, wholesalers and even large industrial buyers realise that shipping materials have value and are developing processes to use these within their own organisation and to reprocess them for recycling (Glenn 1996).

Other initiatives, such as integrated transportation systems and even the use of the Internet, have reduced the overall environmental impact of transportation activities, as fewer modes of transportation are involved (Schegelmilch *et al.* 1995; Wu and Dunn 1995). Organisations can reduce the number of intermediaries and thus reduce the length of distribution networks, which frequently reduces the overall negative environmental impact of transportation as well (Campbell and Green 1999).

However, the most complex advances are in the area of reverse logistics, where organisations have chosen or been forced to move packaging and used goods from the consumer back to the producer (Tibben-Lembke 1998). The regulatory push to take back packaging started in the early 1990s in Germany (*Economist* 1993; Micklitz 1992). These requirements have expanded to require firms to take back unwanted or obsolete products as well. For example, according to the ETMUEL project,[4] European countries have developed a range of requirements relating to waste from electrical and electronic equipment (WEEE). At the time of writing, there were no consistent EU-wide regulations and member countries had varying requirements for producers to collect unwanted goods or subsidise the cost of these goods' collection, although in some countries these costs were shared by firms, consumers and local government.

However, reverse logistics is not simply a legislated activity that places costs on organisations, it is also a flow of inputs to production, as well as a flow of 'goods' to new customers. In this way, organisations can turn 'returned' goods into major cash flows. For example, Xerox reprocesses parts from returned machines; it uses them either to repair other machines or to remanufacture photocopiers for further marketing (Ottman 1997b). Executives at Fuji-Xerox's Australian remanufacturing plant have suggested that this process has generated financial returns in the order of tens of millions of dollars. As such, reverse logistics is not a cost but is an opportunity to generate additional revenue and recover valuable assets, thereby reducing waste, parts and improving performance (Ayres *et al.* 1997), although there are also substantial costs involved with reverse logistics and asset recovery management. Organisations need to develop comprehensive testing procedures to ensure remanufactured products (or recovered components) meet appropriate performance standards. Without developing such procedures organisations risk marketing substandard products, which would adversely affect brand image and thus long-term profitability of new and remanufactured goods.

Integrated reverse logistics requires extensive commitment in terms of strategic focus as well as in terms of financial and human resources. If it is done well, it is a strategic activity requiring extensive changes to organisational processes. Giuntini and Andel (1995) suggest that once organisations have decided to undertake reverse logistics they must consider six Rs (recognition, recovery, review, renewal, removal, re-engineering) when developing strategies and processes to facilitate reverse logistics activities.

4    See Chapter 5, footnote 7, page 112.

● Recognition involves the acknowledgement of the receipt of goods from customers. This requires that there is a monitoring system in place to ensure that all goods flow through the reverse logistics process effectively.

● Recovery is the physical collection of goods for reprocessing to ensure that they are received in good order. For example, when remanufacturing toner cartridges Fuji-Xerox has one channel through which they deliver cartridges to customers and at the same time collect used cartridges for reprocessing.

● Review of materials collected is needed as they will be in various conditions. For example, at Fuji-Xerox they have developed a complete testing system to evaluate whether materials received meet appropriate standards for remanufacturing. Defective goods might be disassembled for component parts or disposed of responsibly.

● Renewal of the goods is sometimes necessary, which may involve reprocessing or remanufacturing. This may mean remanufacturing the product up to its original standards, reclaiming appropriate parts for re-use, or redesigning the product for some other use. It is essential that products are brought up to an appropriate standard, for if they become 'second-quality' goods it could adversely effect the overall image of the company, even if they are branded differently from the company's 'main' line.

● Removal of materials may be necessary. There must be processes in place to dispose of materials that cannot be remanufactured; there may, in fact, be new types of hazardous waste that must be dealt with. In addition, there must be systems and processes in place that market the remanufactured goods to new or existing customers.

● Re-engineering is needed to evaluate how existing goods are produced to identify if they can be designed better. This process should be ongoing, for advances in technology will be taking place both in the initial manufacturing process and in the remanufacturing process. For example, Fuji-Xerox actually found that processes used to remanufacture some components resulted in them outperforming 'original' parts and, thus, they modified the manufacture of the original parts as well.

Green logistics is becoming a substantially more complex strategy but one that provides unique opportunities for organisations. The commitment of organisations to greening their activities, as well as their position within product value chains, may determine the organisation's ability to undertake activities that develop less environmentally harmful logistics. In cases where they do not have the ability or motivation to undertake reverse logistics, organisations may rely on marketing waste, which is discussed next.

## 15.3.6 The marketing of waste

The previous section discussed reverse logistics, where organisations reprocess packaging and products that are no longer needed by consumers. The marketing of waste is sometimes considered to be a different activity, where organisations have products composed of materials they may not be able to reprocess or of materials not traditionally considered to have value. This perspective is incorrect and needs to be changed, for as was discussed in the previous section organisations need to identify how they can recover value from all 'assets', even 'waste'. That is, waste is a product of organisational activities and, like all products, has value (Reynnells 1999). At the most basic level, organisations frequently attempt to develop internal processes that either reduce waste, which improves efficiency, or reprocess their own waste for internal consumption (Ottman 1993). Thus, the marketing of waste may be a precursor to developing reverse logistics or to the redesigning of products and processes to recover the value in 'waste'.

However, in some cases existing technologies are not sufficient to enable waste products to be processed for original use. For example, there are presently no approved technologies that enable sewage to be reprocessed into potable drinking water. The technologies are in place, however, that allow initial treatment of sewage, though to a non-potable standard, which is then used for industrial and commercial purposes (e.g. for watering fairways at golf clubs or tree plantations, with the biosolids used as fertiliser).

In other cases, new markets are developed for waste, which might even involve waste suppliers being customers for the processed waste. For example, in the USA, some wineries pay to have their post-production waste collected, which is then processed and bought by the supplying wineries as fertiliser (Tom 1999). It might also be possible to find new markets for waste, which is how traditional consumer recycling works at the most basic level. In other cases, waste products are used as inputs into other production processes or as completely new products. For example, there have been experiments in the use and marketing of compost as a natural, agricultural pest-control product (Segall 1995).

The marketing of waste is a strategic green marketing activity for the organisation marketing these new goods and may in fact be their sole reason for existing. For example, some Australian councils have banded together to form co-operatives to market waste and achieve economies of scale that make recycling practices economically viable (NCC 1999). For those supplying the waste, marketing that waste is most probably tactical green marketing at best, unless the organisations involved change the way in which they operate (i.e. the collection of waste within the organisation is modified to meet specific standards). For example, the wineries who sell the waste and then buy back the processed fertiliser might be consider to be greener than organisations who simply 'sell' their waste to another organisation that then reprocesses it.

## 15.3.7 *The greening of promotion*[5]

The promotional alternatives available to organisations are increasing and many organisations still seem to be communicating substantive and superficial information (Drumwright 1996). One of the most difficult issues to address concerns what environmental information should be communicated and how it should be communicated (Shrum *et*

5 The term 'promotion' is used in the broadest sense and includes advertising, sales promotions (i.e. competitions, cause-related marketing), personal selling and publicity.

*al.* 1995). In answering this question organisations must have something environmentally worthwhile and meaningful to 'talk about'. Much of the criticism of green marketing has arisen because much of what originally was communicated had little, if any, relevant environmental meaning or because the information provided was not clearly understood by consumers (Carlson *et al.* 1996b; Davis 1994; Mohr *et al.* 1998). As mentioned in the introductory section, green hype, or 'greenwash'—broad-based, meaningless statements—was used extensively in the early 1980s (Easterling *et al.* 1996; Carlson *et al.* 1996b), although this superficial tactical greening is no longer appropriate, nor are consumers or regulators willing to accept it.

Organisations need to consider what types of things consumers perceive to be environmental information and what environmental information consumers will actually understand (Mohr *et al.* 1998). The US EPA has suggested that environmental information needs to educate consumers, to enable them to make more effective decisions (EPA 1999). Although this seems reasonable, one might ask whether this is the domain of marketers and whether giving them the information will simply result in information overload on the part of consumers (Kangun and Polonsky 1995). Some activities may require extensive integrated communication from multiple sources. For example, getting consumers to switch from buying a car to participating in an integrated transportation system would require extensive long-term communication. This will only be possible if firms and governmental bodies adopt strategic greening, such that there is a shift both in corporate activities and in governmental expenditure.

As suggested in the introductory text, many organisations are realising that green promotional campaigns are generally becoming less effective and are shifting to promoting environmental attributes in addition to other product and organisational attributes. Although most people think about advertising when discussing green marketing, there are other promotional tools that are being used. For example, there are a growing number of environmental sponsorships and cause-related marketing programmes where organisations give money to environmental causes and then promote this fact (Mendleson and Polonsky 1995). It is questionable whether such programmes will be effective, especially if they are seen to be unrelated to an organisation's core marketing activities or unrelated to environmental issues related to the product or organisation (as in the case of the jeans manufacturer, discussed in Section 15.2). In addition some recent research suggests that the success of these programmes varies across consumer types and thus may have little impact on the specific market targeted if the consumers in question are not positively disposed to these types of appeal (Webb and Mohr 1998). Thus, all green promotional activities need to be carefully developed and evaluated, and organisations need to be sure that these programmes result in some meaningful environmental benefit and that they are not simply opening themselves up to criticism for promulgating greenwash.

When using green promotion there is also some debate as to whether green appeals actually work at all in changing all consumers' preferences (Mohr *et al.* 1998; Shrum *et al.* 1995). Work by Schuhwerk and Lefkoff-Hagius (1995) suggested that environmentally oriented consumers are not influenced by environmental claims as they have extensive understanding and knowledge of the issues being discussed. However, non-environmentally oriented consumers did not have extensive information and used these claims to evaluate organisational performance. However, others, such as Manrai *et al.* (1997), found that there was some generally positive effect when green claims were used. As such, the overall benefit of using green claims might be questionable, especially if there is any chance that these claims might be deemed to be misleading or superficial.

Green promotion needs to communicate some substantive environmental information to consumers in a way that is meaningful (Carlson *et al.* 1996b). As such, it must be linked with some organisational activity or it will probably be an ineffective tool if used on its own. Thus, promoting some real environmental attribute of a product, service or organisation requires a change in the product, production process or organisational focus. However, these changes need not be strategic in nature; they may be tactical activities, such as engaging in relevant environmental sponsorships or carrying out minor product modifications (i.e. reducing the packaging content or shifting to post-consumer recycled packaging material). Of course, there is the risk that consumers might identify such tactical activities as such and thus may discount their use.

## 15.3.8 Green alliances

As discussed in the previous sections, the greening of marketing activities is complex. Unfortunately, it is unclear whether organisations, especially those that operate for profit, have all the necessary expertise to implement green tactics and strategies within their core activities and/or more traditional marketing activities (Polonsky and Ottman 1998). Environmental groups can be invaluable in assisting organisations in understanding the issues, in developing appropriate solutions and in implementing associated strategies and tactics across a diverse range of functions, not just marketing (Crane 1998; Hartman and Stafford 1998; Lober 1997). Given the multi-dimensional scope of many environmental issues they might only be comprehensively addressed when all relevant stakeholder groups are involved in developing and implementing the solution (Lober 1997).

Extensive research has discussed green alliances (Crane 1998; Hartman and Stafford 1997, 1998; Hartman *et al.* 1999; Lober 1997; Mendleson and Polonsky 1995; Polonsky and Ottman 1998; Stafford and Hartman 1996; Westley and Vredenburg 1991). In short, these works all suggest that green alliance partners can assist in organisations to address and/or incorporate environmental issues within their activities. That is, they can assist organisations of all types in developing less environmentally harmful products by identifying new approaches, products and processes that will enable the organisation to better address various environmental issues by adopting a more responsible philosophy (Polonsky and Ottman 1998). Green groups can assist organisations marketing waste and developing green logistics systems by identifying uses for the materials or assist the organisation in improving production processes (Hartman and Stafford 1998). Environmental alliance partners can improve the quality of communication as well as give it more credibility (Crane 1998; Mendleson and Polonsky 1995). They can also be used to target specific environmental segments of the community, as their membership base can be tapped as a potential market (Mendleson and Polonsky 1995; Westley and Vredenburg 1991).

Although environmental groups can add value to all activities, organisations have frequently had difficulty opening themselves to these new ideas, especially from outside sources. There are several approaches that can be used to include these external stakeholders. These include: formally 'hiring' environmental experts as consultants; forming roundtables from a diverse range of expert interest groups; developing citizen panels involving local constituents; or holding consensus conferences that involve firms, consumers, governmental bodies and other stakeholders (Polonsky and Ottman 1998; Zöller 1999).

However, working through green alliances does not come without potential problems. For, in many cases, these groups have different objectives from those of their organisational partner, which may impact on the organisation's ability to achieve outcomes (Hartman *et al.* 1999). An environmental group's value is not only in its expertise but also in its image. Thus it is unrealistic to expect these groups to simply 'toe the corporate line'. Any problems that arise from the alliance not only reduce organisational benefits from working with these groups but tarnish the group's image, which may negatively impact on their ability to achieve their long-term objectives (Westley and Vredenburg 1991). Green groups may therefore be hesitant to work with organisations that seek to achieve only tactical green outcomes, unless in doing so the green group believes that its own longer-term interests are also being achieved. For example, a tactical programme may raise the profile of the group or issue well beyond what could be achieved by the group alone (Mendleson and Polonsky 1995).

Although green alliances may be an effective method of achieving green marketing outcomes, these alliances may take more time and effort to develop than traditional business-to-business (B2B) alliances (Milne *et al.* 1996). In addition, organisations have traditionally been hesitant to involve external groups, especially environmental groups, which may obtain access to internal information (Polonsky and Ottman 1998). As such, there may need to be a shift in organisational thinking, as well as environmental group thinking, which will enable alliances to develop effective green marketing outcomes.

## 15.4 Implications for green marketing

The previous sections have identified that green marketing has come of age as a sophisticated marketing tool. However, to be used effectively it requires an integrated approach that involves extensive co-ordination across functional areas within the organisation (Carlson *et al.* 1996a). This includes functions that 'produce' the organisation's products, those traditionally marketed and those traditionally considered not to have value (i.e. 'waste') as well as strategic units within the organisation that shapes its direction and thus determine whether greening issues are to be strategic, quasi-strategic or tactical in nature. In addition, there needs to be more input from other functional areas, such as marketing, that are frequently not as actively involved in environmental strategic decision-making as they should be. Thus environmental issues are not simply the domain of an environmental management unit but should become a focus or at least be considered by all functional areas.

The level of greening—strategic, quasi-strategic and tactical—dictates exactly what underlying activities need to be undertaken. Strategic greening within one area may or may not be effectively leveraged in other areas. For example, organisations may make substantial changes in production processes but might choose not to leverage these innovations by positioning the organisation as an environmental leader. As such, 'strategic greening' is not necessarily strategically integrated into all marketing activities but is nevertheless strategic green marketing within the product area. From an organisational perspective this is not problematic and such a decision may make good marketing sense, for organisations that purport to be environmental stewards are sometimes criticised more than other 'traditional' organisations. Thus, some organisations may choose to limit their exposure, even though they have shifted to sustainable activities.

In contrast, tactical greening in promotions might involve minimal, if any, greening of other areas but, rather, might be used purely to exploit a short-term opportunity. For example, an organisation might simply choose to sponsor a local environmental programme without modifying its other activities. Although this may be an 'effective' strategy from a broader perspective, it is not necessarily effective from a green marketing perspective. If consumers are sceptical of the organisation's motives, such sponsorships could actually backfire. Publicity generated in relation to a given environmental sponsorship may in fact make consumers more critical of the organisation's other less environmentally friendly activities.

The overriding implication is that organisations need to ensure that all green marketing activities are integrated across functional areas, especially if they are used for positioning or promotional activities. In this way, organisations should not over-emphasise their actions, as organisational exaggerations may have unanticipated negative consequences. However, it is not necessary for organisations to actively promote all green marketing activities. Although from a strategic perspective this may seem to be ignoring opportunities, careful evaluation of overall organisational activities might identify that such opportunities are illusionary (i.e. not all activities support the same environmental focus).

Problems associated with a non-integrated green marketing approach have occurred in the past. Take, for example, the case of 'biodegradable' rubbish sacks. Hefty spent vast sums developing and marketing these bags. Although the claims were technically true, on closer inspection it was soon realised that conditions within landfills would not allow decomposition to occur (Jay 1990). The result was an extensive public backlash against this product and the firm's other products. In addition, several US states actually sued Hefty for misleading advertising (Lawrence 1991). The problem was not that Hefty had 'lied' but that they had exaggerated their claim. Well-intentioned green marketing activities failed to generate the desired outcomes and, in fact, resulted in a financial loss as well as a loss in corporate credibility because of over-zealous tactical green promotion.

The complex nature of environmental issues associated with green marketing requires that an organisation progress only after it has carefully considered all potential ramifications. Some 'dos' and 'don'ts' of green marketing are provided in Box 15.1. These are based

**DO:**

- Use strategic green marketing as an opportunity to consider innovative ways of satisfying customers' needs
- Identify both the short-term and long-term implications of adopting specific green marketing activities
- Understand what is necessary to develop integrated green marketing activities, at whatever level—strategic, quasi-strategic or tactical
- Expect strategic green marketing to be a long-term, ongoing process

**DON'T:**

- Think that all types of green marketing, especially tactical marketing, will generate extensive competitive advantages, at least not in the short term
- Allow marketing hype to overemphasise the true impact of your green marketing activities
- Think that once you make changes the organisation can relax, as green marketing requires continual improvements
- Try to push green initiatives in your organisation simply on emotional grounds; rather, communicate in the language of business, as in the long term both environmental and business benefits can be obtained

*Box* 15.1  **Some 'dos' and 'don'ts' of green marketing**

on examples discussed in the popular press and in the green marketing literature. However, they are by no means meant to reflect all activities associated with green marketing but rather to identify some critical issues that need to be considered.

## 15.5  Conclusions

Green marketing is a complex tool which has evolved substantially since its was first used in the early 1970s primarily to target environmentally oriented consumers. Organisations have now moved to developing integrated green marketing activities involving cross-functional areas within the organisation and sometimes even involve external bodies as well (i.e. other for-profit organisations, non-profit organisations or governmental agencies). Organisations have moved beyond simply targeting green consumers and recognise that the greening of activities is an essential strategy no matter whom they target and provides a competitive advantage within the marketplace.

This shift in thinking has also resulted in some organisations questioning their core activities, with some realising that they can satisfy customer needs without 'selling' them goods but rather by purchasing or renting want-satisfying capabilities. This shift involves organisations broadening their view of creating organisational value, such that they also attempt to minimise the negative impact that all aspects of organisation–consumer exchanges have on the natural environment. Thus, organisations have rethought all aspects of their activities, ranging from the initial phases of strategic planning to the final stages of actually satisfying consumers' needs, and all activities in between. The natural environment needs to be considered a core component of this exchange process and not something that 'exists' outside of it (Starik 1995). As such, consumer needs are not the sole focus of organisational activities; instead the focus is on satisfying consumer needs while making a profit and ensuring that organisational activities are sustainable and do not cause environmental harm.

Innovative organisations choosing to adopt a strategic environmental marketing focus need to continually re-evaluate and improve their overall performance, as they would with any activity. This is necessary, as knowledge and acceptable environmental practices are continually changing. Thus, when adopting a strategic green marketing philosophy there is no room for complacency. Unfortunately, such a focus requires extensive commitment in terms of resources and top-management support, which may be difficult to maintain, especially in times of broader turbulence within the business environment.

Organisations expecting short-term results may be less committed to making the necessary changes to achieve substantive change and thus will be less likely to maintain a strategic green approach to green marketing. Therefore, green marketing is like any worthwhile strategic activity requiring a change in organisational thinking and, as such, takes time, commitment and resources before meaningful results are achieved. Organisational greening is an imperative for organisations, whether they are for profit, non-profit or not-for-profit or are governmental. Organisations that 'go green' usually have a first-mover advantage over those that do not do so and, if appropriately implemented, greening activities should improve an organisation's environmental performance and its profitability.

# Part 3
# CASE STUDIES

# MAXIMISING ENVIRONMENTAL QUALITY THROUGH ECOREDESIGN™

*John Gertsakis*
RMIT University, Australia

Demonstrating how the design process can integrate environmental factors within a commercial context is a critical step towards reconfiguring the psyche of product designers, engineers, companies, educators and students. It can also directly articulate that ecodesign or design for environment (DfE) does not have to result in inferior, odd or undesirable products plagued by clichéd colours, textures and forms.

Internationally, the demonstration or 'do, show and tell' approach to ecodesign has helped shorten and steepen the learning curve for designers and the companies who rely on them. With support from governments, research institutions and industry associations, countries such as the Netherlands, Norway and Denmark have aimed to encourage greater enthusiasm and more on-the-ground action ahead of policy and regulatory change that, without this proactive approach, would leave industry floundering.

An essential objective of demonstration programmes is to assist individual companies with the know-how required to design greener products with reduced life-cycle environmental impacts. Ensuring that the products move beyond slick renderings and glossy models is paramount as is the need to blend a stronger design and environmental philosophy into company culture and into the mind-set of key decision-makers involved in product development. Documenting the entire process and generating information materials for dissemination to the broader design community directly fulfils the demonstration objective. 'How to' manuals, design guides, videos and computer software collectively provide first-hand knowledge, methods and guidelines based on specific product case studies and real-life commercial experiences.

In Australia, the national Centre for Design (CfD) at the Royal Melbourne Institute of Technology (RMIT) operates a national demonstration initiative known as the EcoReDesign™ programme.[1] EcoReDesign™ provides Australian companies with design support and

1 EcoReDesign™ is a registered trademark of the Centre for Design at RMIT University, Melbourne, Australia.

environmentally related research and development (R&D) to help ensure that greener products reach the market in Australia and overseas. The EcoReDesign™ programme was funded by the commonwealth government through Environment Australia as well as EcoRecycle Victoria, the New South Wales Environment Protection Authority and the now-defunct Energy Research and Development Corporation. Over the past few years, ecodesign work with seven companies has been documented with a view to producing a comprehensive EcoReDesign™ information kit for those involved in product design and development. The kit includes a video and a detailed 'how to' manual explaining the process and discussing case studies based on the products, people and companies involved in the programme. Interviews with company executives, designers and environmental specialists combine with images and data to illustrate the products before, during and after the EcoReDesign™ process. Some examples are given in Box 16.1.

- Axis electric kettle by Kambrook Pty Ltd (commercialised): ecodesign features include improved energy efficiency, materials consolidation and identification and a design that facilitates disassembly and recycling (see Plate 16.1).
- Dishlex dishwasher by Email Major Appliances Ltd (commercialised): ecodesign features include improved energy efficiency, reduced water consumption, reduced materials consumption and 'lightweighting', materials consolidation and identification and a design that facilitates disassembly and recycling (see Plate 16.2).
- Swap Shop business vending machine by Zoom Systems Pty Ltd (commercialised): ecodesign features include reduced materials consumption and 'lightweighting', improved energy efficiency, a facility for the return of used toner cartridges and the use of communications technology to optimise restocking (see Plate 16.3).
- Eco Packaging range by Blackmores Pty Ltd (advanced prototypes and patented designs): ecodesign features include reduced materials consumption and 'lightweighting', long-life and durable outer packaging with disposable primary packaging film (see Plate 16.4).
- Eco Vend cold drinks machine by NIDA Technology Group Pty Ltd (limited production currently under trial): ecodesign features include reduced materials consumption and 'lightweighting', improved energy efficiency, use of communications technology to optimise restocking and improved security to minimise vandalism and extend operational life.
- Water-conserving shower head by Caroma Industries Ltd (detailed design and working prototypes): ecodesign features include improved energy efficiency, reduced water consumption and reduced materials consumption and 'lightweighting' (see Plate 16.5).
- HOTdesk™ workstation system by Schiavello Commercial Interiors Pty Ltd (limited production): ecodesign features include reduced materials consumption and 'lightweighting', materials consolidation and identification and a design that facilitates disassembly and recycling and that accommodates changing work practices and emerging information technology (see Plate 16.6).

For more detailed information about these EcoReDesign™ case studies and other projects and research at the Centre for Design (CfD), go to the CfD website: www.cfd.RMIT.edu.au.

*Box* 16.1 **EcoReDesign™ products**

*Plate* 16.1  **Kambrook Axis electric kettle: reducing energy consumption by insulating design features**

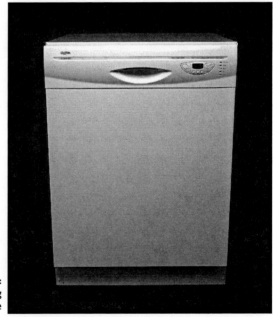

*Plate* 16.2  **Dishlex Global dishwasher: energy-efficient, water-conserving and recyclable**

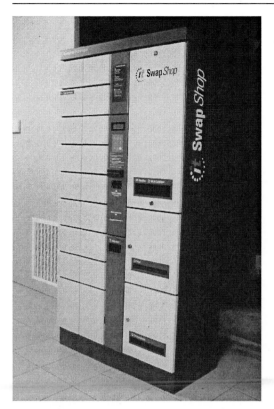

*Plate* 16.3 **Swap Shop vending machine: dematerialising the retail process and maximising energy efficiency**

*Plate* 16.4 **Blackmores Eco Packaging: optimising re-usability and lightweighting**

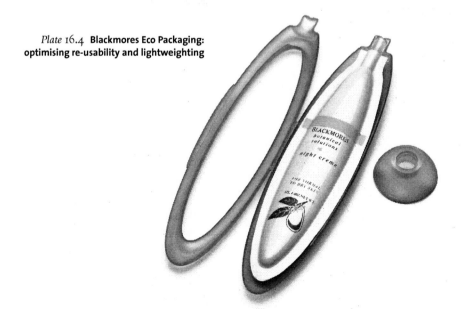

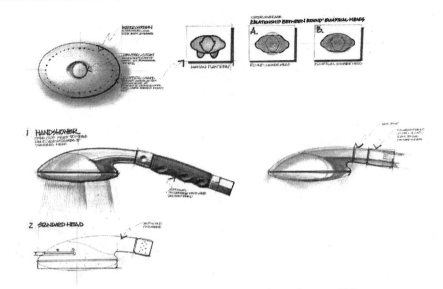

*Plate* 16.5 **Low-flow showerhead: maximising water conservation and energy efficiency**

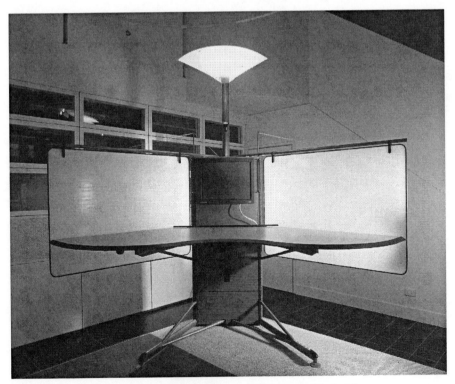

*Plate* 16.6 **HOTdesk™ workstation: reconfigurable, recyclable and overall materials
consolidation and minimisation**

Many lessons were learned during the development and implementation phase of the EcoReDesign™ programme (phase 1). One of the main observations was need to support small and medium-sized enterprises (SMEs) to adopt and apply ecodesign. During the process of inviting Australian companies to join the first phase of the EcoReDesign™ programme (involving Email Major Appliances and Kambrook, and others; see Box 16.1) there was a considerable wave of interest shown by smaller companies. This resulted in the development of the EcoReDesign™ 2 Industry Assistance programme which involved 14 Australian companies and essentially applied the preliminary steps of the EcoReDesign™ methodology (i.e. ideas workshops, streamlined life-cycle assessment [LCA], ecodesign brief development, limited concept designs and other environmental improvement recommendations). The programme concluded in 1999 and a series of case studies are soon to be released via the CfD's website (the address is given at the foot of Box 16.1). This process proved successful with manufacturers and retailers, spanning products such as:

- Office furniture
- Glass, plastic and cardboard packaging for wine
- Carpet and flooring products
- Biodegradable packaging for personal care products
- Textiles for office partitions and seating
- Packaging for pharmaceuticals
- Refilling systems for cosmetics and body care

The business benefits for most of the companies have been directly proportional to the energy, enthusiasm and investment of each of the companies: that is, the more committed to ecodesign the participant, the greater the commercial and public relations outcome for that participant. In free advertising terms alone, virtually all of the companies attracted significant and very positive attention from all sectors of the Australian media. The EcoReDesign™ approach seemed to capture the imagination of journalists, writers and editors across Australia, with numerous features appearing in the major daily papers, segments on television lifestyle programmes and seemingly never-ending radio interviews to hear more about 'green' kettles and 'squeaky' green dishwashers. At the harder end of the balance sheet, those companies that progressed the designs through to commercialisation seem to have outperformed most of their competitors in the same price bracket, especially the Dishlex dishwashers and the Zoom Systems business vending machine (Box 16.1).

Another indirect benefit has been the comprehensive yet informal training and re-education of the designers, engineers and marketers in the participating EcoReDesign™ companies, all of whom experienced one-on-one guidance and support on ecodesign methods and tools, including on the role and judicious application of LCA. This in-house professional development focused on ecodesign translated into a direct investment in building up company knowledge and capabilities in an area that is set to become more and more valued by executives, shareholders, investors and consumers. There is no doubt that the EcoReDesign™ programme in both phases provided a high level of 'on-site' training for all company personnel involved.

The following case study illustrates the design and development of the Dishlex dishwasher range, providing a glimpse of what can be achieved through a collaborative process that adopts the environment as a critical design focus.

## 16.1 EcoReDesign™ case study: an ecologically advanced dishwasher

### 16.1.1 Background, drivers and key players

While many appliance manufacturers are actively addressing environmental issues, Email Major Appliances (EMA), Australia's largest manufacturer and distributor of white goods, has taken the lead in terms of innovation and environmental performance. EMA owns a range of appliance brands in Australia, including Dishlex, Simpson, Chef, Kelvinator and Hoover. EMA's products are market leaders in Australia, with the Dishlex brand dominating the local dishwasher market.

Energy efficiency has been a key driver of new appliance design over the past decade, but water efficiency has also emerged as an important factor in appliances such as dishwashers and washing machines. The presence and consumer popularity of Australian eco-labels for energy-using and water-using products has reinforced the importance of ensuring appliance design strives for high levels of efficiency as a way of remaining competitive. Although Australia's overall performance on minimising greenhouse gas emissions has been relatively low, there are significant pockets of company activity that seek to minimise energy use through the design and production of energy-efficient products. EMA is such a company.

EMA joined the EcoReDesign™ programme to enhance its existing expertise in dishwasher design and therefore realise the commercialisation of an ecologically advanced dishwasher. It was a unique opportunity for EMA to collaborate with a national research centre in pursuit of sustainable product development and corporate environmental responsibility. EMA responded quickly to adverts inviting Australian companies to join the CfD at RMIT's EcoReDesign™ programme.

### 16.1.2 The partnership and the EcoReDesign™ process

The collaboration between EMA and the CfD received the right approval from the outset. EMA executive management endorsed the joint project and thus provided clear and direct signals for all other staff (both within the company and at the CfD) that the EcoReDesign™ project was to be taken seriously at the company. The majority of subsequent activities involved EMA's product development team and ecodesign researchers from RMIT, but the demonstration of executive commitment was always a positive presence in the project. The team involved with the project is given in Box 16.2.

## Team

- **Manufacturer:**
  - Email Major Appliances Ltd (EMA), Australia
- **Core product development team, from EMA:**
  - Rick Boykett, research and development manager
  - Clinton Graham, business manager, dishwashers
  - Peter Riddell, design engineer
  - John Schmidli, design engineer
  - Simon Coultas, group product development manager
- **Core product development team, from the Centre for Design at RMIT:**
  - John Gertsakis, acting director
  - Helen Lewis, former programme manager
  - Chris Ryan, international projects director
  - Henry Okraglik, former associate director
  - Andrew Sweatman, former research assistant
- **Other RMIT associates involved in the project:**
  - Mark Armstrong, Blue Sky Design
  - Alan Pears, Sustainable Solutions
  - Deni Greene, Deni Greene Consulting
  - Edward Kosior, RMIT Polymer Technology Centre

## Awards received

- **1998 Galaxy Award for Innovation in Energy Efficiency**
  - 1997 Australian Design Award
  - 1998 Mingays Industry Awards: Best New Appliance

*Box* 16.2 **The EcoReDesign™ Dishlex project: the team, and awards won**

Streamlined knowledge-transfer underpinned the collaboration rather than a client–consultant relationship. EMA's design office was often a second home to RMIT researchers, and EMA designers, engineers and marketers freely sought input and advice about 'environmental' questions in general. Questions, queries and open discussion were encouraged at all times, with no request considered too trivial. Over the duration of the dishwasher project, this philosophy created a climate of great professional cohesion between parties and also led to increasing enthusiasm for the project's environmental aspects and the desire to meet and beat best available technologies of the day.

The CfD introduced a range of tools, approaches and skills to the EMA Dishlex product development team. These are discussed in more detail in RMIT's EcoReDesign™ manual, 'Good Design, Better Business, Cleaner World: A Guide to EcoReDesign™' (RMIT 1997). Many of the standard tools were applied, albeit in a streamlined process that exploited the notion of ecodesign 'champions' within the company. So, although technical approaches to ecodesign were critical, their application and resultant output was heavily determined by the extent to which individuals and teams at EMA were empowered and encouraged to engage with the priorities and imperatives associated with the broad objective of achieving environmentally oriented product development. People were always considered to be a key element in achieving ecodesign success and thus relationships within the collaborative process were fostered. The haphazard pursuit of ecodesign principles and specification of benign or recyclable materials in isolation, without the will to break unproductive and environmentally indifferent attitudes to product development, rarely generates sustainable outcomes.

Brainstorming workshops and ideas sessions took place throughout the dishwasher project, as did experimentation with ecodesign strategies related to energy and water efficiency, the production of toxic substances and recyclability; importantly, their use was enhanced through the nurturing of individual aptitude and group dynamics. LCA, design for disassembly and recycling and materials specialists were also accessed through the EcoReDesign™ programme, enabling EMA to incorporate the latest thinking on how and when recycled polymers could be used and also how these materials and components could be recovered at end of life.

Streamlined LCA also played a meaningful role in benchmarking and quantifying environmental performance and improvements and was also important in highlighting the benefits of following one design strategy or material type over another. It needs to be stressed that the LCA results were carefully communicated to all team members (technical and non-technical) in a way that avoided using LCA as a powerful sedative. The EcoReDesign™ process always reinforced the role of LCA as a useful support tool as opposed to an essential tool in its own right. LCA for LCA's sake does not result in environmentally improved products! Beware LCA practitioners who are blind to other approaches! Having said this, an environmental assessment of existing Dishlex dish-washers conducted early in the process highlighted the key areas in need of environmental redesign. More importantly, it provided specific performance targets and parameters to guide the design team in its focus on maximising the energy and water efficiency of the dishwasher in operation. Global policy trends in waste avoidance, resource recovery and other market intelligence suggested that attention to design for recycling should also be actively pursued. This substantial body of research undertaken through the EcoReDesign™ programme provided EMA with specific environmental knowledge and data.

Application of ecodesign in the Dishlex project was akin to a strategic product development process; the focus was not on specific details such as how to redesign a dishwasher pump. EMA's in-house product developers were extremely well equipped on the design and engineering front and thus were very productive when provided with specific ecodesign targets or objectives. For example, the EcoReDesign™ dishwasher brief aimed to communicate ideal and optimum end-point scenarios by specifying ecodesign considerations, 'no- or low-cost' objectives and other strategies related to how various control panel designs might facilitate consumers to maximise their dishwasher's eco-performance. Nowhere in the brief was it stipulated that 'the designer shall not specify an "exotic" polymer under any circumstances' or 'the designer must at every opportunity design components to save energy even if it results in a dishwasher that fails to effectively wash dishes' and so on.

It should also be noted that the EcoReDesign™ project was a mutual learning experience; much was learned from EMA by RMIT researchers and associates, especially in relation to how the ecodesign process relates to the production process and supply chain management issues. What became acutely apparent was how superficial the general rhetoric of ecodesign (especially guidelines and principles) can be in a real-life exercise governed by design targets, available technologies, R&D budgets, supplier constraints and the associated time-lines. The lessons learned span both RMIT's position to further develop and refine its EcoReDesign™ methodology as well as EMA's capacity to apply newly discovered and acquired ecodesign and LCA knowledge, not to mention insights into and independent analysis of their competitors' environmental progress.

The eco-redesigned Dishlex dishwashers represent a new benchmark in energy and water efficiency. It is staggering to think that, if the new Dishlex Global 500 were to replace every dishwasher in current use in Australia, approximately 10 billion litres of water could be saved per annum; and 700,000 tonnes of carbon dioxide emission would be cut per annum (see Plate 16.2).

Product features enabling such environmental improvements include:

- A six-star energy rating: the highest rating ever achieved by an Australian-designed and -manufactured 14-place dishwasher; actual energy consumption is 256 kWh on the most efficient wash programme[2]

- Wash programmes compatible with enzyme-based detergents, making low-temperature cycles highly efficient at cleaning while using minimal energy

- An AAA water-conservation rating: the highest rating ever achieved by an Australian-designed and -manufactured dishwasher; actual water consumption is 17.9 l on the most efficient wash programme

- A four-stage, stainless steel, microfiltration system, which contributes to using less water more efficiently

A list of awards won by the dishwasher is given in Box 16.2.

The Dishlex Global range has also integrated a suite of waste-avoidance and resource-recovery features directly aimed at using materials more intelligently from the outset as well as keeping discarded dishwashers out of landfill when they reach end of life. The following Dishlex features increase the possibility of cost-effective recycling:

- Major components are designed for easier disassembly and recycling.

- Plastic components are coded to enable easier identification during disassembly, sorting and recycling.

- Fewer material types are used, increasing recycling efficiencies.

- Waste avoidance is achieved through greater material efficiencies (i.e. the new dishwashers are on average 7 kg lighter than previous EMA models).

2   Actual energy use and running cost will depend on the programme used, water connection and the cost of hot water. Energy consumption of some competitors ranges from 273–330 kWh.

Furthermore, EMA have recently completed a pilot 'take-back' study to further develop their product stewardship policies.

## 16.1.3  Difficulties in hindsight

The Dishlex dishwasher exercise was by far one of the most successful EcoReDesign™ projects in terms of achieving the desired ecodesign outcomes and in terms of the continuing commercial returns the company is experiencing. The fact that the product was commercialised is a major achievement, as is the acknowledgement that has come through design and environmental awards given by the Australian design community, by the white goods industry and by government. The Global range of Dishlex dishwashers is also exported to North America and there are no signs of the product losing its leadership role in the Australian dishwasher market.

From an EcoReDesign™ perspective there are nonetheless aspects that in retrospect could have been improved or done differently. It is always easier to be clever in hindsight. Much closer involvement should have been sought and demanded of the detergent manufacturers from the outset of the project. The need to rethink the type and quantity of detergents used and the associated dispensing mechanisms remains an under-explored area of environmental improvement and design attention.

Another lost opportunity related to user interface design, and the extent to which consumer feedback could have been better addressed as a way of directly informing dishwasher users about their wash cycle choices and how they rate from an energy and water use perceptive. The initial concept designs addressed the issue of 'environment-based' user feedback, but low-risk company views crept into the detailed design stages, resulting in a less radical user-interface design.

By far the most frustrating barriers to the ongoing implementation of ecodesign in Australia relates to all companies and not just to appliance manufacturers. They are best described as structural and involve the usual restructuring and takeovers that confront all actors in the private sector. The constant volatility in the Australian appliance sector has seen companies and brands come and go on a regular basis. From an ecodesign perspective, and seen in light of the earlier reference to the value of ecodesign 'champions' (Section 16.1.2), this results in experienced designers and engineers experiencing a 'revolving-door syndrome' in their employment pattern. This changing industrial context and its undervaluing of experienced ecodesign practitioners ultimately represents a poor use of knowledge and expertise that could otherwise be exploited to maximise profitability and status in a global marketplace constantly reminded of the need for greener products.

The further barrier, which applies across all product sectors, is Australia's relaxed approach to developing sophisticated environmental policies. Although some federal and state government agencies are proactively supporting voluntary measures toward achieving higher levels of eco-efficiency, there is still very much an 'end-of-pipe' approach to environmental management. Policies and programmes that could dramatically facilitate—and help make mainstream—ecodesign, LCA and product stewardship need much more attention, be it in terms of industry assistance, funding support or regulatory development.

## 16.1.4 Beyond the EcoReDesign™ Dishlex demonstration project

The EcoReDesign™ programme together with other drivers and trends in the marketplace have had an enduring and positive impact on EMA's product development activities. EMA continue to address environmental factors during the design process, with a focus on energy efficiency, water conservation and recyclability. The company has also recently introduced a re-usable packaging system for its refrigerators, with a view to implementation across all product lines.

EMA has also commenced the process of looking beyond mere appliance recyclability and has just conducted a pilot project reflecting producer responsibility principles. The EMA take-back pilot programme seeks to gather critical data and information about the environmental and economic viability of white goods take-back, disassembly, and re-use and recycling. In their ongoing commitment to total life-cycle management of their appliances, EMA has also collaborated with the CfD at RMIT in producing a new booklet to raise wider industry awareness about the importance of producer responsibility and ecodesign. The publication, *Appliance Reuse and Recycling: A Product Stewardship Guide* (1999), was jointly sponsored by EMA and EcoRecycle Victoria, a Victoria State government agency.

Ecodesign now seems to be moving closer to becoming yet another core element that must be integrated into the design of every new EMA appliance, and, although more can always be done to improve the life-cycle environmental performance of its products, the company has made significant progress in demonstrating its commitment to conceiving, designing, commercialising and recovering its appliances in an environmentally sensitive manner. Ecodesign is a business strategy that EMA is unlikely to abandon as it further expands its white goods business in Australia and the Pacific region.

## 16.2 Conclusions

In terms of modifying the EcoReDesign™ process, much can be done to further streamline the methodology and to communicate a simpler step-wise view of how to realise an environmentally improved product or service. Although there are some who are eager for the diminutive detail that some manuals and handbooks may offer, our experience has been that overly detailed manuals are not the preferred vehicle for reconfiguring the psyche of product developers, let alone those involved in the cut and thrust of taking products from concept to market within ever-reducing time-lines. So, in short, any third phase of EcoReDesign™ would necessarily involve more intimate discussions not only with hands-on product designers but also those players pivotal in the overall product development process (i.e. senior executives, company accountants and chief financial officers, suppliers, approvals bodies, buyers and so on). EcoReDesign™ 3 would provide a unique opportunity to cut through the peripheral elements of the current EcoReDesign™ manual (despite its continuing popularity) and produce an even more succinct guide (both as hard copy and online) on how companies can further enhance their profitability through designing environmentally improved products.

Most importantly, EcoReDesign™ 3 would have to pay even greater attention to dealing with ecodesign within a global context and start to recognise and act on the need for movement from ecodesign to the sustainable development of products and services. Although the standard suite of ecodesign approaches are valid and critical first steps in 'greening' many a consumer product, there is no doubt that the move to more sustainable patterns of production and consumption will require more than just design for disassembly and recycled plastic content. Genuinely sustainable 'products' of the near future might not even be products, given the current momentum and interest in ecodesigning services. However, regardless of whether the focus is on products or services, someone, somewhere, beyond research centres and universities, needs to introduce social and ethical factors into mainstream business (and the design process) so that the enthusiasm for recyclable chairs or refillable packaging can be tempered. There is a vital need to seriously work towards creating outcomes that are environmentally necessary, socially desirable, culturally acceptable and economically appropriate. These are the harder questions, often quickly dismissed by the 'commercial pragmatists', that must be addressed by the now growing global collective of ecodesign practitioners, researchers, consultants, entrepreneurs and policy-makers. Contemporary ecodesign must transcend and exceed the achievements made in cleaner production and pollution prevention during the 1980s and 1990s!

# TELEWORK AND THE
# TRIPLE BOTTOM LINE*

*Braden R. Allenby*
AT&T and Columbia University, USA

*Deanna Richards*
private consultant, USA

There has been a lot of ink spilled recently about the potential environmental and sustainability benefits of services as opposed to products, with some authors going so far as to imply that a service economy is, virtually by definition, a sustainable economy. These projections are generally not supported by existing data, which is often sparse and contradictory, and tend to draw broad generalisations from remarkably little actual research. Accordingly, this chapter will focus on a case study of one service, telework, to determine whether broader generalisations are supportable and appropriate. Telework has been chosen because it is a familiar concept to most people, and, compared with other services such as e-commerce, has been studied for some time. Even so, the most obvious conclusion is that, even with telework, many of the potential implications are difficult to evaluate. This strongly implies that the service sectors, although potentially critical in achieving a higher quality of life with smaller environmental footprints, are still not sufficiently well understood for generalisations to be any more than highly speculative at this point.

This is not to be wondered at, for the concept of 'service' is itself ambiguous. Depending on how it is defined, service sectors contribute some 70%–80% of gross domestic product (GDP) and employment in developed economies. The scope of activity covered by these sectors is, however, both huge and highly varied. Thus, for example, if one takes the US Standard Industrial Classification (SIC) codes, one finds that division E includes transportation, communications, electric, gas and sanitary services; division F includes wholesale trade; division G includes retail trade; and division H includes finance, insurance and real estate services. Then, to top it off, division I is 'services'. This category includes everything from hotels and rooming houses (major group 70), automotive repair (major group 75), health services (major group 80), museums and art galleries

---

* The views in this chapter are those of the authors alone, and not necessarily those of any institutions with which they are affiliated.

(major group 84) and legal services (major group 81), to motion pictures (major group 78) and social services (major group 83). To try to make valid generalisations across these categories is obviously impossible, doubly so given the paucity of data and lack of analysis of the environmental and social dimensions of these activities.

So, should we think of some of these as 'eco-services', or, perhaps, 'sustainable services'? With the exception of those services associated with traditional environmental activities such as clean-up and remediation, the answer is almost certainly not. The problem is that the analytical capability to understand the environmental impacts of these kinds of offering—much less the social implications—is so attenuated as to be virtually non-existent. Is the Internet an 'eco-service' or 'sustainable'? What does it mean even to ask such a question? What are the boundaries of the analysis? This is particularly problematic because many services (e.g. retailing, information and entertainment offerings, e-commerce and medical services) have a significant cultural component and are so tightly coupled with other elements of the culture (e.g. consumption patterns) that any analysis along those lines is likely to be either superficial or entirely ideological. This is especially true because many of the impacts of services become apparent only after long time-lags, and then only in complex cultural patterns mediated not only by the service but also by many other dimensions of historical and social evolution. Moreover, services in particular offer difficult-to-evaluate multiplier effects: the introduction of telework not only affects the company offering the service but also ripples through the economy and culture in many different ways. Services thus offer the potential for discontinuous shifts in social behaviour—think of how rapidly business-to-consumer (B2C) e-commerce has expanded over the past few years in terms of gift-giving, and how powerfully business-to-business (B2B) e-commerce is dematerialising inventory supply systems.

That does not mean that we cannot evaluate the triple-bottom-line (economic, social and environmental performance) implications of particular services, such as telework. But, particularly with services, we must always respect our ignorance and the lack of definitive data or analysis. Moreover, services always presuppose some sort of technology platform. Thus, for example, telework is an additional capability on a system of networks that use technological artefacts such as routers, switches and cables and consume energy in the process of supporting telework. Here, also, analytical questions arise. How should one allocate the environmental and social costs and benefits arising from infrastructure creation, maintenance and operation to various services that may use it as a platform? Should it be on a marginal basis? That is, should only the marginal energy and equipment expenditures required to perform the specific tasks associated with the services be considered? Alternatively, should it be done on some sort of allocative basis, all of which methods are essentially arbitrary?

Thus, at this point, any evaluation of a service case study, including this one, should be regarded as preliminary, based on the best data and analysis we may have now, subject to change. With these caveats, we can proceed to evaluate telework as a case study in services.

Telework, driven by a wide array of information and telecommunications technologies, is one element in a complex social, environmental and economic evolution of the manufacturing economy of the Industrial Revolution into the new 'knowledge economy'.

It effectively de-couples work from place, redefining work as what one does rather than where one works. In this, of course, it parallels the shift in modern economies from manufacturing, necessarily place-based, to thinking, which is person-based. In doing so, telework contributes to the increased economic, environmental and social efficiency of people, firms and institutions—a concept referred to by some advocates as the 'triple bottom line'.

## 17.1 Telework: an overview

Telework comes in many forms. In some businesses, such as those that require work to be done at a client's location (e.g. management consultancies, marketing and sales, financial planning, installation and maintenance) telework is increasingly the norm, even a necessity. Other professional activities, such as editing and writing, are also knowledge-intensive and are thus ideal for telework. Accordingly, activities such as these have had a long history of telework, but it has usually been informal, ad hoc and frequently discouraged by management. This historical pattern is now being changed because of employee desires for increased personal freedom, better management systems, greatly enhanced technologies such as broad-band telecommunications pipes to the home, increased urban traffic congestion and the resultant poor air quality and a more sophisticated understanding of the benefits that accrue to employees, firms and society as a result (Allenby and Richards 1999).

'Telework' is a generic term that may be defined as the performance of work at any location other than the heretofore normal, white-collar office-building work location. In essence, the worker is removed from a central workplace, with work going to the worker instead of the worker going to the work in the traditional sense. 'Telecommuting', a more familiar related term, refers to that class of telework that is done at home (or a nearby 'satellite office'), eliminating the daily commute.

In many cases, teleworking situations will not involve a complete break from the traditional office (particularly at first, such a change may be too difficult for managers and teleworking employees to handle). Most firms and employees find a telecommuting arrangement of two or three days a week optimal—a schedule that allows the individual to enjoy the freedom of telework without being too disconnected from the office. In some situations, however, certain workers are set up with a 'virtual office'. These workers include those who operate in regions where the firm may not have central offices, or those who have moved with their spouses or partners to areas far from central offices but who are considered critical to the operation of the company. Such employees may never report to a formal office. Although feasible, a virtual office arrangement can make management of the absent employee difficult (the manager of such a worker, for example, needs to be able to understand and measure his or her output for pay, counselling and promotion reasons, to ensure fair evaluation and treatment compared with on-site peers). Moreover, the employee can end up feeling alienated from the firm, which can undercut the employee retention rationale that may have been a primary reason for the programme in the first place. Hence, it is not as common as telecommuting.

There are many reasons for the increase in telework in recent years. The most obvious are the rapid spread of new telecommunications technologies (e.g. satellites, fibre optics and wireless networks), the proliferation of improved electronics and communication devices (cell phones and palm-top and lap-top computers), the growth of the Internet and corporate intranets and improvements to e-mail and voice mail, and an increase in the availability of broad-band telecommunications pipes to the home. This stands to reason: if teleworkers are knowledge workers, they require and generate large volumes of information, and high-capacity telecommunications systems and instant connectivity are important enablers for their productivity. Two other factors have also been critical. The first factor concerns regulatory and legislative requirements directed at reducing urban traffic congestion and improving air quality. Examples are the US Clean Air Act Amendments of 1990 and 1995 that establish stringent air-quality requirements that can be met only by reducing traffic on the roads. The second, and perhaps most important, factor, however, is the slow erosion of the management style inherited from the manufacturing floor, which evaluates output even from white-collar workers by the amount of time spent at a desk 'under management supervision'. The irony of applying management techniques appropriate to a factory environment to knowledge workers is obvious—but this is a strong and subtle cultural barrier that has significantly impeded, and continues to impede, implementation of telework.

Among large firms, AT&T has been a leader in deploying telework, so its experience is somewhat instructive. AT&T began a telework programme in 1992. Today, about half of all managers regularly engage in some form of telework activity. A 1999 survey of AT&T management employees found that 49% teleworked at least one day a month, about 24% teleworked at least one day a week, and about 10% had full-time virtual office arrangements (AT&T 1999).[1] These figures are slightly less than those reported in 1998 (AT&T 1998). Several factors appear to have contributed to this dip. For one, over the past year AT&T has acquired new units that do not have the same history of telework. Another, more subtle, factor is that, like many companies in its sector, AT&T is in the midst of radical change, which puts more of a premium on direct human interaction (and raises anxiety levels in employees, which might incite them to spend more time in the workplace to obtain information and to protect their interests). There are technological factors as well: employees cited inadequate bandwidth and technical support as barriers to increased telework (the more employees rely on intranets and other information-intensive tools, the more they need high-capacity, dependable telecommunications infrastructure).

In general, however, there is a national upward trend in numbers of workers teleworking. Although estimates vary, in 1990 there were some 3.6 million telecommuters. This number grew to about 9.3 million by 1995, accounting for 10% of the US workforce.

---

1   This survey (AT&T 1999) consisted of interviews with 1,106 AT&T managers from a statistically reliable, stratified random sample. All activities were conducted under the professional guidelines of the Council of American Survey Research Organisation (CASRO). The error range was ±2% at the 95% level of confidence.

A 1997 survey found that over 11 million Americans telework—three times the number that did so in 1990. It is projected that there will be 14 million teleworkers by 2000. Other surveys have shown that the average teleworker telecommutes approximately three days a week, and would like to do so four days a week (see AT&T 1997;[2] WRI 1998).

## 17.2 Telework and the 'triple bottom line'

How does this expanding business practice contribute to the 'triple bottom line' of economic, environmental and social performance? We will begin our examination with economic metrics (the most well-understood metrics), followed by environmental metrics (these have been emerging over the past 30 years, but in some instances they are not agreed to) and, finally, social metrics (the latest addition to the mix, which we clearly need to include if progress toward sustainable development goals is to be measured and realised).[3]

As with all emerging information technologies, however, it must be understood that there are significant uncertainties about all these dimensions, for at least two reasons. First, the data that has been gathered is patchy and tends to be culturally and geographically specific, and the extent to which it can be validly extrapolated is unclear. Second, like all fundamental technologies, information technologies result in both short-term and long-term cultural, economic and demographic adjustments; if, as is the case, the short-term effects are only poorly understood, it is clear that the long-term effects will be impossible to predict with any degree of certainty at this point.

### 17.2.1 *Economic factors*

The most obvious benefit to the corporation or government agency is the elimination of unnecessary office space and associated overhead costs. AT&T, for example, estimates that its implementation of teleworking has resulting in an additional US$550 million in cash flow from 1991 to 1998. IBM estimates that its mobility initiatives saved it approximately US$1 billion in real estate costs from 1992 to 1997 (Apgar 1998). This economic benefit accrues to corporations, but it also represents an economic efficiency for society, in that less building infrastructure is required for a given level of economic productivity. Freed real estate becomes available, and new businesses are able to move in, without the additional costs of building new structures.

Three other related benefits concern employee productivity, retention and job satisfaction, all of which seem to increase with teleworking. The respondents to the 1999 AT&T

2   In this survey approximately 12,000 US households were contacted during the period 1–26 May 1997; 8.2% of these households had telecommuters in them, of which 400 were randomly selected for in-depth interviews. The margin of error for the finding was ±4.9%. Although sponsored by AT&T, the survey was national in scope and not limited to any geographic area or particular employee body.

3   For more on sustainability metrics, see Richards and Gladwin 1999.

Employee Telework Survey, for example, claimed to work one hour more per day, equivalent to about 250 hours or 6 weeks of additional work per year (in general, employees seem to allocate the time saved from commuting between personal and work activities). Not only can extra time be allocated to work but, on a per unit basis, telework appears to be more efficient for knowledge work. In the same survey, 68% of the teleworkers said they were able to get more done at home than when in the office. Regarding job retention, 65% of all AT&T managers report that telework provides an advantage in keeping and attracting good employees, an especially important finding because knowledge workers, who are the most difficult to find and keep, are also those most likely to be able to telework and to value that option. Accordingly, it is no surprise that job satisfaction also improves with telework: 76% of teleworkers claim to be more satisfied with their job, and 79% are more satisfied with their career. The most interesting aspect of these statistics is their upward trend each year.

This data also tends to indicate that the argument sometimes heard that telework is an effort to shift costs from companies to teleworkers is invalid. Certainly, one would not expect to find employees so positive about telework if they felt the costs of the firm were being shifted to them. Moreover, any successful telework programme is voluntary (except, perhaps, in certain categories such as marketing representatives, where telework, if required, would be understood as a condition of employment). This mechanism is also a protection against such a shift in costs (indeed, most companies that support telework programmes pay for the telecommunications services and most of the equipment involved—as one would expect if teleworking were being used as an element of employee retention programmes).

Finally, it is apparent that firms that are in the business of providing platforms and services that promote telework, such as AT&T, derive direct revenue streams attributable to teleworking practices. More broadly, however, telework supports the creation of new e-businesses and consulting firms, generating high-paying, high-technology jobs and infrastructure which are, in turn, critical to continued evolution of modern, knowledge-based economies.

## 17.2.2 Environmental factors

The most cited environmental benefit of telework is that associated with telecommuting, which eliminates the daily commute and thus saves energy, reduces emissions contributing to global climate change and the production of photochemical smog and air pollution and reduces traffic congestion. These savings can be significant. Consider an average round-trip commute of 40 miles; this journey consumes approximately 1.6 gallons of petrol per day (assuming a 40-mile commute in a Ford Taurus [the best-selling sedan in the US in 1999], which averages 25 miles per gallon). As the combustion of one gallon of petrol produces 19 lb of carbon dioxide ($CO_2$), each round trip that is eliminated has the potential to reduce $CO_2$ loads by 30.4 lb of $CO_2$. Under these assumptions, based on the number of teleworkers at AT&T and the days of teleworking that occurred, in 1999 alone AT&T reduced $CO_2$ emissions by 41,000 tons.

Telework in 1999 for one company alone, then, resulted in avoiding 87 million miles of driving to the office, saving 4.2 million gallons of petrol and avoiding emissions of 18,000 tons of hydrocarbons, 1.4 million tons of carbon monoxide (CO) and 93,000 tons of nitrogen oxides ($NO_x$). These estimates are based on reasonable assumptions and point to the magnitude of reductions in carbon emissions and other pollutants that teleworking might support if practised more widely.

It has been argued that teleworking results in little net benefit, because teleworkers do errands from their home, which to a large extent negates the benefits of avoided commutes. This conceptual argument is not supported by the available data. An evaluation of nine studies of this issue, for example, reported that all of demonstrated significant absolute reductions in driving, with two, looking at Puget Sound in Washington State, and at California, showing that teleworking actually resulted in total travel savings greater than the commute travel savings alone (Shirazi 2000; see also Allenby and Richards 1999).[4]

There are also indirect environmental effects of telework. For example, by reducing traffic congestion in general, teleworkers contribute to greater efficiency and less energy consumption by those workers that do commute. If teleworking becomes widespread, it may even result in less demand for office buildings and vehicular infrastructure, thus reducing consumption of building materials and generating less land-use impacts (roads are often designed for peak-period loads, which occur during heavy commute periods). Conversely, it might be possible that teleworking, by delinking work from place, will contribute to urban sprawl or different patterns of built environment: it is impossible at this time to know whether, on balance, this would be better or worse for the environment, and, if known, how and to what extent.

### 17.2.3 Social factors

Although teleworking is not for everyone, those employees who successfully telework report an enhanced quality of life. In the 1999 AT&T Employee Telework Survey, 79% were more satisfied with their personal and family lives since they began teleworking (stress reduction as a result of not having to commute on congested highways was not measured, but, as any commuter will attest, it could also be significant). Moreover, not just the teleworker but family members reported increased satisfaction. Teleworkers also stay in their communities, providing enhanced security and presence. Moreover, reduced traffic congestion not only has environmental benefits but also results in a higher quality of life (an easier commute) for those that must drive.

At this point, teleworking is best viewed as a voluntary, not mandatory, programme where it is available. First, there are people who, for psychological reasons or because of situations in their home, do not wish to telework; unless it is in their job description (e.g. as a marketing representative) they should not be forced to do so. This is especially true

---

4 Such studies are beset by methodological difficulties, of course, and reflect the geographical area they are drawn from. That all of them came to the same conclusion, however, gives some credibility to the trend.

if the teleworking situation is anticipated to be for more than two or three days a week on average; some individuals become concerned with social isolation under such circumstances. Moreover, some have raised the possibility that telework services could be abused by employers who, for example, exploit workers by allocating piecework (e.g. typing assignments) and measuring output in such a way as to generate inappropriate pressure and stress on the worker. Although this is conceivable, it is certainly not unique to telework; such exploitation is possible regardless of where the individual works, and can be addressed through the same regulatory and legislative processes that apply to the workplace.

## 17.3  Impediments to telework

Telework appears to be a practice that aligns well with the triple bottom line and its three dimensions: economic, environmental and social. Yet, despite the positive incentives that support the implementation of telework, it has taken a long time for it to become an accepted work option in the USA and it has yet to reach even that level in most other countries. Why is this?

The main reasons seem to be cultural and to stem from two factors. The first is that every organisation is limited in its perception. Thus, not all opportunities are apparent, especially if they are unusual (and often relegated to overhead costs). For example, the US Clean Air Act Amendments of 1990 included a requirement for reducing commuting in areas with poor air quality. This provision essentially created a large captive market for firms producing the hardware and software necessary for telecommuting and for the telecommunications firms that would provide supporting services. Yet none of these firms recognised the opportunity. Why? It was because business managers and marketing personnel in such firms were unable to perceive such a market, because it was driven by environmental regulations. They had a mental model that relegated all things environmental to overheads. It was a profound, if understandable, lack of perception.

The second factor involves institutional culture. Most firms, and especially older managers within them, tend to equate time at work, under supervision, with productivity. This mental model arose in the context of a manufacturing line, where the equation may arguably be reasonable (if you are not on the line, you are not producing). In these authors' view, application of these principles to the modern service-oriented economy is ridiculous. It degrades performance by unnecessarily reducing innovation, risk-taking and morale. Yet old patterns die hard and form resistance to change, even when external indicators argue that it is economically, environmentally and socially preferable. People, employees and managers alike make assumptions about what work is and how it is defined that are rigid and unquestioned and which form powerful cultural barriers to any change, however desirable that change may be.

## 17.4 Conclusions

Telework is a technology that offers significant environmental, social and economic benefits. Although adoption of telework has been slow, it is increasing in the USA; but uptake has been slower elsewhere. Technologies facilitating telework, such as broad-band telecommunications pipes to the home, are rapidly being deployed, so the platforms for telework are increasingly robust.

As with other aspects of sustainable development, however, and given our understanding of the triple bottom line, our greatest challenges lie in cultural barriers to change and the need to integrate technology and management practices to speed our way toward sustainable futures.

# THE UNPREDICTABLE PROCESS OF IMPLEMENTING ECO-EFFICIENCY STRATEGIES

*Jacqueline Cramer*
Cramer Environmental Consultancy and
Erasmus University, Netherlands

*Ab Stevels*
Technical University of Delft and
Philips Consumer Electronics, Netherlands

## 18.1 The promise and potential of eco-efficiency

A growing number of companies are aware of the need to take the environment seriously. They realise that the environment should not be seen as a threat but as a challenge for business. Some scientists even argue that we are on the eve of an 'industrial transformation' that may lead to sustainable development for society. These predictions are perhaps too optimistic, but, undoubtedly, companies are currently making tremendous strides towards sustainable development.

The most important sustainable development trend within industry is the increasing attention being paid to eco-efficiency (DeSimone and Popoff 1997). This concept of eco-efficiency was introduced by the World Business Council for Sustainable Development (WBCSD), a group of prominent companies. It defines the concept as follows:

> Eco-efficiency is reached by the delivery of competitively-priced goods and services that satisfy human needs and bring quality of life, while progressively reducing ecological impacts and resource intensity throughout the life-cycle, to a level at least in line with the Earth's estimated carrying capacity (WBCSD 1995: 9).

So eco-efficiency means not only ecological efficiency but also economic efficiency. It makes a direct connection between ambitious environmental targets and enhanced market opportunities.

A number of companies, including Philips Electronics, Akzo Nobel and Dow, are making efforts to put the eco-efficiency approach into practice (Cramer 2000; Cramer and

Stevels 1997; Fussler with James 1996). Their experiences teach us that this approach fundamentally differs from the environmental management approach that is pursued by most companies. First of all, it involves a chain-oriented approach requiring more communication and co-operation between partners in the product chain (e.g. between suppliers and customers). The eco-efficiency approach is also much more strategic in nature than the more operational environmental management approach currently in place in most companies. More eco-efficient products should also be economically attractive as well as serve long-term goals. Consequently, the environment becomes part of a company's strategic planning and requires a greater involvement of management in environmental policy.

Experiences gained so far with the eco-efficiency approach have shown that it is perfectly possible to create win–win situations. Eco-efficiency improvements can lead to cost reduction, strengthen the market position of existing products, extend the product range and create new markets, avert criticism from external stakeholders and increase the possibility of a company's survival in the long term.

There are many examples of companies that grasp these market opportunities. For instance, automobile manufacturers are investing in research and development (R&D) on fuel efficiency and vehicle recycling in order to strengthen their competitiveness and improve their environmental image. Societal pressure to reduce the environmental burden of vehicles has forced the industry to develop such innovative solutions. As a result, competitive advantages can be gained by seeking eco-efficiency improvements.

In other cases, the eco-efficiency approach has led to substantial cost reductions. For example, Philips Medical Systems has realised a tremendous reduction in material consumption for one of its medical instruments, the magnetic resonance imager. This redesigned instrument weighs 35 tonnes less than it did prior to redesign, resulting in a 50% reduction in transportation costs. Moreover, the product is easier to dismantle and recycle than the original instrument. Another example is the carpet producer Interface. A total of 40 factories have saved about US$60 million by re-using and reducing waste. The Canadian electricity company Ontario Hydro was also able to save US$37 million through energy efficiency improvements alone (Cramer 1999).

A final important example is Xerox, a major producer of photocopiers. The company set a goal of using as few natural resources as possible, which meant focusing on re-using and recycling waste materials. Old copiers are now being 'remanufactured' and their spare parts re-used. In 1995 this strategy led to a cost savings of US$12 million in the recycling programme and US$50 million in the spare-parts recycling programme (Elkington 1997: 314).

These examples illustrate the potential of eco-efficiency. However, it is not possible to determine in advance what marketing and strategy opportunities will ultimately present themselves. This will only become evident during the change process, as this involves innovations for which the outcome is often unpredictable. The identification of promising eco-efficiency improvements is, therefore, more of a search process than a well-defined development path. This point will be illustrated below on the basis of experience gained by Philips Consumer Electronics in strategic environmental product planning.

## 18.2 Strategic environmental product planning within Philips Consumer Electronics

Since the early 1990s the environmental policy of the Philips Consumer Electronics (PCE) division has evolved from having a purely process orientation towards a focus on consumer electronics products themselves. An initial driving force for this was the corporate environmental policy formulated by the former chief executive officer (CEO), Mr Timmer. Another reason was the growing public pressure to find socially responsible ways of disposing of used consumer electronics goods. Additional factors were the demands made by professionals and consumers regarding the use of certain chemical substances and the short-term cost-effectiveness of some environmental improvements (i.e. through material reduction and the application of recycled material).

Since 1990 PCE has introduced a number of measures to improve its consumer electronics products incrementally. For instance, a major project was carried out to reduce the number of environmentally harmful substances. Based on this experience, PCE turned its attention in 1995 to further-reaching, strategic environmental improvements aimed at product alternatives and a radical redesign based on existing concepts. To structure this strategic approach a methodology was developed, called STRETCH, an acronym for Selection of sTRategic EnvironmenTal CHallenges (Cramer and Stevels 1997).

STRETCH represents a similar view to the one expressed by Hamel and Prahalad in their book *Competing for the Future* (1994). Instead of looking defensively for the right 'fit' among its own business operations and between them and external environmental demands, a company must make room in its business strategy for 'stretched' objectives (Cramer 1999). Therefore, the basic idea behind the STRETCH approach is that the selection of promising eco-efficiency improvements over the whole life-cycle should be attuned closely to the business groups' (potential) business strategy and to the future demands of external stakeholders, including those of its suppliers and customers. In order to ensure that the STRETCH approach becomes an integral part of general business planning, it must be embedded structurally in the organisation and attuned to related activities (i.e. as in ISO 14001). The STRETCH approach was tested first at PCE and later at Akzo Nobel. It can be stated, based on their learning experiences, that the STRETCH approach consists of six steps, as listed in Box 18.1.

The implementation of STRETCH started at PCE with the collection and integration of available data (steps 1–3). Subsequently, representatives of strategy development and environmental experts from the consumer electronics division and representatives of Philips Corporate Design made an initial selection of promising project themes.

Nine project themes related to the following technological options were selected for further investigation:

- Minimising the use of raw materials and toxic substances and minimising energy consumption
- Increasing further material recycling

- Step 1: survey the unit's (potential) product and market strategies and the most important driving forces determining business strategy in general
- Step 2: monitor new developments and trends in the environmental debate and changes in influence exerted by external stakeholders
- Step 3: identify potential eco-efficiency improvements that can be made in the product chain
- Step 4: in light of steps 1–3, select eco-efficiency improvements leading to the development of promising market opportunities or preventing potential market threats, then formulate an action plan for short-term and long-term eco-efficiency improvements in the product chain
- Step 5: embed the STRETCH approach in the organisation
- Step 6: bring the results in line with related business-group activities (i.e. ISO 14001 compliance, product stewardship and product development)

*Box 18.1* **The STRETCH (Selection of sTRategic EnvironmenTal CHallenges) approach**

- Optimising product life (e.g. by recycling product components and by upgrading technically)

- Improving product distribution efficiency

- Finding alternative ways of performing the present function of the product (either by applying further eco-efficiency physical principles or looking at more service-oriented systems)

These themes were discussed with representatives of the three main business groups of the PCE division: television (TV), audio and monitors. Each business group had to select four or five themes for further investigation. Within the framework of each business group, brainstorming sessions were organised with relevant persons from the particular business group, including product managers, marketing personnel and technical experts.

The brainstorming technique used was the one developed by Dow (Fussler with James 1996). It centres on brainstorming sessions for teams of experts from different backgrounds and is aimed at generating promising eco-efficiency strategies. During each brainstorming session, ideas are generated that will substantially reduce the environmental burden of the new product and lead at the same time to promising market opportunities.

Separate brainstorming sessions were held on the particular themes selected by each of the three main business groups. On the basis of the results of each session, business-group representatives formulated priorities for the development of new, more eco-efficient products. Most of these priorities could not be implemented immediately but needed further study from both a technical and a business perspective. As will be shown below, it sometimes took two to three years after the first brainstorming sessions before results became visible in the regular product planning process. It was impossible to predict which of the ideas generated during these sessions would finally be implemented.

It appeared that the pace and success of the implementation process depended mainly on the following five factors:

- The organisation's culture (i.e. internal factors such as management interest, environmental skills, cross-functional linkages, personnel motivation)

- Business conditions (i.e. profitability, market share)

- The degree of environmental influence exerted by external stakeholders (customers, authorities)

- The available room to manoeuvre regarding product housing and functionality in relation to combined environmental and economic gain

- The degree to which the environment can be used to gain a competitive edge

The relevance of the five factors mentioned above could be assessed by each business group at the introduction of the eco-efficiency approach. However, this information was insufficient to formulate firm conclusions about the success or failure of some of the promising eco-efficiency improvements selected during the brainstorming sessions. For each case considered, the road towards implementing eco-efficiency improvements turned out to be a special journey with its own specific characteristics. As will be shown in the PCE cases (i.e. for the monitors, audio and TV business groups) the results were quite unpredictable both in terms of achievement and time.

# 18.3 Catalysts for eco-efficiency improvements at the start of the brainstorming sessions

In order to clarify the potential responsiveness to eco-efficiency improvements within the monitors, audio and TV business groups, we present in Table 18.1 an overview of the main catalysts for eco-efficiency improvements at the start of the STRETCH brainstorming sessions during 1996–97. It can be concluded from Table 18.1 that internal factors differed greatly in the three business groups. In the monitors group a member of the management team made himself a 'defender of the environment' and pushed hard for results, in particular for combined customer and environmental benefit. Owing to the high degree of motivation of the employees involved, good cross-functional linkage could be established and the existing backlog in environmental skills could be reduced. This led to an acceleration in eco-efficiency activities over a short period of time.

During 1996–97, management interest in eco-efficiency activities was weak in the audio group. At that time, major attention was being paid to the first results of a turnaround programme. All efforts were being put into further implementation of the restructuring programmes. The environment issue was 'alive' but had a low profile. However, after business results had become healthier, effective product and programme managers stepped in and achieved good results.

| | Monitors | Audio | TV |
|---|---|---|---|
| **1. *Internal factors (culture)*** | | | |
| Management attention | Strong | Weak | Moderate |
| Environmental skills | Fair | Fair | Good |
| Cross-functional linkages | Good | To be improved | To be improved |
| Are eco-efficiency activities already in place? | Limited programme | Small programme | Extensive programme |
| Personnel motivation | Good | Good | Good |
| **2. *Business conditions*** | | | |
| Profitability | Good | Marginal | Moderate |
| Market share | High, growing | Low, recovering | High, stabilising |
| **3. *External influences*** | | | |
| Customer pressure | Strong | Absent | Moderate |
| Legislation | Weak | Absent | Strong |
| **4. *Room for manoeuvre*** | | | |
| Product functionality | Good prospects for win–win | Moderate scope for win–win | A lot of improvements already realised |
| Product alternatives | Alternative is different (LCD screen) | Different physical principle (wind-up radio) | Physical principle (LCD screen) |
| **5. *Competitive edge*** | | | |
| Is competitive environmental benchmarking done? | Yes | No | Yes |
| Is competition active? | Yes | No | Starting |

*Table* 18.1 **Catalysts for eco-efficiency at the start of STRETCH brainstorming sessions (1996–97) in the monitors, audio and TV business groups of Philips Consumer Electronics division**

The TV group had already an extensive eco-efficiency programme in place. As a result the group scored well in environmental benchmarking. However, this turned out to be more of a disadvantage than an advantage for further progress: apart from a strongly motivated environmental manager located in the development department, the TV group showed otherwise moderate interest, particularly in the marketing department.

Furthermore, the business situation of the three business groups was completely different in 1996. That of monitors had developed a profitable business, enjoyed growing value and market share and had created a good investment position. The audio business group, however, was still recovering from a slump that occurred over the period 1992–95. Its restructuring process absorbed almost all the resources and attention of management.

The TV business group viewed the environment from a different perspective: owing to the significant emphasis on environmental performance already in place, this business group could differentiate itself in a market with stabilising volume and overcapacity.

With regard to external influences, the monitor group customers—major computer companies—exerted strong, tangible pressure both for environmental improvement and for lower retail prices; the main customers of audio and TV products are private households, who exert only a diffuse pressure. An influential external pressure on TV products are the European consumer test magazines, which introduced an environmental section in their television evaluations. However, since Philips TVs scored well in these surveys, these tests did not engender further action.

In the field of legislation the debate about manufacturer responsibility and take-back obligations was very heated for the TV business group, marginal for that of monitors ('the TV issue has not yet been solved; only afterwards will it be our turn') and non-existent for the audio business group ('our products are much smaller and represent a low percentage of electronic waste').

Management's room to manoeuvre on this issue was determined to a large extent by the physical, chemical and electronic prerequisites for realising a certain functionality (pictures, sound, etc.). The environmental improvement potential is therefore dependent on the housing resulting from these factors. Products containing a cathode-ray tube (CRT) generally offer the best scope for eco-efficiency gains because of their relatively high energy consumption and weight. An important difference was that the TV group development department had already taken many initiatives and was even considering aiming to achieve an environmental breakthrough by initiating an environmentally friendly TV project.

The area of monitors was less advanced but, as such, the housing offered more potential. Liquid crystal display (LCD) screens are an alternative for CRTs, and this technology will be environmentally friendlier at a later stage of development. Owing to the fact that LCD screens are substantially easier to view, the monitors business group decided to push ahead with this technology. In the TV application, the prospect of such a 'flat' screen is attractive. However, for the time being, brightness and contrast challenges, combined with a high price, are serious obstacles to the introduction of an LCD TV screen as a consumer commodity on the mass market. Products were planned to be introduced slowly to the market and for high-end (superior quality) products only.

For the audio business group, human-powered radios were a viable alternative for portable products. In 1996, only the 'BayGen' human-powered radio (see Chapter 6) was on the market but was seen by industry leaders as being too heavy, unattractive and difficult to operate. The real message ('there are other ways to realise audio functionality') that this product was sending to the market was not perceived as such by the audio management. After a heated debate in the environmental team, the product manager involved decided not to follow up the human-power avenue for the time being.

Competitive benchmarking had been undertaken during 1996–97 for TVs and monitors with completely opposite results. Most TVs scored well in environmental and efficiency performance tests against the competition. For monitors, the competitive benchmarking results showed an urgent need for improvement. This was even more pressing when the competition started to include environmental arguments in their sales pitches (this was not the case for TV.) Audio started benchmarking two years after the eco-efficiency brainstorming sessions. At this time, a successful turnaround had been achieved and the eco-efficiency success of the other consumer electronics groups had been made public.

## 18.4 Eco-efficiency brainstorming sessions and their impact on product development

To generate ideas for eco-efficiency improvements, the management of each business group organised brainstorming sessions during 1996–97. These sessions were prepared by the authors of this chapter, as at that time both were affiliated to the Environmental Competence Centre of Philips Consumer Electronics.

### 18.4.1 *The monitors business group*

The eco-efficiency brainstorming session for the monitors business group, on the basis of the STRETCH approach, took place on 9 September 1997. The message of the CEO of that business group at that time was that 'all relevant items had to be considered'. The management had already approved the inclusion of an environmental paragraph in the business-group strategy and, on the basis of this approval and other considerations, the monitors business group had decided also to develop and market LCD-based monitors.

Other than this strategic information, data obtained through a thorough environmental benchmark on 17-inch monitors formed a solid basis for a creative brainstorming session. In total some 25–30 main environmentally friendly options were generated and ranked in a so-called ecodesign matrix (Table 18.2). In this matrix, the columns were

| Green options | Environmental benefit | Business benefit | Customer benefit | Societal benefit | Feasibility technical | Financial |
|---|---|---|---|---|---|---|
| First option | | | | | | |
| Second option | | | | | | |
| Third option | | | | | | |
| • • • | | | | | | |
| *N*th option | | | | | | |

*Table* 18.2 **The ecodesign matrix**

filled in from left to right. First, management checked whether the proposed environmentally friendly options actually contributed in a positive manner to the environmental performance of its product. A positive score was preferred for the other columns as well, which served primarily as a tool for ranking priority from a business and feasibility perspective.

With the aid of the ecodesign matrix, management selected 12 main options for further investigation, of which seven were incorporated in a new product concept approved in January 1998. Owing to the fact that the concurrent engineering started in the autumn of 1997, the product creation period was to be fairly short. In May 1998 the new product, the A580BQ Brilliance monitor, was launched. It was a huge success as a result of its favourable product and environmentally friendly characteristics (Table 18.3).

Based on the results in Table 18.3 it can be concluded that an extremely good result has been achieved with the 17-inch monitor. Contributing to this success (in terms of the factors illustrated in Table 18.1) were favourable business conditions, strong management support and the positive advantages that could be derived from the ecodesign matrix. These conclusions could be drawn only at the end of the implementation process.

| Area of improvement | Improvement achieved |
| --- | --- |
| *Specification:* | |
| Scanning range | 8% increase |
| Maximum resolution | 5% increase |
| Brightness | 15% increase |
| Bill of materials (including cathode ray tube) | 12% decrease |
| Component count | 32% decrease |
| Assembly time | 35% decrease |
| Energy consumption | 6% decrease |
| *Materials:* | |
| Weight of plastics | 18% decrease |
| Weight of metals | 42% decrease |
| *Hazardous substances:* | |
| Number of printed circuit boards | decrease from 8 to 6 |
| Component count | 32% decrease |
| Packaging weight | 10% decrease |
| *Recyclability:* | |
| Screw total | 40% decrease |

*Table* 18.3 **Improvements in the 17-inch monitor as a result of an eco-efficiency brainstorming session** (based on the STRETCH approach; see Box 18.1)

## 18.4.2 The audio business group

The brainstorming sessions for the audio business group took place 21–24 May 1996. The initiative for holding these sessions had been taken by the Environmental Competence Centre of Philips Consumer Electronics. The Centre had detected a high eco-efficiency potential for audio products. The organisation itself was, however, rather indifferent about the idea. In contrast to the monitors business group, the audio business group decided from the very beginning to focus on three areas:

- Standby energy reduction for audio sets

- Replacement of batteries with human power for portable audio units

- Durability improvement (in particular for audio sets, defined in the meeting as a decrease in environmental load over the life-cycle per hour of use)

The brainstorming sessions on the standby energy reduction yielded initially 20 reduction options, of which four were selected. Since the brainstorming session had a more voluntary character compared with that of the monitors business group, the results were not phrased as clear proposals to management. This resulted in serious delays in the standby energy reduction programme. Environmental benchmarks in 1997 and 1998 indicated that Philips's audio market position was slightly better than that of the competition (see Stevels 2000). Nevertheless, there was still substantial unrealised potential.

Similar conclusions were drawn in 1996, but in 1997 business conditions were more favourable for change. New product and programme managers had effectively taken over and aimed to realise good business results. Moreover, the environmental 'technicalities' were better elaborated and put in clear management perspective: it could finally be shown that the substantial standby reductions were feasible and cost-effective. In 1999, the FW870 audio set was launched with very low energy consumption (0 W in the power-save mode; 2 W in the passive standby mode). Moreover, other energy improvements were made with respect to on-mode energy consumption, weight and packaging reduction, and so on. The resulting life-cycle environmental load of this product is 15% lower than the best competitor in its range. On a life-cycle basis, the cost of ownership for the user is approximately US$35 less than that of a product of the best competitor.

It can be concluded, based on the standby power example, that—apart from more favourable business conditions and motivated managers—technological progress, the definition of an appropriate business rationale and a value proposition to the customer were crucial to realising the eco-efficiency potential.

In 1996 the ideas for human-powered portable products were examined in a pre-development study by Philips Corporate Design. This study showed good prospects for audio products. However, this concept was not developed further because of the lack of interest from the audio business group. Almost simultaneously, a human-powered radio named BayGen was launched. This radio was intended for the reception of information broadcasts in third world countries where batteries and/or electricity are not available or are too expensive. However, this product was soon also marketed as an environmentally friendly product in the electronics mass market. Although the first product was attractive from the point of view of avoiding the hassles associated with battery use, it received negative reviews from professionals in the field. They talked about the unattractive design, the high weight resulting from the heavy metal spring storing the energy and the winding crank, which did not look very durable, and expressed doubts about its environmental friendliness on a life-cycle basis (Jansen and Stevels 1998). This movement in the market, combined with the restructuring of the audio business and the revamping of the product line, put on hold the development of a human-powered product within the Philips audio business group.

However, since that time the human-powered radio has been intensively discussed within the audio business group. After the business group had gone through the turnaround process, the business prospects became more favourable and led to new initiatives. As a result, the decision was made in 1999 to develop a product for mass markets. In February 2000, the Philips AE1000 wind-up radio was launched (for characteristics, see Table 18.4).

| | Philips AE1000 (wind-up) | Philips AE2130 (conventional) | Competitors' product (wind-up) | BayGen product latest version (wind-up) |
|---|---|---|---|---|
| Energy consumption (W) | 57 | 58 | 90 | 57 |
| Product weight (g) | 350 | 600 | 1,500 | 900 |
| Hazardous substance | 0 | 0 | contains Ni–Cd cell | Wiring contains cadmium |
| Packaging | Cardboard only | Cardboard and one type of plastic | Cardboard and one type of plastic | Cardboard and two types of plastic |
| Life-cycle load (eco-indicator, mPt) | 20 | 40 | 25 | 49 |

Ni–Cd = nickel–cadmium; mPt = millipoints

*Table* 18.4 **Characteristics of newly developed (2000) Philips AE1000 wind-up radio**

It can be concluded from Table 18.4 that the Philips human-powered portable audio product is very competitive in terms of environmental load compared with both conventional and other wind-up products, including the latest version of BayGen. In the case of this human-powered product, the progress in product development has been strongly influenced by competitors' behaviour and internal issues.

As far as durability and possible durability strategies for audio products are concerned, it was concluded in 1996 that insufficient insight existed in these matters. Also, as a result of the input from the audio business group, it was decided at the division level to financially support a research project at the Design for Sustainability Lab at the Delft

University of Technology. By then, definitions, conceptual models for the influence of product characteristics on replacement decisions and the impact of intensity of use had been published (Van Nes *et al.* 1999).

Recently, a case study on audio product durability has been carried out (Smeels *et al.* 2000). Smeels *et al.* proposed conceptual designs that have a 60%–75% lower environmental load over a period of 15 years for all audio functions (including digital video disc-player [DVD]) compared with traditional products with the same functions.

In conclusion, the audio case study shows how unpredictable the eco-efficiency improvement process can be. At the start of the brainstorming sessions the potential was high, but the interest of management was limited. Over the course of time, the responsiveness of the business group increased as a result of a combination of factors, as described above.

## 18.4.3 The television business group

The eco-efficiency brainstorming sessions for the TV business group, initiated by the development department, took place on 2 February 1996 and 10 May 1996. An important catalyst for organising these sessions was the participation of one of the preferred suppliers of plastic materials. In these brainstorming sessions, Fussler and James's approach was closely followed (Fussler with James 1996). All fields of the eco-fitness compass were considered: raw materials, manufacturing, distribution, use and end of life. The following subjects were prioritised:

● Materials and manufacturing: future housing designs

● Materials and manufacturing: alternatives for the current glass-based CRT

● Recyclability: a 100% recyclable TV

Some 38 ideas were generated in the field of future housing designs. In the first session, these were reduced to 24, and a further selection brought this number down to seven. The endeavour to find alternatives for the current glass-based CRT resulted in the proposal to investigate the feasibility of a plastic picture tube. For this project, 21 items to be researched were defined. For full recyclability there were initially 12 ideas.

By the summer of 1996 further progress on the eco-efficiency brainstorming sessions and other related efforts were strongly influenced by TV management, who decided to consolidate all eco-efficiency efforts into one effort: the 'green TV' project. In this project the chemical, physical and electronic limitations were to be explored based on the existing concept of a glass CRT.

As a result of this decision, the proposals for future housing and for 100% recyclability received a clear boost. However, the planned feasibility study on a plastic CRT was replaced by efforts to reduce the energy consumption of products. The output of the eco-efficiency brainstorming sessions and the contributions from other sources (e.g. the TV development department) led to the huge success of the 'green TV'. Performance results are listed in Table 18.5.

The strategic success of the 'green TV' was primarily that 'it could be done'. As such, it was one of the powerful impetuses for the Philips-wide 'Eco Vision' programme (Stevels

| Area of improvement | Percentage improvement |
|---|---|
| Energy consumption reduction | 39 |
| Plastic weight reduction | 32 |
| Hazardous substance reduction | 100 |
| Recycled material use | 69 (of total weight) |
| Recycling potential | 93 |
| Reduction of life-cycle environmental load | 30 |
| Reduction of cost price | 5 |

*Table 18.5* **The environmental performance of the 'green TV' compared with a standard TV (1996)**

2000). The technical success of the 'green TV' was that after 1996 many inventions and improvements to the 'green TV' concept were introduced to conventional products, qualifying the best of them now as 'green flagships'—products with superior environmental performance. However, the 'green TV' was never brought to the market owing to the fact that the environment value chain had not been properly addressed (Ishii and Stevels 2000). The reasons for this were:

- A lack of clear value propositions to the potential customer

- An unclear product line-up positioning at that time

- Insufficient involvement of suppliers

- Insufficient attention to the consequences for production (investment, factory layout)

- Problems with logistics (e.g. availability of recycled material)

For the TV business group, it can be concluded that the brainstorming sessions for implementing eco-efficiency strategies worked out in a different way from that originally anticipated. Instead of leading to technology-oriented projects, the improvement options were merged into advanced product development activities. Moreover, corporate strategy and programme development were strongly affected by the outcomes of the brainstorming sessions and other related activities.

## 18.5 Conclusions

The examples from Philips Consumer Electronics presented in this chapter show that processes of implementing eco-efficiency strategies have resulted in a positive but unpredictable outcome. In terms of achievements, internal factors ('culture') had a strong influence in all three cases studied. Particularly, management interest, decision-making and cross-functional capabilities were major determinants. This 'internal value chain' seemed, in fact, to be more important than the external value chain. Moreover, it can be concluded from this study that business conditions, external influences and the possibility of achieving a competitive edge influenced particularly the time-scale on which eco-efficiency was realised. Room for manoeuvre on the issue of product functionality did not play a major role in the case studies. However, if the main thrust is to realise eco-efficiency through radical changes to housing systems this aspect may become very dominant.

In hindsight, four years after the eco-efficiency programmes actually started at Philips Consumer Electronics, it can be concluded that although the paths taken by the various business groups were different, good results were obtained. Finally, an assessment of the catalysts for a change to eco-efficiency and the creation of an appropriate structuring of the potential environmental and economic benefits within company strategy can contribute positively to the process of change. However, such activities cannot predict the real outcome of the eco-efficiency programmes. In this respect, the implementation of the eco-efficiency approach will remain a real adventure.

# ENVIRONMENTAL TECHNOLOGIES AND THEIR BUSINESS DRIVERS*

*Andrew Baynes, Christian Ridder and Lutz-Günther Scheidt*
Sony International (Europe) GmbH

## 19.1 Implementing environmental technologies at Sony

Electronic products and networks are vital elements of modern society. They offer virtually unlimited possibilities to communicate, create, enjoy, play, inform and do business: so much 'value' is created with increasingly smaller and lighter products. Product miniaturisation across product categories can give the impression that the electronic sector is not the cause of significant environmental impacts. However, the accumulating presence of small products in our households and workplaces is giving rise to questions from private and professional customers over the current and future accumulated environmental impact of electronics—even small electronics.

Recognising that environmental protection is one of the most pressing issues facing humankind today, Sony incorporates a sound respect for nature in all of its business activities. Signed by the president of Sony in December 1998, Sony's environmental action plan, 'Green Management 2002', was established to bring environmental issues into practical developments within Sony's management systems, as well as its products, engineering, marketing, recycling and distribution functions.

The Sony corporate environmental report[1] gives an elaborate overview of targets for the reduction of the environmental impact of different business processes and products. In addition, it shows many actual developments in research, design, service and recycling. In the words of Nobuyuki Idei, president of Sony, 'The 21st century is already being coined the age of the environment. I am determined to see Sony become a significant force in this area through the development of unique and distinctly "Sony-like" environmental innovations.'

---

* The content of this chapter reflects the personal perspective of the authors.
1 www.world.sony.com/eco

The environmental conservation committee (ECC) leads Sony's global environmental network from its headquarters in Tokyo. Four regional environmental conservation committees support the global ECC. Their main task is to implement the global strategy within each geographical zone (Japan, USA, Europe, and Asia outside Japan).

The national facilities and business units in Europe are supported through specific research and development (R&D) activities and through different working groups related to, for example:

- Environmental management systems

- Product planning, engineering and marketing

- Take-back and recycling activities

In the end, it is the facilities and business units that have to put conservation activities into practice. In their day-to-day operations, environmental measures have to be considered in relation to economic and social drivers—case by case, for each new technology, process or procedure. Once the decision to implement a specific measure is positive, it is applied consequently, step by step, horizontally through the product group or even company-wide.

The focus of this chapter will be on the economic and social drivers that influence that decision process in Europe. Different technologies and processes will be categorised according to the type of environmental burden they reduce at different stages of the product life-cycle. It will be explained how conservation measures at each of these stages are effected by different types of economic driver. This will be illustrated with examples of environmental technologies that are implemented, or in discussion, at Sony.

### 19.1.1 Technologies to reduce the consumption of material and energy resources during the production process

The business driver for material- and energy-saving measures is a simple one: return on investment. In some cases, this economic benefit can also exist in combination with functional benefits. A good example is air-moulding technology. This technology was first introduced for one television (TV) model in 1995. Now it is used for the production of all cabinets for large Sony televisions that are manufactured in Europe. An initial modest investment is needed for the more complicated moulds used for the air-moulding process. Nitrogen gas is injected together with the melted plastic to make housing parts of higher mechanical stiffness and of lower plastic content. Smaller machines with a lower clamping force can be used in the process. Air-moulding technology also improves the surface quality of the finished plastic as sink marks—which can arise near points of high material concentration—are eliminated.

Legislative developments may also give rise to increasing return-on-investment efforts. In some European countries manufacturers have to provide a return option for consumer packaging. This resulted in collective systems such as the Duales System Deutschland (Green Dot system), where manufacturers pay for the collection and recycling of all packaging material that they bring to the market.

The recycling of cardboard is cheaper than the recycling of plastic. Sony therefore has reduced its use of expanded polystyrene foam by replacing it with paper-based shock-absorbing support. Sony has co-operated with external partners to develop leading protective paper-based packaging such as one-piece boxes, pulp-mould, cellu-mould and Beeboard® (Plate 19.1) cushioning. In Europe, carton packaging has now been implemented for a broad range of products (e.g. mobile phones, TVs, videocassette recorders [VCRs], loudspeakers and monitors) for some models.

*Plate* 19.1 **Beeboard® packaging used for Super Trinitron 29" TV**

A first priority is to ensure that products do not get damaged while being transported to the distributor or customer. The environmental impact, inefficiency and inconvenience associated with having to replace a damaged product should definitely be avoided. Sony therefore strives to reach an optimal balance between packaging material and protection quality. Drop tests are performed to monitor stringent quality standards.

The worldwide implementation of environmental management systems (EMSs) at manufacturing facilities helps Sony to identify most of the production processes that should and could be improved. In engineering, years of product optimisation and fine-tuning have left little room for further material savings. As a result, further improvements depend on new technological innovations.

## 19.1.2 *Technologies to reduce hazardous emissions from production or products*

Two strong drivers to reduce hazardous emissions are compliance with legislation and responsibility for the health of employees and users. The 'problem' of activities that go beyond compliance is that they often result in higher costs without showing a concrete financial benefit or an added value for the end-users. Here, the business drivers are more indirect, anticipating potential future benefits such as:

- Reduced risks of future customer claims
- Readiness for future legislation
- Ability to meet market requirements (consumer tests, labels)

The most obvious European example from recent years concerns the use of halogenated flame-retardant substances. To provide and ensure the best security for customers, products are required to meet strict safety guidelines. The fire-resistant properties of product parts (i.e. housings as well as circuit boards) come from the application of certain brominated and chlorinated (halogenated) flame-retardant substances. Uncontrolled burning and incineration of plastics containing halogenated flame-retardants can cause dioxins, which are suspected carcinogens, to be released to the atmosphere. The undesired side-effects of these flame-retardants led Sony to intensify its research activities to use a more efficient and safer additive.

Sony first started the application of alternative flame-retardant in plastic cabinets and since 1998 single-sided printed wiring boards (PWBs) have been treated with bromine-free and chlorine-free flame-retardants. Considering the broad industrial application of multi-layer boards, further efforts were undertaken to find new solutions for multi-layers as well. Sony contributed to solutions for the new glass epoxy multi-layer PWBs, containing flame-retardant based on phosphorus and nitrogen compounds. Currently, halogen-free flame-retardants are used for the housing and/or PWBs of some models of Sony digital video disc-player (DVD) players, computer displays, TVs, VCRs, audio appliances and electronic notebooks distributed in Europe.

The draft directive on Waste Electrical and Electronic Equipment (WEEE) has fuelled the discussion on the ban on lead in electronic products. In 1999 Sony set up a special committee to support the development and introduction of lead-free solder. One of the committee's first results arrived in April 2000 with the introduction in Japan of the digital camcorder DCR-TRV20. This is the world's first digital camera in which lead-free solder has been used in the reflow soldering process for all the main PWBs.

The implementation of technologies that reduce hazardous emissions from production or products goes hand in hand with strong internal and external discussion and lobbying: first, because the benefits of the 'soft' business drivers are difficult to express in figures; second, because the environmental benefits of the substitute technology is not always evident.

## 19.1.3 Technologies that reduce energy and material use during the use phase of the product

In theory, technologies that save on the use of energy and materials during the use phase of the product should appeal to the consumer because of the potential cost savings. In practice, private customers do not always make 'rational' purchasing decisions. Technologies that add a small additional cost to the purchase price are not easily accepted, even if the initial cost is 'paid back' over the lifetime of the product. Therefore, at present, it tends to be pressure from governments, non-governmental organisations (NGOs) and consumer organisations that drive energy-saving advances.

The reduction of standby power consumption has been one of the major priorities to reduce the environmental impact of the electronic industry. In Europe, the present power consumption by office equipment is about 50 TWh and is forecasted to grow to 80 TWh by 2010.[2] Home consumer electronics consume 36 TWh and are forecasted to grow to 62 TWh by 2010 (DG XVII-C1 2000). About 11% of the total power used by electronic devices is consumed while the appliance is on standby (based on figures relating to German private households; GFEA 1999). Modern product technologies enable products to interact and communicate with other equipment. This technology may encourage users to permanently leave their products on standby mode to enable incoming signals to be detected. As more products incorporate this type of technology, the issue of standby power consumption will become more pressing.

The European Commission tries, in light of the Kyoto Protocol, to encourage manufacturers to decrease the standby losses of their products through voluntary agreements (through a code of conduct). Furthermore, labels—such as energy labels (GEA [European Group for Efficient Appliances] or EnergyStar) or environmental labels (TCO [Swedish confederation of professional employees] for monitors, PCs and notebooks; Blue Angel, for PCs and notebooks)—are concerned with power consumption of electronic equipment. Sony strongly supports many activities to decrease the power consumption of appliances on standby and in use. Sony has so far achieved a standby power consumption of less than 1 W for a significant model share of its European TV models, DVD players, new audio models (single-function and multi-function sets) and battery chargers for mobile phones, camcorders and Walkman®s.

During product use, environmental impacts arise not only from energy consumption but also through the use of the product's so-called 'consumables' (e.g. batteries and recording media). Batteries regularly have to be replaced, creating waste. Even many types of rechargeable battery have to be disposed of after a while, as their energy capacity decreases because of the so-called 'memory effect'.

Battery-return systems have been introduced in many countries to reduce and avoid the hazardous contamination derived from household waste. Many European countries[3] have introduced laws to prohibit the use of quicksilver (mercury), cadmium and lead in batteries. However, Sony has phased out these substances worldwide. Sony is one of the most advanced developers and promoters of rechargeable lithium-ion batteries. This type of battery can be recharged many times without losing its exceptionally high energy capacity. Lithium-ion batteries are available for almost all portable products: camcorders, mobile telephones, portable audios and digital cameras.

Active users of audio and video devices buy a large collection of videotapes, cassettes, compact discs (CDs) or other recording media. Tape and disc production uses large quantities of water and causes emissions. At Sony's European production facility for batteries and recording media (in Dax, France), the plant's air emissions are purified by a system that burns solvent vapours. The smoke from the incinerator is purified in a smoke washer before the emissions are released to the atmosphere. At Sony's CD plant (Salzburg, Austria) a 'biofilter' has been installed which reduces emissions from solvents by 96%.

Generally, these improvements will result in a higher cost price for the product. The market has to be convinced of the mix of functional, financial end environmental benefits over the full product lifetime via appropriate marketing communication.

2   One terawatt-hour (TWh) is a billion ($10^9$) times greater than a kilowatt-hour.
3   Belgium, Finland, France, Germany, Italy, the Netherlands, Spain, Sweden and the UK.

## 19.1.4　Technologies and services that contribute to product lifetime extension

It is sometimes suggested that the product lifetime is intentionally designed to be short, to stimulate sales of new products. For companies that want to sustain their position in the market this is not an option. In order to maintain the Sony brand name (viewed as one of the company's most valuable assets), Sony must take care to ensure it manufactures products that are highly reliable and that involve consumer-friendly repair procedures.

Products should not need to be replaced, as long their technology is up to date. That is why Sony places emphasis on creating durable products with a long lifetime. Products are designed according to stringent standards and have to pass drop tests and durability tests. The user is advised on the proper use and maintenance in the user manual.

Miniaturisation and the shift to digital technologies have made product repair an increasingly difficult and specialised job. In Europe, Sony has introduced an exchange and refurbishing programme (Fig. 19.1), an innovative service concept for the efficient repair of products that have a large sales volume, such as the Walkman®, Discman®, PlayStation® and mobile phones. In the case of a defect, customers can exchange their products at the dealer for a refurbished model, or even for a new one (if a defect is found within the three-month period from purchase). All defective products from the same type are collected and refurbished (broken parts are repaired or exchanged, and cosmetic parts are checked) at a central European location. As the 'factory-like' repair is more efficient, average costs of repair have been reduced by 25%, and more products get the chance of a second life. ABS (acrylonitrile butadiene styrene) housing parts recovered in the PlayStation® refurbishment process are recycled.

It is already understood in business that a long product lifetime and a high customer satisfaction is key to long-term success. Service activities, however, are too often considered to be a burden. This requires a change of mind-set to the view that many services

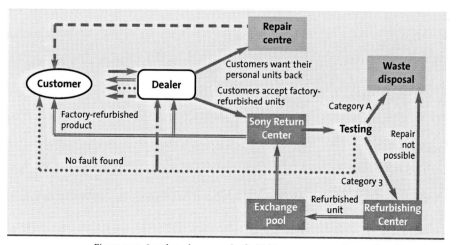

*Figure* 19.1 **Sony's exchange and refurbishing programme for small audio products**

could be considered as a good business opportunity. For example, new revenue can be generated from new software to upgrade a product's functionality, or new cosmetic parts can be sold to adapt the product to changes in the consumer's taste.

### 19.1.5 Technologies and services that contribute to the re-use of components and the recycling of components and materials

If a product becomes obsolete, it should be easy for the consumer to return the product for recycling. Otherwise the product may be disposed of in a municipal landfill site. Professional customers who buy products in large quantities see it as an advantage to know where they can dispose of their old products. Since March 1996 all Sony computer monitors sold in Germany are sold with a specific label that guarantees take-back and recycling free of charge. Any monitor with this label can be returned to one of the 500 return points. The returned monitors are recycled by co-operating recycling firms in an environmentally sound manner.

The European Commission is pushing proposals for a European directive that will make manufacturers (and importers) responsible for the collection and recycling of waste electronics and electrical equipment (WEEE). As one of many contributions to future recycling, Sony has developed an innovative technology for the identification of plastic materials and flame-retardant used in home electronic appliances. Material types are distinguished within a few seconds, greatly simplifying the mechanical recycling of plastics, while manifesting economic benefits. This technology is already being tested for implementation in Japan.

The cost-effectiveness of these technologies relies on a combination of controlling the product during its full lifetime, increasing the scale of operation, internalising recycling costs and benefits, involving suppliers and so on. This combination of activities will require new systems and relationships, such as the leasing and rental of equipment, the establishment of second-hand markets, the offering of refunds for old products and the introduction of 'two-way' contracts with suppliers.

### 19.1.6 Technologies that fulfil the same needs with radically new, less harmful solutions

Radically new technologies and products have always been a strong economic driver because they open the door to new business opportunities. They can be considered as environmental technologies if they replace existing technologies with a higher environmental impact.

Approximately 7,000 copies of the film *Independence Day* were distributed to cinemas all over Europe, consuming approximately 28,000 km of celluloid film. Some 95% of these copies are destroyed and disposed of after a few weeks. The concept of e-cinema involves moving films from analogue celluloid rolls to digital files and moving from conventional to electronic projection. High Definition (HD) technology, with a higher- and better-quality picture, is suitable for cinema projection and could be the solution for celluloid film. The introduction of this new technology could save the use of film material and reduce the chemical emissions related to the production and development of celluloid films, thereby also reducing transport energy and emissions.

Another example of a new market that potentially could reduce the use of fossil fuels is that for video-conferencing systems, to be used in place of face-to-face meetings that require participants to make business trips.

The problem with radically new technologies is that it is very difficult to estimate their net ecological effect. Will they really replace existing solutions, or will they just add to current business? What unexpected 'rebound effects' could occur? Will the (financial) benefits result in an unexpected intensive use of the new technology?

## 19.2 Conclusions and comments

Depending on the type of environmental technology concerned, implementation is driven by different economic and social drivers. In this chapter, examples have been given for:

- Return on investment

- Responsibility for the health of employees and users

- Reducing the risks of future claims

- Complying with and anticipating (future) legislation

- Requirements resulting from consumer tests and eco-labels

- Pressure from governments, NGOs and consumer organisations

- Increased customer satisfaction and maintenance of the Sony brand name

- Sales advantages for professional customers

- New business opportunities

In the public's opinion, products with environmentally sound technologies that show obvious financial benefits are often not regarded as 'truly green products'. Also attempts to achieve an image advantage by the promotion of technologies that contribute to environmental conservation are often observed very critically. This is difficult to understand. Why should it hurt to be 'green'?

In some cases of eco-product design very different materials can sometimes be used compared with products commonly found on the market. Criticism can often arise when the infrastructure needed to treat the new materials in an environmentally sound and economically attractive way does not (yet) exist. Also, qualifications such as 'easy to disassemble and recycle' have little value if nothing is done to ensure that the product is actually supported with a disassembly and recycling system.

Sony aims not to develop single 'green' products in isolation but instead to implement new technologies horizontally across the European product groups. To avoid working on isolated solutions that are not supported by the necessary infrastructure, Sony is in permanent dialogue with its stakeholders: not only its suppliers, dealers and recyclers but also policy-makers and competitors. Those who co-operate and work together today may reap the rewards of the sustainable world of tomorrow.

# 'AWARENESS'
## Sustainability by industrial design

*Philip Thompson*
**Electrolux Industrial
Design Centre, UK**

*Chris Sherwin*
**Cranfield University, UK**

## 20.1 Background

The 'Awareness' project aimed to explore and define industrial design for sustainability. At Electrolux, sustainability is seen as an equation that balances production and consumption—the demands of modern living and the need for company profitability—with the environmental limits of sustainable development. This balances 'desirables' (what is appealing and enjoyable to consumers) with 'sustainables' (what is environmentally acceptable and can continue indefinitely) and demands participation from all actors within the production and consumption chain, not least design professionals.

### 20.1.1 Ecodesign at Electrolux

Electrolux is recognised for its corporate excellence and best-practice policies in the development of environmentally sound processes and systems and for the launch of leading environmentally sensitive products to market. The company's 'total approach' to environmental management and ecodesign represents a search for continuous environmental improvements to all business operations and requires a proactive approach and market stance (Electrolux 1999).

Adoption of this incremental approach to ecodesign integration (step-by-step improvements to existing product and processes) leads the company to strive for increasing and systematic improvement. The recognition that, for instance, 80%–90% of the impacts of its products occur during 'use' and that these impacts are largely determined by how products are designed (Electrolux 1997; Design Council 1997) has led the company to look to integrate ecodesign at the 'early stages' of the product development process. Many of these early design stages are conducted at the Electrolux Industrial Design Centre.

### 20.1.2 *Sustainability by industrial design*

With some 100 in-house designers working across the product development spectrum, the Industrial Design Centre is now recognised as being of central importance to Electrolux's overall corporate environmental performance and is challenged to engage with key company concerns and contribute to its environmental success. Initially, however, there was some uncertainty as to the nature, contribution and approach of industrial designers to ecodesign. Though designers were committed and motivated, ecodesign was viewed within the department as engineering-based, data-intensive and scientifically oriented, to be integrated at later product development stages and in which industrial designers could have little involvement. This 'technology-led' approach had been the major corporate ecodesign driver and practice to date.

Designers, however, felt they could engage with ecodesign, holding the view that there is 'potential for green design that makes it much more than green technology' (Ryan 1993). Current ecodesign practice was viewed as blinkered and limiting, and it was felt there are other, more appropriate, ecodesign pathways for designers to follow.

### 20.1.3 *Ecodesign and industrial design*

The domain of industrial design is usually understood to involve the proposal of new and innovative ideas and to deal extensively with consumption-oriented design dimensions such as behaviour and desire in relation to products and services. Described as a bridge or link between producers and the market, industrial designers have the ability to propose not only what is technically possible but also what is socially acceptable and culturally desirable (Manzini 1993), marrying the 'sustainables' with 'desirables' mentioned above.

Two emerging 'sustainability' principles have enormous implications and potentiality for industrial design. 'Factor 20' and the sustainable consumption debate suggests that ecodesign innovations need to be both radical (beyond the redesign of what exists) and oriented to lifestyle and the demand side (UNEP 1992; von Weizsäcker *et al.* 1997), both of which comfortably fit industrial design skills and practice. There is clearly great potential within the discipline, and to better understand and exploit this the Industrial Design Centre turned to the research community for direction and guidance.

## 20.2 The collaborative process

The collaborative project described here began during a two-day workshop in the Derbyshire countryside of England, attended by four members of the Electrolux industrial design team and three ecodesign researchers from Cranfield University. Here, the parties familiarised themselves with each other and the project in question.

For Electrolux, ecodesign (or any novel or exploratory subject) falls within the remit of concept design. The concept design team is a global, strategic team within the Electrolux group. The mission of the team is to focus on enhanced living, combining design and knowledge of customer needs as future users. The team generates proposals and marketing messages, designed to create innovative and unique product solutions for the future.

Concept design projects do not feed directly or automatically into product development; rather they stimulate secondary-stage development through parts of projects or ideas being taken forward for consideration at a later stage. This allows the project to develop in an open and unqualified manner.

## 20.2.1 *The design project*

The project selected was the 'Ecodesign Kitchen of the Future' (an international design competition), which contained a number of critical factors of relevance to this collaborative project:

- It was 'live', helping to make the concept project more real and focusing discussions within a specific time-frame and towards a specific goal

- The project was concept-based and therefore open and innovative

- The kitchen was seen as an ideal way to embrace both technological and supply-side issues (such as how it is made and what it contains) as well as lifestyle and demand-side ecodesign issues (such as how it is used and what are its energy and material throughputs), essential requirements for both sustainability and for industrial designers

## 20.2.2 *Aims and responsibilities*

The aims, responsibilities and competences of the collaborators, though convergent, were inevitably different. For Electrolux this project was seen as exploratory design research to develop relevant ecodesign working methods and practice. Electrolux brought design capabilities, skill and experience to the project. It had responsibility for conducting all design and development stages of the project, including definition of the project brief, concept generation, design development and detailing as well as responsibility for producing models and making the final presentation.

For Cranfield University this was a chance for involvement in 'live' design activities as well as an opportunity to understand and describe the design and collaborative process. After initiating the project, Cranfield had responsibility for introducing ecodesign and helping to direct the early stages of the project. This role extended to further project stimulation as well as input, validation and feedback on the concept, detail and presentation stages of the design process.

In this sense, the role of research was not to help conduct operational design activities or resolve specific industrial problems; rather it was to propose and push new ideas and to move designers into new and uncharted waters. Research was therefore aimed at introducing novel concepts, new perspectives and approaches and at stretching the boundaries of current design practice. That such activities are located outside the organisational boundaries is of central importance to this process.

## 20.3 **Workshop process**

The workshop aimed to result in three key outcomes:

- A collaborative relationship
- A design brief consisting of the main project aims and focus
- A project agenda describing the tasks to follow the workshop

The design brief is described in more detail below, but the project required further collaborative interaction and other tasks. Within the workshop these were identified and led as shown in Table 20.1.

| At workshop | Led by |
| --- | --- |
| 1. Introduction to ecodesign: some introductory models and tasks | Cranfield |
| 2. Examination of the possibilities of eco-design: some case studies and examples of best and future practice | Cranfield |
| 3. Definition of the project focus: time-frame and target audience | Electrolux and Cranfield |
| 4. Definition of the project brief: a statement of intent | Electrolux with Cranfield |
| **After workshop** | |
| 5. Summarising of ecodesign knowledge into manageable form to aid the designers' idea generation | Cranfield |
| 6. Idea generation | Electrolux |
| 7. Project review | Electrolux with input and feedback from Cranfield |
| 8. Concept development and design | Electrolux |
| 9. Project review | Electrolux with input and feedback from Cranfield |
| 10. Detailing of concepts and production models | Electrolux |

*Table* 20.1 **The workshop process: collaboration between Cranfield University and the Industrial Design Centre, Electrolux**

### 20.3.1 *Workshop tools and methods*

Acting as the project stimulus, Cranfield University began by introducing general ecodesign strategies (such as the 3 Rs—reduce, re-use, recycle) and models of ecodesign innovation (repair, refine, redesign, rethink) followed by some more specific ecodesign information for kitchen products, services and consumer behaviour.

Brainstorming techniques (challenging designers to develop and propose ideas for a sustainable kitchen) aimed to familiarise industrial designers with ecodesign and to empower them to apply it. This introduced participants to the limitations and possibilities of ecodesign and also developed group dynamics.

More specific presentations were then introduced, highlighting domestic and kitchen information in terms of resource and material use and human factors. These were presented as case studies and examples as industrial designers respond best to visible and tangible examples, especially when presented visually.

The exploratory nature of the project and the working practice of the concept design team meant that no analytical tools were used or required. Industrial design is a non-prescriptive process and the design team was encouraged to find its own path and to define its own agenda. The workshop was an opportunity to think freely and creatively and thus broaden the design space.

After the initial introduction to ecodesign and various ecodesign tasks, designers began to fit the project to existing industrial design practice, taking ownership of the project. Here the central project tenet was identified and developed—that industrial design could empower consumers to engage in more environmentally conscious behaviour through sensitive design and responsible production. Industrial design could facilitate and raise *awareness*.

### 20.3.2  The design brief: a partnership of awareness

The collaborative workshop resulted in a design brief, which was a basic statement of intent for the design project. Within this it was felt necessary to place environmental issues as a core theme, using them as the major innovation driver for design and concept development. If environmental issues are included as a peripheral issue, they will be lost to the process, as environment is always the first thing forgotten.

The design brief and project approach was based around the following premise: 'Good corporate citizenship will provide willing consumers with "facilitators" (products and services) to enable them to act responsibly.' This was seen as a 'partnership' between producers and consumers. Here, producers are conscious of their responsibilities and provide consumers with solutions enabling them to manage their actions responsibly—a 'partnership of awareness'.

## 20.4  The design process

Real-world constraints ensured that design processes and the resultant innovations were tangible and comprehensible to consumers and producers alike. The focus of this project was embodied within a design brief, key aspects of which included:

- Use of real behaviour
- The need to balance quality and environment

- The use of (future) support systems for consumers (waste collection, home delivery)

- The need to support and enhance consumer opportunities, not to force the adoption of a particular behaviour

It was also necessary to identify the proposed time-frame (15–20 years in the future) and the target audience (responsible and hedonistic consumers) at these stages.

The design brief and project specifications—the key outcomes from the workshop—are visually represented in the following sections. Figure 20.1 illustrates the focus on producer and consumer. Profiles of (responsible and hedonistic) consumers come from existing Electrolux information and market awareness (Fig. 20.2). This provided descriptions of lifestyles as well as of domestic needs and expectations. The kitchen map provides a universal audit of domestic behaviour (buy, store, prepare, etc.) followed within the kitchen (Fig. 20.3). The diagram of the kitchen boundaries helped visualise the project and represent its tangible nature through product concepts (Fig. 20.4). Within the project, factors outside the boundaries could be considered (food delivery and waste collection), but the proposals should be product concepts that fit within the kitchen boundaries. Finally, the design team chose 'awareness' to focus on both producer and consumer and that 'real' consumer behaviour is a critical factor (Fig. 20.5).

## 20.4.1 Approach

After the workshop, the project moved on to idea generation and concept development stages, conducted at Electrolux. To facilitate this, Cranfield University mapped all eco-design strategies, ideas and case studies into a manageable and usable form to aid concept generation. From these the designers generated ideas, working through concept development to detailed concepts to the production of scale models.

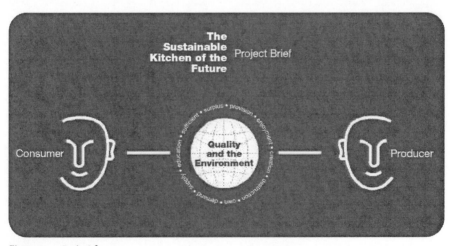

*Figure* 20.1 **Project focus**

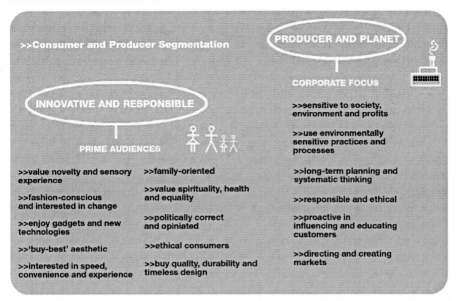

*Figure* 20.2  **Target audience and corporate values**

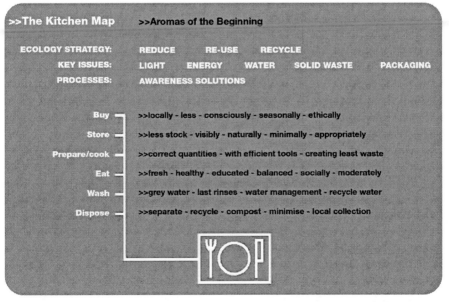

*Figure* 20.3  **Kitchen processes**

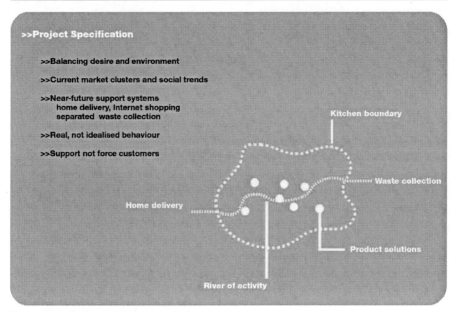

*Figure 20.4* **Kitchen and project boundaries**

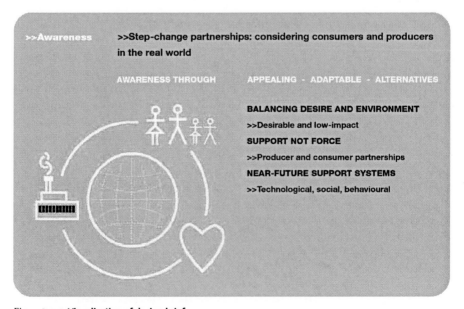

*Figure 20.5* **Visualisation of design brief**

The approach aimed to propose 'one-off' innovative products facilitating 'awareness'. The latest and best environmentally sound technologies were used and market acceptance was also a key consideration. Environmentally sensitive consumer awareness is developed by providing consumers with information on the products' efficient resource use and their benefits. Smarter, educational and informative tools permit willing users to follow better environmental practice within their domestic environment.

## 20.5 The product concepts

The project focus—awareness—was synthesised within design ideas which, after iteration, feedback and validation from Cranfield and after further development, resulted in seven visionary product concepts, described as 'facilitators'. These explore new types of behaviour and lifestyle options in the kitchen and represent new business concepts for the company, as well as indicating new and future areas for ecodesign to explore. The seven product concepts—the smart sink, the datawall, the cooker, chest freezer, light plants, passive coolers and portion projector—are described and illustrated below. These have been described more extensively in Sherwin and Bhamra 1999 and Sherwin *et al.* 1998.

### 20.5.1 The smart sink

The smart sink is the centre of household water management (Fig. 20.6; Plate 20.1). The membrane sink expands to minimise water use, and the smart tap switches from jet, to spray, to mist to suit user needs. A consumption meter and water-level indicator in the main basin give feedback on rates and level of water usage. Household grey water is managed visibly by using an osmosis purifier and a cyclone filter located in the pedestal, both of which are linked to a household grey-water storage unit.

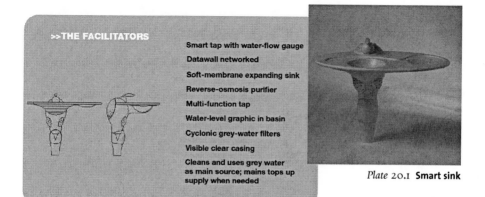

>>THE FACILITATORS

Smart tap with water-flow gauge
Datawall networked
Soft-membrane expanding sink
Reverse-osmosis purifier
Multi-function tap
Water-level graphic in basin
Cyclonic grey-water filters
Visible clear casing
Cleans and uses grey water as main source; mains tops up supply when needed

*Plate* 20.1 **Smart sink**

*Figure* 20.6 **Smart sink: design specification**

## 20.5.2 *The datawall*

The datawall is the 'brain' of the kitchen, an information product that helps manage and communicate domestic resource use (Fig. 20.7; Plate 20.2). It is connected to other kitchen products, giving feedback on levels of resource usage. It also holds an inventory of food stock, communicating quantities, freshness and use-by dates. It is a link to the supermarket for home shopping and delivery services and contains the 'menu master'—advice on recipes, cooking techniques and health and dietary issues. Behind this information interface is a storage area consisting of refillable and re-usable containers of attractive design.

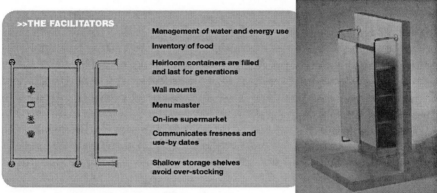

>>THE FACILITATORS

Management of water and energy use

Inventory of food

Heirloom containers are filled and last for generations

Wall mounts

Menu master

On-line supermarket

Communicates fresness and use-by dates

Shallow storage shelves avoid over-stocking

*Figure* 20.7 **Datawall: design specification**

*Plate* 20.2 **Datawall**

## 20.5.3 *The cooker*

The cooker uses steam and gas under an insulted cover; it also provides heating for space and water (Fig. 20.8; Plate 20.3). The base, of thermal bricks, incinerates waste to provide extra domestic heat.

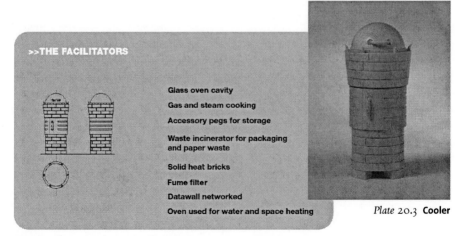

>>THE FACILITATORS

Glass oven cavity

Gas and steam cooking

Accessory pegs for storage

Waste incinerator for packaging and paper waste

Solid heat bricks

Fume filter

Datawall networked

Oven used for water and space heating

*Plate* 20.3 **Cooler**

*Figure* 20.8 **Cooler: design specification**

## 20.5.4  The chest freezer

The strength of some products is their simplicity and elegance. As cold air falls, it is not efficient to have front-door access to freezers, because cold air falls out. As with traditional chest freezers, the principle of this chest freezer is that it is much more efficient to have access from above (Fig. 20.9; Plate 20.4). The body is ceramic, to increase thermal mass, and is raised so that the top becomes a work surface. The lower section is then utilised as a domestic recycling unit.

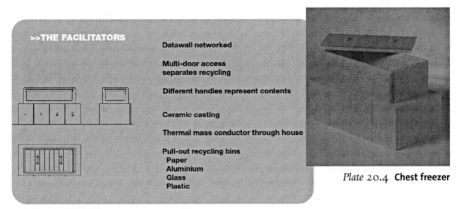

*Plate* 20.4  **Chest freezer**

*Figure* 20.9  **Chest freezer: design specification**

## 20.5.5  Light plants

The light plants are communicators of environmental principles, a functional reminder of resource use (Fig. 20.10; Plate 20.5). Left on a windowsill or in a place where there is good daylight, they collect and store solar energy, to be emitted as light when required.

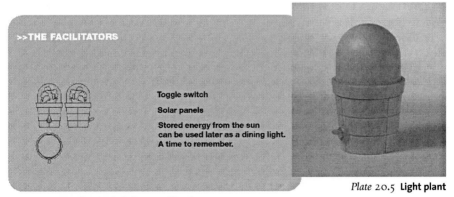

*Plate* 20.5  **Light plant**

*Figure* 20.10  **Light plant: design specification**

## 20.5.6 Passive coolers

Passive cooling is an age-old technology. The newly designed cooler stores food in net bags inside the unit, which are 'planted' in syntho-soil (Fig. 20.11; Plate 20.6). This symbolic act aims to reconnect us to ecological principles and processes in a contemporary interpretation of an environmentally benign technology.

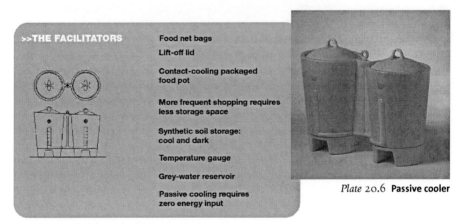

>>THE FACILITATORS

Food net bags

Lift-off lid

Contact-cooling packaged food pot

More frequent shopping requires less storage space

Synthetic soil storage: cool and dark

Temperature gauge

Grey-water reservoir

Passive cooling requires zero energy input

*Plate* 20.6 **Passive cooler**

*Figure* 20.11 **Passive cooler: design specification**

## 20.5.7 The portion projector

The portion projector eliminates excessive or wasteful preparation and cooking (Fig. 20.12; Plate 20.7). Connected to the datawall information network, the portion projector dials up meals, and the correct quantities are projected onto the underplate. This reduces waste and ensures enough food is prepared and cooked for all.

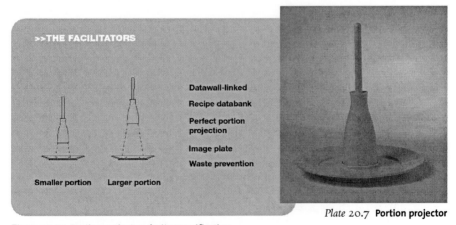

>>THE FACILITATORS

Datawall-linked

Recipe databank

Perfect portion projection

Image plate

Waste prevention

Smaller portion    Larger portion

*Plate* 20.7 **Portion projector**

*Figure* 20.12 **Portion projector: design specification**

## 20.5.8 The kitchen ecosystem

Though each product stands alone, by considering the kitchen as a system, designers create kitchen products that are interconnected and networked to share information and resources. The 'kitchen ecosystem' (Fig. 20.13) illustrates information and resource flows through the kitchen and throughout the household more generally.

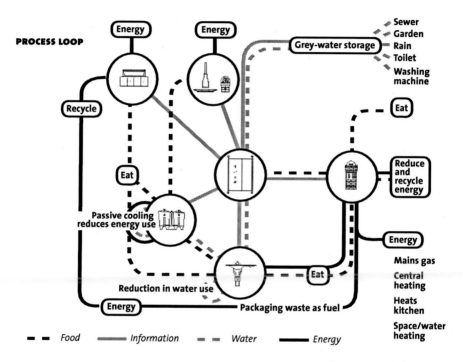

*Figure* 20.13  **Kitchen system**

## 20.6 Conclusions

This project suggests that industrial design is a good place to integrate ecodesign where innovative approaches and new ideas are required (Sherwin and Bhamra 1999). To do this it seemed unnecessary to assess what is environmentally 'bad' about existing products as no comprehensive environmental studies were used here. Such 'corrective' ecodesign (Ryan *et al.* 1992) usually leads to product improvement (with reduced environmental impact) rather than new product innovation (Hook 1995) as in the outcomes described above. This might suggest that environmental audits of product performance (such as life-cycle assessment) are not essential for ecodesign innovation, in turn raising questions of the real benefit of the current life-cycle orientation of ecodesign (Sherwin *et al.* 1998).

Furthermore, this project indicates the importance of the sustainable lifestyle agenda both to ecodesign innovation and to the working practices of industrial designers. Within the project, the designers highlighted two fundamental ecodesign factors:

- Product efficiency, dealing with 'eco-production'

- Use efficiency, dealing with 'eco-consumption'

It is use efficiency, dealing more with the realms of sustainable consumption and 'greening' consumer behaviour, that is more within the remit of industrial designers. Sustainability requires consumption-oriented and lifestyle-focused innovations, mirroring the design orientation of industrial design. So perhaps industrial designers will play a central role in the transition towards this sustainable future, bringing great opportunities and challenges as well as great responsibility which the design profession must respond to.

Similarly the project challenged designers to innovate by using Charter's four-step model of ecodesign innovation (Charter and Chick 1997)—repair, refine, redesign, rethink. The Awareness project and the designers working within it suggested that it is to the redesign and rethink of new product concepts (rather than repair and refine of existing products) that industrial designers can best contribute (Fig. 20.14).

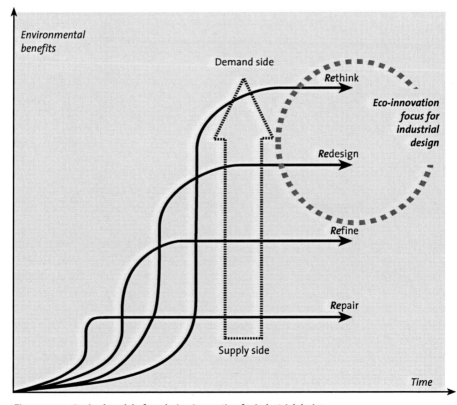

*Figure* 20.14 **Revised model of ecodesign innovation for industrial design**

## 20.7 Discussion and implications

This section discusses the implications of the project with the benefit of hindsight and reflection. The exploratory nature of the project and of the concept design team means the outcomes are used for educational, exploratory or awareness-raising purposes and are unlikely to feed directly into product development. For example, this project is now being used to raise the profile of ecodesign within the department and to stimulate and motivate designers into individual action as well as being used as a facilitator for stakeholder communication. As a concept demonstrator the Awareness project has helped build and strengthen relationships with other internal functions (e.g. the new business and the environmental affairs departments) as a visible means of explaining the role of the industrial design department. The outcomes have also appeared in the Electrolux corporate environmental report (Electrolux 1999), were exhibited at the annual corporate design exhibition in Paris and were profiled in the Young Foresight 'Techno' series produced for the BBC (Young Foresight Ltd 2000). The project's success is its ability to embody and express certain principles to stakeholders (producers, consumers, other departments and industrial design itself) and to visibly and tangibly explain 'eco-industrial design' while also providing stimulus for the ecodesign community.

The project also fits into the 'redesign' stages of the ecodesign innovation model, matches the existing practice of industrial designers and can be managed and conducted by industrial designers alone. When designers move beyond this, towards 'rethink' (as with service and dematerialisation concepts), they begin to redefine and rethink stakeholder roles and company boundaries. This begins to question the existing skills of industrial design (ideas, sketching, model making, etc.) and calls for more strategic insight and planning. Here, uncomfortable questions are asked of the capabilities and practice of design itself, while those involved are forced further outside the day-to-day activities of design operation. However, it is along this path that design must go. Designers must question the existing views of both industrial design and ecodesign and constantly create new languages of what is acceptable and desirable in terms of technology and behaviour, balanced with what is environmentally sustainable. Increasing *awareness* by industrial design will be of central importance to this.

# SUSTAINABLE PRODUCT DESIGN AND RESOURCE MANAGEMENT AT THE KAMBIUM FURNITURE WORKSHOP

*Holger Rohn*
Trifolium—Sustainable
Management Consulting, Germany

*Angelika von Proff-Kesseler*
Kambium Furniture Workshop Inc., Germany

Kambium Möbelwerkstätte GmbH (Kambium Furniture Workshop Inc.) is a medium-sized company in Lindlar near Cologne, Germany. The enterprise was founded in 1991 and presently employs 38 people. The organisational structure is relatively horizontal and is typical for a business of this size. In 1998, approximately 150 kitchens (and some furniture for other areas) were produced, yielding gross revenues of DM7.0 million (about US$3.5 million). Since November 1997, office-fitting under the name 'Working Class' has also been available. In March 1999 a branch was opened in Düsseldorf, with a planning office and showrooms.

From the outset the design of all Kambium kitchens (Plate 21.1) was oriented towards high quality and longevity of the furniture. From the beginning, ecological goals were placed at the core of many of Kambium's activities. These goals have been reached and are now a natural part of all business activities. From 1995 Kambium began increasingly to think about achieving a distinct design profile. The main reason was that it became obvious that all potential customers were convinced of Kambium's product quality and planning competence but not always with the product design of the furniture. Furthermore, the kitchen sector has changed tremendously in recent years: many factories have entered the market with so-called 'new kitchen concepts'. The background to this development is a change in the way in which consumers view kitchens. In the past the kitchen was generally regarded as a 'working room' in which generally good functions were performed. Today the kitchen is developing increasingly into a communication and multi-functional centre in the home.

In reaction to these trends Kambium has worked more on different aspects of design and has become engaged in different projects. The new orientation of the whole

*Plate 21.1* **Kitchen made by Kambium**

*Source:* Kambium

company illustrates the need to fulfil the demand for high-quality products in terms of design. The goals are being reached step by step; some are still in progress. An important role is being played by the interdisciplinary Kambium design team, in which architects, designers, engineers and dieticians are working successfully together.

Kambium kitchens are situated at the high end of the market in every respect. The use of modern computer technologies (computer-aided design [CAD] and computer numerically controlled [CNC] instruments) facilitates the production of very individual kitchens, tailored to each customer's specifications. One of the methods employed in the assembly derives from a traditional construction method (*Hirnleistenbauweise*) which guarantees integral structural stability, despite the characteristic of solid wood to shrink and swell over time.

Kitchens made by Kambium are manufactured from solid wood and are produced and distributed to the highest standard of environmental compatibility. In 1995 the Kambium Furniture Workshop formulated a ten-point environmental policy document (Kambium 1995) which contains ambitious demands such as an examination of the environmental effects of the products spanning the entire product life-cycle, the regional focus of the firm and its source of energy (to be environmentally benign). Examples of Kambium's deep commitment to environmental principles include:

- The choice of a site suitable the use of wind energy (see Plate 21.2)

- Two block-type thermal power plants to heat the buildings and meet the energy needs of drying the wood

*Plate 21.2* **Kambium Furniture Workshop in Lindlar, Germany**
*Source:* Kambium

- The use of ecologically oriented architectural construction methods
- The use of rainwater to meet some water requirements
- The use of direct marketing, with a focus on local markets and therefore on avoiding the need for packaging for transportation
- The use of wood from European sources as the primary raw material
- The use of natural oils to impregnate furniture surfaces
- A commitment to manufacturing products that have a long lifetime
- The offer of re-orders, repairs as well as conversions and modifications
- The requirement that all parts of the kitchen should be easily returned to natural cycles

Several scientific studies and projects have been carried out in co-operation with Kambium (e.g. Liedtke *et al.* 1995). As a result of this commitment the 'Eco-Manager of the year 1996' award from the World Wide Fund for Nature (WWF) and *Capital* (a large-circulation business magazine produced in Germany) was presented to the managers and owners (A. von Proff-Kesseler and C. Gehrt).

In 1993 Kambium Furniture Workshop Inc. searched for a useful, simple, practice-oriented and directionally stable method to gain a better understanding of the environmental impacts of its activities and products. After an extended examination and consultation with the Wuppertal Institute, Kambium decided to evaluate its environmental impact by means of the MIPS (material input per unit service) approach and to improve its performance in this area by using a resource management programme.

In a case study on eco-audits and resource management (Liedtke *et al.* 1995) the Wuppertal Institute, in co-operation with the Kambium Furniture Workshop Inc., tested a resource management programme 'in real life' and analysed whether the programme satisfied the requirements of the European Union's Eco-management and Audit Scheme (EMAS; see CEC 1993). In this chapter, we present some of the results of that project as well as aspects of resource management and ecological design in general, particularly with regard to the Kambium Furniture Workshop.

## 21.1 Ecodesign and resource management

The resource management programme was developed at the Wuppertal Institute on the basis of the MIPS concept (Schmidt-Bleek 1994). It is a management system designed to decrease costs and improve material flows throughout the product life-cycle, with the overall goal of increasing resource efficiency by a factor of 10 (see FIoC 1997; OECD 1997b; Weizsäcker *et al.* 1997). Resource management represents a fundamental instrument for use in environmental audits. It is focused on the life-cycle of products and is site-specific. It combines an input–output analysis of the firm, an analysis of the resource demands of products during their life-cycle and the firm's cost accounting procedures.

It includes three complementary and interlinked components:

- Material flow management
- Product management
- Ecodesign

Material flow management focuses on the life-cycle phases of manufacturing, recycling and disposal of the materials used to produce a product and of the final product itself. Product management has the goal of improving the environmental performance of the product during use (i.e. to design a use phase that is resource-efficient). The ecodesign component aids in product development through specific resource-efficiency criteria (see Schmidt-Bleek and Tischner 1995). The type of resource management to be implemented will depend on the situation—that is, on whether redesign is required (case 1) or whether a new design must be found for a product (case 2).

In case 1—the redesign of an existing product—the product is already on the market, the production site is already installed and consumers (enterprises and final consumers) are in tune with their behaviour in relation to the product. Steps for resource management include:

- **Material flow management.** Different processes will be analysed in terms of their cost and resource efficiency potential; plans for improvement will be developed.

- **Product management.** Consumers will receive advice on the extent to which their behaviour influences the resource efficiency of the product; a channel of communication will be opened so that new ways of product use can be conveyed.

- **Ecodesign.** The product's weaknesses will be analysed with use of a resource-efficiency criteria list; the extent to which resource-efficient product design is possible given the existing production infrastructure will be examined (Liedtke *et al.* 1998).

In case 2—the design of a new product—because the product is new, consumers (enterprises and final consumers) are not in tune with their behaviour in relation to the product. Steps for resource management include:

- **Material flow management.** For a new product new production processes and new production technologies are needed. Often it will be necessary to find and include new companies in the manufacture and operation of the product (e.g. suppliers or for maintenance).

- **Product management.** The service the product needs to deliver will be closely defined with the final consumer, paying special attention to resource efficiency (e.g. providing the cooling function for fresh food in a household with reduced energy and material consumption).

- **Ecodesign.** By using the resource-efficiency criteria list a new consumer-oriented product will be developed; in order to design a product that needs fewer resources throughout its life-cycle entails altering how the consumer uses the product (Liedtke *et al.* 1998).

The resource management concept is based on information on material intensity. To analyse material intensity, the MIPS approach was developed (Schmidt-Bleek 1994). The MIPS approach is a methodology to measure material input at all levels (product, company, national economy, regional) and has two components: material input and service units (Liedtke *et al.* 1994).

## 21.2 Ecodesign at the Kambium Furniture Workshop

Ecodesign, the third component of resource management, determines the ecologically relevant characteristics of products throughout their entire life, from production to re-use or disposal. A product that has been conceived according to ecological considerations will place less of a burden on the environment than will technology concerned with avoiding or removing such damage after it has occurred. The relevant product characteristics, determined with the help of the MIPS approach, that should be considered in devising a new product are, above all: construction, material, longevity, re-use and continued use.

Products are rarely optimised for long life. Defective parts often cannot be repaired because they are inseparable from the rest of the device. Very few products can be adapted to the changing patterns of a user's life. Modular furniture, on the other hand, permits the user to follow fashions by facilitating the exchange of accessories as well as adapting to the changing spatial circumstances of a particular person (Liedtke *et al.* 1998).

Ecodesign aims to contribute to a system-wide increase in resource productivity. Here, we focus on examples of the search for dematerialisation potential through an examination of Kambium products according to various criteria for ecodesign—one very important part of Kambium's design strategy.

The strengths and weaknesses of Kambium's kitchen concept were examined by using the checklist shown in Table 21.1, which enumerates the environmentally relevant product characteristics (Schmidt-Bleek and Tischner 1995). Not all the characteristics mentioned are relevant to kitchen design. Those relevant were selected and then assessed for the Kambium product. The assessment of the ecological design characteristics of the Kambium kitchen reveals a favourable profile: almost 60% (25) of the 42 parameters examined were 'well met or solved', just over 9% (4) were 'not well met or not solved', 19% (8) were 'in part well met but in other respects less well met' and almost 12% (5) were 'not relevant'.

According to this first assessment, made during the period 1994–95, the design aspects that Kambium should improve on in the future include (Liedtke *et al.* 1995):

- In production: material input, energy input, transport intensity and, most importantly, waste generation

- In the use phase: size and weight, use of an 'afashionable' or neutral design, ease of disassembly, modular construction and degree of standardisation, combination possibilities, capability to vary the design in response to different customer preferences

- In the return phase: ease of disassembly, separability, material labelling, re-use and continued use, possibility of collection and sorting

## 21.3 Results and conclusions

The Kambium project is able to demonstrate that qualitatively demanding resource management offers numerous opportunities for reducing environmental burdens at the company level while facilitating companies' participation in the market. Within four years (1994–98) Kambium had an increase in turnover of 35% and improved its customer loyalty considerably. Both can partly be put down to the fact that Kambium had extensively communicated its overall product quality and environmental activities and therefore was able to attract new customers (110 kitchens in 1994 up to 150 in 1998). Moreover, most of its customers have a high regard for the role of Kambium as a local producer. This means, for example, that customers can come anytime to the workshop and see or even feel how their furniture is manufactured.

| Phase and characteristics | Assessment |
|---|---|
| **Production phase** | |
| ▶ Low material or energy input* | +/– |
| ▶ Low waste intensity | – |
| ▶ Low scrap rate* | + |
| ▶ High productivity or output* | o |
| ▶ Low materials diversity* | + |
| ▶ Low transport intensity* | +/– |
| ▶ Low packaging intensity* | + |
| ▶ Minimised appropriation of land area | o |
| ▶ Minimised use of harmful substances | + |
| **Use or consumption phase** | |
| ▶ Low material or energy input* | + |
| ▶ Minimised size and weight* | +/– |
| ▶ Minimised appropriation of land area | o |
| ▶ Low cleaning effort* | + |
| ▶ High multi-functionality* | o |
| ▶ High opportunity for repeated use* | + |
| ▶ High opportunity for joint use* | + |
| ▶ Low waste intensity | + |
| ▶ Minimised use of harmful substances | + |
| ▶ High durability* | + |
| ▶ Non-fashion-oriented design* | +/– |
| ▶ High value estimation | + |
| ▶ High corrosion resistance* | + |
| ▶ High maintenance possibilities* | + |
| ▶ Easy repairability* | + |
| ▶ Easy disassembly* | – |
| ▶ High reliability* | + |
| ▶ High robustness* | + |
| ▶ Low material fatigue and susceptibility to wear* | + |
| ▶ Modular construction and degree of standardisation* | +/– |
| ▶ High adaptability to technical progress* | + |
| ▶ Options for recombination, variability* | +/– |
| **Recycling phase** | |
| ▶ Easy disassembly or separability* | +/– |
| ▶ Low cleaning effort* | + |
| ▶ Clear material labelling* | – |
| ▶ High possibility of disposal* | o |
| ▶ Continued use, re-use* | +/– |
| ▶ Recycling of component parts; secondary utilisation of materials* | + |
| ▶ Possibility of collecting and sorting* | – |
| ▶ Low material or energy input* | + |
| **Disposal phase** | |
| ▶ High compostability or fermentability | + |
| ▶ Positive combustion characteristics | + |
| ▶ Low environmental consequences of landfilling | + |

+   well met or solved     +/–   in part well met but in other respects less well met
–   not well met or solved     o    not relevant

Characteristics marked with an asterisk are taken into account in the material input per service unit (MIPS) approach (Liedtke *et al.* 1995).

*Table* 21.1 **Environmentally relevant product characteristics, as assessed for Kambium kitchens**

The three elements of resource management—material flow management, product management and ecodesign—encourage a high standard in terms of cost and eco-efficiency of products and production patterns. The MIPS approach is an assessment tool well suited to surveying the environmental character of products and to developing a resource management plan spanning the entire life-cycle of a product.

As an example, Kambium made different improvements to the production phase—saving both resources and costs. Compared with conventional energy management, Kambium has reduced its energy-dependent resource consumption by a factor of nearly 4. Resource savings on the input side necessarily lead to a reduced level of air pollution on the output side (e.g. just over 50 tons less $CO_2$ per year were emitted into the atmosphere).

One result of the co-operation with the Wuppertal Institute was that Kambium has started to offer its customers the option to choose locally quarried rock (*Grauwacke*) for counter tops rather than the transport-intensive imported granite (e.g. from India or Brazil). First tests were carried out with *Grauwacke* in 1995; today about 30% of all counter tops are made of *Grauwacke*.

Another result of the ecodesign analyses has been the development of further case studies on and prototypes of kitchen furniture and a complete office furniture pro-gramme (introduced in 1997). In 1998 Kambium started a project in collaboration with the Faculty of Design (Fachbereich Design) of the Cologne University of Applied Science (Fachhochschule Köln) with the aim of developing new concepts for 'The solid wood kitchen of the future' (FoD 1999). Kambium's goal was to receive support to achieve a design unique to Kambium, to prepare it for the requirements of the market in the new millennium.

# MANUFACTUM
## Sustainability as an elementary part of the marketing concept

*Uli Burchardt*
**Manufactum Hoof & Partner KG, Germany**

Since it was founded in 1989 Manufactum Hoof & Partner KG has experienced rapid development. From its first fiscal year, the net turnover has soared from around € 375,000 to over € 45 million today. The company has been declaring a profit since its third year of business. At the end of 2000 Manufactum had around 1,100,000 addresses on its books, of which approximately 500,000 are active customers, making it one of the most successful new companies in recent decades in the booming industry of specialist mail-order companies. Today, the company headquarters, in the former Waltrop mine on the northern periphery of the Ruhr, employs an administrative staff of 120; the warehouse is managed by an external service provider.

To a certain extent, the overall image of Manufactum appears to be contrary to current trading principles:

- The product range of around 5,000 articles in a wide range of categories exclusively comprises items crafted from such 'classical' materials as glass, iron, wood, natural fibres, ceramics, and so on.

- The majority of products are made by craftspeople and all products are made to last, being of a durable nature and repairable if necessary.

- There is a total absence of cheap, imported goods, most notably from countries in the Far East, and the product range includes a large number of products that are no longer available anywhere else in the world, such as: a hand-forged steel pan; 'Hoechl' cutlery; a bakelite telephone; 'Shannon Registrator' furniture; and porcelain and bakelite plugs and switches.

- Some of the products offered in the catalogue do not produce any profit; these are products that Manufactum does not wish to exclude from its range, regarding them as 'political products' (in a sense, these represent the company's philosophy).

- Manufactum products generally carry a high price tag as a result of the production processes used to craft them; in many cases, it was the price in particular that was responsible for the disappearance of these products in the first place, products that today are once again successfully marketed by Manufactum.

- Manufactum does not use many of the currently available and widely used methods of customer acquisition; today, the company continues to canvass the majority of its new customers through recommendations from existing customers.

- Manufactum presents its range of products in what is believed to be an attractive catalogue; the high standard of the accompanying text and the detail of the descriptions and information regarding the composition of the products has—in recent years—found recognition in numerous press reports and reviews published in newspapers[1] throughout the German-speaking world.

- The owner and managing director, Thomas Hoof, is a personally liable shareholder, demonstrating the corporate philosophy of openness and integrity, not only towards customers but also with regard to Manufactum's business partners.

I would suggest that the company's success indicates that there is a target market that prefers Manufactum's approach to trading and advertising and is drawn to the character and long-lived nature of the products offered.

## 22.1 Can an economic enterprise be sustainable?

If 'sustainability' is taken to be a measure of how long it takes before a human action is either terminated through its own damaging influence or as a result of the depletion of the resources required for that action, then few economic enterprises in Central Europe can be described as sustainable. For example, few industries today could survive without energy produced from fossil fuels such as oil or coal. Fossil fuels are not endless resources and their utilisation can by no means be deemed as sustainable. Strictly speaking, sustainable business in the literal sense is practically impossible today. However, this term should be put into context, and when evaluating the sustainability of an action or of a product one should ask oneself whether the existing possibilities for greater sustainability are being utilised.

---

1 *Frankfurter Allgemeine* Sunday edition, Frankfurt, 11 April 1993: 34; *Die Zeit*, Hamburg, 16 December 1994: 32; *Süddeutsche Zeitung*, Munich, 17 January 1995: 3; *Frankfurter Rundschau*, Frankfurt, 5 July 1997: 9; *Der Standard*, Vienna, 23 April 1997: 5; *Badische Zeitung*, Freiburg, 22 November 1997: 7; *Handelsblatt*, Düsseldorf, 28 October 1998: 36; *Welt am Sonntag*, Hamburg, 1 February 1998; *Tages-Anzeiger*, Zurich, 23 October 1999: 75.

One of the very few industries in which the term 'sustainability' is already determining the business processes is forestry. Here, the term sustainability is considered to be a compromise between short-term profit and simultaneous consideration for the long-term ecological consequence of each action: the felling of each tree within a forest represents the removal of biological mass and hence resources from the forest ecosystem. However, based on current knowledge, we can for each forest assume there is a certain measure of exploitation that is tolerable to the ecosystem in the long term. Foresters refer to this level as being 'sustainable'. Adherence to this level presupposes a willingness to view economic enterprise in the long term and to accept that, frequently, long-term profit can be achieved only by sacrificing short-term, 'maximum' economic success (hence, one achieves economic sustainability through ecological sustainability). For the forestry industry, this means that, if viewed in terms of a one-year period, maximum financial success would be achieved by total deforestation. However, viewed in terms of decades or even centuries, this course of action (because it would destroy the forest and thus the basis for economic action) is economically speaking considerably inferior to consistent, measured utilisation. Hence, in this sense, economic action is more sustainable the more rationally and prudently the resources (e.g. materials and energy) are used and the more limitations are imposed and accepted.

## 22.2 Examples of sustainability aspects within the Manufactum concept

It has never been Manufactum's intention to achieve sustainability benefits—and Manufactum has never utilised the adjective 'sustainable' in its advertising. The demands Manufactum has made and still makes on products has resulted, in the course of the past ten years, in an assortment of goods that can, in its entirety, be described, I believe, as 'unusually sustainable' because

- The products are of high quality.
- The products are durable and can be repaired.
- In the selection of products, Manufactum pays particular regard to their origins; the preference is for goods produced in keeping with local culture and which promote local or other European manufacturers and industries—an estimated 95% of the products come from Germany or other European countries, the majority of the remainder coming from North America, with a few items from Japan.

This broadly outlined philosophy is also reflected, for example, in the corporate marketing: Manufactum catalogues are not distributed on a wide scale; they are discreetly marketed, via existing customers, and dispatched only on request. In this way, the quantity of paper and energy required to achieve a sufficient response to keep the company functioning, and the associated wastage of paper and energy, is kept to a minimum.

## 22.3  Benefits for manufacturers

Owing to its success and therefore constant growth, Manufactum is increasingly benefiting smaller companies that had lost their former market position. With the catalogue, Manufactum has marketed their products to thousands of customers, allowing them to continue making products that might otherwise not have been viable economically. For example, in partnership with Manufactum, a traditional German manufacturer of wooden-handled carbon steel knives, which had almost disappeared from the market prior to the foundation of Manufactum, has registered a considerable increase in sales and has become better known. Its knives, although requiring more maintenance than stainless steel equivalents, are considerably less expensive and remain sharper for longer than stainless steel knives and have made a comeback in the retail trade and into the awareness of the consumer. Today it is once more a significant force in the German knife market.

## 22.4  Alternative avenues: developing Manufactum's own products

After more than ten years in the market, Manufactum now perceives an increasingly apparent necessity to develop its own products or to begin producing for itself products that have already been developed. A subsidiary company[2] was set up at the beginning of 1999 for this very purpose, with the objective of looking for, and producing, products that are no longer available. This subsidiary also sells its products through distribution channels other than the catalogue of the parent company. This allows greater batch sizes to be produced than would have been possible by distribution exclusively through the catalogue. It is the very combination of these sales channels that permits efficient production and, in turn, competitive pricing.

The first larger project undertaken by this product research company was the development of a re-creation of the 'Wanderer' bicycle which, like its predecessor, the famous 'Wanderer' bicycle which was produced up to the 1950s by the German Wanderer Works, offers superlative standards of quality: first-class mechanical components (instead of disposable parts), saddles and handlebar grips made of leather (instead of plastic), hand-soldered, sleeved frames, manufactured in Europe (instead of unstable and cheap imported frames) and, finally, assembly in Germany (Plate 22.1). A nationwide distribution network has meanwhile been set up with the specialist bicycle retail trade. The retailers benefit from the advertising impact of the catalogue, while Manufactum benefits from the service provided by retailers and their ability in interfacing with customers.

---

2   Manufactum Thomas Hoof Produkt-GmbH, D-45729 Waltrop, Germany.

*Plate 22.1* **The 'Wanderer' bicycle**

## 22.5 Limits to growth

In spite of all the optimism that this success could reasonably inspire, one fact remains: Manufactum's size is not always adequate, from an economic point of view, to achieve a satisfactory market presence for products that are expensive to manufacture (complete with all their competitive disadvantages). For example, the premium customer segment interested in Manufactum's Wanderer bicycles as a percentage of the bicycle market as a whole tends to be so small that all available distribution channels (including external ones) must be combined to ensure that the product can be manufactured and marketed profitably.

The Manufactum catalogue on its own is particularly successful in promoting products that in a large market (i.e. for products that everyone needs, such as kitchen equipment or clothing) are positioned at the high-quality end of the market. Or, to put a finer point on it, if the market for a product or product group is generally very small (e.g. products for left-handed people), it becomes practically impossible to reach within this consumer group the even smaller group of customers interested in buying products at the high end of the market in such a way as to market the products successfully. It is, then, of little importance whether the product is to be sold via high-street retail outlets or a catalogue: the retail industry cannot achieve the necessary number of customers without increasing the fixed costs; a catalogue has no restrictions with regard to range, but the costs are nevertheless uneconomically high because of the losses caused by large-scale marketing. Hence, the question arises: is the consumer group that is quality-conscious in the sense described here and thus interested in 'good' products in the Manufactum sense, really that small, and, if so, should this simply be accepted as 'a matter of fact'?

Today, the situation seems to be as follows: most people these days have little or no knowledge of the composition of products and are therefore at a disadvantage when it comes to discerning the quality of a product on offer (when related to all product groups required by one person).[3] It is therefore frequently no longer possible for the customer to make an informed judgement concerning the price–performance ratio. An example may help to illustrate this. A customer who is unable to discern the type of steel that has been used to manufacture a kitchen knife, and the way in which it has been manufactured, is also unable to judge whether a knife that is twice the price might also last three times as long—ultimately making it a better deal with regard to the price–performance ratio. The decision to opt for a highly priced product is thus increasingly becoming a matter of trust, which—in the final analysis—is tantamount to these products being perceived as part of a premium product segment.

Modern advertising campaigns conducted by discount stores and retailers of mass-produced goods aggressively assert the price of a product as the only important criterion (*ich bin doch nicht blöd*[4]) and are highly successful in so doing. Durability, the possibility of repair, the quality of specialist advice and the origin of products are increasingly being attributed a secondary role. Swimming against such a tide (as a customer) requires self-confidence and access to information; the part of the population that tends to analyse things critically represents a minority. A concept such as that of Manufactum is therefore not suitable for reaching broad sections of the population.

Market research studies have ascertained the size of Manufactum's potential interest group to be around 20% of all German households,[5] a figure that does not, however, take into consideration the 'propensity for mail order' (i.e. the willingness to purchase goods by mail order). Manufactum's potential customer group is thus without doubt considerably smaller than this 20%, although it is becoming increasingly apparent that the propensity for mail order plays a subordinate role in the characterisation of Manufactum target groups.

Even if it were possible, through an aggressive advertising campaign, to have a substantial effect on the way in which people think, which in turn would create increasing demand for high-quality products, the question of purchasing power still remains: the fact is—returning to the example of the knife—at the point of purchasing, the more durable knife is nevertheless considerably more expensive. Because these days Germans (and probably most other Europeans) prefer to spend their money on cars and holidays than on articles for daily use, the group of potential buyers is restricted to those with above-average education and above-average purchasing power.

---

3   In many cases, hobbies and professions mean that consumers do have specialist knowledge with regard to individual products or product groups.

4   This is an advertising slogan used by a discount store selling electric appliances, referring to the unbeatably low prices: 'I'm not stupid'—in other words, 'Why pay more than you have to?'

5   AZ Bertelsmann, RegioPlus analysis carried out for Manufactum Hoof & Partner KG, 1995–2000.

This raises a fundamental question, posed at the end of the following text of the Manufactum catalogue referring to a bread-slicing machine no longer produced, going on to introduce a similar product, the 'Graef Silber' (Plate 22.2):

> One glance at this hand-held slicer reveals something of the long development towards ugliness that so many household utensils around us today seem to have undergone in next to no time at all. Nothing about this machine is the result of any special design efforts; it would appear that its attractiveness lies solely in the fact that it has evidently been designed to last longer—expressed in the choice of materials, the manufacturing details and the fact that all parts subject to wear can be replaced, in short: in the proverbial passion for detail. Just in case you are already grabbing a pen, anxious to soon become the proud owner of this machine, I'm afraid we will have to disappoint you: this product no longer exists (but fortunately, we have the Graef Silber on the next page). Nobody—it is claimed—would be prepared to pay what a product like this would cost. Apparently, this is 'just the way it is', a phenomenon worthy of a Nobel Prize, for which economists and social psychologists should put their heads together to provide a conclusive answer: Why was this machine attainable for large parts of the population in the 1950s, and yet is deemed no longer affordable—despite considerably higher incomes today?

*Plate* 22.2 **The 'Graef Silber' slicing machine**

## 22.6 Manufactum: the beginning of the wind of change?

Of all the various forms of retail trade, mail order constitutes the best option for effectively addressing special target groups. Mail-order marketing offers the opportunity to approach minority consumer groups from any given location and with as little wastage of resources as possible. Examples such as 'mail-order products for left-handers' demonstrate this most clearly: a high-street retail outlet exclusively marketing products for left-handers would have a very low chance of survival in view of the fact that only 2%–5% of the population is left-handed. However, a specialised concept of this nature can be successful if marketed through mail order.

In a somewhat more complex way, this also rings true for Manufactum. As a result of purchasing power and level of education, the target group is extremely limited. One must also add to this the fact that a large part of this potential target group will not consider mail order as a viable option. Thus, growth for the Manufactum concept is limited because it cannot compete on price against other suppliers of comparable products manufactured where labour costs are lower, hence permitting such products to be sold for less. Manufactum anticipates continued growth in Germany, and initial experience with catalogues elsewhere (in Austria since 1998; in Switzerland since 1999) has shown that the success of the company in Germany is feasible in other European countries. This strategy to move into other European markets and perhaps further afield will continue to be implemented; predominantly English-language catalogues and e-commerce is to be introduced in the near future.

Nevertheless, 'Manufactum' will remain a niche market concept, regardless of which country it is introduced to and regardless of the time-scale. This will be true until consumer behaviour in Europe undergoes a radical change (barely conceivable today) or until world trade and labour costs are harmonised so that products of European origin are able to compete in terms of price. Throughout Europe, trade imbalances have caused the disappearance of trades and industries and with them precious know-how, so that the demise of these trades and industries would appear to be irreversible. However, Manufactum continues to support existing trades and industrial knowledge by offering a market for their products.

## 22.7 Conclusions

By distributing high-quality, durable consumer products, the Manufactum concept has been successful for many years now. The products and the marketing strategies have amply proven that consideration for sustainability is possible in economic enterprises. This success is not so much carried by the principle of 'sustainability' but is supported more by an overall concept of integrity and sincerity, homogeneous from the purchasing phase right through to the distribution and has as such been able to achieve the high levels of trust and loyalty among customers and suppliers alike.

From today's perspective, both the concept and the success of Manufactum are possible only in a niche market (but also outside Germany), because the 'obsession with low prices' and the trend towards discount and mass-produced goods seems to be unwavering. In these sectors, sustainability benefits will only be possible through political intervention, such as resource-related (i.e. higher) taxation of fossil fuels and the resulting price increase for long-distance transportation.

# HESS NATUR: ACTING FOR THE WORLD OF TOMORROW
## Resource management in the textile chain

*Katharina Paulitsch*
**Hess Natur-Textilien GmbH, Germany**

## 23.1 Successful in the eco-niche

Hess Natur-Textilien GmbH (hereafter referred to as Hess Natur) is an award-winning mail-order business offering natural textile products. The company, founded in 1976, is located in Butzbach (central office) and Bad Homburg (store), both close to Frankfurt, Germany. In addition there are is one subsidiary in Switzerland. Today, the company has about 320 employees, 150 suppliers and partners worldwide. Starting with a collection of clothes only for babies, the collection now encompasses fashion for babies, children, adults of both sexes, including casual wear, outfits suitable for business wear, as well as underwear and nightwear, shoes, accessories and home textiles. Each season the catalogue presents an average of 1,800 products. Nearly four million catalogues and almost a million parcels leave the building every year. Hess Natur has grown into Germany's largest supplier in the natural textile sector.

Hess Natur specialises in the distribution of clothing and textiles that are made entirely of natural and predominantly organically grown fibres. Individual items are manufactured by like-minded producers. Through these partnerships Hess Natur exercises influence on the entire textile chain, ranging from fibre production, through processing, to ready-made garments. Altogether, about 90% of the items are produced in Europe, with a focus on Germany, Switzerland and Denmark, with the aim of strengthening local economic cycles. Currently, no more than 5% of raw fibres are derived from Germany. In order to increase the number of locally grown fibre resources in the future, Hess Natur is seeking co-operation in and partnership with various scientific projects (e.g. the re-cultivation of old domestic cultivars in Middle Europe, optimising resource efficiency in production, etc.).

Further, Hess Natur is co-founder of the International Natural Textile Association (Internationaler Verband der Naturtextilwirtschaft [IVN]). Since the foundation of the association in January 1999 the 'Better' and 'Best'[1] label has been launched on the market. Approximately 1,400 products are certified by the Institute for Market Ecology (IMO) as meeting the IVN standard. Almost 25% of Hess Natur articles carry the IVN label. Some of the awards received by Hess Natur are listed in Box 23.1.

---

- In 1996 Hess Natur was the nominated winner of the International Organic Cotton Award, issued by the International Federation of Organic Agriculture Movements (IFOAM).
- In 1997 Hess Natur received the International Award for Design from the state of Baden-Württemberg for a bride's costume the company successfully launched on the market.
- In 1998 the 'Longlife' collection of Hess Natur was presented with the international 'Factor 4 Plus' award in Klagenfurt, Austria, as a model of resource-efficient and innovative product design.
- In 1999 Hess Natur received the 'Hidden Champions' award issued by the state of Hessen, acknowledging the company's global approach as well as its innovation and entrepreneurship.
- Hess Natur was shortlisted for the 1999 Design-Sense award launched by the Design Museum, London, for the sustainable concept behind the wedding dress.

*Box 23.1* **Awards received by Hess Natur-Textilien GmbH**

---

Hess Natur's philosophy is that all its products should be environmentally sound but must also be economically acceptable. Credibility and transparency plays an important role in ecological marketing. The use of organic textiles needs to find ways out of its eco-niche. This provides one of the future challenges for Hess Natur.

The foundations of the Hess Natur business are the four pillars of: ecology, quality, market and society. Each of these pillars has associated guidelines, which were also taken as the base for the so-called Factor 4 Plus project (see Box 23.2).

---

**Hess Natur**
- Insists that—along with price and quality—a holistic ecological perspective is a decisive competitive factor
- Promotes and pursues intensive ecological R&D
- Sets new ecological standards in the market and, in doing this, heightens the environmental awareness of all concerned
- Provides the correct balance between financial and environmental demands through holistic management

*Box 23.2* **Hess Natur's guidelines for the Factor Four Plus project**

---

1   See www.naturtextil.com.

## 23.2 Milestones on the way to sustainable solutions in textiles

The trader who is acting as mediator between supplier and customer has a key role in the textile chain. The philosophy of Hess Natur includes close co-operation with its suppliers in order to improve product quality and to raise the ecological standards of those suppliers. The challenge is to offer a sustainable collection according to customer demands but without minimising prosperity. This can be guaranteed only through an intensive dialogue with consumers. In the following sections some examples of the sustainable activities of Hess Natur are presented (for a summary, see Box 23.3).

**Hess Natur**

- Conducts organic fibre projects
- Provides a declaration, to offer transparent product information
- Offers the 'Longlife' collection, with a three-year guarantee on material, fit and processing quality
- Offers products with a service package
- Carries out research and development in textile ecology (e.g. resource management)
- Imposes quality standards, from fibre production to garment production
- Reduces and re-uses packaging material
- Aims to minimise customer complaints and returns
- Uses new communication systems such as the Internet to increase eco-efficiency
- Has an ecological product information hotline
- Optimises customer service through its highly educated employees

*Box 23.3* **The sustainable concepts of Hess Natur**

### 23.2.1 *Certified organic cotton for a cleaner environment*

Hess Natur exclusively uses renewable raw materials. The company emphasises its strong partnership with growers, investing in its own organic cotton projects since 1990 (e.g. in Turkey, Senegal and Peru) to ensure the high ecological quality of its raw materials. Today, the result is that more than 95% of the Hess Natur cotton articles are produced to organic standards. In accordance to organic cultivation standards (such as EU 2092/91, the Demeter standards, etc.), the use of artificial fertilisers, chemical pesticides and defoliants are prohibited and the soil must have been free of artificial chemicals for at least three years. One certified Hess Natur organic cotton t-shirt keeps approximately 7 m² of soil clean and free of chemicals.[2] Through such activities it is possible to control and influence the cultivation and the requirements of raw materials. Within all these projects Hess Natur is able to fulfil the ecological, economic and social needs of all parties concerned.

---

2   Weight of one t-shirt is approximately 250 g, yield of an organic cotton field is approximately 350 kg/ha; 0.25 kg × 10,000 m²/350 kg = 7 m².

## 23.2.2 *Declaration for transparency*

A further step within the development of Hess Natur was the introduction of a product declaration. Since 1997 the customer has been able to verify the ecological life-cycle of every garment through information given in the catalogue (see Plate 23.1 and accompanying text). It is evident that this service is possible only in close co-operation and communication with all producers in the supply chain. For each article a detailed product document has to be filled in. This data sheet enables Hess Natur to inform customers about the origin, cultivation of raw materials and further treatment (such as bleaching, dyeing, finishing) and the location of production. Such a declaration makes the whole textile supply chain totally transparent to the customers. Hess Natur was a trend-setter in practising such an 'open-book' policy, a policy that used to be daring and unique. Other companies have taken this strategy as an example and have followed the same idea.

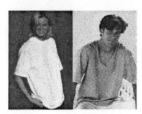

**Hess-cotton from Peru; organic**
**Unbleached/chlorine-free bleached**
**Undyed, synthetic dyes**
**Mechanical finishing, Denmark**
**Meet the requirements of the label 'Naturtextil Better'**

*Plate* 23.1 **Long-life t-shirt and product declaration**

## 23.2.3 *Long-life products as a sustainability strategy*

A very important part of ecologically sound clothing is the efficient use of resources, which means much more than production efficiency. Hess Natur addressed this by introducing its 'Longlife' collection, which consists of 200 articles, each item carrying a three-year guarantee on fit, material and processing quality. The three-year guarantee (in contrast to the six-month guarantee required by law in Germany) contributes to an ecological, comprehensive, preservation of the natural environment through a holistic concept in which fewer natural resources are used (both in manufacturing and in product consumption). These resources spend at least six times longer in use compared to other similar products.

The 'Longlife' collection consists of classical clothing that is unlikely to go out of style and which can be combined with other items over a much longer time-span. These items are produced to the highest quality standards. Long-lasting clothes preserve the use of resources by taking the place of clothes with a shorter life-span. An article of clothing is added to the 'Longlife' collection only after a series of internal testing and evaluations have been performed.

A good example of a clothing item in the Hess Natur 'Longlife' collection is the double-knit Troyer sweater, which represents the Hess Natur Factor 4 Plus concept (see Section 23.2.4). It is:

*Plate 23.2* **Double-knit Troyer sweater and the product-line logo**

- A unisex pullover available in sizes for the whole family
- Available in the colours navy blue and anthracite grey, with a contrast colour in the collar
- The fabric is a double-knit construction
- Made with an exterior of impervious wool for warmth
- Has an interior of cotton yarn, making it soft against the skin
- Permeable to the air

In particular:

- It is robust: the Troyer is a sturdy textile product of exceptionally high durability.
- It possesses flexibility, versatility and good matching abilities: as a unisex article, shared usage is possible; it provides optimal freedom of movement, an adjustable collar (which can be turned up against bad weather), versatility and year-round use, among other advantages.
- It is made to high eco-production standards, both in terms of transparency in the textile chain and in terms of social aspects: the whole textile chain is subject to ecological criteria in accordance to Hess Natur standards:

- Harmful substances have been avoided by use of eco-friendly finishing methods and no chemical treatments are used; only mechanical finishing treatments are used such as washing and tumbling.
- It is made from naturally regenerating, ecologically produced raw materials (100% wool from South America; pesticide-free and 100% certified organic cotton from Peru).
- The above property results in enormous reduction of toxic waste through crop rotation, natural pest control (through use of pheromones, predators, bio-soap, neem) and so on; any use of pesticides, synthetic fertiliser, defoliants, seed mordants or conservation agents for transport and storage are prohibited.
- By-products are gathered for secondary use and/or are composted, as biologically degradable materials.
- Ecologically, from cultivation to the final product, the environment and the people who live and work in it are protected.

## 23.2.4 Factor 4 Plus: resource management in the textile chain

Today 20% of the world's population, located in Western countries, consumes 80% of available materials to creating their material wealth. Sustainability—based on a fair share of environmental resources—requires that Western countries lower their material consumption drastically, e.g. through increased resource productivity in all economic activities (Rohn 1999). To aid in increased resource productivity, the Wuppertal Institute in Germany has developed a resource management programme based on the MIPS[3] concept. This resource management programme is designed to improve life-cycle-wide cost and material flows with the overall goal of increasing resource efficiency by a factor of at least 4. It includes three different components, which complement one another and are interlinked: ecodesign, material flow management and product management. The ecodesign component aids in product development through specific resource efficiency criteria. Material flow management focuses on the life-cycle phases of manufacturing, recycling and disposal of the materials used to produce a product and the final product itself. Product management has the goal of improving the environmental performance of the product during use by designing a resource-efficient use phase (Rohn 1999). This project transfers the philosophy and vision of Hess Natur into practice by using the guiding principle of factor 4 and resource efficiency.[4]

The aim is to point out new ways of designing and manufacturing products in the textile industry that will help save resources. With regard to harmful substances, the

3  Material input per service unit: the measurement of material and energy consumption of a product or service; the quantity of resources used (material input) in relation to the service provided by a product. See Schmidt-Bleek (1994) or visit the Wuppertal Institute's web page, at http://wupperinst.org/Projekte/mipsonline/grundlagen/bausteine.html.

4  The project is carried out by the internal group on Innovation and Ecology of Hess Natur and by two external partners: econcept (a consultancy for ecology and design, Cologne) and the Wuppertal Institute for Climate, Environment and Energy, Wuppertal.

company had already achieved a high level of environmental protection before the project started. During the project environmental strategies to minimise ecological problems downstream have been developed as well as upstream along the textile chain (e.g. from the cotton field, through all production steps and the use phase, to recycling and disposal) with special attention to the reduction of resources used. In particular (Fig. 23.1):

- Retail and supply concepts will be applied to pay heed to individual customer demands.

- Service concepts are applied as well as production concepts.

- A reliable, transparent, holistic description is provided of the ecological impacts along the textile chain.

- Further development of ecological standards is carried out.

- Resources are managed within the textile chain by means of alliances with suppliers.

- The design is ecologically and qualitatively convincing.

The main areas of investigation are ecological product design and process control along the whole length of the textile chain. Based on the information obtained, processes

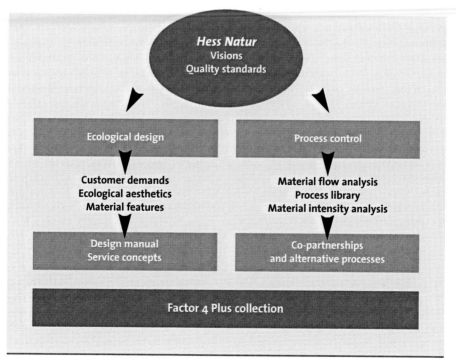

*Figure 23.1* **Factor 4 Plus project components**

and products are optimised. A system-wide resource management has been installed with the aim of reducing the use of resources in Hess Natur garments and increasing their yield by a factor of 4 by optimising the products.[5] 'Factor 4' means half the input, double the benefits (von Weizsäcker 1997).

### 23.2.4.1 A focus on process control[6]

In order to optimise the processes and the ecological quality standards at Hess Natur, the investigation of process control covers a detailed description of the textile chain. This includes material flows of different process technologies , studies regarding the uses, care, recycling and disposal of specific cotton and wool products and their related material flows. For the purposes of the Factor 4 Plus project, a material flow library for each case study is to be compiled to help to assess the overall use of resources. A lot of data was collected for each case study, but this data has not yet been collated into a single resource library: this could be a next step. Material intensities (inputs) for each process in the textile chain of the chosen wool and cotton products have been analysed. The next step required the material input per service unit (MIPS) of these products to be calculated (see Zeunert 1999; Wiegmann 2000).

On the basis of the MIPS concept, development and efficiency potentials as well as possibilities for innovation throughout the entire product line can be assessed. As a result, it is possible for Hess Natur and its suppliers to search for resource-efficient processes and to establish index figures for products, processes, transportation and production sites.

The ultimate goal is to determine the so-called 'ecological rucksack'[7] carried by Hess Natur garments. This 'detective work' will enable Hess Natur to identify and also quantify areas of improvement. The meaning of this ecological rucksack has to be clearly communicated as an indicator to distinguish the good from the better and to give customers an added and easily understandable value to a simple t-shirt or other garment.

### 23.2.4.2 A focus on ecological design[8]

For the first time in the clothing sector, where fashion plays an important role, the impact of design on ecology is being examined and controlled. In order to formulate ecological

---

5  On Factor 4, see von Weizsäcker (1997); on the application of Factor 4 at Hess Natur, see Rohn (1999) and Tischner (1999).
6  Further information on process control is found in the following internal documentation of the project: Rohn 1999 (resource efficiency criteria); Paulitsch 1999 (workshop proceedings on 'process control'; and the case studies (final theses) of Christian Zeunert (use phase; Zeunert 1999); Helmut Bernardy (disposal, recycling; Bernardy 1999); Silke Pütz (material flow analysis of a wool product; Pütz 1999); Anke Üffing (material flow analysis of a cotton product; Üffing 1999); and Kirsten Wiegman (searching for optimisation potential through material flow analysis, Wiegman 2000).
7  The idea of an ecological rucksack was developed at the Wuppertal Institute to describe the life-cycle-wide material and energy consumption of a product (Rohn 1999; von Weizsäcker et al. 1997).
8  For further information, see Tischner 1999; Paulitsch 2000a, 2000b.

product design strategies, customer demands (Tischner 1996, 1998), ecological aesthetics, material features and material flows have been analysed. It was necessary to collect information about the technical properties of the raw materials (yarns, fabrics and knitwear as well as dyes and finishing treatments) in order to determine the typical features of organically grown natural fibres (such as wool, cotton and linen) and their appropriate uses.[9]

Research into the demands of existing and potential Hess Natur customers has revealed that they prefer durable garments that will stay fashionable over a long time. Past catalogues and buying preferences have been also analysed, forming the basis from which the Hess Natur design style will be further developed.[10]

Based on this information, a design manual was produced which included several tools for eco-product development, design and marketing at Hess Natur. Once this manual is brought into use within the company, it will support the supply of products in an ecological and customer-oriented way. Thus the right balance between emphasising ecological qualities (durable design from 'healthy', natural materials) and fashionable, aesthetic, requirements (innovative, experimental articles) will be taken into consideration. The results of the ecodesigned processes and products are, by definition, high-quality products since they need to be long-lived and robust, and easy to use, maintain, update and repair. The design of eco-intelligent products requires, among other factors, improved overall quality for 'long-life' products, multi-functionality, redesign, appropriate information for consumers and/or other follow-up service concepts.

The basic requirement for ecodesign is to generate as many units of service or utility (fun) as possible out of the smallest possible quantity of natural resources for the longest possible time-period. The focus of innovation must shift from constructing better products to the provision of dematerialised technical and managerial answers to social needs and wants (Schmidt-Bleek 1994).

### 23.2.5 *Offering a service instead of mass-producing goods*

The concept of a lending service is unusual for Germany (the purchase of second-hand dresses is more common); and for a mail-order company to offer a lending service for wedding outfits was unique. Also unique was the idea of presenting the lending service as a part of a holistic ecological concept, focusing particularly on resource efficiency. So the Hess Natur wedding outfits for bride and groom represent a successful sustainable concept not mirrored elsewhere in the (conventional) textile business. Of note is the fact that the design fulfilled ecological design criteria and managed to avoid the normal 'rough' look of eco-friendly clothes, creating affordable, attractive fashion made from natural materials (Plate 23.3). But more important is that this is an example illustrating how service can replace production. The outfits are of high ecological value because they

9   Case studies, final theses of: Mareike Lehr (technical material features of knitted fabrics; Lehr 1999); Karin Ratovo (technical material features of woven fabrics; Ratovo 1999); Ursula Scholz (technical features of dyeing agents; Scholz 2000); Bettina Gräf (technical features of cotton, wool, linen yarn; Gräf 1998).

10  Tischner project documentation (Tischner 1996, 1998).

*Plate 23.3* **Wedding outfits for bride and groom**

are lent to brides and grooms. Costly wedding outfits—normally used only once—are thus used for more than one day by different persons. To fulfil the same demand, fewer outfits had to be produced. The lending-service campaign emphasises durability, multiple usage and resource efficiency.

To co-ordinate the lending, Hess Natur created a wedding telephone service and a special lending logistic supported by a computer programme to assist in co-ordinating the distribution of the outfits as well as the required timetable. In the Hess Natur shops in Germany and Switzerland, consultants assisted couples in choosing the correct size. The outfits were sent to the customers, who wore and enjoyed them on their wedding day. The clothes were then returned to Hess Natur for cleaning and sent to the next couple. The company limited this lending campaign to one year because it was developed on the occasion of its 20th anniversary and was free of charge. Still in a good condition, the outfits were then sold.

The response to the unusual offer greatly exceeded the company's expectations. It started with 50 outfits and soon added an additional 15 outfits, which were specially made in a small workshop. This was still too few to fill the demand, so Hess Natur had to disappoint 140 couples. From September 1996 until June 1997 more than 200 couples wore Hess Natur fashion on their wedding day.

The motivation was to illustrate the company's philosophy and in particular Hess Natur wished to:

- Show the versatility of hemp, a rough fibre (at its peak of popularity in 1995 when the outfits were created) generally used for sports garments; the hemp was woven together with silk into a transparent fabric suitable for use in elegant clothing

- Illustrate the simple elegance of unbleached, undyed 'natural' fabrics, that is, fabrics that have not been subject to conventional chemical treatments and finishing processes

- Prove that an alternative method of textile distribution was indeed possible, consistent with a sustainability and Agenda 21

Also of utmost importance to Hess Natur was the dialogue the company established with its customers during the course of this offer.

At each production step the wedding outfit had to meet Hess Natur standards. The following examples of specification for the clothing focuses on different steps in the life-cycle in order to illustrate measurable data:

- **Raw materials**
  - Product weight: 940 g
  - Composition: 40% hemp, 60% silk; all cotton used was certified organic.
  - Recyclability: as only natural raw materials have been used, everything is biodegradable and compostable.
  - Further ecological aspects: 1 kg of organic cotton fabric keeps approximately 40 m$^2$ soil free of artificial chemicals.[11]

- **Process**
  - Treatment: the dress is almost entirely untreated (no bleaching, dying, optical brightening, softening, lustre finish, etc.); the omission of bleaching alone results in saving a huge quantity of material inputs.
  - Material inputs: depending on the method used, for each kilogram of textile produced approximately 15 l water, 45 g chemicals and 1.5 kWh energy are used, indicating a very low material input.

- **Packaging**
  - Quantity: the quantity of packaging is a carefully considered part of the concept and is substantially reduced compared with items produced for sale in a conventional market.
  - Packaging materials: a cotton bag and/or a paper band only

- **Use**
  - Rate of re-use: over the lending period (September 1996 to June 1997) this service required 65 dresses for approximately 200 persons.
  - Efficiency factor: simply calculated, this represents an efficiency factor of 4 at the use stage alone.

This sustainable concept includes social aspects as well.

- The first environmentally sensitive alternative of a wedding dress for sufferers of allergic reactions (to treatment chemicals, synthetic fibres and/or nickel) has been created.

11    See footnote 2, page 383.

- The style and the material of the dress allows the bride to feel comfortable. Pregnant women can also feel comfortable in it.

- The clean working environment in the cotton fields and throughout the processing benefits workers and their communities.

- A premium price for organic cotton growers is paid to compensate yield loss and additional cost of production; this is necessary for the farmers to stay independent to obtain bank loans (often given only to buy pesticides) and to remain economically viable.

- Production in small manufacturing ateliers could support local craftspeople and at the same time save their jobs.


## 23.3 Conclusions

The above-described examples and concepts illustrate that ecology is more than just the need to work with toxic-free substances or to consider human health aspects. Sustainability means not only the production and selling of eco-products: the selling of a service instead of products is one suggestion to improve sustainability. It has been shown that ecology and economy are two parameters in the same world. The economy of the future should bring together both aspects—with the moderate use of resources as a supreme rule. In this context, Factor 4 Plus can be understood as an innovative and extended concept of ecology. An efficiency factor of 4 can be reached through the provision of high-quality (durable) products and/or the replacement of products with services to eliminate unnecessary production and by using a design that conforms with the sustainability concept.

Hess Natur pursues a corporate philosophy that stresses consistent environmental optimisation to a point where it is also economically acceptable. The company is convinced that real sustainable success cannot be achieved at the expense of the natural environment. Hess Natur has taken what it believes to be an exemplary path, 'acting for the world of tomorrow', thus aiming to be a trend-setter for other companies in the textile sector.

# THE DEVELOPMENT OF CLIMATEX® LIFECYCLE™
## A compostable, environmentally sound upholstery fabric*

*Albin Kälin*
**Rohner Textil AG, Switzerland**

Since 1980 the European textile industry has suffered an enormous decline, particularly in Germany and Switzerland. A large number of companies closed their businesses because severe competition drove prices downwards. In addition, textile firms faced more stringent environmental regulations and costs for emissions to air, for noise pollution and for the creation of waste-water.

Rohner Textil AG (hereafter referred to as Rohner), a textile company located in the Rhine Valley near St Gallen and Lake Constance, Switzerland, faces these same market conditions. In 1999 the firm employed 30 people. It manufactures 'high-end' designs of upholstery fabric, creating new designs in-house and also working with outside designers. It dyes yarns in its dye facility and produces textiles in its weaving mill. Many of Rohner's customers (e.g. Designtex, Herman Miller, Giroflex, Girsberger, Sitag, JAB Anstoetz and Team 7) are known globally.

In addition to facing productivity and waste emission issues common to the textile industry in the 1980s, Rohner faced additional local challenges. The company is located in a building constructed in 1911 and having historical building status—a condition that subjects the firm to scrutiny over any proposed architectural changes. Also, the building is situated in a neighbourhood that is both residential and a small business district. The firm is thus subjected to strict noise restrictions which, if violated, result in having night shifts banned. These noise restrictions also hampered efforts at improving productivity because newer, higher-capacity looms generate more vibrations, which would be trans-

* I would like to acknowledge assistance received from Matthew M. Mehalik (Department of Systems Engineering and Darden Graduate School of Business, University of Virginia, Charlottesville, VA) in writing this chapter.

mitted throughout the neighbourhood through the air and, more importantly, through the clay on which the mill and residential structures are built.

The firm had already decided to eliminate the use of cotton from its product line because the cotton dyes would have required Rohner to install special waste-water treatment equipment. Moving the firm was not an economically acceptable option. By 1989 Rohner, like other firms, was facing an increasingly complex situation involving economic and environmental requirements.

In 1992 the company set out a new strategy: to move from reactive to proactive management. The first step involved subjecting all of Rohner's products to tests to obtain the eco-label Oeko-Tex Standard 100. Rohner's products passed these tests; however, the tests did not resolve all of the environmental issues involved with the dyeing process and other manufacturing processes, as only the remaining chemical compounds in the finished products were analysed.

The severe market conditions of the early 1990s forced companies to boost investments in new equipment to increase productivity. These investments left little margin for extra investments to offset increasing governmental regulations on air pollution, waste-water treatment, noise reduction, solid waste disposal and resource efficiency. At that time, the business community tended to focus on profit, market positioning, quality, return on investment, just-in-time inventory management, competitiveness and globalisation.

It was in this context that Rohner built a strategy to balance economic and ecological requirements in order to survive as a company. Rohner articulated this strategy in its internal management document system, 'Eco-eco Concept 1993–2000' (see Steger 1999a, 1999b). At the heart of the challenge was the search for a way to allocate funds for investment in ecological efforts while simultaneously investing in new equipment for productivity gains. Over 10% of Rohner's turnover had to be invested in new equipment in order to increase competitiveness. There were few resources to spare for the ecological initiatives. The restrictions on noise production and on changes to the historic building also needed to be satisfied.

Management at Rohner struggled with these questions. It needed to answer:

- How can management convince the board of directors to accept investments in environmental projects in addition to the productivity investments of over 10% annually to be made over the next eight years?
- Was it management's job to change the board's thinking to make it conform to an environmental ideology?
- Would it be better to make special agreements with governmental institutions?
- What actions are the board responsible for and what actions should it take?

The answers lay in finding a solution couched in the common language of business: economic advantage. Rohner's tax consultant discovered that the canton St Gallen provided special tax concessions for depreciation of capital related to environmental investments. This tax incentive provided Rohner's management with its justification for environmental investments, and Rohner's board agreed to them. Investments had to be planned ahead of time. Beginning in 1993 Rohner included environmental investments in its annual budgets. The amount of investment consisted of 1% of the total budget. In addition, an environmental cost was included in calculating the cost of manufacturing each product. The existing accounting systems were modified to incorporate these two measures. The first environmental investments were realised in 1995 (Mehalik *et al.* 1996–1998: Rohner case study E).

During this time management recognised another necessity: the company needed a full and clear understanding of environmental concerns and resources in order to improve management decisions and provide better management tools of dealing with environmental issues (air, water, waste, noise). The company conducted an inventory and analysis of its environmental resources. In addition, each department measured and catalogued its environmental problems and proposed solutions and set priorities for implementing those solutions. In 1994 Rohner certified its quality management according to the ISO 9001 system.

The company needed to understand the interaction of its management systems (ISO 9001, ISO 14001, eco-eco concepts) in order to make its solutions effective. As an extension, management realised it needed to encourage transparency about what its products were made of. Rohner developed 'eco-controlling'—a quantitative assessment of each product's overall environmental impact—for all its products to promote a long-term focus on ecological product development for the entire product line, enabling the research and development (R&D) department to focus more on environmental issues (Riess 1998).

Customer reactions followed these initiatives. Susan Lyons, design director of the firm Designtex Inc., a subsidiary of Steelcase Inc. and located in New York, approached Rohner in autumn 1993. She found it necessary to search beyond the USA as her investigations on environmentally sound textiles did not suggest many other alternatives. Lyons requested that Rohner collaborate with Designtex, with architect William McDonough and with chemist, former Greenpeace activist and head of the Hamburg-based EPEA Internationale Umweltforschung GmbH, Michael Braungart. Lyons proposed that the vision for the project team should be to develop an 'environmentally intelligent' line of textiles.

## 24.1 Design vision

The project started in early 1994 using the design principles and criteria for products and production systems that McDonough and Braungart developed in 1992 (see Chapter 7; see also Braungart and Engelfried 1991; McDonough 1992, 1993).

### 24.1.1 Product redesign for nature

#### 24.1.1.1 Sustainable design

The development of a compostable, environmentally sound upholstery fabric presented a perfect opportunity to demonstrate a redesign process. The process began with the examination of raw materials used in a previous design of a Rohner product, Climatex®. This product, originally developed in 1988 with 'climate-control' seating features, contains wool, ramie and polyester—materials with properties for humidity absorption and transport. According to the Intelligent Product System™ and the McDonough Braungart Design Protocol™, this combination was neither a biological nor a technical nutrient and therefore presented an opportunity for redesign.

### Step 1: the fibres

Ramie, a plant similar to linen, was found to be an excellent alternative to polyester in Climatex® fabrics. When combined with wool, another natural fibre, the resulting fabric transported moisture away from the skin, allowing a person to remain comfortable when seated for a long period of time. This patented process is registered under the brand name Climatex® Lifecycle™.

### Step 2: the dyes and textile auxiliary chemicals[1]

Braungart, his assistant Alain Rivière, and their associates at EPEA requested 60 major chemical suppliers to submit information relating to their dye chemicals and auxiliaries. They were unwilling to open their books to share the information on their 'deep' chemistry—except Ciba, which co-operated with the requests. From the information submitted on about 1,600 dye chemicals, Braungart and EPEA selected 16 dye chemicals according to the guidelines of their design criteria, which addressed effects on human health and the environment. These design criteria include a requirement that the chemicals selected for the product must be free of mutagens and carcinogens and must not be bioaccumulative or persistent toxins, heavy metals or endocrine disrupters.

The approved chemicals also performed well according to industry standards for upholstery fabrics such as light-fastness, rub test durability, perspiration test durability and manufacturing process colour reproducibility. All colours, with the exception of black, could be developed from the 16 dyes selected.

### Step 3: Manufacturing[2]

The team needed to overcome many additional hurdles, and in some cases unorthodox solutions were adopted. McDonough, Braungart and their colleagues at EPEA conducted a comprehensive assessment of:

- Raw materials, the agricultural production of fibres and their extraction and purification

- Spinning mill processes, and auxiliaries, which were either approved by the EPEA or not used at all for ramie

- Twisting mill processes, for which no auxiliaries were used

- Yarn-dyeing procedures, with waste-water analyses and water and energy reduction programmes

---

1   For further information, see Mehalik et al. 1995: Designtex case studies A and B.
2   For further information, see Gorman 1998; Gorman et al. 1999; Hawken et al. 1999: 72; Mehalik et al. 1996–1998: Rohner case studies A–D.

- Weaving techniques, with no coating of the warp yarns—instead, water was used in combination with spinning and twisting alternatives to strengthen the yarns for the weaving process

- The company's performance in relation to ISO 14001 and the European Union's Eco-management and Audit Scheme (EMAS), with the implementation of an environmental management system, certified in 1996

### Step 4: the final product

It took 18 months of research to create the product, which is highly optimised with respect to

- Minimisation of material streams

- Ability to meet the goal to close biological cycles

- Promotion of soundness of health

The final product, Climatex® Lifecycle™, is competitive with standard upholstery fabrics in terms of:

- Aesthetic criteria: any design and most colours can be constructed.

- Industrial technical criteria: all performance tests are met or exceeded.

- Cost criteria: it is the same price as other high-end products that use similar raw materials.

- Functional criteria: it is suitable for use in climate-control seating (successfully used in extreme conditions, such as in gliders).

- Environmental soundness: it is compostable and biodegradable.

Upon introduction of the finished product to the marketplace, at the Solomon Guggenheim Museum, McDonough commented, in his speech to architects and interior designers, 'This is the first product of the Next Industrial Revolution. What we are now saying is that environmental quality can be an integral part of the design of every product. It's no longer just a wishful option.'

### 24.1.1.2 Beyond recycling

Even with the environmental optimisation associated with Climatex® Lifecycle™, the production process still generates solid waste.

### Step 5: the felt[3]

In the case of textiles, there is waste as a result of trimmings from both sides of the fabric and from the cutting of the seat covers produced from the fabric. This solid waste can be manufactured into felt for upholstery interliners or for use as a mulch for strawberry

---

3  For further information, see *International Journal of LCA* 1996 and Rivière *et al.* 1997.

plants. According to a old saying of farmers, the felt is a perfect fertiliser: 'hair and nail fertilise your ground for seven years'.

**Step 6: ready for nature (composting and biodegrading)**
According to the McDonough Braungart Design Protocol™ of McDonough Braungart Design Chemistry (MBDC), this fabric is designed to be safe for humans and can become safe food for other organisms when it is no longer useful and is 'consumed by natural systems'. When properly used, the fabric is compostable when removed from the chair frame: it will decompose naturally and return to the ecosystem.

# 24.2 The marketing and communication system

A marketing and communication system had to be developed for the US and European markets. The perceptions of different people, such as architects, end users, customers, and the media, had to be taken into consideration in communicating the product and in achieving credibility for the product. This was accomplished through the sensitive selection of designs and colours for each individual market and through careful attention to the marketing language and tools. In addition, Rohner has patented and trademarked Climatex® Lifecycle™.

## 24.2.1 The US market concept

In the USA Rohner's customer, Designtex, decided to use the well-known name of architect William McDonough and his 'Second Industrial Revolution' concept as its marketing tool. The first collection was launched in autumn 1995. The collection was called the William McDonough collection and was released with an information booklet titled *Environmentally Intelligent Textiles*. The collection was launched at the Solomon Guggenheim Museum in New York.

In 1998 Designtex supported the development of a new design tool to improve the environmental soundness of products—an 'index of sustainability'—for items designed by MBDC. In 1999 Designtex and MBDC enabled Carnegie, one of its major business competitors, to market the product and to develop Carnegie's own colours and designs to increase availability to the design community. The extension to diversify product designs and customers remains a natural wish of offering choice with fair competition. All three companies agreed to jointly advertise and market Climatex® Lifecycle™ upholstery fabrics as the 'fabric for the future'. Some of the awards won by Rohner Designtex, Carnegie and William McDonough are listed in Box 24.1.

## 24.2.2 European market concept

In Europe, Rohner hired a marketing and communication expert, René Eugster, to help with the launching of the product in 1996. Upholstery fabric manufacturers are always

## USA

**1995** At the first office furniture trade exhibition at the Neocon convention in Chicago, IL, Designtex's William McDonough collection received the 'Best of Neocon' award.

**1996** William McDonough received a Presidential Award from President Clinton for his work in sustainable design.

**1999** At the annual Neocon convention Carnegie was awarded 'Gold of Neocon' for its Climatex® Lifecycle™ upholstery collection.

**1999** William McDonough was proclaimed the 1999 Designer of the Year in *Interiors* magazine.

**1999** William McDonough received recognition in *Time* magazine as a 'hero for the planet'.

## Europe

*Rohner received*

**1996** The Arge Alp (Community Alpine Countries) Environmental Award

**1997** Support from the non-governmental organisation Deutsche Umwelthilfe

**1998** First prize in Austria's Eco design contest

**1999** The iF (Industrial Forum, Hannover, Germany) ecological design 'best of category' award

**1999** Registration as one of the 450 worldwide international projects as part of World Expo 2000, Hannover

*Box 24.1* **Awards for Climatex® Lifecycle™: products and designers**

sub-suppliers to the furniture industry or to textile merchandisers, as furniture is the final product. Rohner, as a small company, was not able to market the products directly to the end user because of the complex nature of European market distribution. Rohner decided to select 16 key customers that had a credible market image or that were capable technologically, e.g. they use no glues for upholstery. Rohner supplied customised marketing documentation for the 16 selected customers to enable individual marketing concepts based on common arguments and language. The environmental institute EPEA functioned as the vehicle for communicating environmental values, even though the institute was little known at that time.

In Europe, the first collection was launched in autumn 1996. The press reacted quickly, and within eight months over 40 newspapers, magazines and television channels presented the innovation. Climatex® Lifecycle™ was awarded several design prizes and awards (see Box 24.1). In 1999 Rohner established a corresponding website on the Internet.[4]

4 www.climatex.com

## 24.3 The path towards a sustainable company

From 1995 to 1998 the implementation of the Eco-eco Concept 1993–2000 at Rohner (balancing economy with ecology) together with the ongoing further development of the product line Climatex® Lifecycle™ took most of the energy of the management team. Rohner agreed to sign a five-year consulting and design contract with EPEA in order to continue their collaboration.

Rohner invested in updated machinery during this period, with new dyeing equipment that possessed environmental advantages and computer-integrated manufacturing (CIM) methods at its weaving facility. Productivity increases and the improved economic performance demonstrated the competitiveness of the company.

The environmental improvements impressed experts. For example, government officials were surprised that subsequent waste-water analyses showed little or no hazardous compounds in the waste-water from Rohner; textile experts were impressed by the efficiencies achieved in the manufacturing processes.

By 1997, Climatex® Lifecycle™ constituted one-third of Rohner's entire production volume, only two years after the product was introduced.

Rohner's management developed several ecological accounting and financial methods and systems for their products and manufacturing processes to gain further transparency in managing their environmental agenda (Mehalik *et al.* 1996–1998: Rohner case study E). A number of academic institutions have examined the structure of Rohner's business network (see e.g. Bosshard 1997; Gorman *et al.* 1999; Mehalik *et al.* 1996–1998: Rohner case-studies A–E; Mehalik *et al.* 1995: Designtex case studies A and B: Riess 1998; Steger 1999a, 1999b).

In the future, the management of Rohner will continue to demand dramatic improvements in the company's economic, environmental and social aspects. Part of this vision has been articulated in its company document, *The Path towards a Sustainable Company: Rohner Textil 1998–2008*. The concept articulates such goals as:

- Balancing economic, environmental and social aspects

- Implementing an employee development programme (EDP) for education, health and profit-sharing

- Analysing the entire product line and modifying it to the standards set by Climatex® Lifecycle™

- Eliminating waste-water in the dyeing process

- Eliminating waste from all of Rohner's products

- Continuously developing management and accounting systems in order to achieve a 'virtual system network' (including ISO 9001, ISO 14001, EMAS, life-cycle development [as opposed to life-cycle assessment], company concepts and so on)

## 24.4 Conclusions

What matters most is credibility. Climatex® Lifecycle™ embodies the results of six years of experience in the ability to create transparency in procedures, to ensure consistency and reliability and to form a network of committed partners. The selection of partners within the network is paramount. Trust, fairness, openness and the ability to change are characteristics the partners must incorporate. Rohner is responsible for building and maintaining this network along the entire supply chain, from raw material extraction, through the spinning, twisting and dyeing of the yarns, to the weaving, finishing and distribution of the fabrics. In addition, it is responsible for chemical inputs, the producers of the felt and for listening to and applying the recommendations received from EPEA and MBDC.

The development process has faced many challenges throughout the years. Several suppliers went out of business as a result of the severe market conditions prevalent in the textile industry. Chemical companies resisted co-operating by refusing to open their books. Also, Rohner needed to come to terms with ISO 14001, the new standard for environmental management systems. It had to develop new management tools, new environmental accounting methods and new life-cycle development processes (defining closed life-cycles in every individual process). In addition, Rohner had to support the development of MBDC's 'index of sustainability' design tool, measuring environmental strengths and weaknesses.

These challenges situated the company within a context of innovation and pioneering work. This atmosphere led to the expansion of the network to include universities and non-governmental organisations that were interested in overseeing and participating in the process. The challenges also led to new arrangements among competitors. MBDC, Designtex and Carnegie agreed to promote Climatex® Lifecycle™ jointly in the USA. These ways of thinking and acting in business have helped to develop credibility. Respecting and reinforcing the contributions of each network partner while maintaining a common vision and commitment to continuous improvements to satisfy customers and the environment was and continues to be Rohner's strategy.

# SLOW CONSUMPTION
# FOR SUSTAINABLE JOBS
## The example of hand-crafted shoes

*Christine Ax*
Institut für Produktdauerforschung, Germany

The development of the clothing industry (footwear, in this case) may be considered as providing a typical example of the social and ecological blindness of a production model based on economies of scale serving an affluent society. The history of shoemaking since the middle of the 19th century illustrates how traditional, regional, crafts have been replaced by globalised mass production. Since World War II German shoe manufacture has been moved systematically to countries with lower labour costs.

During the first half of the 20th century shoes for day-to-day wear were still considered an investment, their repair deemed worthwhile. However, they have turned into a cheap, disposable, article to be thrown out after a short period of use instead of being mended and worn again. More often than not their low price (usually around DM 50) renders repair uneconomical, or their poor quality even makes repair technically impossible. For both East and West Germany (before reunification) this meant that 300 million shoes were bought and subsequently thrown away with the household waste. About 25% of all purchased shoes were never or only rarely worn, which might be a result of the fact that they did not fit comfortably in the first place or that fashion had changed (Ax 1998a). Since World War II the significance of the shoemaker's trade, traditionally one of Germany's biggest craft trades, has diminished drastically (Fig. 25.1).

Other social and ecological costs of this production model are the problematic circumstances of leather production, particularly in third world countries in Asia. A high level of unnecessary pollution is produced, toxicological residues in the leather are hazardous to health and working conditions in the factories are often poor (low wages, use of child labour, etc.). Other subsequent problems include the destruction of markets in developing countries as a result of the import of 'recycled' shoes to Africa.

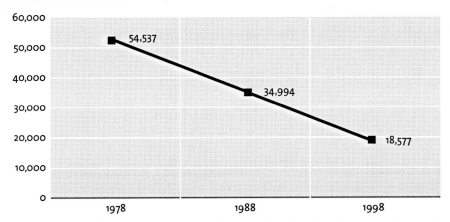

*Figure 25.1* **German shoe industry: number of employees between 1978 and 1998**

*Source:* Statistisches Bundesamt

The blindness of this production model regarding its ecological cost is in keeping with its blindness to its real objective: the protection and support of human feet, which come in many shapes and sizes. It is no wonder that during the second half of their life most people (especially women) suffer from deformations in their lower outer extremities—in short, their feet hurt. In severe cases, they go from the regular shoe shop to an orthopaedic surgeon to a specialised manufacturer of orthopaedic shoes—all at the expense of public health organisations.

Considering these manifold disadvantages it became evident to some that a sustainable alternative had to be found, a 'counter-model' to anonymous mass production. Made-to-measure shoe manufacture seemed to be a promising solution, because of the following assumed advantages:

- The production method is local and labour-intensive, which results in the preservation and/or creation of jobs in a decentralised craft trade.

- The hand-crafted made-to-measure shoe is very resource-efficient because of its high durability.

- The customer can become involved in the production process, thus getting the chance to influence the design of the shoe and thereby enjoy an aesthetically satisfying as well as healthy solution to the problem of footwear.

There were, however, apparent disadvantages: because of the high labour intensity and the high wages in Germany, the made-to-measure shoe has always been a luxury article for the rich enthusiast.[1]

1   There are some people on average wages who purchase made-to-measure shoes if their job puts a lot of strain on their feet (e.g. in the case of postpersons and sales assistants), but they are the exception rather than the rule.

In 1996 the project 'Made-to-Measure instead of Mass Production' was launched in collaboration with several German shoemakers and other firms and agencies.[2] Its objectives were as follows:

- To find out if the hand-crafted made-to-measure shoe is a sustainable alternative to mass-produced footwear

- The reduction of production costs for the made-to-measure shoe by making use of new technologies (such as computer-aided manufacturing) and developing adequate but cheap tools for measuring foot sizes and for making the individual lasts on which the shoes are built up

- The development of sensible concepts for organisation, production, sales and marketing, with the help and input of small manufacturing firms and individual craftspeople

## 25.1 Custom-made shoes: a product-oriented ecological evaluation

With the help of the Wuppertal Institute and by the application of the MIPS (material input per service unit) method,[3] shoes of different qualities were compared in relation to their resource efficiency. As Table 25.1 shows, the reparability and durability of shoes proved to be of crucial importance for the rucksack factors.[4] Owing to the short life of men's shoes, the ecological rucksack of simple men's shoes are much higher than serially custom-made shoes[5] or made-to-measure shoes.

A comparison of these selected shoe varieties leads to the conclusion that the production of high-quality and durable ready-made shoes and serially custom-made shoes is the most resource-efficient.[6] According to the MIPS analysis the production of hand-crafted made-to-measure shoes is slightly less efficient. However, it must be taken

---

2   The project is funded by the Bundesforschungsministerium as part of the PIUS programme. The following manufacturers and institutions took part in phase 1 of the project (development of a scanner-based last construction and production): nine shoemaking firms (regular and orthopaedic); the University of Münster (Klaus Nicol); the scanner and software-development firm GeBioM; the shoe-tree producer Orthops, Flensburg; the Institute for Product Durability Research (Willy Bierter); the Wuppertal Institute for Climate, Environment and Energy (Michael Ritthof); and the Future Workshop of the Handwerkskammer, Hamburg (Christine Ax, Mathias Hartmann).

3   MIPS is a measure that counts all material and energy inputs needed to offer a defined unit of service (see Schmidt-Bleek 1994).

4   The rucksack factor is another word for the MIPS of products (see Schmidt-Bleek 1994).

5   Serially custom-made shoes are high-quality customised shoes, but they are not produced on an individual last.

6   In the case of ready-made footwear thousands of shoes are produced from one last (e.g. a size 8 model).

| | Abiotic material (kg/pair) | Biotic material (kg/pair) | Soil movement (kg/pair) | Water (kg/pair) | Air (kg/pair) |
|---|---|---|---|---|---|
| Simple | 6.13 | 1.16 | 0.40 | 687.81 | 0.92 |
| Medium-quality | 2.14 | 2.79 | 0.13 | 264.34 | 0.55 |
| High-quality | 1.10 | 2.80 | no details | 54.26 | 0.29 |
| Serially custom-made* | 0.97 | 2.55 | no details | 47.97 | 0.26 |
| Made-to-measure | 1.43 | 2.60 | no details | 62.67 | 0.42 |

\* High-quality customised shoes; not produced on an individual last

*All figures were standardised on the basis of a useful life of one year.*

Table 25.1 **Resource intensity of men's shoe varieties in relation to durability**
*Source:* Zukunftsveranstalt eV/WUPI 1999

into account that the individual last needed for the production of hand-crafted shoes was not considered in the evaluation. By inclusion of the individual last the service value of the product is increased considerably, and thus a comparison with ready-made shoes is all but impossible.

The results of the analysis show that the use of resources is slightly lower in the production and repair of serially custom-made shoes than of hand-crafted made-to-measure shoes. High-quality ready-made footwear and hand-crafted shoes show a slightly higher use of resources. This is mainly because of the use of wood in the production of the necessary lasts and to the higher use of energy per workshop place. In comparison, industrial shoe production requires less energy because of the high number of pieces produced per worker. Shoes of medium and low quality, which dominate today's market, 'bring up the rear' of the ecological balance.

Comparison of the production of hand-made shoes with industrially made shoes according to MIPS analysis proved to be problematic, because different production methods as well as services of varying qualities had to be weighed against each other.[7] In addition, neither the increased cost for public health caused by ill-fitting shoes nor the greater social benefits of the regionalisation of shoe production was taken into account.

7  The very singular quality of made-to-measure shoes is that they are individual shoes for individual feet. Neither mass-produced shoes nor high-end quality shoes have this special quality; thus the service value of made-to-measure shoes is not readily compared with that of other shoes.

## 25.2 Custom-made shoes: preserving resources in the workplace

The comparison of industrially mass-produced footwear with hand-crafted made-to-measure shoes was not merely of interest regarding the product as such. If one considers the need to bear in mind all dimensions of sustainability in a global sense—social as well as economic—made-to-measure shoe production proves to be the better alternative. The worldwide dilemma of jobless growth could be counteracted by allowing for an evaluation of production methods that considers resource intensity not only per production unit but also per worker. The social and economic dimensions of the paradigm of sustainability require solutions that counteract jobless growth with an increasing number of growthless jobs.

A look at the use of resources per shoeworker shows that in made-to-measure shoe production only 2–2.5 tonnes of material (abiotic and biotic) are needed per worker per year, whereas in industrial shoe production 11–16 tonnes are used per worker per year.

In 1990 the average material input per worker in the former German Democratic Republic was 213 tonnes. Although the numbers are not directly comparable, it is still clear that the production of made-to-measure shoes can be counted among the number of material-extensive craft trades. It would be difficult to find a production method within the industry that is more resource-efficient.

The correlation between the quality and durability of products and the use of resources for their production becomes evident in an exemplary calculation developed by the Wuppertal Institute. This calculation shows the possible saving of resources as a result of even the smallest increase in the market segment of durable high-quality shoes. The calculation proceeds by assuming a future 1% market share for serially custom-made shoes, up from substantially less than 1% in 1997 (Table 25.2). The higher durability of these shoes in contrast to the mass-produced footwear they replace is taken into account in the calculation for the total number of shoes sold. Given these assumptions, the amount of material used would be reduced from 302,000 tonnes to 282,900 tonnes, which equals a 6.3% decrease in material use.

## 25.3 The shoemakers' trade: future challenges

To establish made-to-measure shoe production in the regional markets the use of new technologies—such as scanner-based last production—is an important but insufficient prerequisite. The high price of made-to-measure shoes is more than many interested customers can afford. With the rationalisation of production costs by means of a unit construction system, made-to-measure shoes or at least serially custom-made shoes would be available for a larger part of society. To provide the customer with options ranging from the individual made-to-measure shoe to the reasonably priced customised shoe, traditional shoemakers must co-operate and develop fairly complex networks for

| Price | 1997 | | Future? | |
|---|---|---|---|---|
| | Share (%) | Pairs (millions) | Share (%) | Pairs (millions) |
| DM 100 | 47.5 | 11.9 | 43.5 | 9.4 |
| DM 200 | 35.5 | 8.9 | 32.5 | 7.0 |
| DM 300 | 14.0 | 3.5 | 17.0 | 3.7 |
| DM 400 | 2.5 | 0.6 | 5.0 | 1.0 |
| DM 500 | 0.5 | 0.1 | 1.0 | 0.2 |
| > DM 500 | <<1.0 | | 1.0 | 0.2 |
| **Total** | **100.0** | **25.0** | **100.0** | **21.5** |
| *Average price* | DM 123* | – | DM 142.5* | – |
| *Turnover* | – | DM 3,075 million | – | DM 3,078 million |

\* The average price was calculated on the basis of the mean price of each class.

*Table 25.2* **Approximate distribution of future market segments in the field of men's shoes**

*Source:* Zukunftsveranstalt eV/WUPI 1999

supply and production. The main objective is the re-establishment of the craftsperson as an expert and service provider in the field of footwear and foot health.

## 25.4 Shoemakers using new technologies go on market . . .

At the end of 1999 the first step of the technical challenge was taken and achieved. A small-scale electronic foot-scanner and accompanying software to enable the construction of an individual last were developed and tested by shoemakers. The next step is now in progress: the system will soon be able to combine last construction with the construction of individual legs. However, the technical side of this development is not sufficient. In order to establish the shoemakers and the bespoke shoe in the market, further support for this kind of production seems necessary. Shoemakers want and will co-operate to develop their own collections and to be able to produce or sell bespoke shoes at a reduced cost. Individual shoes in Germany currently cost between DM 1,500 and DM 3,000; the use of new technology and the establishment of new co-operations will help shoemakers to sell made-to-measure shoes for less than DM 1,000. In spring 2001 a network of shoemakers in North Rhine–Westphalia using the foot scanner and the last-construction software will start to offer their made-to-measure shoes to the market.

## 25.5 Slow consumption for growthless jobs

The example of made-to-measure shoes shows that individual hand-crafted products are an adequate response for the realisation of sufficiency strategies (better instead of more), even if they are unsuitable for the pursuit of efficiency strategies. The labour-intensive production in the craft trade allows for the creation of eco-efficient, decentralised and resource-preserving jobs. At the same time, durability and reparability and an appreciation of the product lead to ecological gains.

New technologies and new forms of co-operation may turn craft trades into interesting 'local players' for sustainable development. Small firms and individual craftspeople have the capacity to offer individual high-quality solutions to the customer, whose high regard for the purchased product adds to its durability (i.e. if the shoes are comfortable and attractive, the customer will wish to have them repaired rather than replaced). The customer's involvement as a 'co-producer' is an important aspect, because it assures the customer's appreciation and willingness to use the product for a long time. To realise such sustainable production strategies it will be necessary to develop new technologies and long-term concepts for organisation, manufacture, distribution and marketing. This holistic approach greatly exceeds purely product-related ecodesign, because it requires the collaboration of craftspeople as well as the creation of strategic co-operation and networks. The biggest advantage of this solution is the increase in regional affluence without inflicting damage to other regions.

## 25.6 Summary and conclusions

The development of the clothing industry—footwear in this case—must be considered a typical example of the social and ecological blindness of a production model based on economies of scale. The history of shoemaking illustrates how traditional regional crafts have been replaced by globalised mass production. The average shoe has become a cheap disposable article to be thrown out after short use instead of being mended and worn again. In the course of the present research project the production methods of hand-crafted made-to-measure shoes were examined, and a new technological basis (e.g. the use of scanner-based last production) was developed.

With use of the MIPS method hand-crafted shoes were compared with industrially produced shoes with regard to their resource efficiency. The example of the made-to-measure shoe shows that reparability and durability are two crucial factors in the resource efficiency of the studied products. Thus durable high-quality ready-made shoes and made-to-measure shoes are the leading products regarding ecological balance. With the production of hand-crafted made-to-measure shoes, it can be concluded, strategies of sufficiency (better instead of more) can be carried out. This labour-intensive production method allows for the creation of eco-efficient, decentralised and resource-preserving jobs. At the same time, durability, reparability and a high level of appreciation for the product lead to ecological gains. The customer's involvement cements his or her willingness to use the product for a long time.

# MICRO ENTERPRISES, LAY DESIGN AND SUSTAINABLE INNOVATION

*Luiz E.C. Guimarães*
Universidade Federal da Pariba, Brazil

*Fred Steward*
Aston Business School, UK

Much of the research on innovation and sustainability in less industrialised countries (LICs) has paid little attention to the role of micro and small entrepreneurial businesses. The term 'micro enterprise' is used by the Brazilian Micro and Small Enterprise Support Service (SEBRAE) to describe firms with up to 20 employees; small enterprises are defined as firms with a maximum of 100 employees (Puga 2000: 9).

The ability of small firms to design and market new products plays an important role within the overall process of innovation. Innovative potential enables ideas and demands from the market to be expressed in material form and translated into hardware. It is a critical requirement where products are to be introduced into a competitive environment. It needs to be expressed in both urban and rural small manufacturing enterprises as well as in large firms. In recent years attention has been drawn to the environmental implications of product design. The United Nations Environment Programme (UNEP), through its Working Group on Sustainable Product Development (WGSPD), has been prominent in this effort.

In LICs, in contrast to goods and services provided by larger enterprises the goods and services provided by small firms are more likely to be appropriate to the customs, needs and financial availability of poor consumers. This advantage is related to the thorough utilisation of available raw materials, capital, etc. and of production techniques where know-how and labour is valued above capital. The flexibility of small firms to adjust themselves when faced with competition is a valuable resource to them.

In the majority of LICs, the product development process has ignored local people's informal innovative capacity (non-professional design) and lay technical know-how. Foreign imports dominate technological development and can discourage innovation conducted by the more vulnerable groups of society.

Recent research on micro and small production units in developing countries is beginning to show that product design activity of a lay and informal nature appears to be widespread. Poston's study of rural manufacturing firms in central Africa (1990: 72) suggests that such design capacity is particularly important in contexts where less technical information and technological resources are available. To innovate, invent and improvise are options when normal commercial resources and market structures are non-existent. Another study reveals parallels in micro and small enterprises in Latin America, where, because of the scarcity of resources, design is used mainly to ensure business survival (Guimarães 1995: 127).

In their preoccupation with survival, micro and small businesses may damage the environment. Owing to their many constraints, competitive contexts and the need for cheap raw materials, they may extract natural resources in an unsustainable manner, and may further affect the environment through the inappropriate disposal of waste.

## 26.1 The role of sustainable product development in micro and small firms in less industrialised countries

Design has an important role to play in small firms in LICs. However, there is evidence that lack of training in product design is a constant feature of small manufacturing firms. Product design praxis in this context emerges from practical experience and informal training, although some methods used by professional designers, such as the use of scale models, can be found.

Concern for the environment does not appear to be a priority for small manufacturers in LICs. For example, salvaging in such a context is not a sign of ecological preoccupation but is mainly related to poverty and deprivation. Paradoxically, the low-income population and the small producers are the ones constantly recycling and re-using waste materials, mainly because of the scarcity or high costs of raw materials. This is common in most LICs where the re-use of waste tyres, tins, plastic bottles and so on is common practice.

One notable aspect is the fact that such products are created by artisans and small entrepreneurs, without any help from government or the private sector. Re-using is thus an important survival strategy, both for excluded groups and for small businesses. The clients for these products are the low-income population but also other strata in society. For example, in north-east Brazil, dustbins made from re-used tyres are bought by consumers of different economic levels because they stand out from similar products (made from plastic or galvanised steel) in terms of function and are sold at much lower prices. Thus, it is clear that there is an informal innovation system, with its own peculiarities, that can be a starting point for the introduction of sustainable product development (SPD) concepts.

According to WGSPD, 'sustainable product development considers the intensity and optimisation of resource use for product design, while developing product concepts within whole systems, that provide a service or function to meet human needs' (Jansen 1995: 3). Thus SPD can be a tool for minimising environmental impact and can contribute to the growth and sustainability of businesses and local societies. It can have a positive impact on micro and small firms. A key question is whether SPD can help in the introduction of commercially viable products.

In the case of capital goods, an effective contribution of SPD can be the design of machines and devices that are appropriate to the needs, size and financial resources of small producers. The design of such capital goods will have an impact on the quality of the products manufactured. Quality can be achieved without the need to buy expensive manufacturing equipment but by 'stretching' the use of existing production machinery, processes and equipment.

SPD can generate more employment and income as well-designed products have the potential of reaching more sophisticated markets. This will require more workers to fulfil growing demand. It can also tailor the design of products to fulfil local and outside demand, considering the needs of specific markets.

The innovative product design activity found in micro enterprises in LICs is usually driven by the goals of survival and the generation of employment, of wages and of sales to low-income consumers. This raises interesting issues regarding environmental sustainability. Can such goals be combined with environmentally friendly innovation in developing countries? This case study shows an example where this is indeed the situation.

## 26.2 The 'ecobroom'

The case study presented here concerns the innovation of a broom made by re-using waste material rather than by the traditional method of using piassava fibre. Joaquim Neto, a 50-year-old farmer from Goiás State, which is located in the centre-west region of Brazil, identified two environmental problems of local concern which he successfully turned into a new business opportunity.

The first of these problems was the threat to the survival of native palm trees from which the piassava, a stout fibre obtained from the leaf stalks, was extracted. In Neto's home town of Itaberaí Municipality there were around 40 small factories making piassava brooms.

The second environmental problem concerned the impact of discarded polyethylene terephthalate (PET) plastic bottles (used to package soft drinks, foods and non-food products) on the local countryside, particularly in terms of the pollution of rivers which are part of the complex ecosystem of the Pantanal wetlands. These bottles cause a number of further undesirable effects: large animals can eat them with fatal consequences, the plastic material takes decades to degrade and large amounts of visible waste accumulates in rural and urban environments. The problem becomes critical in urban areas where bottle disposal may block sewer systems and be responsible for severe floods. The accumulation of water in the interior of PET bottles can also be responsible for the spread of infectious diseases (typhoid fever, break bone fever, cholera, etc.) as they provide an ideal environment for the dissemination of insect larvae.

The production and consumption of PET bottles is large. In 1997, three billion units were consumed in the country. Approximately 15% have been recycled. In Rio de Janeiro alone, consumption reached 300 million bottles per annum.[1] Even small towns are affected by bottle pollution. For example, in Frederico Westphalen, a town in the southern region of Brazil with a population of 25,000, approximately 60,000 bottles are disposed of per month. In Itaberaí, Neto estimates that 72,000 bottles per month are disposed of into the environment.

The idea for a new product, the so-called 'ecobroom', emerged during trips to a local river, where the environmental damage caused by PET bottles was witnessed. The inspiration was its practical use for broom bristles where the durability of the waste plastic would be an advantage rather than a problem.

A prototype was then constructed by using a simple pocket knife. The top and the bottom of a cylindrical two-litre bottle were cut off. The remaining PET cylinder was cut with the knife into vertical shreds for most of its length, leaving one end intact. The result was a set of plastic bristles on the lower part of the cylinder held together at the upper end. Over this first bottle were placed 19 other 'topped and tailed' shredded bottles. Finally, one of the cut-off bottle tops was used to hold all the others together and to enable a wooden stick handle to be attached.

The product appeared feasible and a machine, to accelerate the production process, was designed. The initial version, which allowed the production of 50 units per day, was developed to use a hydraulic system, which produces 300 units per day. The acceptance of the product by the local population endorsed the quality of the design. At the end of the production cycle, plastic waste material from the manufacturing process is collected and sold to rope and plastic utensils manufacturers for use as raw material. Used brooms from consumers are collected and the plastic recycled in the same way, and the wooden handle is re-used in new brooms. One interesting aspect of the commercial relationship of the franchisee with the franchiser is that royalties can be paid directly for the waste plastic from the production process.

According to the designer, tests made with a local refuse collector have shown the superiority of the ecobroom compared with piassava straw brooms. The plastic broom lasted 28 days compared with 3 days for the straw broom (under normal working conditions) when used for public cleaning. The plastic broom was also cheaper than the piassava and other brooms. For example, the selling price of the ecobroom was US$1.00 against US$2.50 for the piassava product.

A factory was set up in July 1998; today, it employs 15 people directly, and over 35 bottle collectors indirectly. The discarded bottles today have a resale value, which means people are cleaning the city as well as selling the bottles. The farmer–designer is satisfied because he has created a product that tidies the environment and has saved the piassava palm

---

1   Figures are from Viva Rio's website (15 May 2000): www.vivario.org.br.

tree from extinction. The factory earns around US$3,000 a month. The main issues in the firm's development were lack of capital to initiate the business and lack of support for product development.

For Neto it was a radical move to become an entrepreneur from his previous occupation as a farmer. Because of shortages of financial resources, the development of the product was slow. The novelty of the product required production machines to be created from scratch. Most of them used scrapped agricultural machine and tractor parts. Initially, few people believed in the product's economic feasibility. The products had to be left at local shops to be sold. Gradually, people bought them and informed others about the broom's qualities. Thus sales took off.

To assist the diffusion of the product, Neto contacted the municipal secretary of Barra do Garças in east of Mato Grosso State, who was very supportive of the project and decided to set up a factory in the municipality. Kits were produced to enable new factories to be set up. Each kit includes a shredding machine, a small guillotine, a drilling machine and a number of small devices and hand-tools.

At a later stage the secretary of development, industry and commerce of Mato Grosso State visited the workshop and perceived the potential of the ecobroom for use in tourist sites for public cleaning. An order for 70 manufacturing kits (US$7,500 per kit) was promised for use in municipalities participating in the National Programme for the Municipalisation of Tourism (Programa Nacional de Municipalização do Turismo). However, this large order never materialised because of a changeover in the State minister's post. Nevertheless, in spite of this setback, within two years Neto sold 16 manufacturing kits to establish new factories.

Another positive development for the factory was the partnership with the National Bank for Family Agriculture (Banco Nacional de Agricultura Familiar [BNAF]). In 1998 the BNAF helped Neto to set up a franchise to sell the production equipment and gave support for raising market awareness and for commercialising and managing the enterprise during the implementation stage. The BNAF, which is in partnership with other Brazilian institutions, finances a number of projects supporting small, family agriculture. Among these projects are training programmes to improve the quality of products from small producers. According to BNAF, the ecobroom has a number of advantages:

- It reduces the presence of plastic waste in the environment.

- It is made from a lightweight material.

- Each factory creates direct employment for a non-skilled workforce of 15 people.

- Each factory creates indirect employment a non-skilled workforce of 35 people, who act as bottle collectors.

- The investment required to set up a factory is low (US$7,500).

- The product is of high durability compared with traditional brooms made from vegetable material.

The partnership with the BNAF will allow wider commercialisation for the ecobroom. The BNAF has established some criteria for the setting up of some of these factories. Cities with more than 45,000 inhabitants or pools of smaller cities are targeted in the marketing strategy. Co-operative ownership of such factories is encouraged by BNAF.

# 26.3 Implications

This case reveals a number of positive aspects related to sustainable product design (SPD) in the context of LICs. It is important to note that the environmentally friendly innovation delivered direct local economic benefits through the generation of employment and wages. Small businesses are responsible for the majority of jobs in LICs and the manufacture of this product creates 50 jobs per factory, with very little investment.

The product uses resources efficiently as it is made mainly from re-used waste material, and its quality and function is superior to existing products. The broom's durability is much greater than competing brooms and can be used for different purposes, such as heavy-duty jobs (e.g. scrubbing the floor with water) or lighter jobs such as sweeping. Production is organised by using simple manufacturing processes and non-polluting appropriate technologies. The product is responsive to local capacities and culture and favours local consumption. There is a wide market to be fulfilled, showing the potential for the diffusion of the product. It also has the advantage of preventing the loss of flora. It has expanded the market for a traditional product by the creation of an alternative design that has given value and quality to otherwise useless material.

The case illustrates the creativity of lay design activity by an entrepreneur and has wider significance for micro enterprises in LICs. Although the innovation is an incremental modification of existing technology the context is such that its environmental consequences are quite radical. Products aimed at the poor population are in general very different from those produced for higher-income groups. Because they use simple technology and use waste as a raw material their finish compared with mass-produced goods is of a different quality. However, this case illustrates that these issues can be effectively combined with the goal of environmental sustainability.

Recognition of the micro and small enterprise sector as an important one for design and innovation in LICs raises the more general issue of appropriate support. There is clearly a role to be played by development agencies and financial institutions. The strengthening of the design and innovation capacity of entrepreneurs and small businesses, whatever the technological sector, needs to receive much higher priority. This raises a challenge for professional designers to develop a new role as social enablers or catalysts. As pointed out by Pacey (1992: 222), to think in these terms is to redefine the role of the professional designer: that of helping people to design for themselves, encouraging participation between the professional and the lay person (see also Chapter 11).

## 26.4 Conclusions and recommendations

Some generic principles can be extracted from the case study. Most importantly, it is clear that to be able to develop SPD capability it is necessary to recognise the role of non-professional designers as a constant source of innovation in micro and small firms in LICs. Developing such capability can be beneficial both for individual firms and for local communities as the success of the product in the market can generate new direct and indirect jobs, increase wages of the low-income population and eliminate waste from the environment. Benefits can also accrue to the consumers, who will have products that function better, that have aesthetic appeal and high durability and that may be purchased at a lower price than other comparable products. As it enhances the value of products, SPD can also be a tool to capture higher-income markets, both at the national level and at the international level.

Another principle is related to the level of support available. Existing support ignores the endogenous knowledge of small firms or inventive individuals. Institutional support has privileged the formal innovation system (universities, research institutes and so on) and ignored the non-institutionalised, informal innovation system. To achieve such recognition will not be an easy task. Institutional bias means that resources, aimed at stimulating innovation, rarely reach the poorest sectors of the business community. Unfortunately, even in institutions that have addressed the problems of micro and small firms, the development of firms' endogenous innovative capability is not at the top of the agenda. Most of the support is related to design for and not design by micro and small firms.

A crucial principle is the interaction with professional designers. This relationship is problematic because micro and small firms have very little financial resources to hire the services of such individuals or agencies. Despite the existence of programmes of support for product development, loans are inaccessible for most smaller firms. This leaves little alternative for innovators but to rely on themselves or on 'loan sharks'.

However, universities, particularly public institutions, might have an important role to play in such a context. Owing to the characteristic of such institutions, students could become involved in schemes similar to teaching company schemes in the UK, where students are placed for a period of 1–3 years in selected enterprises. Such schemes use a mixture of public and private funds to support the transfer of academically acquired know-how. Graduates are located in firms with a brief to develop an agreed project. Universities can, with relatively few resources, intervene in this context. The involvement of students and lecturers in extension programmes may prove an effective form of co-operation.

For the diffusion of SPD, in micro and small production units in LICs, some priorities have to be considered, as follows.

- **Research on innovation and design processes.** More research is necessary to understand the dynamics of product design activity in micro and small businesses in LICs; research is also required in relation to informal training methods for technical subjects.

- **Relevant technology.** The design of capital goods and consumer products that use waste materials and are appropriate to the needs of micro and small businesses should be stimulated; information about the use of waste materials should be disseminated.

- **Learning.** Training in SPD, based on existing knowledge and local peculiarities, should be a priority but should occur in an informal atmosphere and 'close to the job'.

- **Microcredit.** Microcredit aimed at the development of innovation and product design should be made available.

- **Networks of information.** A constant influx of SPD and market information should be available by means of alternative forms of dissemination; mobile units with exhibitions and tools for product design and other forms of transmitting information should be considered; it is crucial to develop access to information technology and to stimulate the use of computers as tools for generating product design.

- **Partnerships.** New relationships between established formal institutions and micro and small enterprises need to be actively promoted; use of local facilities and human resources can minimise costs and create innovative interactions.

Each of these areas needs to be approached in an interactive and interdisciplinary way. Environmental sustainability and economic competitiveness need to be integrated rather than dealt with in separate compartments.

Enhancing the internal capability of design in such a context would put the innovative firm in an advantageous position in the market, thus augmenting its chance of survival and potential for growth. The gains to the manufacturer of having this enhanced ability are evident, ranging from the better use of raw materials, a reduction in the costs of production, a reduction in development time and a consequent increase in profit margins. There are also advantages for the user such as the availability of a wider variety of products of better quality in the market, designed to satisfy local needs and accessible to the low-income consumer.

# 27

# CARVING IN KENYA

*Diego Masera*
EU Micro-Enterprises Support Programme
and Ecodesign Consultant

In Kenya the production of handicrafts makes a significant contribution to the national economy. Many types of Kenyan handicrafts are known around the world, but of all these crafts wood carving may be the most famous. Carving in Kenya is a relatively new phenomenon, derived from the woodworking traditions of the Makonde people of Tanzania and Mozambique. Mutisya Munge, an Akamba man from a small village in Kenya, is credited with introducing carving to his people after returning home from Tanzania at the end of the World War I. Since then, carving in Kenya has become an important source of income, of foreign exchange and of labour.

The Kenyan wood-carving industry is expanding at a high rate both in the volume of trade, the number of people involved and the carving wood requirements. An estimated 80,000 carvers are currently active (Plates 27.1 and 27.2), and their work feeds nearly half a million people. The annual export earnings from the wood-carving industry are as high as KSh264 million per year (approximately US$30 million; see People and Plants 1999: 2).

Traditionally, Kenyan carvers have preferred a few selected hardwood tree species for carving. Unfortunately, these species tend to be slow-growing and have become over-exploited because of increasing demands from harvesters seeking wood for construction, furniture and fuel purposes as well as for carving.

The challenge that Kenya is now facing is that the current demand for indigenous hardwoods far outstrips supply. Today, wood resources are in a critical state of over-exploitation. The future of the wood-carving industry is therefore threatened. Carvers depend on wood from local forests and farms for their raw materials. So far, most of the wood used for carving comes from indigenous hardwood species such as mahogany (*muhuhu; Brachylaeno hulliensis*) and ebony (*mpingo; Dalbergia melanoxylon*) which are not produced on a sustainable basis. Selective harvesting of these species has a severe impact on forest structure and species composition and renders the populations of these species vulnerable as increasingly smaller, immature trees are being cut. The industry uses

*Plate* 27.1  **Carver in Nairobi**

*Plate* 27.2  **Carver at the Malindi co-operative**

approximately 7,000 m³ of wood per annum, and about 50,000 trees are felled each year to supply carvers (Plate 27.3). This is equivalent to ten trees per hectare of natural closed-canopy forest in Kenya (People and Plants 1999: 2). The future of the industry is at stake if the current products, consumption pattern and use of raw materials does not change. This situation is particularly dramatic in a country such as Kenya where employment opportunities are extremely limited and where 500,000 people enter the labour market each year.

*Plate 27.3* **Logs for carving**

For a meaningful shift to environmentally sustainable carving, it is essential to create awareness and to educate the producers and the consumers of carved wood products. In order to satisfy current and future demand, efforts must be made to manage and utilise natural resources on a sustainable basis. To reverse this trend of progressive forest degradation and reduced incomes from sales of carvings, the implementation of a sustainable product development (SPD) strategy is essential. Within the wood-carving sector, producers and traders must work together to develop strategies that ensure a sustainable supply of raw materials if there is to be a future for this important sector. However, the activities carried out so far to this end have focused on mainly research and public awareness campaigns without an integrated strategy for SPD.

## 27.1 Carving out a future

An important effort is being made by a group of organisations[1] that have decided to embark on a campaign to promote 'good wood' carvings to highlight the problem of over-exploitation and to identify possible solutions. The 'good wood' terminology comes from initial research efforts that concentrated on searching for and experimenting with fast-growing non-forest species as a substitute for endangered indigenous species. Research findings indicate the following species are the best alternatives: neem (*Azadirachto indica*), mango (*Mangifera indica*), grevillea (*Grevillea robusta*) and jacaranda (*Jacaranda mimosifolia*). Other species such as coconut (*Cocos nucifera*), casuarina (*Casuarina equisetifolia*), melia (*Melia azedarach*), eucalyptus (*Eucalyptus* spp.) and *Prosopis* spp. are being tested. As most of these species have multiple uses and are fast-growing they have a good potential for being raised in local farms and plantations. The practical use of these woods for carvings has shown that they are equally good and—if accepted—will relieve the pressure from the declining and already over-exploited indigenous carving species.

The main objective of the 'good woods' campaign is to establish a market for sustainably sourced carvings. To achieve this it will concentrate on:

- The introduction of an independently certified 'good wood' label for carvings from sustainable supplies and a system to monitor the use and production of 'good wood' carvings

- The promotion of certified carvings within Kenya and abroad

- Establishing a market share of 10% for certified carvings by 2004

Activities related to SPD have just started; a new project, funded by the European Union under the Micro Enterprises Support Programme and implemented by the Mennonite Central Committee, will focus on SPD as a main area of intervention. The project will tackle three main areas simultaneously:

- Sustainable product development (SPD)

- Reforestation

- Marketing

### Sustainable product development

Under this component SPD training will be provided to local artisans. It aims at diversifying the current production and creating a series of new products, made out of 'good woods', that are attractive to customers and easily identifiable as 'green' products (Plate 27.4).

1 These are National Museums of Kenya (NMK), the Kenya Forestry Research Institute (KEFRI), the Mennonite Central Committee (MCC) and the Kenya Crafts Co-operative Union (KCCU), co-ordinated by the People and Plants project of the United Nations Educational, Scientific and Cultural Organisation (UNESCO); see Nafzinger and Snider 1998.

*Plate* 27.4  **Some 'good wood' products**

### Reforestation

In favourable conditions, 'good wood' tree seedlings can be harvested within 10–15 years after planting. Reforestation is urgent and needs to be done on a scale sufficient to ensure a sustainable source of raw materials for future generations. The project will promote the establishment of tree nurseries within each carver co-operative and the distribution of seedlings to farmers and carvers. The reforestation approach will enhance the sense of ownership of the trees among the carvers. Reforestation of indigenous forest areas is not contemplated by the project because it is the exclusive work of the forestry department of the Kenyan government.

### Marketing

Securing a sustainable source of raw materials and achieving the necessary product innovations required by the alternative materials will not address the challenges facing the wood-carving industry unless there is a corresponding market demand for products made with the new materials. To this end, the project will link to the 'good wood' campaign to create awareness among customers and producers. Furthermore, local and foreign market requirements will be closely researched and followed.

## 27.2 Sustainable product development implementation

Master craftspeople have been selected from the different co-operatives in Kenya to undergo a course in product diversification and in the use of 'good woods' (Plate 27.5). These artisans will then introduce the new ideas to their fellow carvers at each co-operative. As part of the course several experiments have been carried out to test the differences among woods and the best way to carve and finish them. Softwoods require a different carving procedure and technique from indigenous hardwoods. Hardwoods are carved while the timber is still fresh because they are softer at this stage whereas softwoods tend to crack if carved when fresh. Thus, for softwoods a seasoning period is required before carving. The adoption of behavioural changes in the carving process have been difficult but they are already taking place.

As a result of market research carried out in North America and Europe the trainees are also exposed to market requirements and trends. Finally, the carvers are trained in product diversification and are presented with visual information that can facilitate the process. It is important to note that carvers that have produced wild animal carvings for decades have never seen a giraffe or an elephant in their natural habitat and have very limited access to visual information. The exposure to visual information will be critical for the generation of new ideas. The project hopes to produce a collection of newly designed items that can be identified with 'good woods' (Plate 27.6).

An important aspect in product development training is to enhance the awareness of its relevance among carvers and to establish a recognition or award mechanism for innovators, such as price awards for the best innovations, acknowledgement certificates and royalties. The current absence of these mechanisms has limited product diversification and innovation dissemination because innovation costs are rarely recovered by the innovator.

## 27.3 Some initial results

In terms of the reforestation activities, 11 tree nurseries have been established, over 35,000 seedlings planted and some 300 people trained in seedling raising and nursery management. The target for each nursery will be to raise 10,000 seedlings each year.

In terms of marketing activities, specially designated areas have been established in the showrooms of each carver association, posters have been printed, leaflets distributed and articles written to sensitise potential customers. In collaboration with the 'good woods' campaign, videos are shown on long-distance flights to Nairobi, and articles will be published in the in-flight magazine of the Kenyan national airline, Kenya Airways.

The initial results of product development training are encouraging and show a very good response from the carvers and the market. Over 1,500 carvers are already using 'good woods' and over 100 new products have been designed. Sales of products made out of

*Plate 27.5* **SPD trainee**

*Plate 27.6* **SPD trainee with 'good wood' product**

'good woods' in the carvers' associations that participate in the project are still low but already 10,100 products made out of neem have been sold (Eby and Mast 2000: 3). However, sales from *muhugu* (*Brachylaeno hulliensis*), an indigenous hardwood tree, still outweigh sales from neem by tenfold.

## 27.4 Conclusions

The carving industry in Kenya provides a clear example of many micro and small enterprises sectors in developing countries whose existence depends on rapidly degrading natural resources. Until recently very little had been done to protect the indigenous forests and the jobs of thousands of artisans that have no alternative source of income. In this context the implementation of SPD strategies can have a substantial social and economic effect.

The 'good wood' campaign and the sustainable carving project represent two important initiatives that are tackling complementary aspects of the SPD process. Although it is too early to draw final conclusions, the initial results are encouraging and show that SPD is a central element for the success of manufacturing activities in developing countries.

# USEFUL WEBSITES

## Ecodesign

**Biothinking International**  www.biothinking.com
*Examples and information about cyclic, solar and safe products, projects and concepts*

**The Centre for Sustainable Design**  www.cfsd.org.uk/
*Offers information, links, conferences, publications and tools for eco and sustainable design*

**Core 77**  www.core77.com/
*Covers lots of standard industrial design issues and links to much of the US's ID community*

**E-Design**  http://energy.DesignCommunity.com/e-design.html
*An organic coalition of individuals and organisations collaborating for the development of excellent practice in sustainable and environmentally conscious design*

**Ecodesign Information Point of the Technical University Vienna**
www.ecodesign.at/ecodesign_eng/main.htm

**econcept**  www.econcept.org
*Agency for ecology and design advice; offers information about the services of the design consultancy and further ecodesign information, links, literature and examples*

**Industrial Designers Society of America**  www.idsa.org/

**O₂ Global Network**  www.o2.org
*This ecodesign association's site has excellent links to green resources.*

**United Nations Environment Programme UN-WG-SPD**  http://unep.frw.uva.nl/
*Working Group on Sustainable Product Development, UN-WG-SPD, Amsterdam, has several networking and research projects; order their magazine,* Way Beyond, *here*

## Websites with guides for ecodesign

**IISD Developing Ideas Digest**  http://iisd1.iisd.ca/didigest/

**Institute of Sustainable Design, University of Virginia**
www.virginia.edu/~sustain/home-mainpage.html

| | |
|---|---|
| **Design Council: Beyond Millennium Products** | www.millennium-products.org.uk/ |
| **Design for Environment Research Group** | www.mech-eng.mmu.ac.uk/pages/projects/dfe/ |
| **PRé Consultants** | www.pre.nl |
| **Centre for Design at RMIT** | www.cfd.rmit.edu.au/dfe/cfd_2_5.html |
| **Carnegie Mellon University Green Design Initiative** | www.ce.cmu.edu/GreenDesign/ |

## Mailing lists; chatrooms; newsletters on ecodesign

**Ecodesign Information Point of the Technical University Vienna**
www.ecodesign.at/ecodesign_eng/main.htm

**O₂ Global Network**
www.o2.org

**The Environmental Mailing List Archives**
www.earthsystems.org/list/

**Sustainable Discussion Groups**
http://csf.colorado.edu/archive/

**University Centre of Human Ecology and Environmental Sciences: Mailing Lists Archives**
http://ecolu-info.unige.ch/archives/

**University of Sydney Faculty of Architecture Mailing List Archives**
www.arch.su.edu.au/kcdc/forum/mailbox/

**EnviroWeb Support**
www.envirolink.org/support/

**Community Eco-Design Network**
www.cedn.org/index.html

***Journal of Sustainable Product Design***
www.cfsd.org.uk/journal

## Sustainable development

**Applying Sustainable Development**
www.applysd.co.uk
*Helps users to learn about sustainable development and undertake activities*

**Linkages: A Multimedia Resource for Environment and Development**  www.iisd.ca/linkages
*Linkages is provided by the International Institute for Sustainable Development; the calendar provides detailed descriptions of events, conferences, and workshops.*

**Solstice: Sustainable Living**  http://solstice.crest.org/sustainable/index.html/#Environment
*Offers resources on sustainability, in a number of categories, and includes a wealth of information on topics related to sustainable living and design, including green products and practices, environmental planning and case studies and an annotated list of links to related websites*

**Sustainable Business**                                     www.sustainablebusiness.com
*Offers information on sustainable business, with fresh news and job listings*

**Sustainable Development Online**                              http://susdev.eurofound.ie
*You can access 657 websites via the SD-ONLINE database*

**Sustainability Web Ring**                          http://sdgateway.net/webring/default.htm
*Links diverse sites with each other; with the help of the Web Ring sign,*
*you can jump from one sustainability-related site to the others*

**World Business Council for Sustainable Development**                    www.wbcsd.ch/


## Diverse sites covering environmental and sustainability issues

**CREST: Center for Renewable Energy and Sustainable Technology**          http://crest.org

**Centre for Alternative Technology**                                    www.cat.org.uk

**EcoIQ**                                                                 www.ecoiq.com
*EcoIQ exists to help local governments and individual local government leaders, managers,*
*programme staff and consultants design and implement more effective resource*
*management, environmental and urban planning programmes and policies.*

**ECONet**                                                        www.econet.apc.org/econet/
*Serves organisations and individuals concerned with environmental preservation and*
*sustainability. It also provides a gopher site where EcoNet members can share information.*

**Eco-Shop**                                                              www.eco-shop.org

**Environmental Health Clearinghouse**                           http://infoventures.com/e-hlth
*Website topics include environmental health effects, worker exposure, environmental justice*
*issues, and information for schools and students.*

**Environmental Protection Agency (EPA)**                                     www.epa.gov
*The US EPA homepage offers information on a broad range on topics*
*and is customised for different audiences.*

**Forum on Developing Countries**                     http://obelix.polito.it/forum/welcome.htm
*A site about sustainability in developing countries*

**Global Environmental Options**                                     www.geonetwork.org
*Has a great library of sustainable design links, and a sustainable design centre, too*

**Green marketing site**                                            www.greenmarketing.com
*Jacquelyn Ottman's US consultancy on green marketing*

**International Development Research Centre**                              www.idrc.ca

**International Institute for Sustainable Development**

http://iisd1.iisd.ca/about/prodcat/default.htm
*Publications catalogue; IISD's information for decision-makers*

**IUCN - The World Conservation Union** www.iucn.org

**Independent Designers' Network** www.indes.net/idnref.html
*Offers resources for eco-packaging design*

**KTH Royal Institute of Technology, Stockholm** www.lib.kth.se/~lg/envsite.htm
*Offers a global overview to environmental sites*

**Liberty Tree Alliance** www.libtree.org/
*Has in-depth information on a number of environmental issues; offers 'high fives'
of best sites picked by experts, and an extensive eco-art gallery called 'The Serpent's Eye'*

**Material ConneXion** www.materialconnexion.com
*Offers a materials database; costs approximately US$135 per year;
and has a list of literature (English) on materials choice*

**New Economics Foundation** www.neweconomics.org
*Whose main concern is a just and sustainable economy*

**OneWorld** www.oneworld.org
*Is an online community of more than 750 organisations, interested in topics from
development to environment and human rights, and reaching from Manhattan to Delhi*

**Recycler's World** www.recycle.net
*Offers information about recycling organisations and products*

**Science Policy Research Unit (SPRU) of the University of Sussex** www.sussex.ac.uk/spru/

**SETAC Foundation Life-Cycle Assessment** www.setac.org

**The Bioneers** www.bioneers.org
*The site of an annual event to consider practical solutions for restoring the Earth*

**UNEP: United Nations Environment Programme** www.unep.ch/

## Environmental news and publications

**Earthscan Publications** www.earthscan.co.uk

**Environmental Journalism homepage** www.sej.org

**Environmental News Network (ENN)** www.enn.com
*In-depth news is available from ENN Daily News, by subscription only,
and produced in association with Reuters, the Associated Press, PR Newswire
and The Los Angeles Times Syndicate.*

**ENDS Environment Daily**                            www.ends.co.uk/envdaily
*Covers European environmental affairs from Brussels and in the
member nations, reporting daily on events that matter to business*

**Greenleaf Publishing**                          www.greenleaf-publishing.com

**Internet Public Library**                              http://ipl.sils.umich.edu/

**The Green Business Letter**                              www.greenbiz.com

# BIBLIOGRAPHY

ADEME (Agence de l'Énvironnement et de la Maîtrise de l'Energie) (ed.) (1999) *Conception de produits et environnement* (Product design and environment: 90 examples of ecodesign; Paris: ADEME).

Adriaanse, A.S., S. Bringezu, A. Hammond, Y. Moriguchi, E. Rodenburg, D. Rogich and H. Schütz (1997) *Resource Flows: The Material Basis of Industrial Economies* (Washington, DC: World Resources Institute).

*Advertising Age* (1991) 'Spurts and Starts: Corporate Role in '90s Environmentalism Hardly Consistent', *Advertising Age* 62.46: GR14-GR16.

Allenby, B., and D.J. Richards (1999) 'Applying the Triple Bottom Line: Telework and the Environment', *Environmental Quality Management*, Summer 1999: 3-10.

Alvarez-Icaza, P., and C. Garibay (1994) 'Producción Agropecuaria y Forestal', in V. Toledo *et al.* (eds.), *Plan Patzcuaro 2000* (Mexico City: Fundación Friedrich Ebert): 91-133.

Apgar IV, M. (1998) 'The Alternative Workplace: Changing Where and How People Work', *Harvard Business Review*, May/June 1998: 121-36.

Armstrong, L.A., and W.S. White (1997) 'Case Study: Chrysler Corporation Life Cycle Management Comparison of Three Engine Oil Filters', in *International Business Communications Environmental Cost Accounting* (conference proceedings; Washington, DC, November 1997).

Arnold, M., and R. Day (1998) *The Next Bottom Line: Making Sustainable Development Tangible* (Washington, DC: World Resources Institute).

Ashley, S. (1993) 'Designing for the Environment', *Mechanical Engineering* 115.3: 52-55.

ASPRI (Proyecto de Asesoria Integrada al Sector Privada)/CNI (Cámara Nacional de Industrias) (1998) 'Politicas Ambientales al Interior de la Industria', *Documentación: Congreso Nacional de Cámaras Departmentales de Industrías/o Industrías de Comercio*, Cochabamba, Bolivia, 26-28 August 1998.

AT&T (1997) *Survey of Teleworker Attitudes and Workstyles* (conducted by FIND/SVP and Joanne H. Pratt Associates).

AT&T (1998) *Employee Telework Survey* (internal survey of A&T managers conducted by Associated Analysts, Inc.).

AT&T (1999) *Employee Telework Survey* (internal survey conducted by Associated Analysts, Inc.).

Auguston, K. (1996) 'In Search of Pallet Solutions', *Modern Materials Handling* 51.9: 38-41.

*Australian Energy News* (1999) 'A Challenge from the US', *Australian Energy News* 12 (June 1999; www.isr.gov.au/aen/aen12/12challenge.html).

Ax, C. (1998a) *Das Handwerk der Zukunft* (Basel/Boston, MA/Berlin: Birkhäuser).

Ax, C. (ed.) (1998b) 'Werkstatt für Nachhaltigkeit: Handwerk als Schlüssel für eine zukunftsfähige Wirtschaft', *Politische Ökologie* 15.9.

Ayres, R.U., and U.E. Simonis (eds.) (1994) *Industrial Metabolism: Restructuring for Sustainable Development* (Tokyo/New York/Paris: United Nations University Press).

Ayres, R.U., L.W. Ayres and K. Martinas (1996) *Eco-thermodynamics: Exergy and Life Cycle Analysis* (working paper 96/1041; Fontainebleau, France: Centre for the Management of Environmental Resources, INSEAD).

Ayres, R., G. Ferrer and T. van Leynseele (1997) 'Eco-efficiency, Asset Recovery and Remanufacturing', *European Management Journal* 15.5: 557-74.

Baker, K. (1999) *The Development of Organisation and Program Performance Indicators* (Richland, WA: Pacific Northwest Laboratory).

Bakker, C. (1995) *Environmental Information for Industrial Designers* (Rotterdam/Technische Universiteit Delft).

Bakker, C. (1997) 'Solar Mower', in *The Journal of Sustainable Product Design* 2 (July 1997): 44.

Balkau, F., and J.W. Scheijgrond (1994) *Cleaner Production: A Training Resource Package* (Paris: United Nations Environment Programme).

Barnet, R., and J. Cavanagh (1994) *Global Dreams* (New York: Simon & Schuster).

Barrett, L., and E. Datschefski (1997) *A Manager's Introduction to Product Design and the Environment* (London: Environment Council Publications).

Barrett, R. (1998) *Liberating the Corporate Soul* (London: Butterworth Heinemann).

Bartelmus, P. (1999) 'Green Accounting for a Sustainable Economy: Policy Use and Analysis of Environmental Accounts in the Philippines', *Ecological Economics* 29.1: 155-70.

Barthel, M. (1999) *Greening the Supply Chain* (London: British Standards Institution).

Bartolomeo, M., M. Bennett, J. Bouma, P. Heydkamp, P. James and T. Wolters (1999) *Eco-Management Accounting* (Dordrecht, Netherlands: Kluwer Academic Publishers).

BATE (*Business and the Environment*) (1999) 'KPMG partners with The Body Shop to offer social auditing and reporting services', *Business and the Environment*, February 1999: 10.

BATE (*Business and the Environment*) (2000) 'Lucent Technologies applies ISO 14001 to Design for Environment functions', *ISO 14001 Update* 6.2 (February 2000).

Beck, U. (1986) *Risikogesellschaft* (Frankfurt-am-Main: Suhrkamp).

Becker, C.D., and E. Ostrom (1995) 'Human Ecology and Resource Sustainability: The Importance of Institutional Diversity', *Ecol. Syst.* 26: 113-33.

Belmane, I., and M. Charter (1999a) 'Scenarios for the Development of an IPP' (unpublished workshop report; Farnham, UK: Centre for Sustainable Design, Surrey Institute of Art and Design, University College).

Belmane, I., and M. Charter (1999b) 'Developing Competences for IPP: A Focus on Electronics and White Goods Sector' (unpublished workshop materials; Farnham, Surrey, UK: Centre for Sustainable Design, Surrey Institute of Art and Design, University College).

Belz, M. (1999) 'Eco-Marketing 2005', in M. Charter and M.J. Polonsky (eds.), *Greener Marketing: A Global Perspective on Greening Marketing Practice* (Sheffield, UK: Greenleaf Publishing): 84-94.

Bennett, M., and P. James (1999) *Sustainable Measures: Evaluation and Reporting of Environmental and Social Performance* (Sheffield, UK: Greenleaf Publishing).

Bernardy, H. (1999) *Materialintensitätsanalyse ausgewählter Recycling- und Beseitigunsprozeß von Alttextilien* (final thesis; Bayreuth, Germany: University Bayreuth).

Bhat, V.N. (1993) 'Green marketing begins with green design', *Journal of Business and Industrial Marketing* 8.3: 26-31.

Birch, P., and B. Clegg (1995) *Business Creativity* (London: Kogan Page).

Blumberg, J., A. Korsvold and G. Blum (1997) *Environmental Performance and Shareholder Value* (Geneva: World Business Council for Sustainable Development).

BMU (Bundesministerium für Umwelt, Naturschutz und Reaktorsicherheit [German Federal Ministry for the Environment, Nature Conservation and Nuclear Safety]) (1999) *Informal Meeting of EU Environmental Ministers on Integrated Product Policy (IPP), Weimar 7th–9th May 1999: Background Paper on Product Related Environmental Policy* (Bonn: BMU, 20 April 1999).

Börlin, M., and W.R. Stahel (1987) *Stratégie économique de la durabilité: éléments d'une valorisation de la durée de vie des produits en tant que contribution à la prévention des déchets* (publication SBS 32; Basel: Société de Banque Suisse).

Bossel, H. (1994) *Umweltwissen: Daten, Fakten, Zusammenhänge* (Berlin: Springer Verlag).

Bosshard, N. (1997) *Die Verbindung von Ökonomie und Ökologie am Beispiel der Rohner Textil AG* (master's dissertation; St Gallen, Switzerland: Universität St Gallen).

Böttcher, H., R. Hartman and C.G. van Hemel (1997) 'Ecodesign: Benefit for the Environment and Profit for the Company', *UNEP Industry and Environment* 2.1–2: 48-51.

Brandsma, E. (1996) 'Consumption Patterns: More or Less Sustainable?', presentation at the Brasilia Workshop, December 1996, United Nations Department for Economic and Social Affairs (DESA).

Braungart, M., and J. Engelfried (1992) 'An "Intelligent Product System" to replace "Waste Management"', *Fresenius Environmental Bulletin* 1: 613-19.

Brezet, H. (1998a) 'Ecodesign: The Need for a Parallel Approach', in *Towards Sustainable Product Design* (proceedings of the 3rd international conference, 26–27 October 1998; Farnham, UK: Centre for Sustainable Design, Surrey Institute of Art and Design, University College).

Brezet, H. (1998b) 'Ecodesign: With the Bear in Mind', paper presented at ERCP '98: European Roundtable on Cleaner Production, Lisbon, 29–30 October 1998.

Brezet, H., and C. van Hemel (1997) *Ecodesign: A Promising Approach to Sustainable Production and Consumption* (Paris: United Nations Environment Programme).

Brezet, H., B. Houtzager, R. Overbeeke, C. Rocha and S. Silvester (2000) *Evaluatie van 55 PMZ-subsidieprojecten* (Design for Sustainability Programme, Delft University of Technology, Netherlands, August 2000).

Brundtland, G.H. (1994) 'The Challenge of Sustainable Production and Consumption Patterns', paper presented at the *Symposium on Sustainable Consumption*, Oslo, January 1994.

BSI (British Standards Institution) (1992) *British Standard BS 7750: 1992. Specification for Environmental Management Systems* (London: BSI).

Bürdek, B.E. (1991) *Design: Geschichte, Theorie und Praxis der Produktgestaltung* (Cologne: DuMont Publishing).

Burger, K. (1995) *Rapid Market Appraisal for Micro and MSEs: Background and First Experiences* (Amsterdam: Farm Implementation Tools Programme).

Campbell, S., and S. Green (1999) 'Net Alters Face of Distribution', *Computer Reseller News* 869 (15 November 1999): 97.

Carley, M., and P. Spapens (1998) *Sharing the World* (London: Earthscan).

Carlson, L., S.J. Grove and N. Kangun (1993) 'A Content Analysis of Environmental Advertising Claims: A Matrix Method Approach', *Journal of Advertising* 22.3: 27-39.

Carlson, L., S.J. Grove, N. Kangun and M.J. Polonsky (1996a) 'An International Comparison of Environmental Advertising: Substantive Versus Associative Claims', *Journal of Macromarketing* 16.2: 57-68.

Carlson, L., S.J. Grove, R.N. Laczniak and N. Kangun (1996b) 'Does Environmental Advertising Reflect Integrated Marketing Communications? An Empirical Investigation', *Journal of Business Research* 37.3: 225-32.

Caro, R. (1990) *La Problemática Forestal en la Meseta Tarasca: Los Problemas Medio-Ambientales de Michoacán Zamora* (Michoacán, Mexico: El Colegio de Michoacán).

Castañon, L.E. (1993) *Artesanos Purépechas: Análisis Económico y Social de los Determinantes de la Productividad* (Pátzcuaro, Michoacán, Mexico: Instituto Nacional Indigenista).

CEC (Commission of European Communities) (1993) 'Council Regulation (EEC) No 1836/93 of June 1993 Allowing Participation by Companies in the Industrial Sector in a Community Eco-management and Audit Scheme', *Official Journal of the European Communities* L168 (10 July 1993): 1-18.

Cernea, M.M. (1995) *Primero la Gente: Variables sociológicas en el desarrollo rural* (Mexico City: Fondo de Cultura Económica).

Charter, M. (ed.) (1992) *Greener Marketing: A Responsible Approach to Business* (Sheffield, UK: Greenleaf Publishing).

Charter, M. (1997a) 'Interview with Professor William McDonough', *Journal for Sustainable Product Design* 3: 35-39.

Charter, M. (ed.) (1997b) *Managing Ecodesign: A Training Solution* (Farnham, UK: The Centre for Sustainable Design, Surrey Institute of Art and Design, University College, www.cfsd.org.uk).

Charter, M. (1998a) *Sustainable Value* (discussion paper on sustainable product development and design; Farnham, UK: The Centre for Sustainable Design, Surrey Institute of Art and Design, University College, www.cfsd.org.uk).

Charter, M. (1998b) *Design for Environmental Sustainability, Foresight, National Resources and Environment Panel: Cleaner Technologies and Processes* (London: Office of Science and Technology, Department of Trade and Industry).

Charter, M. (2000a) 'Product-Related Environmental Communications' (unpublished workshop proceedings; forthcoming; Farnham, UK: Centre for Sustainable Design, Surrey Institute of Art and Design, University College).

Charter, M. (2000b) *Ecodesign Management Systems* (special report on environmental policy and procedures; Farnham, UK: The Centre for Sustainable Design, Surrey Institute of Art and Design, University College).

Charter, M. (2000c) *Smart ecoDesign©: Electronics* (unpublished; Farnham, UK: The Centre for Sustainable Design, Surrey Institute of Art and Design, University College).

Charter, M., and A. Chick (1997) 'Editorial Notes', *Journal of Sustainable Product Design* 3: 5-6.

Charter, M., and T. Clark (2000) *Management of Ecodesign amongst Fortune 500 Companies* (Farnham, UK: The Centre for Sustainable Design, Surrey Institute of Art and Design, University College).

Charter, M., and M.J. Polonsky (eds.) (1999) *Greener Marketing: A Global Perspective on Greening Marketing Practice* (Sheffield, UK: Greenleaf Publishing).

Charter, M., and C. Sherwin (1996) *Environment, Design and Electronics* (Farnham, UK: The Centre for Sustainable Design, Surrey Institute of Art and Design, University College, July 1996).

Chick, A., and C. Sherwin (1997) *Environmental Issues and the Designers* (Farnham, UK: The Centre for Sustainable Design, Surrey Institute of Art and Design, University College, February 1997).

*CHOICE* (1990) 'Green Cleaners', *CHOICE*, September 1990: 10-14.

CICA (Canadian Institute of Chartered Accountants) (1994) *Reporting on Environmental Performance* (Toronto: CICA).

Clark, T., and M. Charter (1996) *'Design for Environment' Survey: A Study of Fortune 500 Companies* (Farnham, UK: Centre for Sustainable Design, Surrey Institute of Art and Design, University College, December 1996).

Clark, T., and M. Charter (1999) *Chain of Uncertainty: A Survey amongst Suppliers of Electrical and Electronic Components, Assemblies and Materials* (Farnham, UK: Centre for Sustainable Design, Surrey Institute of Art and Design, University College, January 1999).

CNI (Cámara Nacional de Industrias) (1998) *Sistema de Información Ambiental: Cómo conseguir más información sobre medio ambiente* (information leaflet; La Paz, Bolivia: CNI, www.bolivia-industry.com/sia/home.html).

Cogoy, M. (1999) 'The Consumer as a Social and Environmental Actor', *Ecological Economics* 28: 385-98.

Colburn, T., D. Dumanoski and J. Peterson Myers (1997) *Our Stolen Future* (New York: Penguin Books, pbk edn [first published 1996]).

Coomer, J.C. (ed.) (1981) *Quest for a Sustainable Society* (New York/Oxford: Pergamon Press in co-operation with The Woodlands Conference).

Cottam, D. (1994) 'A Green Policy Committed to Print: Kyocera's Cartridge-Free Laser Printer', *Greener Management International* 5 (January 1994): 61-66.

Cowe, R. (1999) 'Turning the Tables on Green Slackers', *The Guardian*, 22 June 1999.

COWI AS/ECON AS/ÖRF (Östfold Research Foundation) (1999) *Proposal for a Common Nordic IPP. Volume 1: Background Documents Prepared for a Nordic IPP-Meeting in Saltsjobaden, February 9–10 in the Year 2000* (Copenhagen: TemaNord 2000:505, Nordic Council of Ministers, February 2000).

COWI AS (2000), 'Economic Instruments in Environmental Protection in Denmark' (Danish Environmental Protection Agency, www.mst.dk/udgiv/publications/2000/87-7909-568-2/html/indhold_eng.htm, January 2000).

Cox, S. (1999) 'Selling Eco-Textiles: Breakthrough on the German Market Still Awaited', *gate* 3: 30-38.

CPE (Centre de Prospective et d'Evaluation) (1986) 'Essai sur l'investissement industriel' (publication 71; Paris: CPE).

Cramer, J. (1997a) *Environmental Management: From 'Fit' to 'Stretch'* (TNO Centre for Technology and Policy Studies report STB/97/45; Apeldoorn, Netherlands, July 1997).

Cramer, J. (1997b) 'Towards Innovative, More Efficient Product Design Strategies', in C. Sheldon (ed.), *ISO 14001 and Beyond: Environmental Management Systems in the Real World* (Sheffield, UK: Greenleaf Publishing): 359-70.

Cramer, J. (1999) *Towards Sustainable Business: Connecting Environment and Market* (The Hague: Stichting Maatschappy en Onderneming [SMO]).

Cramer, J. (2000) 'Responsiveness of Industry to Eco-efficiency Improvements in the Product Chain: The Case of Akzo Nobel', *Business Strategy and the Environment* 9: 36-48.

Cramer, J., and J. Schot (1993) 'The Greening of Interfirm Relationships', in K. Fischer and J. Schot (eds.), *Environmental Strategies for Industry: International Perspectives on Research Needs and Political Implications* (Washington, DC: Island Press).

Cramer, J.M., and A.L.N. Stevels (1997) 'Strategic Environmental Product Planning within Philips Sound and Vision', *Environmental Quality Management*, Autumn 1997: 91-102.

Crane, A. (1998) 'Exploring Green Alliances', *Journal of Marketing Management* 14.4: 559-80.

CTC (Centre for Tomorrow's Company) (1998) *Sooner, Sharper, Simpler* (London: CTC).

Cude, B.J. (1993) 'Consumer Perceptions of Environmental Marketing Claims: An Exploratory Study', *Journal of Consumer Studies and Home Economics* 17.3: 207-25.

Daly, H.E., and J. Cobb. (1990) *For the Common Good: Redirecting the Economy towards Community, the Environment and a Sustainable Future* (London: Green Print).

Daniels, B. (1999) 'Integration of the Supply Chain for Total Through-Cost Reduction', *Total Quality Management* 10.4/5: S481-90.

Datschefski, E. (2000) *The Biothinker* 58 (Internet newsletter; BioThinking International, London, UK, www.biothinking.com, 7 May 2000).

Davis, J.J. (1994) 'Consumer Responses to Corporate Environmental Advertising', *The Journal of Consumer Marketing* 11.2: 25-37.

de Bruijn, T.J.N.M., F.H.J.M. Coenen, S.M.M. Kuks and K.R.D. Lulofs (1992) *Milieuzorg in opbouw* (Enschede, Netherlands: Centrum voor schone technologie en milieubeleid).

den Hond, F. (1996) *In Search of a Useful Theory of Environmental Strategy: A Case Study on the Recycling of End-of-Life Vehicles from Capabilities Perspective* (PhD thesis; Amsterdam: Free University).

DEPA (Danish Environmental Protection Agency) (1997) *A Product-Orientated Environmental Initiative* (Copenhagen: DEPA).

DEPA (Danish Environmental Protection Agency) (1998) *Status of Environmentally Friendly Public Procurement in Denmark* (Copenhagen: DEPA).

DEPAP (Danish Electronics Product Area Panel) (1999) *Action Plan 1999: A Plan for the Production and Use of More Environmentally Sound Electronic Products in Denmark* (Copenhagen: Elektronik-industrien, May 1999).

Design Council (1997) *More for Less: Design for Environmental Sustainability* (London: Design Council).

Designtex (1995) *Environmentally Intelligent Textiles* (product information booklet; New York: Designtex).

DeSimone, L.D., and F. Popoff (1997) *Eco-efficiency: The Business Link to Sustainable Development* (Cambridge, MA: MIT Press).

DETR (UK Department of Environment, Transport and the Regions) (1999) 'Responses to the Consultation Paper "Consumer Products and Environment"' (London: DETR, www.environment. detr.gov.uk/consult/consumerprod/response/index.htm).

DGXI (Directorate General for the Environment of the Commission of the European Communities) (1998) *Workshop on Integrated Product Policy: Final Report* (Brussels: DGXI, December 1998).

DGXI (Directorate General for the Environment of the Commission of the European Communities) (2000) *Draft Proposal for a Directive on Waste from Electronic and Electrical Equipment* (Brussels: DGXI).

DG XVII-CI (Directorate-General for Energy and Transport of the European Commission) (2000) *The European Union Policies and Programmes for Reducing Stand-by Consumption* (2nd International Energy Agency International Workshop on Standby Power, Brussels, 17–18 January 2000).

*Dialog* (1999) 'Economy and Ecology: Environmentally Sound and Economically Acceptable', *Dialog* 4: 12-14.

Dixon, F. (1999) 'Environmental Leaders Achieve Superior Stock Market Performance in the Electric Utility Sector', paper presented at the *Annual Public Utility Reporters Environmental Conference*, New Orleans, LA, 25 May 1999.

Dogson, M., and E. Rothwell (1994) *The Handbook of Industrial Innovation* (Aldershot, UK: Edward Elgar).

Drumwright, M.E. (1994) 'Socially Responsible Organisational Buying: Environmental Concern as a Noneconomic Buying Criterion', *Journal of Marketing* 58.3: 1-19.

Drumwright, M.E (1996) 'Company Advertising with a Social Dimension: The Role of Noneconomic Criteria', *Journal of Marketing* 60.4: 71-87.

Earl, G., and R. Clift (1999) 'Environmental Performance: What is it Worth? A Case Study of "Business-to-Business" Consumers', in M. Charter and M.J. Polonsky (eds.), *Greener Marketing: A Global Perspective on Greening Marketing Practice* (Sheffield, UK: Greenleaf Publishing): 255-74.

Easterling, D., A. Kenworthy and R. Nemzoff (1996) 'The Greening of Advertising: A Twenty-Five Year Look at Environmental Advertising', *Journal of Marketing Theory and Practice* 4.1: 20-34.

Eby, C., and R. Mast (2000) *Technical Report on Sustainable Wood Carving* (Nairobi: Mennonite Central Committee).

*Economist* (1993) 'Rubbish: Green Behind the Ears', *The Economist* 328.7818: 46-47.

Eder, P., and M. Narodoslawski (1999) 'What Environmental Pressures are a Region's Industries Responsible For? A Method of Analysis with Descriptive Indices and Input–Output Models', *Ecological Economics* 29.3: 359-74.

EEA (European Environment Agency) (2000) *Environmental Signals 2000: European Environment Agency Regular Indicator Report* (Copenhagen: EEA).

Ehrlich, P.R., G. Wolff, G.C. Daily, J.B. Hughes, M. Dalton and L. Goulder (1999) 'Knowledge and the Environment', *Ecological Economics* 30.2: 267-84.

Einstein, A. (1934) *Out of My Later Years* (New York: Philosophical Library).

ELCI (Environment Liaison Centre International) (1997) Special Issue Rio+5, *EcoForum* 20.4: 1-37.

Electrolux (1997) 'Electrolux: The Integration of Environmentally-Sound Technologies into Product Design', in M. Charter (ed.), *Managing Ecodesign: A Training Manual* (Farnham, UK: Centre for Sustainable Design, Surrey Institute of Art and Design, University College).

Electrolux (1999) *Environmental Report* (www.electrolux.com).

Elkington, J. (1997) *Cannibals with Forks: The Triple Bottom Line of 21st Century Business* (Oxford, UK: Capstone Publishing).

ENDS (Environmental Data Services) (1999), 'Volvo issues externally verified product profile based on LCA', *ENDS Report*, January 1999.

EP3 (1997) *ISO 14000 y Sistemas de Gerencia Ambiental: La Paz, Bolivia Julio 1 y 2, 1997* (Arlington, VA: Hagler Bailly Services Inc.).

EPA (US Environmental Protection Agency) (1999) *Consumer Labeling Initiative: Phase 2 Report* (Washington, DC: EPA).

EPRI (Electric Power Research Institute) (1996) *Environmental Performance Measurement: A Framework for the Utility Industry* (publication TR-106078; Palo Alto, CA: EPRI).

EPRI (Electric Power Research Institute) (1998) *Environmental Performance Measurement: Design, Implementation, and Review Guidance for the Utility Industry* (publication TR-111354; Palo Alto, CA: EPRI).

Epstein, M.J. (1996) *Measuring Corporate Environmental Performance: Best Practices for Costing and Managing an Effective Environmental Strategy* (Institute of Management Accountants, Foundation for Applied Research; Chicago, IL: Irwin).

Ernst & Young/SPRU (Science Policy Research Unit, University of Sussex, Brighton, UK) (1998) *Integrated Product Policy* (Brussels: European Commission, DGXI [Directorate General on the Environment], March 1998).

EuroStat (European Statistical Office) (1999) *The Environmental Pressure Index Programme* (Luxembourg: Office for Official Publications of the European Communities).

F10C (The Factor 10 Club) (1994) *Carnoules Declaration of the Factor 10 Club* (Carnoules, France: F10C).

F10C (The Factor Ten Club) (1997) *The Carnoules Declaration: Statement to Government and Business Leaders* (Wuppertal, Germany: Wuppertal Institute for Climate, Environment and Energy).

Fava, J., and J. Smith (1998) 'Integrating Financial and Environmental Information for Better Decision Making', *Journal of Industrial Ecology*, Winter 1998.

Feldman, S.J., P.A. Soyka and P. Ameer (1997) 'Does improving a firm's environmental management system and environmental performance result in a higher stock price?', *Journal of Investing*, January 1997.

Fiksel, J. (1995a) 'Metrics, Decisions, and Strategies: Environmental Performance Measurement in the Electric Utility Industry', *Total Quality Environmental Management*: 63-70.

Fiksel, J. (1995b) 'Design for Environment' (unpublished survey results; Mount View, USA: Decision Focus, October 1995).

Fiksel, J. (1996) 'Practical Issues in Environmental Performance Evaluation', in T. Tibor and I. Feldman (eds.), *Implementing ISO 14001* (Chicago: Irwin): 145-65.

Fiksel, J., J. McDaniel and C. Mendenhall (1999) 'Measuring Progress towards Sustainability Principles, Process, and Best Practices', paper presented at the *Eighth International Greening of Industry Network Conference*, Chapel Hill, NC, 14–17 November 1999.

Fiksel, J., J. McDaniel and D. Spitzley (1998) 'Measuring Product Sustainability', *The Journal of Sustainable Product Design*, July 1998: 7-18.

*Financial Times* (2000) ' "Third way" guru attacks Blair', *The Financial Times*, 6 July 2000: 5.

FoD (Faculty of Design, Cologne University of Applied Science [Fachbereich Design, Fachhochschule Köln]) (eds.) (1999) *Die Vollholzküche der Zukunft: Ein Gemeinschaftsprojekt des Kölner Fachbereich Design mit der Firma Kambium* (Cologne: Walter König).

Frankel, C. (1998) *In Earth's Company: Business, Environment and the Challenge of Sustainability* (Stony Creek, CT: New Society Publishers).

Fukuyama, F. (1995) *Trust: The Social Virtues and the Creation of Prosperity* (London: Hamish Hamilton).

Funtowicz, S.O., and J.R. Ravetz (1993) 'Science for the Post-Normal Age', *Futures* 25.7: 739-55.

Fussler, C., with P. James (1996) *Driving Eco-innovation: A Breakthrough Discipline for Innovation and Sustainability* (London: FT/Pitman).

*Gaceta Oficial de Bolivia* (1992) 'Ley Nr° 1333: Medio Ambiente', *Gaceta Oficial de Bolivia* 1740.

Gaffard, J.L. (1990) 'Innovations et changements structurels', *Revue d'Economie Politique* 3: 325-82.

Galbraith, J.K. (1958) *The Affluent Society* (Harmondsworth, UK: Penguin).

Gertsakis, J., H. Lewis and C. Ryan (1997) *Good Design, Better Business, Cleaner World: A Guide to EcoReDesign™* (Melbourne: Centre for Design at RMIT University).

Gertsakis, J., S. Reardon and A. Sweatman (1999) *Appliance Reuse and Recycling: A Product Stewardship Guide* (Melbourne: Centre For Design at RMIT University/EcoRecycle Victoria).

GFEA (German Federal Environmental Agency) (1999) *Climate Protection through Reduction of No-Load Losses in Electric Appliances and Equipment* (GFEA, December 1999).

Ghazi, P., and J. Jones (1997) *Downshifting* (London: Coronet).

Giarini, O., and H. Louberge (1978) *The Diminishing Returns of Technology* (Oxford: Pergamon Press).

Giarini, O., and W.R. Stahel (1989) *The Limits to Certainty: Facing Risks in the New Service Economy* (translations available in French, Italian, Romanian, Japanese and German; Dordrecht, Netherlands/Boston, MA/London: Kluwer Academic Publishers, rev. edn 1993).

Giddens, A. (1996) 'Leben in einer posttraditionalen Gesellschaft', in U. Beck, A. Giddens and S. Lash (eds.), *Reflexive Modernisierung* (Frankfurt: Suhrkamp): 113-94.

Gifford, B. (1991) 'The Greening of the Golden Arches: McDonald's teams with environmental group to cut waste', *The San Diego Union*, 19 August 1991: C1, C4.

Giuntini, R., and T. Andel (1995) 'Master the Six R's of Reverse Logistics: Part 2', *Transportation and Distribution* 36.3: 93-98.

Glenn, J. (1996) 'Keeping the Defense Department out of the Landfill', *BioCycle* 37.4: 46-47.

Gonella, C., A. Pilling and S. Zadek (1998) *Making Values Count: Contemporary Experience in Social and Ethical Accounting, Auditing and Reporting* (London: Association of Chartered Certified Accountants).

Gong, Y. (1999) 'Anomaly of Consumption: Asian's Extravagance in Luxury Goods', in Sang-Whan Lho, Hyun-Jung Im and Ross W. Kim (eds.), *Sustainable Consumption Patterns* (Seoul: Korea Environment Institute).

Gooley, T.B. (1996) 'Is there hidden treasure in your packaging?' *Logistics Management* 35.12: 19-23.

Gorman, M. (1998) *Transforming Nature, Ethics, Invention and Discovery* (Dordrecht, Netherlands: Kluwer Academic Publishers).

Gorman, M., M.M. Mehalik and P. Werhane (1999) *Ethical and Environmental Challenges to Engineering* (New York: Prentice–Hall).

Gouldson, A., and J. Murphy (1998) *Regulatory Realities: The Implementation and Impact of Industrial Environmental Regulation* (London: Earthscan).

Gräf, B. (1998) *Rohstoff und Garnrecherche von Baumwolle, Wolle und Leinen* (case study; Reutlingen, Germany: University Reutlingen).

Gray, R., D. Owen and C. Adams (1996) *Accounting and Accountability: Changes and Challenges in Corporate Social and Environmental Reporting* (Hemel Hempstead, UK: Prentice–Hall).

Greider, W. (1997) *One World Ready or Not* (New York: Simon & Schuster).

Groen, A.J. (1995) *Milieu en MKB: Kennis en Kennissen. Milieu-innovatie in de grafische industrie: modelmatig verklaard* (Groningen, Netherlands: Wolters-Noordhof).

Gross, P. (1995) *Die Multi-Options-Gesellschaft* (The Multi-Option Society; Bern; Frankfurt: Suhrkamp).

Gruhler, W. (1990) *Dienstleistungsbestimmter Strukturwandel in deutschen Industrieunternehmen* (Cologne: Deutscher Instituts Verlag).

Guimarães, L.E.C. (1995) *Product Design in the Context of the Social Needs in Less Industrialised Economies* (PhD thesis; Birmingham, UK: Aston University, School of Engineering).

Guinomet, I. (1999) *The Relationship between Indicators of Sustainable Development* (overview provided on behalf of the United Nations Conference on Sustainable Development; New York: United Nations).

Hamel, G., and C.K. Prahalad (1994) *Competing for the Future* (Schieden: Scriptum Management).

Hanssen, O.J. (1997) *Sustainable Industrial Product Systems* (PhD thesis, AR 20.97; Trondheim: Østfold Research Foundation, Norwegian University of Science and Technology).

Hart, S.J. (1996) 'Beyond Greening: Strategies for a Sustainable World', *Harvard Business Review*, January/February 1997: 66-76.

Hartman, C.L., and E.R. Stafford (1997) 'Green Alliances: Building New Business with Environmental Groups', *Long Range Planning* 30.2: 184-96.

Hartman, C.L., and E.R. Stafford (1998) 'Crafting Enviropreneurial Value Chain Strategies through Green Alliances', *Business Horizons* 41.2: 62-72.

Hartman, C.L., E.R. Stafford and M.J. Polonsky (1999) 'Green Alliances: Environmental Groups as Strategic Bridges to Other Stakeholders', in M. Charter and M.J. Polonsky (eds.), *Greener Marketing: A Global Perspective on Greening Marketing Practice* (Sheffield, UK: Greenleaf Publishing): 201-17.

Hawken, P., A.B. Lovins and L.H. Lovins (1999) *Natural Capitalism: Creating the Next Industrial Revolution* (Boston, MA: Little, Brown & Co.; London: Earthscan).

HBS (Hans Böckler Stiftung) (2000) *Arbeit und Ökologie: Endbericht* (Düsseldorf: HBS).

Herrera, A., and G. Skolnik (1976) *Die Grenzen des Elends: Das Bariloche-Modell* (*Limits to Misery: The Bariloche Model*) (Frankfurt-am-Main: Suhrkamp).

Hildebrandt, E. (1999) 'Flexible Arbeit und nachhaltige Lebensführung', *Wissenschaftszentrum für die Sozialwissenschaften Berlin WZB Papers* (Berlin): 42.

Hillary, R. (1996) 'The Eco-management and Audit Scheme: Progress and Outstanding Issues', *EEMA Review: Journal of the European Environmental Association* 7 (May 1996): 8-10.

Hinterberger, F., F. Luks and F. Schmidt-Bleek (1997) 'Material Flows vs Natural Capital: What Makes an Economy Sustainable?', *Ecological Economics* 23.1: 1-14.

Hook, E. (1995) 'LCA: Help or Headache?', *Co-Design* 05 06 (01 02 03): 18-22.

Hopkinson, P., and P. James (2000) *A Typology of Eco-Efficient Services* (working paper; Bradford, UK: University of Bradford).

Hutchinson, A., and I. Chaston (1994) 'Environmental Management in Devon and Cornwall's Small and Medium-sized Enterprise Sector', *Business Strategy and the Environment* 3.1: 15-22.

Hutchinson, A., and F. Hutchinson (1995) 'Sustainable Regeneration of the UK's Small and Medium-sized Enterprise Sector: Some Implications of SME Response to BS 7750', *Greener Management International* 9 (January 1995): 73-84.

*Industry and Environment* (1995) 'Environmental Management Tools', *Industry and Environment: A Publication of the Environmental Programme of the United Nations* 18.2-3.

INEGI (Instituto Nacional de Estadística Geografía e Informática) (1986) *Michoacán Hablantes de Lengua Indígena* (Mexico City: INEGI).

INEGI (Instituto Nacional de Estadística Geografía e Informática) (1988) *Encuesta Nacional Ejidal. Vol. II* (Mexico City: INEGI).

*International Journal of LCA* (1996) 'EPEA and Rohner Textil', *International Journal of LCA* 1: 119-20.

Ishii, K., and A. Stevels (2000) 'Environmental Value Chain Analysis: A Tool for Product Definition in Eco-design', in G. Pitts (ed.), *Proceedings of the ISEE Conference 2000, San Francisco* (Piscataway, NJ: IEEE): 184-90.

ISO (International Organization for Standardization) (1996) *ISO 14001: Environmental Management Systems: Specification with Guidance for Use* (Geneva: ISO).

ISO (International Organization for Standardization) (1998) *ISO/FDIS 14031: Environmental Management: Environmental Performance Evaluation: Guidelines* (final draft international standard; Geneva: ISO).

ITF (Indicators Task Force) (1991) *A Report on Canada's Progress Towards a National Set of Environmental Indicators* (Ottawa: Environment Canada).

IUCN (International Union for the Conservation of Nature)/UNEP (United Nations Environment Programme)/WWF (World Wide Fund for Nature International) (1980) *World Conservation Strategy* (Gland, Switzerland: IUCN/WWF; Nairobi: UNEP).

Jackson, T., and N. Marks (1994) *Measuring Sustainable Economic Welfare: A Pilot Index: 1950-1990* (Stockholm: Stockholm Environmental Institute).

James, P. (1997) 'The Sustainability Cycle: A New Tool for Product Development and Design', *The Journal of Sustainable Product Design* 2 (July 1997): 52-57.

Jansen, A., and A. Stevels (1998) 'Renewable Energy and the Road towards "Green" for Portable Audio Products', in A. Rintahuhta (ed.), *Proceedings of the International Conference on Engineering Design, ICED 97, Tampere. Vol. III* (Tampere, Finland: Tampere University): 577-82

Jansen, L., and P. Vergragt (1992) *Sustainable Development: A Challenge to Technology* (Leidschendam, Netherlands: Ministry for Housing, Physical Planning and Environment).

Jansen, M. (1995) *Influences upon Sustainable Product Development in the Developing World* (Amsterdam: Working Group on Sustainable Product Development, United Nations Environment Programme).

Jay, L. (1990) 'Green about the Tills: Markets Discover the Eco-consumer', *Management Review* 79.6: 24-28.

Kambium (Kambium Möbelwerkstätte) (1995) *Environmental Policy* (Lindlar, Germany: Kambium).

Kangun, N., and M.J. Polonsky (1995) 'Regulation of Environmental Marketing Claims: A Comparative Perspective', *International Journal of Advertising* 14.1: 1-24.

Kapelianis, D., and S. Strachan (1996) 'The Price Premium of an Environmentally Friendly Product', *South African Journal of Business Management* 27.4: 89-95.

Kiernan, M., and J. Martin (1998) 'Wake-up Call for Fiduciaries: Eco-efficiency drives shareholder value', *Today's Corporate Investor*, December 1998.

Kilburne, W. (1998) 'Green Marketing: A Theoretical Perspective', *Journal of Marketing Management* 14.6: 657-77.

Kilburne, W., and S. Beckmann (1998) 'Review and Critical Assessment of Research on Marketing and the Environment', *Journal of Marketing Management* 14.6: 513-32.

King, J., and M. Slesser (1994) 'Can the world make the transition to a sustainable economy driven by solar energy?' *International Journal of Environment and Pollution* 5.1: 14-29.

Klein, N. (2000) *No Logo* (London: Flamingo).

Kruijsen, J. (1997) 'Sustainable Product Innovation: The Introduction of New Technologies Like Solar Cell Technology', paper presented at the *6th Greening of Industry Network Conference*, Santa Barbara, CA, USA, 16-19 November 1997.

Lafferty, W.M. (1994) *Steps towards Sustainable Consumption: A Presentation of Selected Norwegian Initiatives* (Oslo: Prosjekt Alternativ Framtid).

Lawrence, J. (1991) 'Mobil', *Advertising Age* 62.5: 12-13.

Lehmann, K. (1999) 'Design for Environment' (speech at International Organization for Standardization [ISO] Environmental Management Seminar, Seoul, Korea, 1999).

Lehr, M. (1999) *Stärken- und Schwächenanalyse von Maschenware* (final thesis; Albstadt-Sigmaringen, Germany: University Albstadt-Sigmaringen).

Lélé, S.M. (1991) *A Framework for Sustainability and its Application in Visualizing a Peaceful and Sustainable Society* (Berkeley, CA: University of California Press).

Lélé, S.M. (1993) *Sustainability: A Plural, Multi-dimensional Approach* (Berkeley, CA: University of California Press).

Lentz, R. (1997) *Umweltmanagement in Bolivien: Status und Aufgaben* [in German]; *La gestión ambiental en la empresa boliviana: Situación y Tareas* [in Spanish] (Eschborn, Germany: Gesellschaft für technische Zusammenarbeit [GTZ]; Cologne: Institut für angewandte Sozialforschung, Beretung, Planung und Entwicklung [ICON]-Institut).

Lentz, R. (1998) *Umweltmanagement in kleinen und mittleren Unternehmen in Bolivien: Rolle der Industriekammer—Informationsinstrumente Aufgaben in der Lederindustrie* [in German]; *La gestión ambiental en las pequeñas y medianas empresas de Bolivia: El rol des las Cámaras de Industria—Instrumentos de información* [in Spanish] (Eschborn, Germany: Gesellschaft für technische Zusammenarbeit [GTZ]; Cologne: Institut für angewandte Sozialforschung, Beretung, Planung und Entwicklung [ICON]-Institut).

Lentz, R., A. Detzel and P. Aldana (1997) *Manual de la Gestión Ambiental* (Wedel, Germany: Fachhochschule Wedel; Frankfurt, Germany: GTZ).

Liedtke, C., C. Manstein and T. Merten (1994) 'MIPS, Resources Management and Sustainable Development', paper presented at the *Conference on the Recycling of Metals*, Amsterdam, October 1994).

Liedtke, C., R. Nickel, H. Rohn and U. Tischner (1995) *Öko-Audit und Ressourcenmanagement bei dem Unternehmen Kambium Möbelwerkstätte GmbH* (*Eco-auditing and Resource Management at the Kambium Furniture Workshop*; final report on behalf of the Ministry of Environment, Land Use Planning and Agriculture in North Rhine Westphalia, Germany; available from The Wuppertal Institute or Kambium Furniture Workshop Inc.).

Liedtke, C., H. Rohn, M. Kuhndt and R. Nickel (1998) 'Applying Material Flow Accounting: Eco-auditing and Resource Management at the Kambium Furniture Workshop', *Journal of Industrial Ecology* 2.3: 131-47.

Lippmann, S. (1999) 'Supply Chain Environmental Management: Elements for Success', *Corporate Environmental Strategy* 6.2: 175-82.

Lober, D.J. (1997) 'Explaining the Formation of Business–Environmentalist Collaborations: Collaborative Windows and the Paper Task Force', *Policy Sciences* 30.1: 1-24

Lorek, S., and J.H. Spangenberg (2001) 'Sustainable Household Consumption: Indicators for Priority Fields of Action', *International Journal of Sustainable Development* 4.4: accepted for publication.

Machiavelli, N. (1513) *Il Principe*, quoted in Associazione Libro d'Oro (eds.) (1999) 'Il Caffè 14, from The Prince' (Milan: Nike Edizioni).

Magretta, J. (1997) 'Growth through Sustainability: An Interview with Monsanto's CEO, Robert B. Shapiro', *Harvard Business Review*, January/February 1997: 82.

Manrai, L.A., A.K. Manrai, D.N. Lascu and J.K. Ryans Jr (1997) 'How Green-Claim Strength and Country Disposition affect Product Evaluation and Company Image', *Psychology and Marketing* 14.5: 511-37.

Manzini, E. (1993) 'Values, Quality and Sustainable Development: The Role of the Cultural Factor in the Environmental Reorientation of the System of Production and Consumption', in T. Jackson (ed.), *Clean Production Strategies* (London: Lewis): 367-86.

Martin, H.-P., and H. Schumann (1998) *The Global Trap* (London: Zed Books).

Masera, D. (1994) 'Product Development for the Informal Sector in Kenya', *Appropriate Technology Magazine* 21.2 (September 1994): 34-35.

Masera, D. (1997) 'Creating Raw Material by Re-using and Recycling', *Appropriate Technology Magazine* 24.1 (June 1997): 32-34.

Masera, D. (1998) *Eco-production, Sustainable Product Development in Small Furniture Enterprises in the Purepecha Region of Mexico* (London: Royal College of Art).

Masera, D., and F. Bedini (1994) 'Local Farmers Innovate in Irrigation: The Development of Low-Cost Sprinklers in Kenya', *Indigenous Knowledge and Development Magazine* 2.1: 20-22.

Masera, D., and M. González (1997) *Aprovechamiento de la Madera en Talleres Artesanales de Carpintería* (Pátzcuaro, Michoacán, Mexico: Grupo Interdisciplinario de Tecnología Rural Apropiada).

Masera, D., and R. Okangaa (1995) *Scrap Metal Recycling: A Product Development Oriented Study of the Informal Sector* (Nairobi: Undugu Society).

Masera, D., and J. Sana (1992) *Product Development Training Module* (Nairobi: International Labour Organisation).

Masera, D., and J. Sana (1994) *Product Development for the Informal Sector* (Nairobi: Undugu Society).

Matthews, E., C. Amann, S. Bringezu, M. Fischer-Kowalski, W. Hüttler, R. Kleijn, Y. Moriguchi, C. Ottke, E. Rodenburg, D. Rogich, H. Schandl, H. Schütz, E. van der Voet and H. Weisz (2000) *The Weight of Nations: Material Outflows from Industrial Economies* (Washington, DC: World Resources Institute, September 2000).

Mayhew, N. (1998) 'Trouble with the Triple Bottom Line', *The Financial Times*, 10 August 1998.

McDaniel, S.W., and D.H. Rylander (1993) 'Strategic Green Marketing', *Journal of Consumer Marketing* 10.3: 4-10.

McDonough, W. (1992) *Hannover Principles: Design for Sustainability*.

McDonough, W. (1993) 'A Centennial Sermon: Design Ecology Ethics and the Making of Things'.

Meadows, D.L. (1972) *Limits to Growth: A Report to the Club of Rome* (New York: Universe Books).

Mehalik, M.M., M. Gorman and P. Werhane (1995) *Business Case Studies* (Designtex, case studies A and B; Charlottesville, VA: Darden Graduate School of Business, University of Virginia).

Mehalik, M.M., M. Gorman and P. Werhane (1996-1998) *Business Case Studies* (Rohner Textil, case studies A-E; Charlottesville, VA: Darden Graduate School of Business, University of Virginia).

Meinders, H. (1997) *Point of No Return: Philips EcoDesign Guideline* (Eindhoven: Philips).

Mendleson, N., and M.J. Polonsky (1995) 'Using Strategic Alliances to Develop Credible Green Marketing', *Journal of Consumer Marketing* 12.2: 4-18.

Menon, M., and A. Menon (1997) 'Enviropreneurial Marketing Strategy: The Emergence of Corporate Environmentalism as Marketing Strategy', *Journal of Marketing* 61.1: 51-67.

Metcalf, K., P. Williams, J. Minter and C. Hobson (1996) 'Environmental Performance Indicators for Enhancing Environmental Management', *Total Quality Environmental Management*, Summer 1996.

MFF (Merck Family Fund) (1996) *Yearning for Balance* (Tacoma, WA: MFF).

Michaelis, L. (2001) *The Ethics of Consumption* (Oxford, UK: Oxford Centre for Environment, Ethics and Society, forthcoming).

Micklitz, H.W. (1992) 'The German Packaging Order: A Model for State-Induced Waste Avoidance?', *The Columbia Journal of World Business*, September 1992: 120-27.

Milne, G.R., E.S. Iyer and S. Gooding-Williams (1996) 'Environmental Organisation Alliance Relationships within and across Nonprofit, Business, and Government Sectors', *Journal of Public Policy and Marketing* 15.2: 203-15.

Mohr, L.A., D. Eroglu and P.S. Ellen (1998) 'The Development and Testing of a Measure of Scepticism towards Environmental Claims in Marketers' Communications', *The Journal of Consumer Affairs* 32.1: 30-56.

Moors, E., K. Mulder and P. Vergragt (1998) 'Transition to Sustainable Industrial Production: Towards a Conceptual Framework for Analysing Incremental and Radical Process Innovations in the Metals Producing Industry', paper presented at the *7th International Greening of Industry Network Conference*, Rome, Italy, 15-18 November 1998.

Nafzinger, L., and J. Snider (1998) *Sustainable Wood Carving* (Nairobi: Mennonite Central Committee).

NCC (Newcastle City Council) (1999) *State of the Environment Report 1998/99* (Newcastle, NSW, Australia: NCC).

NCM (Nordic Council of Ministers) (1999) *Factor 4 and 10 in the Nordic Countries* (Copenhagen: NCM).

Nelson, J. (1998) *Building Competitiveness and Communities: How World Class Companies are Creating Shareholder Value and Societal Value* (London: The Prince of Wales Business Leaders' Forum).

Noordhoek, M., and C. van Hemel (1999) *Productgericht milieuzirg bij de Atag Group: Een model voor het productgericht milieuzorgsystem* (September 1999).

North, K. (1992) *Environmental Business Management* (Geneva: International Labour Office).

NRTEE (National Round Table on the Environment and the Economy) (1999) *Measuring Eco-efficiency in Business: Feasibility of a Core Set of Indicators* (Ottawa: Renouf Publishing).

Oakley, B.T. (1993) 'Total Quality Product Design: How to Integrate Environmental Criteria into the Production Realisation Process', *Total Quality Environmental Management* 2.3: 309-21.

Obunga, R. (1995) *Sustainable Development of Woodcarving Industry in Kenya* (Nairobi: National Museums of Kenya).

Odum, H.T. (1996) *Environmental Accounting, Emergy and Environmental Decision Making* (New York: John Wiley).

OECD (Organisation for Economic Co-operation and Development) (1997a) *Sustainable Consumption and Production* (Paris: OECD).

OECD (Organisation for Economic Co-operation and Development) (1997b) *Meeting of the OECD Council on Ministerial Level, May 1997* (Paris: OECD).

OECD (Organisation for Economic Co-operation and Development) (1998) *Towards Sustainable Development: Environmental Indicators* (code 971998031P1; Paris: OECD, July 1998).

OECD (Organisation for Economic Co-operation and Development) (1999a) 'Sustainable Development and its Economic, Social and Environmental Indicators' (OECD Document ENV/EPOC/SE/CONF[99]7), *Towards Sustainable Development Indicators to Measure Progress*, Rome, 15–17 December 1999, OECD.

OECD (Organisation for Economic Co-operation and Development) (1999b) 'Environmental Performance Indicators: OECD Overview' (OECD Document ENV/EPOC/SE/CONF[99]4), *Towards Sustainable Development Indicators to Measure Progress*, Rome, 15–17 December 1999, OECD.

Oleck, J. (1992) 'The Great Clamshell Debate', *Restaurant Business* 91.16: 68-72.

Oosterhuis, F., F. Rubik and G. Scholl (1996) Product Policy in Europe: New Environmental Perspectives (Dordrecht, Netherlands: Kluwer Academic Publishers).

Ottman, J. (1993) 'Source reduction will be more valuable in years ahead', *Marketing News* 27.23: 10.

Ottman, J. (1997a) *Green Marketing: Opportunity for Innovation* (Lincolnwood, IL: NTC Business Books).

Ottman, J. (1997b) 'Product take-back is a new marketing tool', *Marketing News* 31.2: 8.

Pacey, P. (1992 ) ' "Anyone Designing Anything?" Non-Professional Designers and the History of Design', *Journal of Design History* 5.3: 217-25.

Packard, V. (1960) *The Waste Makers* (Harmondsworth, UK: Penguin Book).

Papanek, V. (1994) *The Green Imperative: Design for the Real World* (London: Thames & Hudson).

Pauli, G. (1998) *UpSizing. The Road to Zero Emissions: More Jobs, More Income and No Pollution* (Sheffield, UK: Greenleaf Publishing).

Paulitsch, K. (1999) *Process Control* (workshop proceedings; Butzbach, Germany: Hess Naturtextilien).

Paulitsch, K. (2000a) *Ergebnisdokumentation der Teilprojekte ökologische Produktgestaltung und Prozeß-steuerung* (final project documentation Butzbach, Germany: Hess Naturtextilien).

Paulitsch, K. (2000b) *Ecological Design* (workshop proceedings; Butzbach, Germany: Hess Naturtextilien).

Pearce, D.W., and R.K. Turner (1991) *Economics of Natural Resources and the Environment* (Hemel Hempstead, UK: Harvester Wheatsheaf).

Pearce. D., E. Barbier and A. Markandya (1990) *Sustainable Development* (London: Earthscan).

Peattie, K. (1999) 'Rethinking Marketing: Shifting to a Greener Paradigm', in M. Charter and M.J. Polonsky (eds.), *Greener Marketing: A Global Perspective on Greening Marketing Practice* (Sheffield, UK: Greenleaf Publishing): 57-71.

People and Plants (1999) 'Carving in Kenya', *Chonga* 1 (November 1999): 1-3.

PLI (Product-Life Institute) (1995a) *Vienna Decision Trees: Strategic Design Tool for Sustainable Solutions* (unpublished research report for the Austrian Federal Ministry of Economic Affairs, Vienna/Geneva: PLI; http://product-life.org).

PLI (Product-Life Institute) (1995b) '300 Examples of Higher Resource Productivity in Today's Industry and Society', in Landesanstalt für Umweltschutz Baden-Württemberg, Karlsruher (ed.), *Intelligente Produktionsweisen und Nutzungskonzepte. Handbuch, Abfall 1: Allgemeine Kreislauf und Rückstandswirtschaft* (vols. 1 and 2; Geneva: PLI, http://product-life.org).

PLI (Product-Life Institute) (2000a) *Cultural Factors of Ecology and their Influence on Competitiveness* (joint research report for the Austrian Federal Ministry of Science and Infrastructures, Vienna, and Amt der Steiermärkischen Landesregierung, Graz; Geneva: PLI, http://product-life.org).

PLI (Product-Life Institute) (2000b) *The Shift from Manufacturing to a Service Economy* (multi-client study, open subscription; Geneva: PLI, http://product-life.org).

Polonsky, M., H. Brooks, P. Henry and C. Schweizer (1998) 'An Exploratory Examination of Environmentally Responsible Straight Rebuy Purchases in Large Australian Organisations', *Journal of Business and Industrial Marketing* 13.1: 54-69.

Polonsky, M.J., and J. Ottman (1998) 'Stakeholders' Contribution to the Green New Product Development Process', *Journal of Marketing Management* 14.6: 533-58.

Porter, M.E. (1985) *Competitive Advantage: Creating and Sustaining Superior Performance* (New York: Free Press).

Porter, M.E. (1990) *The Competitive Advantage of Nations* (New York: Free Press).

Porter, M.E., and C. van der Linde (1995) 'Green and Competitive: Ending the Stalemate', *Harvard Business Review* 73.5: 120-34.

Poston, D. (1990) *The Development of Rural Manufacturing Industry in Central Africa, with Special Reference to Metal Working* (PhD thesis; Coventry, UK: Department of Engineering, University of Warwick).

Princen, T. (1999) 'Consumption and Environment: Some Conceptual Issues', *Ecological Economics* 31.3: 347-64.

Puga, F.P. (2000) *Experiências de apoio às micro, pequenas em médias empresas nos Estados Unidos, na Itália e em Taiwan* (discussion paper 75; Rio de Janeiro: Departamento Econômico, BNDES).

Putz, F.E. (1994) *Approaches to Sustainable Forest Management* (Indonesia: Center for International Forestry Research [CIFOR]).

Pütz, S. (1999) *Materialintensitätsanalyse der Hess Natur spezifischen Porduktline Wolle* (final thesis; Mönchengladbach, Germany: University Mönchengladbach).

Ranganathan, J. (1998) *Sustainability Rulers: Measuring Corporate Environmental and Social Performance* (Washington, DC: World Resources Institute, Sustainable Enterprise Initiative, May 1998).

Ranganathan, J., and D. Ditz (1997) *Measuring Up: Toward a Common Framework for Tracking Corporate Environmental Performance* (Washington, DC: World Resources Institute, Sustainable Enterprise Initiative).

Rathenau Institute (1996) *A Vision on Producer Responsibility and Ecodesign Innovation* (The Hague: Rathenau Institute, April 1996).

Ratovo, K. (1999) *Stärken- und Schwächenanalyse von Geweben* (final thesis; Albstadt-Sigmaringen, Germany: University Albstadt-Sigmaringen).

RBI (Reed Business Information) (1998) *Profile of the European Consumer Electronics Industry* (Sutton, UK: Reed Electronics Research, www.rer.co.uk).

Redclift, M. (1987) *Sustainable Development: Exploring the Contradictions* (London: Routledge).

Rees, W., and M. Wackernagel (1994) 'Ecological Footprints and Appropriated Carrying Capacity: Investing in Natural Capital', in A.M. Jansson, M, Hammer, C. Folke and R. Costanza (eds.), *The Ecological Economics Approach to Sustainability* (Washington, DC: Island Press): 504ff.

Regan, M.B. (1996) 'The Dustup over Dust', *Business Week*, 2 December 1996: 119.

Rejeski, D. (1997) 'Clean Production and the Post Command and Control Paradigm', in R. Hillary (ed.), *Environmental Management Systems and Cleaner Production* (Chichester, UK: John Wiley): 143-55.

Reynnells, R.D. (1999) 'Turning Animal By-products into Resource', *Biocycle* 40.6: 48-49.

Rice, F. (1990) 'How to Deal with Tougher Customers', *Fortune* 122.14: 38-48.

Richards, D.J., and T.N. Gladwin (1999) 'Sustainability Metrics for the Business Enterprise', *Environmental Quality Management*, Spring 1999: 11-21.

Riess, G. (1998) 'Rohner Textil massgeschneidertes Beurteilen', *Bulletin ETH Zürich* 268 (January 1998).

Rivière, A., B. Soth and R. Ketelhut (1997) *From LCA to LCD (Life-Cycle Development)* (Hamburg: EPEA Internationale Umweltforschung GmbH).

Robins, N., and S. Roberts (1998) *Upshifting? Sustainable Consumption and the South* (London: International Institute for Environment and Development).

Robinson, S. (1998) *Beyond the Twilight Zone: Defining and Managing Key Survival Issues for Corporate Environmental Sustainability* (London: The Environment Council).

Rocha, C., and H. Brezet (1999) *Review of DAF Trucks' NV Environmental Management Systems and EcoDesign Activities, Including Recommendations for DAF's Product Oriented Environmental Management System* (internal report; Design for Sustainability Programme, Delft University of Technology, Netherlands, July 1999).

Roddick, J. (1998) *El Niño, El Viejo, and the Global Re-shaping of Latin America: Surviving the UNCED Coups* (Edinburgh, UK: Department of Sociology, University of Edinburgh).

Rohn, H. (1999) *Documentation of Factor 4 Plus Project at Hess Natur: Entwicklung von Erfolgskriterien* (Wuppertal, Germany: Wuppertal Institute, http://wupperinst.org/Projekte/mipsonline/grundlagen/bausteine.html).

Rohner (Rohner Textil AG) (1995) *Eco-eco Concept 1993–2000* (Heerbrugg, Switzerland: Rohner).

Rohner (Rohner Textil AG) (1997) *The Path towards a Sustainable Company: Rohner Textil 1998–2008* (Heerbrugg, Switzerland: Rohner).

Romm, J. (1994) *Lean and Clean Management: How to Boost Profits and Productivity by Reducing Pollution* (New York: Kondasha America).

Romm, J. (1999) *Cool Companies* (London: Earthscan).

Roome, N. (1992) 'Developing Environmental Management Strategies', *Business Strategy and the Environment* 1.1: 11-24.

Roos, G. (1999) 'Lucent touts lead-free soldering', *Electronic Buyers' News* 1151 (15 March 1999): 30.

Rowledge, L., R. Barton, and K. Brady (1999) *Mapping the Journey: Case Studies in Strategy and Action toward Sustainable Development* (Sheffield, UK: Greenleaf Publishing).

Roy, R. (1997) *Proposal for an Educational Module on Sustainable Product Development* (Amsterdam: United Nations Environment Programme Working Group on Sustainable Product Development).

Roy, R. (1999) 'Designing and Marketing Greener Products', in M. Charter and M.J. Polonsky (eds.), *Greener Marketing: A Global Perspective on Greening Marketing Practice* (Sheffield, UK: Greenleaf Publishing): 126-42.

Russel, T. (1998) *Greener Purchasing: Opportunities and Innovations* (Sheffield, UK: Greenleaf Publishing).

Ryan, C. (1993) 'Design and the Ends of Progress', *Striking Visions O$_2$ Conference*: 5-6.

Ryan, C., M. Hoskens and D. Greens (1992) 'Ecodesign: Design and the Response to the Greening of International Markets', *Design Studies* 13.1: 3-22.

Sachs, W., R. Loske and M. Linz (1998) *Greening the North* (London: Zed Books).

Schegelmilch, B.D., A. Diamantopoulos and G.M. Bohlen (1995) 'Environmental Issues in the Freight Transport Industry: A Qualitative Analysis of Key Stakeholders' Perceptions', in M.J. Polonsky and A.T. Mintu-Wimsatt (eds.), *Environmental Marketing: Strategies, Practice, Theory and Research* (New York: The Haworth Press): 363-88.

Schmidheiny, S., with the Business Council for Sustainable Development (1992) *Changing Course: A Global Perspective on Development and the Environment* (Cambridge, MA: MIT Press)

Schmidheiny, S. (1996) 'Eco-efficiency and Sustainable Development', *Risk Management* 43.7 (Risk Management Society Publishing; Information Access Company, a Thomson Corporation Company): 51.

Schmidt-Bleek, F. (1994) *Wieviel Umwelt braucht der Mensch? MIPS: Das Mass für ökologisches Wirtschaften (The Fossil Makers: Factor 10 and More)* (Berlin/Basel: Birkhäuser, German edn 1994; English trans. 1996).

Schmidt-Bleek, F., and U. Tischner (1995) *Produktentwicklung: Nutzen gestalten, Natur schonen* (Schriftenreihe 270; Vienna: Wirtschaftsförderungsinstitut).

Schmidt-Bleek, F., S. Bringezu, F. Hinterberger, C. Liedtke, J.H. Spangenberg, H. Stiller and M.J. Welfens (1998) *MAIA Einführung in die Material-Intensitäts-Analyse nach dem MIPS-Konzept* (Berlin/Basel: Birkhäuser).

Scholz, U. (2000) *Schwermetallfreies Färben von Wolle: Farbstoffscreening* (final thesis; Münchberg, Germany: University Münchberg).

Schor, J. (1998) *The Overspent American* (New York: Basic Books).

Schuhwerk, M.E., and R. Lefkoff-Hagius (1995) 'Green or Non-Green? Does type of appeal matter when advertising a green product?', *Journal of Advertising* 24.2: 45-54.

Schwepker, C.H., and B.T. Cornwell (1991) 'An Examination of Ecologically Concerned Consumers and their Intention to Purchase Ecologically Packaged Products', *Journal of Public Policy and Marketing* 10.2: 77-101.

Segall, L. (1995) 'Marketing Compost as a Pest Control Product', *Biocycle* 36.5: 65-67.

Sharfman, M., R.T. Ellington and M. Meo (1997) 'The Next Step in Becoming "Green": Life-Cycle Oriented Environmental Management', *Business Horizons* 40.3: 13-22.

Shell (1998a) *Profits and Principles: Does there have to be a choice?* (London: Shell International).

Shell (1998b) *The Triple Bottom Line in Action* (London: Shell International).

Sherwin, C., and T. Bhamra (1999) 'Beyond Engineering: Ecodesign as a Proactive Approach to Product Innovation', paper presented at *Ecodesign '99: 1st International Symposium on Environmentally Conscious Design and Inverse Manufacturing*, Waseda University International Conference Centre, Tokyo, Japan, 18–20 February 1999.

Sherwin, C., T. Bhamra and S. Evans (1998) 'The "Eco-kitchen" Project: Using Ecodesign to Innovate', *Journal of Sustainable Product Design* 7: 51-57.

Shirazi, E. (2000) *Impact of Teleworking on Vehicle Miles Saved and Trip Reduction: A Review of Existing Research* (report to the National Telecommuting and Air Quality Act Steering Committee, 18 February 2000, available from International Telework Association and Council, Washington, DC).

Shrum, L.J., J.A. McCarty and T.M. Lowrey (1995) 'Buyer Characteristics of the Green Consumer and their Implications for Advertising Strategy', *Journal of Advertising* 24 (Summer 1995): 21-31.

Skandia (1994) *Visualising Intellectual Capital in Skandia: Supplement to Skandia's 1994 Annual Report* (Stockholm: Skandia).

Smeels, E. (2000) *Sound 2000: A Durable Audio System* (graduation report; Delft, Netherlands, March 2000).

Smith, M.T., R. Roy and S. Potter (1996) *The Commercial Impacts of Green Product Development* (report DIG.05; Milton Keynes, UK: Design Innovation Group, The Open University).

Spangenberg, J.H. (ed.) (1995) *Towards Sustainable Europe: A Study from the Wuppertal Institute for Friends of the Earth Europe* (Luton, UK/Brussels: FoE Publications).

Spangenberg, J.H. (2001a) 'Investing in Sustainable Development', *International Journal of Sustainable Development* 4.2.

Spangenberg, J.H. (2001b) 'The Environmental Kuznets Curve: A Methodological Artefact', *Population and Environment*, accepted for publication.

Spangenberg, J.H., and O. Bonniot, (1998) 'Sustainability Indicators: A Compass on the Road Towards Sustainability' (paper 81; Wuppertal, Germany: Wuppertal Institute).

Spangenberg, J.H. and M. Kuhndt (1996) *Ökobilanz für Geschirrsysteme im Cateringbereich* (Wuppertal, Germany: Wuppertal Institut für Klima, Umwelt, Energie).

Spangenberg, J.H., and S. Lorek (2001) 'Reichtum und Umwelt', in K. Stadlinger and R. Rilling (eds.), *Reichtum in Deutschland* (Münster, Germany: Westfälisches Dampfboot): in press.

Spangenberg, J.H., F. Hinterberger, S. Moll and H. Schütz, H. (1999) 'Material Flow Analysis, TMR and the MIPS Concept: A Contribution to the Development of Indicators for Measuring Changes in Production and Consumption Patterns', *International Journal of Sustainable Development* 2.4: 491-505.

SSA (Sustainable Systems Associates Ltd) (1998) *Applying Sustainable Development to Business: Realising the Benefits* (Ottawa: Queen's Printer for Ontario, May 1998).

Stafford, E.R., and C.L. Hartman (1996) 'Green Alliances: Strategic Relations Between Businesses and Environmental Groups', *Business Horizons* 39.2: 50-59.

Stahel, W.R. (1982) 'The Product-Life Factor', in O.S. Grinton (ed.), *An Inquiry into the Nature of Sustainable Societies: The Role of the Private Sector* (The Woodlands, TX: Houston Area Research Center, repr. 1984).

Stahel, W.R. (1986a) 'Hidden Innovation, R&D in a Sustainable Society', in 'The Hidden Wealth' (special issue), *Science and Public Policy: Journal of the International Science Policy Foundation, London* 13.4 (August 1986): 196-203.

Stahel, W.R. (1986b) 'Product-Life as a Variable: The Notion of Utilisation', *Science and Public Policy* 13.4 (August 1986): 185-93.

Stahel, W.R. (1991) *Langlebigkeit und Materialrecycling: Strategien zur Vermeidung von Abfällen im Bereich der Produkte* (Essen, Germany: Vulkan Verlag).

Stahel, W.R. (1994) *The Impact of Shortening (or Lengthening) of Life-time of Products and Production Equipment on Industrial Competitiveness, Sustainability and Employment* (unpublished report to the European Commission, DGIII, 1 November 1994).

Stahel, W.R. (1997a) 'Some Thoughts on Sustainability, Insurability and Insurance', in The Geneva Association (ed.), *Geneva Papers on Risk and Insurance: 85* (October 1997; Geneva: The Geneva Association): 417-95.

Stahel, W.R. (1997b) 'The Service Economy: Wealth without Resource Consumption?', *Philosophical Transactions of the Royal Society London*, A355 (June 1997): 1309-19.

Stahel, W.R., and G. Reday (1976) *Jobs for Tomorrow: The Potential for Substituting Manpower for Energy* (report to the Commission of the European Communities, Brussels; New York: Vantage Press, repr. 1981).

Stapleton, P.J., A.M. Cooney and W.M. Hix Jr (1996) *Environmental Management Systems: An Implementation Guide for Small and Medium-Sized Operations* (Ann Arbor, MI: NSF International).

Starik, M. (1995) 'Should trees have managerial standing? Toward Stakeholder Status for Non-Human Nature', *Journal of Business Ethics* 14.3: 207-17.

Steger, U. (1999a) *Surviving the Impossible* (Rohner Textil, case study A; Lausanne, Switzerland: IMD Business School Lausanne).

Steger, U. (1999b) *Leveraging Sustainability* (Rohner Textil, case study B; Lausanne, Switzerland: IMD Business School Lausanne).

Stevels, A. (1997) 'Moving Companies towards Sustainability through Ecodesign: Conditions for Change, *The Journal of Sustainable Design* 3: 47-55.

Stevels, A. (2000) 'A 2000 Application for Eco-design in the Electronics Industry', in *The Mechanical Life Cycle Handbook* (New York: Marcel Dekker): ch. 19.

Suranyi, M. (1999) *Blind to Sustainability? Stock Markets and the Environment* (London: Forum for the Future).

SustainAbility (1999) 'Integrity at Work', *SustainAbility Headlines*, March 1999: 3.

SustainAbility and UNEP (United Nations Environment Programme) (1996a) *Engaging Stakeholders. I. The Benchmark Survey: The Second International Progress Report on Company Environmental Reporting* (Paris: UNEP; London: SustainAbility).

SustainAbility and UNEP (United Nations Environment Programme) (1996b) *Engaging Stakeholders. II. The Case Studies* (London: SustainAbility/UNEP).

SustainAbility and UNEP (United Nations Environment Programme) (1997) *Engaging Stakeholders: The 1997 Benchmark Survey* (London: SustainAbility/UNEP).

SustainAbility and UNEP (United Nations Environment Programme) (1998a) *Engaging Stakeholders. The CEO Agenda: Can business leaders satisfy the triple bottom line?* (London: SustainAbility/UNEP).

SustainAbility and UNEP (United Nations Environment Programme) (1998b) *Engaging Stakeholders. The Non-Reporting Report* (London: SustainAbility/UNEP).

SustainAbility and UNEP (United Nations Environment Programme) (1999a) *Engaging Stakeholders. The Social Reporting Report* (in association with Royal Dutch/Shell Group; London: SustainAbility/UNEP).

SustainAbility and UNEP (United Nations Environment Programme) (1999b) *Engaging Stakeholders. The Internet Reporting Report* (London: SustainAbility/UNEP).

Sweatman, A., and J. Gertsakis (1997) 'Mainstream Appliance Meets Ecodesign', *Journal for Sustainable Product Design*, July 1997: 31-37.

TERI (Tata Energy Research Institute) (1998) *Looking Back to Think Ahead* (New Delhi: TERI).

Tibben-Lembke, R.S. (1998) 'The Impact of Reverse Logistics on the Total Cost of Ownership', *Journal of Marketing Theory and Practice* 6.4: 51-60.

Tischner, U. (1995) 'Sustainability by Design?', in Friends of the Earth Europe and J.H. Spangenberg (eds.), *Towards Sustainable Europe* (Wuppertal, Germany: Wuppertal Institute): 214-19.

Tischner, U. (1997) *Kundenbedürfnisse im Bereich Bekleidung* (Documentation of the Factor 4 Plus Project at Hess Natur; Cologne: econcept).

Tischner, U. (1998) *Hess Natur Designstil: Statusquo und Entwicklungspotentiale* (Documentation of the Factor 4 Plus Project at Hess Natur: Cologne: econcept).

Tischner, U. (1999) *Documentation of the Factor 4 Plus Project at Hess Natur* (Cologne: econcept, www.econcept.org).

Tischner, U., and F. Schmidt-Bleek (1993) 'Designing Goods with MIPS', *Fresenius Environmental Bulletin* 2.8: 479-84.

Tischner, U., E. Schmincke, F. Rubik and M. Prösler (2000) *How to do EcoDesign? A Guide for Environmentally and Economically Sound Design* (Frankfurt a.M.: form publisher).

Tom, P.A. (1999) 'From Dirt to Dollars', *Waste Age* 30.8: 54-62.

Toyota (1997) *Care for the Earth* (Tokyo: Toyota Motor Corporation).

Tukker, A., and E. Haag (eds.) (2000) *Ecodesign: European State of the Art* (completed for IPTS, Seville, Spain; European Science and Technology Observatory [ESTO]).

Turaga, J. (1998) 'A Ringside Seat at the Conference', in *Development Alternatives Newsletter* (New Delhi), May 1998.

TWN (Third World Network) (1997) *The Need to Channel Globalisation towards Sustainable Development* (Penang, Malaysia: TWN).

Üffing, A. (1999) *Materialintensitätsanalyse der Hess Natur spezifischen Porduktline Baumwolle* (final thesis; Mönchengladbach, Germany: University Mönchengladbach).

UN (United Nations) (1991) *Audit and Reduction Manual for Industrial Emissions and Wastes* (Technical Report Series No. 7, publication 91-III-D6; Vienna/Paris: United Nations).

UN (United Nations) (1992) *Agenda 21: The Earth Summit Strategy to Save Our Planet* (document E.92-38352; New York: UN).

UN (United Nations) (1993) *Results of the World Conference on Environment and Development, Rio de Janeiro, June 1992* (document A/CONF.151/4; New York: United Nations).

UNCSD (United Nations Conference on Sustainable Development) (1996) *Indicators of Sustainable Development: Framework and Methodologies* (New York: United Nations).

UNCSD (United Nations Commission on Sustainable Development; Secretariat) (1997) *CSD Update* 4.1 (September 1997).

UNCSD (United Nations Commission on Sustainable Development) (1999) *Comprehensive Review of Changing Consumption and Production Patterns: Report of the Secretary-General* (New York: United Nations Department for Economic and Social Affairs).

UNDESA (United Nations Department of Economic and Social Affairs) (1998) *Measuring Changes in Consumption and Production Patterns: A Set of Indicators* (ST/ESA/264; New York: Population Division, UNDESA).

UNDP (United Nations Development Programme) (1994) *Human Development Report: An Agenda for the Social Summit* (New York/Oxford, UK: Oxford University Press).

UNDP (United Nations Development Programme) (1998) *Human Development Report 1998* (New York: UNDP).

UNEP (United Nations Environment Programme) (1992) *The Rio Declaration on Environment and Development* (The Earth Summit; London: UNEP): 11-13.

UNEP (United Nations Environment Programme) (1999a) *International Expert Meeting Report: Advertising and Sustainable Consumption* (Paris: UNEP, January 1999).

UNEP (United Nations Environment Programme) (1999b) *Youth and Sustainable Consumption* (programme brochure; Nairobi/Paris: UNEP, November 1999).

UNIDO (United Nations Industrial Development Organisation) (1999) *Supporting the Private Sector* (Vienna: UNIDO)

Upton, C, and S. Bass (1996) *The Forest Certification Handbook* (London: St Lucie Press).

US Clean Air Act (Amendment) (1990) 42 USC, secs. 7511a(d)(1)(B) (Washington, DC: US Government Printing Office).

US Clean Air Act (Amendment) (1995) 42 USC, secs. 7511a(d)(1)(B) (Washington, DC: US Government Printing Office).

van Dam, Y.K., and P.A.C. Apeldoorn (1996) 'Sustainable Marketing', *Journal of Macromarketing* 16.2: 45-59.

van Dieren, W. (ed.). (1995) *Taking Nature into Account: A Report to the Club of Rome* (New York: Springer; Basel: Birkhäuser).

van Gelder, B., and P. O'Keefe (1995) *The New Forester* (London: IT Publications).

van Hemel, C.G. (1994) 'Lifecycle Design Strategies for Environmental Product Development', paper presented at *Workshop Design-Konstruktion*; Copenhagen, Denmark: Institut Produkt Udvikling, Technical University of Denmark.

van Hemel, C.G. (1998) *Ecodesign Empirically Explored: Design for Environment in Dutch Small and Medium-Sized Enterprises* (PhD thesis; Design for Sustainability Research Programme, publication no. 1; Delft, Netherlands: Delft University of Technology).

van Hemel, C.G., and J.C. Brezet (1997) *Ecodesign: A Promising Approach to Sustainable Production and Consumption* (Paris: United Nations Environmental Programme).

Van Nes N., J. Cramer and A. Stevels (1999) 'A Practical Approach to the Ecological Optimisation of Electronic Products', in H. Yoshikawa, R. Yamamoto, F. Kimura, T. Suga and Y. Umeda (eds.), *Proceedings of Eco-design 99, Tokyo* (Los Alamitos, CA: IEEE Computer Society): 108-11.

VDI (Verein Deutscher Ingenieure) (ed.) (1993) *VDI-Richtlinie 2221 Methodik zum Entwickeln und Konstruieren technischer Systeme und Produkte* (Düsseldorf: VDI).

von Weizsäcker, E.-U. (1994) *Earth Politics* (London: Zed Books).

von Weizsäcker, E.-U, A.B. Lovins and L.H. Lovins (1996) *Faktor Vier: Doppelter Wohlstand; Halbierter Naturverbrauch* (Munich: Droemer Knaur).

von Weizsäcker, E.U., A.B. Lovins and L.H. Lovins (1997) *Factor Four: Doubling Wealth, Halving Resource Use* (London: Earthscan).

VROM (Ministerie van Volkshiusvesting, Ruimtelijke Ordening en Miieubeheer) (1995) *Facilities for a Sustainable Household* (workshop report; The Hague: VROM).

VROM (Ministerie van Volkshiusvesting, Ruimtelijke Ordening en Miieubeheer) (1998) *Product-Oriented Environmental Management: Its Theory and Practice* (The Hague: VROM, October 1998).

Wackernagel, M., and W.E. Rees (1996) *Our Ecological Footprint: Reducing Human Impact on Earth* (Gabriola Islands, BC, Canada: New Society Publishers).

Walker, S. (1998) 'Experiments in Sustainable Product Design', *Journal of Sustainable Product Design* 7 (October 1998): 42-50.

Walley, N., and B. Whitehead (1994) 'It's Not Easy Being Green', *Harvard Business Review* 72.3: 46-52.

Walz, R., K. Ostertag and N. Block (1995) *Synopsis of Selected Indicator Systems for Sustainable Development* (Karlsruhe, Germany: Fraunhofer Institute for Systems and Innovation Research).

WBCSD (World Business Council for Sustainable Development) (1995) *Eco-efficient Leadership for Improved Economic and Environmental Performance* (Geneva: WBCSD).

WBCSD (World Business Council for Sustainable Development) (1999) *Working Group on Metrics, Eco-Efficiency and Reporting: Report on the Statistics Projects* (Geneva: WBCSD).

WCED (World Commission for Environment and Development) (1987) *Our Common Future* (report of the Brundtland Commission; Oxford, UK: Oxford University Press).

Webb , D.J., and L.A. Mohr (1998) 'A Typology of Consumer Responses to Cause-Related Marketing: From Skeptics to Socially Concerned', *Journal of Public Policy and Marketing* 17.2: 226-38.

Wehrmeyer, W. (1996) *Greening People: Human Resources and Environmental Management* (Sheffield, UK: Greenleaf Publishing).

Welford, R. (1996) 'Hijacking Environmentalism', in J. Ulhøi and H. Madsen (eds.), *Industry and the Environment* (Aarhus, Denmark: University of Aarhus).

Westley, F., and H. Vredenburg (1991) 'Strategic Bridging: The Collaboration between Environmentalists and Business in the Marketing of Green Products', *Journal of Applied Behavioral Science* 27.1: 65-90.

Weterings, R., and H. Opschoor (1992) *The Ecocapacity as a Challenge to Technological Development* (ed. Raad voor ruimtelijk, milieu- en natuuronderzoek [RMNO] [Advisory Council for Research on Nature and the Environment]; publication 74A; Rijswijk, Netherlands: RMNO).

Wiegmann, K. (2000) *Ökobilanz eines Longlife T-Shirts: Bewertung und Optimierung der Produktlinie* (final thesis; Braunschweig, Germany: University Braunschweig).

Wijkman, A. (1999) 'The good life does not equal wasteful lifestyles', in Sang-Whan Lho, Hyun-Jung Im and Ross W. Kim (eds.), *Sustainable Consumption Patterns* (Seoul: Korea Environment Institute).

Wilkhahn (1996) *Wilkhahn Awarded the German Ecology Prize 1996* (Bad Münder, Germany: Wilkhahn).

Willums, J.-O., with the World Business Council for Sustainable Development (1998) *The Sustainable Business Challenge: A Briefing for Tomorrow's Business Leaders* (Sheffield, UK: Greenleaf Publishing).

Wilson, C. (1995) 'Peitsche oder Zuckerbrot? Wie läßt sich die Abfallwirtschaft umstrukturieren?', *Warmer Bulletin* 46: 16-20.

Winter, G. (1996) *Blueprint for Green Management* (New York: McGraw–Hill).

Winter, L., and G. Ledgerwood (1994) 'Motivation and Compliance in Environmental Performance for Small and Medium-Sized Businesses: A Model Based on Empirical Evidence from a Pilot Investigation of Small Businesses in the English West Midlands', *Greener Management International* 7 (July 1994): 62-72.

Wong, V., W. Turner and P. Stoneman (1996) 'Marketing Strategies and Market Prospects for Environmentally-Friendly Consumer Products', *British Journal of Management* 7.3: 263-82.

World Bank (1995) *Monitoring Environmental Progress: A Report on Work in Progress* (Environmentally Sustainable Development [ESD] Series, No. 14; Washington, DC: World Bank).

World Bank (1997) *Expanding the Measure of Wealth* (Environmentally Sustainable Development [ESD] and Monographs Series, No. 17; Washington, DC: World Bank).

WRI (World Resources Institute) (1998) *Taking a Byte out of Carbon: Electronic Innovation for Climate Protection* (Washington, DC: WRI).

Wu, H.J., and S.C. Dunn (1995) 'Environmentally Responsible Logistics Systems', *International Journal of Physical Distribution and Logistics Management* 25.2: 20-38.

Young Foresight Ltd (2000) 'Designing our Future' ('Techno' series for BBC Schools, screened on 7 March 2000, BBC 2).

Zadek, S., P. Pruzan and R. Evans (eds.) (1997) *Building Corporate AccountAbility: Emerging Practices in Social and Ethical Accounting, Auditing and Reporting* (London: Earthscan).

Zeunert, C. (1999) *Stoffstromnalyse in der Gebrauchsphase* (final thesis; Bayreuth, Germany: University Bayreuth).

Zöller, K. (1999) 'Growing Credibility through Dialogue: Experience in Germany and the USA', in M. Charter and M.J. Polonsky (eds.), *Greener Marketing: A Global Perspective on Greening Marketing Practice* (Sheffield, UK: Greenleaf Publishing): 196-206.

Zuckerman, A. (1999) 'Using ISO 1400 as a Trade Barrier', *Iron Age New Steel* 15.3: 77.

# ABBREVIATIONS

| | |
|---|---|
| ABS | acrylonitrile butadiene styrene |
| ACCA | Association of Chartered Certified Accountants |
| ADEME | Agence de l'Énvironnement et de la Maîtrise de l'Energie (France) |
| ASDI | Swedish society for international development co-operation |
| ASPRI | Proyecto de Asesoría Integrado al Sector Privado (Bolivia) |
| B2B | business to business |
| B2C | business to consumer |
| *BATE* | *Business and the Environment* |
| BBC | British Broadcasting Corporation |
| BCSD | Business Council for Sustainable Development |
| BMU | Bundesumweltministerium für Umwelt, Naturschutz und Reaktorsicherheit (German Federal Ministry for the Environment, Nature Conservation and Nuclear Safety) |
| BNAF | Banco Nacional de Agricultura Familiar (Brazil) |
| BNDES | Banco Nacional de Desenvolvimento Econômico e Social (Brazil) |
| BS | British Standard |
| BSE | bovine spongiform encephalopathy |
| BSI | British Standards Institution |
| BSI | Body Shop International |
| BTU | British thermal unit |
| CAD | computer-aided design |
| CASRO | Council of American Survey Research Organisation |
| CD | compact disc |
| CED | cumulative energy demand |
| CEO | chief executive officer |
| CEP | corporate environmental policy |
| CEP | Council on Economic Priorities |
| CERES | Coalition for Environmentally Responsible Economies |
| CFC | chlorofluorocarbon |
| CfD | National Centre for Design, RMIT University, Australia |
| CfSD | The Centre for Sustainable Design, Surrey Institute of Art and Design, University College, Farnham, UK |
| CHDI | corporate human development index |
| CIM | computer-integrated manufacturing |
| CNC | computer numerically controlled |
| CNI | Cámara Nacional de Industrias (Bolivia) |
| CO | carbon monoxide |
| $CO_2$ | carbon dioxide |
| COSUDE | Swiss Agency for Development and Co-operation in Bolivia |
| CPE | Centre de Prospective et d'Evaluation (France) |
| CPU | central processing unit |

| | |
|---|---|
| CRT | cathode-ray tube |
| CTC | Centre for Tomorrow's Company (UK) |
| DEPA | Danish Environmental Protection Agency |
| DEPAP | Danish Electronics Product Area Panel |
| DETR | Department for the Environment, Transport and the Regions (UK) |
| DfE | Design for environment |
| DfS | Design for sustainability |
| DKr | Danish krone |
| DM | deutsche mark |
| DTIE | Division of Technology, Industry and Economics, UNEP |
| DVD | digital video disc-player |
| EAP | Environmental Action Programme |
| ECC | environmental conservation committee |
| ECECP | Engineering Centre for Environmentally Conscious Products (USA) |
| ECP | environmentally conscious product |
| EDIP | Environmental Design of Industrial Products |
| EDP | employee development programme |
| EEA | European Environment Agency |
| EEE | electrical and electronic equipment |
| EEEI | European Eco-Efficiency Initiative |
| EIA | environmental impact analysis |
| ELCI | Environment Liaison Centre International |
| EM | environmental management |
| EMA | Email Major Appliances (Australia) |
| EMAS | Eco-management and Audit Scheme |
| EMS | environmental management system |
| ENDS | Environmental Data Services (UK) |
| EOLM | 'end-of-life' management |
| EOLV | end-of-life vehicles |
| EP3 | Environmental Pollution Prevention Programme |
| EPA | Environmental Protection Agency (USA) |
| EPD | eco-product development |
| EPEA | Environmental Protection Encouragement Agency (Germany) |
| EPP | environmental product policy |
| ESMAP | Energy Sector Management Programme |
| ETA | environmental trends analysis |
| ETMUEL | Ecodesign and Training for Manufacture, Use and 'End-of-Life' for SMEs |
| EU | European Union |
| EVA | economic value added |
| F10C | Factor 10 Club |
| FoD | Faculty of Design, Cologne University of Applied Science |
| FSC | Forest Stewardship Council |
| GAAP | generally accepted accounting principle |
| GDDS | Grupo de Design e Desenvolvimento Sustentável (Design and Sustainable Development Group, Universidade Federal da Paraíba, Brazil) |
| GDR | German Democratic Republic |
| GEA | European Group for Efficient Appliances |
| GFEA | German Federal Environmental Agency |
| GMO | genetically modified organism |
| GNP | gross national product |
| GPS | global positioning system |
| GRI | Global Reporting Initiative |
| GTZ | Gesellschaft für technische Zusammenheit (Germany) |
| HBS | Hans Böckler Stiftung (Germany) |

| | |
|---|---|
| HD | High Definition |
| HDI | human development index |
| HoEQ | house of environmental quality |
| HP | Hewlett-Packard |
| HSE | health and safety executive |
| IC | innovation centre |
| ICT | information and communication technologies |
| IFOAM | International Federation of Organic Agriculture Movements |
| IIED | International Institute for Sustainable Development |
| IIIEE | International Institute for Industrial Environmental Economics |
| IMO | Institute for Market Ecology |
| INETI | Instituto Nacional de Engenharia e Tecnologia Industrial (National Institute of Engineering and Industrial Technology, Portugal) |
| IPD | integrated product development |
| IPM | integrated product management |
| IPP | integrated product policy |
| ISEA | Institute of Social and Ethical Accountability |
| ISEE | International Society for Environmental Ethics |
| ISO | International Organization for Standardization |
| IVN | Internationaler Verband der Naturtextilwirtschaft |
| KCCU | Kenya Crafts Co-operative Union |
| KEFRI | Kenya Forestry Research Institute |
| KSh | Kenyan shilling |
| LCA | life-cycle assessment |
| LCC | life-cycle costing |
| LCD | liquid crystal display |
| LDC | less developed country |
| LETS | local exchange trading scheme |
| LIC | less industrialised country |
| LiDS | Life-cycle Design Strategy |
| MAI | mean annual increment |
| MBDC | McDonough Braungart Design Chemistry |
| MCC | Mennonite Central Committee |
| MEDMIN | Manejo Integrado del Medio Ambiente en la Peque (Bolivia) |
| MET | Material and Energy inputs/outputs, Toxic emissions output |
| MFF | Merck Family Fund (USA) |
| MIPS | material input per unit of service |
| MITI | Ministry of International Trade and Industry (Japan) |
| MNC | multinational corporation |
| mPt | millipoint |
| MSE | micro or small enterprise |
| NCC | Newcastle City Council (Australia) |
| NCM | Nordic Council of Ministers |
| NGO | non-governmental organisation |
| Ni–Cd | nickel–cadmium |
| NMK | National Museums of Kenya |
| $NO_x$ | nitrogen oxide |
| NRTEE | National Round Table on the Environment and Economy (Canada) |
| OECD | Organisation for Economic Co-operation and Development |
| OEM | original equipment manufacturer |
| OPEC | Organisation of Petroleum Exporting Countries |
| ÖRF | Östfold Research Foundation |
| PAIB | Protección Ambiental en la Industría Boliviana |
| PCE | Philips Consumer Electronics |

| | |
|---|---|
| PDP | product development process |
| PERI | Public Environmental Reporting Initiative |
| PET | polyethylene terephthalate |
| PLI | Product-Life Institute (Switzerland) |
| PMAIM | Proyecto Medio Ambiental de Industría y Minería (Bolivia) |
| PMZ | *Productgerichte milieuzorg* |
| POEMS | product-oriented environmental management system |
| POS | point-of-sale |
| PS | product stewardship |
| PSC | product stewardship council |
| PSS | product service system |
| PTS | plane transport system |
| PVC | polyvinyl chloride |
| PWB | printed wiring board |
| R&D | research and development |
| RBI | Reed Business Information (UK) |
| RSA | Royal Society of Arts |
| SA | social accountability |
| SCM | supply chain management |
| SEBRAE | Serviço Brasileiro de Apoio à Micro e Pequenas Empresas (Micro and Small Enterprise Support Service, Brazil) |
| SEEA | system of integrated environmental and economic accounting |
| SEEBA | South-East Environmental Business Association (UK) |
| SEK | Swedish kronor |
| SIC | Standard Industrial Classification |
| SIPP | sustainable integrated product policy |
| SME | small or medium-sized enterprise |
| SOCOG | Sydney Organising Committee for the Olympic Games |
| SPD | sustainable product design |
| SPDD | sustainable product development and design |
| SPI | sustainability performance indicator |
| SPI | sustainable process index |
| SPM | sustainability performance measurement |
| SPRU | Science Policy Research Unit of the University of Sussex (UK) |
| STRETCH | Selection of sTRategic EnvironmenTal CHallenges |
| SWOT | strengths, weaknesses, opportunities, threats |
| TCO | Tjänstemännens Centralorganisation (Confederation of Professional Employees, Sweden) |
| TERI | Tata Energy Research Institute (India) |
| TMR | total material requirement |
| TNC | transnational corporation |
| TNO | Netherlands Organisation for Applied Scientific Research |
| TQEM | total quality environmental management |
| TQM | total quality management |
| TV | television |
| TWN | Third World Network |
| UN | United Nations |
| UNAM | Universidad Autónoma del Estado de México |
| UNCED | United Nations Conference on Environment and Development |
| UNCSD | United Nations Commission on Sustainable Development |
| UNDP | United Nations Development Programme |
| UNEP | United Nations Environment Programme |
| UNESCO | United Nations Educational, Scientific and Cultural Organisation |
| UNIDO | United Nations Industrial Development Organisation |

| | |
|---|---|
| uop | unit of performance |
| VCR | videocassette recorder |
| VDI | Verein Deutscher Ingenieure |
| VOC | volatile organic compound |
| VROM | Ministerie van Volkshiusvesting, Ruimtelijke Ordening en Miieubeheer (Ministry of Housing, Spatial Planning and the Environment, Netherlands) |
| WBCSD | World Business Council for Sustainable Development |
| WCED | World Commission on Environment and Development |
| WEEE | Waste from Electrical and Electronic Equipment |
| WGSPD | Working Group on Sustainable Product Development, UNEP |
| WRI | World Resources Institute |
| WTO | World Trade Organisation |
| WWF | World Wide Fund for Nature |
| ZBIA | zero, basic, intermediate, advanced |
| ZERI | Zero Emissions Research Institute |

# AUTHOR BIOGRAPHIES

**Braden R. Allenby** is the Environment, Health and Safety Vice-President for AT&T and an adjunct professor at Columbia University's School of International and Public Affairs. He graduated *cum laude* from Yale University in 1972, received his Juris Doctor from the University of Virginia Law School in 1978, his Master's in economics from the University of Virginia in 1979, his Master's in environmental sciences from Rutgers University in the spring of 1989 and his PhD in environmental sciences from Rutgers University in 1992. He is co-author or author of several engineering textbooks, including *Industrial Ecology* (Prentice–Hall, 1995), *Industrial Ecology and the Automobile* (Prentice–Hall, 1997), and the first policy textbook on industrial ecology, *Industrial Ecology: Policy Framework and Implementation* (Prentice–Hall, 1998).
ballenby@att.com

**Christine Ax** holds a Master's degree in politics and philosophy. She is a scholar and journalist and the mother of two children. She has specialised in the field of ecology and economy for more than 20 years. From 1991–99 she worked as head of the at Zukunftswerkstatt eV of the Handwerkskammer, Hamburg. Since 1999 she has headed the Institut für Produktdauer-Forschung, Hamburg.
Christine.ax@t-online.de

**Andrew Baynes** graduated from King's College, London, with a BSc honours degree in geology and geomorphology. He then went on to complete a Master's degree in environmental technology at Imperial College, London. His experience in business and environment issues was initially developed in the field of auditing, followed by a brief introduction to credit risk assessment and 'Superfund' strategies in California, USA. Prior to joining Sony International (Europe) he developed his knowledge in two main fields relating to UK and US environmental law and technologies for industrial and vehicle emissions. He now works for Sony International (Europe) GmbH where he is responsible for European take-back policy, environmental reporting and communication. In addition he has been instrumental in the set-up of joint producer projects for ecodesign and end-of-life management of electronic products.

**Inga Belmane** worked as a researcher at the Centre for Sustainable Design (CfSD; Surrey Institute of Art and Design, University College, Farnham, UK) on a number of projects related to integrated product policy, eco-product development and ecodesign. She has a BA in business administration and has worked for both government and private business in Latvia. She holds an MSc in environmental management and policy from the International Institute for Industrial Environmental Economics (Lund University, Sweden).
ibelmane@lppc.lv

**Michael Braungart** is a chemist and co-founder of McDonough Braungart Design Chemistry (Charlottesville, VA, USA), founder of EPEA (Environmental Protection Encouragement Agency), Hamburg, Germany, International Umweltforschung GmbH and professor of Process Engineering at the Technical University of Northeast Lower Saxony (Fachhochschule Nordostniedersachsen). He also serves as President of the Hamburg Environmental Institute (Germany), which produces the 'Top 50' Study of the chemical industry.
mb@mbdc.com

**Han Brezet** holds an MSc in electrical engineering from Delft University of Technology, Netherlands, and a PhD in environmental sciences from the Erasmus University of Rotterdam. He is professor of sustainable product development at Delft University of Technology and the co-ordinator of the Design for Sustainability (DfS) programme at the Sub-faculty of Industrial Design Engineering of the same University. In addition, since 1997 he has held a position as Scientific Director of Kathalys, the joint Centre for Sustainable Product Innovation of TNO—Netherlands Organisation for Applied Scientific Research and Delft University of Technology. Via the DfS programme he is actively involved in several international projects and institutes, including the National Institute of Engineering and Industrial Technology (INETI), Lisbon, Portugal.
j.c.brezet@io.tudelft.nl

**Uli Burchardt**, born 1971, a forestry engineer and farmer, was a Manufactum buyer and product manager from 1997–99. In this time he established the Manufactum special catalogue, 'Plants and Gardening', and today is a member of the Manufactum management board, responsible for buying, marketing and public relations. He is married and lives with his wife and daughter in Reckling-hausen, Germany.
uli.burchardt@manufactum.de

**Martin Charter** is a visiting professor in sustainable product design. He has held management positions in financial services, trade exhibitions and consultancy and, over the past ten years, has established various organisations in the business and environment field, in publishing, training, research and consultancy. He is currently Co-ordinator of The Centre for Sustainable Design (CfSD) at the Surrey Institute of Art and Design, University College, and South-East Environmental Business Association (SEEBA), UK. At CfSD, he is responsible for the strategic direction and management of international training and the research centre, which covers environmental communications, managing ecodesign and sustainable product development and design. He is a Fellow of the Royal Society of Arts (RSA) and has completed two books on environmental issues and marketing—including two editions of *Greener Marketing* (Greenleaf Publishing, 1992, 1999)—and a number of publications on managing ecodesign and electronic environmental reporting. He has edited a range of green management publications and is currently Editor of *The Journal of Sustainable Design*, as well as acting as the UK expert to and chairman of the ISO and BSI sub-groups on 'Integrating Environmental Aspects into Product Development'.
mcharter@surrart.ac.uk

**Jacqueline M. Cramer** is professor of environmental management at Erasmus University, Rotter-dam, and director of Cramer Environmental Consultancy, Arnhem, the Netherlands. After working as an associate professor at the University of Amsterdam (1976–89) she joined the Strategy, Technology and Policy Centre of the Netherlands Organisation for Applied Scientific Research (TNO; 1989–99). From 1995–97 she worked at Philips Consumer Electronics as a senior consultant on the integration of environmental issues into business strategy, detached from TNO, and from 1997–99 she worked with Akzo Nobel in a similar position. Since then she has started her own consultancy company, Cramer Environmental Consultancy. In addition, she worked as part-time professor in

environmental science at the University of Amsterdam (1990–96) and in environmental management at the Tilburg University (1996–99). Since 1999 she has worked at Erasmus University. She is
member of various national and international advisory boards to the government, to industry and
to non-profit organisations, e.g. she is a member of the Dutch council for transportation and
waterworks, of the Dutch Social–Economic Council and of the Board of the World Wide Fund for
Nature (WWF) in the Netherlands.
jmcramer@xs4all.nl

**Bas de Leeuw** is senior advisor at the Dutch Ministry of Housing, Spatial Planning and the
Environment and since 1998 has been working with the United Nations Environment Programme
(UNEP)'s Division of Technology, Industry and Economics (DTIE), where he initiated UNEP's
Sustainable Consumption Programme. Before joining UNEP he worked in several areas, including
six years (1985–91) for the Dutch Ministry of Economic Affairs (on business, technology, energy and
environmental issues), followed by another six years (1991–97) for the Dutch Ministry of Housing,
Spatial Planning and the Environment. In this function he was deputy head of the Consumer and
Product Policy Department, responsible for Dutch consumption and product policies.
bas.leeuw@unep.fr

**Joseph Fiksel** is vice-president in charge of Battelle's life-cycle management group, helping clients
achieve both sustainability and profitability by incorporating life-cycle thinking into their business
processes. Previously, he was the founding director of the Decision and Risk Management group at
Arthur D. Little Inc. He holds a BSc in electrical engineering from the Massachusetts Institute of
Technology, Cambridge, MA, a PhD in operations research from Stanford University, Stanford, CA,
and a graduate degree from La Sorbonne, Paris, France. He has published extensively, and his book
*Design for Environment: Creating Eco-efficient Products and Processes* (McGraw–Hill, 1996), has been
translated into Spanish and distributed worldwide. Currently, he serves on the editorial board of
*The Journal for Sustainable Product Design.*
fiksel@battelle.org

**John Gertsakis** is acting director of the Centre for Design at RMIT University, Australia. He is
responsible for managing a range of projects related to ecodesign and product stewardship,
including EcoReDesign™ and EcoSpecifier, as well as other industry and consulting projects. He has
written widely on 'green products' and has worked exclusively on the policy and practice of
ecodesign since 1991. He has also co-authored and published some key handbooks, reports and
websites directly related to ecodesign and product stewardship, including *Good Design, Better
Business, Cleaner World: A Guide to EcoReDesign™* (Centre for Design at RMIT University, 1997),
*Appliance Reuse and Recycling: A Product Stewardship Guide* (Centre For Design at RMIT University and
EcoRecycle Victoria, 1999) and *Return to Sender: An Introduction to Extended Producer Responsibility*
(Centre For Design at RMIT University and EcoRecycle Victoria, 1998).
john.gertsakis@rmit.edu.au

**Luiz Eduardo Cid Guimarães** is a lecturer at Universidade Federal da Paraíba, Northeast Brazil. He
is head of the Design and Sustainable Development Group (GDDS). He is an industrial designer
with a special interest in ecodesign and innovation in micro and small businesses in less
industrialised countries.
adocid@aol.com

**Peter James** has worked as a consultant, business school researcher, teacher and professor, and as
a manager and journalist in the areas of management of technology and environmental manage-

ment. This has included positions with BBC Television Science Features department and as senior research fellow at the University of Warwick Business School, Professor of Management and MBA director at the University of Limerick and Assistant Director, Research, at Ashridge Management College. He is currently Visiting Professor of Environmental Management at the University of Bradford and a research associate of Ashridge and the UK Centre for Environment and Economic Development. His publications, with co-authors, include *Sustainable Measures: Evaluation and Reporting of Environmental and Social Performance* (Greenleaf Publishing, 1999), *The Green Bottom Line: Environmental Accounting for Management* (Greenleaf Publishing, 1998), *Driving Eco-innovation* (FT Pitman, 1996), *Corporate Environmental Management in Britain and Germany* (Anglo-German Foundation, 1997) and *Environment under the Spotlight: Current Practice and Future Trends in Environment-Related Performance Measurement in Business* (ACCA, 1998), as well as many articles on environmental management, environmental accounting, performance evaluation and product evaluation for environmental and business journals.
sustainablebusiness@compuserve.com

**Albin Kälin**, textile entrepreneur, is CEO of Rohner Textil AG. The company was rewarded in the 1990s with several international design awards, and it has taken a pioneering role in economic and ecological issues. In 1996 Rohner Textil was certified to ISO 14001 and EMAS. The development of Climatex® Lifecycle™ has generated press features in *Time*, *The Wall Street Journal*, *Manager* magazine, *Facts*, *Schöner Wohnen* and *Arte*.
Albin.Kaelin@ria.com

**Aleksandra Kielkiewicz-Young** holds an MSc in landscape ecology from the Department of Geography and Natural Sciences, University of Gdansk, Poland. She has worked for the Polish Ecological Club, co-ordinating a nationwide programme to promote consumer awareness of the environmental impacts of products; she has also worked with consultancies and academic institutions on various environmental projects. In 1999 she was granted her second MSc, in environmental management and policy, from the International Institute for Industrial Environmental Economics (IIIEE), Lund University, Sweden. Currently, she works at The Centre for Sustainable Design (CfSD; Surrey Institute of Art and Design, University College, Farnham, UK), researching ecodesign and eco-innovation through supply chain management.
oyoung@surrart.ac.uk

**Roland Lentz** studied biology in Germany, with a focus on ecology and physiology. In 1988 he received a PhD in eco-toxicology at the University of Mainz, Germany. He worked for seven years for the international company Procter & Gamble at the European headquarters, with responsibility for cradle-to-grave environmental product evaluation. At a the University of Applied Sciences, Wedel, Germany, he developed a postgraduate curriculum in environmental management for engineers and for four years taught resource flow management at that university. Currently, he is director of innovation management at a German chamber of industry and commerce. He spent some years in Ecuador and other parts of South America as a naturalist and during his professional career conducted several projects in the area of environmental management in Mexico and Bolivia.
Roland.Lentz@t-online.de

**Diego Masera** studied industrial design in Italy. After working for several years with international development organisations in Africa and Latin America, in 1998 he received a PhD from the Royal College of Art in London on sustainable product development. He is the author of several articles and manuals on product development for small enterprises in developing countries.
diegomasera@hotmail.com

**William McDonough** is an architect and co-founder of McDonough Braungart Design Chemistry (Charlottesville, VA, USA), a product and systems development firm, and is founding principal of William McDonough & Partners. He teaches at the University of Virginia, Charlottesville, VA. *Time* magazine recently honoured him as a 'hero for the planet'.
william@mcdonough.com

**Katharina Paulitsch** received a diploma in garment engineering in 1995 at the University of Albstadt-Sigmaringen. From 1995 to 1997 she worked in the Textile Department of the Institute of Market Ecology in Switzerland as an administrator, co-ordinator and inspector. She developed an international inspection and certification system for organic textiles and organised the second International IFOAM (International Federation of Organic Agriculture Movements) Conference on Organic Textiles, Intercot, in Bingen, Germany, 1996. Since November 1997 she has worked as project manager for Hess Natur-Textilien GmbH in Germany in the Department for Innovation and Ecology. Here, she has responsibility for the Factor 4 Plus project on resource management in the textile chain and has acted as an internal consultant and expert in the subjects of cotton, silk and certification systems.
kpaulitsch@t-online.de

Dr **Michael Jay Polonsky** is an Associate Professor in marketing within the School of Management, University of Newcastle, Newcastle, Australia. He has taught in Australia, New Zealand, South Africa and the USA. One of his main research areas concerns environmental marketing and management issues. He has edited three books, and has published a number of book chapters and articles on environmental topics. In addition, he has presented environmentally oriented papers at numerous conferences. He has also been an invited speaker at SOCOG (Sydney Organising Committee for the Olympic Games)'s Environmental Forum, EcoBiz 98, EcoBiz 99, The Sustainable Futures workshops and was (and is to be again) the keynote speaker at environmental marketing conferences in Mexico and Colombia.
mgmjp@alinga.newcastle.edu.au

**Deanna J. Richards** is an independent consultant working on technology and environmental corporate and public policy matters for a range of clients. Previously, for ten years until December 1999, Dr Richards directed the Technology and Sustainable Development programme of the National Academy of Engineering, USA, where she oversaw efforts to address policy and management issues related to technology, environment and economic growth, and directed the most recent study on 'Industrial Environmental Performance Metrics: Challenges and Opportunities'. Before this, she spent several years consulting as an environmental engineer.
richards_dj@home.com

**Christian Ridder** graduated in 1996 at the Delft University for Technology in the Netherlands, specialising in environmentally sound product development. As a project manager at Sony's Environmental Centre Europe he evaluated many products, in terms of their environmental quality, in co-operation with European product planning and engineering groups. Current activities relate to the internal communication and implementation of corporate environmental targets and to involving European marketing groups in ecodesign.

**Nick Robins** is former Director of the Sustainable Markets Group at the International Institute for Sustainable Development (IIED), London, and is now Head of Research in the Socially Responsible Investment team at Henderson Global Investors, also in London. He has more than ten years of experience with international environment and development issues, focusing on EU policy-making and business practice. He is co-author of a number of recent IIED publications, including *The Reality* *of Sustainable Trade* (2000), *Consumption in a Sustainable World* (1998) and *Unlocking Trade Opportunities* (1997). Before joining IIED he worked at the European Commission in the run-up to the 1992 Rio Earth Summit and also contributed chapters on corporate strategy and clean technology to the World Business Council for Sustainable Development's *Changing Course* report (MIT Press, 1992). Nick.Robins@henderson.com

**Cristina Rocha** graduated in environmental engineering at the Faculty of Sciences and Technology, New University of Lisbon, in 1992. She was awarded a postgraduate qualification in sanitary engineering from the same university in 1992. She currently holds a position as researcher at the National Institute of Engineering and Industrial Technology (INETI), Lisbon, and, since 1993, has been involved in national and international projects in the areas of cleaner production, environmental management systems and ecodesign. In 1998/99 she was a research fellow at Delft University of Technology on the Design for Sustainability programme, where she started her PhD project on product-oriented environmental management systems. cristina.rocha@mail.ineti.pt

**Holger Rohn** holds a diploma in engineering. Since 1994 he has worked as a freelance researcher at the Wuppertal Institute for Climate, Environment and Energy for the working group on 'Eco-efficiency and Sustainable Enterprises'. In 1997 he became a partner of Trifolium—Sustainable Management Consulting. He works in the fields of sustainable enterprises, environmental management, resource management, material flow accounting (processes, products, enterprises), environmental information systems, qualification and organisational learning. Trifolium.Rohn@t-online.de

**Lutz-Günther Scheidt** joined Sony Europe in April 1990 and holds a doctorate in information technology from Dresden University. He is the responsible director of the Environmental Centre Europe and procurement officer of Sony International (Europe) GmbH. He is developing, among other things, comprehensive environmental management systems and environmental research and development for Sony in Europe. He represents Sony in the World Business Council for Sustainable Development, acting as liaison delegate, and is actively involved in several working groups and is a member of the Earth Summit 3 team. He is one of the directors of the Foundation for Business and Sustainable Development (Geneva and Oslo). Furthermore, he is a member of the EEEI (European Eco-Efficiency Initiative) steering committee. In 1994 he initiated the Eureka umbrella CARE 'VISION 2000'. Further activity has included time as a visiting/guest professor at the Technical University of Vienna.

**Chris Sherwin** has undergraduate and postgraduate (MA) degrees in furniture design and in furniture design and technology, respectively. He has worked in ecodesign research for six years, with experience at organisations such as: The Centre for Sustainable Design, the Design Council, the Chartered Society of Designers and, most recently, with the Industrial Design Centre at Electrolux. He has taught ecodesign and sustainability-related design subjects and projects at the Surrey Institute of Art and Design, University College; Goldsmiths College; and the Royal College of Art, among other places. He is currently undertaking PhD studies on exploring innovative ecodesign (methods and techniques) at the 'early' concept-design stages of industrial design projects. Chris has published works in a number of ecodesign and design-related conferences and publications over recent years. He recently accepted a job as an ecodesign consultant at Philips Environmental Services in the Netherlands. chris.sherwin@philips.com

**Joachim H. Spangenberg**, born 1955, studied biology and mathematics in Cologne and environmental sciences in Essen. He worked as an expert advisor to several MPs from 1985–91 before joining the German Environmental Convention team as Programme Director in 1991/92. Experience as a senior research fellow includes the Institute for European Environmental Policy, Bonn, and the Wuppertal Institute. From 1995–99 he was director of the Sustainable Societies Programme in the Department for Material Flows and Structural Change. In 2000 he worked with the LEAD Europe team as Fellows Programme Director. Currently he is self-employed, working as a freelancing expert and for the Sustainable Europe Research Institute, Vienna, in his capacity as Vice-President of the Institute and director of its Cologne office. Voluntary activities include work with NGOs (e.g. the European Environment Bureau in the 1980s and Friends of the Earth Europe in the 1990s), as well as scientific affiliations (INES, ESEE, ISEE) and advisory functions, particularly on sustainable development indicators, e.g. to the UNCSD, OECD, European Commission, the German government and a number of trade unions and environmental NGOs.
Joachim.Spangenberg@seri.de

**Walter R. Stahel**, born in 1946 in Zurich, is an alumnus of ETH (Eidgenössische Technische Hochschule Zürich), the Swiss Federal Institute of Technology, where he studied architecture. He has worked in industry, research centres and universities in European, Asian and North American countries. Since 1982 he has been the founder director of the Product-Life Institute in Geneva, an institute that undertakes contract research, the focus of which is to develop strategies and policies leading to a more sustainable society.
wrstahel@vtx.ch

**Ab Stevels** is senior advisor at the Environmental Competence Centre of Philips Consumer Electronics and professor of Environmental Design and part-time professor in applied ecodesign at Delft University of Technology in Delft, the Netherlands. He has done trail-blazing work on how to make ecodesign in day-to-day business really happen. For this purpose, tools and management procedures have been developed which have proven their strength through their practical success. He is the author of some 80 journal articles and conference contributions. His training courses on applied ecodesign have been held at Philips departments and divisions, at other companies and at various universities around the globe (Delft University of Technology, Delft, the Netherlands; Stanford University, CA; Technical University Berlin, Germany; UNAM [Universidad Autónoma del Estado de México], Mexico City; Technical University, Vienna; Hong Kong Polytechnic).
Ab.Stevels@philips.com

**Fred Steward** is reader in Innovation and director of the Innovation Research Centre at Aston Business School, Birmingham, UK. He has led a number of international projects on innovation and environmental sustainability and also has research interests in innovation networks and small firms.
h.f.steward@aston.ac.uk

**Philip Thompson** has worked for Electrolux Industrial Design Centre for ten years. After working up to senior designer level, Phil managed to merge an interest in environmental design with his work responsibilities, becoming the first full-time environmental design co-ordinator in Electrolux Industrial Design. This position balances more innovative and strategic design and sustainability projects with more operational forms of ecodesign. Since writing the chapter in this volume, Phil has accepted a design management post with Whirlpool.
Philip_M_Thompson@email.whirlpool.com

**Ursula Tischner** studied architecture and industrial design in Aachen and Wuppertal, Germany, and specialised in ecodesign and sustainable design. From 1992–96 she worked as a researcher at the Wuppertal Institute for Climate, Environment and Energy in the field of ecology and design. There she was engaged in theoretical and practical projects and wrote a guide for environmentally conscious product design on behalf of the Austrian Ministry for Science and Research (Schmidt-Bleek and Tischner, *Produktentwicklung: Nutzen gestalten, Natur schonen*, Wirtschaftsförderungs-institut, 1995). In 1996 she founded 'econcept', the ecology and design consultancy in Cologne. With econcept she advises companies in the field of eco- and sustainable design of products and services; and she is engaged in research projects, teaches ecology and design at various schools and universities and undertakes development of environmentally sound products and service concepts.
u.tischner@econcept.org

**Carolien van Hemel**, born in 1967, completed her MSc studies on industrial design engineering at the Delft University of Technology in 1992. In 1998 she obtained a PhD at the Delft University of Technology, with her thesis on *Ecodesign Empirically Explored: Design for Environment in Dutch Small and Medium-Sized Enterprises*. In 1997 she started working in industry for ATAG Home Products Group as project manager for research. One of her tasks was co-ordinating the development of five eco-innovations for this Dutch manufacturer of domestic kitchen appliances. She is research fellow at the Delft University of Technology. From 2000, she has been employed as product manager at Nefit Buderus, a leading Dutch producer of efficient central heating equipment.
c.van.hemel@wxs.nl

**Angelika von Proff-Kesseler** holds a diploma in business management. In 1991 she became manager and owner of the Kambium Furniture Workshop Inc. in Lindlar, Germany.
info@kambium.de

**Alex Young** received his BA in environmental studies from the University of California, Santa Cruz, USA, and then worked for almost ten years in industry before moving full time into the environmental field. More recently, he has worked in Poland developing campaigns to raise consumer awareness of the environmental aspects of products. He is also author of a number of articles and reports and was the editor of *Tools for Change*, a newsletter focused on Central and Eastern European consumption and production policy issues. In 1998 he received an MSc in environmental management and policy from the International Institute for Industrial Environmental Economics (IIIEE), Lund University, Sweden. He is currently working as a researcher on integrated product policy at The Centre for Sustainable Design (CfSD; Surrey Institute of Art and Design, University College, Farnham, UK).
ayoung@surrart.ac.uk

# INDEX